On This Day
in
Tudor
History
II

MadeGlobal
Publishing

On This Day in Tudor History II
Copyright © 2022 Claire Ridgway

ISBN: 978-84-125953-0-7

MadeGlobal Publishing

For more information on
MadeGlobal Publishing, visit our website:
www.madeglobal.com

Dedication

To Christian, Kira & Iden,
with love,
Mum/Claire/Бабушка
Xxx

For Erin Marie Hill,
keep your passion for history!

Introduction

It's been ten years since the publication of *On This Day In Tudor History*, so it's about time I wrote and published a second helping! Thank you to all those who bought book one and have followed my "on this day" videos on the Anne Boleyn Files and Tudor Society YouTube channel and urged me to get on with this book. I've finally done it!

In the first book, I gave multiple events per day, whereas, in this book, I focus on one event and give detailed information. It's the perfect complement to the first book, and I hope it will introduce you to lesser-known – but oh-so-interesting – Tudor people and events.

Using this Book

This book is set out chronologically like a diary, taking you through the modern calendar year daily from 1st January to 31st December. However, you don't need to read it in order, it's perfect for dipping into.

On This Day in Tudor History 2 can also be used for:

- Educational Purposes – I know from comments on my videos that teachers found book one a useful resource in history lessons, giving their students an "on this day" fact each lesson.

- Reading cover to cover – You can treat it like a normal book and read cover to cover and immerse yourself in Tudor history.

- Competitions, quizzes and trivia nights – It's a great resource for putting together quiz nights or trivia competitions.

- Birthdays – I do love sharing with my loved ones an "on this day" event on their birthday. Why not add a piece of Tudor trivia to friends' birthday cards?

- Wowing acquaintances and your friends and family with your Tudor knowledge – Use a piece of Tudor trivia as an icebreaker in a conversation or to change the subject!

However you use this book, I do hope you enjoy it.

Calendar of Feast Days and Special Days

January

1 January – New Year's Day - New Year was a time for the nobility and monarchy to exchange gifts.

1 January – Feast of the Circumcision of Christ.

5 January – Twelfth Night - Twelfth Night was a time to celebrate, and it was marked at the royal court with entertainment like masques, plays and pageants, and the people might also share a communal bowl of wassail or Lambswool.

6 January – Epiphany - This feast day brought the Twelve Days of Christmas to a close and celebrated the visit of the Magi to the Christ child.

Plough Monday – First Monday after 6th January. The day on which things would return to normal after the Twelve Days of Christmas.

7 January – St Distaff's Day - The day on which women would resume their spinning following the Twelve Days of Christmas.

13 January – Feast of St Hilary of Poitiers, patron saints of lawyers.

25 January – Feast of the Conversion of St Paul. In Queen Mary I's reign, the Feast of St Paul's was celebrated with torchlit processions and bonfires.

February

1 February – Candlemas Eve - The traditional day for removing the greenery, such as laurel, holly, ivy and rosemary, and other objects that decorated homes over the Christmas period.

2 February – Candlemas, the Feast of the Presentation of Christ in the Temple and the Purification of the Blessed Virgin - Candles were blessed in church services and then carried around the parish, their light symbolising Christ lighting the way for his followers.

13 February – Feast of St Blaise, patron saint of wool-combers, waxchandling and wild animals. Wool combers would have special processions to celebrate their craft. St Blaise is also the patron saint of those with sore throats.

14 February – Valentine's Day - It was custom on Valentine's Day for people to choose their love and buy their Valentine a gift.

24 February – Feast of St Matthias the Apostle.

March

1 March – Feast of St David (Dewi Sant), patron saint of Wales.

25 March – Lady Day, or the Feast of the Annunciation of the Blessed Virgin – The first day of the new calendar year in Tudor times.

April

23 April – Feast day of St George, patron saint of England from 1552. The Order of the Garter was established under his banner in 1348 by Edward III, and an annual chapter meeting always took place on 23rd April.

24 April – St Mark's Eve - St Mark's Eve was all about divining the future.

25 April – Feast of St Mark the Evangelist - St Mark's Day was the traditional day for praying for fertile land and a good harvest.

May

1 May – May Day, the first day of summer - It was celebrated with special processions, plays and pantomimes, pageants, Morris dancing, the crowning of a May Queen, and bringing in the May (collecting flowers and branches to make garlands and wreaths).

19 May – Feast of St Dunstan, the patron saint of goldsmiths, silversmiths, musicians, locksmiths and blacksmiths. The traditional day to do spring-cleaning.

June

2 June – Feast of St Elmo or St Erasmus, the traditional time for shearing sheep.

11 June – Feast of St Barnabas, a day for decorating churches with garlands of flowers.

24 June – Feast of St John the Baptist and Midsummer's Day - Fire was at the heart of the celebrations, and people back then would jump through the fires to bring good luck. Evil spirits were also believed to be roaming free, and the fires would ward them off. There was also plenty of dancing, drinking of ale and socialising.

29 June – Feast of St Peter and St Paul, the traditional time for the "rushbearing" ceremony, a feast of dedication when the parishioners would process to the church and strew the church floor with newly cut rushes, new-mown hay from the hay-making, and wildflowers.

July

2 July – The Visitation of the Virgin – This commemorated the pregnant Virgin Mary visiting her cousin Elizabeth, who was pregnant with John the Baptist.

15 July – Feast of St Swithin – If it rained on St Swithin's Day, it was said that it would rain for 40 days, but if the weather was fair, it wouldn't rain for 40 days.

20 July – Feast of St Margaret of Antioch, one of the Fourteen Holy Helpers, saints who are venerated because their intercession is believed to be particularly powerful.

22 July – Feast of St Mary Magdalene. She was the patron of many guilds, and many chapels and buildings were named after her. She was the most widely venerated saint in the Medieval period after the Virgin Mary.

25 July – Feast of St James the Great the Apostle, Feast of St Christopher the Martyr - It was traditional to eat oysters on St James's Day, and St Christopher is the patron saint of travellers

August

1 August – Lammas or "Loaf Mass", the start of the wheat harvest. After the first crops were safely brought in, the first loaves baked with the wheat from this harvest in each household would be taken to church and blessed as a thanksgiving for the harvest.

This would be followed by a celebratory feast.

1 August – Feast of St Peter in Chains (St Peter ad Vincula).

15 August – Assumption of the Virgin or Assumption of Our Lady.

24 August – Feast of St Bartholomew.

29 August – Feast of the Beheading of St John the Baptist.

September

Harvest Home – Celebrated when the harvest was done. A thanksgiving for God's help with the harvest and the crop. Harvest Home marked the end of the agricultural year.

29 September – Michaelmas or the Feast of St. Michael and All Angels, Protector of the Church. The first day of the agricultural year. It was traditional to enjoy a feast of goose at this time of year. The geese had been fattened on the stubble land left over from the harvest and so were now perfect for slaughtering and cooking.

October

First Sunday of October – In the medieval period, wakes were held to mark the end of summer and to dedicate the local church.

13 October – Feast of St Edward the Confessor. The traditional day for the mayor of London to be chosen by the freemen at Guildhall.

18 October – Feast of St Luke the Evangelist, patron saint of artists, physicians and surgeons, brewers, notaries, students and butchers.

25 October – Feast of St Crispin and St Crispinian, patron saints of shoemakers, saddlers and tanners. The day also celebrated the English victory at the Battle of Agincourt on 25th October 1415. Celebrations included bonfires, revelry and the crowning of a King Crispin.

28 October – Feast of St Simon and St Jude. St Simon is the patron saint of tanners, and St Jude is the patron saint of hope and hopeless/desperate cases.

31 October – All Hallows Eve (Halloween) - On that night, it was believed that the veil between the world of the living and that of the dead was at its thinnest and that the souls of the dead and evil spirits could walk the earth. Church bells were rung, bonfires were lit, and people wore masks to ward off these spirits and to send them on their way. Farm buildings and homes were also blessed to protect them from evil spirits and witches.

November

1 November – Feast of All Saints. It was a feast day in honour of all the saints and martyrs and was established because there were not enough days in the year to commemorate the lives of all the saints.

2 November – Feast of All Souls - A time to remember the souls in Purgatory who might not have masses or prayers being said for them, the forgotten souls.

11 November – Martinmas, the Feast of St Martin of Tours, the traditional day for slaughtering animals.

17 November – Accession Day. Accession Day was celebrated throughout the reign of Elizabeth I and the reigns of many of her successors. It commemorated the day Elizabeth I came to the throne in 1558.

30 November – Feast of St Andrew the Apostle, patron saint of Scotland.

December

6 December – Feast of St Nicholas, or St Nicholas of Myra, patron saint of children, sailors, merchants, archers, repentant thieves, brewers, pawnbrokers and students. It was traditional for a choirboy to be chosen on 6th December, or Childermas (Holy Innocents' Day) on 28th December, as "Boy Bishop" to act as bishop. He would lead processions around communities collecting money for the church and parish funds and would also lead some religious services.

8 December – Feast of the Immaculate Conception

21 December – Feast of St Thomas the Apostle, also known as Didymus and "Doubting Thomas". It was traditional for old women, children and the poor to "go Thomasing", i.e. walk the streets collecting alms.

24 December – Christmas Eve - The Yule log was brought into the home.

25 December – Christmas Day - The fasting of Advent was now over, and this was a day to celebrate. Christmas Day was the first day of the Twelve Days of Christmas. A day to celebrate the coming of Jesus Christ, our Saviour and to eat, drink and be merry.

26 December – Feast of St Stephen, the first Christian martyr or protomartyr. It was the traditional day for bleeding horses and cattle, and was also a day associated with hunting.

28 December – Childermas (Children's Mass) or Holy Innocents' Day. It commemorates the massacre of the baby boys which King Herod ordered in Bethlehem in an attempt to kill the infant Jesus Christ. The Catholic Church saw the innocent babies as the very first martyrs.

Moveable Feasts

See "On This Day in Tudor History" (book 1) for details on these.

Spring
> Shrovetide and Lent
> Palm Sunday
> Maundy Thursday
> Good Friday
> Easter Sunday

Summer
> Rogationtide
> Feast of the Ascension
> Whitsun
> Trinity Sunday
> Corpus Christi

1 January

On 1st January 1540, King Henry VIII met his bride-to-be, Anne of Cleves, for the first time. Anne would be his fourth wife.

It was a rather disastrous meeting, and, as historian Amy Licence notes, Henry VIII really should have learned from the disastrous first meeting of King Henry VI and Margaret of Anjou.

Henry VI was desperate to see his future bride, Margaret, who'd been fetched from France by William de la Pole, but Margaret was ill. The king just couldn't wait, so he disguised himself as a squire bearing a letter from the king. He knelt in front of her, and she completely ignored him, leaving him on his knees while she read the letter. After the king had left, de la Pole had to explain to Margaret that the squire had been the king. Margaret was described as being "vexed... because she had kept him on his knees." Of course, as historian Lauren Johnson has pointed out, Margaret may have been fully aware of what was going on and was just playing the innocent lady as part of this game of courtly love. It's hard to say, but history repeated itself on 1st January 1540 when Henry VIII decided to play the game of courtly love.

Like Henry VI before him, Henry VIII was excited about meeting his bride-to-be for the first time and couldn't wait for her official reception at Greenwich, so he decided to disguise himself and travel to Rochester to surprise her.

Chronicler and Windsor Herald Charles Wriothesley gives an account of this first meeting:

"[...] and on New Year's day at afternoon, the King's Grace, with five of his Privy Chamber, being disguised with cloaks of marble with hoods, that they should not be known, came privily to Rochester, and so went up into the chamber where the said Lady Anne looked out at a window to see the bull baiting that was that time in the court, and suddenly he embraced her and kissed, and showed her a token that the King had sent her for her New Year's gift, and she being abashed, not knowing who it was, thanked him, and so he communed with her, but she regarded him little, but always looked out of the window on the bull baiting, and when the King perceived she regarded his coming so little, he departed into another chamber and put off his cloak and came in again in a coat of purple velvet, and when the lords and knights did see his Grace they did him reverence, and then she, perceiving the lords doing their duties, humbled her Grace lowly to the King's Majesty, and his Grace saluted her again, and so talked together lovingly, and after took her by the hand and led her into another chamber where they solaced their graces that night and till Friday at afternoune [...]"

As we can see from this account, Anne was not expecting a visit from the king, Henry was in disguise, and she did not realise who he was and so treated him just like a servant. However, it doesn't sound like it was too disastrous as the king and Anne then talked lovingly together after the misunderstanding.

But, in the depositions taken a few months later, during the annulment proceedings, Sir Anthony Browne, Henry VIII's Master of the Horse, gave a slightly different account:

"The said Sir Anthony saith how at the arrival of the Queen at Rochester, the King's Highness appointed to go thither to see her upon New Year's day, and ordered the said Anthony to wait upon him: and at his coming thither, to go before him with this message, how he had brought her a New Year's gift, if it liked her to see it. And when the said Sir Anthony entered the chamber where she was, and having conceived in his mind, what was by pictures and advertisements signified of her beauty and qualities, at the general view of the ladies he thought he saw no such thing there, and yet were thother of better favour than the Queen. But when he was directed unto herself, and advisedly looked upon her, he saith, he was never more dismayed in all his life, lamenting in his heart, which altered his outward countenance, to see the Lady so far and unlike that was reported and of such sort as he thought the King's Highness should not content hiself with her. Nevertheless, at his return to the King's Majesty with her answer, the said Sir Anthony said nothing, he durst not. Then when the King's Highness entered to embrace her, and kiss her, the said Sir Anthony saith, he saw and noted in the King's Highness countenance such a discontentment and misliking of her person, as he was very sorry of it. For the said Sir Anthony saith, he much marked that the King's Highness tarried not to speak with her twenty words, but called for her council, and with his council and them devised communication all that night, the King's Highness without showing any cheerful or merry countenance disclosed not his heart. But whereas the King's Majesty had brought with him a partlet furred with sables and richly garnished, sable skins garnished to wear about her neck, with a muffle furred, to give the Queene, and a cap, the King's Highness passed over the execution of his intent that night, and in the morning sent them by the said Sir Anthony Browne with as cold and single a message as might be.

The said Sir Anthony saith also, how the King's Majesty returning in his barge from thence to Greenwich, said to the said Sir Anthony, by his Highness's commandment, then sitting by him, these words very sadly and pensively: I see nothing in this woman as men report of her; and I marvel that wise men would make such report as they have done. With which words the said Sir Anthony was abashed, fearing lest anything should be objected to my Lord of Southampton his brother, for that he had written to her praise."

So, this first meeting was used as evidence of the king's unhappiness and his view that he had been deceived into marrying Anne by those who had made false reports about her.

So which account is true?

Well, the king was likely humiliated by this meeting. According to chivalric tradition, the woman was meant to be able to see through a disguise and recognise her true love. Anne was meant to fall in love with Henry at first sight, she was meant to be bowled over by him, but she had ignored him and carried on watching the bull-baiting.

This must have been a blow to Henry VIII's pride, particularly as this happened in front of Anne's ladies and the king's men. He may have been able to cover up his embarrassment, but I think this impacted how he felt about Anne.

However, I don't think he'd been deceived at all. Nobody else found Anne unattractive or questioned Holbein's depiction of her or reports on her looks and personality. I'm sure those who fetched her from Calais would have been worried and done something to warn the king if they had found anything wrong with his bride-to-be. After all, those sent to greet her in Calais had included the king's best friend, Charles Brandon, Duke of Suffolk. Surely he would have sent an urgent message to the king if something had been wrong.

I believe Henry VIII needed to blame someone else for setting him up with a woman who hadn't been 'wowed' by him on their first meeting. He couldn't get over that initial humiliation, which left him unable to consummate the marriage, which was even more humiliating. It couldn't be his fault!

If only Anne had been warned of Henry VIII's love of dressing up. If only someone had whispered in her ear that the servant in front of her was the King of England. If only Anne had swooned and sunk to her knees, recognising her husband to be. If only… I'm sure she would have made a wonderful queen consort if the king had given her a chance.

2 January

On 2nd January 1536, Catherine of Aragon, who had been abandoned by her husband, King Henry VIII, lay dying at Kimbolton Castle. Her dear friend and ally, Eustace Chapuys, the imperial ambassador, arrived at her bedside. He'd travelled there by horse immediately after hearing news of Catherine's decline. In a letter to Emperor Charles V, Catherine's nephew, Chapuys wrote that

"After making my reverence, and kissing the Queen's hand, she was pleased, out of sheer kindness and benevolence, and without any occasion or merit it on my part, to thank me for the many services which, she said, I had rendered her on former occasions, as well as the trouble I had taken in coming down to visit her, at a time too when, if it should please God to take her to Himself, it would at least be a consolation to die as it were in my arms, and not all alone like a beast."

He goes on to say that he gave her "all-possible hope of a speedy recovery" and of being moved somewhere more comfortable. He describes how he "entreated her to take courage, and do her best to get well, If not entirely for her own sake, I said she ought at least to consider that on her recovery and life depended in a great measure the union, peace, and welfare of Christendom."

Chapuys visited Catherine every afternoon for two hours at a time, over four days, and left for London on 6th January 1536, believing her to be on the mend. Unfortunately, Catherine died the next day.

3 January

What a difference a year a year can make, and did in the life of Anne of Cleves! On 3rd January 1540, Anne of Cleves was officially received by her soon-to-be husband, Henry VIII, at a spectacular pageant that spread from Greenwich Park to Blackheath. From chronicler Edward Hall's account, we know that tents and pavilions had been erected, one being made from rich cloth of gold. Hall describes how at midday, Anne, accompanied by the Dukes of Norfolk and Suffolk, the Archbishop of Canterbury and other bishops, lords and knights, and people from her own country, came down the hill towards the tents. She was met by a company including the Earl of Rutland, her Lord Chamberlain; Sir Thomas Dennis, her chancellor; and Dr Day, her almoner, who then made what Hall described as an eloquent oration in Latin. Following her official welcome, Anne and her ladies warmed themselves in the tents.

On hearing of her arrival at the tents, the king set off from Greenwich Palace. His courser was, according to Hall, "trapped in ryche cloth of golde traversed lattice wise square, all over enbroidered with gold of damaske, pearled on every side of the enbroderye, the buckles and pendentes were all of fine golde". Hall goes on to say that:

"His persone was apparelled in a coate of purple velvet, somewhat made lyke a frocke, all over enbroidered with flat golde of Dammaske with small lace mixed betwene of the same gold, and other laces of the same so going traverse wyse, that the ground little appered: about whyche garment was a rvche garde very curiously enbriodered, the sleeves and breast were cut lined with cloth of golde, and tied together with great buttons of Diamondes, Rubyes, and Orient Perle, his swoorde and swoorde girdle adorned with stones and especiall Emeraldes, his night cap garnished with stone, but his bonnet was so ryche of jewels that fewe men coulde value them. Besyde all this he ware in baldricke wise a collar of such Ballasts and Perle that few men ever saw the lyke: and aboute his persone ran. x. footemen all rychely apparelled in goldsmythes worke."

Hall adds, "his Princely countenaunce, his goodly personage and royall gesture so farre exceded all other creatures beyng present, that in comparyson of his persone, all his ryche apparell was lytle estemed."

Hall also describes Anne's appearance that day. She was "apparelled in a ryche goune of cloth of golde raised, made rounde without any trayne after the Dutche fashion, and on her head a call, & over that a rounde bonnet or cappe set full of Orient Perle of a very propre fassyon, & before that she had a cornet of blacke veluet, & about her necke she had a partelet set full of riche stone which glystered all the felde."

Anne came out of the tent, mounting a horse at the door of her tent, and rode out to meet Henry VIII. Hall describes how the king "put off his bonnet came foreward to her, & with most lovely countenance and Princely behauyour saluted, welcomed & embrased her to the great reioicing of the beholders: and she lykewyse not forgettyng her duty, with most amiable aspecte & womanly behaviour receyved his Grace with many sweete wordes and great thankes and praisynges given to hym."

They then rode through the crowds to Greenwich Palace, where they dismounted in the outer courtyard, and the king "lovyngly embrased her and kissed her" before escorting her through the hall and to her privy chamber.

Henry VIII married Anne of Cleves on 6th January 1540 in the Queen's Closet at Greenwich Palace.

Things were very different a year later. The king had had his marriage to Anne annulled on 9th July 1540 and had married one of Anne's maids of honour, Catherine Howard, on 28th July. On 3rd January 1541, Anne of Cleves visited the royal court at Hampton Court Palace to greet her former husband and his new wife. She came bearing New Year's gifts for the king: "two fine and large horses caparisoned in mauve velvet, with trappings and so forth to match".

Chapuys describes how she was taken to the queen's apartments but had to wait a while while the new queen was instructed regarding how to receive and treat the former queen. A tricky situation! Chapuys records their meeting:

> "Having entered the room, Lady Anne approached the Queen with as much reverence and punctilious ceremony as if she herself were the most insignificant damsel about Court, all the time addressing the Queen on her knees, notwithstanding the prayers and entreaties of the latter, who received her most kindly, showing her great favor and courtesy."

The king then entered the room, making a low bow to Anne and embracing and kissing her. Anne then joined them for supper, although she was seated near the bottom of the table.

After supper, the three conversed for a while before the king retired for the night. Anne and Catherine stayed up a while, dancing together and separately. They did this again the next night.

While Anne was at Hampton Court, the king sent Catherine a ring and two small dogs. Chapuys records that Catherine gave her gifts to Anne, adding, "whether in the King's name or in her own I cannot say, though, most likely, as is generally believed, it was in her own, since the King has separately presented Lady Anne with an annual rent of one thousand ducats."

What could have been a very uncomfortable visit to the royal court seemed to go incredibly well for all concerned.

4 January

On 4th January 1575, in the reign of Queen Elizabeth I, courtier and diplomat Sir William Pickering died in London.

He was buried in the chancel of St Helen's Church, Bishopsgate, in London, along with his father, who was moved there to be with him. Pickering had ordered a tomb to be made, instructing it to be "garnished and decked with the armes coates of me and my auncestors".

Pickering is an interesting man in that he was involved in a failed rebellion, but unlike some of his fellow rebels, he kept his head.

Let me share a few facts about this Tudor courtier, diplomat and rebel.

- Pickering was born around 1516/17 and was the son of Sir William Pickering, knight marshal to King Henry VIII.
- He was educated at St John's College, Cambridge, by Sir John Cheke.
- In 1538, Pickering was recorded as being at the royal court and serving the king as one of his "daily waiters".
- Henry Howard, Earl of Surrey, acted as his patron. The two men, along with Sir Thomas Wyatt the Younger, had to appear before the royal council in April 1543 charged with eating meat during Lent and committing vandalism by breaking house and church windows at Candlemas. Pickering confessed and was committed to the Tower of London for just over a month.
- Pickering served his king in Calais during Henry VIII's French Wars in the 1540s.
- John Dudley, Viscount Lisle and the future Earl of Warwick and Duke of Northumberland, served as Pickering's patron following the execution of the Earl of Surrey in 1547. Dudley's patronage helped Pickering rise during Edward VI's reign.
- Following Edward VI's accession, Pickering was made a Knight of the Carpet.
- He undertook diplomatic missions to France in Edward VI's reign, where, according to his biographer, Susan Doran, he

earned the respect of King Henry II. Pickering didn't enjoy his time there, though.

- In Edward VI's reign, the imperial ambassador wrote of Pickering being a creature of Warwick's, unlettered, a novice diplomat, and a zealous Protestant.
- He escaped involvement in the events of 1553, when Lady Jane Grey was proclaimed queen and removed, because he was still serving in France.
- After the accession of the Catholic queen, Mary I, Pickering was one of a number of men, including his friend, Sir Thomas Wyatt the Younger, who became worried about Mary's plans to marry Philip II of Spain, and the religious changes her reign was bringing. They decided that a military coup might be the only way to prevent her marriage and so planned a series of uprisings. The aim of Wyatt's Rebellion, as it became known, was to depose Mary I and replace her with her half-sister Elizabeth, who would then marry Edward Courtenay, Earl of Devon. The rebellion failed and although Wyatt was apprehended and executed, Pickering, along with Sir Peter Carew, were able to flee to Normandy, where it was said that they were planning to intercept Philip of Spain on his way to England. In April 1554, Pickering was indicted, although he was safely in Paris. In France, Pickering changed sides and started giving information on the surviving rebels to Dr Nicholas Wotton. He was now in danger of assassination by those he had betrayed, so he kept on the road, travelling from Paris to Italy and Germany.
- Pickering was pardoned on 4th December 1554 thanks to his decision to betray the rebels and the intercession of Wotton, Sir John Mason and Sir William Petre. He returned to England in 1555.
- In 1558, he was away from England when he was sent to recruit soldiers in Germany to defend Calais. Of course, Calais ended up being lost to the French.
- Shortly after Elizabeth I's accession, it was rumoured that Pickering was a suitor for the hand of the queen, and bets in London were said to be at 25 to 100 that he would be Elizabeth's

king. However, he made it clear that he thought the queen would never marry. Pickering also never married.

- In 1569, during the Northern Rebellion, he was appointed as one of the queen's lieutenants, and in 1570, he was on the commission that tried Catholic martyr John Felton.
- He died on this day in 1575 at his home, Pickering House, in London. He was about 58 or 59 years of age.
- He left an illegitimate daughter, Hester.
- In his will, he left instructions for a jewel worth 200 marks to be given to the queen by his executors. He also left money to the poor in his parish, money to St Bartholomew's Hospital, and bequests to his daughter and friends. To William Cecil, Lord Burghley, he left his "papers of Antiquities", along with globes, compasses, and a horse. He also instructed that his library would be passed on to his daughter's husband. His bequests show that Pickering died a wealthy man.

So, a rebel who survived not only being indicted as a traitor but also the vengeance of those he betrayed. A rebel who died a natural death on 4ᵗʰ January 1575 - quite an achievement!

5 January

On 5ᵗʰ January 1546, in the reign of King Henry VIII, geographer and poet Richard Willes was born in Pulham, Dorset.

He was educated at Winchester College, under headmaster and Neo-Latin poet Christopher Johnson, then New College, Oxford, and Louvain, in Belgium. In 1565, he joined the Society of Jesus, i.e. he became a Jesuit, at Mainz, obtaining his Master there in 1568, and in 1569, in Trier, he began training to be a priest. After going on a pilgrimage to Rome and working as a professor of rhetoric at Perugia, he returned to England in late 1572. Even though he'd been a Jesuit, he became loyal to the Church of England and was incorporated at both Oxford and Cambridge Universities on his return to England.

Willes is mostly known for his geographical works, including the 1577 "History of Travayle", but his contemporary authors respected him as both a poet and geographer. His biographer, Anthony Payne, notes that his "History of Travel" included a treatise on navigator

Martin Frobisher and the North-West Passage, and new material on Asia, which Payne describes as "nearly all derived from continental sources and including accounts of China and Japan translated by Willes and never before printed in English".

Librarian William Poole described Willes as a "Sixteenth-Century Religious Renegade and Concrete Poet" and "One of the quirkier figures in the literary history not only of the college but of the Elizabethan period as a whole". Some of the quirky things about him include:

- His change of religious stance, from Jesuit novice to Protestant
- He wrote a poem in Egyptian hieroglyphics

Poole notes that Willes's poems are "the first extensive examples in England (although written mainly in Latin) of what would today be called concrete poetry".

6 January

6th January is Epiphany or Twelfth Night, and it was celebrated at the Tudor court with feasting, games and entertainment.

In 1494, in the reign of King Henry VII, Epiphany was celebrated at Westminster Hall with what was described as "a greate banquett... where there was a play, with a pageant of St George with a castle, and also 12 lords, knights and Esquires with 12 disguised which did dance."

In 1512, in Henry VIII's reign, something very exciting happened at court, an entertainment that chronicler Edward Hall described as "a thing not seen afore in England". It was a masque. Here is Edward Hall's account:

> "On the day of the Epiphany at night, the king, with 11 other, were disguised, after the manner of Italy, called a maske, a thing not seen afore in England. They were apparelled in garments long and broad, wrought all with gold, with visers and caps of gold, & after the banquet done, these Maskers came in, with six gentlemen disguised in silk, bearing staff torches, and desired the ladies to dance, some were content, and some that knew the fashion of it refused, because it was not a thing

commonly seen. And after they danced and commoned together, as the fashion of the Maske is, they took their leave and departed, and so did the Queen, and all the ladies."

On Twelfth Night 1552, in the reign of King Edward VI, a tourney was held during the day, and that evening, following a play performed by the King's Players, there was a contest or feat of arms between Youth and Riches, with them arguing over which of them was better. The men in these teams were described as fighting "two to two at barriers in the hall". After that, according to a contemporary account, "Then came in two apparelled like Almains (Germans). The Earl of Ormonde and Jacques Granado, and two came in like friars, but the Almains would not suffer them to pass till they had fought. The friars were Mr. Drury and Thomas Cobham." This mock combat was followed by a mask of men, a mask of women, and then a banquet of 120 dishes.

In 1553, in the reign of Queen Mary I, Twelfth Night was celebrated with "The Triumph of Cupid, Venus and Mars", a play devised by Sir George Howard. Venus entered in a triumphal chariot accompanied by a mask of ladies, followed by the marshal and his band. Venus rescued Cupid from the marshal, with some mock combat being performed, and at some point, Mars also made his triumphal entry.

These celebrations brought the Twelve Days of Christmas to an end.

In his book "The Stations of the Sun", Ronald Hutton explains how it was traditional by the Tudor period for monarchs to make offerings at Epiphany, just like the Wise Men did to the Christ child. Hutton writes of how Henry VII made offerings of gold, frankincense and myrrh and that King James IV of Scotland gave three gold crowns. This tradition is continued today. The official website of the British Monarchy states, "A service of Holy Communion is celebrated on 6 January (Epiphany) each year in the Chapel Royal, St James's Palace, when an offering of gold, frankincense and myrrh is made on behalf of The Queen".

7 January

On 7th January 1558, England lost Calais. The Lord Deputy of Calais, Thomas Wentworth, was forced to surrender when French troops led by the Duke of Guise stormed the castle.

The Pale of Calais on the coast of Northern France had become an English territory in 1347 after a siege following the English victory at the Battle of Crécy in 1346. This was in the reign of King Edward III. It became increasingly important as, by the mid-15th century, it was the only English possession in mainland France, and became the main port for exporting English wool abroad.

In 1554, Queen Mary I, eldest daughter of King Henry VIII, married Philip of Spain, and in 1557 England became involved in Philip's war with France, which Henry II ruled. The French king, concerned about English troops supporting those of Spain, secretly planned an attack on Calais. Philip of Spain got wind of this attack and warned the English government, who set about raising troops to send across the channel. However, historian Richard Cavendish noted in an article for History Today that England was in the grips of an influenza epidemic, so it was hard to find men fit enough to go.

On 31st December, Thomas Wentworth, Lord Deputy of Calais, wrote to King Philip reporting that the French were camped three leagues from Calais and that he was concerned about them launching an attack.

On 1st January, Philip sent the following message to Wentworth:

"We have had sure information to-day that the French are about to make an attack with all their forces on Calais. We wish to inform you by this messenger, in order that you may urgently take all possible precautions, with your customary vigilance, for the defence of that fortress and the frustration of the enemy's designs. It is desirable that you should report by special messenger to the Queen, our consort, informing her of everything that you require from that kingdom. If there is anything else we can do to contribute to the defence of Calais and defeat of the enemy, we will gladly use our best efforts, for there is nothing of greater importance for our interests and those of the Kingdom of England."

On 2nd January, Wentworth reported to Philip that "The enemy is by the bridge very near this town. He has 20,000 men, foot and horse, and is skirmishing with us all the time" and begged the king for help. The following day, he wrote again, saying "They have set their batteries in position, and have stormed the castle at the entrance to the port, and also the other castle on the road leading to France. Thus they have occupied all our territory, and nothing remains for them to do except to take this town" and concluding that "We have little hope, unless your Majesty sends us relief". Wentworth added, "Whatever befalls, I am determined to die at my post."

English troops under the leadership of the Earl of Rutland arrived at Dover on 3rd January, ready to set off across the Channel to Calais, but discovered that Calais could not be reached because the French were occupying the beaches. England could not help.

On 6th January, 200 of Philip's soldiers from Gravelines tried to enter the Pale of Calais but were unsuccessful, being driven off by the French. Calais was on its own.

On 7th January 1558, Philip wrote to Don Luis Carvajal telling him that the harbour castle had fallen and that Calais was besieged and being shelled. He ordered him to move the Spanish fleet out of the harbour to stop the French from seizing their supplies, and join the English fleet out at sea. Philip added, "If the English go on requesting you to throw troops into Calais, and you see that this can be done without taking too great risks or loss of reputation, I will leave the decision to you; but you yourself are not to leave the fleet, and you will take the greatest pains to keep me informed of what happens." The fleet had luckily already been moved out of the port

The French siege was successful, and Calais fell to the French on this day in 1558. Here is an account by JeanPerdrix, who is described as "townsman of Calais" who "came to this town of Gravelines" where he declared:

> "On 7 January, at 2 o'clock after midnight, the French entered the castle of Calais by a breach which they had opened in it.
>
> The French had entered the castle before the townsmen knew they were there.
>
> At about three o'clock, a parley began with the French. At about 6 o'clock, it was learnt that an agreement had been reached and that the town had been surrendered, the garrison's lives being spared, but every one taken prisoner.
>
> As soon as the town was surrendered, it was sacked by the French, and all the inhabitants were taken prisoner.
>
> As the defenders were only 2,000 strong, they were compelled to surrender.
>
> Within the castle, there was a man-at-arms of Calais called Middleton, having about 20 men-at-arms with him, who had entered the town."

The loss of Calais, a territory which had been held for over 500 years, was a huge blow for Mary I and England, and it is said that Mary exclaimed to one of her attendants, "When I am dead and opened, you shall find 'Philip' and 'Calais' lying in my heart".

8 January

Henry VIII's first wife, Catherine of Aragon, had died on 7th January 1536. She had died away from the royal court, at Kimbolton Castle, where she'd been living since April 1534.

News of her death might have been a blow for her daughter, Mary, and people like Eustace Chapuys, the imperial ambassador and Catherine's good friend and ally, but for King Henry VIII, it was good news. Catherine had defied him by refusing to accept the annulment of their marriage and her new title of Dowager Princess of Wales. Henry must have viewed her as a thorn in his side, particularly as Emperor Charles V was her nephew, so Henry's treatment of Catherine affected his diplomatic relationship with the powerful Emperor.

So how did Henry VIII react to the news of Catherine's death?

When a messenger came to court with the news, the king cried out, "God be praised that we are free from all suspicion of war!". Eustace Chapuys records that on Sunday 8ᵗʰ January 1536 "the King was clad all over in yellow, from top to toe, except the white feather he had in his bonnet, and the Little Bastard [i.e. his daughter Elizabeth] was conducted to mass with trumpets and other great triumphs."

The king was celebrating.

In "The Tudors" series, we see Anne Boleyn dressed in yellow and celebrating, but is this true?

Chronicler Edward Hall writes that "Queen Anne wore yellow for the mourning", but chronicler and Windsor Herald Charles Wriothesley makes no mention of what happened. Chapuys, who was there at court, makes no mention of Anne wearing yellow, just the king. The Spanish Chronicle, which generally has to be taken with a pinch of salt due to its numerous inaccuracies, corroborates Chapuys' account: "Couriers were at once sent off to the King informing him of her death; and as soon as the King heard of it he dressed himself in yellow, which in that country is a sign of rejoicing, and ordered all his grandees to go thither, and that she should be buried very sumptuously."

I would think that if Anne *had* worn yellow, Chapuys, who didn't like her and saw her as usurping the true queen's place, would have mentioned it.

It is sometimes said that yellow was a mourning colour in Spain at the time. This just isn't true. Black was associated with death, mourning and burial, not yellow.

9 January

On 9ᵗʰ January 1539, Henry Courtenay, Marquess of Exeter and first cousin of King Henry VIII, and Henry Pole, 1ˢᵗ Baron Montagu and son of Margaret Pole, Countess of Salisbury, were executed on Tower Hill.

The two men were arrested in November 1538 and found guilty of high treason in December 1538 for denying the king's supremacy, desiring the king's death, and favouring and promoting Cardinal

Reginald Pole, Montagu's brother, "in his traitorous proceedings" to restore papal authority in England.

Others caught up in the same alleged plot, known as the Exeter Conspiracy, were Montagu's brother-in-law, Sir Edward Neville, who was beheaded on 8th December 1538, and Geoffrey Pole, Montagu's brother, who was pardoned on 2nd January 1539, after attempting suicide in prison for the third time. Montagu's chaplain, Doctor George Croft, who chancellor of Chichester Cathedral, was hanged, drawn and quartered at Tyburn on 9th December 1538 along with Hugh Holland, a servant of Geoffrey Pole, and John Collins, a chaplain of the Pole family.

Margaret Pole, Countess of Salisbury, had also been arrested in 1538 and imprisoned in the Tower of London. She was attainted in May 1539 for supporting her sons, Montagu and Cardinal Pole, and she was executed on 27th May 1541.

10 January

On 10th January 1532, Protestant martyr Thomas Dusgate, also known as Thomas Benet, was burnt at the stake at Livery Dole in Heavitree, near Exeter.

In the Records of the City of Exeter is the following record of this execution:

"Md. that this present yere (23 Henry VIII, 1531–32) a little before Christmas their was one Thomas Benet that dwelled in the butcher row, was arrested by Mr. Mayor for heresy, and he was born at Cambridge and he was condemned by the Clergy to be burned for his opinions the 15 day of December, the year above written [i.e. 1531], and so he remained in the bishop prison until the 10th day of January [1532], that he was delivered by Chancel of the Church to Sir Thomas Denis, knight, then sheriff of Devonshire, and he would have burned the same heretic in Southinghay, Southernhay, and they had brought wood and put up a post, but he was compelled by Mr. Mayor and others to remove away the post and wood and so burned the heretic at Liverydole, where the place of execution for the sheriff is accustomed to be had."

How did Thomas Benet or Dusgate come to this end?

While studying at Cambridge, Thomas, an ordained priest, became friends with Reformer and preacher Thomas Bilney. This friendship led to Thomas also becoming a Reformer. After suffering problems with lust, "and stryvyng gretely to suppresse the same", he travelled to the Continent to seek the advice of Reformer Martin Luther. Luther advised him to leave the priesthood and marry, which he did in 1524. He also left Cambridge, where he'd been a fellow at Corpus Christi. He changed his name from Dusgate to Benet and moved to Devon. In Torrington and then Exeter, he kept a school for young children and taught there.

In October 1531, his evangelical zeal led to him posting bills on Exeter Cathedral's door, saying, "The pope is antichrist; and we ought to worship God only, and no saints." An investigation was launched into the writer of these bills, and Thomas was arrested and imprisoned. Martyrologist John Foxe records how a Grey Friar named Gregory Basset, who "not long before, was revolted from the way of righteousness, to the way of Belial", i.e. had recanted his reformed faith, tried to persuade Thomas also to recant, but Thomas refused. Basset said of him, "that there never was so obstinate a heretic."

On 22nd December 1541, Thomas was tried, condemned for heresy and turned over to the secular powers. The Records of the City of Exeter state that the sheriff wanted him to be burnt at Southernhay, but the mayor refused permission. He was burnt at Liverydole in Heavitree on either 10th or 15th January 1532.

Here is John Foxe's account of his execution:

"The mild martyr, rejoicing that his end was approaching so near, as the sheep before the shearer, yielded himself with all humbleness to abide and suffer the cross of persecution. And being brought to his execution, in a place called Livery-dole, without Exeter, he made his most humble confession and prayer unto Almighty God, and requested all the people to do the like for him; whom he exhorted with such gravity and sobriety, and with such a pithy oration, to seek the true honouring of God, and the true knowledge of him; as also to leave the devices, fantasies, and imaginations of man's inventions, that all the hearers and beholders of him were astonied and in great admiration; insomuch that the most part of the people, as also the scribe who wrote the sentence of condemnation against him, did pronounce and confess that he was God's servant, and a good man.

Nevertheless two esquires, namely, Thomas Carew and John Barnehouse, standing at the stake by him, first with fair promises and goodly words, but at length through rough threatenings, willed him to revoke his errors, and to call to our Lady and the saints, and to say, I pray holy Mary, and all the saints of God, &c. To whom, with all meekness, he answered, saying, "No, no; it is God only upon whose name we must call; and we have no other advocate unto him, but only Jesus Christ, who died for us, and now sitteth at the right hand of his Father, to be an advocate for us; and by him must we offer and make our prayers to God, if we will have them to take place and to be heard." With which answer the aforesaid Barnehouse was so enkindled, that he took a furze-bush upon a pike, and having set it on fire, he thrust it unto his face, saying, "Ah! whoreson heretic! pray to our Lady, and say, Holy Mary, pray for us, or, by God's wounds, I will make thee do it." To whom the said Thomas Benet, with a humble and a meek spirit, most patiently answered, "Alas, sir! trouble me not". And holding up his hands, he said, "Father, forgive them." Whereupon the gentlemen caused the wood and furzes to be set on fire, and therewith this godly man lifted up his eyes and hands to heaven, saying, "O Lord, receive my spirit." And so, continuing in his prayers, did never stir nor strive, but most patiently abode the cruelty of the fire, until his life was ended. For this the Lord God be praised, and send us his grace and blessing, that at the latter day we may with him enjoy the bliss and joy provided and prepared for the elect children of God."

11 January

On 11th January 1579, courtier, member of Parliament, Lord of Misrule and poet George Ferrers was buried at Flamstead, Hertfordshire.

Ferrers is known for the Ferrer's Case, when he was arrested for debt and fought with the arresting officers. Ferrers also contributed works to "A Mirror for Magistrates", which the British Library describes as "a collaborative collection of poems in which the ghosts of eminent statesmen recount their downfalls in first-person narratives called 'tragedies' or 'complaints' as an example for magistrates and others in positions of power".

Here are some facts about this colourful character:

- George Ferrers was born in St Albans in around 1510.
- In the early 1530s, according to antiquary John Leland, he joined the service of Thomas Cromwell.
- In 1534, he was admitted to Lincoln's Inn, an inn of the court in London, where, according to Leland, he gained a reputation for his oratory prowess at the bar.
- In 1534, Ferrers also published the first printed English translation of Magna Carta.
- By 1541, he had married Elizabeth Bourchier, a widow.
- From 1542-7, he was a page of the chamber for Henry VIII and attended the king on his campaign in France in 1544. His service saw him being rewarded in the king's will on his death in 1547.
- In the 1540s, he was a member of Parliament and while on his way to the House of Commons in 1542, he was arrested for debt of 200 marks. He was taken to the Counter, a debtor's prison. The House of Commons was sitting at the time, and the UK Parliament website explains that Ferrers' arrest interrupted the business of the House, so the Serjeant at Arms was commanded to have Ferrers released from prison. Trouble then broke out. According to William Cobbett, in his

"The Parliamentary History of England", "The serjeant went immediately to the counter, but the clerks and officers there were so far from delivering the prisoner, that they forcibly resisted him; broke the serjeant's mace, and knocked down his servant." The serjeant declared to the Speaker of the House of Commons "all the circumstances of his ill usage", but the whole House would not sit without their fellow MP and so went to the House of Lords to air their grievance. To cut a rather long story short, Ferrers was released, and the man to whom Ferrers owed the debt, along with the sheriffs, were charged with breach of parliamentary privilege for arresting and imprisoning an MP while the House was sitting. They ended up in the Tower of London for a couple of days.

- In 1546, Ferrers married his second wife, Jane Southcote, and the couple went on to have a son, Julius.
- In 1547, he served in the Scottish campaign.
- Ferrers was the Lord of Misrule for Christmas 1551/2 and 1552/3 in Edward VI's reign. As Lord of Misrule, in January 1553, he entered London in a huge procession which mimicked that of a monarch – his large retinue included councillors, fools, jugglers, tumblers, a divine, a philosopher, an astronomer, a poet, a physician, an apothecary, a Master of Requests, a civilian, friars, two gentleman ushers and others. He also processed into the royal court at Greenwich palace under a canopy, like a royal canopy of estate. The revels he presided over included a tourney, a drunken mask, a mock joust with hobby horses, a mock Midsummer Night festival, a variety of other masks, plays, banquets, mock combats, and hunting and hawking.
- Ferrers also played Lord of Misrule for Mary I's first Christmas.
- In 1555, Ferrers and John Prideaux accused John Dee of conjuring, casting nativities and plotting against Mary I and her husband, Philip of Spain. These accusations led to Dee's imprisonment. However, not long after, the privy council was looking for Ferrers, who lay low for a time.
- In 1569, he married his third wife, widow Margaret Preston, and they had at least five children.

- In the 1570s, he is said to have supported Mary, Queen of Scots' claim to the throne, and the Bishop of Ross, with whom he corresponded, was under the impression that Ferrers had written a work in Latin on Mary's claim.
- Ferrers wrote the words for the recitation of King Arthur's Lady of the Lake, for the entertainment for Queen Elizabeth's famous visit to Kenilworth Castle in 1575.
- Ferrers was buried on this day in 1579 at Flamstead, Hertfordshire. He died intestate.

12 January

On Thursday 12th January 1559, Queen Elizabeth I travelled by barge from Whitehall to the Tower of London to prepare for her coronation, which was scheduled for the 15th January, an auspicious date chosen by her astrologer and advisor, John Dee.

The Venetian ambassador gave an account of Elizabeth's journey along the River Thames:

"Her Majesty, being pleased to follow the example of her ancestors about the Coronation, determined to have it performed on the 15th January of this year 1559; so she left her palace of Whitehall on Thursday the 12th to go to the Tower by water. The necessary ships, galleys, brigantines, &c, were prepared as sumptuously as possible to accompany her Majesty and her Court thither by the Thames, which reminded me of Ascension Day at Venice, when the Signory go to espouse the sea.

At 2 p.m., the flood-tide then serving to pass under London Bridge, her Majesty, accompanied by many knights, barons, ladies, and by the whole Court, passing through the private corridor, embarked in her barge, which was covered with its usual tapestries, both externally and internally, and was towed by a long galley rowed by 40 men in their shirts, with a band of music, as usual when the Queen goes by water. Her Majesty having passed the bridge, in sight of the Tower, some pieces of artillery were fired; she landed at the private stairs, and, entering by a little bridge, was seen but by very few persons."

Another contemporary account can be found in Raphael Holinshed's chronicles:

"On thursday the twelf of January, the queen removeth from her palace of Westminster by water unto the tower of London, the lord mayor and aldermen in their barge, and all the citizens with their barges decked and trimmed with targets and banners of their mysteries accordingly attending on her grace.

The bachelors' barge of the lord mayor's company, to wit, the mercers had their barge with a foist trimmed with three tops, and artillery aboard, gallantly appointed to wait upon them, shooting off lustily as they went, with great and pleasant melody of instruments, which played in most sweet and heavenly manner. Her grace shut the bridge about two of the clock in the afternoon, at the still of the ebb, the lord mayor and the rest following after her barge, attending the same, till her majesty took land at the privy stairs at the tower wharf: and then the said lord mayor with the other barges returned, passing through the bridge again with the flood, and landed at the wharf of the three cranes in the Vintrie."

The Vintrie was a large wine store located in the City of London.

As was traditional during coronation celebrations, on the following day, 13th January, at the Tower of London, Elizabeth I created 11 Knights of the Bath: John Darcy, 2nd Lord Darcy of the North; John Sheffield, 2nd Lord Sheffield of Butterwick; John Darcy, 2nd Lord Darcy of Chiche; Robert Rich; Roger North; John de la Zouche of Zouche; Nicholas Poyntz; John Berkeley; Edward Unton; Henry Weston, and George Speke.

Her coronation procession through the streets of London from the Tower to Westminster took place on 14th January 1559, and then she was crowned on 15th.

13 January

On 13th January 1547, Henry Howard, Earl of Surrey, poet and soldier, and son of Thomas Howard, 3rd Duke of Norfolk, was tried for treason in front of a common inquest at Guildhall, London.

Surrey had been arrested on 2nd December 1546 after his former friend, Richard Southwell, gave evidence against him. It was alleged that on 7th October 1546 at Kenninghall, he had displayed the arms of his ancestor Edward the Confessor in his heraldry, in a shield he'd had painted, something which only the king was entitled to do, and that he had placed the arms of England in the first quarter of his shield, indicating that he had a direct claim to the crown. But as Edmond Bapst, Surrey's 19th-century biographer, points out, this last accusation was false: "Surrey had placed the royal arms in the second quarter, and had been careful to differentiate them by collaring the leopards." Southwell's information, though, was enough for Surrey's enemies to use against him. It convinced an already paranoid Henry VIII, who only had a few weeks left to live, that Surrey and his father, Norfolk, who had also been arrested, had designs on the regency.

At his trial, Surrey pleaded not guilty to the charge of high treason. Chronicler and Windsor Herald Charles Wriothesley records that Surrey "had such pleading for himself that he kept the Commissioners from nyne of the clocke in the forenoune till five of the clocke at night or he had judgment." His efforts were in vain. He was found guilty and sentenced to be "led through the city of London to the gallows at Tiborne [Tyburn], hanged, disembowelled, &c. (as usual)."

As he was a gentleman, Surrey's sentence was commuted to beheading, and he was executed on Tower Hill on 19th January 1547.

14 January

On 14th January 1589, physician Francis Kett was burnt for heresy near Norwich Castle.

Francis Kett was born around 1547 in Wymondham in Norfolk, East Anglia. He was the nephew of Robert Kett, leader of the famous Kett's Rebellion in Norfolk in the reign of Edward VI. Francis was educated at Clare College and Corpus Christi College, Cambridge, attaining his BA and MA in 1570 and 1573 respectively. He became a fellow of Corpus Christi in 1573 and was ordained as a priest. He graduated MD in 1581, and in 1585 he published his work "The Glorious and Beautiful Garland of Mans Glorification", which he dedicated to Queen Elizabeth I. In the same year, he published "An epistle to divers papistes in England, proving the Pope to be the beast in the XIII Revelations, and to be the man exalted in the temple of God, as God, (2 Thess II. 4) whereby the true Christ is knowen from the evil".

Three years later, in 1588, Edmund Scambler, Bishop of Norwich, brought Articles of heretical pravity against Francis. On 7th October 1588, the bishop wrote to William Cecil, Lord Burghley, telling him that he had "lately condemned for heresy Francis Ket, M. A. whose blasphemous opinions he had thought good to acquaint his honour with; and referring to his wisdom the speedy execution of, he being so dangerous a person." According to the articles brought by the Bishop of Norwich, Kett was accused of believing:

"That the new Covenant promised is not yet established, and that the Covenant, which you mean, is the Lawe of God written in our hearts and the forgiveness of our sinnes.

That there is no sufficient sacrifice past for the sinnes of the worlde, but that Christ shall offer it at the ende of the worlde.

That the Christ hath suffered only as Jesus allready and shall suffer hereafter as Jesus Chryste. That Chryste is now in his human nature gathering a church here in earth in Judea.

That this yeare of our Lord 1588 divers and Jewes shall be sent into dyvers countryes to publishe the new covenant.

That Chryste shall againe suffer and gyve his soule for the synne of the worlde before the last daye.

That Chryste shall comme before the ende of the world, before the last daye."

There was a further list of "blasphemous heresies of one Kett". William Burton, a minister in Norwich, also recorded that Francis believed that "Christ is not God, but a good man as others be". However, Burton added that Francis's tongue never ceased praising God, that he was always in prayer, and that "The sacred Bible almost never out of his hands".

On this day in history, 14th January 1589, Francis Kett was taken to the ditch of Norwich Castle to be burnt at the stake. The minister William Burton recorded that "when he went to the fire he was clothed in sackecloth, he went leaping and dauncing: being in the fire, above twenty times together clapping his hands, he cried nothing but blessed bee God … and so continued until the fire had consumed all his nether partes, and untill he was stifled with the smoke."

15 January

On 15th January 1569, Catherine Knollys (née Carey), wife of Sir Francis Knollys, daughter of Mary Boleyn, and cousin of Queen Elizabeth I, died at Hampton Court Palace. She was about 45 years old.

Catherine had been at court since late 1539, when she had been appointed to serve Anne of Cleves, Henry VIII's fourth wife, and she had risen to become Chief Lady of the Bedchamber in Elizabeth I's reign. She married a fellow courtier, Sir Francis Knollys, in 1540, and they had a happy and successful marriage.

In late 1568, the royal court moved to Hampton Court for Christmas, and Catherine accompanied the queen there as one of the queen's most trusted friends and ladies. However, she became seriously ill over the Christmas period. Her husband, Sir Francis Knollys, was acting as custodian of Mary, Queen of Scots, who was being held in North Yorkshire, at Bolton Castle, at the time, and he asked permission to leave his post and be with his sick wife, but the queen refused. When Catherine rallied, she asked the queen to release her so that she could travel to be with her husband, but again the queen refused, reasoning that the journey might endanger Catherine's health. Francis was angry and frustrated that he was not allowed to be with his wife, writing of the queen's "ungrateful denial of my coming to the court this Christmas". At the end of December, he wrote to his wife with the idea of them retiring to the country. Sadly, Catherine went downhill again. The queen had her moved to a chamber near her own and regularly visited her ailing cousin.

Catherine died on this day in 1569 while her husband of nearly 29 years was still in Yorkshire. It is unclear whether any of her children were with her, but her daughter, Lettice, was not at court at the time. Francis received news of his wife's death from his brother, Henry, on his arrival at Bolton on 20th January. In a letter to William Cecil, Lord Burghley, Henry wrote that Francis was "distracted with sorrow for his great loss". Francis himself wrote of the melancholy humour that "grows daily on me since my wife's death" and described his pitiful case, noting that "my wife disburdened me of many cares, kept all the monuments of my public charges, as well as my private accounts – now, my children, my servants and all other things, are loosely left without good order." It is clear, as historian Nicola Tallis points out in her book on Catherine's daughter, Lettice, that "Katherine had been the glue that held the Knollys family together."

Queen Elizabeth I was grief-stricken at the death of her cousin and friend and even became ill herself: "forgetful of her own health, she took cold, wherewith she was much troubled". Privy councillor, Nicholas White, wrote of how the queen "returned back again to talk of my Lady Knollys" and that she would "harp much upon her departure". She also admitted that "the long absence of her husband… did greatly further her end", so the queen must have also been guilt-ridden that she kept Francis and Catherine apart.

Elizabeth gave Catherine a lavish funeral at Westminster Abbey, spending £640 2s. 11d on her burial, which in today's money, is about £150,000, or over $190,000. A huge amount. Catherine was buried in the floor of St Edmund's Chapel in the abbey, and her beautiful coloured alabaster monument can be seen on the chapel wall. The four shields on it include the arms of the Knollys, Carey, Spencer, Beaufort and Boleyn families, and it also features crests of a maiden's head, bull's head, and swan.

The Latin inscription translates to read:

"O, Francis, she who was thy wife, behold, Catherine Knolle lies dead under the chilly marble. I know well that she will never depart from thy soul, though dead. Whilst alive she was always loved by thee: living, she bore thee, her husband, sixteen children, equally female and male (that is, both gentle and valiant). Would that she had lived many years with thee and thy wife was now an old lady. But God desired it not. But he willed that thou, O Catherine, should await thy husband in Heaven."

Catherine is also remembered in the Knollys Chapel of St Nicholas' Parish Church, Rotherfield Greys in Oxfordshire, where there is a Knollys family tomb with effigies of Sir Francis and Catherine Knollys.

Some people believe that Catherine may have been the daughter of King Henry VIII. However, although we know that her mother, Mary Boleyn, was the king's mistress at some point, we do not know when or for how long, and Mary was married to William Carey at the time of Catherine's birth.

16 January

On 16th January 1572, Thomas Howard, 4th Duke of Norfolk, eldest son of the late Henry Howard, Earl of Surrey, was tried and found guilty of treason at Westminster Hall.

Norfolk had been arrested and imprisoned in the Tower of London in October 1569 and questioned about his plans to marry Mary, Queen of Scots. Norfolk denied involvement in the 1569 Rising of the North, which sought to depose the queen and replace her with Mary. However, he secretly corresponded with Mary in cypher and sent her gifts at Christmas and during the summer of 1570.

In June 1570, Norfolk begged Elizabeth I's forgiveness and vowed: "never to deale in that Cause of Mariage of the Quene of Scottes, nor in any other Cause belonginge to her, but as your Majestie shall commaund me". In August 1570, he was released into house arrest at Howard House, formerly London Charterhouse, in London.

It wasn't long before he was in trouble again, having broken his promise to Elizabeth. When the Ridolfi Plot, a plot to free Mary and put her on the throne of England, came to light in 1571, it was found that Norfolk, who had initially refused to support the plot, had met with Roberto Ridolfi, a Florentine banker and papal agent, given his approval of the plot, and signed letters to the pope,

Philip of Spain, and the Duke of Alva, Philip's commander in the Netherlands. The latter was going to launch an invasion of England. Under interrogation, Norfolk's servants confessed to their involvement and implicated the duke, who was apprehended and taken to the Tower in September 1571.

In December 1571, the Grand Jury of Middlesex, headed by Norfolk's friend, Thomas Gresham as foreman, drew up an indictment against him. Norfolk was charged with "having conspired and imagined to deprive the queen of her crown and dignity, and compassed to excite sedition, to cause great slaughter amongst the queen's lieges, to levy war and rebellion against the queen, to subvert the government, to change and alter the pure religion established in the kingdom, and to bring in strangers and aliens to invade the realm, and to carry on a bitter war against the queen." The acts of treason were:

- Seeking to marry the pretender, the Queen of Scots, and sending to and receiving from her tokens, and sending money to her.
- Corresponding with the Earls of Northumberland and Westmorland and others, who were described as traitors and fugitives from justice.
- Aiding, adhering to and comforting several named Scottish lords, who were described as "enemies of England"
- And corresponding with the pope, Philip of Spain and the Duke of Alva "in order that the king of Spain might invade England and deprive the queen of her royal dignity".

On this day in 1572, Norfolk was tried at Westminster Hall by a jury of 26 of his peers, with George Talbot, Earl of Shrewsbury, acting as High Steward. Norfolk maintained his innocence, but his own admissions and the written confessions of others involved were used against him. The jury was unanimous in finding him guilty of high treason. He was sentenced to death, and on 26th January 1572, he was degraded from the Order of the Garter.

Queen Elizabeth I, however, was reluctant to sign Norfolk's death warrant – he was, after all, the highest peer of the land - and over the next few months, Norfolk took the opportunity to plead his loyalty to the queen by letter. In May 1572, Parliament pressured the queen to act against Mary, Queen of Scots, and Elizabeth finally signed Norfolk's death warrant. He was beheaded on Tower Hill on

2nd June 1572 and his remains were buried in the Chapel of St Peter ad Vincula at the Tower of London.

17 January

On 17th January 1541, courtier, diplomat and poet Sir Thomas Wyatt the Elder was arrested and sent to the Tower of London after being accused of corresponding with Cardinal Pole and referring to the prospect of Henry VIII's death.

It wasn't his first time in the Tower. He'd been imprisoned there in May 1536 after the fall of Anne Boleyn but was eventually released without charge.

But what happened in 1541?

Well, claims made by Edmund Bonner, who had been sent along with Simon Heynes to France in 1537 to help Wyatt with diplomacy there, came back to haunt Wyatt. In 1538, Bonner wrote to Thomas Cromwell claiming that Wyatt was trying to contact Cardinal Reginald Pole, the king's enemy, AND that he had also wished for the king's death, saying, "By goddes bludde, ye shall see the kinge our maister cast out at the carts tail, and if he soo be served, by godds body, he is well served", i.e. that he wanted the king hanged. At this point, nothing happened to Wyatt, but Cromwell, who acted as Wyatt's patron, kept hold of Bonner's letter.

Cromwell was executed as a traitor in July 1540, and Wyatt retired from court, probably to his family seat of Allington Castle in Kent. However, Bonner's previous claims were resurrected, and on this day in 1541, Wyatt was taken to the Tower of London. Orders were given for his plate and horses at Allington to be confiscated and his household to be dismissed. It was not looking good for him.

An oration prepared for his trial by Wyatt during his imprisonment shows that he denied verbal treason, claiming that his words about the king were simply him using a common proverb and referring to the fact that the king was going to be left out of an alliance between Francis I and the Holy Roman Emperor. Wyatt concluded, "The labour be took in the King's affairs is proof that he meant not that naughty interpretation." As for the accusation regarding Pole, he claimed that he was seeking contact with Cardinal Pole to spy on him and that the king and council knew that Wyatt wasn't a papist as they knew "the hazard he was in in Spain with the Inquisition for speaking against the bishop of Rome".

In "A declaration made by Sir Thomas Wiatt, knight, of his innocence being in the Tower upon the false accusation of Dr. Bonarde, bishop of London, made to the Council", Wyatt declared that he had "never offended" and had never communed or sent messages to "any known traitor". The letter he sent was a detailed rebuttal of the accusations against him.

Although Wyatt was evidently prepared to plead his case in court, he was never tried, and on 19th March 1541, Queen Catherine Howard interceded with her husband, the king, on Wyatt's behalf, asking for mercy. Eustace Chapuys, the imperial ambassador, recorded this in a letter to Mary of Hungary:

> "The King lately took his queen to Greenwich, and as it was the first time after her marriage that she had to pass through London by the Thames, the people of this city honored her with a most splendid reception, the Tower saluting her with salvoes of artillery. From this triumphal march the Queen took occasion and courage to beg and entreat the King for the release of Maistre Huyet (Whyat), a prisoner in the said Tower..."

The king granted his wife's petition, and Wyatt was summoned to appear before the king at Dover later that month. He was granted a full pardon and released from the Tower, but at a price. Chapuys explained what he described as "hard conditions":

> "The first of them being that the said What should confess the guilt for which he had been arrested; and, secondly, that he was to resume conjugal relations with his wife, from whom he had been separated for upwards of fifteen years. What had cast her away on account of adultery, and had not seen her for many years; he will now be obliged to receive her, and should he not do so, and not lead a conjugal life with her, or should he be found to keep up criminal relations with one or two other ladies that he has since loved, he is to suffer pain of death and confiscation of property."

Wyatt had separated from his unfaithful wife, Elizabeth Brooke, as Chapuys states, many years before and was living with his mistress, Elizabeth Darrell, the mother of his illegitimate son, Francis. He may have set Darrell aside, but he bequeathed land to her and their son when he wrote his will in June 1541.

In 1542, Wyatt was back in favour and had been restored to his office of ambassador. However, his return to favour was short-lived. He was taken ill with a fever after receiving the emperor's envoy at Falmouth, in Cornwall, on 3rd October 1542. Sir Thomas Wyatt died on the 11th October 1542 at Clifton Maybank House, the home of his friend Sir John Horsey, in Sherborne, Dorset. He was buried at Sherborne Abbey.

18 January

On 18th January 1510, eighteen-year-old King Henry VIII and twelve of his men disguised themselves as outlaws, or Robin Hood and his merry men, and surprised Queen Catherine of Aragon and her ladies. Chronicler Edward Hall records this event:

"The king soon after, came to Westminster with the Queen, and all their train: And on a time being there, his grace the Earls of Essex, Wiltshire, and other noble men, to the number of twelve, came suddenly in a morning, into the Queen's Chamber, all apparelled in short coats, of Kentish Kendal, with hoods on their heads, and hosen of the same, every one of them, his bow and arrows, and a sword and a buckler, like outlaws, or Robin Hood's men. Whereof the Queen, the Ladies, and all other there, were abashed, as well for the strange sight, as also for their sudden coming. And after certain dances and pastime made, they departed."

It sounds like it was quite a surprise for Catherine and her ladies, but one that was fun and which was followed by dancing and entertainment.

Henry VIII enjoyed this chivalric tradition of disguising, but it didn't go so well when he disguised himself to surprise his future bride, Anne of Cleves, in January 1540. Anne did not know who he was and was rather dismissive. It was a rather humiliating episode for the king. See 1ˢᵗ January entry.

19 January

On 19ᵗʰ January 1601, Henry Herbert, 2ⁿᵈ Earl of Pembroke, died at Wilton, the family home near Salisbury. He had been suffering from ill health for about five years.

Let me give you a few facts about this Tudor nobleman.

- Henry Herbert was born around 1538 and was the eldest son and heir of William Herbert, 1ˢᵗ Earl of Pembroke, and his wife, Anne Parr, sister of Queen Catherine Parr.
- He was married three times: On 25ᵗʰ May 1553, at the same ceremony that Lady Jane Grey married Lord Guildford Dudley, Herbert married Jane's sister, Lady Catherine Grey. It wasn't consummated, and just a year later, in 1554, following the fall of Lady Jane Grey, it was annulled. Herbert married Catherine Talbot, daughter of George Talbot, Earl of Shrewsbury, in 1563, but she died childless in 1576. In April 1577, Herbert married Mary Sidney, daughter of Sir Henry Sidney and sister of poets Sir Philip Sidney and Sir Robert Sidney. The couple had three surviving children: William, Philip and Anne. Mary was a literary patron, and their home of Wilton was described as "like a college".
- Herbert was made a Knight of the Bath as part of Mary I's coronation celebrations in 1553, and after Mary married Philip of Spain, he was made one of the king's gentlemen of the bedchamber.
- He served the queen in France in 1557, being present at the Siege of St Quentin with his father.
- He became Earl of Pembroke on his father's death in 1570 and became Lord Lieutenant of Wiltshire.
- In 1586, he succeeded his father-in-law, Sir Henry Sidney, as Lord President of the Council in the Welsh Marches.
- Herbert could speak Welsh.
- He could be rather rash. A messenger once refused to deliver a letter from Herbert to Queen Elizabeth I because "he found it

would be his Lord's overthrow to have so passionate a letter delivered unto the queen."

- He was a good friend of Robert Dudley, Earl of Leicester, and patron of the theatre company Pembroke's Men.
- In the 1590s, he had a feud with Robert Devereux, Earl of Essex, and his rival faction in Wales.
- He died at Wilton on this day in 1601, and although John Chamberlain wrote of him "leaving his lady as bare as he could and bestowing all on the young lord, even to her jewels", his biographer Penry Williams points out that Herbert's will shows that he left Mary substantial rents, as well as jewels and plate to the value of 3000 marks.
- Herbert was laid to rest in Salisbury Cathedral.
- A suit of armour made for Herbert by the royal workshops at Greenwich in around 1585/6 is in the collection of the Met Museum in New York. It is decorated with his coat of arms and the Order of the Garter, which he was awarded in 1574.

20 January

On 20th January 1557, Queen Mary I's pensioners "did muster in bright harnesss" before the queen at Greenwich Park.

Henry Machyn, a merchant-tailor of London, records the event in his diary:

> "The 20th day of January at Greenwich Park the queen grace('s) pensioners did muster in bright harness and many barbary horses. And every pensioner had 3 men in green coats guarded with white. So they rode about the park, 3 in rank, upon great horses with spears in their hands painted white and green, and afore rode trumpeters blowing; and next a man of arms bearing a standard of red and yellow, in the standard a white hart, and on the other side a black eagle with gilded legs. And between 2 and 3 of the clock they came down and mustered afore the Queen('s) grace afore the park gate, for there stood the Queen('s) grace on high,

and my lord cardinal, and my lord admiral, and my lord Montagu, and diverse other lords and ladies.

And so afore the pensioners rode many gentlemen on Jennets and light horses, but especially there rode one gentleman, his name is master [the name is missing], upon the least mule that ever I saw. And so they rode to and fro afore the Queen. And there came a tumbler, and played many pretty feats afore the Queen and my lord cardinal, that her grace did like heartily. And so her grace did thank them all for their pain. And so after they parted, for there were of the pensioners 50 and more, beside their men of arms; and there were of people of men and women above ten thousand and more."

But who were these pensioners assembled for the queen's inspection on this day in 1557? The Honourable Band of Gentlemen Pensioners were the monarch's personal bodyguards. They were formed in 1509 when Mary's father, Henry VIII, came to the throne. They were a mounted escort, whose job was to protect the monarch. They still exist today as Her Majesty's Body Guard of the Honourable Corps of Gentlemen at Arms. However, their duties are now only ceremonial, whereas, in Henry VIII's time, they accompanied the king into battle.

21 January

On 21ˢᵗ January 1542, a bill of attainder against Catherine Howard, Henry VIII's fifth wife, and Jane Boleyn, Lady Rochford, widow of George Boleyn, Lord Rochford, was introduced into the House of Lords. According to this bill, the women were guilty of treason and could be punished without needing a trial.

Historian Retha Warnicke points out that although the bill was introduced into Parliament on 21ˢᵗ January 1542, it was not passed. She writes that there seemed to have been "uncertainty among the judges, however, about whether the former queen's offence constituted treason", so it was read again on the 28ᵗʰ January and again postponed. It finally "received the king's assent, given in absentia by letters patent, on 11 February".

Here is an extract from the record of the attainder in the Letters and Papers of Henry VIII's reign:

"Attainder of Katharine Howard and others.— Katharine Howard whom the King took to wife is proved to have been not of pure and honest living before her marriage, and the fact that she has since taken to her service one Francis Dereham, the person with whom she "used that vicious life before," and has taken as chamberer a woman who was privy to her naughty life before, is proof of her will to return to her old abominable life. Also she has confederated with lady Jane Rocheford, widow, late wife of Sir Geo. Boleyn, late lord Rocheford, to "bring her vicious and abominable purpose to pass" with Thos. Culpeper, late one of the King's Privy Chamber, and has met Culpeper in "a secret and vile place," at 11 o'clock at night, and remained there with him until 3 a.m., with only "that bawd, the lady Jane Rocheford." For these treasons, Culpeper and Dereham have been convicted and executed, and the Queen and lady Rochford stand indicted."

The attainder went on to say that both women were "by authority of this Parliament, convicted and attainted of high treason" and that they would suffer accordingly.

As an eye-witness to the proceedings later pointed out, Catherine was not attainted for adultery but rather for her "dissolute life previous to her marriage". This bill of attainder also made it high treason for "an unchaste woman" to marry the king.

Francis Dereham and Thomas Culpeper had already been found guilty of high treason and executed at Tyburn on 10th December 1541, Culpeper being beheaded and Dereham being hanged, drawn and quartered. Catherine and Jane were beheaded at the Tower of London on 13th February 1542 and laid to rest in the Chapel of St Peter ad Vincula.

22 January

On 22nd January 1554, Thomas Wyatt the Younger, son of poet and diplomat Thomas Wyatt the Elder, met with fellow conspirators at his home of Allington Castle in Kent. Their meeting was to make final plans for their uprising against Queen Mary I and her decision to marry Philip of Spain, an uprising that would become known as Wyatt's Rebellion.

As historian Ian W. Archer explained in an article on Thomas Wyatt the Younger, "The anomalous position of a king regnant crystallized fears about how Philip might use his powers within England; the possibility that England might become another Habsburg milch cow was very real; and there was a real risk of a succession struggle on Mary's death", and even members of Mary I's privy council were concerned about the Spanish match and were putting forward Edward Courtenay, Earl of Devon, as a match.

In November 1553, Parliament had tried to dissuade the queen from her marriage plans, but she had made up her mind and wouldn't budge. Some men decided that a military coup might be the only way to prevent the marriage. On the 26th November 1553, a group of men including Wyatt, Sir Peter Carew, Sir Edward Rogers, Sir Edward Warner, Sir William Pickering, Sir Nicholas Throckmorton, Sir James Croft, Sir George Harper, Nicholas Arnold, William Thomas, and William Winter, met in London. Archer writes that the leader at this point was probably Croft and not Wyatt.

In December 1553, Henry Grey, Duke of Suffolk, father of the imprisoned former queen, Lady Jane Grey, joined the rebel group, and plans were implemented. The rebels planned a simultaneous rising in four locations on Palm Sunday, 18th March 1554. Sir Peter Carew was to lead a rising in the West Country, Sir James Croft was to lead one in Herefordshire, the Duke of Suffolk was to lead one in the Midlands, and Wyatt was to lead one in Kent. All agreed to this plan, but there were disagreements over Mary's fate. William Thomas wanted Mary assassinated, whereas others, like Wyatt, just wanted her deposed. Mary would then be replaced with her half-sister, Elizabeth, who would marry Englishman Edward Courtenay, Earl of Devon.

Unfortunately for the rebels, the privy council had got wind of trouble brewing by the end of December 1553. On 21st January 1554, Edward Courtenay told Stephen Gardiner, Bishop of Winchester and Mary I's Lord Chancellor, of the rebels' plans. This meant that the rebels were forced into action earlier than planned. While Carew was busy spreading dissent in Devon, Wyatt called a meeting at Allington Castle on this day in 1554 to organise the Kent part of the rebellion. Three days later, on 25th January 1554, Wyatt raised his standard in the town of Maidstone, while his fellow Kentish rebels proclaimed for the rebellion in Rochester, Tonbridge, Malling and Milton.

On 28th January, the government sent 600 men from London to Kent under the leadership of Thomas Howard, 3rd Duke of Norfolk. It wasn't enough. Wyatt's forces far outnumbered them, and many men mutinied, joining the rebel cause. On 30th January, Wyatt and his men besieged Cooling Castle, owned by George Brooke, 9th Baron Cobham, who had withdrawn to his castle after the Duke of Norfolk's forces had mutinied and dispersed. According to historian C S Knighton, Cobham claimed that he had fought valiantly against the rebels for seven hours before surrendering to them. Still, Knighton points out that his resistance was actually a "pretence" and he joined the rebels willingly. At this point, things were looking very good for Wyatt and his men, who then marched on to London.

On 1st February 1554, Mary I gave a rousing speech at Guildhall in London to rally Londoners to her cause. When Wyatt and his men reached London on 3rd February, they found the City guarded and barricaded. Wyatt changed his plan, moving from Southwark to Kingston, and successfully entered Kingston on 6th February. But there, he encountered problems: the bridge over the Thames needed repairing before it could be crossed, and his siege artillery became bogged down and had to be abandoned. Archer writes, "Some observers doubted the loyalty of the queen's commanders, as they apparently let Wyatt advance unmolested", but Wyatt was left alone because he was being "lured into a trap". By the time Wyatt and his troops reached Ludgate, Mary's force had barred the gates, and the rebels were forced into turning around and heading to Temple Bar, where Mary's troops were waiting for them. With his men surrendering and swearing allegiance to the queen, Wyatt was forced to surrender, and he was arrested by Sir Maurice Berkeley and taken to the Tower of London.

On 15th March 1554, Thomas Wyatt the Younger was tried for high treason at Westminster Hall. He denied plotting the assassination of Mary I and refused to implicate Mary's half-sister, Elizabeth. He was found guilty of treason and was executed by beheading on 11th April 1554. His body was quartered before his head and body parts were taken to Newgate, where they were parboiled. His body parts were nailed up around the city, and his head was placed on a gibbet at St James's. It is not known what happened to his head, as it was subsequently stolen from the gibbet.

On 18th March 1554, Mary I's half-sister, Elizabeth, was escorted to the Tower of London and imprisoned there while Mary's council tried to implicate her in the rebellion. Fortunately, they couldn't, and she was released in May 1554. However, Lady Jane Grey, whose father had been involved in Wyatt's Rebellion, was not so lucky. Jane and her husband Guildford Dudley were executed on 12th February 1554. Her father was executed on the 23rd February 1554.

23 January

On 23rd January 1516, King Ferdinand II of Aragon died in Madrigalejo, Extremadura. He was laid to rest in La Capilla Real, the Royal Chapel of Granada.

Ferdinand was the husband of Isabella I of Castile and, of course, the father of Catherine of Aragon, Henry VIII's first wife. Ferdinand was succeeded by his daughter, Juana (Joanna), who ruled jointly with her son, Charles, or Carlos, who became King Charles I of Spain. This same Charles would become Charles V, Holy Roman Emperor, in 1519.

Here are some facts about the Capilla Real, Isabella and Ferdinand:

- Granada became part of the Kingdom of Castile under Ferdinand and Isabella.
- Isabella and Ferdinand are known for uniting all Spanish states under one monarchy and linking Spain to Portugal, England and Austria through arranged marriages.
- The conquest of Granada in 1492 and the defeat of the Moors by Isabella and Ferdinand led to the expeditions of Christopher Columbus, which, in turn, opened up the New World. This is

why 1492 is seen as the start of the beginning of the Modern Era in history.

- The Capilla Real was founded as the mausoleum of Ferdinand and Isabella by Royal Warrant on 13th September 1504. Construction began in 1506, and the chapel was completed in 1517.
- The tomb of Ferdinand and Isabella was sculpted in 1517 by Italian Domenico Fancelli. Bartolomé Ordóñez was responsible for the tombs of Juana and Felipe, which date to 1520.
- The sacristy museum houses the Royal Warrant commissioning the chapel's building, tapestries, Isabella's crown and sceptre, Ferdinand's sword, liturgical items and personal items belonging to Isabella (Gothic altar cross, chalice, peace-offering, chalice, girdle, rosary and mirror). The Queen's Missal, a work on vellum by Francisco Flores (1496), is also on display, as is a statue of St Catherine.
- The Capilla is home to a collection of paintings which once belonged to Isabella. Artists include Botticelli, Perugino, Berrugueti and Bermejo.
- Jacob Florentino made the Passion Altarpiece in 1521, and on each side of it are carvings by Felipe Vigarny of Ferdinand and Isabella kneeling in prayer.
- The outside of the Capilla features crests with the repeated letters of "F" and "Y" for Ferdinand and Isabella/Ysabel.
- The Capilla is still a place of worship where the Eucharist is celebrated daily.

24 January

On 24th January 1555, in the reign of Queen Mary I, a great joust was held at Westminster between English and the Spanish knights.

Merchant-tailor and citizen of London Henry Machyn recorded it in his diary, writing, "The 24th day of January there were great running at the tylt at Westmynster with spears, both English men and Spaniards."

There were Spaniards there because Queen Mary I had married Philip of Spain, son of Charles V, Holy Roman Emperor, in July 1554. Philip had brought Spaniards over to England with him.

Philip was a keen sportsman, but he also, as historian David Loades pointed out in his book "Intrigue and Treason: The Tudor Court, 1547-1558", wanted to build bridges between his Spanish household and the English aristocracy, particularly as there was some anti-Spanish feeling in London at the time and trouble between Spaniards and Englishmen. Mary may have rallied the citizens of London against Wyatt and his men earlier that year, but that didn't mean that her marriage to Philip was popular with her people and courtiers. Machyn recorded in his diary that on 26th October, a Spaniard was hanged at Charing Cross for killing a servant of Sir George Gifford by Temple Bar. On 4th November 1554, there was "a great fray at Charing Cross at 8 of the clock at night between the Spaniards and Englishmen, the which through wisdom there were but a fewe hurt".

What better way to bring Spaniards and English courtiers together than sports like jousting?

On 18th December 1554, Machyn recorded that there

> "was a grett tryhumph at the court gatte, by the Kyng and dyvers lordes boyth English-men and Spaneards, the wyche the Kyng and his compene [were] in goodly harnes, and a-pon ther armes goodly jerkyns of bluw velvett, and hosse in-brodered with sylver and bluw sarsenett; and so thay rane on fott with spayrers and swerds at the tornay, and with dromes and flutes in whyt velvet [drawn] owt with blu sarsenett, and ther wher x aganst [the King] and ys compene, the wher xviij in odur colers."

But there was more trouble to come. On New Year's Day 1555, some "insolent and drunk Spaniards" caused "great uproar" with some whores in the cloisters of Westminster Abbey. They'd left other Spaniards guarding the passageway while they had fun, and there was violence when the dean's men encountered them. John Strype records, "some of the Dean's men happened now to come into the cloister, at whom these Spaniards discharged their pistols, and wounded some of them: whereat began a fray. A Spanish friar gets presently into the church, and rings the bell for alarm. This called all the street together, and much blood had like to have been spilt. But the tumult at length ceased, and no more harm done than the great fright and disturbance which it occasioned." But eight days later, Henry Machyn recorded that "certain Spaniards killed an Englishman basely: two held him while one thrust him through, and so he died."

So, the 24th January jousts were important for bringing the two sides together. David Loades also notes that Philip "honoured the nuptials of one of his English chamberlones, Lord Strange, with a tournament, banquet, masque and juego de cañas", in which he participated. This was a diplomatic move from Philip, showing that he was making an effort with the English courtiers. "Juego de cañas", or game of canes, appears to be a sport where teams on horseback threw cane javelins at each other. The riders had to dodge or deflect these javelins. A bit different to jousting.

Philip himself was also recorded as running at the tilt against other Spaniards on the 19th March, probably practising for the big joust organised for Lady Day, 25th March, which Machyn also recorded:

> "The 25 day of Marche, the which was our lady [day,] there was as great jousts as you have seen at the tilt at Westmynster; the challengers was a Spaniard and Sir George Howard; and all their men, and their horses trimmed in white, and then came the King and a great many all in blue, and trimmed with yellow, and their helmets with great tufts of blue and yellow feather, and all their whifflers and their footmen, and their armorers, and a company like Turks rode in crimson satin gowns and capes, and with falchions, and great targets; and some in green, and many of diverse colours; and there was broken 200 staffs and above."

It must have been a wonderful sight.

So English and Spanish relations could be difficult at times, but it appears that Philip of Spain tried his best to bring the two sides together in fun events.

25 January

On 25th January 1540, St Edmund Campion, Jesuit and martyr, was born in London.

Campion was hanged, drawn and quartered on 1st December 1581 for treasonable conspiracy. He was beatified in 1886 by Pope Leo XIII and canonized in 1970 by Pope Paul VI.

Let me tell you a bit more about this Catholic martyr.

- Campion was the son of a London bookseller.
- On 3rd August 1553, when the queen, Mary I, made her official entry into the city of London and stopped near St Paul's School, it was St Paul's pupil, thirteen-year-old Campion who made an oration to her. His oration was well received by the listening crowd and the queen herself.
- Before St Paul's, Campion had been educated at Christ's Hospital. In 1558, under the patronage of the Grocers' Company, he entered St John's College, Oxford, where he studied philosophy and theology, attaining a BA and then, in 1564, an MA.
- In 1560, when he was twenty, Campion delivered an oration in English at the funeral of Amy Dudley, wife of Robert Dudley, Earl of Leicester, and then, in 1567, an oration in Latin at the funeral of Sir Thomas White.
- At Queen Elizabeth I's visit to Oxford in August 1566, Campion welcomed her and participated in a debate in front of her and the university chancellor. His eloquence impressed Robert Dudley, who became his patron.
- In 1569, Campion was ordained as a deacon and given a living in Gloucestershire by Richard Cheyney, Bishop of Gloucester, who became good friends with Campion.
- Even though Campion was close to the Earl of Leicester and William Cecil, Baron Burghley, it appears that he'd taken the oath of supremacy against his conscience and conformed only so he could enjoy public speaking.
- In August 1570, troubled by his conscience, Campion left England for Ireland, going to Dublin at the invitation of his student Richard Stanihurst's father, James Stanihurst, speaker

of the Irish House of Commons and Recorder of Dublin. In Dublin, Campion worked on two books, "De homine academic" and his "History of Ireland", which he dedicated to the Earl of Leicester.

- Campion's now Catholic faith became a danger to him following the pope's excommunication of Elizabeth I in 1570, so he was smuggled out of Dublin by the Stanihursts. In 1571, he was smuggled into England, disguised as one of the Earl of Kildare's steward's servants.

- From England, Campion tried to flee into exile on the Continent but was captured on his way across the Channel. A second try saw him successfully making it across and entering the English College at Douai. He recanted his Protestant faith, became ordained as a subdeacon, and attained his Bachelor of Theology there in 1572. He also taught rhetoric there.

- In 1573, he left Douai for Rome to become a Jesuit novice. He then served in Moravia and Prague, teaching philosophy and rhetoric. In 1578, while still in Prague, he was ordained deacon and priest, and he also wrote Latin dramas that were performed at the imperial court.

- In December 1579, he was recalled from Prague to Rome by William Allen. In March 1580, Allen chose Campion to serve on a mission, with Father Robert Persons, in England to convert English people to the true faith.

- On 24th June 1580, Campion arrived in England, disguised as a jewel merchant. He was with fellow Jesuit Ralph Emerson. Persons had travelled separately. Campion and Emerson were apprehended at Dover and taken before the mayor, who then released them. They then made their way to London, where Person's friend, George Gilbert, sheltered them. Just a few days later, Campion preached at Smithfield at the invitation of devout Catholic Thomas, Lord Paget. The Jesuits then moved to Hoxton, where Campion wrote his "Challenge to the Privy Council", also known as his Brag. His biographer, Michael A R Graves, writes that this "was a challenge to debate religion with councillors, university scholars, and lawyers, confident that 'no one Protestant nor all the Protestants living … can maintain their doctrine in disputation'". Thomas Pound, a Catholic on parole, printed and circulated copies of it, and prominent Protestants called Campion a traitor.

- In August 1580, Campion left London, travelling through Berkshire, Oxfordshire, Northamptonshire, then later, Nottinghamshire, Derbyshire, Yorkshire and Lancashire, preaching, ministering to Catholics and writing his "Rationes Decem", or ten reasons, which presented the Catholic case against the Anglican Church. He completed it in March 1581, and it was published by Persons on his own press at Stonor Park, Oxford, and abroad.

- On 17th July 1581, Campion, two other priests and seven laymen were arrested at Lyford Grange in Berkshire, home of Edward Yates, after they were betrayed by Catholic informer George Eliot. They were taken to London, Campion being forced to wear a hat inscribed "The Seditious Jesuit". On arrival at the Tower of London, Campion was put in the Little Ease, a cell beneath the White Tower so-called because its size prevented a person from being able to stand, sit, or lie down. It is said that Campion spent four days in it, which must have been truly awful.

- Campion was then escorted by river to the home of Lord Chancellor Thomas Bromley to be questioned by him, the Earl of Leicester and Sir Christopher Hatton. Campion refused to answer the men's questions, so the privy council ordered a further examination and, if Campion still refused, the use of the rack. Campion was racked during his interrogations which took place over three months, and the Venetian and Spanish ambassadors recorded that he was also tortured by having iron spikes driven "between the nails and the quick". It is little wonder that at his trial in November 1581, Campion had to be helped to raise his hand to make his plea.

- In her excellent book "God's Traitors", Jessie Childs explains that during the interrogations, Campion stayed firm to his Catholic faith and refused to say where he said Mass or provide the government with any new information. Childs notes, however, that he confessed in a letter to Thomas Pounde, giving his interrogators the names of those who had sheltered him.

- Campion was tried with seven other priests at Westminster Hall on 20th November 1581. Campion defended himself so well that it was expected that the jury would acquit him. Campion declared that it was not treason for him and the other priests to adhere to their faith and that they were still the queen's loyal subjects, but they were willing to die for their faith if it came to it. The jury found Campion and his fellow priests guilty of treason, and as Sir Christopher Wray, Lord Chief Justice, condemned them to be hanged, drawn and quartered, Campion began singing the Te Deum and his fellow priests joined in.

- On 1st December 1581, forty-one-year-old Campion and priests Ralph Sherwin and Alexander Briant were drawn on hurdles to Tyburn for execution. Campion begged the forgiveness of those he had named during his interrogations, saying that he had only named them after being promised that no harm would come to them. He kept being interrupted by Sir Francis Knollys, who questioned him on his opinions on the pope's bull of excommunication against the queen and his loyalty to the pope. Thomas Alfield, a Catholic present at Campion's execution, recorded that he "was asked for which queen he prayed ... [H]e answered, yea for Elizabeth your queen and my queen ... And so he meekly and sweetly yielded his soul unto his Saviour, protesting that he died a perfect catholic."

- Campion's feast day is celebrated on 1st December, and the rope that tied Campion to the hurdle that dragged him from the Tower to Tyburn is used in Campion Day masses said on his feast day at St Peter's Church, Stonyhurst College. Pupils also sing the Te Deum. An order of service from the Stonyhurst College website explains that a Catholic bribed the executioner into selling the rope and that it was later presented to Father Robert Persons, who wore it around his waist for the rest of his life. The rope, along with a corporal used in the Tower by five martyred priests, is placed on the high altar of the chapel at the college on 1st December each year.

- In the order of service is this quote from Campion's "Challenge to the Privy Council": "And touching our Society, be it known to you that we have made a league - all the Jesuits in the world, whose succession and multitude must overreach all the practices of England - cheerfully to carry the cross you shall lay upon us, and never to despair your recovery, while we have a man left to enjoy your Tyburn, or to be racked with your torments, or consumed with your prisons. The expense is reckoned, the enterprise is begun; it is of God, it cannot be withstood. So the Faith was planted: so it must be restored."

26 January

On 26th January 1554, Queen Mary I wrote to her half-sister, the future Elizabeth I, summoning her to court and warning her about Wyatt's Rebellion. Elizabeth did not obey the summons, pleading illness as an excuse.

But why? What was all this about?

Let me give you some background.

In 1553, after coming to the throne of England, Mary I decided to marry Philip of Spain, her cousin Charles V's son. Parliament had tried to dissuade Mary from her marriage plans, knowing that an alliance with the man who would become King of Spain and rule both countries would not be popular with everyone, but Mary was determined to go ahead. In late November 1553, a group of men decided that a military coup was the only way of stopping Mary from marrying Philip. Unfortunately for the conspirators of Wyatt's Rebellion, by the end of December, rumours that trouble was brewing had reached Mary's privy council, and in January 1554, Edward Courtenay spilt the beans to Stephen Gardiner, Bishop of Winchester.

On 26th January, the day after the rebels had raised their standards, Mary wrote to Elizabeth, who was away from court at Ashridge. Elizabeth was, of course, implicated in this plot as the rebels sought to put her on the throne, but Mary didn't openly accuse Elizabeth. She told her of the rebellion and asked her to come to court, saying it was for her protection. Elizabeth must have been worried, and she replied straight away. Here is an excerpt from a record of her letter from the Calendar of State Papers, Spain:

"Although by neglect of my duty, most noble Queen, I might incur blame for not having sent your Highness any news of my doings since I left your Court, yet I trust that your Grace, of your noble nature and inclination, will excuse me and attribute this shortcoming to its true causes. I have been troubled, since my arrival at my house, with such a cold and headache that I have never felt their like, and especially during the last three weeks I have had no respite because of the pain in my head and also in my arms. I have several times had occasion to offer your Highness my humble thanks for having sent to inquire after my health and for the plate that you gave me, but I now have a still more pressing call to do so, for you have been pleased not only to write me a letter with your own hand, which I know is tedious to you, but also to tell me of the conclusion of your marriage and of the articles to accompany it. This is a deep and weighty matter, but I have no doubt that it will redound to the glory of God, the repose of your Majesty and the safety and preservation of your kingdoms."

She finished by saying:

"And as I know of no one more bound by duty and inclination to wish your Highness all prosperity, than myself, so no one shall be found, though comparisons be odious, more ready to pray God for you or more desirous of your greatness.

And so, Madam, fearing to importune your Majesty, I will consign you to the Creator's keeping and make an end to this letter."

Elizabeth was excusing herself from appearing at court due to illness. She just couldn't travel. Mary sent the royal physicians to check Elizabeth's story, and they found her ill in bed.

As Elizabeth kept a low profile at Ashridge, Mary rallied her troops. The rebellion known as Wyatt's Revolt was a complete failure, and Mary was victorious. Although Wyatt refused to implicate

Elizabeth in any way, Elizabeth, who was still pleading sickness, was forced to travel to London after Mary sent three of her councillors to escort her. She was taken to Whitehall Palace, where she stayed until Palm Sunday, 18th March 1554, when she was taken to the Tower of London.

Wyatt was executed on the 11th April 1554, after giving a rousing speech proclaiming Elizabeth's innocence. Elizabeth was interrogated several times but stuck to her story, i.e. that she was innocent. On 19th May 1554, just over two months after she'd entered the Tower confines and on the anniversary of her mother Anne Boleyn's execution, Elizabeth was released into house arrest. She may have got away with her life, but her half-sister didn't trust her.

27 January

On 27th January 1556, in the reign of Queen Mary I, Protestant Bartholomew or Bartlet Green was burnt at the stake at Smithfield with six other Protestants. Green, who martyrologist John Foxe describes as a gentleman and lawyer, "saw the true light of God's gospel" when listening to lectures given by Peter the Martyr while studying at Oxford. Foxe writes, "Whereof when he had once tasted, it became unto him as the fountain of lively water, that our Saviour Christ spake of to the woman of Samaria, so as he never thirsted any more, but had a well springing unto everlasting life". Green studied law at the Inner Temple in London.

At Easter 1554, Green received communion according to the Protestant rites of the late King Edward VI's reign at the home of John Pullain, rector of St Peter Cornhill, with his friend, Christopher Goodman, who was just about to leave England to go into exile. He did it a second time with Michael Renniger, and continued celebrating this way and refusing to attend the Catholic mass or confession. As his biographer Thomas S Freeman points out, he might have got away with this if it hadn't been for the fact that he appears to have been behind the circulation of a bill in 1555 which was smuggled into London from the Continent. It denounced Philip of Spain and Mary I and supported Elizabeth. Also, in a letter to his friend, Goodman, he reported, "the queen is not yet dead", which could be twisted to be treasonous.

Green was apprehended and imprisoned in the Fleet and then in the Tower of London, and when a charge of treason could not stand up, he was questioned on matters concerning religion. In his confession, he confessed to not attending mass and receiving both the bread and wine. He denied the real presence in the Eucharist, saying that he "received material bread and material wine, no substance thereof changed, and so no real presence of the body and blood of Christ there being, but only grace added thereto". This was heresy.

While he was examined by Edmund Bonner, Bishop of London, he was held at the bishop's palace, sharing a room with John Dee and being treated well, so well, in fact, that it was rumoured that he'd recanted. He didn't recant, though, not even when his grandfather tried to bribe him with a large amount of money. On 15th January 1556, after an examination by Bishop Bonner and John Feckenham, Abbot of Westminster, Green was found guilty of heresy and condemned to death. He was taken to Newgate to await his death. There, he was visited by friends including William Fleetwood and Thomas Hussey.

On 27th January 1556, he was taken to Smithfield with priest Thomas Whittle, artificers John Tudson and John Went, Thomas Browne, Isabel Foster and Joan Warne or Lashford. Merchant-tailor and diarist Henry Machyn recorded that "they were all burned by nine at 3 posts; and there were a commandment through London overnight that no young folk should come there, for there the greatest number was as has been seen at such a time." Foxe writes of how they were burnt on one fire and that they "went most cheerfully unto the place of their torments, often repeating, as well by the way, as also at the stake, these verses following:

O Christ, my God, sure hope of health, besides thee
have I none:
The truth I love, and falsehood hate, be thou my Guide
alone."

And that was the end of Bartholomew Green.

28 January

On 28th January 1598, diplomat Edward Barton died of dysentery on the island of Heybeli Ada, in the Sea of Marmara, off the coast of Istanbul. He was buried on the island in the Christian cemetery.

Barton was just thirty-five years old at his death but had had quite a career. He worked his way up from serving merchant and ambassador William Harborne, as his assistant and secretary, in Istanbul, known as Constantinople then, when Harborne was working there as an agent of the Turkey Company of Merchants and first English ambassador, to succeeding Harborne in both those positions when Harborne left in 1588. Although he'd been recognised as ambassador by the Ottoman Empire from 1588, it took until 1593 for him to be officially granted the title of ambassador by Elizabeth I. His biographer, Christine Woodhead, explains that the delay was "caused largely by the necessity to send a suitably expensive present (on this occasion mainly of garments and lengths of cloth) without which it was unlikely that his official credentials would be favourably received."

Barton was very useful in Turkey, more useful than many other agents sent there, because he could speak Turkish and deal directly with the Ottomans.

Elizabeth I had a very positive relationship with the Ottoman Empire, and this alliance was sensible following her excommunication from the Catholic Church, which isolated her from Catholic Europe. Her excommunication also freed her and English merchants from the pope's ban from trading with what he called the Infidel. As Jerry Brotton, author of "This Orient Isle: Elizabethan England and the Islamic World", points out, the Ottoman Empire was a 16th-century global superpower, which, like Elizabeth, had been condemned as heretical by the papacy. In 1578, Elizabeth I's advisor and spymaster, Sir Francis Walsingham, recommended Elizabeth send a merchant to also act in an ambassadorial role to Constantinople. That man was William Harborne, Edward Barton's boss, and he was sent to Turkey in 1579.

Here are a few facts about diplomacy between Elizabeth I and the Ottomans at this time:

- Harborne's first mission was to help set up trading between Turkey and England, and in 1581, Elizabeth gave royal assent to the Levant Company, or Turkey Company, to do this.
- Historian Jerry Brotton explains that William Harborne and his men, like Edward Barton, were accepted in Turkey by the Ottomans as "dhimmi ('zimmi'), protected guests who paid a tax to remain unmolested in Muslim territory."
- Much to Spain's fury, England shipped cloth for soldiers' uniforms and scrap tin and lead taken from the roofs and bells of deconsecrated Catholic churches and monasteries to Constantinople, where it was then turned into munitions. The Ottomans used these in their wars against Spain and the Shia Persian Empire. In return, she received spices, pistachio nuts, currants, Turkish carpets, ceramics, damasks, and embroideries. Elizabeth did the same with the Barbary States, swapping metals for gold and sugar, and with Morocco, she sent ship timbers in exchange for saltpetre.
- Between 1585 and 1587, Sir Francis Walsingham wanted Harborne to persuade the Sultan to attack the Spanish fleet in the Mediterranean to try and prevent them from attacking England. They didn't do this, but Harborne's diplomacy did prevent a peace treaty between the Ottomans and Spain.
- Elizabeth I had a good relationship with Sultan Murad III throughout the 1580s, and it was also a political alliance. Both of them saw Spain as the enemy, with Elizabeth seeing Spaniards as idolatrous Catholics who falsely professed the name of Christ, and feeling that she had more in common with the Ottomans. The Sultan called her Sultana Isabel and viewed England's Protestantism as "the most sound religion" in Christianity. Elizabeth sent him an elaborate mechanical clock "beset with jewels". Above it "was a forest of trees of silver, among which were deer chased with dogs, and men on horseback following, men drawing water, others carrying mine ore in barrows: on top of the clock stood a castle, and on the castle a mill. All these were of silver."
- In 1588, Edward Barton encouraged the queen to correspond with, and send gifts to, Walide Safiye, the Sultana,

which she did from 1593. The first gifts were "a jewel of her majestie's picture, set with some rubies and diamants, 3 great pieces of gilt plate, 10 garments of cloth of gold, a very fine case of glass bottles silver and gilt, with 2 pieces of fine Holland." The Sultana reciprocated with a gown of cloth of gold, an undergown of cloth of silver, and a girdle of Turkish work. Elizabeth continued corresponding with her after Murad's death, when Walide's son became Sultan. Later gifts from Elizabeth included a clockwork musical organ and a beautiful carriage.

- By the 1580s, as well as having Harborne and Barton in Turkey, Elizabeth had consuls throughout the Middle East and North Africa.
- Barton's boss, William Harborne, signed the first English alliance with the Sultan, known as the Capitulations. This alliance remained in place until 1922 when the Ottoman Empire fell. According to the terms of this alliance, English merchants could trade freely throughout Ottoman territories.
- Jerry Brotton notes that in the late 16th and early 17th-century, 62 plays contained Islamic characters, themes or settings due to England's links with the Muslim world, including William Shakespeare's Othello, The Merchant of Venice, and Titus Andronicus.

I love how pragmatic Elizabeth I could be and how she turned her excommunication into a positive. They do say that the enemy of your enemy is your friend, and it was so true in this instance. It may have been a beneficial relationship in terms of trade and politics, but it was also a relationship of mutual respect.

29 January

On 29th January 1536, the same day that her predecessor, Catherine of Aragon, was laid to rest at Peterborough Abbey, Queen Anne Boleyn, second wife of King Henry VIII, suffered a miscarriage.

Eustace Chapuys, the imperial ambassador, reported the miscarriage to his master, Charles V:

"On the day of the interment the Concubine had an abortion which seemed to be a male child which she had not borne 3½ months, at which the King has shown great distress. The said concubine wished to lay the blame on the duke of Norfolk, whom she hates, saying he frightened her by bringing the news of the fall the King had six days before. But it is well known that is not the cause, for it was told her in a way that she should not be alarmed or attach much importance to it. Some think it was owing to her own incapacity to bear children, others to a fear that the King would treat her like the late Queen, especially considering the treatment shown to a lady of the Court, named Mistress Semel, to whom, as many say, he has lately made great presents."

The Mistress Semel referred to by Chapuys here is, of course, Jane Seymour.

On 25th February, Chapuys mentioned the miscarriage again:

"I learn from several persons of this Court that for more than three months this King has not spoken ten times to the Concubine, and that when she miscarried he scarcely said anything to her, except that he saw clearly that God did not wish to give him male children; and in leaving her he told her, as if for spite, that he would speak to her after she was "releuize." The said Concubine attributed the misfortune to two causes: first, the King's fall; and, secondly, that the love she bore him was far greater than that of the late Queen, so that her heart broke when she saw that he loved others. At which remark the King was much grieved, and has shown his feeling by the fact that during these festive days he is here, and has left the other at Greenwich, when formerly he could not leave her for an hour."

Catholic recusant Nicholas Sander, while in exile during Elizabeth I's reign, wrote of how Anne Boleyn blamed her miscarriage on catching the king with Jane Seymour on his lap, and "The Life of Jane Dormer", who served as lady-in-waiting to Queen Mary I, which was described as being transcribed from an ancient manuscript, recorded that "there was often much scratching and bye-blows between the queen and her maid."

Nicholas Sander also wrote that the foetus Anne miscarried was a shapeless mass of flesh, giving rise to the idea that Anne had miscarried a "monster". However, there is no contemporary evidence to support this idea.

30 January

On 30th January 1520, in the reign of King Henry VIII, member of Parliament, Protestant, landowner and administrator Sir William More was born.

More was the only surviving son of Sir Christopher More of Loseley, a powerful administrator in Henry VII's reign, and his wife, Margaret Mudge.

The Protestant More came to the forefront in the reign of Queen Elizabeth I, serving her as Constable of Farnham Castle, Treasurer of the Lottery, Commissioner for Ecclesiastical Causes, Collector of the Loan, Chamberlain of the Exchequer, Master of Swans and Deputy Custos Rotulorum. He was also a commissioner on various commissions of oyer and terminer during her reign.

More was a member of Parliament for Reigate in 1547, Guildford in Mary I's reign, and then Grantham, Surrey and Guildford in Elizabeth I's reign.

More was married twice, first to Mabel Digneley of the Isle of Wight, and then to Margaret Daniel of Swaffham in Norfolk, with whom he had a son and two daughters. His daughter, Elizabeth, served Elizabeth I as one of her ladies.

More was close friends with William Cecil, Lord Burghley, the Earl of Leicester, the 1st Earl of Lincoln, and the queen herself. More's son-in-law, who was the queen's Latin secretary, told More that the queen "fell in speech of you, with great good liking and commendation, willing me to send you word that she did perceive that where the young sort of men, wanting experience and trust, did forget their duties, such old servants as you are would remember themselves."

More was also close to Sir Thomas Cawarden, a man involved in Wyatt's Rebellion in 1554.

Between 1562 and 1568, More built Loseley House using stone from Waverley Abbey, and the queen stayed there on several occasions. She knighted More in 1576.

More was taken ill suddenly in 1594, causing his daughter, Elizabeth, to leave her duties at court, and he never recovered properly. He died on 20th July 1600 and was laid to rest at the Loseley Chapel at St Nicholas's Church, Guildford. An epitaph there includes the words "evermore a zealous professor of true religion, and a favourer of all those ... truly ... religious, spending his days in the service of our late sovereign of blessed memory, Queen Elizabeth, in whose favour he lived and died ..." His heir was his son, George, who became chancellor of the Order of the Garter and Lieutenant of the Tower of London. He was also survived by his daughters Elizabeth and Anne.

31 January

31st January 1547 was the day Henry VIII's Lord Chancellor, Thomas Wriothesley, announced the death of Henry VIII to Parliament. The king had died on 28th January.

Chronicler and Windsor Herald Charles Wriothesley records the late king's nine-year-old son, Edward, being officially proclaimed king:

"Imediatlie the said lordes in their ordre, with Garter, the King of Haroldes [heralds], and other, in their cote armors, came out of the Perliament Chambre into the Palace of Westminster Hall with a trumpett, and their proclamation was made by the said Garter under the Kinges brode seale. Edward the Sixth, sonne and heire of our late Soveraigne Lord, to be King of this realme of England, France, and Ireland, Defendour of the Faith, &c., and of the churches of England and also of Ireland the Supream Head, ymediatlie under God, on earth.

Also that daie, at tenne of the clocke, the major and aldermen assembled in the Guildhall in their skarlett gownes, and Clarentius, one of the kinges of haroldes, with tow other haroldes and a trumpeter, and so rode from thence with my lord major and aldermen to Sainct Magnus Church corner, where proclamation was made by Clarentius, after the blowing of the trumpett tow tymes, under the Kinges broade seale, Edwarde the Sixth, with the death also of Henry the Eight, the Kinges Majestys father, and so from thence they rode in order to Leaden Hall [by] the Standard in Cheepe to the conduite in Fleet Streete, where also the said proclamation was made."

The crown had been successfully passed to the king's son, but the instructions given in Henry VIII's will regarding 16 executors acting as a council of equals to help his son reign until his majority, were not followed. Edward's uncle, Edward Seymour, became Lord Protector and Governor of the King's Majesty, instead.

1 February

On 1st February 1587, Queen Elizabeth I called her secretary, William Davison, to her and asked him to bring her the death warrant of Mary, Queen of Scots. She then signed it.

Mary, Queen of Scots, was tried in October 1586 for her involvement in the Babington Plot, a plot to assassinate Queen Elizabeth I and replace her with Mary as queen. As the trial closed, Mary demanded that she should be heard in front of Parliament or the Queen, but she was fighting a losing battle. Sentencing was delayed as long as possible by order of Elizabeth, but on 25th October, the commission reconvened and found Mary guilty. On 29th October, Parliament met to discuss Mary, the Babington Plot and her role in the murder of her second husband, Henry Stuart, Lord Darnley. Parliament decided that they should petition Elizabeth to execute Mary. This put Elizabeth in a difficult position. Mary was family, being descended from Margaret Tudor, Elizabeth's aunt, and she was a fellow monarch. Elizabeth did not want to be accused of regicide. On 4th December, Mary was publicly proclaimed guilty.

On this day in 1587, Elizabeth signed Mary's death warrant. Still, she told William Davison to ask her spymaster Sir Francis Walsingham to write to Sir Amyas Paulet, Mary's gaoler, in his own name, asking him to kill Mary. This would enable Elizabeth to be rid of Mary without taking any responsibility for her death. Instead, Paulet would be acting privately under the Bond of Association. Historian John Guy describes the Bond of Association as "a licence to kill". Anyone signing the Bond, which was drawn up by Walsingham and William Cecil, Lord Burghley, in 1584 after the 1583 Throckmorton plot, was swearing to "pursue as well by force of arms as by all other means of revenge" anyone plotting to cause harm to the queen.

Paulet was understandably horrified, protesting, "God forbid that I should make so foul a shipwreck of my conscience." Meanwhile, Cecil called a secret meeting of Elizabeth's Privy Council, and they agreed to send the signed warrant to Fotheringhay Castle, where Mary was being held. Cecil appointed the Earls of Shrewsbury and Kent to direct the execution, and the council agreed to keep Elizabeth in the dark until the deed was done.

On 8th February 1587, Mary Queen of Scots was executed at Fotheringhay. Although Elizabeth was furious with her council, so much so that Cecil fled to his home and Davison was thrown into the Tower, John Guy points out that whatever happened to Mary, whether she was assassinated or executed, Elizabeth could deny any responsibility: "She had carefully contrived things so that she would win whatever happened. If Mary was killed under the Bond of Association, Elizabeth could disclaim responsibility. If Cecil covertly sealed the warrant and sent it to Fotheringhay behind her back, she could claim she had been the victim of a court conspiracy." Clever.

We'll never know the truth of what happened, but Elizabeth was finally free of her enemy.

2 February

On 2nd February 1508, in the reign of King Henry VII, physician and provost of King's College, Cambridge, John Argentine died at King's College. He was about sixty-five years of age at his death. He was laid to rest in the Chantry Chapel at the college.

Cambridgeshire man Argentine was educated at Eton and King's College, Cambridge, studying theology, before spending three years studying medicine in Italy. On his return to England, he began practising medicine at the royal court.

According to Domenico Mancini, Argentine attended King Edward V and his brother, Richard of Shrewsbury, Duke of York, commonly known as the Princes in the Tower, and was said to be the last person to attend them before their disappearance. In Henry VII's reign, he was physician to the king's eldest son, Arthur Tudor, Prince of Wales, who sadly died in 1502.

Argentine was appointed as provost of King's College in 1501. In his will, he left 100 marks to King's, as well as a silver basin and ewer.

Argentine wrote two works, a poem in Latin and a medical commonplace book.

3 February

On 3rd February 1537, in the reign of King Henry VIII, Thomas Fitzgerald, 10th Earl of Kildare (known as Silken Thomas), his five uncles and Sir John Burnell were executed at Tyburn in London. Thomas was hanged and beheaded, but his uncles and Burnell were hanged, drawn and quartered.

What had led these men to their rather sticky ends?

Thomas's father, Gerald Fitzgerald, 9th Earl of Kildare and Lord Deputy of Ireland, had been called to the royal court in London in 1534. According to the Annals of Ulster, the summons were due to accusations by "Foreigners of Ireland" regarding "excess of his illegality and his injustice on them". The Annals say that they planned to put him in the Tower of London "in anticipation of his ruin". Kildare answered the summons, leaving his twenty-one-year-old son Thomas in charge of things in Ireland as Vice-Deputy. Kildare was indeed imprisoned in the Tower, where he died in September 1534.

While his father was imprisoned in the Tower, Thomas, known as Silken Thomas after the silk fringes he and his men wore on their jackets, heard a rumour that his father had been executed in London. Thomas publicly renounced his allegiance to King Henry VIII, who was Lord of Ireland, at St Mary's Abbey in Dublin in June 1534 and asserted his allegiance to the pope. He then launched a rebellion against King Henry VIII. Chronicler Edward Hall records that "he took all the king's ordinance, and sent ambassadors to the Emperor to have entreated to him to take part with him. Also he slew the Bishop of Dublin and burnt and robbed all such as would not obey him."

It is not known who exactly murdered Archbishop John Alen, but Thomas got the blame. Unfortunately for Silken Thomas, an English army under the command of the newly appointed Lord Deputy of Ireland, Sir William Skeffington, recaptured Dublin and then, in March 1535, attacked Silken Thomas and his forces who'd holed up at Maynooth Castle. In the summer of 1535, after realising that no Spanish or imperial forces would be sent to help him, Silken Thomas surrendered to the English forces led by Lord Leonard Grey, who guaranteed his safety. He was escorted to London, where he was imprisoned in the Tower. While a prisoner there, he wrote a letter to his friend O'Brien asking him for money for food and clothes, writing, "I never had any money since I came into prison, but a noble, nor I have had neither hosen, doublet, nor shoes, nor shirt but one; nor any other garment but a single frieze gown, for a velvet furred with a budge, and so I have gone wolward (shirtless) and barefoot and barelegged diverse times (when it hath not been very warm); and so I should have done still, but that poor prisoners of their gentleness hath sometimes given me old hosen and shoes and shirts."

Worse was to come, though. Despite the promise of safety and the hope of mercy, Silken Thomas and his five uncles, who'd been implicated in the rebellion, were executed as traitors. "The Chronicle of the Grey Friars" records:

> "Also the 3rd day of February [1537] the lorde Garrad with his five uncles of Ireland—these were their names, Thomas lorde Fytzgarrard, sir James Fytzgarrard, sir John Fytzgarrard, sir Richard Fytzgarrard lord of St Johns in Ireland, sir Oliver Fytzgarrard, and sir Watter Fytzgarrard—were drawn from the tower unto Tyburn, and there all hanged and hedded and quartered, save the lorde Thomas, for he was but hanged and hedded and his body buried at the Crost Freeres in the quire, and the quarters with their heads set up about the city."

Thomas's family's lands were confiscated.

In 1541, Parliament declared King Henry VIII King of Ireland, stating that Ireland was now "knit forever to the imperial crown of the realm of England." King Henry was determined to dominate Ireland completely.

4 February

On 4th February 1555, John Rogers, a Protestant clergyman and Biblical editor, was burnt at the stake at Smithfield. Rogers was the first English Protestant burnt in Mary I's reign after being condemned as a heretic. He refused the chance of a last-minute pardon if he recanted. He died with courage.

Rogers had met Bible translator William Tyndale in Antwerp while Rogers was serving as a chaplain to English merchants there. After

Tyndale's execution, he was able to save Tyndale's work and assemble a complete Bible using it and work by Myles Coverdale. It was printed in Antwerp in 1537 as the Thomas Matthew's Bible, taking its name from two of Christ's disciples.

Rogers returned to England in 1548, and when Mary I came to the throne, Rogers' protestant faith led to him being ordered to remain in his house and then imprisoned. He was eventually tried and condemned as a heretic.

Martyrologist John Foxe recorded John Rogers' execution:

"Now when the time came that he, being delivered to the sheriffs, should be brought out of Newgate to Smithfield, the place of his execution, first came to him master Woodroofe, one of the aforesaid sheriffs, and calling master Rogers unto him, asked him if he would revoke his abominable doctrine, and his evil opinion of the sacrament of the altar. Master Rogers answered and said, "That which I have preached I will seal with my blood." "Then," quoth master Woodroofe, "thou art a heretic." "That shall be known," quoth Rogers, "at the day of judgment." "Well," quoth master Woodroofe, "I will never pray for thee." "But I will pray for you," quoth master Rogers; and so was brought the same day, which was Monday the 4th of February, by the sheriffs toward Smithfield, saying the psalm "Miserere" by the way, all the people wonderfully rejoicing at his constancy, with great praises and thanks to God for the same.

And there, in the presence of master Rochester, comptroller of the queen's household, sir Richard Southwell, both the sheriffs, and a wonderful number of people, the fire was put unto him; and when it had taken hold both upon his legs and shoulders, he, as one feeling no smart, washed his hands in the flame, as though it had been in cold water. And, after lifting up his hands unto heaven, not removing the same until such time as the devouring fire had consumed them - most mildly this happy martyr yielded up his spirit into the hands of his heavenly Father. A little before his burning at the stake, his pardon was brought, if he would have recanted, but he utterly refused. He was the first proto-martyr of all the blessed company that suffered in queen Mary's time, that gave the first adventure upon the fire. His wife and children, being eleven in number, and ten able to go, and one sucking on her breast, met him by the way as he went towards Smithfield. This sorrowful sight of his own flesh and blood could nothing move him; but that he constantly and cheerfully took his death, with wonderful patience, in the defence and quarrel of Christ's gospel."

5 February

On 5th February 1537, diplomat Sir Henry Brooke was born. His father was George Brooke, 9th Baron Cobham, owner of Cooling Castle, and his mother was Anne Bray, a woman who had served Queen Anne Boleyn as one of her ladies. She had served as an attendant horsewoman at the queen's coronation on 1st June 1533. There is controversy over whether she was the "Nan Cobham" who Sir John Husee named as one of the queen's accusers in 1536 when he wrote, "the Lady Worcester, and Nan Cobham and one maid more."

Sir Henry Brooke, or Henry Cobham as he was known, was the couple's fifth surviving son, and was one of ten children. He was educated at Trinity College, Cambridge, and then joined the household of Edward Courtenay, Earl of Devon. His biographer, Julian Lock, notes that this is when Elizabeth, the future Queen Elizabeth I, noticed him and he came to her "liking". Shortly after Elizabeth became queen, he was made a gentleman pensioner, and in 1561, he began his diplomatic career, accompanying Sir Thomas Chaloner to Spain. He carried out embassies for Elizabeth to the Low Countries and France, and in October 1579, Elizabeth appointed him as her resident ambassador in France. He remained in that position until he was recalled and replaced by Sir Edward Stafford in 1583.

Cobham was also a Justice of the Peace and Deputy Lieutenant for his home county of Kent, where he acted against Catholic recusants, and in the late 1580s, he was also a knight of the shire. In Parliament, he was one of the members who petitioned for the execution of Mary, Queen of Scots.

Cobham died on 13th January 1592 at his home, Sutton-at-Hone, the residence his wife, Anne Sutton, had brought to their marriage. He died heavily in debt. He and his wife had three sons and two daughters.

6 February

On 6th February 1561, poet Tailboys Dymoke (pseudonym Thomas Cutwode) was baptised at Kyme in Lincolnshire. He was the son of Sir Robert Dymoke and his wife, Bridget (née Clinton).

Dymoke is known for his allegorical poem, *Caltha poetarum*, or "The Bumble Bee", which he published in 1599 under the name of Thomas Cutwode, "cut wood" being the English translation of Dymoke's first name, the French "taille-bois". The poem comprises 187 seven-line stanzas, so it is rather long.

Julie M. Walker, in "Dissing Elizabeth: Negative Representations of Gloriana", describes it as a "pornographic political satire" and explains that the Lincolnshire garden setting of the poem "is populated by a series of plants representing royal houses, monarchs and court flatterers". Leslie Hotson, a scholar of Elizabethan literary puzzles, speculated that the bumblebee was Dymoke; Caltha, the marigold, was one of Queen Elizabeth I's maids of honour; and Diana was the queen.

Other works by Dymoke include a slanderous poem he and his brother Edward were accused of writing about their uncle, Henry Clinton, Earl of Lincoln. It was called "Faunus his Four Poetical Furies". Unfortunately, that poem does not survive. Dymoke also wrote a play in which he acted: "The Death of the Lord of Kyme", performed at Kyme in August 1601. Dymoke and his brother were charged with "contriving and acting a stage play ... containing scurrilous and slanderous matter", amongst other things, after the Earl of Lincoln complained. The earl won his case, and according to Dymoke's biographer, Eleri Larkum, although those involved suffered severe penalties, "Dymoke, however, escaped the judgment".

Dymoke died before February 1603.

7 February

On 7th February 1526, the traditional annual Shrovetide joust took place at Greenwich Palace.

The joust's theme was unrequited love. Henry Courtenay, Marquess of Exeter, and his team of men wore green velvet and crimson satin embroidered with burning hearts. Above these hearts, a lady's hand was depicted coming out of a cloud and holding a watering can, which dropped silver droplets on the burning hearts to quench them. Henry VIII's team wore cloth of gold and silver richly embroidered with a man's heart in a press, surrounded by flames and bearing the motto *Declare ie nose*, Declare I dare not. The theme was unrequited love, and some historians have linked it with the beginning of Henry's interest in Anne Boleyn, who initially rejected the king's advances.

Chronicler Edward Hall records how "many a spere" was broken at the joust, and one of these breaks ended up being rather nasty for Sir Francis Bryan. According to Hall, the "shiueryng [shivering]", i.e. splintering, of a spear caused Bryan to lose an eye. Bryan was lucky, though, as Henry II of France had the same happen to him in June 1559, and the splinters pierced his eye and entered his brain, causing him to die a few days later. In 2007, re-enactor Paul Allen was killed while re-enacting a joust when a splinter sheared off a lance, entered his visor's eye slit, and penetrated his eye and brain. A tragic accident. Bryan suffered no long-term ill effects and lived until 2nd February 1550.

8 February

On Sunday 8th February 1601, Robert Devereux, 2nd Earl of Essex, Queen Elizabeth I's former favourite, gathered at his home, Essex House in London, with his supporters and two hundred soldiers. They then marched into the city with Essex crying, "For the Queen! For the Queen! The crown of England is sold to the Spaniard! A plot is laid for my life!"

Essex believed that he had enemies at court, like the faction led by Robert Cecil, who was trying to bring him down, so he aimed to seize control of the royal court, the Tower of London and the City, and remove his enemies from power.

Thomas Birch gives an account of the rebellion in his book "Memoirs of the Reign of Queen Elizabeth: From the Year 1581 Till Her Death", Volume II, which is based on original papers from Anthony Bacon and other documents. He also shares this letter written by Robert Cecil, Secretary of State, to Sir George Carew, Lord President of Munster:

"Sir George Carew,

Because I am not ignorant, that greatest accidents are most subject to be misreported by such, as are either in passion or ignorance, I have thought it very fit, with all convenient speed to acquaint you with a most dangerous attempt, which hath happened on Sunday last, wherein both her majesty's own person and the usurpation of this kingdom was openly shot at. By this proclamation the proceedings of this earl of Essex will appear, and therefore I shall only need say this unto you, that I think, by that time my letters shall come unto you, both he and the earl of Southampton, with some others of the principals, shall have lost their heads, I send you the note of most of them, that were in open action with, them. If the queen had not put herself in strength that very morning and barricaded Charing-cross and other places of the back parts of Westminster, their resolution was to have been at court by noon: whereof when they understood, they put themselves into London, and from thence (hoping to have been followed by the city) they resolved to come back; but being repulsed at Ludgate by a stand of pikes, and the city holding fast for the queen, they and some fifty of their complices ran to the water, and put themselves into Essex-house, which the earl had furnished with all manner of warlike provisions, and then defended them-selves till towards six o'clock in the evening; at which time the lord admiral sent unto them, that if they would not yield, he would blow up the house, which he might have done sooner, but that the lady Essex and the lady Rich were within it. Whereupon, notwithstanding their great batteries, they all yielded to her majesty's mercy. Thus you have a true relation of this dangerous accident, unto which I will only add this, that even when a false alarm was brought to the queen, that the city was revolted with them, she never was more amazed than she would have been to have heard of a fray in Fleet-street. And thus much for this time I thought good to let you know till farther opportunity, committing you to God's protection.

Your loving and assured friend,

From the court at Whitehall,

Feb. 10, 1600. R O. CECIL."

The letter is dated February 1600, rather than 1601, because the Tudor new calendar year did not begin until Lady Day on 25th March.

As Cecil states, Essex's Rebellion was a complete failure. The citizens of London did not come out and support him; instead, they ignored him and his men and stayed indoors. His supporters deserted him, and Essex finally surrendered after Lord Admiral Nottingham threatened to blow up Essex House if the earl did not give himself up. Birch records that Essex and his friend and fellow rebel, Henry Wriothesley, 3rd Earl of Southampton, were taken first to Lambeth Palace, the London residence of the Archbishop of Canterbury, due to stormy weather preventing them from travelling on the River Thames to the Tower of London, but were taken to the Tower as soon as was possible. The other rebels were "committed to the public prisons".

Essex was executed for treason on 25th February 1601.

9 February

On 9th February 1542, Jane Boleyn, Lady Rochford, widow of George Boleyn, was rowed to the Tower of London to prepare for her execution.

Jane, who had served as one of Queen Catherine Howard's ladies, had been arrested and taken to the Tower in November 1541 after her mistress's colourful past and secret assignations with Thomas Culpeper had come to light, along with Jane's involvement in helping the couple meet. However, on the third day after her imprisonment, according to imperial ambassador Eustace Chapuys, Jane was "seized with a fit of madness by which her brain is affected." Chapuys explains that she was moved from the Tower to the home of Sir John Russell, the Lord Admiral, on the Strand, where she was put under the care of his wife, Anne. King Henry VIII was concerned that Jane's breakdown might prevent her from being punished, so he arranged for his physicians to visit her.

By the beginning of December 1541, Jane appeared to be improving. Chapuys described how "now and then she recovers her reason", but the king wanted to be in no doubt that she would suffer for her crime. On 11th February 1542, an Act of Attainder against Catherine and Jane "received the royal assent". The act stated that the two women were "convicted and attainted of high treason, and shall suffer accordingly". On that same day, an act for "due process to be had in high treason in cases of lunacy or madness" received royal assent in the House of Lords. It stated that "a person becoming insane after the supposed commission of treason, might be tried; or losing his rational faculties after attainder, might be executed". So, regardless of her mental state, Jane Boleyn would be executed.

Jane Boleyn, Lady Rochford, and Queen Catherine Howard were executed by beheading at the Tower of London on 13th February 1542 and laid to rest in the Chapel of St Peter ad Vincula.

Trivia: when she came to the throne, Mary I repealed not only the legislation regarding insane people and high treason, but also the Act of Attainder against the two women. She wasn't saying that they were innocent, it was because Henry VIII had not signed the attainder, it only bore the great seal.

10 February

On 10th February 1542, Catherine Howard, King Henry VIII's fifth wife, was taken from Syon House, where she'd been kept since November 1541, to the Tower of London in preparation for her execution.

Chronicler Charles Wriothesley recorded Catherine's move to the Tower on this day in 1542:

"The 10th of February the Queen was had by water from Syon to the Tower of London, the Duke of Suffolk, the Lord Privy Seal, and the Lord Great Chamberlain having the conveyance of her."

Eustace Chapuys, the imperial ambassador, also recorded Catherine's journey:

"Some days after, that is to say on the afternoon of the 10th, the Queen after some difficulty and resistance was conducted to the Tower by the river. The Lord Privy Seal, with a number of privy councillors and a large retinue of servants, went first in a large oared barge; then came a small covered boat with the Queen and four ladies of her suite, besides four sailors to man the boat. Then followed the duke of Suffolk in a big and well-manned barge, with plenty of armed men inside. On their arrival at the Tower stairs the Lord Privy Seal and the duke of Suffolk landed first; then the Queen herself, dressed in black velvet, with the same honors and ceremonies as if she were still reigning."

So, Catherine was escorted by Charles Brandon, Duke of Suffolk; William Fitzwilliam, who was 1st Earl of Southampton and Lord Privy Seal; and Robert Radcliffe, 1st Earl of Sussex and Lord Great Chamberlain.

Catherine's time at the Tower was short. She was executed on 13th February 1542.

11 February

On 11th February 1531, the ecclesiastical assembly known as convocation granted King Henry VIII the title of "singular protector, supreme lord, and even, so far as the law of Christ allows, supreme head of the English church and clergy".

This was during the King's Great Matter, Henry VIII's quest for an annulment of his marriage to Catherine of Aragon so that he could marry his sweetheart, Anne Boleyn. The king had come to believe that as a ruler and God's anointed king, he was answerable only to God and not the pope.

Anne Boleyn's brother, George Boleyn, Lord Rochford, played a prominent role in persuading convocation of the scriptural case for the king's supremacy. I'd like to share an excerpt from George Boleyn: Tudor Poet, Courtier and Diplomat, a book I co-wrote with my dear friend, Clare Cherry, to explain a bit more about this.

"The Convocations of Canterbury and York were the English Church's legislative body which, like Parliament, was made up of two houses: the upper house of bishops and the lower house of general clergy. The Convocation of Canterbury ran at the same time as Parliament, and the King's articles were introduced to them on 7 February 1531, following which Convocation met on five consecutive days between 7 and 11 February.

George Boleyn, by now a member of the Privy Council, was chosen by Henry to express his growing anti-papal sentiments and Parliament's arguments in favour of supremacy. He was sent to Convocation on the afternoon of Friday 10 February and delivered various tracts, one of which still survives today. George announced to the legislative body that the King's 'supreme authority grounded on God's word ought in no case to be restrained by any frustrate decrees of popish laws or void prescripts of human traditions, but that he may both order and minister, yea and also execute, the office of spiritual administration in the church whereof he is head".

Convocation did not want to deal with this 26-year-old envoy, they wanted to deal directly with the King but when they sent members of the lower house to see the King, they were turned away and instructed to deal with George. Henry, ever the coward, was happy to use the inexperienced young man as a buffer between himself and Convocation, and this was no doubt to the extreme satisfaction of the Boleyns. The position in which Henry was happy to put George can have done nothing to temper the young man's pride, and it is hard to imagine that Thomas Boleyn was unmoved by his son's extraordinary prominence at such tender years.

Convocation initially balked at the idea of recognising Henry as head of the church, and eventually a suggestion was made, either by Cromwell, Thomas Audley or even George Boleyn himself, to qualify the demand with the words 'as far as the law of Christ allows'. The following day, upon hearing the King's agreement to the limitation clause, the clergy agreed the amended wording, thereby accepting royal demands to recognise Henry as 'Head of the Church of England, as far as the law of Christ allows'. Although this was a victory for the Boleyns and their supporters, verbal acceptance by the clergy and actual compliance were two different matters, and any act of Convocation had to be agreed on by Parliament to be enforced."

In November 1534, the Act of Supremacy was passed, declaring, "Albeit the King's Majesty justly and rightfully is & oweth to be supreme head of the Church of England and so is recognised by the Clergy of the Realm in their convocations." On 15th January 1535, in the presence of Sir Thomas Audley, Lord Chancellor; Thomas Howard, Duke of Norfolk and treasurer of England; Thomas Boleyn, Earl of Wiltshire and keeper of the Privy Seal, and Thomas Cromwell, chief secretary, Henry VIII proclaimed that he was now Supreme Head of the Church of England. The Act of Supremacy came into force in February 1535. With the act came the Oath of Supremacy which the nobility and anyone taking public or church office in England were required to take. Some people, like the Carthusian monks of London Charterhouse and Sir Thomas More, refused to sign the oath, believing that only Christ could be head of the church, and they ended up being executed as traitors.

Today, Queen Elizabeth II is the Supreme Governor of the Church of England, a title which Elizabeth I chose to use rather than supreme head.

12 February

On 12th February 1590, Blanche Parry died at the age of 82. She had served Queen Elizabeth I loyally as Chief Gentlewoman of the

Privy Chamber, Keeper of the Queen Jewels and Furs, and Keeper of the Queen's Books.

Here are some facts about this woman who was also a mother figure, friend and confidant to the queen:

- Blanche was born around 1507/1508 and was the daughter of Henry Myles of Bacton, Herefordshire, Sheriff of Herefordshire, and his wife, Alice Milborne. Her family were of the gentry class from the border between England and Wales. Her paternal grandparents were from Glamorgan in Wales, her grandfather being Miles ap Harry, i.e. Miles, son of Harry.
- Blanche was related to the Herbert family and the Earls of Pembroke, and William Cecil, Lord Burghley, was her cousin and a good friend.
- In 1533, she was one of baby Princess Elizabeth's rockers, i.e. a lady who rocked the princess's cradle. She went on to serve the princess as a lady-in-waiting.
- Her appointment to the princess's household is thought to have been due to the influence of her maternal aunt, Blanche Herbert, Lady Troy, who was the Lady Mistress in charge of Elizabeth's household.
- Blanche spoke Welsh and English, and it is thought that she may have taught the young Elizabeth Welsh.
- Blanche Parry was appointed a gentlewoman of the privy chamber when Elizabeth became queen in 1558. She succeeded Katherine Ashley as Chief Gentleman of the Privy Chamber after Ashley's death in 1565. It is not known when Blanche became the queen's keeper of the jewels, but she served in that position until 1587. She was also in charge of the books presented to the queen.
- Her position in the queen's household meant she was intimate with the queen, helping her wash and dress, and sleeping in her chamber. She also wrote letters on behalf of the queen.
- Blanche's close relationship with the queen meant that she was often used as an intermediary for those wanting something from the queen, and she certainly was able to help her relatives.
- Blanche never married.

- She lost her sight towards the end of her life, forcing her to pass on the responsibility of looking after the queen's jewels to another lady, Mary Radcliffe.
- Blanche died on this day in 1590 and was buried in St Margaret's, Westminster, on the evening of 27th February. The queen, whom she had served for 57 years, paid for her funeral, and she was given funeral rites usually reserved for a baroness. The chief mourner at her funeral was her great-niece, Frances, Lady Burgh.
- She has a marble and alabaster monument in St Margaret's, and the inscription on it reads:

  "Hereunder is entombed Blanche Parry, daughter of Henry Parry of New Court in the county of Hereford, Esquier, Gentlewoman of Queen Elizabeth's most honourable bedchamber and Keeper of her Majesty's jewels, whom she faithfully served from her Highness' birth. Beneficial to her kinsfolk and countrymen, charitable to the poor, insomuch that she gave to the poor of Bacton and Newton in Herefordshire seven score bushels of wheat and rye yearly for ever with divers sums of money to Westminster and other places for good uses. She died a maid in the eighty-two years of her age the twelfth of February 1589."

  As she died before Lady Day, 25th March, the start of the new calendar year, in Tudor times, her death is recorded as 1589 rather than 1590.
- Blanche also has a stone and alabaster monument in Bacton Church, her home village in Herefordshire, which features the figure of Elizabeth I with Blanche kneeling beside her and holding a book. It bears an inscription of twenty-eight lines of verse, thought to have been written by Blanche herself, recording her long service to her beloved queen. It includes the line, "With maiden queen a maiden did end my life."
- In her will, which Lord Burghley helped her write, she left her best diamond to the queen and "a pair of sables garnished with 8 chains of gold". Her bequests show that she was a wealthy woman at her death.

- The Bacton Altar Cloth is thought to be part of the dress worn by Queen Elizabeth I in the famous Rainbow Portrait and is thought to have been sent to Bacton Church by order of the queen in memory of Blanche.

13 February

On 13th February 1608, in the reign of King James I, the prominent Tudor noblewoman and one of the richest people in England, Elizabeth Talbot, Countess of Shrewsbury, more commonly known as Bess of Hardwick, died at her home at Hardwick. Her body lay in state at Hardwick until her funeral at All Hallows, Derby (now All Saints' Cathedral), on 4th May 1608.

Here are some facts about this interesting Tudor lady:
- Bess was born around 1527 and was the daughter of John Hardwick of Hardwick in Derbyshire, and his wife, Elizabeth Leake.
- Even though the family was of the gentry class and had been moderately wealthy, circumstances changed when Bess's father died and the Crown seized much of his land. Until his eldest son came of age, this land and the money it made would be controlled by those who held the boy's wardship. This made things financially hard for the family.
- Bess was married to her first husband, Robert Barlow, by May 1543, when she was around 16. It seems, however, that the marriage was not consummated before Barlow died in December 1544.
- In August 1547, Bess married her second husband, widower Sir William Cavendish, Treasurer of the King's Chamber, in the chapel at Bradgate Manor, the home of the Grey family in Leicestershire. Historian Elizabeth Goldring writes that the pair were well-matched, as they "shared a fierce ambition for social advancement". Bess had eight children by Cavendish, and six of them survived childhood. Godparents to their children included Princess Elizabeth, the future Elizabeth I; John Dudley, Duke of Northumberland; William Herbert, Earl of Pembroke, and Lady Jane Grey.

- Bess is today remembered for her building projects, and these projects started in 1549 when Cavendish bought the Chatsworth estate, and the couple began rebuilding it. They also bought further land and properties in Derbyshire and in joint names, which Goldring points out was a shrewd move as it prevented the problem that Bess's own family had experienced, i.e. lands and properties falling into wardship if Cavendish died before his eldest son reached his majority, which he did in 1557 when his son, Henry, was just 7. However, Cavendish left Bess with a debt of over £5,000 owed to the crown.
- Due to her financial situation, Bess married again quickly, marrying her third husband, wealthy widower and nobleman Sir William St Loe, sometime in 1557 or 1558.
- St Loe served Queen Elizabeth I as Captain of the Guard, and Bess was appointed as a gentlewoman of the queen's privy chamber. However, Bess ended up being dismissed by the queen after she supported the secret marriage of Katherine Grey, sister of the late Lady Jane Grey, and Edward Seymour, Earl of Hertford.
- The St Loe marriage was childless, and Bess was the main beneficiary of St Loe's estate when he died around 1565.
- In November 1567, Bess married for a fourth time, marrying the rich and powerful George Talbot, 6th Earl of Shrewsbury, owner of Tutbury Castle, Pontefract Castle, Sheffield Castle, Sheffield Manor, and other manors, lodges and properties. As well as Bess marrying Shrewsbury, Bess's daughter, Mary, married Shrewsbury's son, Gilbert, and Bess's son, Henry, married Shrewsbury's daughter, Grace.
- In 1568, a year after Bess married him, Shrewsbury was appointed as Mary, Queen of Scots' keeper, and in 1569, Mary was installed with the couple at Tutbury. Shrewsbury acted as Mary's keeper from 1568 to 1584, with Mary being kept at Tutbury on four separate occasions and his properties of Wingfield Manor, Chatsworth, Rufford Abbey and Sheffield.
- When Margaret Douglas, Countess of Lennox, visited Mary, Queen of Scots, and the Talbots at Rufford Abbey in 1574, Bess took the opportunity to arrange a match between Margaret's

son, Charles Stuart, and her daughter Elizabeth Cavendish. The two married and had a daughter, Arabella or Arbella Stuart, in 1575. Both Shrewsbury and the queen, who were both in the dark concerning the marriage, were furious.

- Bess and Shrewsbury had a troubled marriage while Mary, Queen of Scots, was in their custody, and Bess even accused her husband of being intimate with Mary. They separated in 1584, and Bess retired to her estate at Chatsworth. However, Shrewsbury took her to court, claiming ownership as per the terms of their marriage agreement, but in 1587 the courts found in Bess's favour, and she was awarded Chatsworth and an income from her husband.

- Shrewsbury died in November 1590, leaving his wife a third of his lands. By 1591, Bess had completed another building project, rebuilding her old family home, Hardwick Old Hall, before building a new property next to it, Hardwick New Hall, which Bess moved into in 1597. She filled it with sumptuous furniture, embroidery, paintings, tapestries and silver, and her initials ES along with a countess's coronet feature on the top of each of the hall's six towers. Another house, Oldcotes in Derbyshire, was also built in the 1590s.

- Bess died on this day in history, 13th February 1608, and by the terms of her will, which was made in 1601, she left Oldcotes and Hardwick Old and New Halls to her second and favourite son, William. She had left the contents of Chatsworth to her eldest son, Henry, but disinherited him in changes made in 1603 following arguments with him. She left bequests for her other children and grandchildren, excluding Arabella, with whom she'd argued, and servants and residents of an almshouse she had founded in Derbyshire. Chatsworth and Hardwick can still be visited today, although Oldcotes no longer exists.

- As well as making her mark with her building projects, Bess is the ancestress of the dukes of Devonshire and Newcastle. Bess is also known for the needlework that she, Mary, Queen of Scots, and the Scottish queen's household worked on during Mary's time as her prisoner. They embroidered over 100 panels, and the Victoria and Albert Museum has some of them in its collection today.

14 February

On 14th February 1539, Sir Nicholas Carew was tried for treason after being implicated in the Exeter Conspiracy. It was alleged that a letter had been found at the Marchioness of Exeter's home. It was evidence of Carew being involved in a conspiracy with the Marquess of Exeter and Baron Montagu, who had been arrested in November 1538. It was alleged that they had been plotting with Cardinal Pole, Montagu's exiled brother, a man who was seen as an enemy of King Henry VIII. Carew was found guilty and sentenced to death. He was executed on 3rd March 1539 at Tyburn.

Carew was a royal favourite for 20 years – surviving even though he'd been a supporter of Princess Mary during the Great Matter - but things started to go wrong for him in late 1538.

Carew was arrested on 31st December 1538. In his book "The History of the Worthies of England", Thomas Fuller explained that according to a Carew family tradition, Carew upset the king during a game of bowls:

"King Henry, then at bowls, gave this knight
opprobrious language, betwixt jest and earnest; to which
the other returned an answer rather true than discreet,
as more consulting therein his own animosity than
allegiance."

Fuller says that the king was so offended that "Sir Nicholas fell from the top of his favour to the bottom of his displeasure, and was bruised to death thereby."

In writing of the fall of Carew, imperial ambassador Eustace Chapuys put it down to his love for Princess Mary, of whom he had "always shown himself a most devoted servant", and the fact that the king and his council wanted to leave Mary with "as few such as possible", i.e. remove her supporters.

Historian Stanford Lehmberg believes that Carew's fall was actually down to Thomas Cromwell, King Henry VIII's right-hand man at this time, who saw Carew as a threat that needed to be removed. And removed he was!

The king seemed to believe that Carew had plotted with the Poles, writing to Sir Thomas Wyatt the Elder on 13th February 1539, "Moreover, after their execution it was found, by their letters, that Sir Nich. Carew was one of the chief of that faction,"

Here is the record of the indictment drawn up against Carew by the Surrey commission:

> "that Sir Nic. Carewe of Bedyngton alias of Westminster, knowing the said Marquis to be a traitor, did, 20 Aug. 28 Hen. VIII., at Westhorseley, Surrey, and at other times, falsely abet the said Marquis, and, 24 Aug. ao 28, and at other times, had conversations with him about the change of the world, and also with his own hand wrote him divers letters, at Bedyngton, 4 Sept. ao 28o and at other times, and the said Marquis at that or other times sent divers traitorous letters to the said Carewe from Westhorseley which the said Carewe traitorously received, which letters they afterwards, to conceal their treason, traitorously burnt at Westhorseley and Bedyngton, 1 Sept. 30 Hen. VIII. and at other times; and afterwards, knowing that the said Marquis was indicted as aforesaid, 29 Nov. ao 30o, the said Carewe at Bedyngton traitorously said these words in English, "I marvel greatly that the indictment against the lord Marquis was so secretly handled and for what purpose, for the like was never seen"; contrary to his allegiance, &c."

At his trial on this day in 1539, Carew pleaded not guilty, but the verdict was guilty, and he was condemned to death.

A favourite for 20 years but, like many others before him, he ended his days being branded a traitor to the crown.

15 February

On 15th February 1564, the Italian physicist, mathematician, astronomer, and philosopher, Galileo Galilei, was born in Pisa, Italy. He was the eldest child of musician, composer and music theorist Vincenzo Galilei and his wife, Giulia.

Galileo considered becoming a priest but instead studied at the University of Pisa, choosing medicine and then changing to mathematics and natural philosophy.

Galileo was one of the central figures of the Scientific Revolution and supported Copernicanism (the heliocentric model). He has been referred to as "the Father of Modern Science", "the Father of Modern Physics", and "the father of modern observational astronomy". He is also known for discovering the Galilean Moons (Jupiter's satellites Io, Europa, Ganymede and Callisto), his improved military compass and his work on the telescope, which allowed Jupiter's satellites to be seen, as well as the moon's mountains.

But what else did Galileo do?

- He created a hydrostatic balance to measure the density of objects.
- He invented the thermoscope, a forerunner of the thermometer.
- He invented Galileo's pump, a device for raising water using only a single horse.
- He began work on a pendulum clock but died before his design was finished.
- He saw that the Milky Way was not just a band of light but was made up of stars.

In 1633, he was tried for heresy by the Inquisition for his view that the Earth revolved around the sun, which he'd made public in his 1632 work "Dialogue Concerning the Two Chief World Systems - Ptolemaic and Copernican". The Catholic Church promoted the belief that the Earth was at the centre of the universe and that all the heavenly bodies revolved around the Earth. He was found guilty, forced to publicly recant and spent the rest of his life under house arrest.

Galileo died in Arcetri, near Florence, on 8th January 1642, aged 77.

This Galileo quote is taken from his 1615 letter to the Grand Duchess Christina, in which he was defending science against those who attacked it on the grounds of religion:

"But I do not feel obliged to believe that that same God who has endowed us with senses, reason, and intellect has intended to forgo their use and by some other means to give us knowledge which we can attain by them. He would not require us to deny sense and reason in physical matters which are set before our eyes and minds by direct experience or necessary demonstrations."

Trivia: Galileo had three illegitimate children, two daughters and a son, by Marina Gamba.

16 February

On 16th February 1495, Sir William Stanley, administrator and landowner, was executed for treason on Tower Hill.

William was born around 1435 and was the second son of Thomas Stanley, 1st Baron Stanley, and his wife, Joan. During the Wars of the Roses, the Stanley's supported the Yorkists, and William ended up being attainted as a traitor following the Battle of Bloreheath in 1459. William's support of the Nevilles and Yorkists led to King Edward IV appointing him as chamberlain of Chester, constable of Flint Castle, and sheriff of Flintshire, and knighting him following his accession in 1461. He served Edward IV loyally even when Richard Neville, Earl of Warwick, rebelled against the king and deposed him, forcing Edward to flee into exile. William also supported Edward when he returned from exile to claim the throne again.

William's biographer, Michael J. Bennett, writes of how William and his younger brother, Thomas Stanley, who'd later become Earl of Derby, "reluctantly acquiesced in the usurpation of Richard III" in 1483 they helped put down the rebellion of the Duke of Buckingham. However, it seems that they were in contact with Henry Tudor regarding his return from exile and his plan to claim the throne. Following Henry's landing in Wales, William set off with 3,000 men from his property of Holt Castle, a few miles from Wrexham in North Wales, while his brother, Thomas, set off with his men from Lancashire.

The Stanley brothers are known for helping Henry Tudor at the Battle of Bosworth Field on 22nd August 1485 by committing their troops to Henry's side, against King Richard III, at a critical stage of the battle and saving the day. The new king, Henry VII, rewarded William for his support by appointing him as Chamberlain of the King's Household. In 1487, William sided with his king during the Lambert Simnel rebellion and, in 1489, helped him put down the Yorkshire Rebellion.

So how did William go from being a loyal supporter of the king to being executed as a traitor?

It was alleged that he supported the pretender Perkin Warbeck, who claimed to be Richard, Duke of York, son of Edward IV and one of the Princes in the Tower. According to the charges against him, William had discussed Warbeck with Robert Clifford and had sent Clifford to Brabant to assure Warbeck of his support. Contemporary historian Polydore Vergil recorded that William had told Clifford, "if he were sure that the man was Edward's son, he would never take up arms against him."

Now, William HAD been a loyal supporter of King Edward IV, as you have heard, and had served his eldest son, Edward, as steward of his household, but as Vergil notes, what he said to Clifford about Warbeck "would indicate lukewarmness towards King Henry rather than treason".

On 6th and 7th February 1495, William was tried for treason. His brother, Thomas, presided over the trial as Constable of England. William confessed to treason, hoping, perhaps, as Vergil states, "that by ready confession he would obtain his life from the king." If that was the plan, it didn't work. Even though William had previously been loyal to Henry VII and was the brother of the king's stepfather, the king had to act. Vergil writes, "Henry feared such leniency to be dangerous to himself – others would be encouraged by William's avoidance of punishment and would undertake similar acts of folly."

Sir William Stanley was found guilty of treason and condemned to a full traitor's death, to be hanged, drawn and quartered. The sentence was, however, commuted to the more merciful method of beheading. William was beheaded on Tower Hill on this day in history, 16th February 1495. He was about sixty years old. He was laid to rest at Syon Abbey.

17 February

On Saturday 17th February 1565, Mary, Queen of Scots, met and fell in love with Henry Stuart, Lord Darnley, at Wemyss Castle in Scotland.

Darnley, son of Lady Margaret Douglas and Matthew Stewart, 4th Earl of Lennox, had met Mary on at least one occasion, having been sent to France in 1559 by his parents to congratulate Mary and her husband, Francis II of France, on their accession. It has also been suggested that he was sent again in late 1560 or early 1561 to offer his condolences to Mary on the death of Francis. This was all part of his father's effort to recover the Scottish estates he'd lost in 1545 when he'd been declared a traitor for supporting the military action of Henry VIII against Scotland in the War of the Rough Wooing. Mary did restore Lennox's lands following the intercession of Elizabeth I in 1564.

Darnley left London for Scotland on 3rd February, after Elizabeth I permitted him to join his father there. He arrived in Edinburgh by 12th February, and on this day in history, 17th February 1565, he presented himself to the Scottish queen at Wemyss Castle in Fife. Sir James Melville, the Scottish ambassador, recorded that Mary "took well with him, and said that he was the lustiest and best proportioned long man that she had seen; for he was of high stature, long and small (meaning slender), even and erect." He was a good-looking man and appears to have been charming and accomplished too. Besides a temporary separation for Darnley to visit his father, the couple were constant companions. Just over seven months later, on 29th July 1565, Mary married Darnley at Holyrood Palace.

Marital bliss didn't last long, with the couple being estranged by Christmas 1565. Things went from bad to worse when Mary's private secretary, David Rizzio, was stabbed to death in front of her by a gang of assassins led by her husband in March 1566. Mary gave birth to Darnley's son, James, the future James VI and James I, on 19th June 1566, but there was no reconciliation. Darnley was murdered on 10th February 1567.

18 February

On 18th February 1612, Italian banker Roberto di Ridolfi died in Florence, Italy, aged 80. He is known for his Ridolfi Plot against Elizabeth I.

Let me tell you a bit more about this plot.

The Ridolfi Plot aimed to launch a Spanish invasion of England to depose Queen Elizabeth I, replace her with Mary, Queen of Scots and restore Catholicism in England. Ridolfi, who had been based in London since 1562 and who had worked for men like William Cecil, Lord Burghley, as a financial agent, had been involved in plans to remove Elizabeth before. He'd been arrested and interrogated by Sir Francis Walsingham, the queen's spymaster, in 1568 after being implicated in the Northern Rebellion after the pope had asked him to distribute money to the Northern lords opposing Elizabeth. The rebellion failed, and Ridolfi was released as no firm evidence of financial support for the rebellion could be found against him.

Those who were involved in the plot which Ridolfi hatched included King Philip II of Spain; Pope Pius V; the Duke of Alba, who was the leader of the Spanish troops in the Netherlands; John Lesley, Bishop of Ross, who was Mary, Queen of Scots' agent; the Spanish ambassador Guerau de Espés del Valle; Thomas Howard, 4th Duke of Norfolk, who was to marry Mary, Queen of Scots, and Mary herself, who gave her consent to this plot against Elizabeth. Ridolfi was in the perfect position to hatch a plot because he had banking connections and could use his banking travels as a cover for conspiring with the Spanish king, pope and the Duke of Alba on the Continent.

Fortunately for Elizabeth, she had an amazing network of spies, and so she received advanced warning of the plot. Ridolfi had also bragged about the plot to the Grand Duke of Tuscany, who passed the information on to Elizabeth. In April 1571, Ridolfi's messenger, Charles Baillie, was apprehended while carrying letters at Dover. He was interrogated and tortured until he gave up information, including the cypher used for the correspondence. In August 1571, more correspondence, along with 600 pounds in gold, made its way into the Crown's possession when draper Thomas Browne, who'd been employed by the Duke of Norfolk's secretaries to take a bag to one of

Norfolk's agents in the North, became suspicious and reported the bag to William Cecil, Lord Burghley, Elizabeth I's chief advisor. Norfolk's secretaries were interrogated, and when Howard House, Norfolk's home, was searched for a cypher to help decipher the letters, a letter from Mary, Queen of Scots, in cypher was found.

Further members of Norfolk's household were interrogated, and Norfolk was also arrested. He was executed for treason in June 1572. The Spanish ambassador was expelled from England, but Ridolfi, who hadn't been in England when the plot was uncovered, escaped punishment and continued working as a special envoy for the pope. Mary, Queen of Scots, was kept under closer surveillance.

Roberto Ridolfi may have been involved in plots to depose Elizabeth I, but he died a natural death at the grand age of 80.

19 February

On 19th February 1547, nine-year-old King Edward VI processed from the Tower of London to Westminster, through the streets of London, in preparation for his coronation, which was due to take place the following day.

The streets were described as being well-gravelled, the walls and windows were hanged with rich cloths of tapestry, arras, cloth of gold, tissue, and streamers and banners, and some streets were also railed so that the horses would not go on the pavements and so people would not get hurt. The conduits were also running with wine.

A College of Arms manuscript describes how there were also "goodly pagents, and devyses, and therein goodly melody and eloquent speches of noble historyes, treating of the joyfull welcominge and recepte of so noble a Kynge".

The procession was huge. On foot were the king's messengers, the king's gentlemen, ambassadors' servants, the king's trumpeters, the chaplains "without dignity", esquires of the body, knights, and chaplains "of dignity". Then after them, on horseback, were the gentlemen and noblemen's sons, barons, bishops, earls' sons, marquesses' sons, dukes' younger sons, earls, marquesses and dukes. Then came members of the council who were paired with foreign diplomats, then "Sir Percevall Hart, knyght harbenger" who bore the king's cloak and hat, gentlemen ushers, then "Garter in the Kynges cote of armes" and the Mayor of London, the sergeants of arms, then the Constable of England (Henry Grey, Marquess of Dorset) bearing the sword of state, the Earl of Warwick (John Dudley), then the Earl of Arundel acting as Earl Marshall in place of Edward Seymour, the Duke of Somerset, who, as Lord Protector, was "a lyttell before the Kyng on the left hande"

And there finally was the young king, who was described as "walking a little before his canopy, because the people might the better see his grace, his highness being richly apparelled with a rich gown of clothe of silver all over embroidered with damask gold, with a jerkin of white velvet, wrought with Venice silver, garnished with precious stones, as rubies and diamonds, with true-loves of pearls, a doublet of white velvet according to the same, with like precious stones and pearls, a white velvet cap garnished with like stones and pearls, and a pair of buskins of white velvet." His horse was described as having crimson satin embroidered with pearls and damask gold.

Six knights carried the king's canopy with assistants. The king was followed by his footmen; his master of the horse, Anthony Browne, leading a goodly courser of honour very richly trapped; his master of the Henchmen, Sir Francis Bryan, leading the henchmen; then the gentlemen and grooms of the privy chamber, followed by the pensioners and men of arms.

The procession paused at several points on their journey to enjoy pageants and entertainment.

At Fenchurch Street, there was a scaffold hung with cloth of arras and with men and children singing and playing music.

At the conduit at Cornhill, there was wine running and a pageant with more music, singing and speeches.

At Cheapside, there were two people described as "resembling Valentyne and wylde Urson, the one clothed with moss and in leaves, having in his hand a great club of yew-tree for his weapon, the other armed as a knight" who made speeches. Another pageant featured a rock decorated with flowers and a fountain and topped by an imperial crown. Wine flowed out of springs, into pipes and out into the street. On the fountain stood children dressed as Grace, Nature, Fortune and Charity, who then gave speeches. There were also eight richly apparrelled ladies who represented "Sapience and the Seven Sciences Liberall", who also made good speeches.

At the end of the conduit was a scaffold with heaven, the sun, stars and clouds, out of which descended a phoenix, which had been the badge of Jane Seymour, the king's mother. The phoenix landed on a mount of red and white roses, gillyflowers and hawthorn bushes – the roses and hawthorn symbolising Henry VIII, the king's father. There was also a gold crowned lion, another symbol of Henry VIII, and a small lion crowned with the imperial crown by two angels. Then the phoenix and the big lion vanished, leaving the small crowned lion alone.

On another scaffold was a throne upon which a child, representing the young king and wearing cloth of gold and a robe of crimson satin, sat. The throne was described as "upholded with 4 other children" dressed as Regality, Justice, Truth and Mercy, who made speeches. Behind the throne, "the golden fleece was kept by two bulls and a serpent casting out of their mouths flaming fire, according to the story of Jason".

At the Standard at Cheap was a pageant with music and speeches.

The Cross at Cheap was painted and gilded, and just beyond it, the Mayor and Aldermen received the king and presented him with a purse containing 1000 gold marks.

The Little Conduit at Cheap had a pageant "garnished with a target of Seint George and the King's arms". There was also a depiction of Edward the Confessor with a golden lion, another of St George on horseback, and a "faire mayden holding a lamb in a stryng." A child pronounced an oration in Latin, and St George gave a speech in English.

At St Paul's Churchyard, there was a tightrope walker who performed for the king.

The Great Conduit in Fleet Street had a stage on which were richly apparrelled children dressed as Truth, Faith and Justice. Truth gave a speech to the king, and then wine was given to the people.

The gate at Temple Bar was decorated and fashioned into battlements and buttresses garnished with standards and flags, and eight French trumpeters blew their trumpets, and children sang.

Then the procession moved on to Westminster, where the king, who must have been tired, thanked the ambassadors and then retired. Edward was crowned the following day.

20 February

On 20th February 1523, Agnes, or Alice, Lady Hungerford, was hanged at Tyburn.

Agnes, the widow of Sir Edward Hungerford, was hanged with her servant William Mathewe after they were found guilty of murdering Agnes's first husband, John Cotell, in 1518. Although Cotell was murdered in 1518, Agnes and her servants were not arrested and imprisoned in the Tower of London until 1522, following the death of her second husband, Sir Edward Hungerford. It may be that her second husband had protected her from trouble.

According to the indictments, on 26th July 1518, Agnes's servants William Mathewe and William Ignes "with force and arms made an assault upon John Cotell, at Farley, in the county of Somerset, by the procurement and abetting of Agnes Hungerford." There, they "feloniously did throttle, suffocate and strangle" Cotell with a neckerchief of linen. Then, they disposed of the body by putting it into "a certain fire in the furnace of the kitchen in the Castle of Farley" where "it did burn and consume". Agnes, according to the indictments, "well knowing that the aforesaid William Mathewe and William Ignes had done the felony and murder aforesaid, did receive, comfort and aid them on 28th December 1518."

On 27th November 1522, they were tried for Cotell's murder and found guilty. Mathewe and Agnes were sentenced to hanging, while Ignes pleaded benefit of the clergy, i.e. that as a member of the clergy, he was exempt from criminal prosecution in the secular courts. However, he didn't get very far with his plea as it was found that he was a bigamist, so his plea was disallowed and eventually, like the others, he was sentenced to be hanged.

Chronicler John Stowe records that in 1523 on "the 20 February the Lady Alice (or Agnes) Hungerford, a knight's wife, for murdering her husband was led from the Tower of London to Holborne, and there put into a cart with one of her servants, and so carried to Tyburn and both hanged." He records that she was buried at Grey Friars, London.

21 February

On 21st February 1568, Katherine Seymour, Countess of Hertford, was buried at Yoxford. Her remains were later re-interred, by her grandson, in the Seymour family tomb at Salisbury Cathedral.

Katherine was the second daughter of Henry Grey, Duke of Suffolk, and his wife, Frances Brandon, and the granddaughter of Charles Brandon, Duke of Suffolk, and Mary Tudor, Queen of France. She was also the younger sister of Lady Jane Grey.

Katherine was only about twenty-seven years of age at her death on 27th January 1568 but had had an eventful life. Here are a few facts about her:

- In May 1553, she married Lord Henry Herbert in a triple wedding service which saw her sister Jane marry Lord Guildford Dudley and Guildford's sister, Catherine, marry Lord Henry Hastings. Katherine's marriage to Herbert was annulled following the accession of Queen Mary I in July 1553.
- Katherine's sister was queen for just thirteen days in July 1553 before being deposed and imprisoned in the Tower of London. Jane was executed in February 1554, and the sisters' father was executed on 23rd February. Katherine was then placed in the household of Anne Seymour, Dowager Duchess of Somerset, wife of the late Edward Seymour.
- Katherine served as a maid of honour to Queen Elizabeth I on her accession in 1558.
- In late 1560, Katherine secretly married the Duchess of Somerset's eldest son, Edward, Earl of Hertford, without the queen's consent, and Katherine quickly became pregnant. When their marriage came to light, Katherine and Hertford were imprisoned in the Tower, where Katherine gave birth to a son, Edward, in September 1561.
- In 1562, the couple's marriage was declared invalid, and their son was declared illegitimate. Katherine and Edward remained in the Tower but were able to see each other, thanks to the

kindness of Sir Edward Warner, Lieutenant of the Tower. Katherine got pregnant again and gave birth to a second son, Thomas, in February 1563.

- After this, Katherine and Hertford never saw each other again. Katherine was released into house arrest in the summer of 1563 due to the plague, but she spent the rest of her life in house arrest due to her royal blood and those who viewed her as the queen's successor.
- She died on 27th January 1568 at Cockfield Hall, Yoxford, in Suffolk, home of Owen Hopton, in whose custody she'd been since October 1567.
- Katherine's widower, Hertford, was released from confinement in 1571 when he was allowed back at court.
- Katherine's younger sister Mary also had a secret marriage and was kept under house arrest while her husband was imprisoned.

22 February

On 22nd February 1540, twenty-four-year-old Marie de Guise, or Mary of Guise, queen consort of King James V of Scotland, was crowned queen at Holyrood Abbey.

Her husband, the king, was the son of King James IV and Margaret Tudor, and Marie was the eldest daughter of Claude of Lorraine, Duke of Guise, and his wife Antoinette de Bourbon, widow of Louis, duc de Longueville. James had previously been married to Madeleine de Valois, but Madeleine died shortly after arriving in Scotland in 1537. James was intent on another French wife and thought of Marie, but his widowed uncle, King Henry VIII, was also interested in taking Marie as his bride. According to the French ambassador, who asked the English king why he was interested in Marie, Henry VIII had explained that Marie was big in person and that he needed a big wife. According to historian Antonia Fraser, Marie was not impressed with the idea of marriage to Henry and commented, "I may be big in person, but my neck is small." She chose to marry James instead, and they were married by proxy in May 1538. In June 1538, following Marie's arrival in Scotland, the couple married in person in a lavish ceremony at St Andrews. Forty days of celebrations followed the wedding and included feasting, hunting and hawking, archery competitions, and tournaments. Marie entered Edinburgh as queen on 16th November 1538.

Following a pilgrimage to the Shrine of St Adrian on the Isle of May in August 1539, a well-known place of pilgrimage for women having trouble conceiving, Marie became pregnant. Her husband, the king, began planning a fitting coronation for the mother of his child. A new crown of 35 ounces of gold decorated with precious stones and pearls was commissioned from the royal jeweller for the ceremony, and a French-style silver-gilt sceptre was made. James also ordered his own crown to be remodelled. Tiered stands were erected in Holyrood Abbey so that spectators could see their queen, who was dressed in a purple velvet robe lined with white corded taffeta. Her husband also wore purple velvet but lined with ermine.

Marie was crowned queen at Holyrood by Cardinal Beaton, and following the mass, the royal couple retired to the state apartments for the coronation banquet and entertainment.

Marie gave birth to a son, James, on 22nd May 1540, and he was followed by a brother, Robert, in April 1541. Unfortunately, both boys died shortly after Robert's birth. They were buried together at Holyrood Abbey.

On 8th December 1542, Marie gave birth to a daughter, Mary, while King James was ill. On 14th December 1542, James died, leaving the throne to his six-day-old daughter, who became Mary, Queen of Scots. Marie was not appointed regent at this time but remained in Scotland to help her daughter. However, she acted as regent from 1554, when her daughter was in France preparing to marry the Dauphin, and remained queen regent until her death on 11th June 1560 at Edinburgh Castle. Her body lay in a lead coffin in the castle's St Margaret's Chapel until March 1561, when it was transported to France and buried in the Convent of St Pierre, Reims. She was given a funeral at Notre Dame in Paris.

Marie's daughter, Mary, Queen of Scots, ended up being forced to abdicate the throne of Scotland in 1567 in favour of her son, James, who became King James VI of Scotland. This boy, Marie's grandson, would, of course, become King James I of England following the death of Queen Elizabeth I in March 1603.

23 February

On 23rd February 1601, religious pamphleteer and member of Parliament Job Throckmorton was buried at Haseley in Warwickshire. Job was the eldest son of Clement Throckmorton of Haseley, Warwickshire, and his wife, Katherine Neville.

It is believed that Throckmorton was one of the men responsible for the "Martin Marprelate tracts". These religious tracts, which attacked the established church, were written under the pseudonym Martin Marprelate (and his sons) and published in 1588 and 1589 by John Penry and Robert Waldegrave. In his article on Throckmorton, Patrick Collinson, writes that a comparison of Throckmorton's 1549 work, "The Defence of Job Throkmorton Against the Slaunders of Maister Sutcliffe", with the Marprelate satires "has persuaded modern critical opinion that if these satires had a single author, that author was Throckmorton", although Throckmorton denied it. Other names linked to the tracts include the publisher John Penry, Sir Michael Hicks, Henry Barrow, Roger Williams, George Carleton and Patrick Collinson.

"The Marprelate Controversy" was a pamphlet war between the writers of the Marprelate tracts and defenders of the Church. It had been sparked off by a Star Chamber decree, championed by John Whitgift, Archbishop of Canterbury, which forbade the publication of any books, pamphlets or tracts which had not been authorised by the archbishop, or his colleague, the Bishop of London. This allowed Whitgift to suppress Puritan works, which he viewed as heresy. In response to the archbishop's censorship, Martin Marprelate and sons printed a series of tracts using private printing presses. These tracts attacked certain bishops and the church as a whole and included "The Epistle", "The Epitome", and "Certain Mineral and Metaphysical School-points". Tracts were written in answer by church defenders, including Thomas Cooper, Bishop of Winchester; writer and playwright John Lyly; writer and playwright Thomas Nashe; and dramatist Robert Greene.

Although Job was tried in 1590 after being implicated in the Marprelate Controversy, he pleaded "I am not Martin, I knewe not Martin", and escaped punishment thanks to his status. His colleague, John Penry, however, wasn't as lucky and was hanged.

Job is also known for what Patrick Collinson describes as his "extraordinary parliamentary speeches", such as when he denounced Mary, Queen of Scots as "the daughter of sedition, the mother of rebellion, the nurse of impiety", and his attacks on England's Catholic neighbours, which included him calling James VI of Scotland "the younge impe of Scotlande", for which William Cecil, Lord Burghley, had to apologise to the Scottish ambassador and promise to imprison Job in the Tower. Job escaped imprisonment, though.

Job Throckmorton seems to have been quite a colourful and lucky character.

24 February

On 24th February 1603, Katherine Howard (née Carey), Countess of Nottingham, died at Arundel House. She was buried at All Saints, Chelsea (Chelsea Old Church) on 25th April 1603.

Katherine was the eldest daughter of Henry Carey, 1st Baron Hunsdon, and his wife, Anne Morgan, making her the granddaughter of Mary Boleyn, sister of Queen Anne Boleyn. Her birthdate is unknown, but must have been between 1545 and 1550.

By 1551, Katherine's father was serving as a gentleman in Elizabeth's household. Her mother also had connections to the princess's household, being the granddaughter of Blanche Herbert, Lady Troy, Elizabeth's Lady Mistress. Elizabeth came to the throne in November 1558, and Katherine was appointed as a gentlewoman of Elizabeth I's privy chamber in 1560. Katherine's biographer, Simon Adams, notes that Elizabeth and Katherine were obviously close friends as the queen disguised herself as one of Katherine's maids so that she could watch Robert Dudley shoot at Windsor in 1561.

Katherine married Charles Howard, 2nd Baron Howard of Effingham and 1st Earl of Nottingham, in 1563, and the couple went on to have at least five children. Katherine's daughters,

Elizabeth and Frances, also served the queen as maids of honour, as did her granddaughter, Elizabeth Southwell.

Katherine also served the queen as her carver, meaning that she was responsible for receiving the queen's food and serving it on plates. From 1572, she was the chief lady of the privy chamber, and in 1598 Katherine was listed as one of the queen's grooms of the stool. She was also one of the queen's ladies trusted with caring for her jewels. Her husband, Effingham, served as a gentleman of the privy chamber, was elected to the Order of the Garter in 1575, and joined the privy council in 1584, becoming Lord Chamberlain. In 1585, Elizabeth appointed him as her Lord High Admiral, and he acted in this role in the 1588 Spanish Armada trouble and 1596 in Cadiz.

In 1591, the queen granted Katherine and Effingham the manor of Chelsea, and in 1597, she made Effingham Earl of Nottingham, the second-highest peer in England.

Katherine became ill in 1601 and never recovered, dying on this day in 1603 at Arundel House, having suffered several "fits". The queen was devastated by her death, with one contemporary noting that she took the news of her friend's death "muche more heavyly" than Katherine's own husband did. A courtier remarked: "The Queen loved the countess well, and hath much lamented her death, remaining ever since in a deep melancholy that she must die herself, and complaineth of many infirmities wherewith she seemeth suddenly to be overtaken." Katherine's brother, Robert Carey, noted that the queen had a "melancholy humour" and that she made more than "forty or fifty great sighs" as she spoke to him. The women had been close for over 40 years, so Katherine's death was a heavy blow for Elizabeth. It is said grief was a factor in the decline of the queen's own health. Elizabeth died just a month later.

Trivia: there is a myth about the Countess of Nottingham. According to this myth, Katherine played a role in bringing down her husband's enemy, Robert Devereux, Earl of Essex. The queen had once promised Essex that if she ever became angry with him, then he was to send her a ring she had given him and that on receipt of it, she would forgive him. It was alleged that following the Essex Rebellion of 1601, Essex tried to send the ring to the queen, but Katherine intercepted it and withheld it from the queen. When Katherine was dying, the queen who had heard of Katherine's part in Essex's fall, said to her, "God may forgive you, Madam, but I never shall." It's a great story, but it has no basis and dates only to the 17th century.

25 February

On 25th February 1570, Pope Pius V issued the papal bull "Regnans in Excelsis". This bull excommunicated Queen Elizabeth I from the Catholic Church. Here are some excerpts from the bull:

"But the number of the ungodly has so much grown in power that there is no place left in the world which they have not tried to corrupt with their most wicked doctrines; and among others, Elizabeth, the pretended queen of England and the servant of crime, has assisted in this, with whom as in a sanctuary the most pernicious of all have found refuge. This very woman, having seized the crown and monstrously usurped the place of supreme head of the Church in all England to gather with the chief authority and jurisdiction belonging to it, has once again reduced this same kingdom- which had already been restored to the Catholic faith and to good fruits- to a miserable ruin."

"She has removed the royal Council, composed of the nobility of England, and has filled it with obscure men, being heretics; oppressed the followers of the Catholic faith; instituted false preachers and ministers of impiety; abolished the sacrifice of the mass, prayers, fasts, choice of meats, celibacy, and Catholic ceremonies; and has ordered that books of manifestly heretical content be propounded to the whole realm and that impious rites and institutions after the rule of Calvin, entertained and observed by herself, be also observed by her subjects."

"Therefore, resting upon the authority of Him whose pleasure it was to place us (though unequal to such a burden) upon this supreme justice-seat, we do out of the fullness of our apostolic power declare the foresaid Elizabeth to be a heretic and favourer of heretics, and her adherents in the matters aforesaid to have incurred the sentence of excommunication and to be cut off from the unity of the body of Christ."

"And moreover (we declare) her to be deprived of her pretended title to the aforesaid crown and of all lordship, dignity and privilege whatsoever."

The pope went on to state that those who had made any sworn oaths to her were now absolved from those oaths, and he called on the English people to disobey her orders, mandates and laws, and threatened excommunication for those who did obey her.

The pope's orders put English Catholics in an impossible situation – if they obeyed the pope, God's representative on Earth, they had to disobey their queen. However, if they continued to be loyal to their queen, they were deemed heretics by the pope and could be excommunicated.

Even though the queen had declared previously that she had "no desire to make windows into men's souls", i.e. she did not want to prescribe what someone's personal faith should be, this bull described her as a usurper and pretender and was supporting rebellions against her. Elizabeth and her government were forced to act against the Jesuits, the Catholic society committed to bringing people back to Catholicism, seeing them as enemies of the state. A number of Jesuits, and those who harboured them, ended up being executed.

The publication of the bull of excommunication was soon followed by trouble for Elizabeth, with the Ridolfi Plot, a Catholic plot to assassinate Elizabeth and replace her with Mary, Queen of Scots, uncovered just a year after Elizabeth was excommunicated.

26 February

On 26th February 1552, Sir Thomas Arundell, Sir Michael Stanhope, Sir Miles Partridge and Sir Ralph Fane were executed. Arundell and Stanhope were beheaded on Tower Hill while Partridge and Fane were hanged. The men had been condemned as traitors after being accused of conspiring with Edward Seymour, Duke of Somerset and former Lord Protector, against John Dudley, Duke of Northumberland.

Edward Seymour, Duke of Somerset, had made himself Lord Protector shortly after the death of King Henry VIII in 1547, taking control of the young boy-king Edward VI's government. But there were tensions between him and John Dudley, Duke of Northumberland, in late 1549 and Somerset had taken the king to Windsor Castle and called on the English people to rise and defend the Crown against those he saw as trying to depose him. He was branded a traitor, arrested and thrown into the Tower of London. Although he was released and pardoned in February 1550, he quarrelled again with the Duke of Northumberland, and it was rumoured that he wanted to regain his former power and get rid of Northumberland. He was arrested once more, tried for treason in December 1551 and executed on 22nd January 1552.

As for those who'd supported him, in his chronicle, John Stow recorded:

> "Upon Friday, being the 26th of february, one sir Raffe a Vane, & one sir Myles Partryge were both hanged [at] the Tower hill upon the gallowes, & sir Michael Stanhope & sir Thomas Arundell were beheaded upon the skaffold there: all which foure were condemned by virtue of the act of unlawful assemblies as accessories to the duke of Somerset."

Merchant-tailor and citizen of London Henry Machyn also recorded their executions in his diary:

> "The 26th day of February, the which was the morrow after saint Matthew's day, was headed on the Tower hill sir Michael Stanhope knight, and sir Thomas Arundell; and incontinent was hanged the self same time sir Raff [a Vane] knight, and sir Miles Parterege knight, of the gallows beside the . . . . and after their bodes were put into diverse new coffins to be buried and heads in to the Towre in cases and there buried."

Arundell's biographer, Pamela Y. Stanton, writes, "During Somerset's protectorate Arundell was not an ambitious power seeker. He was an intelligent and experienced politician with decades of proven loyalty to the Tudor crown; though he had ample opportunity, there was no hint of a dangerously ambitious man. His loyalty to the king remained intact. However, he was embroiled in circumstances beyond his control, and his political and religious status played against him in a struggle that he lost."

All these men had served their monarch loyally. Arundell had served as a Justice of the Peace and was, as Stanton describes, "one of the most experienced government officers in the country". Sir Michael Stanhope was Edward Seymour's brother-in-law and probably owed his rise at court to Seymour. He served Edward VI as the chief gentleman of the privy chamber and had attended the king when Seymour had retreated to Windsor Castle with the king in 1549. Sir Miles Patridge had also been an active supporter of Somerset, and contemporary historian John Strype wrote of how he was little pitied since he was credited with the duke's evil deeds. Vane was also a loyal supporter of Somerset. Their only crime, it seems, was supporting a man who had now fallen from power, and his enemy, the man now on the rise, the Duke of Northumberland, needed them gone.

Stow went on to say, "all which four persons took on their death that they never offended against the king's majesty, nor against any of his council." It didn't matter, they were deemed traitors.

27 February

On 27th February 1601, Mark Barkworth (also known by the alias Lambert), a Benedictine monk, was hanged, drawn and quartered, dressed in the habit of the Benedictine order, at Tyburn. Two others died that day: Jesuit Roger Filcock and Anne Line, a widow who had harboured priests. Barkworth was beatified in 1929, Line was canonised in 1970, and Filcock was beatified in 1987.

Bishop Richard Challoner gives a biography of Barkworth in his book "Memoirs of missionary priests, and other Catholics of both sexes, that have suffered death in England on religious accounts from the year 1577 to 1684". He explains that Barkworth was a Lincolnshire man brought up as a Protestant. He converted to Catholicism when he went abroad at twenty-two and was instructed in the faith by a Flemish Jesuit at Douai. Barkworth travelled on to Spain and was ordained at the English College at Valladolid in 1599. He was then sent on a mission to England but was apprehended as soon as he had arrived there. He was tried for treason, for being a priest, and was found guilty and condemned to death.

Roger Filcock, who also died that day, hailed from Sandwich in Kent. Challoner writes that he was educated at Douai or Reims and then Valladolid, where he was ordained. He wanted to become a Jesuit priest, so he was sent on a mission to England in 1598 to prove himself. After two years in England, Father Henry Garnet agreed to admit him into the Society of Jesus, and it was planned that Filcock would travel to Flanders to be admitted as a Jesuit novice. However, he was arrested and imprisoned in Newgate. He was tried on 23rd February 1601 and found guilty of treason for being a priest. He was condemned to death.

On 27th February 1601, Barkworth and Filcock were drawn from Newgate to Tyburn on the same hurdle. Challoner gives an account of what happened then:

> "When they were put up into the cart, Mr. Barkwork, with a joyful accent, sung those words of the royal prophet, hoec dies quam fecit Dominus, exultemus; and Mr. Filcock went on in the same tone, & loetemur in ea. Then Mr. Barkworth declared how ready he was to lay down, even a thousand lives, if he had them, for his faith; and protested, that he forgave, with all his heart, the queen, and all that were any ways accessary to his death, and wished to have them with him in eternal glory. Then he recommended himself to the prayers of the catholics, and the cart was drawn from under him. Here some cruel wretch, fearing lest the weight of his body should put the martyr too soon out of his pain, for he was tall and bulky, set his shoulders under him to bear up, at least, some part of that weight; so that he was cut down whilst he was yet alive; and even when the butcher was seeking for his heart, he pronounced these words, O God be merciful to me."

Challoner goes on to say that Barkworth's head was kept by the English Benedictines at their convent in Douai.

Regarding Filcock's end, Challoner records that Barkworth

"was first butchered, before the eyes of father Filcock; who, so far from being discouraged or terrified with that scene of blood, took occasion from thence of more heartily aspiring after the like felicity; crying out with the apostle, I desire to be dissolved, and to le with Christ. His desire was not long deferred: when, after a short prayer, he chearfully yielded himself up to the executioner; and the cart being drawn away, he was hanged, and then cut down, dismembered, bowelled and quartered."

Anne Line was a widow who suffered with regular headaches and "dropsy", but whose "soul was strong and vigorous". On Candlemas Day 1601, 2nd February, Anne's house was raided after it was suspected that she was harbouring priests. Father Francis Page, who had been about to celebrate mass with her, was able to escape, but Anne was still taken to prison. She was tried at the Old Bailey by judge Sir John Popham, and she was so weak that she had to be carried to her trial in a chair. She was sentenced to death for harbouring a priest, although no priest had been found at her house. She was executed before Barkworth and Filcock, and Challoner writes:

"At Tyburn, when she was just ready to die, she declared to the standers-by with a loud voice: 'I am sentenced to die for harbouring a catholic priest; and so far I am from repenting for having so done, that I wish, with all my soul, that where I have entertained one, I could have entertained a thousand'. She suffered before the two priests; and Mr. Barkworth, whose combat came on the next, embraced her dead body whilst it was yet hanging, saying, 'O! blessed Mrs. Line, who hast now happily received thy reward. Thou art gone before us; but we shall quickly follow thee to bliss, if it please the Almighty.'"

Filcock had been Anne's confessor and friend.

So, on this day in 1601, three Catholics were executed in the reign of Queen Elizabeth I.

28 February

On 28th February 1540, Protestant Thomas Forret was burnt at the stake in Castle Hill, Edinburgh, in the presence of King James V. John Knox and David Calderwood record the year of his execution as 1539, but John Foxe and George Buchanan, who had actually spent time with Forret, recorded it as 1540.

Let me tell you more about Forret and what led to his sad end.

Thomas Forret was the son of Thomas Forret, a man who worked as master stabler to King James IV of Scotland. Forret studied on the Continent, in Cologne, before joining Inchcolm Augustinian Abbey in the Firth of Forth in Scotland. As an Augustinian monk, he became the vicar of Dollar, in Clackmannanshire, near Stirling, being recorded as "showing the mysteries of the Scriptures to the vulgar people in English", teaching his parishioners the ten commandments and showing them that the only way to salvation was through the blood of Jesus Christ. He also spoke out against the sale of indulgences. He was a pious man, aiming to memorise three chapters of the Bible every day and then getting his servant, Andrew Kirkie, to test him. When he visited sick parishioners, as well as feeding their souls with the bread of life, he would take with him bread and cheese and give them silver out of his purse.

David Calderwood quotes martyrologist John Foxe in stating that Forret was summoned before the Bishop of St Andrews and Dunkelden several times "to give account of his doctrine", but that he managed to escape until the rise of Cardinal David Beaton.

In 1538, he was summoned to trial for heresy due to his teachings and to him using the New Testament in English. He had also attended the wedding of Thomas Cucklaw, a fellow vicar, during Lent and broke the Lent fast by eating meat there. He was condemned as a chief heretic and teacher of heresy, with four other men: Friar John Beverage, Sir Duncan Simpson, Robert Forrester and friar John Kelowe, "without permission to recant" and burnt on this day in 1540.

At the place of execution, Forret was asked to say that he believed in God and Our Lady, but that he replied, "I believe in God" and "I believe as our Lady believeth". They also took his New Testament from where he'd been holding it to his chest and cried, "Heresy, heresy", the people replying "burn him! Burn him!". At his burning, he cried in Latin and then English, "God be merciful to me, a sinner", and then "Lord Jesus, receive my spirit" before he recited the 51st psalm in Latin and continued doing so until they pulled the stool from under his feet.

And that was the end of martyr Thomas Forret.

29 February

On 29th February 1604, John Whitgift, Archbishop of Canterbury, died at Lambeth Palace, the archbishop's palace in London. He was the last Archbishop of Canterbury in Queen Elizabeth I's reign and had been in office since 1583.

Here are some facts about this Archbishop of Canterbury:

- John Whitgift was born around 1530/1531 and was the eldest son of Henry Whitgift of Great Grimsby, Lincolnshire, and his wife, Anne Dynewell.
- Whitgift's uncle, Robert, provided for the boy's education, first at the Augustinian house where he was abbot in Wellow, then at St Anthony's School in London, Queen's College, Cambridge, and Pembroke College. He graduated BA in 1554.
- In 1555, he became a fellow at Peterhouse College, obtaining his MA in 1557, rather than fleeing into exile as other Protestants did in Mary I's reign. He appears to have been protected by the Vice-Chancellor Andrew Perne, his good friend.
- In 1560, following the accession of Queen Elizabeth I, he was ordained deacon at Ely and then a priest, and he also acted as the Bishop of Ely's chaplain. He regularly denounced the pope as the Anti-Christ in his sermons.
- He obtained his Bachelor of Theology from Peterhouse in 1563 and was appointed Lady Margaret Professor of Divinity, becoming known for his anti-papal stance.
- Although he was originally against the wearing of the surplice, he eventually sided with government policy and preached in its defence. His support of the government brought him favour from William Cecil and helped his career enormously. He obtained his doctorate in theology in 1567 and was made regius

professor of divinity. He was also master of Pembroke College temporarily before becoming master of Trinity College.

- Queen Elizabeth I called him her "White gift" because of his talent for preaching. She also called him "her little black husband".

- In 1571, he was elected Dean of Lincoln and became Vice-Chancellor at Cambridge in 1573. He became Bishop of Worcester in 1577.

- He is known for his religious disagreements, in the pulpit and in pamphlets, with Puritan Thomas Cartwright, who was forced into exile.

- As far as Whitgift's personal faith is concerned, his biographer William Joseph Sheils writes of his Calvinist theology and how he believed that scripture was central to defining the nature of the Church.

- During his time as Bishop of Worcester, he was very concerned with recusancy and acted against Catholics in his diocese.

- On 14ᵗʰ August 1583, following the death of Edmund Grindal, Whitgift was nominated as Archbishop of Canterbury. He was eager to reform the church and take action against Catholics and those who did not attend church. He upset Puritans in the church by endorsing the Book of Common Prayer as the only prayer book that should be used in public worship. Further anti-Puritan measures followed.

- In 1588, Whitgift was one of those targeted in the Marprelate Controversy, with the tracts attacking the established church referring to him as "that miserable, and desperate caytiffe wicked John Whitgift, the Pope of Lambehith".

- He cared for the poor. One Christmas, he and his household sat down to eat with the poor, and he would top up the poorer livings in his diocese. He founded an almshouse in 1595 and then a school. He also encouraged bishops to remind their clergy and the wealthy in their areas of their duty to the poor.

- Whitgift was at Queen Elizabeth's bedside when she died on 24ᵗʰ April 1603 and acted as chief mourner at her funeral. He was also at the council that proclaimed King James VI of

Scotland as king of England and provided the new king with a report on the church in England.

- In February 1604, he caught a cold and suffered a stroke while dining at Whitehall. He died on this day in history, 29th February 1604. He was buried on 27th March 1604 in the Chapel of St Nicholas at Croydon Minster. He made significant bequests to the poor in his will, and left provisions for his school and hospital.

1 March

For today's "on this day in Tudor history", I'm taking you back to King Henry VIII's reign, but to something that happened in Scotland while James Hamilton, 2nd Earl of Arran, was acting as regent for 3-year-old Mary, Queen of Scots.

On this day in Tudor history, 1st March 1546, Scottish evangelical preacher and martyr George Wishart was hanged and burnt at St Andrews, Scotland.

In his preaching, Wishart had denounced the Pope and had continued preaching contrary to Cardinal Beaton's orders. He was tried on 1st March 1546, or 28th February according to John Knox, eighteen charges being levelled against him, and was condemned to death. He went to his death with courage, asking Christ's forgiveness for those who had condemned him to death "ignorantly".

It is not known when George Wishart was born, but it is thought to have been around 1513. He is believed to have been the son of John Wishart of Pitarrow and Janet Lindsay of Edzell. Wishart fled from Scotland to England in 1538 after being accused of heresy for teaching his students the Greek New Testament while working as a teacher. In Bristol, in 1539, he was forced to make a public recantation after preaching against the worship and veneration of the Virgin Mary. He then fled into exile abroad, to Germany and Switzerland, until the death of King James V. In 1543, he was at Corpus Christi College, Cambridge. In 1544 or 1545, he returned to his homeland of Scotland, where he preached in different parts of the country.

On 16th January 1546, he was arrested at Ormiston in East Lothian, Scotland, and imprisoned first in Edinburgh and then transferred to St Andrews. At his trial, either on 28th February or 1st March, he was charged with 18 articles, accusing him of:

- Refusing to desist from preaching, which he answered by saying that it is written, "We shall rather obey God then men".
- Preaching against the sacraments
- Teaching that confession wasn't a sacrament
- Saying openly that it wasn't necessary for a man to know and understand his baptism
- Saying that the sacrament was just a piece of bread

- Saying that Holy Water is "no so good as wash" and that the Pope had no more power than any other man
- Saying that man has no free will and that meat could be eaten in Friday, just like on Sunday
- Saying that we should not pray to saints but only to God
- Saying that there is no Purgatory
- Saying that it was lawful for priests to marry
- Condemning fasting
- Teaching that souls sleep until Judgement day and do not obtain eternal life until that day.

After he had been charged with these counts of heresy and had answered each one, he was condemned to be burnt as a heretic.

Here is an account of his execution from The Works of John Knox:

"He was led to the fire, with a rope about his neck, and a chain of iron about his middle.

When that he came to the fire, he sat down upon his knees, and rose again; and thrice he said these words, "O thou Saviour of the world, have mercy upon me: Father of heaven, I commend my spirit into thy holy hands." When he had made this prayer, he turned him to the people, and said these words: "I beseech you, Christian brethren and sisters, that ye be not offended at the word of God, for the affliction and torments which ye see already prepared for me. But I exhort you, that ye love the word of God, your salvation, and suffer patiently, and with a comfortable heart, for the word's sake, which is your undoubted salvation and everlasting comfort. Moreover, I pray you, show my brethren and sisters, which have heard me oft before, that they cease not nor leave off to learn the word of God, which I taught unto them, after the grace given unto me, for no persecutions nor troubles in this world, which lestith nott. And show unto them, that my doctrine was no wives' fables, after the constitutions made by men; and if I had taught men's doctrine, I had gotten greater thanks by men. But for the word's sake, and true Evangell, which was given to me by the grace of God, I suffer this day by men, not sorrowfully, but with a glad heart and mind. For this cause I was sent, that I should suffer this fire for Christ's sake. Consider and behold my visage, ye shall not see me change my colour. This grim fire I fear not; and so I pray you for to do, if that any persecution come unto you for the word's sake; and not to fear them that slay the body, and afterward have no power to slay the soul. Some have said of me, that I taught, that the soul of man should sleep until the last day; but I know surely, and my faith is such, that my soul shall sup with my Saviour this night, or it be six hours, for whom I suffer this." Then he prayed for them which accused him, saying, "I beseech the Father of Heaven to forgive them that have of any ignorance, or else of any evil mind, forged lies upon me; I forgive them with all mine heart: I beseech Christ to forgive them that have condemned me to death this day ignorantly." And last of all, he said to the people on this manner, "I beseech you, brethren and sisters, to exhort your Prelates to the learning of the word of God, that they at the least may be ashamed to do evil, and learn to do good; and if they will not convert themselves from their wicked error, there shall hastily come upon them the wrath of God, which they shall not eschew."

"Many faithful words said he in the meantime, taking no head or care of the cruel torments which were then prepared for him. Then, last of all, the hangman, that was his tormentor, sat down upon his knees, and said, "Sir, I pray you, forgive me, for I am not guilty of your death." To whom he answered, "Come hither to me." When he was come to him, he kissed his cheek, and said, "Lo! here is a token that I forgive thee: My heart, do thine office." And then by and by, he was put upon the gibbet, and hanged, and there burnt to powder. When that the people beheld the great tormenting of that innocent, they might not withhold from piteous morning and complaining of the innocent lamb's slaughter."

Knox goes on to say, "After the death of this blessed martyr of God, began the people, in plain speaking, to dampen and detest the cruelty that was used. Yea, men of great birth, estimation, and honour, at open tables avowed, That the blood of the said Master George should be revenged, or else they should cost life for life", so it's clear that the common people were unhappy about Wishart's execution.

Wishart's biographer, Martin Holt Dotterweich, writes of Wishart: "To contemporaries Wishart was personally gentle and generous, austere but forgiving; however, his vehemence from the pulpit could also show him to be harsh and vindictive, and thus he had both close friends and bitter enemies." Those bitter enemies that had their say in the end, but Wishart seems confident of his salvation, and that must have been a comfort to him.

2 March

On 2nd March 1545, scholar, diplomat and founder of the Bodleian Library, Sir Thomas Bodley, was born in Exeter.

Thomas was the son of John Bodley, a Protestant merchant who took his family into exile to Germany during Mary I's reign, and his wife, Joan Hone. The family returned to England during Queen Elizabeth I's reign, and Bodley was able to study at Magdalen College, Oxford, where he graduated BA in 1563 and MA in 1566. He then lectured at Merton College and was elected junior proctor. He left Oxford in 1576 and began a diplomatic career for Elizabeth I's government, under the patronage of Robert Dudley, Earl of Leicester, and Sir Francis Walsingham. He also served as a member of Parliament for Portsmouth.

In 1583, Thomas began serving Elizabeth as a gentleman usher, and in 1585, he carried out his first major diplomatic mission in Denmark and Brunswick. In 1588, he carried out a further diplomatic mission to Henry III in France, followed by another to Denmark and the merchants at Hamburg. However, his most important diplomatic mission was when he was appointed as the queen's ambassador to the United Provinces, i.e. the Netherlands, where he was resident ambassador at the Hague from late 1588 to early 1597.

Thomas returned to England in 1597 in ill health and disillusioned by his time as ambassador. At that point, he retired from public service and began the project for which he is known today, the foundation of the Bodleian Library. In 1598, he restored, refurbished and re-founded the Oxford University library, and it was re-opened on 8th November 1602 as Bodley's Library, or the Bodleian Library. This library had been begun in around 1320 but was rescued by Bodley, who had married a rich widow, Anne Cary, widow of Nicholas Ball, a wealthy fish merchant who had made his fortune in trading pilchards. Bodley wrote that in his retirement, he wanted to "set up my staff at the library door in Oxon; being thoroughly persuaded, that in my solitude, and surcease from the Commonwealth affairs, I could not busy myself to better purpose, than by reducing that place (which then in every part lay ruined and waste) to the public use of students". By the time the library opened in 1602, it had over 2,500 books and soon became world famous.

In 1604, Bodley was knighted by King James I, who was a patron of the library. In 1610, Bodley came to an agreement with the Stationers' Company, London, that every book published in England and registered with the Stationers would have a copy deposited at the Bodleian.

Sir Thomas Bodley died at his home next to St Bartholomew's Hospital in London on 29th January 1613, shortly after work started on an extension to the library. He was buried in Merton College Chapel on 29th March 1613. He left most of his fortune to Oxford University, as he had no children.

The Bodleian Library had further work carried out in the 17th, 18th and 19th centuries, and it is a wonderful place and an important Oxford landmark.

3 March

3rd March 1515 is one of the dates given in the contemporary sources for the secret marriage of Henry VIII's sister, Mary, Dowager Queen of France, and Charles Brandon, Duke of Suffolk, the king's best friend.

18-year-old Mary had been widowed on 1st January 1515 when her first husband, 52-year-old King Louis XII of France, died after less than three months of marriage. When the marriage match had been negotiated between Mary and the French king, Mary had made her brother, Henry VIII, promise that Henry would allow her to marry a man of her choosing if Louis died. Mary reminded her brother of this deal in a letter: "I beseech your grace that you will keep all the promises that you promised me when I take my leave of you by the waterside" and added that she wished to marry where "my mind is". She also threatened to enter a convent if the king reneged on his promise, which would mean the king would lose control of her dower. Mary had, of course, fallen in love with Suffolk, the man her brother had sent to escort her back to England.

Suffolk had promised Henry VIII that he would not marry Mary without permission, but he broke that promise. He excused his actions in a letter to Cardinal Thomas Wolsey, explaining that he'd had to rescue Mary, that she was a veritable damsel in distress. He wrote, "When he came to Paris he heard many things which put him and the Queen in great fear. And the Queen would never let me [be] in rest till I had granted her to be married; and so, to be plain with you, I have married her."

We don't know for sure when this marriage took place. A contemporary French chronicle records the secret marriage taking place on 3rd March 1515, and Louise of Savoy, mother of the new French king, Francis I, records it as taking place on Saturday, the last day of March, i.e. Saturday, 31st March 1515. However, in his letter to Wolsey, in which he confesses their secret marriage, Suffolk wrote that he and Mary had consummated the marriage and he feared that she was pregnant, so it was important for them to have a more public marriage. The letter was dated 5th March 1515, so the couple must have married earlier than 3rd March.

Are there any records that can help us narrow it down?

Well, we have a record of a meeting between Francis I and Suffolk on Thursday 1st February, and at that meeting, the French king accused Suffolk of coming to France "to marry the Queen, your master's sister." Suffolk denied it, saying that it would be a "great folly" for him to come to France to marry the dowager queen without Francis's knowledge or the permission of Henry VIII. He assured Francis that it was not his or his king's intention. However, Francis caught him in a lie, for the French king had already spoken to Mary, and she "had broken her mind unto him" and told him of the couple's plan. Francis had said to Mary "that he would help her and do what was possible in him to help her to obtain her heart's desire." Suffolk thanked the king "for the great goodness he intended to show to himself and the Queen". Suffolk recorded this meeting in a letter to Wolsey on 3rd February 1515, written ten leagues from Paris, so we know that Mary and Suffolk had not married at this point but were planning to do so.

As Mary Croom Brown points out in her book on Mary, Suffolk must have been overjoyed that the French king had pledged his support. Croom Brown writes of how Suffolk reached Paris on 4th February, and Mary sent for him. He was greeted by an emotional Mary, who begged him to marry her before their return to England.

Although Francis I offered his support for the marriage, he didn't expect the couple to marry while he was trying to help them, but they did. In the "Chronicle Louis XII", Robert III de La Marck, Seigneur of Fleuranges and Marshal of France, records Francis I's subsequent fury at Suffolk:

> "I am advertised of this thing: I did not think you had been so base, and if I chose to do my duty, I should, this very hour, have your head taken off your shoulders; for you have failed of your faith; and, trusting to your faith, I have not had watch kept over you. You have secretly, without my knowledge married Queen Mary."

Robert de la Marck does not date Francis I's reaction to the news of the couple's secret marriage. This section of his chronicle simply says March 1515 in the margin. Suffolk's biographer, Steven Gunn, dates the secret marriage to mid-February, Mary Croom Brown, in her biography of Mary, dates it to "about the second week of February", and Mary Anne Everett Wood and Agnes Strickland date it to taking place in Lent, which started on 21st February, citing the French chronicle that states the 3rd March 1515.

We can conclude that the couple married secretly sometime after 3rd February when Suffolk wrote to Wolsey of his meeting with the French king, and at least a couple of weeks before Suffolk's 5th March letter to Wolsey when he writes of his fear that Mary could be pregnant. A date of mid-February makes sense, then. This secret marriage would have taken place at the chapel at the Hôtel de Cluny in Paris, where Mary was staying. This secret marriage was then followed by the more public marriage that Suffolk wanted, which took place on 31st March 1515.

These two weddings in France were followed by an official wedding in England, at Greenwich, on 13th May 1515 in the presence of Henry VIII and Queen Katherine of Aragon. Henry may have been furious with the couple at the time, but he did go on to forgive them. Suffolk's biographer, Steven Gunn, writes, "Henry's displeasure was mollified by the surrender of Mary's jewels and plate, half her dowry, the wardship of the now redundant Lady Lisle, and a further £24,000 payable over twelve years from the profits of Mary's dower lands in France."

Mary and Suffolk went on to have four children: Henry, Frances, Eleanor, and a second Henry, the first Henry having died by his birth. They were married for 18 years, and their marriage ended when Mary died on 25th June 1533. Suffolk went on to marry his ward, Catherine Willoughby.

4 March

4th March 1522 was Shrove Tuesday and the date of a special pageant that was part of the Shrovetide celebrations of that year.

As well as marking Shrovetide, the three days before Lent which were the last opportunity to eat well and have some fun before the abstinence of Lent, the entertainment at court in March 1522 also celebrated the negotiations between Charles V, Holy Roman Emperor, and Henry VIII for a joint attack on France. This alliance was to be sealed by the agreement of a marriage between Charles V and Princess Mary, daughter of Henry VIII.

There had been a lavish joust on 2nd March, and then on 3rd March 1522, Cardinal Thomas Wolsey had hosted "a great and costly banquet" for Henry VIII and Charles V's ambassadors. A play and a masque followed it.

Then, on the night of Shrove Tuesday, 4th March 1522, at York Place, the home of Cardinal Wolsey, the cardinal, king and ambassadors supped together and then enjoyed a spectacular pageant.

Here is chronicler Edward Hall's account of the Château Vert, or Green Castle, pageant:

"After supper they came into a great chamber hanged with arras, and there was a cloth of estate, and many branches, and on every branch 32 torchettes of wax. And in the nether end of the same chamber was a castle, in which was a principal tower, in which was a cresset burning: and two other lesser towers stood on every side, warded and embattled. And on every tower was a banner, one banner was of 3 rent (torn) hearts, the other was a lady's hand gripping a man's heart, the third banner was a lady's hand turning a man's heart. This castle was kept with ladies of strange names, the first Beauty, the second Honour, the third Perseverance, the fourth Kindness, the fifth Constance, the sixth Bounty, the seventh Mercy, and the eighth Pity. These eight ladies had Milan gowns of white satin, every lady had her name embroidered with gold, on their heads cauls, and Milan bonnets of gold, with jewels.

Underneath the base fortress of the castle were other eight ladies, whose names were Danger, Disdain, Jealousy, Unkindness, Scorn, Malbouche [evil speaking], Strangeness, these ladies were attired like women of India.

Then entered eight Lords in cloth of gold caps and all, and great mantel cloaks of blue satin. These lords were named Amorous, Nobleness, Youth, Attendance, Loyalty, Pleasure, Gentleness, and Liberty. The king was chief of this company. This company was led by one all in crimson satin with burning flames of gold, called Ardent Desire, which so moved the Ladies to give over the Castle, but Scorn and Disdain said they would hold the place. Then Desire said the ladies should be won and came and encouraged the knights, then the lords ran to the castle, (at which time without was shot a great peal of guns) and the ladies defended the castle with Rose water and Comfits and the lords threw in Dates and Oranges, and other fruits made for pleasure, but at the last the place was won. But Lady Scorn and her company stubbornly defended them with bows and balls, till they were driven out of the place and fled.

Then the lords took the ladies of honour as prisoners by the hands, and brought them down, and danced together very pleasantly, which much pleased the strangers, and when they had danced their fill then all these unmasked themselves and were known. And then was there a costly banquet, and when all was done, the strangers took their leave of the king and the Cardinal and so departed into Flanders, giving to the king much commendation."

The torn hearts on the banners of this pageant continued the theme of unrequited love from the 2nd March joust, where Henry VIII had appeared with the motto "Elle mon coeur a navera", she has wounded my heart. It is not known whether Henry VIII's heart was really wounded or whether it was simply a theme that had been picked.

Henry VIII's future wife, Anne Boleyn, was present at this pageant. She had been recalled from the French court in late 1521 to serve Catherine of Aragon and because of negotiations for her to marry James Butler of Ireland. We don't know exactly when Anne arrived in England, but the Château Vert pageant is the first recorded appearance of her at court. She played the part of Perseverance, while her sister, Mary, played Kindness; Mary Tudor, the king's sister, played Beauty, and Jane Parker, Anne's future sister-in-law, played Constancy.

The Showtime series "The Tudors" depicted Henry VIII falling in love with Anne Boleyn at this pageant, but we don't know when Henry first noticed Anne. The earliest that historians date Henry's interest to is around 1524, so not this early. Anne was yet to be involved with Henry Percy, the Earl of Northumberland's son.

5 March

On 5th March 1549, the bill of attainder introduced into Parliament on 25th February received royal assent. This attainder was against King Edward VI's uncle, Thomas Seymour, Baron Sudeley and Lord Admiral, who had been arrested on 17th January 1549 and charged with 33 counts of treason. As well as being the king's uncle, he was, of course, the brother of Edward Seymour, Lord Protector, who was the leader of the king's government at this time.

An act of attainder was an Act of Parliament by which a named person, or a list of people, was found guilty of a serious crime, such as treason, felony or misprision. Instead of the person being tried for their alleged crimes, Parliament ruled on their guilt. The Act of Attainder provided for their punishment and included the forfeiture of lands to the crown and the corruption of blood, meaning that they couldn't inherit lands or transmit them, i.e. leave them to their heirs.

So, Thomas Seymour wasn't tried for his alleged crimes; he was found guilty by Parliament.

A record in the Acts of the Privy Council for 23rd February states that on that day, the Lord Chancellor and the council had visited Thomas Seymour in the Tower of London and "declared to the said Lord Admiral that great and heinous matters and articles of high treason were objected and laid unto his charge, and by manifest means and witnesses confessed and approved." They then went on to list the 33 charges, which included Seymour being accused of:

- Attempting to get his hands on the government of the king's majesty "to the great danger of his highness's person".
- Using gifts and "fair promises" to "allure" the young king to his "heinous and perilous purposes".
- Intending and trying to take the king into his own hands and custody, i.e. that he had attempted to kidnap the king.
- Promising the marriage of the king at his will and pleasure.
- Retaining young men and yeomen "to a great multitude and far above such number as is permitted by the laws and statutes of the realm" to help him in his evil intents and purposes.
- Attempting to marry the Lady Elizabeth, the king's sister, both before and after his marriage to Catherine Parr.

There were also charges relating to his position as Lord Admiral, accusing him of maintaining pirates, taking the spoils, and distributing them among his servants and friends.

When the council laid the charges before the young King Edward VI, he said, "We perceive that there is great things which be objected and laid to my Lord Admiral, mine uncle, and they tend to treason, and we perceive that you require but justice to be done. We think it reasonable, and we will well that you proceed according to your request."

The bill was then put before Parliament. Parliament heard the examinations, depositions and witnesses and declared that the offences were "in the compass of high treason".

The record then states: "when no man was able to say the contrary, being diverse times provoked thereunto by the Speaker, the Nether House being marvellous full almost to the number of 400 persons, not 10 or 12 at the most giving their nays thereunto, the bill was there likewise passed and assented unto the 5th March".

Thomas Seymour was executed by beheading on Tower Hill on 20th March 1549.

6 March

On 6th March 1536, the "Act for the Suppression (or Dissolution) of the Lesser Monasteries" was introduced into the Parliament known as the Reformation Parliament. This was the beginning of the Dissolution of the Monasteries.

The Reformation Parliament had first sat in October 1529 and is referred to as the Reformation Parliament because it was responsible for passing the legislation, leading to the break between Rome and the English Reformation. As Clare Cherry and I wrote in our book "George Boleyn: Tudor Poet, Courtier and Diplomat":

> "The Reformation Parliament was established on the theory that England was governed by one supreme head, namely the King, and that all jurisdiction in the land, including that of spiritual matters, belonged to the King. It naturally followed that no foreign power could dictate English public policy – specifically, the Pope. It established that only law enacted by a monarch within a sovereign state was binding; hence, this sovereign power was supreme and gave the King and Parliament authority over church law."

The Reformation Parliament was recalled in February 1536, and met until it was dismissed on 14th April 1536.

The Act for the Suppression (or Dissolution) of the Lesser Monasteries affected monasteries with fewer than twelve members and those worth less than £200 per year. They were to be dissolved, their heads pensioned off, and their members to become secularised or moved to larger monasteries "where they may be compelled to live religiously for reformation of their lives".

This dissolution followed visitations ordered by Thomas Cromwell and authorised by King Henry VIII in 1535. By the 1520s, there was widespread indignation at how some abbots and monks were behaved - their vice, immorality, hypocrisy and wealth. Religious tracts had been written against them. In 1535 the king authorised his right-hand man, Thomas Cromwell, to carry out visitations to religious institutions and gather evidence of any irregularities and abuses. However, the concern about abuses was only one reason for the visitations and was probably only a pretext; it was more about King Henry VIII wanting to get his hands on the wealth of the monasteries. Some of the scandals and abuses uncovered were true, but others were completely made up to justify the monastery's closure.

Dissolving the lesser monasteries wasn't enough for the king. In 1539, the remaining monasteries were dissolved, with most of the land and profits going to the Crown and then land being resold to nobles and gentry.

The monasteries weren't just communities of religious people; they were the social welfare system of the day. They fed the poor, cared for the elderly and infirm, acted as hospitals, orphanages, schools and care homes, and provided accommodation for travellers and pilgrims. Their closure impacted both the English landscape and the English people.

7 March

This day in Tudor history, 7th March 1556, was one of the days when the Great Comet, or the Comet of Charles V, was seen and recorded by Paul Fabricius, mathematician and physician at the court of Charles V, Holy Roman Emperor.

In the 1848 book, "On the expected return of the great comet of 1264 and 1556", J. R. Hind writes of how the comet is thought to have been visible in some places by the end of February, "but it was not generally observed until the middle of the first week in March." He explains that "its apparent diameter was equal to half that of the moon" and that its tail, according to a contemporary observer, "resembled 'the flame of a torch agitated by the wind". Physician, astronomer and astrologer Cornelius Gemma described the head of the comet as being as large as Jupiter, its colour resembling that of Mars, and its tail facing East.

In March 1556, the comet's course was observed by Fabricius, and his observations were published in a pamphlet dated 14th March 1556, along with a map of the comet's course. Sadly, his pamphlet is no longer extant, and Hind explains that all that remained of it was "a small rough chart" which other authors used in their works.

Hind writes that the chart shows that "On the 7th it was in 5° of Libra, and had the same declination as epsilon Virginis; consequently the north latitude would be about 17°." He adds, "On March 15th, Fabricius observed the comet for the last time, in about 20° of Aries, with a north latitude of 72° or 74°."

C.D. Hellman notes that another observer of the comet of 1556 was Joachim Heller, who recorded first seeing it while travelling on 27th February. However, he did not see its tail and so was unsure of what he'd seen until he reached Nuremberg when he was told that a comet with a tail had been observed there on 3rd March. His observations in March and April 1556 were used together with those of Fabricius in 1857 by Dutch astronomer and physicist Martin Hoek in his PhD dissertation "The comet of the years 1556, 1264 and 975, and its alleged identity" to make a new computation of the orbit of the 1556 comet and to prove that the comets of 1264 and 1556 were not identical.

At this time, comets were seen as portents of natural disasters, and theologian and historian David Chytraeus recorded Emperor Charles V's reaction to this comet's appearance. The emperor said: "By this dread sign my fates do summon me". That year, he left the Low Countries, having abdicated his various offices and titles, and travelled to Spain to spend his final two years in a monastery.

8 March

On 8th March 1516, Sir John Wiltshire wrote to King Henry VIII from the English territory of Calais.

It's not an important letter; it's just interesting. In the letter, Wiltshire is giving the king warning of some gifts that are on their way to England, and it's the gifts that are interesting. Wiltshire writes:

> "A gentleman of the Duke of Ferrara is coming with presents to Henry, a dark grey courser of Naples, and a 'lebard,' a marvellous dangerous beast to keep. The keeper saith a will kill a buck or doe or roe and an hare, which is a marvellous thing if it be so."

I assume that the lebard is a leopard. A courser was a type of horse that was fast and strong and had good endurance. Knights often used them in battle.

Although the letter appears in the archives for Henry VIII's reign in 1516. This gift is mentioned in the Venetian Archives for the year 1515. There are two mentions:

> "announced the arrival in London on the 18th March of an ambassador from the Marquis of Ferrara, by name Hironimo de Strozi; and in the said Duke's name he presented the King with a horse, said to be very handsome, and a live leopard. According to report, the King was much pleased with this present."

Then, the second mention:

> "Exhibited letters from his Duke Don Alfonso, announcing the return of the envoy sent by him to England with a horse and a live [leopard]. The envoy was much favoured by the King, who reciprocated the presents."

King Henry VIII seemed to like his horse and leopard!

Antonio Frizzi, in his "History of Ferrara", gave more details on these gifts, describing the horse as having gold trappings and stating that as well as the horse and the leopard, the duke sent three trained falcons.

Animal gifts, particularly exotic ones, were all the rage at the time, and the duke obviously wanted to impress. The Tower of

London's website states that there was a royal menagerie at the Tower to house these animal gifts from the 1200s to 1835. It was started when Henry III was sent what was described as three leopards, but which might have been lions, in 1235 by Frederick II, Holy Roman Emperor. In 1252, the King of Norway sent a polar bear, and in 1255 the King of France sent an elephant. Lions at the Tower gave their name to the Lion Tower, which is no longer standing. By the way, the polar bear (with a chain securing it) was able to fish and swim in the River Thames.

Fast-forward to the Tudors, and as well as marmosets and monkeys being kept as pets by wealthy Tudors, including Catherine of Aragon, Henry VIII and Edward VI, visitors to the menagerie at the Tower in the 1540s recorded seeing lions, leopards, an eagle and a lynx, all belonging to the royal family. In 1592, a visitor saw six lions and lionesses and "a lean, ugly wolf" kept by the queen. In 1598, there were three lionesses, a lion, a tiger, a lynx, a wolf, a porcupine and an eagle. Henry VII gave his wife, Elizabeth of York, a lion.

In 1826, 150 of the menagerie's animals were re-homed at Regent's Park, founding London Zoo, and the rest were re-homed when the menagerie closed in 1835.

9 March

On 9th March 1589, Lady Frances Radcliffe, Countess of Sussex, wife of Sir Thomas Radcliffe, Lord Fitzwalter and 3rd Earl of Sussex, died at her home in Bermondsey. She was buried at Westminster Abbey in the Chapel of St Paul.

Here are some facts about this Tudor lady:

- Frances was born around 1531 and was the fourth daughter of Sir William Sidney and his wife, Anne Pagenham.
- Poets Sir Philip Sidney and Sir Robert Sidney were her nephews.
- In 1555, Frances married Thomas Radcliffe, Lord Fitzwalter, as his second wife, at Hampton Court Palace. Mary I's husband, Philip of Spain, participated in the celebratory jousts for the wedding.
- Frances's husband was made Earl of Sussex in 1557.

- Frances resided in Ireland when her husband was Lord Deputy and Lord Lieutenant there between 1556 and 1564. She also accompanied him to Berwick after he was appointed as President of the North in 1568. She caught smallpox there, but fortunately survived.
- In 1571, Frances and Thomas played host to Queen Elizabeth I at their home in Bermondsey.
- In 1572, Thomas was made Lord Chamberlain of the Household, and in 1574 he was rewarded with New Hall in Essex, along with a number of manors.
- It is not known exactly when Frances was appointed as one of Queen Elizabeth I's ladies of the bedchamber, but it was probably in the late 1570s.
- In the early 1580s, Frances had three works dedicated to her.
- Frances did not have any children with Thomas, and he died in June 1583. Frances's biographer, Mary Prior, writes of how "In his last months the countess's enemies (unspecified) alienated his affections from her, and turned the queen against her", and that Frances ended up turning to royal favourite, Sir Christopher Hatton, to intercede with the queen, asking him to deliver a letter to the queen in which she expressed her loyalty to both the queen and to Thomas. Unfortunately, she could not recover her husband's affections, but she inherited his wealth.
- Following Thomas's death, she was pursued by politician Arthur Hall, who had a reputation for trouble. Frances rebuffed him, and as revenge, he attacked her in his book. He ended up being imprisoned for impugning the authority of Parliament and defaming some of its members.
- Frances made her will in December 1588 and died on this day in 1589. She is known for being the benefactor of Sidney Sussex College at Cambridge, and left £5,000, plus plate and other possessions, for a "good and godly monument for the mayntenance of good learning": Lady Sidney Sussex College.
- Frances also left bequests for her Sidney family, poor Puritan preachers in London, and a lectureship at Westminster Abbey.

Frances's monument, which is 24 feet high and made from alabaster, can be found in the Chapel of St Paul in Westminster Abbey. It features an effigy of her wearing a long, red robe lined with ermine and wearing a gilded countess's coronet. The Sidney family crest of a blue and gold porcupine made in wood is at her feet.

The inscription on her tomb, translated from Latin, reads:

"Here lyeth the most honorable lady Frances, sometime Countess of Sussex daughter of Sir William Sidney of Penshurst, Knight; wife and widow to ye most noble, most wise and most martial GentlemanThomas Radclif Earl of Sussex; a woman while she lived adorned with many and most rare gifts both of mind and body, towards God truly and zealously religious: to her friends and kinsfolk most liberal: to the poore, to prisoners and to the ministers of the word of God, always most charitable. By her last will and testament she instituted a divinity lecture to be read in this Collegiate Church and by the same her testament gave also five thousand pounds towards the building of a new college in the University of Cambridge, with sufficient yearly revenue for the continual maintenance of one Master, 10 Fellows, and 20 Scholars, either in ye same College or else in another house in ye said University already builded, commonly called Clare Hall. She lived 58 years and died ye 9 of March, and was buried ye 15 of Aprile 1589."

10 March

On 10th March 1513, magnate John de Vere, 13th Earl of Oxford, died at Castle Hedingham in Essex.

Let me give you some facts about this Earl of Oxford, a key figure in the Wars of the Roses.

- John de Vere was born on 8th September 1442. He was the second son of John de Vere, 12th Earl of Oxford, and his wife, Elizabeth Howard, daughter of Sir John Howard.
- The 12th earl and his eldest son were executed for treason in 1462. John, however, did not suffer. He was granted licence of entry on his father's lands and created Knight of the Bath at the

coronation of Elizabeth Woodville, Edward IV's queen consort, in 1465. He also served as great chamberlain of England and the queen's chamberlain at the proceedings.

- In November 1468, Oxford was imprisoned in the Tower of London for plotting with Lancastrians but was released in early 1469 and pardoned in April 1469.
- In the summer of 1469, he plotted with George, Duke of Clarence, brother of Edward IV, and Richard Neville, Earl of Warwick, against King Edward IV. The latter was then captured at the Battle of Edgecote Moor on 26th July following the defeat of his royal army. However, Edward was released in September 1469 and took back his throne.
- Oxford was unpopular with the king now and so fled into exile at the court of Margaret of Anjou, wife of King Henry VI. He joined Warwick, Clarence and the Lancastrians in planning an English invasion to put Henry VI back on the throne. They successfully restored Henry to his throne, and on 13th October 1470, John bore the Sword of State before King Henry VI in a procession to St Paul's. On 15th October, he presided over the trial of John Tiptoft, Earl of Worcester, who was condemned for high treason. As Lord High Constable, Worcester had presided over the trials of Oxford's father and brother.
- Oxford helped prevent the landing of the former king, Edward IV, in Norfolk in 1471 and commanded the force that defeated that of Lord Hastings at the Battle of Barnet on 14th April 1471. However, after this initial victory, bad visibility due to mist caused Oxford's badge, with its star with rays, to be confused with Edward IV's sun in splendour badge, and Lord Montagu's men, who were actually on the same side as Oxford, attacked Oxford's force, causing them to flee in panic. Edward's Yorkist side had the final victory, and Oxford fled to Scotland and then France, where he focused on privateering, or piracy for a time.
- In September 1473, Oxford was able to seize St Michael's Mount in Cornwall but was forced to surrender on 15th February 1474 after a siege and having been hit in the face by an arrow.
- Oxford was imprisoned at Hammes Castle in the Pale of Calais and attainted for treason. In 1478, Oxford either tried to escape

or attempted suicide by scaling the castle's walls and jumping into the moat. In 1484, the new king, Richard III, ordered him to be transferred from Calais to England, but Oxford had escaped, and he and his gaoler, James Blount, joined Henry Tudor, who was planning an invasion of England. Oxford helped Henry by bringing a force from Hammes.

- Henry Tudor and his forces met those of Richard III at the Battle of Bosworth Field on 22nd August 1485, with Oxford commanding Henry's archers and his vanguard against Richard's vanguard led by John Howard, Duke of Norfolk, who was killed in the battle. Henry and his forces were victorious in the battle, Richard III was killed, and Henry became King Henry VII.
- King Henry VII rewarded Oxford's loyalty with offices including Lord Admiral, Constable of the Tower of London, Captain of the Yeoman Guard and Lord Great Chamberlain of England. He was also a member of the king's council and was elected a Knight of the Garter in 1486. He also stood as godfather at Prince Arthur's christening in 1486 and commanded the vanguard at the 1487 Battle of Stoke.
- In 1489 and 1497, Oxford led forces against the Yorkshire and Cornish Rebellions, and in 1499, he presided over the trial of Edward, Earl of Warwick. Oxford was a powerful man in East Anglia, holding many offices there.
- Oxford was married to Margaret Neville, sixth daughter of Richard Neville, Earl of Salisbury, and sister of Warwick the Kingmaker. His wife was adversely affected following the Battle of Barnet in 1471 when her husband's estates were confiscated. Things didn't improve until 1482, when she was granted an annuity. Margaret died in 1506, and Oxford went on to marry again, marrying Elizabeth Scrope, daughter and co-heir of Sir Richard Scrope and widow of William, 2nd Viscount Beaumont.
- Oxford died on this day in 1513, in the reign of King Henry VIII, leaving his wife, Elizabeth, but no children. He was buried alongside his first wife, Margaret, in the Lady Chapel of Colne Priory, the traditional burial place of the de Veres, on 24th April 1513.

11 March

On this day in history, 11th March 1609, Tudor poet and lawyer William Warner was buried at the Church of St John the Baptist at Great Amwell in Hertfordshire.

Warner's works included "Albion's England" and "Pan his Syrinx, or Pipe, Compact of Seven Reedes".

Let me tell you a little bit more about this Tudor poet.

- William Warner was born around 1558/1559 in London.
- Little is known of his background, but from his work we know that his father accompanied navigator Richard Chancellor on his voyage to Russia in 1553. He died while accompanying William Towerson to Guiana in 1577.
- Nothing is known about Warner's education, but he worked as an attorney in London's court of common pleas.
- Warner married Anne Dale, a widow, in October 1599 at Great Amwell in Hertfordshire, and the couple had a son, William, who was born in 1604.
- Warner published his first work, "Pan his Syrinx, or Pipe, Compact of Seven Reedes" in 1584, which is described as an episodic prose romance. His best-known work is "Albion's England, or, Historicall Map of the same Island", which was published in 1586 and dedicated to Henry Carey, Lord Hunsdon, Queen Elizabeth I's cousin and the son of Mary Boleyn. It's a long poem in 14-syllable couplets, and the first edition told the history of England from the time of Noah to the Norman Conquest. It was expanded in later editions to the reign of Elizabeth I. Warner's biographer Katharine A. Craik describes Albion's England as "an eclectic mixture of classical mythology and Christian legend, together with episodes from the English chronicles and theological debate".
- The vicar of Great Amwell, Warner's local church, recorded that Warner died "suddenly in the night in his bedde without any former complaynt or sicknesse on Thursday night, beeinge the 9th daye of March."

- William Warner was well-known and well-respected as a poet in his lifetime, being described by Francis Meres as "our English Homer", but sadly not many today have heard of him.

12 March

On 12th March 1537, Cistercian monk William Haydock was hanged for treason at Whalley.

Haydock was a senior monk at Whalley Abbey, Lancashire, which had been caught up in the 1536 Pilgrimage of Grace Rebellion, a rebellion of the common people of parts of Northern England against Henry VIII's new religious policies, the dissolution of the monasteries and the advice the king was receiving from some of his senior advisors.

"A History of the County of Lancaster" explains, "At the end of October, 1536, Nicholas Tempest, one of the Yorkshire leaders of the rising, came to Whalley with 400 men and swore the abbot and his brethren to the cause of the commons." It goes on to say that John Paslew, abbot of Whalley, was alleged to have lent Tempest a horse and some plate. It is also said that Paslew refused to sign the oath of allegiance and that an unnamed monk at the abbey had declared that no secular knave should be head of the church. After the rebellion had been successfully put down, King Henry VIII wanted the abbey punished.

Whalley monks Haydock, Abbot Paslew and John Eastgate, were tried for high treason in March 1537 at the spring Lancashire Assizes, along with Eastgate's brother, Richard. He had joined the abbey following the dissolution of nearby Sawley Abbey. John Eastgate was acquitted, but Richard Eastgate, the abbot and William Haydock were found guilty. Eastgate and Abbot Paslew were hanged at Lancaster on 10th March, and their bodies quartered and displayed in various towns in Lancashire. William Haydock was hanged at Whalley in a field adjoining his abbey on 12th March. He wasn't dismembered like the others, and his nephew, also called William Haydock, was able to save Haydock's body and hide it at the Haydock family home, Cottam Hall. Haydock's remains were found when part of the hall was demolished in the 19th century.

13 March

On 13th March 1601, Henry Cuffe and Sir Gelly Meyrick were hanged at Tyburn for their part in Essex's Rebellion of February 1601.

Cuffe had served as secretary to Robert Devereux, 2nd Earl of Essex, and Meyrick had been the earl's steward. Essex himself had been executed by beheading on 25th February 1601.

Henry Cuffe was a scholar who hailed from Somerset originally. He'd been born around 1562/3. He was educated at Trinity College, Oxford, after securing the patronage of Lady Elizabeth Paulet, and graduated BA before becoming a Fellow of the college. In 1586, he became a fellow of Merton College, where he took his MA. In 1590, he was appointed as regius professor of Greek and delivered a speech for Queen Elizabeth I on her visit to Oxford in 1592. Between 1593 and 1594, he was a university proctor, and then he moved into the service of Robert Devereux, becoming one of his secretaries.

He accompanied Essex on his expedition to Cadiz in 1596, and over the next two years, he carried out missions to Florence and Paris for the earl. In Paris, he struck up a friendship with Henry Wriothesley, Earl of Southampton, a good friend of Essex. In 1599, he accompanied his employer, the earl, to Ireland after Essex was appointed Lord Lieutenant of Ireland. Cuffe was sent to argue Essex's case to the queen back in England after Essex's failure there. Cuffe carried on as the earl's secretary after the earl's arrest and confinement following his return from Ireland.

Sir Gelly Meyrick was born around 1556 and was the eldest son of Rowland Meyrick, Bishop of Bangor. He was named Gelly after his grandfather's estate of Gelliswic. Following his father's death, nine-year-old Gelly entered the service of George Devereux, the Earl of Essex's uncle who lived in Pembrokeshire. He served Essex when the earl was studying at Cambridge in 1579, being in charge of hiring and keeping his horses. When the earl came of age, Meyrick managed his estates and financial affairs. His links to the Welsh gentry were also useful to the earl, who wanted a Welsh power base. In turn, Essex helped Meyrick with building up lands and offices.

Meyrick accompanied his master warring in France and Cadiz, helping organise supplies, and he was knighted after the capture of

Cadiz in 1596. Like Cuffe, he accompanied Essex on the expedition to Ireland. And, like Cuffe, he viewed the earl's subsequent troubles as unfair and wanted the earl vindicated.

While some of the earl's supporters advised him that he should seek the queen's forgiveness for his actions in Ireland, Cuffe, Meyrick, and the Earl of Southampton encouraged the earl in the idea that he should remove his enemies at court, those who had spoken ill of the earl while he was in Ireland. According to William Camden, a contemporary source, Cuffe kept on at Essex, saying that he should "resolve upon somewhat worthy of himself, for the perfect recovery of his lost reputation and liberty, for the delivering of his friends from slavery, and the kingdom from the corrupt managery of certain persons." It was then that Essex opened his door to "all comers" and Meyrick entertained at the earl's table "all swordmen, bold confident fellows, men of broken fortunes, discontented persons, and such as saucily used their tongues in railing against all men." Essex also reached out to Scotland for the Scottish king's support and Meyrick began rallying Welsh support.

On 7th February 1601, the day before Essex's rebellion, Meyrick went to watch a performance of Shakespeare's Richard II at the Globe Theatre with a group of Essex supporters. Sir Charles Percy had apparently requested the play, but at his trial, Meyrick was accused of procuring it to be played, and it was said that the play about the deposing of King Richard II was even a play bespoke by Meyrick.

On 8th February 1601, Essex and his supporters marched out of Essex House with his supporters and nobles. They entered the city of London, Essex crying out, "For the Queen, For the Queen, a plot is laid for my life." He planned to force an audience with the queen, but he failed and was denounced as a traitor. Historian Paul Hammer writes that Cuffe "remained entirely aloof from the disaster, reading books and bewailing his master's precipitate action" and when he was arrested, claimed innocence. Essex, however, accused Cuffe of being "a principall instigator to these violent courses".

Cuffe was tried for high treason with Sir Christopher Blount, Sir Charles Danvers, Sir John Davis and Sir Gelly Meyrick at Westminster on 5th March 1601. At his trial, Cuffe said, "If my being within Essex House the day of the rebellion be a foundation to charge me with High Treason, you may as well charge a lion that is within a grate with treason". It was pointed out that he was there that day of his own volition. He was also accused of being "the very seducer of the earl".

The evidence against Meyrick that proved him guilty of open rebellion was that he had acted as captain or commander over the house and had been involved in fortifying and barricading it and providing munitions for the earl's men. It was alleged that he had also removed some men from a property near Essex house and replaced them with some of the earl's supporters. He was also accused of extorting protection money from Catholic recusants in Wales. Meyrick did not try to defend himself. He said only, "I have little to say, but let what I have done be considered, and my offence will be found less than others: But the law hath adjudged it treason, and I must die, and not unwillingly; for the tree being fallen, the branches must not stand".

The jury went away to deliberate and found all of the men guilty. They were sentenced to death – Blount and Danvers to be beheaded on Tower Hill, "being nobly descended", and the others to be hanged, drawn and quartered at Tyburn.

On 13th March 1601, Cuffe and Meyrick were drawn to the gallows at Tyburn. At the gallows, Cuffe gave a long speech, finishing it by proclaiming his innocence:

> "But to come to the cause of my death, there is nobody here can possibly be ignorant what a wild commotion was raised on the 8th of February, by a particular great, but unadvised earl. I do call God, his angels, and my own conscience to witness, that I was not in the least concerned therein, but was shut up that whole day within the house, where I spent the time in very melancholy reflections."

Then, after an interruption, he carried on:

> "I confess it as a crime as black as treason for a subject who lost his prince's favour, to force his way to the royal presence: for my own part, I never persuaded any man to take up arms against the queen."

One account of his speech has him saying, "I am here adjudged to die for plotting a plott never acted [and] for acting an act never plotted".

He carried on but was interrupted again. He finally gave up on his speech and made a profession of his faith, asking pardon of God and the queen. He was then dispatched by the executioner.

It was then Meyrick's turn. His speech was brief, but he used it to clear Charles Blount, Lord Mountjoy, of any involvement in the rebellion.

The two men were then hanged. They were allowed to die by hanging rather than being cut down and disembowelled while still alive. At least there's that mercy.

Trivia: Cuffe doesn't seem to have liked women very much. His biographer Paul Hammer notes that in his work "In The Differences of the Ages of Mans Life" (1607), "he mentions women only in connection with 'the woman's treacherous seduction by the divel in the serpent' and their physical inferiority to men. He also described sex as "'death's best harbinger'" and thought semen conservation was good.

14 March

On 14th March 1540, judge Sir John Port died.

Port is best known for mumbling in a court case and being counted on the wrong side. The case in question was the case of Lord Dacre of the South. Diarmaid MacCulloch explains in his biography of Thomas Cromwell that this was a case that attacked family trusts that Lord Dacre of the South had set up before his death in 1533. MacCulloch explains that the Crown brought its case against Lord Dacre's trust before Chancery but that the judges there adjourned the matter, and it went before the common law judges in the Court of Exchequer in 1535. The Crown won by a narrow margin, and the Dacre trust was declared fraudulent. Port's mumbling gave the Crown a majority in the case.

Sir John Spelman, in his report of the case, recorded, "Port, another Justice of the King's bench, was of the same opinion, but he spoke so low that the said chancellor and secretary understood him to be of the other opinion, and therefore they thought that the greater number of justices were of the same opinion as themselves."

The moral of this tale is that you should always speak clearly in court!

But let's not only remember Sir John Port for this mistake, but also let's look at what else we know about him:

- He was born around 1472 and was from Chester.
- He was practising the law by 1503.
- He was attorney-general in the county palatine of Chester by 1509.
- He was appointed one of the justices of the king's bench in 1525 and served as a member of Princess Mary's council in the Marches.
- He was knighted in 1525.
- He was married twice: to Jane Fitzherbert, who died c.1520, and then to Margery Trafford. He had a son and three daughters with Jane, but his second marriage was childless.
- He was given an estate in Etwall, Derbyshire, by his first father-in-law, and that became his seat.
- He was on the commission of oyer and terminer that tried John Fisher, Bishop of Rochester, and Sir Thomas More in 1535.
- In 1536, he was on the Middlesex and Kent commissions that drew up the indictments against Anne Boleyn and the five men accused with her.
- He was an assize judge.
- He gave Brasenose College, Oxford, an endowment for scholarships.
- His notebook of reports of legal cases and notes came to light at an auction in 1979, and some of it was published in 1986.

He was taken ill at Worcester during the Lent assize of 1540. He was taken to Bewdley and died there on or around 14th March. His remains were taken to Etwall in Derbyshire and buried there. An effigy depicting him wearing judicial robes was erected there.

15 March

On 15th March 1532, King Henry VIII used what was described as "foul language" to William Warham, Archbishop of Canterbury, after the archbishop criticised him in the House of Lords. Warham's criticism of the king came when Parliament discussed the proposed annulment of the king's marriage to his first wife, Catherine of Aragon.

Carlo Capello, the Venetian ambassador, recorded what happened in a letter to the Council of Ten, the government of Venice:

"On the 15th instant the Parliament met to discuss the affair of the divorce, and the Archbishop of Canterbury spoke against the King much to the indignation of his Majesty, who used foul language to him, saying that were it not for his age, he would make him repent of having said what he did against his Majesty."

I'd love to know what the king said to Warham that day. It must surely have shaken the archbishop, who was in his 80s.

Warham died five months later, on 22nd August 1532, while visiting his nephew in Hackington, Kent. He'd served as Archbishop of Canterbury from Henry VII's reign in 1503 and had also served Henry VIII as Keeper of the Great Seal and Lord Chancellor. He was laid to rest in Canterbury Cathedral, having left instructions to be buried near the spot where Thomas Becket was killed. On 30th March 1533, the office of Archbishop of Canterbury was filled by Thomas Cranmer. While Warham had opposed the annulment, Cranmer supported it wholeheartedly and was able to declare the annulment on 23rd May 1533, pleasing the king and his new wife, Anne Boleyn, who was crowned queen on 1st June 1533.

At least Warham kept his head!

16 March

On 16th March 1589, or possibly the day before, Roman Catholic priests Robert Dalby and John Amias were executed at York as traitors.

Dalby was originally from the East Riding of Yorkshire, and he'd been a Protestant clergyman before he was converted to Catholicism. He studied at the English College, the Catholic Seminary at Reims, and was ordained as a Catholic priest in 1588 at Châlons. In August 1588, he arrived back in England on a mission but was arrested soon after arriving at Scarborough. He was taken to York Castle, where he was imprisoned. He was tried and condemned to death for being a priest.

There is little known about John Amias, and it's not even known whether Amias was his real name. In his "Memoirs of missionary priests", Bishop Richard Challoner writes that Amias was a Yorkshire man who studied at the English College at Reims, just like Dalby, and that he was ordained in 1581. In June 1581, he was sent back to England on a mission with a Mr Edmund Sykes but was apprehended, tried and condemned to death for what Challoner describes as his "priestly character".

Why would these men be tried and condemned to death for being a priest?

Elizabeth I was excommunicated by the pope in 1570, and the pope released all her Catholic subjects from their allegiance to her and from obeying her laws. This meant that Catholics and Jesuit priests coming to England to convert people to Catholicism were seen as threats, as traitors. In 1584, the Act against Jesuits ordered Jesuit priests to leave the country. Those who didn't leave or arrived in England after that point and didn't swear an oath of allegiance to the queen were guilty of high treason. So, Dalby and Amias, as priests on a mission, were traitors according to the law of the land.

Bishop Challoner gives an account of their executions from a manuscript by Dr Champney:

> "This year on the 16th of March, John Amias and Robert Dalby, priests of the college of Douai, suffered at York, as in cases of high treason; for no other cause, but that they were priests ordained by the authority of the see of Rome, and had returned into England, and exercised there their priestly functions for the benefit of the souls of their neighbours. I was myself an eye-witness of the glorious combat of these holy men, being at that time a young man, in the 20th year of my age, and I returned home confirmed by the sight of their constancy and meekness, joined with a singular constancy, that you would easily say, that they were lambs led to the slaughter.
>
> They were drawn about a mile out of the city to the place of execution, where being arrived, and taken off the hurdle, they prostrated themselves upon their faces to the ground, and there employed some time in prayer, till the former "Mr Amias" being called upon by the sheriff,

rose up, and , with serene countenance, walked to the gallows and kissed it; then kissing the ladder, went up. The hangman having fitted the rope to his neck, bid him descend a step or two lower, affirming, that by this means he would suffer the less. He then turning to the people declared, That the cause of his death was not treason, but religion, but here he was interrupted, and not suffered to go on. Therefore composing himself for death, with his eyes and hands lifted up to heaven, forgiving all who had any ways procured his death, and praying for his persecutors, he recommended his soul to God, and being flung off the ladder, quietly expired; for he was suffered to hang so long till he seemed to be quite dead. Then he was cut down, dismembered and bowelled, his bowels cast into a fire that was prepared hard by for that purpose, his head cut off, and the trunk of his body quartered.

All this while, his companion "Mr Dalby" was most intent on prayer; who being called upon, immediately followed the footsteps of him that had gone before him, and obtained the like victory."

Champney goes on to say that a gentlewoman caused a scene by breaking through the crowd and making her way to where the bodies were being quartered. She then fell on her knees, joined her hands, looked up to heaven and "declared an extraordinary motion and affection of soul" and then spoke some words which Champney couldn't hear. "Immediately a clamour was raised against her as an idolatress", and she was driven away. Champney wasn't sure if she was taken to prison.

Pope Pius XI beatified both Amias and Dalby on 15th December 1929, so they are known as Bless Robert Dalby and Blessed John Amias.

17 March

On 17th March 1554, two of Mary I's councillors, the Marquess of Winchester and Earl of Sussex, were sent to escort Elizabeth, daughter of Henry VIII and Anne Boleyn, to her prison at the Tower of London. It was alleged that she was involved in Wyatt's Rebellion, a rebellion which sought to depose the Catholic Mary I, who was planning to marry Philip of Spain, and replace her with her Protestant half-sister, Elizabeth.

Mary had written to Elizabeth on 26th January, summoning her to court and warning her about the rebellion, but Elizabeth didn't obey, pleading illness. Elizabeth was finally forced to travel to London, and then on the 17th, Winchester and Sussex turned up at her door at Whitehall Palace.

This was when Elizabeth wrote what David Starkey calls "the letter of her life", the famous Tide Letter, so-called because as Elizabeth wrote this letter to her sister, the tide of the Thames turned, making it impossible to escort Elizabeth to the Tower of London by barge that day.

The letter was written in haste, but Elizabeth still managed to write an eloquent and well-argued letter, which unfortunately went ignored by Mary. It did, however, delay her imprisonment by one day. On Palm Sunday, 18th March 1554, Elizabeth was taken to the Tower, where she was imprisoned until 19th May 1554, the anniversary of her mother's execution.

Here is the famous Tide Letter:

"If any ever did try this old saying, 'that a king's word was more than another man's oath', I most humbly beseech your majesty to verify it to me, and to remember your last promise and my last demand, that I be not condemned without answer and due proof, which it seems that I now am; for without cause proved, I am by your Council from you commanded to go to the Tower, a place more wanted for a false traitor than a true subject, which though I know I desire it not, yet in the face of all this realm it appears proved.

I pray to God I may die the shamefullest death that any ever died, if I may mean any such thing; and to this present hour I protest before God (Who shall judge my truth, whatsoever malice shall devise), that I never practised, counselled, nor consented to anything that might be prejudicial to your person any way, or dangerous to the state by any means. And therefore I humbly beseech your majesty to let me answer afore yourself, and not suffer me to trust to your councillors, yea, and that afore I go to the Tower, if it be possible; if not, before I be further condemned. Howbeit, I trust assuredly your highness will give me leave to do it afore I go, that thus shamefully I may not be cried out on, as I now shall be; yea, and that without cause.

Let conscience move your highness to pardon this my boldness, which innocency procures me to do, together with hope of your natural kindness, which I trust will not see me cast away without desert, which what it is I would desire no more of God but that you truly knew. Which thing I think and believe you shall never by report know, unless by yourself you hear. I have heard in my time of many cast away for want of coming to the presence of their prince; and in late days I heard my Lord of Somerset say that if his brother had been suffered to speak with him he had never suffered; but persuasions were made to him so great that he was brought in belief that he could not live safely if the Admiral lived, and that made him give consent to his death. Though these persons are not to be compared to your majesty, yet I pray God the like evil persuasions persuade not one sister against the other, and all for that they have heard false report, and the truth not known.

Therefore, once again, kneeling with humbleness of heart, because I am not suffered to blow the knees of my body, I humbly crave to speak with your highness, which I would not be so bold as to desire if I knew not myself most clear, as I know myself most true. And as for the traitor Wyatt, he might peradventure write me a letter, but on my faith I never received any from him. And as for the copy of the letter sent to the French king, I pray God confound me eternally if ever I sent him word, message, token, or letter, by any means, and to this truth I will stand in till my death. Your highness's most faithful subject, that hath been from the beginning, and will be to my end, Elizabeth I humbly crave but only one word of answer from yourself.

Your highness's most faithful subject that hath been from the beginning, and will be to my end. Elizabeth."

18 March

On 18th March 1554, Palm Sunday, the twenty-year-old Lady Elizabeth (the future Queen Elizabeth I) was escorted by barge from her home at Whitehall Palace along the River Thames to the Tower of London and imprisoned there.

John Foxe, in his Book of Martyrs, includes a tract called "The miraculous preservation of the Lady Elizabeth, now Queen of England, from extreme calamity and danger of life; in the time of Queen Mary, her sister", and here is an excerpt regarding Elizabeth's apprehension:

"About nine of the clock, these two [Winchester and Sussex] returned again, declaring that it was time for her Grace to depart. She answered, 'If there be no remedy, I must be contented;' willing the lords to go on before. Being come forth into the garden, she did cast her eyes towards the window, thinking to have seen the queen, which she could not: whereat she said, she marvelled much what the nobility of the realm meant, which in that sort would suffer her to be led into captivity, the Lord knew whither, for she did not. In the mean time, commandment was given in all London, that every one should keep the church, and carry their palms, while in the mean season she might be conveyed without all recourse of people into the Tower.

After all this, she took her barge with the two foresaid lords, three of the queen's gentlewomen, and three of her own, her gentleman-usher, and two of her grooms, lying and hovering upon the water a certain space, for that they could not shoot the bridge, the bargemen being very unwilling to shoot the same so soon as they did, because of the danger thereof: for the stern of the boat struck upon the ground, the fall was so big, and the water was so shallow, that the boat being under the bridge, there staid again awhile. At landing she first stayed, and denied to land at those stairs where all traitors and offenders customably used to land, neither well could she, unless she should go over her shoes. The lords were gone out of the boat before, and asked why she came not. One of the lords went back again to her, and brought word she would not come. Then said one of the lords, which shall be nameless, that she should not choose: and because it did then rain, he offered to her his cloak, which she, putting it back with her hand with a good dash, refused. So she coming out, having one foot upon the stair, said, 'Here landeth as true a subject, being prisoner, as ever landed at these stairs; and before thee, O God! I speak it, having no other friends but thee alone.' To whom the same lord answered again, that if it were so, it was the better for her.

At her landing there was a great multitude of their servants and warders standing in their order. 'What needed all this?' said she. 'It is the use,' said some, 'so to be, when any prisoner comes thither.' 'And if it be,' quoth she, 'for my cause, I beseech you that they may be dismissed.' , Whereat the poor men kneeled down, and with one voice desired God to preserve her Grace; who the next day were released of their cold coats.

After this, passing a little further, she sat down upon a cold stone, and there rested herself. To whom the lieutenant then being said, 'Madam, you were best to come out of the rain; for you sit unwholesomely.' She then replying, answered again, 'It is better sitting here, than in a worse place; for God knoweth, I know not whither you will bring me.' With that her gentleman-usher wept: she demanding of him what he meant so uncomfortably to use her, seeing she took him to be her comforter, and not to dismay her; especially for that she knew her truth to be such, that no man should have cause to weep for her. But forth she went into the prison.

The doors were locked and bolted upon her, which did not a little discomfort and dismay her Grace: at what time she called to her gentlewoman for her book, desiring God not to suffer her to build her foundation upon the sands, but upon the rock, whereby all blasts of blustering weather should have no power against her. The doors being thus locked, and she close shut up, the lords had great conference how to keep ward and watch, every man declaring his own opinion in that behalf, agreeing straitly and circumspectly to keep her."

It's a wonderfully descriptive account, but we have to take it with a hefty pinch of salt, for, as David Starkey points out, we know from other sources that Elizabeth was not taken through Traitors' Gate, but instead was taken to Tower Wharf. The tract also states that Elizabeth was kept in a dungeon, and some books and websites state that she was imprisoned in the Bell Tower, but this isn't true. Elizabeth was confined in the royal palace in the inner ward of the Tower of London, the palace renovated by her father, King Henry VIII, for her mother Anne Boleyn's coronation in 1533. The royal apartments there served as Anne Boleyn's prison in May 1536 and Elizabeth's prison in 1554. Elizabeth's prison was not a cold, damp horrible dungeon or prison cell, and she was attended by servants. However, she was still a prisoner and was accused of being a traitor to the crown.

On 23rd March 1554, Good Friday, Elizabeth was interrogated by the queen's council. Rebel leader Thomas Wyatt the Younger had refused to implicate Elizabeth in his plot during his interrogations, so the council hoped they could break Elizabeth and that she'd implicated herself. However, the princess kept her wits about her.

At his execution on 11th April 1554, Wyatt gave a rousing speech proclaiming Elizabeth's innocence. There was just no evidence against her. David Starkey writes of how Mary's council "bickered and debated" over what to do with Elizabeth and how Mary herself "dithered". Mary may have seen Elizabeth as a threat, but Elizabeth was her half-sister and the daughter of Bluff King Hal. There may well have been trouble if Mary had executed her. Simon Renard, the imperial ambassador, recorded in a dispatch to the emperor that "even if there were evidence, they would not dare to proceed against her because her relative, the Admiral, has espoused her cause, and controls all the forces of England". He was referring to William Howard, 1st Baron Howard of Effingham, who was Lord Admiral to Mary I but also Elizabeth's uncle.

With no evidence of treason, Elizabeth was granted more freedom and, although still a prisoner, was permitted to walk in the palace's privy garden. The story in "The Miraculous Preservation" of a boy, the son of an officer of the Tower, bringing flowers to Elizabeth, and Elizabeth's fellow prisoner, Edward Courtenay, Earl of Devon, trying to communicate with her through this boy, is true as it is confirmed in a report by Simon Renard. Renard reported to the emperor, "It is proved that Courtenay has sent a child of five, the son of one of the soldiers in the Tower, to present his commendations to Elizabeth." The Earl of Devon was, of course, the man that the rebels had wanted Elizabeth to marry when they put her on the throne after deposing Mary I. Elizabeth was also permitted to walk in the great gallery. This extra freedom must have given Elizabeth hope that Mary was going to release her and spare her life.

Elizabeth must have been stricken with fear, though, on 4th Mary when Sir Henry Bedingfield, Constable of the Tower of London, was ordered to raise a hundred troops. Were these men for crowd control at her execution? Fortunately for Elizabeth, the queen decided to release her into house arrest, and on 19th May 1554, the anniversary of her mother's execution, Elizabeth was released from the Tower.

19 March

On 19th March 1568, Elizabeth Seymour, Lady Cromwell, died. She was around fifty years old at her death.

Let me give you a few facts about this Tudor lady.

- Elizabeth Seymour was born around 1518 and was the daughter of Sir John Seymour of Wolfhall in Wiltshire and his wife, Margery Wentworth. Her siblings included Jane Seymour, third wife of King Henry VIII; Edward Seymour, Lord Protector Somerset; and Thomas Seymour, 1st Baron Seymour of Sudeley.

- Elizabeth was married three times. She was married to Sir Anthony Ughtred by 1530 as his second wife and had two children with him. He was appointed Captain and Governor of Jersey in 1532, taking Elizabeth with him to the island, but died in 1534. Following his death, Elizabeth returned to England. In 1537, the widowed Elizabeth wrote to Thomas Cromwell for help. She wrote, "please it you to be so good unto me as through your means I might be holpen to obtain of the king's grace to be farmer of one of these abbeys, if they fortune to go down." She hoped to have her precarious financial situation eased with the granting of a dissolved abbey. Instead, Thomas Cromwell arranged for her to marry his son and heir, 17-year-old Gregory Cromwell, who would later become Baron Cromwell. The couple married at Mortlake in August 1537. It was a happy and successful marriage, resulting in three sons and two daughters. Sadly, Gregory died of sweating sickness in 1551. In 1554, Elizabeth married her third and final husband, Sir John Paulet, later Lord St. John and 2nd Marquess of Winchester. Two of Elizabeth's sons, Henry Ughtred and Henry Cromwell, married Paulet's daughters, Elizabeth and Mary. Elizabeth did not have any children with Paulet.
- Elizabeth served three of Henry VIII's wives: Anne Boleyn, Anne of Cleves and Catherine Howard.
- Elizabeth was laid to rest on 5th April 1568 at St Mary's Church, Basing in Hampshire, the Paulet family church.

Trivia: a portrait by Hans Holbein the Younger found in the collections of the Toledo Museum of Art and Hever Castle and once thought to be Catherine Howard, Henry VIII's fifth wife, is now believed by several historians to be Elizabeth Seymour.

20 March

On 20th March 1544, Cuthbert Mayne, Roman Catholic priest and martyr, was baptised on the Feast of St Cuthbert in Youlston in North Devon.

Cuthbert Mayne has gone down in history as the first seminary priest to be martyred. He was hanged, drawn and quartered at Launceston on 30th November 1577.

Let me tell you a bit more about this man.

- Cuthbert Mayne was born in 1544 and was the son of farmer William Mayne.
- Cuthbert was educated at Barnstaple Grammar School. His father's boss, Sir John Chichester, acted as Cuthbert's patron, and in 1561, when Cuthbert was just 17, Chichester got him installed as rector of Hutshaw in Devon. In 1565, he went to St Alban Hall, Oxford, and in 1566 he graduated BA. He then became a chaplain at St John's College and obtained his MA in 1570.
- During his time at St John's, Gregory Martin, Edmund Campion and others warned him of the "evil state he stood in" and encouraged him to convert to the Roman Catholic faith and travel to Douai. One of their letters to Cuthbert was seen by the Bishop of London, who sent men to Oxford in search of Cuthbert. However, Cuthbert had already managed to flee to Douai, and there was admitted to the English College, the Jesuit seminary college.
- He was ordained as a priest there in 1575 and obtained his Bachelor in Theology in 1576.
- Cuthbert returned to England in 1576 and became chaplain and steward to Francis Tregian, a recusant gentleman of Golden Manor, near Probus in Cornwall. He celebrated mass at several of Tregian's family estates in Cornwall, but in June 1577, after the Bishop of Exeter and Sheriff of Cornwall had decided to crack down on Catholics in Cornwall, Golden Manor was surrounded by several Justices of the Peace and a hundred armed men. They were intent on searching the property on the pretext that they had heard that a Mr Bourne, who had committed a crime in London, had fled to Cornwall and was holed up in the house. After being threatened by the sheriff with a dagger, Tregian allowed the men into his house, and they went straight to Cuthbert's room. Cuthbert, who was wearing a prohibited wax Agnus Dei, was arrested, and his papers were seized and sent

to the bishop. A wax Agnus Dei was a wax disc usually made from the previous year's Easter candles and imprinted with a lamb, the lamb of God, on one side and figures of saints on the other.

- Cuthbert was paraded through several Cornish villages on his way to his prison at Launceston Castle, where he was imprisoned for three months before being tried at the Michaelmas Assizes. The charges against him included him traitorously getting hold of a papal bull and publishing it at Golden Manor, defending the authority of the pope, purchasing a number of Agnus Dei and giving them to people, and celebrating the Catholic mass. Cuthbert was found guilty of treason and sentenced to be hanged, drawn and quartered, while his master, Francis Tregian, had his property seized and was sentenced to life imprisonment. Bishop Richard Challoner notes that "there were no sufficient proofs of any of these heads of the indictments" and that the bull was simply "a printed copy of the grant of the jubilee of the past year" and had not been procured by Cuthbert.

- On 29th November 1577, Cuthbert was allegedly offered mercy if he would renounce his Catholic faith, which he refused to do. He also refused to name any other Catholic recusants. He was asked to swear on the Bible that Queen Elizabeth I was the Supreme Head of the Church in England: "Upon this he took the Bible into his hands, made the sign of the cross upon it, kissed it, and said, "The queen neither ever was, nor is, nor ever shall be, the head of the church of England".

- On 30th November 1577, Cuthbert was drawn on a hurdle to the marketplace of Launceston for his execution. Bishop Challoner drew on an account published in 1582 and a Latin Manuscript from Douai in his account of Cuthbert's life and execution. Here is the account of his execution:

"When he came to the place of execution, which was the market-place of the town, where they had on purpose erected a gibbet of unusual height, being taken off the sledge, he kneeled down and prayed: when he was on the ladder, and the rope about his neck, he would have spoken to the people, but the justices would not suffer him, but bid him say his prayers, which he did very devoutly. And as the hangman was about to turn the ladder, one of the justices spoke to him in this manner: 'Now villain and traitor, thou knowest that thou shalt die, and therefore tell us whether Mr Tregian and Sir John Arundel did know of these things which thou art condemned for: and also what thou dost know by them?' Mr Main answered him very mildly: 'I know nothing of Mr Tregian and Sir John Arundel, but that they are good and godly gentlemen; and as for the things I am condemned for, they were only known to me, and to no other' - Then he was cast off the ladder saying 'in manus tuas', etc. and knocking his breast. Some of the gentlemen would have had him cut down strait away, that they might have had him quartered alive; but the sheriff's deputy would not, but let him hang till he was dead. The Latin manuscript says, "he was, indeed, cut down alive, but falling from the beam, which was of an unusual height, with his head upon the side of the scaffold, on which he was to be quartered, he was by that means almost quite killed; and therefore but little sensible of the ensuing butchery. His quarters were disposed of, one to Bodwin, one to Tregny, one to Barnstable, and the fourth to remain at Launceston castle: his head was set upon a pole at Wadebridge, a noted high-way. The hangman, who embrued his hands in his innocent blood, in less than a month's time became mad, and soon after miserably expired. And it is particularly remarked, that not one of those whom Mr. Maine reconciled to the church, could ever be induced to renounce the catholic truth, which they had learned from so good a master."

- Cuthbert was canonized on 15th October 1970 by Pope Paul VI as one of the forty martyrs of England and Wales. St Cuthbert Mayne's feast day is celebrated on 30th November.

21 March

On 21st March 1603, a dying Queen Elizabeth I finally took to her bed.

Elizabeth had been deeply depressed following the death of her close friend and lady, Katherine Howard, the Countess of Nottingham, on 25th February, and was feverish and had trouble sleeping at the beginning of March 1603.

When Sir Robert Carey, the countess's brother, visited the queen at Richmond on 19th March, he found her sitting on cushions in one of her withdrawing chambers. When he entered, she took him by the hand, said, "No, Robin, I am not well", and gave 40-50 sighs. He described her "melancholy humour" that was "too deep rooted in her heart" for him to do anything about. Soon, she stopped eating but refused to see a physician. An anonymous contemporary recorded how the queen "could be prevailed on neither by entreaties, arguments, nor artifices, to take the least medicine and scarcely sufficient nourishment to support life" and said, "She could get no sleep whatever. Dreading her bed, she sat up whole days supported by pillows, mostly awake, and speaking not at all."

Her coronation ring had to be sawn off as it was digging into her flesh, and historian J. E. Neale writes of how this "was a symbolic act; as though her marriage with the realm was to be destroyed." And a new monarch was waiting in the wings: the son of Mary, Queen of Scots: King James VI of Scotland. On 19th March, Robert Carey wrote to James, telling him that Elizabeth would not live more than three days, and on 20th March, he sent a draft proclamation of James's kingship.

On 21st March 1603, the day of the Countess of Nottingham's funeral, the queen's physicians and privy council sent for the countess's husband, Charles Howard, Earl of Nottingham and Lord High Admiral. By this point, the queen had, according to Robert Carey, "remained upon her cushions four days and nights at least", although de Beaumont recorded that she'd been sitting on cushions for ten days. Everyone was concerned. Nobody could persuade her to go to bed, but, according to Carey, on 21st March 1603, his brother-in-law, the Lord Admiral, was able to get the queen to bed "what by fair means, what by force". Elizabeth would never leave her bed.

Although the queen seemed to rally at first, asking for meat broth, Carey described how, on 23rd March, the queen "grew speechless". Although she couldn't speak, she was able "by signs" to call for her council and then "by putting her hand to her head when the king of Scots was named to succeed her" to choose James VI of Scotland to be her successor.

At least during her final days, the queen was comforted by religious men she trusted, like John Whitgift, her Archbishop of Canterbury and the man she called her little black husband, and also the Bishop of London, Bishop of Chichester and other royal chaplains. In fact, Elizabeth wouldn't let Whitgift leave. John Chamberlain recorded that the queen "would not suffer the archbishop to depart as longe as she had sence, but held him twise or thrise when he was going and could not indure both by reason of his own weakenes and compassion of hers." John Manningham recorded how she hugged his hand when he spoke of heaven but would not let the archbishop speak of her surviving to have a longer life. She knew she was dying and appears to have been ready for it.

22 March

22nd March 1519 is the traditional date given for the birth of Katherine Willoughby (married names Brandon and Bertie), Duchess of Suffolk, a woman known for her patronage of the reformed religion and reformists.

Let me tell you a few facts about this Tudor woman.

- Katherine was the daughter of William Willoughby, 11th Baron Willoughby de Eresby, and Lady Maria de Salinas, lady-in-waiting to Catherine of Aragon.
- She became Charles Brandon, Duke of Suffolk's ward in 1529, following her father's death, and married him in September 1533, just three months after the death of his previous wife, Mary Tudor. Suffolk was about 49, and Katherine was 14.
- Suffolk and Katherine went on to have two sons, Henry and Charles, born in 1535 and 1537. Unfortunately, they both died of sweating sickness on 14th July 1551.

- Katherine served Catherine Parr, Henry VIII's sixth and final wife, as one of her ladies. In the queen's household, the evangelical Katherine could mix with like-minded women like Anne Seymour, Countess of Hertford; Lady Elizabeth Tyrwhit; Jane Dudley, Lady Lisle; and Lady Joan Denny; and evangelical men like Dr Robert Huick, Sir Philip Hoby and John Parkhurst.
- Katherine named her dog Gardiner after Bishop Stephen Gardiner, and it is said that she dressed the dog in a vestment and processed in "a mock parade" to humiliate the bishop and to show her opposition to such vestments. Some say that she called the dog Gardiner so that she could enjoy calling him to heel!
- Katherine's first husband, the Duke of Suffolk, died in August 1545, and in around 1552, Katherine married her gentleman usher, Richard Bertie. She had two children with him: Susan and Peregrine.
- In Edward VI's reign, Katherine was an active patron of Protestants and theologians.
- Katherine and Bertie went into exile on the Continent during the Catholic Mary I's reign.
- Although the couple returned to England when Elizabeth I came to the throne, Katherine, who believed that Elizabeth's religious settlement did not go far enough, chose to keep away from the royal court and spend her time in Lincolnshire, where she promoted her religious views.
- Katherine employed Bible translator Miles Coverdale as a tutor to her children.
- Katherine died on 19th September 1580 and was buried in Spilsby Church, Lincolnshire.

23 March

On 23rd March 1540, Waltham Abbey, an Augustinian house in Essex, was surrendered to the Crown. It was the last abbey to be dissolved in Henry VIII and Thomas Cromwell's dissolution of the monasteries. It was the richest religious house in Essex, with the net value of its 1150 acres listed as £900 4s. 3d., and the gross value as £1,079 2s. 1d. yearly.

Henry VIII rewarded his friends and favoured courtiers with monastery lands. It was Anthony Denny, a member of the king's privy chamber who later became his groom of the stool, who benefitted from the dissolution of this house, being granted in April 1541, a 21-year lease of the property of Waltham Abbey. He received other Waltham assets following the death of the king in 1547.

I want to share with you an extract from my book "Tudor Places of Great Britain" on Waltham Abbey:

"Today, the Abbey Church, gatehouse and bridge, and a few ruins are all that remain of Waltham Abbey, an abbey whose origins dated back to the 11th century, when a church was re-founded at Waltham after Harold Godwin, Earl of Wessex, father of Harold II, was healed of paralysis after praying before the Holy Rood at Waltham. The church was refounded in 1177 as an Augustinian priory, as part of Henry II's penitence for the murder of Thomas Becket. It was raised to the status of an abbey in 1184 and became one of the most important monastic house of England.

The church is the resting place of King Harold II and the abbey library was home to the 13th century Waltham Bible. The church was a major site of pilgrimage in the medieval and Tudor periods. Waltham was the last abbey to be surrendered to the crown during the Dissolution of the Monasteries, and was dissolved in 1540 and granted to the Denny family. It was at this time that the monastic buildings and the parts of the church that stood east of the crossing were sadly demolished. Visitors to the church today, which is known as the Abbey Church of Waltham Holy Cross and St Lawrence, and which serves as the parish church of Waltham Abbey town, can still see the Norman nave, the 14th century Lady Chapel and west wall, and the 16th century west tower. It still has plenty of fine Norman architecture and is well worth a visit.

The gatehouse dates back to the 14th century as does "Harold's Bridge", which crosses Cornmill Stream. The gatehouse's west wall has two beautiful arched gateways that are dressed in limestone: one for pedestrians and one for carriages. Also visible on the site are some remains of the cloister and chapter house walls, along with remains of a post-medieval house."

24 March

On 24th March 1619, Robert Rich, 1st Earl of Warwick, nobleman and politician, died at his London home, Warwick House in Holborn. He was laid to rest at Felsted Church in Essex.

Robert Rich was the second son of Robert Rich, 2nd Baron Rich, and his wife, Elizabeth, and grandson of Richard Rich, 1st Baron Rich, who served King Edward VI as Lord Chancellor but is more famous for being involved in the torture of Protestant Anne Askew in Henry VIII's reign.

Robert Rich succeeded his father as Baron Rich in 1581 as his older brother, Richard, had died without issue the previous year.

His biographer Brett Usher points out that Rich was the most eligible bachelor in England since he owned estates worth around £5,000 per annum. William Cecil, Lord Burghley, and Henry Hastings, Earl of Huntingdon, the guardians of Robert Devereux, Earl of Essex, and his sister, Penelope Devereux, respectively, arranged a marriage match between Rich and Penelope. Penelope was the daughter of the late Walter Devereux, 1st Earl of Essex, and his wife, Lettice Knollys, and she is thought to have been the inspiration or muse for Sir Philip Sidney's "Astrophel and Stella". Although Penelope did not want to marry Rich, she was forced to marry him in November 1581. It was not a happy marriage. Penelope's second husband, Charles Blount, Lord Mountjoy, recorded that following the marriage, Rich "did study in all things to torment her".

Rich and his wife separated in 1590 after the birth of their second son, and Penelope began a relationship with Charles Blount, the future Lord Mountjoy. Their resulting children were brought up as Rich's as the couple did not divorce until 1605. Even though they'd been desperately unhappy and Penelope was involved with Mountjoy, when Rich was seriously ill in 1600, Penelope nursed him through it. In 1601, following her brother's failed rebellion, Penelope was imprisoned briefly and interrogated before being sent home to her husband. There was no loving reunion; their divorce was granted in November 1605 after Penelope admitted to adultery. Penelope married Mountjoy in December 1605, but he died in April 1606.

In 1608, Rich was appointed as a privy councillor, and in 1618, he was made Earl of Warwick after paying the exchequer £10,000 for the privilege. Rich made his will in September 1617, appointing his eldest son, Robert, as executor and leaving instructions to be buried at Felsted. He died on this day in 1619, leaving somewhere in the region of £5000 plus properties in London, Essex, Norfolk and Suffolk. His eldest son inherited the earldom of Warwick, and his second son, Henry, became Earl of Holland.

25 March

On 25th March 1586, Good Friday and Lady Day, the Feast of the Annunciation, Catholic martyr Margaret Clitherow (née Middleton), known as "the Pearl of York", was pressed to death at the toll-booth on Ouse Bridge in York, under 7 or 8 hundred-weight. She was executed for harbouring Catholic priests.

Margaret Clitherow had previously been imprisoned for helping and harbouring priests, hiding them in two chambers, one connected to her house and another in another part of York. Margaret refused a trial by jury as she did not want her children to be forced to testify and possibly tortured, so she was automatically sentenced to death. Her family and friends claimed she was pregnant with her fourth child, but Margaret would not confirm it.

In his "Life of Margaret Clitherow", Margaret's confessor, John Mush, writes of her martyrdom:

"The place of execution was the tollbooth, six or seven yards distant from the prison. There were present at her martyrdom the two sheriffs of York, Fawcet and Gibson, Frost, a minister, Fox, Mr. Cheeke's kinsman, with another of his men, the four sergeants, which had hired certain beggars to do the murther, three or four men, and four women.

The martyr coming to the place, kneeled her down, and prayed to herself. The tormentors bade her pray with them, and they would pray with her. The martyr denied, and said, 'I will not pray with you, and you shall not pray with me; neither will I say Amen to your prayers, nor shall you to mine.' Then they willed her to pray for the Queen's majesty. The martyr began in this order. First, in the hearing of them all, she prayed for the Catholic Church, then for the Pope's Holiness, Cardinals, and other Fathers which have charge of souls, and then for all Christian princes. At which words the tormentors interrupted her, and willed her not to put her majesty among that company; yet the martyr proceeded in this order, 'and especially for Elizabeth, Queen of England, that God turn her to the Catholic faith, and that after this mortal life she may receive the blessed joys of heaven, For I wish as much good,' quoth she, 'to her majesty's soul as to mine own.' Sheriff Gibson, abhorring the cruel fact, stood weeping at the door. Then said Fawcet, 'Mrs. Clitherow, you must remember and confess that you die for treason.' The martyr answered, 'No, no, Mr. Sheriff, I die for the love of my Lord Jesu'; which last words she spake with a loud voice.

Then Fawcet commanded her to put off her apparel ;

'For you must die,' said he, 'naked, as judgment was given and pronounced against you.'

The martyr with the other women requested him on their knees that she might die in her smock, and that for the honour of womanhood they would not see her naked; but that would not be granted. Then she requested that women might unapparel her, and that they would turn their faces from her for that time.

The women took off her clothes, and put upon her the long habit of linen. Then very quietly she laid her down upon the ground, her face covered with a handkerchief, the linen habit being placed over her as far as it would reach, all the rest of her body being naked. The door was laid upon her, her hands she joined towards her face. Then the sheriff said, 'Nay, you must have your hands bound.' The martyr put forth her hands over the door still joined. Then two sergeants parted them, and with the inkle strings, which she had prepared for that purpose, bound them to two posts, so that her body and her arms made a perfect cross. They willed her again to ask the Queen's Majesty's forgiveness, and to pray for her. The martyr said she had prayed for her. They also willed her to ask her husband's forgiveness. The martyr said, "If ever I have offended him, but for my conscience, I ask him forgiveness.'

After this they laid weight upon her, which when she first felt, she said, 'Jesu! Jesu ! Jesu ! have mercy upon me!' which were the last words she was heard to speak.

She was in dying one quarter of an hour. A sharp stone, as much as a man's fist, put under her back; upon her was laid to the quantity of seven or eight hundredweight at the least, which, breaking her ribs, caused them to burst forth of the skin.

Thus most victoriously this gracious martyr overcame all her enemies, passing [from] this mortal life with marvellous triumph into the peaceable city of God, there to receive a worthy crown of endless immortality and joy.

This was at nine of the clock, and she continued in the press until three at afternoon."

And that was the awful end of Margaret Clitherow, the Pearl of York.

26 March

26th March 1609 is the date of death given for John Dee, astrologer, mathematician, alchemist, antiquary, spy, philosopher, geographer and adviser to Elizabeth I, by John Pontois, a merchant who inherited some of Dee's books. This date was backed up by Dee's son, Arthur, in a letter, and by Anthony Wood, who told Elias Ashmole that Dee had died at Pontois' house in Bishopsgate Street. Dee was buried in Mortlake Church.

The traditional date for Dee's death, however, is December 1608. Let me tell you some facts about this fascinating Tudor man.

- John Dee was born in London on 13th July 1527 and was the son and only child of Rowland Dee, a merchant and chief sewer to King Henry VIII, and his wife, Joan or Joanna.
- His father's family were from Wales.
- He studied at St John's College and Trinity College, Cambridge, obtaining an MA in 1548, and then studied maths, geography, astrology, astronomical observation and civil law at the University of Louvain.
- When he returned to England, the Earl of Pembroke, the Grey family and John, Dudley, Duke of Northumberland, acted as his patrons, and he was a tutor to Robert Dudley, the future Earl of Leicester, and also to King Edward VI.
- He also worked as a rector.
- After the fall of the Duke of Northumberland, he worked as a maths teacher in London and also taught merchants mathematical and navigational skills.
- He was arrested in 1555, in the reign of Queen Mary I, for casting horoscopes – the nativities of Mary, her husband, Philip, and Princess Elizabeth - and was later charged with witchcraft and conjuring. Fortunately, he convinced the Bishop of London of his religious orthodoxy, so he was only imprisoned for a short while.
- His career took off in Elizabeth I's reign thanks to his patrons, Robert Dudley and William Herbert, Earl of Pembroke.
- He drew up a special astrological chart to find the most auspicious time and date for Queen Elizabeth's coronation.

- He built up an extensive library, one of the most extensive in Europe, at his home Mortlake in Surrey. In 1592, Dee claimed it held 3000 books and 1000 manuscripts.
- He practised alchemy and wrote books on maths, astronomy and navigation.
- In the 1580s, he worked with apothecary, alchemist and medium Edward Kelley. They travelled around Europe, holding seances and allegedly communicating with angels in a special angelic language. In Prague, they worked under the patronage of the Rosenberg family, experimenting with alchemy and continuing their work with angels.
- He received a doctorate of medicine from the University of Prague in the 1580s, hence his title Dr John Dee.
- In 1589, Dee returned to England and lived in Manchester until 1605, acting as warden of the Collegiate Church at Manchester.
- He returned to Mortlake in 1605, spending his last years with his daughter, Katherine, and carrying on his work with angels with scryer Bartholomew Hickman.
- He was married three times and shared his third wife, Jane, with Edward Kelley. Kelley claimed that it was the angels' wish for him to do that!
- He had eight children.
- His son, Arthur Dee, was a writer on alchemy and acted as physician to Queen Anne, wife of James I, and Tsar Michael Romanov.
- Although Dee had been a royal favourite in Elizabeth I's reign, this did not continue into James I's reign, and Dee died in poverty and obscurity.

27 March

On 27th March (some sources say 26th), nineteen-year-old William Hunter was burnt at the stake for heresy in Brentwood, Essex.

His story is told in John Foxe's Book of Martyrs, and here is a brief overview.

William Hunter was an apprentice to silk-weaver Thomas Taylor in London when the Catholic Queen Mary I came to the throne.

After refusing to attend mass and receive communion at Easter 1554, Hunter was threatened with being hauled before Edmund Bonner, Bishop of London. At this point, his master, Taylor, dismissed him "lest that he should come in danger because of him, if he continued in his house."

Hunter returned to his home in Brentwood, Essex, but got into trouble when Father Atwell of Brentwood Chapel found Hunter reading the Bible to himself in the chapel. An argument between the priest and Hunter then ensued. The priest reported Hunter to Justice Anthony Browne, who called Hunter's father before him and ordered him to find his son and bring him to Browne. Hunter voluntarily came home and was put in the stocks by the local constable before being taken to Browne.

After an argument over communion, and Hunter's refusal to accept the Catholic doctrine of transubstantiation, believing communion to be solely "in remembrance" of Christ's sacrifice rather than changing into Christ's body and blood, Hunter was sent to the Bishop of London. Hunter refused to recant his beliefs. He was put in the stocks for two days and nights but refused to recant. He was then sent to prison, and the bishop "commanded the keeper to lay irons upon him as many as he could bear". Foxe writes that Hunter was kept in prison for nine months and that he was called before the Bishop of London five times during that time. He still refused to recant. Foxe records that he was condemned with five others in the consistory of St Paul's on 9th February 1555.

After his condemnation, Hunter was sent to Newgate and then to Brentwood. His parents were proud of their son's faith. Foxe records:

> "In the mean time William's father and mother came to him, and desired heartily of God that he might continue to the end in that good way which he had begun: and his mother said to him, that she was glad that ever she was so happy to bear such a child, which could find in his heart to lose his life for Christ's name's sake.
>
> Then William said to his mother, 'For my little pain which I shall suffer, which is but a short braid, Christ hath promised me, mother,' said he, 'a crown of joy: may you not be glad of that, mother?' With that his

mother kneeled down on her knees, saying, 'I pray God strengthen thee, my son, to the end. Yea, I think thee as well bestowed as any child that ever I bare.'"

Foxe records that just before his burning, Hunter said, "Son of God, shine upon me", and "immediately the sun in the element shone out of a dark cloud so full in his face, that he was constrained to look another way: whereat the people mused, because it was so dark a little time afore. Then William took up a faggot of broom, and embraced it in his arms."

He went to his death courageously, assuring his brother that he was not afraid of death. Foxe writes: "Then lift he up his hands to heaven, and said, 'Lord, Lord, Lord, receive my spirit;' and, casting down his head again into the smothering smoke, he yielded up his life for the truth, sealing it with his blood to the praise of God."

An elm tree was later planted on the spot and became known as the Martyr's Elm. A plaque at the spot where Hunter was burnt reads:
"WILLIAM HUNTER. MARTYR. Committed to the Flames March 26th MDLV (1555)."

28 March

On 28th March 1552, John Skip, Bishop of Hereford, died in London.

Skip is known for being the chaplain and almoner of Queen Anne Boleyn, second wife of King Henry VIII, and preaching a controversial Passion Sunday sermon on 2nd April 1536, just under a month before Anne was arrested.

Skip's theme was "Which of you can convict me of sin?" According to an account of his sermon, Skip "explained and defended the ancient ceremonies of the church... defending the clergy from their defamers and from the immoderate zeal of men in holding up to public reprobation the faults of any single clergyman as if it were the fault of all". He also used the example of the Old Testament story of King Ahasuerus, who was persuaded by his wicked minister, Haman, to order the killing of the Jews. However, Queen Esther stepped in and managed to change her husband's mind and therefore save the Jews.

In Skip's sermon, Henry VIII was Ahasuerus, Anne Boleyn was Queen Esther, and Thomas Cromwell, who had just introduced the Act of Suppression of the Lesser Monasteries into Parliament, was Haman, the "wicked minister".

As Anne's almoner, Skip must have had the queen's blessing to preach this sermon. It may even have been her idea. Anne believed in reform and tackling abuse and corruption, but felt that reform should only be carried out where necessary and that the money from dissolved monasteries should be spent on poor relief and education rather than going into the Crown's coffers. She did not agree with what was going on and the advice the king was received from advisors like Cromwell. The sermon was a public attack on Cromwell and an attack on what had been debated in Parliament. It was also a statement on Anne's stance and her beliefs.

Predictably, Skip did get into a spot of bother with his sermon. He was interrogated for preaching seditious doctrines and slandering "the King's highness, his counsellors, his lords and nobles, and his whole Parliament", but managed to escape punishment.

In May 1536, he visited Anne Boleyn in the Tower as her almoner and was with her in the early hours of 19th May 1536, the day of her execution, helping her prepare for her death.

Anne's fall did not adversely affect his career, and he became Bishop of Hereford in 1539 when Edmund Bonner became Bishop of London.

After his death on 28th March 1552, he was buried at St Mary Mounthaw, London.

29 March

Mary Dudley and Henry Sidney got married on this day in Tudor history, 29th March 1551, in the reign of King Edward VI.

Mary was the eldest daughter of John Dudley, Duke of Northumberland, and his wife Jane Guildford, and Henry was the eldest son of Sir William Sidney of Penshurst. The bride was between 16 and 21, while the groom was 21. They were married at Esher in Surrey and then had a more public ceremony at the Dudley family home, Ely House in London, on 17th May 1551.

It is not known whether the marriage was a love match, but it was a good match for both families. Henry Sidney had been a constant companion to the young Edward VI since 1538 and was one of his principal gentlemen of the privy chamber. Mary's father was Lord President of the Council, the man in charge of leading Edward VI's government. Henry was knighted in October 1551.

The marriage appears to have been happy and successful. Mary and Henry had seven children together, although only four survived childhood. Their children included Mary Herbert, Countess of Pembroke, and the poets Sir Philip Sidney and Robert Sidney, 1st Earl of Leicester.

Mary was very well educated and is known for her intellect. She knew French, Latin and Italian, and she corresponded with and visited John Dee, the famous Elizabethan scholar, mathematician, astronomer, astrologer and alchemist. She began serving in Queen Elizabeth I's privy chamber in 1559 and was with the queen when Elizabeth became ill at Hampton Court Palace in October 1562. What was thought to be a heavy cold turned into smallpox, a highly contagious and often fatal disease. Mary nursed her royal mistress through her illness and contracted it herself. While Elizabeth was lucky to survive it and got off lightly with light scarring, Mary was badly scarred. Her husband, Henry, recorded:

> "When I went to Newhaven [Le Havre] I left her a full fair Lady, in mine eye at least the fairest, and when I returned I found her as foul a lady as the smallpox could make her, which she did take by continual attendance of her majesty's most precious person (sick of the same disease). The scars of which (to her resolute discomfort) ever since hath done and doth remain in her face, so as she liveth solitarily *sicut Nicticorax in domicilio suo* [like a night-raven in the house] more to my charge then if we had boarded together as we did before that evil accident happened."

Sadly, Mary suffered due to her loyal service to the queen.

Although her husband's words suggest that Mary hid away, she continued in her service to the queen at court, and she accompanied her husband to Ireland in 1565 when he travelled there as Lord

Deputy. The couple also accompanied their mistress, the queen, on her famous 1575 visit to Kenilworth Castle, the home of Mary's brother, Robert Dudley, Earl of Leicester.

Henry died on 5th May 1586, and Mary died on 9th August the same year. They share a tomb at Penshurst Church.

Mary's biographer, Simon Adams, writes of the couple: "The Sidneys were in some respects the golden couple of the court in the early years of Elizabeth's reign. But from the end of the 1560s they became increasingly embittered by what they regarded as shabby treatment at the queen's hands." They felt unappreciated for their long and loyal service.

30 March

In January 1558, Mary I had written to her husband, Philip of Spain, believing herself to be six months pregnant, to tell him of the joyous news, which she said had "gone far to lighten the sorrow I have felt for the loss of Calais." Then, on this day in Tudor history, 30th March 1558, Mary sat down to write her will, believing the birth of her child to be imminent.

She started with the words, "Thinking myself to be with child in lawful marriage between my said dearly beloved husband and lord, although I be at this present (thanks be unto Almighty God) otherwise in good health, yet foreseeing the great danger which by God's ordinance remain to all women in their travail of children, have thought good, both for the discharge of my conscience and continuance of good order within my realms and dominions, to declare my last will and testament."

In her will, Mary left the crown to her child, with Philip acting as guardian and regent. She stated that her mother Catherine of Aragon's remains should be moved from Peterborough and laid to rest with Mary and for her executors to commission an honourable tomb or monument for them both. Mary also ordered the restoration of lands formerly belonging to the Church and taken during the Dissolution. She left money for alms for the poor and needy, for the religious houses of Sheen and Syon (which she had re-established), and the Observant Friars of Greenwich, the Black Friars at St Bartholomews, and various other orders and establishments with requests for them to say "daily Masses, Suffrages, and Prayers".

Among the other provisions, she also requested that her Archbishop of Canterbury, Reginald Pole, continue his "good work in this realm" and warned that her executors should follow the terms of her will because they would be answerable to God at Judgement Day.

Of course, Mary never gave birth because she wasn't pregnant. Her health deteriorated over the next few months, and she died on 17th November 1558. Her archbishop died on the same day.

There was no heir to inherit her throne; instead, her half-sister Elizabeth became queen, and Mary was buried at Westminster Abbey. Catherine of Aragon's remains were never moved to join those of Mary, but in 1603 Mary's vault was opened, and a coffin containing the remains of Elizabeth I were lowered in.

31 March

On 31st March 1631, in the Stuart period, metaphysical poet, satirist, lawyer and clergyman John Donne died. Donne served as a member of Parliament, royal chaplain and Dean of St Paul's, but is best known for his poems, sonnets and epigrams, which included the meditation "For whom the bell tolls" and the erotic metaphysical poem "The Flea", which is thought to have been written in the 1590s.

Here are some facts about this famous metaphysical poet:

- John Donne was born in Bread Street, London, in his father's house, in 1572, although his exact birth date is unknown.
- He was the son of John Donne, warden of the Ironmongers' Company, and his wife, Elizabeth Heywood.
- His maternal grandfather was John Heywood, the Tudor playwright and poet.
- Donne was brought up as a Catholic.
- He was educated at Hart Hall, Oxford, and then studied at Thavies Inn, an inn of the chancery, before being admitted to Lincoln's Inn, one of London's inns of court.
- In 1596, he joined the expedition led by the Earl of Essex and Lord Howard of Effingham to Cadiz, then again in 1597 to

the Azores. On his return, he worked as secretary to Sir Thomas Egerton, Lord Keeper of the Great Seal.

- By 1601, Donne was serving as a member of Parliament and had embraced the Protestant faith.
- In December 1601, Donne secretly married seventeen-year-old Ann More, the niece of Lady Egerton. When her father, Sir George More, found out about the marriage, he had Donne arrested and imprisoned in the Fleet. Donne was soon released, though, and was able to prove that the marriage was valid. Ann's father cut her off financially as punishment. They had their first child, a daughter, Constance, in early 1603.
- In January 1615, Donne was ordained as a Church of England deacon and priest and served as a royal chaplain to King James.
- Donne's wife, Ann, died in 1617 after giving birth to their twelfth child, who was stillborn. Donne preached the funeral sermon.
- Donne was also a diplomat, being sent on an embassy to Germany in 1619.
- In 1621, he was made Dean of St Paul's.
- Following King Charles I's accession in 1625, Donne was made a prolucator to the king.
- Donne died on this day in 1631 at the deanery of St Paul's. He was laid to rest in St Paul's Cathedral on 3rd April 1631.
- His memorial thankfully survived the Great Fire of London and can now be seen in the present St Paul's Cathedral.
- Donne didn't just write poems; he also wrote sermons, religious verse and treatises, epigrams, songs, satires and translations.
- His poem "The Flea" is about the writer, the man, trying to persuade a woman to have sex with him. The Guardian Newspaper described it as "sharp romantic comedy".
- His meditation XVII, which begins with the words, "PERCHANCE he for whom this bell tolls may be so ill as that he knows not it tolls for him", is also very famous. My favourite bit is this:

"No man is an island, entire of itself; every man is a
piece of the continent, a part of the main; if a clod be

washed away by the sea, Europe is the less, as well as if a promontory were, as well as if a manor of thy friend's or of thine own were; any man's death diminishes me, because I am involved in mankind, and therefore never send to know for whom the bell tolls; it tolls for thee." (Meditation 17)

1 April

On 1st April 1578, English physician William Harvey was born in Folkestone, Kent. Harvey has gone down in history as the man who discovered blood circulation, and he was also physician extraordinary to King James I and King Charles I.

Let me tell you more about his work on the heart and circulation.

In 1615, William Harvey was elected to the Lumleian lectureship in the College of Physicians and prepared a course of lectures. His preparation included vivisectional experiments on the heart. As his biographer, Roger French, notes, Harvey's findings were "inconsistent with the Galenic doctrine that blood moved into the arteries as the heart passively contracted after its forcible diastole." "Harvey concluded", explains French, "that the active phase of the heart's action was a forceful systole—its rising up in the vivisected animal—which produced the pulse by pushing the blood into the arteries as it contracted."

Of course, the doctrine of Galen, the famous Greek physician and scholar, had been long accepted, so Harvey's findings were greeted with scepticism for quite a time, although by his death in 1657, they'd been accepted.

Now, I'm not a scientist at all, so here's an explanation of Galen's theory from the National Geographic magazine:

> "According to Galen, dark, venous blood formed in the liver and then travelled through the veins throughout the body to deliver nourishment and build and maintain tissues. Some blood would come into contact with air in the lungs and go to the heart. From there, this bright red blood went to the brain to form "pneuma," a substance responsible for sensation and feeling. According to Galen's theory, the blood did not return to the liver or the heart. Instead, it would be consumed by the body, which meant that it needed to be constantly replenished."

- Galen believed that the liver could produce too much blood, which had to be alleviated by blood-letting.
- Harvey challenged Galen's doctrine by laying out the evidence for his view that blood moved throughout the body in a circle. It

circulated. His experiments on live animals had shown him their beating hearts, and this observation caused him to conclude that it was the heart that was responsible for moving the blood around the body and that it did this by pumping it. The heart moved the blood out through the arteries, and the blood was pumped back to the heart through the veins. After rigorous research and experiments, Harvey published his findings in 1628 in his book "On the Motion of the Heart and Blood in Animals", which was first published in Latin. This wasn't new. Centuries before that, manuals on Chinese medicine had mentioned blood being pumped around the body by the heart in a circle, and a 13th-century Arab doctor had written about circulation. In England, however, Galen's doctrine was still believed.

- Harvey also did experiments like applying tourniquets to the arm and showing that there must be valves in the veins.
- Harvey was also responsible for another medical work, this time on embryology, a book called "On Animal Generation".
- Harvey died on 3rd June 1657 from a stroke.

Trivia: in Charles I's reign, he was involved in investigations into alleged witchcraft. As a physician, he examined some women from Burnley accused of being witches. Still, they were pardoned after he and his colleagues concluded that they were normal women without extra nipples to feed their familiars. In one witchcraft trial, he dissected a toad to prove that it was a normal dead toad, not a demon in disguise.

2 April

On this day in Tudor history, 2nd April 1552, fourteen-year-old King Edward VI recorded in his journal: "I fell sick of the measles and the smallpox."

In his book "Pustules, Pestilence and Pain", which is about Tudor Treatments and the ailments of Henry VIII, Seamus O'Caellaigh, describes the development of smallpox. After an incubation period of around 12-14 days, a person would start to develop symptoms:

"The symptoms can include high fever, weakness, head and body aches, and vomiting. This may last for

2 to 4 days. After the high fever spots start to appear in the mouth. These spots develop into sores that break open and spread large amounts of the virus into the mouth and throat. When the sores in the back of the throat start to breakdown a rash starts to appear on the skin and moves from the face, to the trunk, and then out the limbs. When the rash starts, the fever usually falls and the person may start to feel better. On the third day of the rash, the rash becomes the well-known raised bumps that are the disease's namesake. The fourth day brings the bumps filling with a thick cloudy fluid. Fever often will rise again and remain high until scabs form. The bumps feel like there are hard objects inside them, like a bead under the skin. The second week, after the rash appears, most of the sores have scabbed over. The scabs begin to fall off, leaving marks on the skin that eventually become pitted scars. Most scabs will have fallen off three weeks after the rash appears."

Once a person had had smallpox and survived, they could not catch it again.

Seamus also describes different treatments for smallpox that he found in contemporary sources. A barley water drink was used to help temper the fever, barley mixed with poppy and wild lettuce was used to help the person sleep, a sulphur-based oil was used on the spots, and a sulphur-based ointment was applied to the scabs that formed.

Ten days after Edward had recorded falling ill, the imperial ambassador recorded:

"I arrived here on the evening of the 12th instant, and the next morning the ambassador and I sent to the Duke of Northumberland to inform him of my arrival and demand audience. He replied that I was very welcome, and informed us that the King had recently had the measles, and was not yet quite recovered, so he feared audience might not be given for five or six days."

He added in a postscript:

"After the above was written, the Council sent Mr. Hoby to tell me that the King was not quite recovered from the small-pox, and as he still bore some marks on his face, he did not wish to show himself to strangers. Hoby therefore saw little chance of my obtaining audience for ten days. He begged me to be patient, but said that if my charge was urgent I might come to the Council to declare it and discuss it with them, until I should be able to make a more ample declaration to the King, when restored to health."

Then, on 21st April, nineteen days after he'd fallen ill, Edward's half-sister, Elizabeth, wrote to him. Here is her letter:

"What cause I had of sorrow, when I heard first of your majesty's sickness, all men might guess, but none but myself could feel, which to declare were or might seem a point of flattery; and therefore I omit to write it. But, as the sorrow could not be little, because the occasions were many, so is the joy great to hear of your good escape out of the perilous diseases. And, that I am fully satisfied and well assured of the same by your grace's own hand, I must need give you my most humble thanks, assuring your majesty, that a precious jewel at another time could not so well have contented, as your letter in this case hath comforted me. For now do I say with Saint Austin, that a disease is to be accounted no sickness, that shall cause a better health when it is past, than was assured afore it came. For afore you had them, every man thought that that should not be eschewed of you that was not escaped of many. But since you have had them doubt of them is past, and hope is given to all men, that it was a purgation by these means for other worse diseases, which might happen this year. Moreover, I consider that, as a good father, that loves his child dearly, doth punish him sharply, so God, favouring your majesty greatly, hath chastened you straitly; and, as a father doth it for the further good of his child, so hath God prepared this for the better health of your grace.

And, in this hope, I commit your majesty to His hands, most humbly craving pardon of your grace that I did write no sooner; desiring you to attribute the fault to my evil head, and not to my slothful hand. From Hatfield, this 21st of April.

Your majesty's most humble sister

to command,

ELIZABETH."

In her letter, Elizabeth mentions Edward writing in his own hand about his illness and recovery, so Edward obviously recovered quickly.

On 3rd May 1552, Edward wrote to his good friend Barnaby Fitzpatrick:

"We have a little been troubled with the smallpox, which hath letted us to write hitherto; but now we have shaken that quite away."

Edward was incredibly lucky. When Elizabeth caught smallpox in 1562, it was feared that she would die. His quick recovery suggested that he only had the diseases lightly or had a very good constitution.

However, in 1553, Edward wasn't so lucky. He was taken ill in January/February 1553 and never got better. His biographer, Chris Skidmore, believes that this April 1552 bout of smallpox and measles suppressed Edward's immune system and led to him dying of some type of pulmonary infection or tuberculosis on 6th July 1553. Kyra Kramer, in her "Edward VI in a Nutshell" book, puts forward the idea that Edward, his half-brother Henry Fitzroy, and his uncle, Arthur Tudor, who died on this day in 1502, all suffered from non-classic cystic fibrosis. It's an interesting theory.

3 April

On 3rd April 1578, Lady Margaret Douglas, Countess of Lennox, daughter of Margaret Tudor and Archibald Douglas, 6th Earl of Angus, and cousin of Queen Elizabeth I, was buried in the south aisle of Henry VII's Chapel in Westminster Abbey.

Margaret died on 9th March 1578. She'd been taken ill at a dinner party attended by Robert Dudley, Earl of Leicester, in February, and this led to rumours that she'd been poisoned, but there's no evidence that she was.

She made her will on 26th February, and in it, she stated that she wanted the remains of her son, Charles, father of Arbella Stuart, to be moved from his resting place at Hackney to share her tomb at Westminster. All of her children had predeceased her.

Although she is said to have died in poverty, Margaret was given a lavish funeral at her cousin Queen Elizabeth I's expense. Thomas Fowler, her former secretary, erected a fine monument to Margaret. Her effigy lies on top of her tomb, and she is depicted wearing a red fur-lined cloak and a gown of blue and gold. There are four weepers (kneeling statues) on each side of her tomb – on the one side, her four sons and the other, her four daughters.

The Westminster Abbey website explains, "At her feet is a crowned lion. Sculpted and painted coats of arms adorn the tomb chest: Darnley impaling Scotland at the east end; a lozenge of Angus and Douglas at the west end and at the sides Lennox impaling Angus and Douglas."

The main inscription which was added in James VI's reign reads:

"Here lyeth the noble Lady Margaret, Countess of Lennox, daughter and sole heir of Archibald Earl of Angus, by Margaret Queen of Scots, his wife that was eldest daughter to King Henry VII, who bear unto Matthew, Earl of Lennox, her husband, 4 sons and 4 daughters.

This lady has to her great-grandfather King Edward IV, to her grandfather King Henry VII, to her uncle King Henry VIII, to her cousin germane King Edward VI, to her brother King James of Scotland the fifth, to her son King Henry I (referring to Lord Darnley, husband of Mary, Queen of Scots), to her grandchild King James VI. Having to her great grandmother and grandmother 2 queens both named Elizabeth, to her mother Margaret Queen of Scots, to her Aunt Mary the French queen, to her cousins germane Mary and Elizabeth queens of England, to her niece and daughter-in-law, Mary Queen of Scots.

Henry, second son to this lady was King of Scots and father to James VI, now king. This Henry was murdered at the age of 21 years, Charles her youngest son was Earl of Lennox, father to the lady Arbella. He died at the age of 21 years and is here entombed."

Another inscription reads:

"Sacred to the memory of MARGARET DOUGLAS, wife of Matthew Stuart, Earl of Lennox, granddaughter to Henry VII, King of England, by his daughter (Margaret Tudor): joined by the closest ties of kinship to most puissant kings, grandmother to James VI of Scotland, a lady of most pious character, invincible spirit, and matchless steadfastness. She died the tenth of March, year of Our Lord 1577. Margaret, mighty in virtue, mightier yet in lineage: ennobled by kings and by her forebears; descended from Scottish and English princes, she was also a progenitor of princes. Those things that belong unto death, she released to death most joyfully, and sought God, for she belonged to God before."

Margaret was survived by her granddaughter Lady Arbella Stuart, who died in the Tower of London in 1615, and by her grandson King James VI of Scotland, who became James I of England.

4 April

On 4th April 1589, scholar and noblewoman Mildred Cecil (née Cooke), Lady Burghley, died at Cecil House in the Strand in London. Mildred, the wife of William Cecil, 1st Baron Burghley and Elizabeth I's right-hand man, was about sixty-three when she died.

Here are some facts about Mildred:

- She was the eldest of nine children born to Sir Anthony Cooke and his wife, Anne Fitzwilliam.
- Her father was a humanist and believed in providing his five daughters with the same classical education he offered to his sons. He was a scholar and taught Mildred himself at home, Gidea Hall in Essex.
- Her father was also a keen reformer.
- On 21st December 1545, Mildred married William Cecil as his second wife. She helped to bring up her stepson, Thomas Cecil, and the couple went on to have five children. Sadly, Mildred

outlived all but one of them: Robert Cecil, 1st Earl of Salisbury, a man who would serve as Secretary of State to both Elizabeth I and James I.

- Mildred was very influential, acting as an intermediary between petitioners and her husband. William Maitland, Lord Lethington and other Scottish leaders corresponded with her when negotiating the Treaty of Edinburgh.

- Mildred was fluent in French, Greek and Latin. She built up a huge library of Greek and Latin texts, including works on medicine, religion, literature and history.

- Towards the end of her life, she donated books to institutions such as Christ Church, Oxford, St John's College, Oxford, and Westminster School. Today, we still have thirty books inscribed with Mildred's name.

- Mildred and Burghley appear to have had a happy marriage. Mildred wrote of her "everlasting comfort... living with this noble man in divine love and charity", and when she died in 1589, in the eulogy he wrote, Burghley described her as "dearest above all" and "far beyond the race of womankind". When he arranged her lavish funeral he said it was "a testimony of my hearty love which I did bear her, with whom I lived in the state of matrimony forty and two years continually without any unkindness". In a letter to their son, Robert, Cecil wrote of "the virtuous inclinations of thy matchless mother, by whose tender and godly care thy infancy was governed, together with thy education under so zealous and excellent a tutor".

- She was laid to rest with her daughter Anne, Countess of Oxford, in St Nicholas's Chapel in Westminster Abbey. Their 24-feet high monument is attributed to sculptor Cornelius Cure. Here is an inscription from her tomb. It was written originally in Latin by Burghley:

"Mildred, first born daughter of the noble Lord Anthony Cooke, Kt. a man of virtue and distinguished learning, a noble Maecenas to all men of letters; her mother was the Lady Anne, daughter of Lord William Fitzwilliams, Kt.: celebrated and high born because of her parents' ancient pedigree, tracing its descent from many of the noble families of the realm, she was no less famed and exceedingly praised by all the learned for her erudition, combined with her steadfast profession of the Christian faith, and her singular knowledge of the Greek and Latin tongues, which knowledge she received solely at the hands of her father, who instructed her. She became, in her 20th year the wife of Lord William Cecil, Lord of Burghley, and afterwards, by reason of her husband's being ennobled with the title of Baron of the realm, she was created Baroness of Burghley and bore him many children, but three only who attained maturity: that is, Anne, Robert and Elizabeth."

5 April

On 5th April 1533, Convocation gave its ruling on King Henry VIII's marriage to Catherine of Aragon. The English Church's legislative body concluded that the pope had no power to dispense in the case of a man marrying his brother's widow and that it was contrary to God's law.

Here is the record from Letters and Papers:

"Notarial attestation of the determination of the Convocation of Canterbury, begun 5 Nov. 1529, on the two points discussed in the King's divorce, determining, 1, that the Pope has no power of dispensing in case of a marriage where the brother's widow has been cognita. The house consisted of 66 theologians. The proxies were 197; the negatives 19. The second question was, whether Katharine was cognita. The numbers present, 44; one holding the proxies of three bishops. Decided in the affirmative against five or six negatives. Dated 5 April 1533."

On the 11th April 1533, the archbishop wrote to the king "Beseeching the King very humbly to allow him to determine his great cause of matrimony, as belongs to the Archbishop's spiritual office, as much bruit exists among the common people on the subject", and the king replied in the affirmative, saying that he was not "displeased with Cranmer's zeal for justice."

On 10th May 1533, the archbishop opened a special court at Dunstable Priory, Bedfordshire, to examine Henry VIII's case for the annulment of his first marriage. After hearing testimonies from people such as Dr John Bell, the king's proctor, and the Dowager Duchess of Norfolk and Lady Jane Guildford; the opinions of universities and Convocation; and examining the proceedings of the Legatine Court at Blackfriars; the court came to a decision and gave their sentence on 23rd May. Cranmer declared the marriage "against the law of God" and annulled the marriage.

King Henry VIII was already married to Anne Boleyn by this point, as he believed his first marriage invalid. On 28th May 1533, the archbishop proclaimed the validity of Henry VIII's marriage to Anne Boleyn following a secret enquiry at Lambeth Palace. The next day, celebrations for Anne Boleyn's coronation kicked off with a lavish river procession, and on 1st June 1533, a pregnant Anne was crowned queen at Westminster Abbey. She gave birth to the couple's daughter, the future Queen Elizabeth I, on 7th September 1533.

6 April

On 6th April 1621, in the Stuart period, Edward Seymour, 1st Earl of Hertford, died at Netley in Hampshire. He was about 81 at his death. He was laid to rest in Salisbury Cathedral.

Hertford is known for secretly marrying Lady Katherine Grey, sister of Lady Jane Grey and a claimant to the throne, in 1560, which led to them both being thrown into the Tower of London. But after Katherine's death, Hertford married twice more, both in secret.

Let me tell you more about this Tudor man.

- Edward was born around 1539 and was the son and heir of Edward Seymour, Duke of Somerset, and his second wife, Anne Stanhope. His father had two sons by his previous marriage, but he'd repudiated his wife, Catherine Filliol, and their sons had been disinherited.
- Edward's father served as Lord Protector in Edward VI's reign until he was brought down and executed. His father's lands

and titles were declared forfeit. Edward was made a ward of the crown until his mother was released from the Tower in Mary I's reign.

- When Elizabeth I came to the throne, Edward's father's lands were restored to him, and he was made Baron Beauchamp and Earl of Hertford.

- In late 1560, Hertford secretly married Lady Katherine Grey, daughter of Queen Elizabeth I's cousin, Frances Grey, Duchess of Suffolk, and a girl who was an heir to the throne. Hertford was recalled from a diplomatic mission to France in August 1561 because his pregnant wife had confessed her secret marriage to the queen's favourite, Robert Dudley. Katherine and Edward were imprisoned in the Tower of London, where, on 24th September 1561, Katherine gave birth to their son, also named Edward. The marriage was ruled invalid by an ecclesiastical high commission in May 1562, making little Edward illegitimate.

- Sir Edward Warner, Lieutenant of the Tower, allowed the couple conjugal visits and Katherine gave birth to another son, Thomas, in February 1563. Hertford was fined £15,000 for this.

- Following the birth of his second son, Hertford was prevented from seeing Katherine, and they never saw each other again. Katherine was eventually released from the Tower but into house arrest, and she died in 1568.

- Hertford was released from the Tower in August 1563 but into the custody of his mother, Anne, and her second husband, Francis Newdigate, at their home at Hanworth. He ended up in the Tower once again, albeit temporarily, after his stepfather was implicated in helping John Hales, who wrote a pamphlet defending Hertford's wife's claim to the throne.

- In 1571, Hertford was allowed back at court, and it was there that he met the woman who'd become his second wife, Frances Howard, a gentlewoman of Elizabeth I's privy chamber and daughter of Lord William Howard of Effingham. It is not known when they got married, but John Dee called her the

Countess of Hertford in 1578. The queen gave her permission for the marriage in 1585.

- In 1581, his eldest son, Edward, Lord Beauchamp, secretly married Honora Rogers, and Hertford rather hypocritically would not accept the marriage and had his son taken into custody at Hertford House. However, Queen Elizabeth I and her council sided with Beauchamp and Honora, and Hertford was forced into accepting his son's marriage.
- In 1591, Queen Elizabeth I visited Hertford and his wife at their home, Elvetham, in Hampshire.
- In late 1595/early 1596, Hertford ended up in the Tower once more for a couple of months after supporting his younger son Thomas's appeal against the ruling that had deemed his parents' marriage invalid.
- In 1598, Hertford's second wife, Frances, died. Their marriage had been childless.
- In 1601, Hertford married Frances, daughter of Thomas, 1st Viscount Howard of Bindon. She was the wealthy widow of Henry Prannell and was twenty-two years of age when she married Hertford, who was in his early sixties. The couple married in secret at Hertford House. The marriage was childless.
- On the death of Elizabeth I in 1603, Hertford supported the claim of King James VI of Scotland rather than promoting the claim of his eldest son, Edward, Lord Beauchamp. He went on to gain favour in James I's reign, serving as an ambassador and high steward of Queen Anne's revenues.
- King James I visited Hertford at Tottenham Lodge, in Wiltshire, in 1603, 1617 and 1620.
- In 1608, King James gave Hertford's son, Edward, the right to inherit the earldom of Hertford. He was still deemed illegitimate, though.
- In 1610, Hertford's grandson, William, secretly married Lady Arbella Stuart, daughter of Charles Stuart, Earl of Lennox, and Elizabeth Cavendish. Both William and Arbella were claimants to the throne, and their marriage led to them being imprisoned. William escaped and fled abroad, but Arbella remained in the Tower, where she died in 1615.

- Although Hertford was angry with his grandson, he gave him an annual allowance while he was abroad. In 1612, William became Hertford's heir after the death of his father, Beauchamp.
- Hertford acted as a patron of the Arts and also had a company of players.
- He died on this day in 1621. Hertford's grandson, William, had the remains of his grandmother, Lady Katherine Grey, moved from her resting place at Yoxford in Suffolk to Salisbury to be buried with Hertford in Salisbury Cathedral. Their tomb can still be seen there today in the south aisle. Katherine's effigy is placed higher than her husband's to reflect her royal status. An inscription in Latin translates to:
"Incomparable Consorts
Who, experienced in the vicissitudes of changing fortune
At length, in the concord which marked their lives,
Here rest together."

7 April

On 7th April 1537, Robert Aske and Thomas Darcy, 1st Baron Darcy, were sent to the Tower of London.

Both men had been involved in the Pilgrimage of Grace rebellion of late 1536. Aske was one of the rebel leaders, and Darcy became involved with the rebels after yielding Pontefract Castle to them. Darcy was beheaded on 30th June 1537, and Aske was hanged in chains on 12th July 1537.

Let me tell you more about Robert Aske and how he got involved in the Pilgrimage of Grace.

Aske was born around 1500 and was a Yorkshire man related to Henry Clifford, 1st Earl of Cumberland. He studied law and, in the late 1520s, was secretary to Henry Percy, 6th Earl of Northumberland, before working as a lawyer, handling cases in the Star Chamber. His biographer R W Hoyle notes that he was on his way to London for the start of the law term, travelling through Lincolnshire when he became involved in the Lincolnshire Rising, which started the Pilgrimage of Grace. The rising was sparked off by:

- A sermon at evensong on the 1st October 1536 at St James's Church, Louth. The vicar preached a sermon which is thought to have "affirmed that the church or its faith, or both, were in danger".
- A visitation from the Bishop of Lincoln's registrar on 2nd October. The registrar tried to read out Thomas Cromwell's commission to the townspeople. His papers were ripped from his hands and burnt. Things escalated very quickly from that point.

On 4th October, Dr Raynes, the chancellor of the Bishop of Lincoln, who was staying nearby at Bolingbroke, after having held a session of the commissionary's court there, was dragged from his sickbed and taken to Horncastle. He was then pulled from his horse and murdered by a rebel mob. One of Thomas Cromwell's men was also hanged by the mob. On 5th October, at Sawcliffe, in North Lincolnshire, Aske, who'd arrived in the area, was taken by the rebels and swore his allegiance to them after hearing their grievances. The rebels sent their grievances in a letter to King Henry VIII. Their complaints included the dissolution of the monasteries, the grant to the king of the tenths and first-fruits of spiritual benefices, the promotion of Thomas Cromwell and Richard Rich to the king's council, and the promotion of the archbishops of Canterbury and Dublin, the bishops of Rochester and St David's, and others, who, in their opinion, had clearly "subverted the faith of Christ".

On 8th October 1536, Aske, who'd gone back to Yorkshire to muster people to the rebel cause, called the people of Beverley together, asking them to be true to "God, the king, the commonwealth" and "to maintain the Holy Church". By the time the king's reply to the rebels arrived with a herald on 11th October, Aske was seen as the rebels' "chief captain". The king was furious with the rebels and did not give in to any of their demands.

R W Hoyle explains, "It was only after the disintegration of the Lincolnshire revolt that Aske wrote his own oath, gave the movement the title of the Pilgrimage of Grace, and shifted it from the broad commonwealth concerns of the Lincoln articles to the critique of Cromwell's religious policies contained in his oath".

On 19th October 1536, Aske and the rebels arrived at Pontefract in Yorkshire and threatened an assault on the castle, which Thomas Darcy, 1st Baron Darcy, owned. Early the next morning, Darcy surrendered his castle to the rebels and swore the rebel oath, along with other castle inhabitants, including Edmund Lee, Archbishop of York. Darcy sympathised with the rebel cause and agreed with their grievances, so no force was necessary. Aske went on to rally other members of the gentry, and by 24th October, the rebel force numbered 30,000 and far outnumbered that of the royal force led by the Duke of Norfolk and Earl of Shrewsbury, which was about a fifth of the size. However, there was no battle as they decided to negotiate. Norfolk gave promises from Henry VIII that the people's demands would be met and that they would be pardoned. Robert Aske then dismissed his troops. Unfortunately, Henry VIII later broke his promises to the rebels after a further rebellion in Yorkshire in January 1537 led by Sir Francis Bigod. Robert Aske tried to prevent it, but he and other men who'd been involved in the Pilgrimage of Grace rebellion - such as Lord Darcy, Thomas Percy and Robert Constable - were arrested and convicted of treason.

On 30th June 1537, Lord Darcy was beheaded on Tower Hill. According to one contemporary source, his head was displayed on London Bridge while his body was laid to rest "at the Crossed Friars beside the Tower of London", although it must have been moved to St Botolph's Aldgate. On 22nd July 1537, Darcy was posthumously degraded from the Order of the Garter. It was Thomas Cromwell who was elected to the Order in his place.

On 12th July 1537, according to chronicler Edward Hall, Robert Aske was hanged in chains at York. He was hanged outside Clifford's Tower, the keep of York Castle. In November 2018, a plaque to Robert Aske was unveiled at Clifford's Tower in York. It reads, "Near this place, Robert Aske leader of the Pilgrimage of Grace died for his faith in 1537, martyred by Henry VIII."

8 April

On 8th April 1608, in the reign of King James I, Magdalen Browne (née Dacre), Viscountess Montagu and patron of Roman Catholics, died at Battle in East Sussex, following a stroke she had suffered in January 1508. She was buried at Midhurst.

Here are some facts about this Tudor lady:

- Magdalen was born in 1538 and was the daughter of William Dacre, 3rd Baron Dacre of Gilsland and his wife, Elizabeth Talbot, daughter of George Talbot, 4th Earl of Shrewsbury.

- She grew up at Naworth Castle in Cumberland, leaving at the age of 13 to join the household of her older sister, Anne, Countess of Bedford.

- In 1554, at 16, Magdalen became a maid of honour to Queen Mary I and attended her at her wedding to Philip of Spain.

- In 1556, when she was 18, she became the second wife of Anthony Browne, 1st Viscount Montagu. Their wedding was attended by Mary I. They went on to have eight children: five sons and three daughters.

- Magdalen's married life was spent at her husband's properties, Battle Abbey, Cowdray House, and Montague House.

- Magdalen had been brought up a Catholic, and her husband was also a staunch Catholic. He served Mary I by being one of three ambassadors who helped negotiate England's return to the Catholic fold.

- Even though she was Catholic, Magdalen had a good relationship with Elizabeth I, following her and her husband's declaration that they would be loyal to the Queen if the Pope invaded or caused trouble. Their properties, however, were known as Catholic centres.

- When the Queen visited the Montagus in 1591, they kept their priests hidden.

- Montagu died in 1592, and Magdalen carried on running a household that was predominantly Catholic. Her property at Battle was known as Little Rome by the local Protestants, and she kept three priests there, one of whom was Thomas More, great-grandson of Sir Thomas More.

- Magdalen used Battle Abbey and Montague House as safe houses for Catholic priests from the Continent. Luckily, many local law enforcers were Catholics, so Magdalen managed to avoid getting into trouble until 1599 when her London property was searched, and again following the Gunpowder Plot.

- Magdalen suffered a stroke on 21st January 1608 and never recovered, dying at Battle on 8th April. She was survived by her children, Sir George Browne, Sir Henry Browne, Elizabeth Dormer and Jane Lacon, and grandchildren.
- Archpriest George Birkhead said of Magdalen that she was "a great mother in Israel, and the priests everywhere did extol her as the worthy patroness of the holy faith and the singular ornament of the Catholic religion in England" and Richard Smith, her confessor, wrote a biography of her, "Life of the most Honourable and Vertuous Lady, the Lady Magdalen Viscountesse Montague" with chapters on her excellent humility, notable chastity, singular patience, prompt obedience, liberality towards others, notable piety towards God, and her zeal and constancy in supporting and professing the Catholic faith.

9 April

On 9th April 1557, Cardinal Reginald Pole's legatine powers were revoked by Pope Paul IV. Pole, who was also Mary I's Archbishop of Canterbury, had served as *legate a latere* to England from March 1554 until the pope deprived him of this power on 9th April 1557.

Pole had a bit of a history with Pope Paul IV. Back in 1549, following the death of Pope Paul III, Pole was a frontrunner to become pope at the papal conclave. However, one factor which prevented his election was Cardinal Gianpetro Carafa denouncing him as a heretic. Pope Julius III was elected instead. When Julius died in 1555, Cardinal Gianpetro Carafa was elected and became Pope Paul IV. Lambeth Palace Library's guide to Cardinal Pole explains: "At first relations between the two men were cordial; but on 9 April 1557, motivated partly by political considerations and partly by mounting charges of heresy against Pole, the Pope revoked the legatine powers of his English archbishop and recalled him to Rome. In the event, however, Pole contracted his final illness before he could be reclaimed by the Inquisition."

Although it was his earlier works, his Catholic humanism, and his belief in justification by faith that had provoked the first accusations of heresy, Pole's downfall with the papacy in 1557 seems to have been down to his close relationship with Mary I, who was supporting her husband, Philip of Spain, in his conflicts with the papacy. The final straw for the pope was Philip's arrival in England in March 1557. In December 1557, the pope sent his nephew Carlo Carafa to King Philip to convince him of Pole's guilt, but Mary I refused to let her archbishop leave England to travel to Rome to face the charges. Pole died of influenza on 17th November 1558; the queen died on the same day.

10 April

On 10th April 1585, Pope Gregory XIII died from a fever. He was succeeded by Pope Sixtus V.

Pope Gregory is known for his reform of the calendar. He introduced what is now called the Gregorian Calendar, or Western or Christian Calendar, by papal bull on 24th February 1582. This calendar replaced the Julian calendar, which had been the official calendar of Europe since 45 BC when Julius Caesar invented it to bring order to the chaos caused by priests adding days to the Roman calendar in his empire.

By 1582, the Julian Calendar was behind the solar calendar by ten days, and Pope Gregory wanted to correct this. His reform meant that the calendar would advance by ten days and included instructions that century years, e.g. 1700 and 1800, would not count as leap years unless they were divisible by 400. It also included a reform of the lunar cycle used by the church to calculate the date of Easter, which was far more accurate than the Julian calendar as it only differed from the solar calendar by 26 seconds, which only adds up to a difference of 1 day every 3,323 years.

The 15th October 1582 was the first day of the Gregorian calendar following the last day of the Julian calendar, 4th October 1582, meaning that the 5th-14th October did not exist in the year 1582 in countries adopting the new calendar. However, many countries ignored the Papal Bull and used the Julian Calendar. England, for example, did not adopt the Gregorian Calendar until 1752, when the British Calendar Act of 1751 meant that people went to sleep on the night of Wednesday 2nd September 1752 but woke up the next day on Thursday 14th September.

I can imagine it was very confusing for people like merchants and diplomats who travelled between countries that used different calendars.

It's also confusing for historians and researchers using archives from different countries after the 1582 change, as dates would differ between English and foreign sources for the same event. As historical novelist Kate Emerson points out on her website: "English reports on the Spanish Armada of 1588 record events as taking place ten days earlier than Spanish reports do". Benjamin Woolley, in his book on John Dee, "The Queen's Conjurer", explains that communications during the period between 1582 and 1752, when England did start using the Gregorian calendar, customarily carried "two dates, one 'O.S.' or Old Style, the other 'N.S.' or New Style". So this double dating and the different dates between countries is something to bear in mind when researching records of different countries between 1582 and 1752, as well as taking into account that the new calendar year started on Lady Day, 25th March, rather than 1st January.

Trivia: the Orthodox Churches still celebrate Easter according to the Julian Calendar because changing it to the Gregorian Calendar would mean that it would sometimes coincide with the Jewish Passover.

11 April

On 11th April 1533, Good Friday, Henry VIII informed his council that Anne was his rightful wife and queen and that she should be accorded royal honours. The following day, the pregnant Anne Boleyn attended Holy Saturday mass "with all the pomp of a Queen, clad in cloth of gold, and loaded (carga) with the richest jewels." A real statement!

While the king was ordering his council to do this, his new Archbishop of Canterbury, Thomas Cranmer, was working on the king's "Great Matter", i.e. the annulment of Henry VIII's marriage to Catherine of Aragon.

Being recognised as queen and appearing in public as queen was a huge deal for Anne, who'd been waiting to be Henry VIII's wife and queen since his proposal in 1527. Neither of them could have known that it would take that long to get the marriage annulled. Henry VIII wasn't asking the pope for anything unusual. In the 12th century, Louis VII of France had asked for his marriage to Eleanor of Aquitaine, which had produced only daughters and no male heir, to be annulled, and the annulment had been granted. In more recent history, Louix XII had had his marriage to Joan of France annulled by the pope so that he could marry Anne of Brittany. Things were different in Henry VIII's case, though. Although he and his canon lawyers could argue that the dispensation that Pope Julius II had issued was not valid because the pope should not overturn God's law, Henry's wife, Catherine of Aragon, was opposed to the annulment and had appealed to the pope and her nephew, Charles V, Holy Roman Emperor. Pope Clement VII could not afford to upset the powerful Holy Roman Emperor.

In 1529, a special legatine court opened at Blackfriars in London. The court's purpose was to hear the case for the annulment. It was presided over by papal legate Cardinal Lorenzo Campeggio and Cardinal Thomas Wolsey, who had been made Pope Clement VII's viceregent in 1528 "to take cognisance of all matters concerning the King's divorce". Unfortunately, the court was adjourned in July 1529 for a summer recess but never reopened as Catherine appealed her case directly to Rome. Henry VIII was bitterly disappointed. His disappointment with his advisor, Cardinal Wolsey, made the cardinal vulnerable. His enemies were able to paint him as someone stalling over the annulment and who was in the pocket of France and not working for the king's best interests. He was called to London to face charges of praemunire but died on the way.

In 1531, with the help of his new right-hand man, Thomas Cromwell, Henry was granted the title of "singular protector, supreme lord, and even, so far as the law of Christ allows, supreme head of the English church and clergy", and in 1532 Anne Boleyn was raised to the peerage, being made Marquess of Pembroke in her own right. The couple then had a successful trip to Calais, gaining Francis I's support for their plans to marry, and they may even have married in secret on their arrival back in England on 14th November 1532.

On 25th January 1533, they had a secret but official marriage ceremony at Whitehall Palace. Although they may not have known at the time, Anne was pregnant.

On 30th March 1533, Thomas Cranmer was consecrated as Archbishop of Canterbury. On 5th April 1533, Convocation determined that the pope was wrong in issuing a dispensation for Henry VIII to marry Catherine of Aragon, his brother's widow. On 9th April, Catherine was informed that she was demoted from queen to Dowager Princess of Wales and on this day in 1533, Henry VIII informed his Council that Anne was his rightful wife and queen and should be accorded royal honours.

On 23rd May 1533, a special court annulled Henry VIII's marriage to Catherine, and on 28th May, the Archbishop of Canterbury proclaimed that Henry's second marriage was valid. It was a victory at last for the king and Anne Boleyn, and they set about celebrating it in style with a lavish coronation at Westminster Abbey, which followed three days of pageantry, processions and celebrations. Sadly, Anne just had three short years as queen.

The 11th April 1533, the date when Anne Boleyn was officially recognised as queen, is recorded in the amazing painting by Hans Holbein the Younger, The Ambassadors, which portrays two ambassadors: Jean de Dinteville, maître d'hôtel to Francis I of France, and George de Selve, Bishop of Lavaur. Those who have analysed the painting have found the date marked on the celestial globe, the quadrant and the cylinder sundial. Historian Eric Ives wonders if Anne Boleyn commissioned this spectacular painting. It is an amazing painting rich in symbolism and messages.

Interestingly, in May 1536, ambassador Jean de Dinteville attempted to intercede on behalf of Sir Francis Weston, who was accused of sleeping with Queen Anne Boleyn, but his petition was unsuccessful.

12 April

On 12th April 1550, in the reign of King Edward VI, courtier and poet Edward de Vere, 17th Earl of Oxford, was born. He was the only son of John de Vere, 16th Earl of Oxford, and his second wife, Margery Golding. Edward became Earl of Oxford in 1562 after his father's death.

Here are some facts about this Tudor man:

- He was made a royal ward after his father's death, and William Cecil, master of the court of wards, became his guardian and appointed tutors to educate him.
- He was granted an honorary MA from Cambridge in 1564 and Oxford in September 1566 as one of Queen Elizabeth I's retinue on her visits to the cities.
- He killed an unarmed man in 1567 while practising fencing, but the coroner's jury found in his favour, ruling that the man had committed suicide by running at Oxford's rapier.
- In 1570, after begging William Cecil for some military experience, he was sent to Scotland with the Earl of Sussex.
- In 1571, he married Cecil's daughter, Anne, but the marriage was unhappy.
- Oxford was not the nicest of men. In the company of friends, he made fun of the queen, then he insulted poet Philip Sidney and may even have plotted his murder. In 1580, he reported his friends, Henry Howard and Charles Arundel, to the queen for their Catholic faith.
- In 1581, he ended up in the Tower of London after his mistress, one of the queen's ladies, Anne Vavasour, gave birth to his son. He was released after a few months and returned to his wife.
- In 1582, Oxford fought a duel with his mistress's uncle, Sir Thomas Knyvet. They were both injured, but not fatally, although servants of theirs would die over the coming months due to their argument.
- In 1586, he served on the commission that tried Mary, Queen of Scots, and in 1589 and 1601, he was one of the peers who sat in judgement on Philip Howard, Earl of Arundel, and Robert Devereux, Earl of Essex.

- His wife, Anne, died in 1588, and in 1592, Oxford married Elizabeth Trentham, who gave him a son, Henry, in 1593.
- In 1603, he was one of those against the succession of the Scottish king, James VI, as King of England.
- Oxford died on 24th June 1604, and he was buried in St Augustine's churchyard in Hackney, London.
- Oxford loved music, was the patron of a company of players from 1580 to 1602, acted as a literary patron, and wrote poetry.
- Oxfordians believe that he wrote the poems and plays attributed to William Shakespeare, but his biographer, Alan H. Nelson, and many others believe this theory is entirely without merit.
- According to some people, Edward de Vere was also the illegitimate son of Queen Elizabeth I. Author Paul Streitz dates Oxford's birth to 1548. He believes Oxford was the result of the young Elizabeth's relationship with Thomas Seymour, husband of her guardian and stepmother, Catherine Parr. The baby, he argues, was placed with John de Vere, Earl of Oxford, He uses the fact that Edward became a royal ward and his education was overseen by people in high places, such as William Cecil, as evidence that Edward was royal. However, Cecil was master of the court of wards, and Edward was the late Earl of Oxford's son. There's nothing at all unusual in what happened.

13 April

On 13th April 1534, Sir Thomas More, Henry VIII's former Lord Chancellor and good friend, was summoned to Lambeth to swear his allegiance to the Act of Succession.

More recorded what happened that day in a letter he wrote a few days later to his daughter, Margaret (or Meg) Roper. Here's an excerpt from that letter:

> "When I was before the Lords at Lambeth, I was the first that was called in, albeit Master Doctor, the Vicar of Croydon, was come before me, and divers others. After the cause of my sending for, declared unto me, (whereof I somewhat marvelled in my mind, considering that they

sent for no more temporal men but me), I desired the sight of the oath, which they showed me under the great seal. Then desired I the sight of the act of the succession, which was delivered me in a printed roll. After which read secretly by myself, and the oath considered with the act, I showed unto them, that my purpose was not to put any fault, either in the act or any man that made it, or in the oath or any man that sware it, nor to condemn the conscience of any other man. But as for myself in good faith my conscience so moved me in the matter, that though I would not deny to swear to the succession, yet unto the oath that there was offered me, I could not swear, without the jeoparding of my soul to perpetual damnation. And that if they doubted whether I did refuse the oath only for the grudge of my conscience, or for any other fantasy, I was ready therein to satisfy them by mine oath. Which if they trusted not, what should they be the better to give me any oath. And if they trusted that I would therein swear true, then trusted I that of their goodness they would not move me to swear the oath that they offered me, perceiving that for to swear it was against my conscience."

More records that he was then shown the roll listing the names of those who had sworn the oath, but More still refused, although he did not say that he blamed any man that had sworn.

Due to his refusal to swear to the oath, More was then "delivered to the abbot of Westminster to be kept as a prisoner" before being taken to the Tower of London on 17th April.

Sir Thomas More would not swear the oath because he believed that "no temporal man may be the head of spirituality", including the king. A commission of oyer and terminer was appointed on 26th June 1535 to try him for "traitorously attempting to deprive the King of his title of Supreme Head of the Church, &c." and he was tried for high treason on 1st July 1535. Unsurprisingly, More was found guilty and sentenced to a full traitor's death, i.e. to be hanged, drawn and quartered, to be carried out at Tyburn. Mercifully, his sentence was commuted to beheading, and he was put to death on Tower Hill on 6th July 1535.

14 April

On 14th April 1565, in the reign of Queen Elizabeth I, astrologer, astronomer, mathematician and magician Edward Gresham was born in Stainsford, Yorkshire.

Gresham is known for his treatise on the planets, "Astrostereon", and astrological almanacks published between 1603 and 1607. Gresham's biographer, Bernard Capp, writes of how his 1605 almanack, which sadly no longer exists, apparently foretold the Gunpowder Plot and was so accurate that Gresham was suspected of being involved in the plot!

Here are some facts about Edward Gresham:

- It is thought that he was educated at Trinity College, Cambridge.
- He had homes in Stainsford, Yorkshire, and Thames Street, London.
- His 1603 treatise "Astrostereon, or a Discourse of the Falling of the Planet" showed that Gresham favoured the heliocentric system put forward by Copernicus.
- When accused of being an atheist, Gresham claimed to have written at least two religious treatises, "Sabbath-dayes exercises" and "Positions in divinitie", although they were never published.
- As well as being a mathematician, astronomer and astrologer, he practised medicine and magic, or perhaps witchcraft.
- In 1611, Frances Howard, wife of Robert Devereux, 3rd Earl of Essex, needed a magician to help her out of her marriage. Her previous magician, Simon Forman, who had allegedly helped make Robert Carr fall in love with her, had just died, and now she needed someone to step in to get her an annulment so she could marry Carr. Gresham is said to have made her husband impotent, and in 1613, the marriage was ruled unconsummated due to Essex's impotence, and an annulment was granted. Frances married Carr, who had just become Earl of Somerset, three months after the annulment.
- It was also said that Gresham used his skills as a magician to get rid of courtier Sir Thomas Overbury who was a friend of Robert Carr, but who was opposed to the idea of him marrying Frances and was vocal in his opposition. After

refusing a diplomatic posting from King James I, Overbury was imprisoned in the Tower of London, and it was there that he died on 15th September 1613. It was rumoured that he was poisoned and that Frances was behind it. It was alleged that the countess had employed Richard Weston and two others to obtain poison and put them into food sent to Overbury. Weston was an associate of Gresham, and before his death, Gresham gathered together his baubles, things he'd used in his magic, such as pictures in lead and wax and plates of gold of naked people, crosses, crucifixes, and other things, wrapped them in a scarf and gave them to Weston with instructions to bury them so "that no man might find them". Weston was obviously a man Gresham was close to. However, Gresham died on 13th January 1613, so he cannot be held responsible for Overbury's death.

- Weston was executed for his involvement in Overbury's death, and the countess and her husband were imprisoned.
- Gresham was buried on 14th January 1613 at All Saints-the-Less, London. The Harleian Miscellany states that he left behind a man and a maid, "the one hanged for a witch, the other for a thief."

15 April

On 15th April 1545, Sir Robert Dymoke, champion at the coronations of Henry VII and Henry VIII, and a man who served in the households of Queens Catherine of Aragon and Anne Boleyn, died .

Here are a few facts about Dymoke:

- Robert was born around 1461 and was the son of Sir Thomas Dymoke of Scrivesby in Lincolnshire, and his wife, Margaret, daughter and co-heir of Leo Welles, Baron Welles. Robert's father was the champion at the coronation of King Edward IV.
- In May 1471, when he was about ten years old, an order was issued to arrest Robert and his mother. This followed a feud that his father had had with Thomas Burgh, Master of the Horse to Edward IV, which resulted in Burgh's manor being attacked

and destroyed. His father was executed, and the Dymoke lands were granted to the king's brother, the future Richard III.

- In 1472, Robert's wardship was granted to Robert Radcliffe.
- In 1482, Dymoke was given licence to inherit his father's lands.
- Dymoke was knighted in 1483 before Richard III's coronation and acted as champion. The champion has to ride into the coronation banquet at Westminster Hall and challenge all those present who might impugn the monarch's title, and Dymoke did this. He is recorded as riding into the hall and challenging anyone who thought Richard wasn't the lawful king to a fight. Nobody spoke against the king and instead cried, "King Richard!"
- He acted as champion at the coronation of Henry VII in 1485 and at that of Henry VIII in 1509.
- He served as Sheriff of Lincolnshire three times between 1484 and 1509, and as Mayor of Boston, in Lincolnshire, in 1520.
- He served the king in his French campaign of 1513 and was rewarded for his service at the siege of Tournai by being made treasurer of Tournai.
- Between 1527 and 1535, he was chancellor to the queen's household and served as almoner and receiver to Catherine of Aragon and as chamberlain to Anne Boleyn.
- In 1536, he was suspected of involvement in the Pilgrimage of Grace rebellion after the rebels used a banner depicting his family's arms. He and his sons were fetched from their home at Scrivelsby by the rebels, but he was not punished.
- Robert was married to Anne Sparrow, and their children included sons Edward and Arthur.
- He died on this day in 1545, in the Catholic faith, leaving instructions for masses to be said daily for his soul, and those of his wife and parents.
- His son, Edward, was the champion at the coronations of Edward VI, Mary I and Elizabeth I.

16 April

On 16th April 1512, Henry VIII's warship, The Mary Rose, began her first tour of duty in the English Channel to hunt for French warships.

The Mary Rose served her king for 34 years. She fought against France in 1512 in the Battle of Saint-Mathieu. She was part of England's victory at Flodden in 1513 as the troop transport ship, and was chosen as the flagship in skirmishes against France in the 1520s.

Sadly, she sank in the Battle of the Solent on 19th July 1545. Over 400 men went down with her.

She was raised in 1982 and can be seen at the Mary Rose Museum in Portsmouth.

17 April

On 17th April 1595 (or, according to some sources, 7th April), in the reign of Queen Elizabeth I, Jesuit Henry Walpole was hanged, drawn and quartered in the city of York. Walpole had been accused of treason on three counts: that he "had abjured the realm without licence; that he had received holy orders overseas; and that he had returned to England as a Jesuit priest to exercise his priestly functions". Walpole was beatified in 1929 and canonised in 1970 by Pope Paul VI, so he is now St Henry Walpole.

Henry Walpole was the eldest child of Christopher Walpole and Margery Warner, and he was baptised in October 1558 in Docking, Norfolk. Walpole was educated at Norwich Grammar School before studying philosophy and languages at Cambridge, at Peterhouse. He also studied at Gray's Inn.

On 1st December 1581, Walpole attended the execution of the Jesuit priest Edmund Campion and was splashed with the priest's blood. He saw this as a sign that he was to carry on Campion's work. He wrote a poem, "An Epitaph of the Life and Death of ... Edmund Campion", which was published anonymously and copies of it were destroyed by Elizabeth I's government. The government suspected Walpole of being the poet, and after the printer was punished by losing his ears, Walpole went into hiding at Anmer Hall in Norfolk, which belonged to his family. He then escaped to France, arriving at the English College in Reims in July 1582. In 1583, he was accepted by the English College, Rome, and was ordained as a Jesuit priest in Paris on 17th December 1588.

Walpole served as a chaplain to the Spanish forces in the Netherlands under Colonel William Stanley and was arrested in Flushing after it fell to the English forces in the winter of 1589. He was released in January 1590 after one of his brothers paid a ransom. He then spent time on the Continent acting as a priest.

In November 1591, Elizabeth I issued an edict against Jesuit seminary priests, which was answered by Robert Persons with his "Responsio ad edictum", published under the name of Philopater. Walpole was tasked to translate it into English as an attack not on the queen but on her advisor, William Cecil. In 1593, Walpole was sent on an English mission by Robert Persons, leaving Dunkirk with his brother, Thomas. He landed at Flamborough Head, near Bridlington in Yorkshire, and he and his party were arrested on 7th December at Kilham and taken to York Castle, where he admitted to being a Jesuit. In February 1594, Walpole was escorted to the Tower of London, where he spent two months in solitary confinement and was tortured at least 14 times. In "Unpublished documents relating to the English martyrs", editor J. H. Pollen writes of how both his thumbs were lamed, and he was put into gauntlets. These iron gauntlets were constricting irons placed on the wrists and tightened by a screw, which was torture in itself, but then chains from a beam were attached to them, and the victim was suspended from the chains without anything under their feet. The gauntlets would cut into the flesh and make the arms swell. He may also have been racked, and he certainly lost proper use of his fingers. All of this torture was to try and get him to give information on seminaries in Spain and their students' names. Although he did give some information, Antony Charles Ryan, his biographer, notes that "One thing he did not do was to compromise anyone in England whose life would have been in peril as the result of revelations."

In early 1595, Walpole was sent to York for trial and was found guilty of high treason. He was executed on 17th April 1595, and Ryan writes, "When the day dawned, Walpole was dragged to the place of execution on a hurdle. Once again, he testified his loyalty to the queen so that some tried to persuade the magistrate to stop the execution. On the scaffold, he was pushed and hanged before he could complete his prayers. He was immediately drawn and quartered."

18 April

On 18th April 1540, King Henry VIII made Thomas Cromwell Earl of Essex.

The previous earl, Henry Bourchier, had died that March after a horse-riding accident. He died childless, so the earldom had become extinct until its new creation for Cromwell.

Cromwell, the man who'd helped the king get rid of Anne Boleyn and dissolve the monasteries, was also made Lord Great Chamberlain.

Cromwell had failed to get the king out of his marriage to Anne of Cleves, but it looked like he was still in favour. However, Cromwell's enemies rose against him. He was arrested at a council meeting on 10th June and executed on 28th July for treason, heresy and corruption.

19 April

On 19th April 1558, fifteen-year-old Mary, Queen of Scots and fourteen-year-old Francis, the dauphin, son of King Henry II of France, were formally betrothed.

The King of France escorted the young Scottish queen into the great hall of the Louvre Palace in Paris, while Anthony Bourbon, King of Navarre, escorted the dauphin into the hall. After the king announced that Mary and Francis would marry in five days, the Cardinal of Lorraine joined the couple's hands. They plighted their troths, with Francis declaring that of "his own free will and with the fullest consent of the King and Queen his father and mother, and being duly authorised by them to take the Queen of Scotland for his wife and consort, he promised to espouse her on the following Sunday April 24." Mary agreed too.

The formal betrothal was celebrated with a lavish ball. Mary danced with her future father-in-law, the king, Francis with his aunt,

Marguerite of Valois, and Francis's mother, Catherine de Medici, with the King of Navarre.

Historian Lady Antonia Fraser doesn't think much of Mary, Queen of Scots' first husband, the dauphin. In writing of his affection for his bride-to-be, she also writes:

> "His mother, Catherine de Medici, and Mary Stuart seem to have been indeed the only two human beings for whom this pathetic, wizened creature felt true emotion."

She says that he had been sickly in his childhood and now, in adolescence, "his physique was scarcely developed and his height was stunted" and that he "showed little enthusiasm or aptitude for learning".

His bride, however, was described by the Venetian ambassador as "the most beautiful princess in Europe" and was tall for a woman of the time, being about 5'11.

On the eve of the wedding, 23rd April 1558, the royal family prepared for the marriage by moving to the bishop's palace near Notre Dame Cathedral, where the ceremony would take place. Historian Retha Warnicke explains that a viewing platform had been erected on the pavement outside the cathedral for important officials and that a 12-foot high arch-shaped gallery had been constructed linking the bishop's palace door to the cathedral door, and that it was decorated with greenery. A pavilion decorated with fleur de lis was also erected near the cathedral door.

Historian John Guy notes that Henry II was determined that his son's wedding "was to be the most regal and triumphant ever celebrated in the kingdom of France" and that there had been secret preparations for it for well over a month, with people from officials to carpenters, dress-makers to pastry chefs, working day and night. This marriage was important to Henry. The agreement for the marriage stipulated that if Mary died without heirs, then Scotland would become a vassal of France, and Mary wasn't just Queen of Scotland; she was also going to be laying claim to England.

20 April

On 20th April 1578, Lady Mary Keys (née Grey), sister of Lady Jane Grey and wife of Thomas Keys, died at her home in the parish of St Botolph without Aldgate, London.

Here are some facts about Mary:

- Mary was born around 1545, probably at the Grey family home, Bradgate Hall in Leicestershire. She was the youngest daughter, after Jane and Katherine, of Henry Grey, Duke of Suffolk, and his wife, Frances Brandon. Through her mother, Mary was the granddaughter of Charles Brandon, Duke of Suffolk, and his wife, Mary Tudor, Queen of France, and the great-granddaughter of King Henry VII.
- In May 1553, when she was about eight years old, Mary was betrothed to Arthur, Lord Grey of Wilton, her cousin. However, the fall of her sister, Lady Jane Grey, in the summer of 1553, followed by the execution of Jane and the sisters' father in February 1554 dashed the family's hopes of a good marriage for Mary, and the betrothal was dissolved.
- The Spanish ambassador described Mary as "little, crook-backed and very ugly".
- Mary was interested in theology and had a collection of religious works.
- Mary served Queen Elizabeth I as a maid of honour and was granted a pension of £80, which was a real help as her late mother's estate had mostly gone to Mary's stepfather, Adrian Stokes.
- In 1565, she angered Elizabeth by marrying the queen's sergeant porter, Thomas Keys, a widower with many children who was twice her age. It was an interesting match, too, in that Mary was tiny, and he was said to be 6ft 8, and he was of the gentry class, and Mary was related to the queen.
- The queen was furious with the couple for marrying without her consent when Mary was so close to the throne. Keys was thrown into the Fleet Prison, and Mary was put into the care of Sir William Hawtrey at Chequers. In 1567, Mary was moved to the home of her stepgrandmother, Katherine Willoughby,

Duchess of Suffolk, and then on to that of Sir Thomas Gresham in 1569. In 1568, Keys was released from prison, but he died in 1571 without ever being reconciled with Mary. Although the queen gave Mary her freedom in 1572, Mary stayed with Gresham voluntarily because she had nowhere else to go and no money. However, Gresham didn't want her, and in 1573 she moved to her stepfather Adrian Stokes' home for a time before setting up her own home in London. At New Year 1578, she is recorded as having exchanged gifts with the queen and so was back at court by that time.

- She died at her home on this day in 1578 at the age of 33 during an outbreak of the plague. In her will, she left her mother's jewellery to her stepgrandmother, Katherine Willoughby, along with a mystic ruby, something that was thought to protect against the plague. She also made bequests to her cousin, Lady Arundell, her stepfather's second wife, Lady Throckmorton, her servants, and her stepdaughter, Jane. The bulk of her estate went to her god-daughter, Mary, her stepdaughter's daughter.
- Mary was laid to rest on 14th May 1578 at Westminster Abbey, with Susan Bertie, Countess of Kent and daughter of Katherine Willoughby, acting as chief mourner. She was laid to rest in the tomb of her mother, Frances.

If you want to know more about Mary, and her sisters Lady Katherine Grey and Lady Jane Grey, I'd highly recommend reading Leanda de Lisle's book "The Sisters Who Would be Queen".

21 April

On 21st April 1581, alchemist Thomas Charnock was buried at Otterhampton in Somerset. He had died at his home in Combwich in Somerset.

Let me tell you a bit more about this 16th-century alchemist.

- Thomas Charnock was born in the mid-1520s in Faversham, Kent.
- He referred to himself as an "unlettered scholar", and he did not receive much in terms of formal education.

- His biographer Robert M Schuler writes that he'd become involved in alchemy by the time he was 12. Alchemy is concerned with changing base substances like metals into other substances, such as silver or gold, or finding a universal elixir. Charnock's uncle, also named Thomas Charnock, who had served King Henry VII as confessor, was also an alchemist. When he died, Charnock had access to his collection of alchemical works.
- He travelled all over England to broaden his alchemical knowledge and collect works on the subject.
- Around 1554, he learned the secret of the philosopher's stone from a priest and an abbot, and he set about applying what he had learned.
- Charnock's alchemical work caused a fire in 1555, which destroyed some of his work.
- In 1557, just after he had allegedly achieved the philosopher's stone, he was drafted into defending Calais. He hadn't wanted to do this, but it seems he'd made an enemy of his local Justice of the Peace, who ensured he was conscripted. In frustration, he smashed up his work and vowed never to work on alchemy again. It is, however, thought that he wrote his work "Breviary of Natural Philosophy", an account of his alchemical experiences, while he was in Calais.
- In 1562, he married Agnes Norden at Stockland Bristol in Somerset, and began an unlicensed medical practice there. He had two children with Agnes, a son, Absolon, who died in infancy, and a daughter Bridget.
- He didn't practise medicine for very long as the alchemy bug bit him, and in 1579, he claimed that he had succeeded in making the stone.
- He offered Queen Elizabeth I the Philosopher's Stone in return for her granting him a 14-year subsidy for his alchemical work. He even said that he would lose his head on Tower Hill if he weren't successful at making her the stone, which would prolong her life and produce gold for her coinage. Unfortunately for Charnock, he was turned down.

- One hundred years after his death, a friend of philosopher and writer John Aubrey visited Charnock's former home at Combwich to see an alchemical scroll discovered hidden in the wall of the property. Nobody had dared live in the house after Charnock's death, as it was believed to be haunted by spirits. There, he found Charnock's intact laboratory painted with alchemical symbols.

Trivia: according to Glyn Parry, author of "The Arch Conjuror of England", a book on John Dee, Charnock claimed that King Henry VII had "possessed the purest stone" by 1504.

22 April

On 22nd April 1598, Justice Francis Beaumont, member of Parliament, Serjeant-at-Law and Justice of the Common Pleas in the reign of Elizabeth I, died. He died from gaol fever at his home in Grace Dieu, Leicestershire, and was buried in Belton Church. His colleague Serjeant Edward Drew also died of the fever they picked up on the Lent circuit in Lancaster.

But what was gaol fever?

It is believed to have been epidemic typhus and was a major killer in medieval and Tudor England. It is louse-borne and is spread through contact with infected body lice. Symptoms included fever, chills, headache, nausea and vomiting, rapid breathing, aches, rash, cough, and confusion. Today, it can be prevented with a vaccine, and it could be treated with antibiotics, but there were no effective treatments in Tudor times.

The disease was common in prisons because body lice thrive in overcrowded places and where people cannot bathe regularly or change their bedding and clothing. When an infected prisoner was brought before a court, the infected lice could find new hosts in members of the court, and the disease would spread.

Several serious outbreaks of gaol fever at prisons and courts in the 16th century caused the deaths of prisoners and magistrates, and these were known as "The Black Assizes". As well as the Black Assize of the Northern Circuit, which saw the deaths of Justice Beaumont and Sergeant Drew in 1598, there were also the Black Assize of Oxford in 1577 and the Black Assize of Exeter Castle in 1586.

Epidemics of gaol fever were common until the 19th century when the Victorians reformed prisons.

23 April

23rd April is St George's Day, the day for announcing new appointments to the Order of the Garter, England's highest order of chivalry. Today, I'm going back to Henry VIII's reign and St George's Day 1536, shortly before the fall of Anne Boleyn.

In 1536, Queen Anne Boleyn's brother, George Boleyn, Lord Rochford, was expected to be elected to the order. He had been nominated in 1535 and had received a reasonable amount of support, but King James V of Scotland had beaten him by two votes. Unfortunately for George, he was to miss out in 1536, too, with the honour going to Nicholas Carew, a known opponent of the Boleyns and the man who was said to be coaching Jane Seymour on how to behave with King Henry VIII. Carew beat George soundly, receiving twice as many votes, and even George's father, Thomas Boleyn, had voted for Carew.

Although some historians see Carew's appointment as a snub to George and the queen, that may well be reading too much into what happened. While it could be taken as a sign that the Boleyns were losing their influence, it is only with hindsight, knowing what would happen to George very soon, that we interpret this appointment as the beginning of the end for him.

The choice of appointment to the Order of the Garter in 1536 was largely dictated by the Henry VIII's earlier promise to King Francis I of France that Carew was next in line for an appointment to the order. This promise is referred to in a 1535 letter from Palamedes Gontier, secretary to Philippe de Chabot, Admiral of France. Gontier had written to his master in February 1535 explaining that he had seen Henry VIII and "Presented the letter in favor of the "Grand Escuyer" of England [Nicholas Carew], to which he replied that the said place of the Chancellor of the Order was filled by the King of Scotland, and the number of 24 could not be exceeded. On the first vacancy he would remember the said Grand Escuyer." Francis I had been favouring an appointment for Carew since at least 1533.

Having researched the voting for appointments to the Order of the Garter, I can say that knights appear to have voted for men for whom the king wanted them to vote. In 1536, quite a few knights voted for both Carew and George Boleyn, as they were in different categories due to their status. Each knight could cast nine votes: 3 "Principes", 3 "Barones" and 3 "Equites". It wasn't a case of Thomas Boleyn voting AGAINST his son, he just didn't vote FOR him. Thomas voted for Delaware, Cobham and Powys as Barons and Carew, Browne and Cheyney as Equites (knights). The Dukes of Norfolk and Richmond voted for both men, as did the Earls of Sussex and Oxford, and William Fitzwilliam.

The king could see by the votes who was popular with his Knights of the Garter, but he was still free to choose whoever he wanted. Hence, Henry VIII could still have chosen George Boleyn even though Carew had proved more popular.

Eustace Chapuys, the imperial ambassador, recorded that "the Concubine has not had sufficient influence to get it for her brother", so he read Carew's appointment as a sign that the queen's power was waning. Whatever the truth, it must have been humiliating for George to have his name put forward for voting and then see a Boleyn opponent win the vote and get chosen by the king.

Nicholas Carew, the knight appointed that year, was a royal favourite until his arrest on 31st December 1538. He was implicated in a plot to depose Henry VIII and replace him with Henry Courtenay, 1st Marquess of Exeter and cousin of the king through his mother, Catherine of York. Carew was tried on 14th February 1539 and executed on 8th March on Tower Hill.

The 23rd April is still the traditional day for new appointments to the order to be announced. The installation ceremonies take place in June, on Garter Day, the Monday of Royal Ascot week. Back in 1536, Nicholas Carew was installed on 21st May at the annual Order feast, just four days after George Boleyn's execution.

24 April

24th April is St Mark's Eve, the day before the Feast of St Mark the Evangelist, one of Christ's apostles and the man who is said to have written the Gospel of Mark. In medieval and Tudor times, St Mark's Day was the traditional day for praying for fertile land and a good harvest, so how was St Mark's Eve celebrated?

In "Folklore of Lincolnshire", Susanna O'Neill writes of how St Mark's Eve was the night for young women to "divine who they were to marry". Ladies in North Kelsey would visit the Maiden Well, "walking towards it backwards and then circling it three times, still backwards, whilst wishing to see their destined husbands. After the third circling, the girl would kneel and gaze into the spring, where she would supposedly see the face of her lover."

Other ways of divining who you were going to marry, according to O'Neill and also Steve Roud, author of "The English Year", included hanging your washed chemise in front of the fire and waiting for a man (your future husband) to turn them; setting the table for supper and leaving the door open and waiting to see which man would come and join you; picking grass from a grave at midnight to put under your pillow so that you would then dream of your future beau; sitting in a barn at midnight and waiting for your future lover to walk through the door, and throwing an unbroken apple peel over your shoulder and then seeing whose name it had spelt out when it landed.

If a man wanted to divine who his future bride would be, he could visit the local church late on St Mark's Eve and see whose reflection he could see in the church window at midnight.

Still another tradition I found on Mostly-Medieval.com, was for a woman to "fast from sunset and then during the night make and bake a cake containing an eggshell full of salt, wheat meal, and barley meal. Then she should open the door of her home. Her future lover should come in and turn the cake."

25 April

On 25th April 1544, an English translation of John Fisher's Latin work, "Psalms or Prayers", was published. It had been translated by Queen Catherine Parr, Henry VIII's sixth and final wife.

The work was published anonymously by the king's printer, Thomas Berthelet, but Janel Mueller, editor of "Katherine Parr: Complete Works and Correspondence", points out that there is "considerable circumstantial evidence" to point to Catherine as the translator.

Here is the evidence:

- On 12th May 1544, Thomas Berthelet submitted a bill to Catherine's clerk of the closet for twenty copies of the book.
- The two extant copies from this print run were gifts from Catherine to her husband, Henry VIII, and her brother, William Parr.
- The book's two concluding prayers appear "timed to coincide with Henry VIII's military expedition against France." "A prayer for the King" was adapted from Fisher's original work, and "A prayer for men to say going into battle" may have been composed by Catherine herself. Mueller points out that these two prayers were contained in the book "Prayers or Meditations", published in 1545 under Catherine's name.
- Nicholas Udall, who worked with the queen on an English translation of a work by Erasmus, praised Catherine in a letter for her work on "godly Psalms", although he could have been commenting on Catherine's other works.

Susan James, Catherine's biographer, concurs with Mueller's conclusion that Catherine was responsible for this translation, writing

> "Fourteen presentation copies 'of the psalm prayers' ordered by the queen from the king's printer, half of them sent to her almoner, who was presumably the inspiration for the project, less than a week after the publication of the English translation of Psalms or Prayers, and including prayers known at court to have been written by the queen, is a fairly strong indication of the royal source of the translation."

James also notes that there were a number of bills in the queen's accounts that summer for further copies of "a book", which were presentation copies that Catherine sent out. James also states that Catherine ordered four crimson velvet-bound copies of the book in June 1546 and kept one of those copies with her until her death in 1548.

Here is one of the prayers said to be Catherine's composition, "A prayer for men to say going into battle":

"Oh Almighty King and lord of hosts,
which by thy angels thereunto appointed
dost minister both war and peace,
and which didest give unto David
both courage and strength,
being but a little one,
unarmed, and unexpert in feats of war
with his ling to set upon and overthrow
the great huge Goliath:
our cause now being just,
and being enforced to enter into war and battle,
we most humbly beseech thee
O Lord God of hosts
so to turn the hearts of our enemies
to the desire of peace,
that no Christian blood be spilt,
or else grant (O Lorde)
that with small effusion of blood,
and to the little hurt and damage of innocents,
we may to thy glory obtain victory:
and that the wars being soon ended,
we may all with one heart and mind,
all knit together in concord and unity,
laud and praise thee:
which livest and reignest, world without end.
Amen."

26 April

On 26th April 1564, the Bard, William Shakespeare, was baptised at Holy Trinity Church, Stratford-upon-Avon, Warwickshire. We don't know the exact date of Shakespeare's birth, but it is traditionally celebrated on 23rd April as babies at that time were usually baptised within a few days of their birth.

The church where he was baptised is also his resting place, and if you visit Holy Trinity, you can see copies of the register entries of his baptism and death in the parish records on the wall and the font which would have been used to baptise Shakespeare in 1564. It's also lovely to pay your respects at his grave and see a bust of Shakespeare on the wall that dates back to 1623 and was erected by his widow Anne and his family and friends.

Shakespeare was lucky to survive the summer of 1564. In July 1564, the plague hit Stratford-upon-Avon, where little William lived with his parents, John Shakespeare and Mary Arden. The first death in the parish was recorded on 11th July 1564 by John Bretchgirdle, vicar of Holy Trinity. The victim's name was Oliver Gunn, an apprentice weaver who died in what is now The Garrick Inn on the town's High Street. The words "*hic incepit pestis*" ("Here begins the plague") are scribbled next to the burial entry, although they may have been added to the burial entry at a later date.

Plague is a bacterial infection caused by the bacterium *Yersinia pestis*, which is spread in various ways:
- in the air,
- by direct contact
- by contaminated food
- and from being bitten by infected fleas.

Bubonic plague was spread via fleas from the black rat, and pneumonic plague was spread via droplets from people coughing. Symptoms included necrosis of the bite, swelling of lymph nodes in the neck and armpits, headache, fever and delirium. Its deadliest form, pneumonic plague, affected the lungs and was highly infectious.

It has been estimated that the Black Death, an epidemic of bubonic plague, wiped out 60% of Europe's population in the 14th century, and the last major English epidemic of bubonic plague was from

1665 to 1666 in London, where it is said to have killed a quarter of London's population. There were numerous outbreaks of "plague" in England throughout the 14th, 15th and 16th centuries. Including the one I mention in Stratford. In Stratford, the bubonic plague epidemic lasted six months and killed over 200 people in the parish, around a fifth (some say a seventh) of the population. William Shakespeare's family were very fortunate to escape the plague.

27 April

On this day in Tudor history, 27th April 1584, Dr David Lewis, a civil lawyer and judge involved in the maritime cases of Elizabeth I's reign, died in London.

He was laid to rest on 24th May in St Mary's Church, Abergavenny, in the part of the church now known as the Lewis Chapel. Lewis had left instructions that he be buried at the church where he was "want to kneel", and he had already prepared his tomb, commissioning sculptor John Gildon of Hereford, who made it from a single piece of stone. Lewis's friend, poet Thomas Churchyard, wrote of Lewis's tomb in his poem "The Worthines of Wales":

"A friend of mine, who lately died
That Doctor Lewis hight
Within that Church his Tomb I spyed
Well wrought and fair to sight"
"hight" here means "was called".

I expect that you haven't heard of David Lewis, so here are some facts about this lesser-known Tudor man:

- He was born around 1520 at Abergavenny in Monmouthshire and was the eldest son of Lewis Wallis, who later became vicar of Abergavenny, and his wife, Lucy. David's surname of Lewis would come from his Welsh name David ap Lewis, meaning son of Lewis.
- David was educated at All Souls College, Oxford, and graduated with a Bachelor of Civil Law in 1540. He became a Fellow of All Souls College in 1541.
- He earned his civil law doctorate in 1548 and became an advocate in the civil law courts.

- He was a member of Parliament for Steyning in 1553 and Monmouthshire from late 1554 to January 1555.
- His legal posts and offices included Master in Chancery, Master of Requests, Judge of the high court of admiralty, joint commissioner of the admiralty, and treasurer of Doctors' Commons.
- He was one of those commissioned to inquire into piracy affecting the King of Spain, and he examined navigators Martin Frobisher and Sir John Hawkins. They were alleged to be planning campaigns of piracy.
- As a civil lawyer, Lewis was one of those who signed a document in 1571 stating that Mary, Queen of Scots' ambassador, John Leslie, Bishop of Ross, was punishable in England for plotting against Elizabeth I.
- Lewis never married.
- As well as his legal work, Lewis was also head of New Inn Hall, Oxford, from 1546-8, and was the first principal of Jesus College, Oxford, from 1571-2.
- At his death, he left property to his sister, Maud Baker; his books on divinity, philosophy, history and art to his nephew, William Pritchard; and rings to his friend Henry Jones and his protégé Sir Julius Caesar.

28 April

On 28th April 1548 (some sources say 6th May), courtier, diplomat, soldier and Keeper of Oatlands Palace, Sir Anthony Browne, died at Byfleet in Surrey. He was around 48 at his death and was one of Henry VIII's most important and richest courtiers.

Browne was the son of another Sir Anthony Browne, who served as King Henry VII's standard-bearer and Lieutenant of Calais Castle. He followed in his father's footsteps as a loyal servant of the monarch. His first appointment at the royal court was in 1518, when he was appointed as surveyor and master of hunting for several Yorkshire properties. The same year, he served in a diplomatic capacity on an embassy to France.

Browne was close to the king throughout Henry VIII's reign,

and his appointments and offices included privy chamberer, knight of the body, Lieutenant of the Isle of Man, ambassador to France, royal standard-bearer, privy councillor, master of the horse, and captain of the gentleman pensioners. His good friend, the king, appointed him as an executor of his will and guardian of Prince Edward and the Lady Elizabeth, and left him the sum of £300. It was Browne who informed Henry VIII that he was dying in January 1547. Along with Edward Seymour, Earl of Hertford, he also informed Edward and Elizabeth that their father had died.

Browne was married twice, first to Alice, daughter of Sir John Gage, who gave him seven sons and three daughters, and then, in 1542, he married fifteen-year-old Lady Elizabeth Fitzgerald, daughter of Gerald Fitzgerald, 9th Earl of Kildare. They had two sons together, Edward and Thomas, but they died in infancy. Browne also had two illegitimate children, Charles and Anne.

Interestingly, Sir Anthony Browne was involved in the falls of two queens. In 1536, according to Lancelot de Carles, secretary to the French ambassador, Browne reported to the Crown that his sister, Elizabeth, Countess of Worcester, who was one of Queen Anne Boleyn's ladies, had defended her own behaviour, possible adultery, saying that it was nothing in comparison to the queen, who allowed members of the court to come into her chamber "at improper hours" and that if her brother did not believe her, then he could find out more from Mark Smeaton. She then said, "I must not forget to tell you what seems to me to be the worst thing, which is that often her brother has carnal knowledge of her in bed."

Then, in 1540, Browne was involved in the fall of Anne of Cleves, Henry VIII's fourth wife, giving a deposition regarding the king's first disastrous meeting with Anne at Rochester on 1st January 1540, when he accompanied the king as his master of the horse. He told of how he was dismayed at Anne's appearance and thought that "the King's Highness should not content hiself with her." According to Browne, when the king met Anne, Browne "noted in the King's Highness countenance such a discontentment and misliking of her person, as he was very sorry of it". The king told him after the meeting that he could see "nothing in this woman as men report of her; and I marvel that wise men would make such report as they have done".

Browne's deposition was used as evidence of the king's unhappiness with Anne and the idea that he had been deceived into marrying her by false reports on her appearance.

Sir Anthony Browne died on either 28th April or 6th May 1548 and was buried with his first wife in a tomb in St Mary's Church, Battle, in Sussex. He was a wealthy man at his death, owning about 11,000 acres of land in Sussex and 8,500 in Surrey.

29 April

On 29th April 1617, Sir Dru Drury, courtier, member of Parliament, friend of Thomas Howard, 4th Duke of Norfolk, and Lieutenant of the Tower of London, died at Riddlesworth Hall in Norfolk. He was buried in Riddlesworth Parish Church.

Drury was aged eighty-five when he died, a very good age. His tomb states that he was 99 when he died, but that is believed to be an error.

Drury died in the Stuart period, but he was prominent in the reign of Queen Elizabeth I. Let me tell you some facts about him.

- He was born around 1531/2, in the reign of King Henry VIII, and was the son of landowner Sir Robert Drury and his wife, Elizabeth.
- He was educated at St Edmund's Hostel, Cambridge.
- In 1559, in the reign of Queen Elizabeth I, Drury was appointed as a gentleman usher of the privy chamber and held this position until his death.
- He was a member of Parliament for Mitchell in Cornwall in 1559, Camelford, Cornwall in 1563, and Norfolk in 1584.
- He was a good friend of Thomas Howard, 4th Duke of Norfolk. He was imprisoned from December 1559 until early 1561 after becoming involved in a brawl to do with his support of Norfolk in his disagreement with Robert Dudley over Elizabeth I's relationship with Dudley. He managed to avoid getting caught up in Norfolk's later plotting.
- He married Elizabeth, daughter of Sir Philip Calthorpe and Jane Boleyn, aunt of Queen Anne Boleyn. Elizabeth had been widowed twice. They set up home at Riddlesworth Hall, which

Drury had built. The marriage was childless. After Elizabeth's death, he married Katherine Finch and had four children with her.

- He served as a Justice for the Peace for Norfolk and Middlesex, was sheriff of Norfolk in 1576/1577, and *custos rotulorum*, or keeper of the rolls, from 1583.
- Drury was knighted in 1579.
- In 1586, Drury and Sir Amyas (Amias) Paulet were chosen to supervise Mary, Queen of Scots, during her imprisonment.
- He served as Lieutenant of the Tower of London from 1595 to 1596.

30 April

On 30th April 1544, in the reign of King Henry VIII, Thomas Audley, Baron Audley of Walden and Lord Chancellor, died at his home, the former Christ Church Priory, in Aldgate, London, at the age of about 56. Audley was Cromwell's right-hand man in 1536, during the fall of Anne Boleyn, and became even more important after Cromwell's fall.

Thomas Audley was born around 1487/8 in Earls Colne, Essex, and was the son of Geoffrey Audley, an administrator. After being educated at Buckingham College, Cambridge, Audley was admitted to the Inner Temple, one of the four inns of the court in London, and in 1514 he served as town clerk of Colchester in Essex, and in 1520 as a Justice of the Peace for Essex.

Audley came to the attention of Henry VIII in 1523 after taking Cardinal Wolsey's side in Parliament when Sir Thomas More defended the rights of the common people. He rose quickly from that point, and on 20th May 1532, he was knighted and made keeper of the great seal after Sir Thomas More resigned as Lord Chancellor. On 26th January 1533, he was officially named Lord Chancellor. Audley is thought to have been responsible for smoothing the passage through Parliament of legislation regarding the king's break with Rome and the supremacy.

On 24th April 1536, Audley was responsible for setting up the legal machinery used in Anne Boleyn's fall: two commissions of oyer and terminer, one for the county of Middlesex and one for Kent. The job of this type of commission was to investigate alleged serious crimes, such as treason, and to determine if there was a case. In 1536, the grand juries of Kent and Middlesex ruled that there was sufficient evidence to send Queen Anne Boleyn, Lord Rochford, Sir Henry Norris, Sir Francis Weston, Willliam Brereton and Mark Smeaton to trial for high treason. Of course, they ended up being found guilty and were executed.

On 17th May 1536, Audley was present at Lambeth when Thomas Cranmer, Archbishop of Canterbury, declared that the marriage between Henry VIII and Anne Boleyn was null and void. On 19th May, he attended the queen's execution at the Tower of London.

On 29th November 1538, Thomas Audley was made Baron Audley of Walden and was elected as a Knight of the Garter in April 1540. The 1539 Parliament's Act of Precedence gave him "precedence over all but dukes of royal blood in parliament, privy council, and Star Chamber."

Although he played a role in negotiating the king's marriage to his fourth wife, Anne of Cleves, Audley survived the fall of Thomas Cromwell and was involved in negotiating the annulment of the Cleves marriage and, later, in interrogating Catherine Howard. Audley was the Privy Council's expert on treason. He was also a commissioner at the trials of Thomas Culpeper and Francis Dereham. Audley was Lord High Steward at the trials of Henry Pole, Baron Montagu, and Henry Courtenay, Marquess of Exeter, in 1538. In 1541, he performed the same role at the trial of Thomas Fiennes, 9th Baron Dacre.

In April 1542, he re-established his former Cambridge college, Buckingham College, as Magdalene College. On 21st April 1544, he resigned the great seal due to illness and died on 30th April 1544 at his home in London. He was buried at Saffron Walden, Essex.

Thomas Audley was married twice, first to Christina Barnardiston, who didn't give him any children, then to Lady Elizabeth Grey, daughter of Thomas Grey, 2nd Marquess of Dorset. Elizabeth gave him two daughters, Mary and Margaret. Margaret married Henry Dudley and then Thomas Howard, 4th Duke of Norfolk.

1 May

On 1ˢᵗ May 1551, Norfolk landowner and member of Parliament, Sir Edmund Knyvet, died.

Before telling you about Knyvet and his hot temper, I want to talk about his surname. I'm not entirely sure how Sir Edmund pronounced it, but it's commonly pronounced "Niv-it", but can also be pronounced "c-niv-it" and even "Nifton".

Here are some facts about Knyvet:

- Sir Edmund Knyvet was the eldest son of Sir Thomas Knyvet of Buckenham Castle, Norfolk, and his wife, Muriel Howard, daughter of Thomas Howard, 2ⁿᵈ Duke of Norfolk, and widow of John Grey, 2ⁿᵈ Viscount Lisle. Sir Thomas Knyvet had served King Henry VIII as his standard-bearer and master of the horse but was killed in the naval battle known as the Battle of St Mathieu with the French in 1512.
- In the 1520s, Edmund married Anne Shelton, daughter of Sir John Shelton of Carrow, Norfolk. The couple went on to have two sons.
- Edmund's wardship, and that of his half-sister, Elizabeth Grey, were purchased by Charles Brandon, Duke of Suffolk, and then sold on to Sir Thomas Wyndham and then Anthony Wingfield.
- Knyvet didn't come into his inheritance until 1533, as his great-grandfather had outlived his father and then left the estate to another family member. Edmund had to wait until that man and his heir had died to enjoy the family lands.
- In late 1536, Knyvet helped his uncle, Thomas Howard, 3ʳᵈ Duke of Norfolk, suppress the Pilgrimage of Grace rebellion.
- He served as Sheriff of Norfolk and Suffolk in 1539 and was knighted in 1538 or 1539.
- Knyvet attended his uncle, the Duke of Norfolk, at the reception of Henry VIII's fourth wife, Anne of Cleves, in January 1540.
- In 1546, he testified against his cousin, Henry Howard, Earl of Surrey, after Surrey was charged with treason. Knyvet was rewarded for his service with the grant of some of the Howard lands in Norfolk.

- He helped John Dudley, Earl of Warwick, suppress Kett's Rebellion in 1549.
- Knyvet was known for his hot temper. In 1539, Knyvet wanted to be elected as a knight of the shire for Norfolk, but Thomas Cromwell preferred Edmund Wyndham and Richard Southwell. Knyvet lost his cool and argued with Southwell. The Duke of Norfolk described what happened in a letter to Thomas Cromwell, saying, "Then he fell in such fume with Richard Southewell that divers of the most worshipful of the shire, fearing a breach of the peace, went to entreat between them". Knyvet and Southwell ended up being called before the Duke of Norfolk, who "desired them to forgive displeasures and be lovers as before", and the duke reported that Southwell was happy with that, but "Knevet said he would never love him, calling him false gentleman, knave, and other opprobrious words". The duke reported that he bound them in £2,000 apiece to keep the peace until they appeared before the Star Chamber. The duke went on to explain to Cromwell that Knyvet "is young and trusts too much to his wit, and will neither follow the advice of his father-in-law, Sir John Shelton, nor me, but is ruled by three or four 'light naughty knaves of Welshmen and others,' and is running into debt. If he comes to you before I do, 'be quick with him and give not too much confidence to his words.'" Another example of his hot temper is from April 1541, when he hit Thomas Clere, a servant of his cousin, Henry Howard, Earl of Surrey, during a game of tennis at the royal court. The law stated that the punishment for an act of violence at court was the loss of the perpetrator's right hand, and Knyvet was condemned to lose his hand, but he was reprieved at the last moment.
- Knyvet died on this day in 1551 in London while there for a session of Parliament as a knight of the shire for Norfolk. His wife and two sons survived him.

2 May

On 2nd May 1568, Mary, Queen of Scots, escaped from Lochleven Castle.

Mary had been a prisoner on the island of Loch Leven since 17th June 1567, following her surrender to the Protestant nobles at the Battle of Carberry Hill on 15th June. Mary's marriage to James Hepburn, Earl of Bothwell, a man implicated in the murder of her previous husband, Henry Stuart, Lord Darnley, had been unpopular with the Scottish Lords, and they had turned against the queen. At Lochleven, it is said that she miscarried twins fathered by Bothwell, and then on 24th July 1567, she was forced to abdicate in favour of her son, James. He became King James VI of Scotland, with his uncle, Mary's illegitimate half-brother, James Stewart, Earl of Moray, acting as Regent.

Mary had tried to escape the island in March 1568, dressed as a laundress, but unfortunately was recognised by the boatman who was to row her across the loch. However, on 2nd May, while a May Day masque took place at the castle, Mary was able to make her getaway. She was helped by a castle page, 16-year-old Willie Douglas, who sabotaged every boat except one. Mary then swapped outfits with her lady, Mary Seton. When the coast was clear, and everyone was enjoying the festivities, Willie rowed the former queen across the loch, where she was met by George Douglas, younger brother of the Laird of Lochleven and a man who had been determined to help the queen after witnessing her forced abdication.

Mary was never able to regain her crown. After being defeated, along with her supporters, on 13th May 1568 at the Battle of Langside, she was forced to flee her homeland into England. Of course, she may have escaped one prison, but she was soon a prisoner again and would be for the rest of her life.

3 May

On 3rd May 1580, poet, farmer and writer on agriculture Thomas Tusser died at sixty-five. He was buried at Manningtree in Essex.

Tusser is known for his poem "A Hundreth Good Pointes of

Husbandrie", which records the country year, and his instructional poem on farming, "Five Hundreth Points of Good Husbandry United to as many of Good Huswiferie".

As we are in May, I thought I would share the verses on May from his poem "A Hundreth Good Pointes of Husbandrie":

"Both Philip and Jacob, bid put off thy lambs:
That thinkest to have any milk of their dams.
But Lammas adviseth thee, milk not too long:
for hardness make poverty, skabbed among.
To milk and to fold them, is much to require:
except thou have pasture, to fill their desire.
But nights being short, and such heed thou mayst take:
not hurting their bodies, much profit to make.
Milk six ewes, for one cow, well chosen therefore:
and double thy dairy else trust me no more.
And yet may good housewives, that knoweth the skill:
have mixed or unmixed, at their pleasure and will.
For greedy of gain, overlay not thy ground:
and they shall thy cattle, be lusty and sound.
But pinch them of pasture, while summer time last:
and pluck at their tails, ere & winter be past.
Pinche weannels at no time, of water nor meat:
if ever thou hope, for to have them good neat.
In summer at all times, in winter in frost:
if cattle lack drink, they be utterly lost.
In May at the furthest, twy fallow thy land:
much drought may cause after, thy plough else to strand.
That tilth being done, thou hast passed the worst:
then after, who plougheth, plough thou with the first.

4 May

On 4th May 1513, in the reign of King Henry VIII, Edmund de la Pole, 8th Earl of Suffolk and claimant to the English throne, was executed by beheading on Tower Hill. He was then laid to rest at Greyfriars without Aldgate in London.

Edmund and Richard were sons of John de la Pole, 2nd Duke of

Suffolk, and his wife, Elizabeth Plantagenet, sister of King Edward IV. They were also the brothers of John de la Pole, Earl of Lincoln, who was killed at the Battle of Stoke in King Henry VII's reign after he had supported the crowning of a boy claiming to be the Earl of Warwick as Edward VI in Dublin in 1487.

Edmund remained loyal to the crown until the late 1490s when he was indicted for murder. He fled to St Omer but was back again in 1500 and then fled again, without royal licence, joining his brother, Richard, at the court of Maximilian, the Holy Roman Emperor. Richard hoped the emperor would support his claim to the English throne and help with an invasion.

Edmund and Richard were attainted by Henry VII's Parliament in 1504, and Edmund was soon taken prisoner by servants of the Duke of Gueldres and then Archduke Philip, son of Maximilian. The archduke handed Edmund over to King Henry VII, who imprisoned him in the Tower of London. He remained in prison on the accession of Henry VIII but was executed after his brother Richard claimed the throne in his own right and was recognised as king by King Louis XII of France. Richard became Earl of Suffolk on Edmund's death and went on plotting. However, he was killed at the Battle of Pavia in February 1525.

5 May

On 5th May 1543, religious radical Adam Damplip, also known as George Bucker, was hanged, drawn and quartered in Calais, which was an English territory.

Nothing is known of this Protestant martyr's early life, but he was in Padua, in Northern Italy, in 1536 with Reginald Pole, who became a cardinal that year. He also became close to Cosmo Gheri, bishop of Fano, who was about to write a biography of John Fisher, the Catholic Bishop of Rochester, who had been executed in London in 1535 for refusing to accept the king as supreme head of the church. Bucker claimed to have served Fisher as his priest. He told of how, after Fisher had been imprisoned in the Tower of London, Bucker took the king's side, but, after Fisher's death, he had a vision in which Fisher confronted him about his desertion, so he repented. Bucker then travelled to Rome on pilgrimage, and there, Gheri had to intercede on his behalf after he killed a man.

By April 1538, he was in Calais as Adam Damplip on his way home to England. Instead of taking a ship on to England, he stayed in Calais preaching, although Cardinal Pole was sending him money to try and get him to go back to Rome. He was also supported financially in Calais by Arthur Plantagenet, Lord Lisle, Deputy of Calais, who recommended Damplip to Thomas Cranmer, Archbishop of Canterbury, and said Damplip's sermon on Romans was the best he'd heard.

Damplip was taken to England by a member of Lord Lisle's household, but he was being investigated, and Cranmer warned him that he could well be imprisoned. Damplip wrote a statement of his religious opinions, and he was eventually able to return to Calais. However, in 1539, it was alleged that he was preaching against the sacrament of the altar and baptism – heresy. In 1540, a royal commission went to Calais to investigate, and they found that Damplip, with his preaching, was causing division there. On 22nd July 1540, Damplip was attainted for treason for his correspondence with the traitor Cardinal Pole. He was imprisoned in London's Marshalsea prison. After Easter 1543, he was released and sent back to Calais on 2nd May to prepare for his execution.

On 5th May 1543, Damplip was hanged, drawn and quartered as a traitor for accepting money from Cardinal Pole, rather than being executed as a heretic. Martyrologist John Foxe explains:

> "The cause whiche firste they layd to his charge, was for heresie. But because by an acte of Parliamente, all suche offences done before a certayne daye, were pardoned (through which Acte he could not be burdened with anye thing that he had preached or taught before) yet for the receiuing of the foresayd French crowne of Cardinall Pole, (as you heard before) he was condemned of treason, and in Calice cruelly put to death, being drawne, hanged, and quartered."

So they couldn't get rid of this man causing trouble in Calais for heresy, so they picked his link to the king's enemy Cardinal Pole. Clever, but nasty.

6 May

On 6th May 1541, Henry VIII issued an injunction ordering "the Byble of the largest and greatest volume, to be had in every churche".

This injunction referred to "The Great Bible", or "Coverdale Bible", the first authorised Bible in English. It had been prepared by Miles Coverdale, who had been commissioned by Thomas Cromwell in 1537 to revise the "Matthew Bible", a Bible which combined the work of William Tyndale and Coverdale, and to print it in Paris. It used Tyndale's New Testament and Pentateuch and then Coverdale's translations of the other books of the Bible. Unfortunately, over 2,000 copies were confiscated by the Inquisition and burnt. Fortunately, some unbound copies were saved, and it was eventually printed in 1539 as the Great Bible.

Here is the injunction that was issued on this day in 1541 by King Henry VIII:

> "Proclamation confirming injunctions heretofore set forth by Royal authority for curates and parishioners to provide, "by a day now expired," and set up in every church, Bibles containing the Old and New Testament in English. By these injunctions the King intended his subjects to read the Bibles for their instruction humbly and reverently; not reading aloud in time of Holy Mass or other divine service, nor, being laymen, arguing thereupon. Many towns and parishes having failed to accomplish this, they are straitly commanded, before All Saints Day next, to provide and set up Bibles of the largest volume, upon penalty of 40 shillings for every month's delay after All Saints Day, half to go to the informer. The sellers of such Bibles are taxed to charge for them not above 10 shillings for Bibles unbound or 12 shillings for Bibles well bound and clasped. Ordinaries having ecclesiastical jurisdiction are to see to this."

The Great Bible is also known as Whitchurch's Bible, as it was printed in London by Edward Whitchurch, who had originally printed it in Paris with Richard Grafton, and the Chained Bible, as it was often chained to stop parishioners taking it out of the church.

It is thought that over 9,000 copies had been printed by 1541.

7 May

On 7th May 1567, eight days before James Hepburn, Earl of Bothwell, married Mary, Queen of Scots, the Catholic court granted him an annulment of his marriage to Lady Jean Gordon on the grounds of consanguinity, with the couple having been related in the fourth degree.

This annulment was granted at the request of Mary, Queen of Scots, as Bothwell was determined to marry her. A Protestant court had annulled the marriage on 3rd May due to Bothwell's adultery with his wife's maid.

Jean Gordon was born around 1546 and was the daughter of Scottish nobleman George Gordon, 4th Earl of Huntly, and his wife, Elizabeth Keith. Her father and two of her brothers and the Clan Gordon rebelled against Mary, Queen of Scots in 1562, and her father died at the Battle of Corrichie against the Earl of Moray, dying of a stroke rather than battle wounds. Following Moray's victory, Jean's brothers involved in the battle were executed, and her father was attainted posthumously for treason. Fortunately for Jean, the queen didn't hold this rebellion against the family, and by 1565, Jean and her mother were serving the queen at court. Her eldest brother, George, was restored to her father's earldom in 1565 and to the Gordon lands in 1567.

Jean fell in love with Alexander Ogilvy, laird of Boyne, but, on 22nd February 1566, Jean, a Catholic, married James Hepburn, Earl of Bothwell, a friend of her brother George, in a ceremony at Holyroodhouse. The ceremony was presided over by Jean's uncle, Alexander Gordon, Bishop of Galloway, a Protestant. This was because Bothwell refused to have a Catholic service. Mary, Queen of Scots, was heavily involved in the marriage, signing the marriage contract on 12th February 1566 and giving Jean twelve ells of cloth of silver to make her wedding dress. John Hamilton, Archbishop of St Andrews, had granted a dispensation to cover consanguinity on 17th February.

Jean and Bothwell set up home at Crichton Castle in Midlothian, but the marriage was short-lived as Jean's husband was determined to marry Mary, Queen of Scots. Bothwell persuaded Jean to begin a suit for divorce on the grounds of adultery. At the same time, with Mary's help, he sought one on the grounds of consanguinity even though a dispensation had been granted just a year earlier. The queen used her influence there!

Bothwell married Mary on 15th May 1567, and in 1573, Jean married Alexander Gordon, 12th Earl of Sutherland, and settled with him at Dunrobin Castle. They went on to have seven children together before Sutherland's death in 1594. In 1599, Jean married her first love, Alexander Ogilvy, and they were married for ten years before Ogilvy died. Jean's eldest son, who had inherited the Sutherland lands from his father, died in 1615, so Jean took over the estates while bringing up her grandson, who became the earl on his father's death.

In Protestant Scotland, Jean held firm to her Catholic faith, and in 1627, when she was about eighty-one, she was excommunicated for harbouring Jesuit priests. Two years later, on 14th May 1629, eighty-three-year-old Jean died. She was buried with her second husband at Dornoch Cathedral.

Her son, Robert, described her as "a virtuous and comelie lady… of great understanding above the capacitie of her sex" so I'm glad she ended up with her first love, a happy end to her life.

Her first husband, the Earl of Bothwell, ended his days in a Danish prison, where he was held in appalling conditions and driven insane.

8 May

On 8th May 1559, just under six months after her accession, Queen Elizabeth I gave her approval to the Acts of Uniformity and Supremacy, which Parliament had passed on 29th April 1559.

The Act of Uniformity made Protestantism England's official faith, established a form of worship still followed in parish churches in England today, and showed the country that Elizabeth was bent on following a middle road where religion was concerned. The monarch was Head of the Church again and still is today.

Elizabeth I was a keen Protestant, having been influenced by her stepmother, Queen Catherine Parr, a zealous reformer, in her formative years in the 1540s. But Elizabeth was no Puritan or Calvinist, and she was against clerical marriage.

Elizabeth had seen the damage that religious divisions had done to the country in her half-sister Queen Mary I's reign and intended to bring peace and tolerance to England once again. Although she had the Protestant faith, she wanted to create a religious settlement that Protestants and Catholics would be happy with, a halfway house, a middle of the road settlement that would allow her subjects to live in peace with each other but which would also allow her to restore Protestantism as the country's faith and restore royal supremacy so she could be head of the Church. Elizabeth declared that she had "no desire to make windows into men's souls" and believed that "there is only one Christ, Jesus, one faith, all else is a dispute over trifles", and her religious settlement was her attempt to show this.

Both Calvinists and Catholics criticised the act, but Elizabeth knew the importance of stability and knew that this religious settlement would achieve it.

So, what did Elizabeth's middle-of-the-road settlement consist of?

- It made Mary I's repeal of Edward VI's Act for Uniformity and Administration of the Sacraments null and void - Elizabeth's Act of Uniformity reinstated the use of the English Book of Common Prayer from 1552. All services were to follow the order of service set out in this book and be in English.
- Elizabeth was made Supreme Governor of the Church of England.
- The Catholic mass was banned.
- Everybody was to attend church on Sundays and holy days or be fined 12 pence.
- There were measures or punishments for clergymen who did not stick to the Act and the Book of Common Prayer.
- And regarding church ornaments, the act stated: "that such ornaments of the church, and of the ministers thereof, shall be retained and be in use, as was in the Church of England, by authority of Parliament, in the second year of the reign of King Edward VI".

Although many people see Elizabeth I's religious settlement as too middle of the road and a sign that Elizabeth's faith was weak, I think that

Elizabeth had to set her personal faith and feelings to one side and act in the best interests of her country. The Marian persecutions and the way that England had bounced from Protestantism to Catholicism had caused much unrest and instability, and Elizabeth had to deal with this. Obviously, she did have to take certain measures against the Catholics later in her reign, following her excommunication by the pope and when she was dealing with plots against her and imminent invasion from Spain, but the start of her reign was all about moderation and tolerance. If only she'd been able to continue in that way.

9 May

On 9th May 1657, in the Stuart period, William Bradford died. He is known as the founder of the Plymouth Colony in America, and he was born in England in the reign of Queen Elizabeth I.

Let me tell you a bit more about him.

- We don't know his exact birthdate, but Bradford was baptised in Austerfield, in the West Riding of Yorkshire, on 19th March 1590, and baptisms usually took place within a few days of birth. He was the only son of William Bradford and his wife, Alice Hanson.

- He lost his father, grandfather, and mother during his early childhood, so he was brought up by his paternal uncles, Robert and Thomas, who were farmers.

- Although there is no record of him attending university, he clearly had some education as he knew Latin, Greek, Dutch and French and went on to learn Hebrew.

- During his youth, he was influenced by puritan ministers Richard Clyfton and John Robinson and William Brewster, in whose home the Scrooby separatist puritan congregation of which Bradford was a part met. Brewster and Bradford became good friends, with Brewster acting as his mentor.

- Things became difficult for the Scrooby congregation after the accession of King James I, who wanted to suppress the Puritan movement, and in 1607, members of the congregation were arrested. Some were imprisoned, and Brewster was fined. This, combined with the treatment of other Puritans in England, led to the congregation deciding to leave England for the Dutch Republic, where there was religious freedom due to a truce with Spain.

- Unfortunately, on their first attempt to cross to the Netherlands, they were betrayed by the ship's captain, and Bradford was one of those imprisoned for a time. They then made a plan to split into groups to travel, and by the summer of 1608, they had all reached Amsterdam.
- In 1609, they moved to Leiden, where Bradford lived with Brewster and his family and worked as a fustian weaver. In 1613, he married sixteen-year-old Dorothy May, originally from Cambridgeshire, but whose family had settled in Amsterdam. They had their first child, John, in 1617.
- In 1611, when Bradford turned 21, he came into his inheritance and sold his property in England to buy a property in Leiden and invest in his business.
- 1621 was the year that the truce with Spain was due to expire, and there was concern among the separatists that their children were being negatively influenced by their Dutch neighbours, so in 1617, Bradford and other members of his church began to look into leaving the Netherlands and establishing a colony in North America.
- In 1619, Bradford sold his home, and the would-be colonists arranged backing from English merchant adventurers.
- In July 1620, around fifty separatists, or "pilgrims" as Bradford called them, sailed from the Dutch port of Delftshaven on board the Speedwell, bound for Southampton. There, they met up with a bigger ship, the Mayflower, which, along with the Speedwell, would take the pilgrims across the Atlantic to North America. However, there were problems with the Speedwell, and the group eventually left aboard the Mayflower from Dartmouth on 6th September 1620. Bradford and Dorothy left their son, John, behind, but he joined his father in America seven years later.
- On 11th November 1620, the Mayflower anchored at what is now Provincetown Harbor on Cape Cod, Massachusetts. On the same day, Bradford and forty other men signed the

Mayflower Compact, the first governing document of the Plymouth Colony.

- Sadly, Bradford's wife, Dorothy, drowned after falling overboard shortly after their arrival while Bradford was off exploring the new land. On 15th December 1620, after explorations of the area, the Mayflower landed at Plymouth.

- The colonists were struck by a sickness their first winter and spring. Bradford was taken ill but survived, but in April 1621, the colony's first governor, John Carver, died, and Bradford was chosen to replace him.

- The colonists were helped with their farming efforts by the local native American Indians, who also helped them establish relations with other Indian groups. Bradford's biographer Sargent Bush Junior notes that Bradford "followed a policy of seeking peaceful relations with the neighbouring American Indians. Throughout his career he enforced a strict policy requiring that all land must be purchased before it could be settled." When an Indian man was murdered in 1638, Bradford ensured that the three Englishmen responsible were tried and executed.

- In 1623, Bradford married his second wife, widow Alice Carpenter Southworth, who he'd known in Leiden and invited to join the colonists in Plymouth. They had two sons and a daughter.

- The colony trusted Isaac Allerton, who, in seeking personal profit, brought the colony into debt, and Allerton had to be dismissed.

- Although, in 1630, Bradford was named by patent as the colony's owner, he signed his privileges away to all of the freemen of the colony.

- As well as being the founder of the Plymouth Colony, Bradford is also known for "Of Plimmoth Plantation", his chronicle of the founding of the colony and its early years, which runs until 1646 and which is described by Sargent Bush Junior as the "fullest history of early American colonial experience".

- William Bradford died on this day in history, 9th May 1657, in Plymouth and was laid to rest on Burial Hill in Plymouth.

10 May

On 10th May 1552, John Clerk, author and secretary to Thomas Howard, 3rd Duke of Norfolk, committed suicide in the Tower of London. Clerk hanged himself with his girdle after books about necromancy were found in his possession, and he was interrogated regarding "lewd prophecies and slanders".

Here are some facts about Clerk:

- He was employed by Thomas Howard, 3rd Duke of Norfolk, as a tutor for the duke's son, Henry Howard, Earl of Surrey.
- From 1530, he acted as the duke's secretary.
- He was a conservative Catholic.
- His works included a translation of a treatise on courtly behaviour, which he translated from a French translation of a Spanish work, and a work which his biographer Seymour Baker House describes as a "Catholic redaction of biblical accounts of the general resurrection of the dead and the last judgment" in which "Clerk urges Christians to ensure their salvation by performing the traditional corporal works of mercy described in Matthew".
- His master, the Duke of Norfolk, was imprisoned from 1546 in the Tower of London, and Clerk joined him in the Tower in 1552 following his examination by members of Edward VI's council.
- His suicide is thought to have been due to him wanting to avoid public shame.

11 May

On 11th May 1560, royal physician Dr Thomas Wendy died at his home, the manor of Haslingfield, in Cambridgeshire. He was in his sixty-first year at his death.

Let me tell you more about Dr Wendy and how he saved a queen from a plot against her.

- Thomas Wendy was born around 1499/1500 as the second son of Thomas Wendy of Clare in Suffolk.

- He was educated at Cambridge University before travelling to Ferrara to study for his MD. He also obtained an MD from Cambridge in 1527.
- In 1534, he was employed by Henry Percy, 6th Earl of Northumberland, and attended Northumberland as his physician when he was dying in 1537.
- He then moved into the service of King Henry VIII, being rewarded for this in 1541 by the grant of the manor of Haslingfield, which became his home.
- In 1546, he was appointed as queen's physician to Catherine Parr, Henry VIII's sixth and final wife. In January 1547, he attended the dying King Henry VIII, along with doctors George Owen and Thomas Huicke. They each received a legacy of 100 pounds.
- Wendy served as king's physician to Henry VIII's son, King Edward VI.
- In 1548, he was appointed as an ecclesiastical visitor of Oxford, Cambridge and Eton, and in 1551 he was made a fellow of the College of Physicians.
- In 1553, Wendy attended the dying King Edward VI and then became royal physician to the king's half-sister, Mary I.
- Wendy was a member of Parliament for St Albans (1554) and Cambridgeshire (1555).
- In November 1558, he attended the dying Queen Mary I, and in 1559 he served Queen Elizabeth I as an ecclesiastical visitor.
- Wendy was married twice: firstly to a woman named Margery and then, in 1552, to Margaret Porter, daughter of John Porter and widow of Thomas Atkins.
- Wendy died on this day in 1560, and on 27th May 1560, he was laid to rest at Cambridge.

According to martyrologist John Foxe, Wendy helped save Queen Catherine Parr from a plot against her. In 1546, the conservative faction, which included the likes of Stephen Gardiner, Bishop of Winchester, and Thomas Wriothesley, Lord Chancellor, decided to move against Catherine Parr, who had been married to the king for three years. These men used the queen's reformed faith against her and persuaded the irritable Henry VIII, who was tired of his wife's debates with him on religion, to sign a bill of articles against the queen. However, while Catherine's enemies planned on questioning the queen's ladies and searching the queen's belongings for heretical books, the king spoke of the matter with his physician, Dr Wendy, and the signed bill of articles was 'accidentally' dropped and found by "some godly person and brought immediately to the queen".

Knowing what had happened to Anne Boleyn and Catherine Howard, Catherine understandably became hysterical. Dr Wendy was sent to attend her, the very man with whom the king had spoken. The physician advised Catherine to "shew her humble submission to the king", who would be "gracious and favourable to her". Fortunately for Catherine, the warning meant that she could get to the king before she was arrested. After ordering her ladies to get rid of any questionable books, she went to the king's chamber. She submitted to him, talking of how she was only a poor woman "so much inferior in all respects of nature" to her husband and that when she uttered her judgement, she was always referring it to the king's wisdom as her "only anchor, supreme head and governor here in earth next under God".

The king disagreed with her. According to Foxe, he said, "Not so by Saint Mary... You are become a Doctor, Kate, to instruct us (as we take it) and not to be instructed, or directed by us."

And here, Catherine completely submitted and explained that she had simply been trying to take the king's mind off his illness and pain while also wanting to learn from him:

> "If your Majesty take it so... then hath your Majesty very much mistaken me, who have ever been of the opinion, to think it very unseemly & preposterous for the woman to take upon her the office of an instructor or teacher to her Lord and husband, but rather to learn of her husband, & to be taught by him. And where I have with your Majesty's leave heretofore been bold to hold talk with your Majesty, wherein sometimes in opinions there hath seemed some difference, I have not done it so much to maintain opinion, as I did it rather to minister talk, not only to the end that your Majesty might with less grief pass over this painful time of your

infirmity, being intentive to our talk, and hoping that your Majesty should reap some ease thereby: but also that I hearing your Majesty's learnéd discourse, might receive to myself some profit thereof. Wherein I assure your Majesty I have not missed any part of my desire in that behalf, always referring my self in all such matters unto your Majesty, as by ordinance of nature it is convenient for me to do."

The king was happy with her speech, commenting that they were "perfect friends" again, and he took her in his arms, embraced her and kissed her.

Henry VIII, however, didn't tell Thomas Wriothesley that he and his queen were friends. As arranged, Wriothesley turned up with forty guards as the king and queen walked in the privy garden at Hampton Court Palace. Wriothesley produced Catherine's arrest warrant, and the king took him to one side, shouting, "Knave! Arrant knave, beast and fool!", and ordering him out of his sight.

It is hard to know whether Catherine was in danger or if her husband just wanted it to serve as a warning to her to keep herself in check. Whatever the case, Dr Thomas Wendy played a part in helping Catherine wriggle out of danger.

12 May

On 12th May 1521, at St Paul's, John Fisher, Bishop of Rochester, preached a two-hour-long sermon against reformer Martin Luther before Cardinal Thomas Wolsey announced the papal bull against Luther. The two men then oversaw the burning of Luther's books on a bonfire.

Antonio Surian wrote to the Signory of Venice on 11th May 1521, saying, "Friar Martin Luther is to be proclaimed an heretic, and his works burnt. He has already been sentenced; and on Sunday Cardinal Wolsey will publish his condemnation by the Councils of Cambridge and Oxford, as a heretic; and that all his books be burnt under penalty of excommunication, according to the brief received from the Pope."

Lodovico Spinelli, Secretary of the Venetian Ambassador in

England, recorded the event in a letter to his brother Gasparo Spinelli, Secretary of the Venetian Ambassador in France:

"On Sunday last, the 12th, the ambassadors, Papal, Imperial, and Venetian, were taken to a palace of the Queen's, and there during two hours awaited the Cardinal of York, the Legate, who came on horseback with a great train of nobility. On his arrival all went processionally to the cathedral church of St. Paul's, where on dismounting they were met by the dean and canons in their copes, and proceeded thus to the high altar.

The Cardinal was under a canopy, an unusual thing, and after the oration gave the blessing, whereupon all went out of the church processionally, into the churchyard, where there was a lofty platform, which we ascended in great confusion. On this stage was a high chair with its canopy of cloth of gold. In this chair Cardinal Wolsey seated himself, having on his right hand the Papal Nuncio and part of the English bishops, and on his left the Imperial and Venetian ambassadors, with the rest of the bishops. In the centre were prelates and lay lords and plebeians. The Cardinal and the others having seated themselves, the Bishop of Rochester ascended a pulpit and delivered an English oration, two hours in length, against Friar Martin Luther, which, being ended, was much commended by Cardinal Wolsey. Then the Cardinal made a speech also in English, excommunicating and cursing Martin and his followers. During the delivery of these speeches, the Lutheran works were burnt.

These ceremonies being concluded, the Cardinal gave the blessing to all present, and everybody returned home. Thus Luther's festival terminated, upwards of 30,000 persons attending its celebration."

13 May

On Sunday 13th May 1515, Mary Tudor, Dowager Queen of France and sister of King Henry VIII, married the king's good friend, Charles Brandon, Duke of Suffolk, at Greenwich Palace. This official marriage followed their earlier secret marriage in France.

The marriage was recorded as taking place in the presence "of the King and Queen and such other nobles and estates of this realm as then were attending in the court", and it was said that "all the said estates and others of this realm be very glad and well pleased."

The Venetian ambassadors, Andrea Badoer and Sebastian Giustinian, who were in London at the time, recorded the event in a letter to the signory written on 15th May 1515:

"On the 13th instant the espousals of Queen Mary to the Duke of Suffolk at length took place; there were no public demonstrations, because the kingdom did not approve of the marriage. Wishing to ascertain whether this marriage had been concluded with the King's consent, were assured by great personages that it had first been arranged between the bride and bridegroom, after which they asked the consent of King Henry, who, however, had maintained his former friendship for the Duke, which would appear incredible, but is affirmed by the nobility at the Court. Have, therefore, abstained from paying any compliments either to the King or to the bride and bridegroom, but have determined to visit his Majesty in a day or two, and congratulate him on his sister's arrival. Should they understand that the great personages of the Court intend to make public mention of the event, and that it was celebrated, they would then offer congratulations in the Signory's name on the marriage, but not seeing it solemnized as becoming, would keep silence, to avoid giving offence."

Mary and Suffolk stayed married until Mary's death on 25th June 1533.

14 May

On 14th May 1538, the French ambassador, Louis de Perreau, Sieur de Castillon, wrote a dispatch regarding King Henry VIII having been dangerously ill. He wrote:

> "This King has had stopped one of the fistulas of his legs, and for 10 or 12 days the humours which had no outlet were like to have stifled him, so that he was sometime without speaking, black in the face, and in great danger."

In his book "The Last Days of Henry VIII", historian Robert Hutchinson explains that "in today's modern medical terms, the king was suffering from a thrombosed vein in his leg and, dangerously, a clot may have detached from this vein."

In November 1538, Geoffrey Pole, brother of Cardinal Reginald Pole, commented on the king's leg problem during interrogations for alleged treason. Pole stated that the king had "a sore leg that no poor man would be glad of and that he should not live long for all his authority next to God." That same autumn, courtier George Constantine commented to the Dean of Westbury on the king's leg problem, saying, "it grieveth me at heart to see his Grace halt so much upon his sore leg."

In March 1541, during Henry VIII's marriage to Catherine Howard, Charles de Marillac, the French ambassador, wrote of the king suffering problems again with one of his legs, saying in one dispatch that "this King's life was really thought to be in danger, not from the fever but from the leg, which often troubles him because he is very stout and marvellously excessive in drinking and eating," and in another dispatch: "one of his legs, formerly opened and kept open to maintain his health, suddenly closed to his great alarm, for, five or six years ago, in like case he thought to have died."

Five or six years previously would have been around 1535/6, but perhaps Marillac remembered wrong and was referring to the 1538 health scare when the king turned black in the face and was in great danger.

In December 1546, the month before the king's death, the privy council informed Nicholas Wotton that "The King lately, 'upon some grief of his leg, was entered into a fever'; but he is now well rid of it and we trust that he will be the 'better for it a great while.'" Of course, the king was dying, and he died on 28ᵗʰ January 1547.

The king had been plagued with leg problems for nearly 20 years at the time of his death. In 1528, physician Thomas Vicary was called "to cure the king of a sorre legge". We don't know the cause of the problem, whether it was a sporting accident, like the year before, when he had hurt his foot playing tennis, or whether this was the start of his long-term problem with leg ulcers. Whatever it was, Vicary was able to help the king, something which led to his advancement as sergeant-surgeon to the Royal Household.

But in April 1537, John Hussee wrote to Lord Lisle of how the king was suffering with his leg once more, reporting that "the king goes seldom abroad, because his leg is something sore". In June 1537, the king confessed to the Duke of Norfolk that he had postponed his trip to York because of his health, writing, "to be frank with you, which you must keep to yourself, a humour has fallen into our legs, and our physicians advise us not to go far in the heat of the day, even for this reason only." Perhaps the king's earlier leg problem had reared its ugly head following an injury from his January 1536 jousting accident?

His sore leg affected his mobility, and this, combined with his jousting accident of 1536, which reminded him of his mortality, led to him giving up his beloved sport. Eating the same amount but giving up his usual sports led him to gain weight, which must have exacerbated his leg and mobility problems.

But what caused his leg ulcers?

The theories include syphilis, which was debunked when the king's medical expenses and accounts were studied and did not include mercury, the standard treatment for syphilis. Other theories include osteomyelitis, an infection of the bone, perhaps caused by an untreated fracture; deep vein thrombosis as a result of his injuries and immobility, and ulceration caused by severe venous hypertension; deep vein thrombosis caused by the wearing of tight garters on his leg; and venous ulceration caused by vascular disease, which in turn could have been caused by Type II diabetes, high cholesterol and hypertension.

Whatever the cause, these leg ulcers would have been itchy, painful and swollen and would have produced a foul-smelling discharge, which must have been awful for the king and those near him. I'm sure the pain and frustration must have affected the king's mood. Being in constant pain, being conscious that you smell awful, and being prevented from things you love doing like sport and hunting, is bound to make you grumpy. Perhaps this pain was one factor in the king's tyranny.

15 May

On 15th May 1537, Thomas Darcy, 1st Baron Darcy de Darcy, and his cousin, John Hussey, 1st Baron Hussey of Sleaford, were tried for treason at Westminster after being implicated in the Pilgrimage of Grace.

Lord Darcy had yielded his castle to the rebels of the Pilgrimage of Grace on 20th October 1536 after they had threatened an assault on it. No violence was necessary, and it is thought that Darcy was sympathetic to the rebel cause because of his reservations about the dissolution of the monasteries and the power of Thomas Cromwell.

John Hussey, 1st Baron Hussey of Sleaford, Lincolnshire, and Chief Butler of England, was a staunch Catholic and supporter of Princess Mary. Still, when rebellion had broken out in his county in late 1536, he told the rebels to "walk home knaves, for the king is used not to condition with no such rebellious", and he refused to betray his king by joining them. He even fled disguised as a priest to try and stop the rebels from taking him. However, his faith, his support for Princess Mary, and what was seen as his inaction against the rebels in his area led to him being implicated in the rebellion and accused of conspiring and rebelling against the king.

Darcy and Hussey were tried on this day in 1537 by a jury of their peers, presided over by the Marquess of Exeter as High Steward of England. A record in the Letters and Papers of Henry VIII's reign shows that both men pleaded not guilty but were both found guilty of high treason. The sentence was "Judgment as usual in cases of high treason. Execution to be at Tyburn", i.e. they were sentenced to the full traitor's death, to be hanged, drawn and quartered. However, their sentences were commuted to beheading due to their status as barons. It was decided that Hussey would be executed in Lincolnshire, so he was escorted to Huntingdon by Sir Thomas Wentworth, who then handed him over to Sir William Parr, who took him to Lincoln and handed him over to Charles Brandon, Duke of Suffolk. He was beheaded in Lincoln on 29th June 1537. Darcy was beheaded on Tower Hill in London on 30th June 1537.

16 May

On 16th May 1620, navigator William Adams died in Hirado, Japan.

Adams is thought to be the first Englishman to have reached Japan (arriving there in 1600) and was the inspiration for the character of John Blackthorne in the famous novel Shōgun.

Let me give you a few facts about this Tudor navigator.

- William Adams was born in September 1564 in Gillingham, Kent, and was the son of John Adams.
- Nothing is known of his early life, except that he worked as an apprentice to shipbuilder Nicholas Diggens in Limehouse, London, between the ages of 12 and 24.
- In 1588, at the time of the Spanish Armada, Adams served as master of a 120-ton supply ship called the Richard Dyffylde.
- After that, he served as a pilot and master for ten years for the Barbary Company, which traded with Morocco.
- In 1589, Adams married Mary Hyn and they had two children together.
- In 1598, when he was 34, Adams was recruited by the Dutch to pilot the Hoop, the admiral's ship, on a voyage via the Strait of Magellan to the East Indies for spices and other products, with the added incentive of attacking Spanish settlements in South America. They left Rotterdam on 27th June 1598 and reached the coast of Brazil on 2nd January 1599 and the Strait of Magellan on 6th April 1599. However, they couldn't pass through due to the winter weather, and it was September when they eventually cleared the strait. Unfortunately, due to Spanish attacks and the weather, only two ships, the Hoop and the Liefde, made the arranged rendezvous in November 1599

off the Island of St Mary, and even they had suffered attacks by Indians, and, sadly, Adams's brother, Thomas, had been killed. By this time, Adams was on the Liefde rather than the Hoop. The remaining crews decided to sail to Japan, where they believed they could sell their cloth. Unfortunately, they encountered trouble again, being attacked while sailing near the Hawaiian Islands, and a storm in February 1600 saw the ships becoming separated and the Hoop perishing.

- In April 1600, the Liefde arrived in Japan, off the coast of Bungo. It was the first non-Iberian European ship to reach the country, and William Adams was the first Englishman to do so.

- In May 1600, Adams was called before regent Tokugawa Ieyasu to explain where he'd come from. Adams persuaded him that he and his crew were not the thieves and robbers that previous European visitors, the Jesuits and Portuguese, had made them out to be and explained that they were there to trade. He hit it off with Ieyasu, which was good because later that year, Ieyasu took power after defeating his opponents in battle, becoming shogun of Japan. Ieyasu was also keen on expanding trade.

- Although Adams was welcomed to Japan, he wanted to go home to his family after the negotiations with Ieyasu. However, his ship had been destroyed, and the Japanese valued his shipbuilding and navigational skills. He became one of the shogun's advisors, helping particularly with European matters, maths and geometry. In return for his service, he was given land.

- Adams became involved with a Japanese woman, and she had two children with him. However, he continued to support his family back in England by sending them money. He also had another child in Japan, but little is known about the mother and child.

- Adams was also able to help Japan by acting as an interpreter between the shogun and the Dutch and the English in trade negotiations.

- After successful negotiations between the English and Japanese in 1613, Adams was employed by the English company in Hirado for three years. During that time, he took two voyages to Siam.

- Adams was eventually given permission to leave for England, but he decided to stay in Japan, and he made three further voyages between 1617 and 1619, two bound for Faifo and one for Tongking.
- Adams died on this day in history, 16th May 1620, in Hirado. According to his will, half his estate went to his wife and surviving child in England, a daughter, Deliverance, and the other half went to his children, Joseph and Susanna, in Japan. Adams was buried in Japan.
- James Clavell's famous novel, Shōgun, which was adapted for TV, was based on Adams' story, which has also inspired many other works of fiction.

This is a very brief overview of William Adams, and if you'd like to know more about him, I'd recommend "Samurai William: The Adventurer Who Unlocked Japan" by Giles Milton.

17 May

On 17th May 1521, the Friday before Whitsunday, Edward Stafford, 3rd Duke of Buckingham, was executed for treason on Tower Hill.

Buckingham was the son of Henry Stafford, 2nd Duke of Buckingham, and Catherine Woodville, the sister of Queen Elizabeth Woodville. He was also the great-grandson of Thomas of Woodstock, Edward III's youngest son, and so had Plantagenet blood. His father rebelled against King Richard III in 1483 and was executed as a result. When Henry Tudor became King Henry VII in 1485, after defeating Richard III at Bosworth, Edward was made a Knight of the Bath.

Although his favour continued into King Henry VIII's reign, with him serving as lord high constable and lord high steward at Henry VIII's coronation and being appointed to the new king's privy council, King Henry VIII came to see Buckingham's royal blood as a threat.

In 1520, he was suspected of treason, so Henry VIII ordered an investigation. Buckingham was summoned to court in April 1521 and arrested. He was imprisoned in the Tower of London and then tried for treason. Chronicler Edward Hall records that he was indicted of high treason for traitorously conspiring and imagining "as far as in thee lay to shorten the life of our sovereign lord the king". Buckingham denied the charges, saying they were false, untrue, conspired and forged. However, witness depositions from his employees Charles Knyvett, Robert Gilbert and Edmund Dellacourt, and monk Nicholas Hopkins were read to the court. According to them, Buckingham had been listening to political prophecies from the monk Hopkins, who had prophesied that he'd be king one day. Buckingham was found guilty of high treason by a jury of his peers and sentenced to be hanged, drawn and quartered.

On 17th May 1521, at about 11am, he was delivered to the sheriffs, who led him to the scaffold on Tower Hill. As a nobleman, he was to be executed by beheading rather than suffering a full traitor's death.

Hall gives the following account of his execution:

"He said he had offended the king's grace through negligence and lack of grace, and desired all noblemen to be beware by him, and all men to pray for him, and that he trusted to die the king's true man. Thus meekly with an axe he took his death, on whose soul Jesu have mercy. Then the Augustine friars took the body and head and buried them. Alas that ever the grace of truth was withdrawn from so noble a man, that he was not to his king in allegiance as he ought to have been, such is the end of ambition, the end of false prophecies, the end of evil life and evil counsel."

18 May

On 18th May 1497, in the reign of King Henry VII, Catherine Woodville, Duchess of Buckingham and Bedford, died.

Here are some facts about this Woodville woman.

- She was the daughter of Richard Woodville, 1st Earl Rivers, and his wife, Jacquetta of Luxembourg.
- Catherine was the sister of Queen Elizabeth Woodville, consort of King Edward IV.
- Her niece, Elizabeth of York, was Henry VII's queen consort.

- She was married three times: to Henry Stafford, 2nd Duke of Buckingham, then, after his execution, she married Jasper Tudor, Duke of Bedford and uncle of King Henry VII, and then, after his death, she married Sir Richard Wingfield. King Henry VII fined her for marrying Richard without royal licence.
- Catherine had four children with her first husband: Edward Stafford, 3rd Duke of Buckingham (see yesterday's "on this day"); Elizabeth Stafford, Countess of Sussex; Henry Stafford, 1st Earl of Wiltshire; and Anne Stafford, Countess of Huntingdon.
- Her resting place is not known.

19 May

On 19th May 1554, on the 18th anniversary of her mother's execution, the future Queen Elizabeth I was released from her prison in the Tower of London and placed under house arrest.

Elizabeth had been arrested and taken to the Tower on 18th March 1554, Palm Sunday, after being implicated in Wyatt's Rebellion. She had been imprisoned in the royal palace in the inner ward of the Tower of London. This palace had been renovated by her father, Henry VIII, for her mother Anne Boleyn's coronation in 1533 and was also where her mother had been imprisoned before her execution in 1536.

Elizabeth was interrogated about the rebellion but did not incriminate herself, and rebel leader, Sir Thomas Wyatt the Younger, went to the scaffold proclaiming her innocence. Mary I's council argued about what to do with Elizabeth, and Mary "dithered", in David Starkey's words, and it was eventually decided that she should be released into house arrest.

On 19th May 1554, Elizabeth was escorted from the Tower and taken by water to Richmond, where she was convinced she'd be assassinated. After all, it would be convenient for Mary if Elizabeth was dispatched by an intruder, which Mary could not be held accountable for. After what must have been a sleepless night, Elizabeth was taken from Richmond to Woodstock in Oxfordshire. On the 4-day journey, Elizabeth's popularity was demonstrated by people lining the streets to see her and giving her gifts.

At Woodstock, Sir Henry Bedingfield was to keep Elizabeth securely under house arrest. She was to be treated well but was not to converse with any suspicious person or be allowed to send or receive any correspondence. Elizabeth was well aware of how closely she would be watched. In a message to her household, she referred to a verse from St Matthew's Gospel:

> "Behold, I send you forth as sheep in the midst of wolves; be ye therefore wise as serpents, and harmless as doves."

Elizabeth knew that both she and her servants would have to keep their wits about them if they were to survive; her enemies would be watching. An etching on a window at Woodstock reads, "Much suspected by me, Nothing proved can be. Quod Elizabeth the Prisoner".

On the 17th April 1555, after nearly a year at Woodstock, Elizabeth was summoned to court to attend her half-sister, the queen, who believed she would soon give birth. The baby never came. Mary had suffered a phantom pregnancy.

On 18th October 1555, Elizabeth was granted permission to leave court for Hatfield, her own estate, where she could get on with her life without being watched. It must have been a huge relief for her.

20 May

On 20th May 1579, wheelwright Matthew Hamont, who is thought to have been from the Netherlands originally, was executed for heresy in the castle ditch at Norwich.

Earlier in the year, he'd been cited before Edmund Freak, Bishop of Norwich, for heresy, for denying Christ and believing him to be "a sinful man and an abominable idol". He was also accused of believing the Bible to be a fable and challenging the existence of the Holy Spirit. Some considered him to be a deist and others an Arian, and local clergyman William Burton said:

> "I have known some Arian heretics, whose life hath been most strict amongst men, whose tongues have been tired with scripture upon scripture, their knees even hardened in prayer, and their faces wedded to sadness,

and their mouths full of praises to God, while in the
meantime they have stoutly denied the divinity of the
Son of God, and have not sticked to tear out of the Bible
all such places as made against them; such were Hamond,
Lewes, and Cole, heretics of wretched memory, lately
executed and cut off in Norwich."

Lewes and Cole were also Arians burnt at Norwich.

A deist at this time was someone who believed in the existence
of God but did not believe that this God interacted with his created
world. An Arian denied the divinity of Christ and believed that as
Christ was the son of God, he was distinct from God and was his
subordinate.

On 18th April 1579, Hamont was condemned for heresy at the
consistory court. Then, at Guildhall, Norwich, he was condemned for
seditious and scandalous speeches against Queen Elizabeth I and her
privy council. The city mayor ordered that he should be punished by
having his ears cut off. On 13th May 1579, Hamont was put on the
pillory in Norwich marketplace and had his ears cut off. Then on
20th May 1579, Hamont was burnt for heresy in Norwich Castle ditch.
He was survived by his wife and a son named Erasmus.

21 May

On 21st May 1535, Bible translator and religious reformer William
Tyndale was arrested in Antwerp after being tricked into leaving the
English House owned by Thomas Pontz.

Although Tyndale's book, "The Obedience of a Christian Man", had
helped King Henry VIII defy papal authority and break with Rome,
his opposition to the annulment of Henry's marriage to Catherine of
Aragon had infuriated the king. In his TV programme on Tyndale,
"The Most Dangerous Man in Tudor England", Melvyn Bragg
explained how heretic hunting began in Antwerp in 1535 because it
was under the control of Emperor Charles V. Tyndale befriended a new
arrival, Harry Phillips. The latter claimed to be an Oxford graduate
interested in Reform. However, Phillips colluded with the Imperial
Court and betrayed Tyndale.

On 21st May 1535, Phillips visited the English House in Antwerp, where Tyndale was living and said he had no money. Tyndale offered to take him out for a meal, and as they walked down an alley, two guards arrested Tyndale. Phillips had acted as Judas.

According to the martyrologist John Foxe, Tyndale was then taken to the "castle of Filford" (Vilvoorde), eighteen miles from Antwerp, and imprisoned there for a year and a half. Thomas Cromwell tried to secure Tyndale's release, but Henry VIII had no sympathy for Tyndale and would not intervene. Tyndale was tried for heresy and "condemned by virtue of the emperor's decree". He was strangled and then burnt in October 1536. The exact date of his execution is not known, but it is traditionally commemorated on the 6th October.

In his documentary, Melvyn Bragg said that Tyndale had translated the New Testament and the first five books of the Old Testament by the time of his death.

22 May

On 22nd May 1538, in the reign of King Henry VIII, John Forest, Franciscan friar and martyr, was burnt at the stake at Smithfield for heresy, for his allegiance to Rome.

Very little is known of Forest's background, but by 1512 he was a member of the Observant Franciscans at Greenwich, and by the early 1530s, he was well-known for his regular preaching at St Paul's Cross. There is no evidence to back up the idea that he acted as a confessor to Queen Catherine of Aragon, but he does appear to have once been a favourite of King Henry VIII and Thomas Howard, 3rd Duke of Norfolk. However, he would have lost the king's favour when he opposed his plans to annul his first marriage to Catherine of Aragon.

Historian Peter Marshall writes of how his fellow observants, John Lawrence and Richard Lyst, denounced him to Thomas Cromwell for his views on the king's annulment and that he was exiled by Francis Faber, the provincial minister of his order, to a religious house in the north of England. However, he was back in London by early 1538, and was soon arrested for heresy. He was accused, Marshall explains, of "identifying the Catholic church of the creed with the Church of Rome" and, according to chronicler Edward Hall, of denying the king's supremacy. He was convicted of heresy and ordered to abjure his beliefs in public at St Paul's Cross.

On 12th May 1538, at St Paul's Cross, he refused to recant, so on 22nd May 1538, he was taken to Smithfield to be executed. Hugh Latimer, Bishop of Worcester and a man who would himself be burnt at the stake in Mary I's reign, preached a sermon declaring Forest's errors.

Edward Hall describes how Forest was "hanged in chains by the middle and armholes" from the gallows at Smithfield, and a fire was lit underneath. A wooden statue of St Derfel taken from a pilgrimage site in North Wales gave extra fuel to the fire. The burning of Forest with this statue was said to fulfil a prophecy saying that the saint's image would one day set a whole forest on fire.

Hall doesn't seem to have thought much of this man, for he writes of his execution that:

> "he so unpatiently took his death, that no man that ever put his trust in God never so unquietly nor so ungodly ended his life: if men might judge him by his outward man, he appeared to have little knowledge of God and his sincere truth, and less trust in him at his ending."

Chronicler and Windsor herald Charles Wriothesley also gives an account of his execution and in it states that when Bishop Latimer asked in what state he would die, Forest replied in a loud voice:

> "That if an angel should come down from heaven and show him any other thing than that he had believed all his life time past, he would not believe him, and that if his body should be cut joint after joint or member after member, burnt, hanged, or what pain soever might be done to his body, he would never turn from his old sect of this Bishop of Rome."

Wriothesley records that the Dukes of Norfolk and Suffolk, the Earls of Sussex and Hertford, the Bishop of London, members of the king's council, the Mayor of London, aldermen, shreeves, and ten thousand persons and more were present at the execution.

In 1886, John Forest was beatified by Pope Leo XIII, so he is Blessed John Forest.

23 May

On 23rd May 1554, Elizabeth, daughter of King Henry VIII and his second wife, Anne Boleyn, arrived at the Palace of Woodstock in Oxfordshire, where she was placed under house arrest.

Elizabeth had been arrested on 18th March 1554, accused of being involved in Wyatt's Rebellion. She was interrogated numerous times during her two-month imprisonment in the Tower of London, but she was firm in her denial of involvement in the plot and was released on 19th May 1554.

After a night at Richmond, she was escorted to Woodstock Palace in Oxfordshire. There, she was lodged in the Gatehouse.

Chronicler Raphael Holinshed wrote of how she was closely guarded at the palace but was allowed to take some fresh air in the gardens. Holinshed wrote, "In this situation, no marvell, if she hearing upon a time out of hir garden at Woodstocke a certain milkmaide singing pleasantlie, wished herself to be a milkmaide, as she was; saying, that her case was better, and life merrier."

However, Bedingfield had a hard time guarding the princess. He'd been instructed to make sure that Elizabeth did not converse with any suspicious person without him being present, and she was also not to receive any gifts or correspondence. Lisa Hilton, in her book "Elizabeth: Renaissance Prince", writes of how the mind of this "honest, dogged, but poorly educated man" was "no match for the quicksilver temperament of his charge". As David Starkey points out, Elizabeth was in a gaol without any locks, and most of her warders were her devoted servants.

Another issue was that Elizabeth's cofferer, Thomas Parry, was not even lodging at the palace. He resided at the Bull Inn at Woodstock, so he was out of Bedingfield's control. And Bedingfield couldn't get rid of him, for the princess needed her cofferer, for she was responsible for paying her household expenses. Hilton writes of how Parry held court at the inn, having up to forty visitors a day, including members of Elizabeth's household. Elizabeth caused problems for Bedingfield by receiving gifts and complaining constantly. It couldn't have been fun for Bedingfield.

Elizabeth wanted to appeal to the queen, but Bedingfield refused to allow her to write to her. He did, however, mention it to the royal council and was informed by them that Mary was pleased that Elizabeth wanted to write to her. Elizabeth's letter has not survived, but Mary replied to her through Bedingfield, pointing out why Elizabeth had been arrested, including that she'd been a figurehead of Wyatt's Rebellion and pointing out the "clemency and favour" with which she had been treated. Elizabeth appealed for a trial or a meeting with the queen in which she could plead her case, or a visit from council members. None of which happened.

In April 1555, after nearly a year of house arrest at Woodstock, where Bedingfield must surely have been driven mad by his charge, Elizabeth finally received a summons to court from her half-sister, the queen. Mary was married to Philip of Spain and believed herself to be pregnant by this time. With linen that she had embroidered for her new niece or nephew, Elizabeth set off for Hampton Court Palace, arriving there at the end of the month. However, she was not called to the queen, and she spent two weeks in the Prince of Wales's Lodgings at the palace before asking to see her half-sister's council. Bishop Stephen Gardiner led the delegation that visited Elizabeth, and asked her to submit to the queen, which she refused to do. Another week went by until Elizabeth was summoned to appear before Mary, who rebuked her for refusing to submit. Still, despite this difficult first meeting, Elizabeth spent the next few months at Mary's side.

Sadly for Mary, there was no baby. On 18th October 1555, Queen Mary I gave permission for Elizabeth to leave the royal court and travel to her estate at Hatfield, where she was reunited with loyal servants like Thomas Parry and Catherine Ashley. She was no longer under house arrest; she was free.

24 May

On 24th May 1546, letters were sent from the privy council to the future Protestant martyr Anne Askew and her estranged husband, Thomas Kyme. The couple was ordered to appear in front of the council within fourteen days.

Twenty-five-year-old Anne Askew was from Stallingborough in Lincolnshire and was the daughter of landowner Sir William Askew and his first wife, Elizabeth Wrottesley. She received an excellent education, and Karen Lindsey, author of "Divorced, Beheaded, Survived: A Feminist Reinterpretation of the Wives of Henry VIII", writes of how Anne was influenced by the Protestant ideas that her brothers, who were students at Cambridge, would discuss when they came home to visit, but that the Askew family were conservatives. Even though he was conservative in his faith, Anne's father opposed the rebels during the Pilgrimage of Grace in 1537, and it was this rebellion that Lindsey believes is a reason for Anne turning her back on the old faith because Anne saw the rebels attack her home and seize her brothers.

At around this time, Anne was forced to marry Thomas Kyme. Kyme had originally been betrothed to Anne's older sister Martha, but Anne was offered as a replacement when she died. It was not a happy union, but it did result in two children. Kyme was traditional in his religious views and Anne, by this time, had strong Protestant views. Lindsey believes that Anne probably survived the early days of her marriage by spending time with her sister Jane, who was married to a Protestant, George Saint Paul. Saint Paul was friends with Charles Brandon, Duke of Suffolk, and his wife Catherine (née Willoughby), a supporter of religious reform. From 1538 to 1543, the law allowed normal parishioners access to the English Bible in churches. Those of Protestant leanings took the opportunity to conduct Bible readings and share their evangelical views. Anne was one of those people.

In 1543, King Henry VIII changed his mind about Bible reading and passed an act which prevented all women (and men below the rank of gentlemen) from reading the Bible. This did not prevent people like Anne from sharing their views and preaching because they had memorised scripture. In fact, this law made Anne even more determined to share her Bible knowledge with those deprived of reading the Bible themselves. Kyme, a traditional conservative, could not and would not cope with his outspoken wife, a woman who even refused to take his name, so, as advised by his local priests, he kicked her out of the family home. Anne moved in with her brother Francis and petitioned for a divorce. Her local court denied her petition, so

Anne headed to London, where she was convinced that she would get her divorce. As Lindsey writes:

"Like the king's new wife [Catherine Parr], Anne revered Henry for freeing his people from the evil of popery. She was certain the king, who had himself disposed of several unworthy spouses, would allow a godly woman to be free of her unbelieving husband."

While in London, Anne met up with an old friend and neighbour, John Lascelles, a man of Protestant persuasion. He introduced her to people like Hugh Latimer, Bishop of Worcester; Nicholas Shaxton, Bishop of Salisbury, and Dr Edward Crome. These men were not only high profile Protestants but they were also connected to Henry VIII's new queen, Catherine Parr. Anne flourished with the support of such friends and the climate of reform in London.

Unfortunately, although some of London was open to reform and fell in love with this passionate woman, Anne was making enemies. Bishop Stephen Gardiner, a Catholic Conservative, was looking to discredit the new queen and deal with the Protestant climate that seemed to surround her. Anne Askew was not only an outspoken heretic stirring up the people of London, but she was also linked to the Duchess of Suffolk, a good friend of the queen. Perhaps Anne could be used to bring down the queen.

In June 1545, Anne Askew, and a few other Protestant sympathisers, were rounded up and arrested for heresy but later released due to a lack of evidence and witnesses. A few months later, in early 1546, Anne's petition for divorce was dismissed, and the court ordered her to return to Kyme, which Anne refused to do. Gardiner was keen to use this refusal against her. Although she had been arrested again in March 1546 and subsequently released, Gardiner summoned her to London to order her to return to her husband. He used this opportunity to question Anne on her religious beliefs. Anne shared her religious views, including her denial that Christ was present in the sacrament, saying that the bread was just bread and that it would go mouldy if it were left for three months. She stated that she believed that "the sacramental bread was left us to be received with thanksgiving, in remembrance of Christ's death, the only remedy of our soul's recovery". This was heresy, and she was tried for it at Guildhall on 18th June 1546, found guilty and condemned to death.

After being condemned to death, Anne Askew was taken to the Tower of London, where she was subjected to torture on the rack at the hands of Gardiner's right-hand men, Sir Richard Rich and Sir Thomas Wriothesley. Even though she had already been condemned to death, she was racked because Gardiner was determined to link Anne to the queen's friends, women like the Duchess of Suffolk, the Countess of Sussex and the Countess of Hertford, and Anne refused to name names during her interrogations.

As Anne had already been condemned and she was a gentlewoman, the Lieutenant of the Tower, Sir Anthony Kingston, refused to continue racking Anne after the first turn. He left the Tower in search of Henry VIII to inform him of this illegal and appalling torture and seek a pardon for letting it happen. This did not stop Rich and Wriothesley; they simply racked the poor woman themselves until they were stopped by Kingston, who informed them that the king had ordered that Anne should be taken off the rack and returned to her prison cell.

Anne was so badly racked that on 16th July 1546, she had to be carried to the stake on a chair, and the stake on which she burnt for heresy had to have a seat attached to support her body.

What happened to Thomas Kyme, her husband? Well, he did turn up in front of the Privy Council with Anne within the stipulated 14-day period. Anne denied that he was her husband, and while she was detained and thrown into the Tower of London to await her trial, he was allowed to go home.

25 May

On 25th May 1551, at around noon, Croydon and several Surrey villages in the south of England experienced a "great shaking of the ground", an earthquake.

Francis Godwin, Bishop of Hereford, recorded in his "Annales of England" that "On the five and twentieth of May, Croydon and seven or eight other Villages in Surrey were terribly shaken with an Earthquake". 17th-century clergyman and historian John

Strype recorded in his "Ecclesiastical Memorials" that on "May 25, about Rygate, Croydon and Dorking was felt an earthquake, and especially at Dorking; insomuch that there, and elsewhere, pots, and pans, and dishes fell down, and moved about."

It was not the only earthquake felt in Tudor England.

On 19th September 1508, in the reign of King Henry VII, an earthquake was felt in England and Scotland. In his Annales of Scotland, Sir James Balfour described it as "a dreadful earthquake... which lasted the 10 part of an hour, to the great terror and astonishment of all the inhabitants."

In July 1534, in the reign of King Henry VIII, an earthquake was felt in North Wales and Dublin, Ireland. It was mentioned in a Welsh poem, and by Sir James Ware in his History of Ireland.

Then, on 26th February 1575, in the reign of Queen Elizabeth I, an earthquake was felt in Yorkshire, North Wales, Herefordshire, and Gloucestershire. The British Geological Survey states that from contemporary sources, we know that Hatfield in Yorkshire suffered the most damage. Their report states, "At this place some old houses and barns were thrown down and part of the gable end of the manor house fell. Near Hatfield, supposedly, churches were "laid flat with the ground" and "great damage was done in all the country over"".

Five years later, on 6th April 1580, the Wednesday of Holy Week, a large earthquake known as the Dover Straits Earthquake was recorded. The British Geological Survey states that its epicentre was between Dover and Calais and it was felt as far as York and possibly even Edinburgh. It was also felt in Northern France, the Low Countries, and Germany. Aftershocks were noted on 1st and 2nd May. There were fatalities in the Low Countries and London, and wall sections fell in Dover. St Peter's Church in Sandwich, Kent, suffered damage, as did Saltwood Castle. In Essex, a portion of Stratford Castle collapsed, and stones fell from Ely Cathedral in Cambridgeshire. The earthquake was seen as a portent, and pamphlets were published urging people to repent.

Here is a description of the London earthquake from Thomas Churchyard's pamphlet "A warning for the wise, a feare to the fond, a bridle to the lewde, and a glasse to the good Written of the late earthquake chanced in London and other places, the. 6. of April 1580. for the glorie of God, and benefite of men that warely can walke, and wisely can iudge":

"On Wednesdaye in the Easter weeke, beyng the sixt day of April. 1580. betwene the houres of fiue and sixe in the euening, hapned generally through all the City of London, & the Suburbes of the same (as it were in a moment and vppon the sodaine) a wonderful motion and trembling of the earth, in somuch, as Churches, Pallaces, Houses, and other buildings did so quiuer and shake, that such as were then present in the same were tossed too and fro as they stoode, and others, as they sate on seates, driuen off from their places: some leaning backewardes, were readye to fall: and manye besides so shaken standing, that it broughte suche terror to those that were in the same houses, that the most part feared, their houses woulde come downe vpon them, and therevppon ranne oute of their doores in greate perplexitie, to see whether their houses were stil standing in their wonted place or no. And some houses did so crackle, that the tables and stooles, with other furniture, as Brasse and Pewter, so tottered, that it was thought they would haue fallen to the ground, and the houses reste insunder. And this chaunced not only in London (& the suburbs of the same) but also in diuers other parts through the nerest places of our knowlege in Englãd. But specially about S. Katherins, the Limehouse, & Radcliffe, where the people were so maruellously amazed, that it was pitifull to beholde how fearefully they ranne oute of their doores, and howe strangely one would beholde an other, thinking verilye, that the latter daye hadde bene come. And the houses on London bridge didde shake euen in the same sort as in other parts of the Citie. Whereby it appeareth, that the sayd trembling and mouing of the earth, did not onely passe vnder the houses on the firme ground, but also vnder the riuers and waters. And to signifie better the generalitie of the same, you shal vnderstãd, that the Abbey Church at Westminster, was there with so shaken, that one of the Pinacles of the same, loste aboue one foote of his toppe, the stones whereof fel to the ground. Also the stéeple in the Pallace so shoke, that the bell of the great Clocke sounded therewith, as thoughe it hadde bene stricken with some hãmmer. Also at White Hall where hir Maiestie lieth, the great Chamber & other parts of the Court so shooke, as séemed strange to such as were present. The new Hall of the middle Témple did so shake also, as it caused a number of Gentlemén (being set to Supper) to run forth with their knives in their hands, fearing that it woulde fall. It chanced also, Tho. Cobhed being in the pulpit in Christes church in Newgate market, preaching to the people, sodenly the church so shooke, that out of the roofe of the same fell certayne greate stones, by the fall whereof, a boy named Thomas Gray, apprentice to Iohn Spurling Shoomaker, was brayned, and Mabell Eueret his fellowe seruaunt, was stricken on the heade with a stone, being daungerously hurt, but is not dead: and a number of the people (by hasting to flee and scape away) were sore brused and hurt, by falles and suche like accidentes."

Churchyard then breaks into verse in which he states that the earthquake was "sent from fathers hand, to make the childe to knowe, The rodde is neare their backes, that out of order goe", and concluding with a call for people to heed this "good warning" from God.

The 1580 earthquake may even have been alluded to in Shakespeare's Romeo and Juliet, when Juliet's nurse says, "Tis since the earthquake now eleven years". However, it could also refer to the 1584 earthquake felt in Western Switzerland.

26 May

On 26th May 1520, in the lead-up to King Henry VIII's meeting with King Francis I of France at the Field of Cloth of Gold, the English king met with his nephew Charles V, Holy Roman Emperor, at Dover Castle on the south coast of England.

Henry VIII and his wife, Catherine of Aragon, had left Greenwich on 21st May 1520, arriving at Canterbury on 25th, intending, as chronicler Edward Hall records, to celebrate Pentecost there. However, shortly after their arrival at Canterbury, they received news that Charles had been sighted off the coast of England. The royal couple made their way to Dover in readiness for his arrival, as did Cardinal Wolsey.

Hall records that Charles arrived at the port of Hythe in Kent at noon on 26th May:

> "where he was hailed by the noble knight sir Willyam Fitzwillyam, vice admirall of Englande, with sixe of the kynges shippes well furnished". The calmness of the weather meant that they could land at Dover, where he was received "with such reverence" by Wolsey. Hall describes how Charles landed "under the clothe of his estate of the blacke Egle all splaied on riche clothe of golde" and that he was accompanied by a retinue of noblemen and "many fair ladies... whiche landed with hym in high and sumptuous maner and great riches in their apparell".

Hall also records how the English people greeted his arrival with "great joy".

Cardinal Wolsey then escorted the emperor to Dover Castle to the marvellous noise of the emperor's fleet firing their guns. King Henry VIII met him there, and they "embraced each other right lovingly" and communed with gladness in the king's chamber. In "Dress at the Court of King Henry VIII", Maria Hayward writes of how Henry VIII was dressed "in a cloth of silver with a raised pile, and wrought throughout with emblematic letters" and "a stiff brocade in the Hungarian fashion". Then later, he wore "white damask in the Turkish fashion... all embroidered with roses, made of rubies and diamonds" along with long royal robes of "gold brocade lined with ermine".

On Whitsunday, the king and emperor rose early and set off for Canterbury to celebrate the Feast of Pentecost and see Queen Catherine, who had remained there. Charles was greeted by the "noble personages of the realme of England and the quene with her beautiful trayne of ladies". Catherine was recorded as wearing "a petticoat of silver lama, the gown of cloth of gold lined with violet velvet with raised pile, on which the roses of England were wrought in gold." Charles, Henry and Catherine remained in Canterbury until the Thursday, when Charles took his leave, rode to Sandwich and sailed from there to Flanders.

Hall records that after the departure of the Emperor Henry VIII sailed from Dover to Calais "and with hym the quene and ladyes and many nobles of the realm" for his next meeting with a European ruler, Francis I.

27 May

On 27th May 1537, Trinity Sunday, there were celebrations in London following the news of the 'quickening', i.e. the first movement, of Queen Jane Seymour's baby.

This was just under a year after King Henry VIII had taken Jane as his third wife following the execution of Queen Anne Boleyn. It was, of course, hoped that this baby would be the prince Henry VIII had longed for since 1509.

Chronicler and Windsor Herald Charles Wriothesley recorded the celebrations in London:

"Also, the 27th day of May 1537, being Trinity Sunday, there was Te Deum sung in Paul's for joy of the Queen's quickening of child, my Lord Chancellor, Lord Privy Seale, with diverse other Lords and Bishops, being then present; the Mayor and Aldermen with the best crafts of the city being there in their liveries, all giving laud and praise to God for joy of the same, where the Bishop of Worcester, called Doctor Latimer, made an oration afore all the Lords and Commons, after Te Deum was sung, showing the cause of their assembly, which oration was marvelous fruitful to the hearers. And also the same night, was diverse great fires made in London, and a hogshead of wine at every fire for poor people to drink as longe as it would last; I pray Jesu, and it be his will, send us a Prince."

The quickening of Jane's baby was a joyous event, and the news also sparked off celebrations in other places. A sermon was preached at Oxford exhorting the people "to give praise, and pray that it may be a prince". Guns were shot at Calais, along with the singing of a Te Deum, fires were lit, and similar celebrations took place in Guînes. According to Thomas Howard, 3rd Duke of Norfolk, the city of York celebrated with a Te Deum and bonfires throughout the city. Norfolk wrote to Cromwell that he had ordered "four hogsheads of wine out of his cellar to be laid abroad at night to be drunk in divers places freely".

And this time, Henry VIII was not to be disappointed. On 12th October 1537, the eve of the Feast of St Edward the Confessor, Queen Jane gave birth to a son. The couple named him Edward. Edward, of course, became king on his father's death in January 1547 and ruled until his death in July 1553 at the age of 15.

28 May

On 28th May 1588, the Spanish Armada set sail from Lisbon in Portugal, bound for the Spanish Netherlands.

King Philip II of Spain had planned his "Enterprise of England", an invasion of England to depose Queen Elizabeth I, in 1587 following the execution of Mary, Queen of Scots. He planned to send a huge fleet, or armada, from Spain to the Netherlands, where he had an army under the control of the Governor of the Netherlands, the Duke of Parma. The fleet would pick up the army and then sail to invade England.

However, Philip's plan had to be postponed following Sir Francis Drake's attack on the fleet in the harbour of Cádiz in southern Spain in April 1587. Drake managed to capture or destroy thirty ships and their supplies. This postponement gave Elizabeth I time to get her navy organised under the control of Lord Admiral Baron Howard of Effingham and Sir Francis Drake.

On 25th April 1588, the Spanish Armada's banner, which displayed images of the Virgin Mary and Crucified Christ on either side of the arms of Spain and with a Latin motto which translated to "Arise, O

Lord, and vindicate thy cause", was blessed in a special ceremony at Lisbon Cathedral. It was then carried out to the fleet, and papal crusader absolution was given to the soldiers and sailors. It was seen as a holy mission against heresy. In "The Defeat of the Spanish Armada", Garret Mattingly explains how all the sailors and soldiers went to confession before they sailed and were warned against bad behaviour such as blasphemous swearing. The ships were also searched to ensure that no women were on board.

Then, on this day in 1588, the fleet of 130 ships left Lisbon harbour for their journey to the Spanish Netherlands. Victorian historian Agnes Strickland wrote that the fleet carried "19,290 soldiers, 8350 mariners, 2080 galley slaves, besides a numerous company of priests to stir up religious fervour in the host." In the Netherlands, 30,000 foot soldiers and 1800 horses awaited them.

In June, the fleet put in at A Coruña in northwest Spain for provisions and water, but a storm scattered some of the ships, and around 6,000 men were lost. There was damage to some of the remaining ships, and many of the men were suffering from dysentery and scurvy. They set off again on 12th July and were spotted by the English just off The Lizard in Cornwall on 19th July 1588. The English fleet set sail on 21st July 1588, and there was a skirmish which saw the Armada having to abandon two of its ships. An inconclusive battle took place between the two fleets on 23rd July, just off the Isle of Portland, and on 25th July 1588, the Battle of the Isle of Wight took place. The Spaniards had planned on taking the island to use it as a base to launch invasions, but a five-hour battle stopped their plans, and the Armada was forced to carry on to Calais.

On 28th July 1588, the English fleet sent eight hell-burners amongst the Spanish Armada anchored just off Calais.. Hell-burners were fire-ships, ships packed with wood and pitch and set alight. The high winds at Calais caused an inferno which resulted in complete chaos, and the Armada's crescent formation was wrecked as galleons scattered in panic. The next day, the English fleet attacked the remaining Spanish Armada in a battle known as the Battle of Gravelines. England was victorious. Spain lost at least five ships, and several others were severely damaged.

On 30th July, the wind changed, and the remaining Spanish ships were forced northwards and scattered. Then, terrible storms caused further damage to the Armada. This wind that saw the end of Spanish hopes of invasion became known as the Protestant Wind, for it was believed that God had helped Protestant England drive off Catholic Spain – "God blew, and they were scattered", is the translation of the Latin motto inscribed on a special medal which was struck.

Although the Armada had been defeated, Queen Elizabeth I still expected an invasion from the Spanish Netherlands and so visited her troops at Tilbury Fort to give a rousing speech to raise morale. Still, by 20th August 1588, it became clear that England was safe for now, and a thanksgiving service was held at St Paul's. The defeat of the Spanish Armada was commemorated in the famous Elizabeth I Armada portrait.

29 May

On 29th May 1593, Welsh religious controversialist, and a man regarded by Welsh historians as the pioneer of Welsh nonconformity, John Penry, was hanged at St Thomas-a-Watering in Surrey.

Penry had been found guilty of "publishing scandalous writings against the church" after being linked to the "Martin Marprelate tracts." These religious tracts, which attacked the established church, were written under the pseudonym Martin Marprelate (and his sons) and published in 1588 and 1589 by John Penry and Robert Waldegrave.

The publication of these tracts resulted in the Marprelate Controversy, a pamphlet war between the tract writers and defenders of the Church, including Thomas Cooper, Bishop of Winchester; writer and playwright John Lyly, writer and playwright Thomas Nashe, and dramatist Robert Greene.

Penry was a Welshman who hailed from Brecknockshire and had been educated at the Universities of Oxford and Cambridge, graduating BA and MA. He would not be ordained as a priest because he believed the present church was insufficiently reformed. Instead, he became a licensed university preacher.

In 1587, he published a treatise on the state of the church in Wales, which, after he and Job Throckmorton, MP for Warwickshire, had pushed for it to be discussed in Parliament, saw Penry being accused of publishing treason and heresy. Penry was found guilty and imprisoned for a month in the Gatehouse Prison.

This trouble didn't put Penry off, and he published a longer work through printer Robert Waldegrave, which, as his biographer Claire Cross points out, "denounced the bishops as soul murderers for their neglect of the people of Wales". Waldegrave's home was raided in April 1588, but Waldegrave published another tract by Penry in August 1588.

Although Penry's supporter Job Throckmorton is thought to have been Martin Marprelate of the Marprelate Tracts, Cross states that most historians believe that Penry played a minor part, if any, in the actual writing of the tracts. However, he is associated with the secret press. The press was moved from place to place, including London, Fawsley and Coventry, to escape detection, and while it was printing the Marprelate tracts, it was also being used to publish works by Penry.

In 1589, Waldegrave left England for France for a few months due to his worries over the Marprelate tracts, and Penry worked with a new printer, John Hodgkins. The press was apprehended on a move to Manchester in August 1589. Penry went into hiding before fleeing to Scotland with his wife, Helen or Eleanor Godley, supported financially by Job Throckmorton, in October 1589. Waldegrave also fled there. Penry published further religious work in Scotland, defending Scottish Presbyterians and also a translation of a work by Theodore Beza. Still, after complaints from the English government, King James VI proclaimed Penry an outlaw in 1590. In late 1592, Penry travelled to London, where he became involved in a separatist church led by Francis Johnson, Henry Barrow, and John Greenwood, preaching there and petitioning to release members who'd been imprisoned. He also published a tract defending the separatists.

On 22nd March 1593, Penry was arrested at Stepney and interrogated after the vicar of Stepney told authorities of his whereabouts. He confessed to publishing two works during his time in Scotland, and then, during his imprisonment, wrote a work in which he made clear his loyalty to Queen Elizabeth despite his views on the church.

Separatist leaders Henry Barrow and John Greenwood were hanged for treason at Tyburn on 6th April 1593. Penry wrote farewell letters to his wife and daughters, Deliverance, Comfort, Safety, and Sure Hope, the eldest being only 4. He also wrote one to the separatist congregation over the next few days. Then, on 21st May, he was tried, accused of sedition, of trying to overthrow religion and incite rebellion. The trial was suspended after Penry appealed to William Cecil, Lord Burghley, against the court using information from private papers he'd had in Scotland. He also defended himself well, pointing out that far from encouraging rebellion, his teaching was "the clean contrary". But when his trial opened again on 25th May, he was found guilty of publishing scandalous writings against the Church. Penry appealed once more to Burghley, but it was no good. Archbishop Whitgift hastened to draw up and sign his death warrant, which was also signed by Sir John Puckering, Keeper of the Great Seal, and Chief Justice Sir John Popham, who had sat in judgement on Penry.

On this day in 1593, thirty-year-old John Penry was just finishing his lunch when he was taken, fixed to a hurdle and dragged to St Thomas-a-Watering in Surrey. There, he was prevented from making a speech before he was hanged. Penry's work wasn't over, though, as a seditious pamphlet was published following his death, stating that it was written by Mr John Penry, a Martyr of Jesus Christ.

30 May

On the night of 30th/31st May 1533, as part of the celebrations for Queen Anne Boleyn's coronation, which was scheduled for 1st June, eighteen men were created Knights of the Bath.

Chronicler Edward Hall records:

"On Friday at dinner served the king all such as were appointed by his highness to be knights of the bath, which after dinner were brought to their chambers, and that night were bathed and shriven according to the old usage of England, and the next day in the morning the king dubbed them according to the ceremonies thereto belonging whose names ensueth.

The Marquess of Dorset, Sir William Windsor, The Earl of Derby, Sir Frances Weston, The Lord Clifford, Sir Thomas Arrundell, The Lord Fitzwater, Sir John

Huddelston, The Lord Hastings, Sir Thomas Poynings, The Lord Mountegle, Sir Henry Savile, Sir John Mordaunt, Sir George Fitzwilliam, The Lord Vaux, Sir John Tyndall, Sir Henry Parker, Sir Thomas Germayne."

A record in Letters and Papers adds further names: "Mr. Corbet, Mr. Wyndham, John Barkely... Ric. Verney of Penley... Rob. Whitneye of Gloucestershire".

Major-General Sir George Younghusband, in his book "The Tower from Within", describes this traditional coronation ceremony in relation to the coronation of King Henry IV, when 46 men were created Knights of the Bath. He writes that forty-six baths were arranged in one of the halls of the White Tower. Each bath had a canopy and was filled with warm water and draped with clean sheets. The forty-six knights bathed, and then the king led a procession into the hall. The king then approached each knight, still in his bath, dipped his finger into the bath water, and made the sign of the cross on the knight's bare back. While he did this, the king said:

"You shall honor God above all things; you shall be steadfast in the faith of Christ; you shall love the King your Sovereign Lord, and him and his right defend to your power; you shall defend maidens, widows, and orphans in their rights, and shall suffer no extortion, as far as you may prevent it; and of as great honor be this Order unto you, as ever it was to any of your progenitors or others."

When he had done this to all forty-six knights, King Henry IV processed out of the hall. The knights then dried themselves off and were put to bed in "beds with rich hangings", which had been placed behind their baths. After they had rested for a while, they were summoned to rise by the curfew bell of the Bell Tower. Their esquires helped them dress as monks in long brown woollen cassocks with cowls, and then they processed into St John's Chapel as music played. Their new helmets, armour, swords and spurs had been arranged around the high altar, "and before these each Knight knelt in devotion, and watched his armour all night".

That is what happened at Henry IV's coronation in 1399, and it gives us a good idea of what took place on the night of 30th May 1533.

Of course, it would have been King Henry VIII as monarch dubbing the knights, not Queen Anne Boleyn.

31 May

On 31st May 1529, a special legatine court opened at Blackfriars in London.

The court's purpose was to hear the case for an annulment of Henry VIII's first marriage, his marriage to Catherine of Aragon, to whom he'd been married for nearly 20 years. The court was presided over by papal legate Cardinal Lorenzo Campeggio and Cardinal Thomas Wolsey.

In early 1528 Cardinal Thomas Wolsey, Henry VIII's Lord Chancellor and chief advisor, had written to Pope Clement VII outlining Henry VIII's demand that the case for an annulment of his marriage to Catherine of Aragon be decided in England by Wolsey and a visiting papal legate, who would act with the full authority of the pope. On the 13th April 1528, a papal bull had empowered Cardinal Wolsey as the Pope's viceregent "to take cognisance of all matters concerning the King's divorce", and Cardinal Campeggio had been made papal legate in June 1528 in preparation for hearing the divorce case.

Campeggio landed at Dover on the Kent coast on 29th September 1528, and on 8th December 1528, he arrived in London. However, at this point, as historian Eric Ives explained, his "powers were not complete", which necessitated "further wearisome and unsatisfactory negotiation with the papal Curia." This lack of authority was a papal stalling tactic.

Things were made worse for Henry VIII and Wolsey when Catherine of Aragon produced Pope Julius II's dispensation for her to marry Henry. This put a spanner in the works and caused delays with the case. In the meantime, Campeggio met with Catherine and advised her to join a convent, which would allow the marriage to be annulled easily. But Catherine believed that she was Henry's true wife and queen, and would not agree to taking the veil. Henry VIII and Wolsey then played dirty, threatening Catherine with separation from her daughter, Mary, if she would not obey the king. Instead of submitting to the king, Catherine fought back by appealing to Rome against the authority of Wolsey and Campeggio to try the case at a Legatine Court. She had the support of the people and men like John Fisher, Bishop of Rochester, Archbishop William Warham and Cuthbert Tunstall, Bishop of London.

Campeggio could only stall for so long, and formal proceedings finally began on this day in 1529 at Blackfriars. On the 21st June, Henry and Catherine appeared at the court, and Catherine gave an impassioned speech at the court, while kneeling at her husband's feet and appealing directly to him. In it, she said that she'd been the king's true wife for twenty years and had given him diverse children, although God had called them out of this world. She claimed that when Henry had taken her as his wife, she had been a true maid, "without touch of man". After stealing the show completely, she left the court, leaving the king to put forward his doubts about the marriage.

Henry VIII had high hopes for this court case, but it came to nothing when the court was adjourned in July 1529 for a summer recess, never to meet again. It took until May 1533, following the break with Rome, for the marriage to be formally annulled.

1 June

On 1st June 1593, the inquest into the death of playwright, poet and translator Christopher Marlowe took place. The coroner was William Danby, coroner of Queen Elizabeth I's household.

Twenty-nine-year-old Marlowe, writer of such famous works as "Tamburlaine", "Dr Faustus", and "The Jew of Malta", had been fatally stabbed at a house in Deptford Strand, London, by a man named Ingram Frizer, but what happened?

Well, J. Leslie Hotson, in his 1925 book "The Death of Christopher Marlowe", has a transcript of the coroner's report in the original Latin and English. The coroner, Willian Danby, recorded what had happened on that fateful day based on witness accounts and the injuries suffered by Marlowe and Frizer:

"When a certain Ingram ffrysar, late of London, Gentleman, and the aforesaid Christopher Morley and one Nicholas Skeres, late of London, Gentleman, and Robert Poley of London aforesaid, Gentleman, on the thirtieth day of May in the thirty-fifth year above named, at Detford Strand aforesaid in the said County of Kent within the verge, about the tenth hour before noon of the same day, met together in a room in the house of a certain Eleanor Bull, widow; & there passed the time together & dined & after dinner were in quiet sort together there & walked in the garden belonging to the "said house until the sixth hour after noon of the same day & then returned from the said garden to the room aforesaid & there together and in company supped, & after supper the said Ingram & Christopher Morley were in speech & uttered one to the other divers malicious words for the reason that they could not be at one nor agree about the payment of the sum of pence, that is, the recknynge, there, & the said Christopher Morley then lying upon a bed in the room where they supped, & moved with anger against the said Ingram ffirysar upon the words as aforesaid spoken between them, And the said Ingrain then & there sitting in the room aforesaid with his back towards the bed where the said Christopher Morley was then lying, sitting near the bed, that is, nere the bed, & with the front part of his body towards the table & the aforesaid Nicholas Skeres & Robert Poley sitting on either side of the said Ingram in such a manner that the same Ingram ffrysar in no wise could take flight: it so befell that the said Christopher Morley on a sudden, & of his malice towards the said Ingram aforethought, then & there maliciously drew the dagger of the said Ingram which was at his back, and with the same dagger the said Christopher Morley then & there maliciously gave the aforesaid Ingram two wounds on his head of the length of two inches & of the depth of a quarter of an inch; where upon the said Ingram, in fear of being slain, & sitting in the manner aforesaid between the said Nicholas Skeres & Robert Poley so that he could not in any wise get away, in his own defence & for the saving of his life, then & there struggled with the said Christopher Morley to get back from him his dagger aforesaid; in which affray the same Ingram could not get away from the said Christopher Morley; and so it befell in that affray that the said Ingram, in defence of his life, with the dagger aforesaid of the value of 12d. gave the said Christopher then & there a mortal wound over his right eye of the depth of two inches & of the width of one inch; of which mortal wound the aforesaid Christopher Morley then & there instantly died."

Danby went on to record that on hearing the accounts of those present, the jury, who had viewed Marlowe's body, taken measurements of his fatal wound, and seen Frizer's wounds, ruled that Frizer had acted "in the defence and saving of his own life, against the peace of our said lady the Queen, her now crown & dignity". They noted that he had not tried to flee the scene. It was ruled that Frizer had killed Marlowe in self-defence after Marlowe attacked him because of an argument over a bill.

On 28th June, Danby and the jury then pardoned Frizer for the breach of the peace caused by the incident.

Marlowe had been involved in fights before. He'd been in a fight using a sword and a dagger in 1589 and a streetfight in 1592, so he could be violent and perhaps this attack isn't out of character. Still, there is also the possibility that the witnesses got together and made up the story, and that Marlowe was murdered. In his book "Christopher Marlowe", Frederick Boas wonders if the jury were prejudiced against the colourful Marlowe, who was said to be an atheist and who'd been recently arrested by order of Elizabeth I's privy council, or whether they'd been misled by witnesses giving false statements. Was Marlowe really the aggressor, or was he the intended victim?

2 June

On 2nd June 1572, at about eight o'clock in the morning, thirty-four-year-old Thomas Howard, 4th Duke of Norfolk, was led up to the scaffold on Tower Hill to be beheaded for high treason.

As you will know from the 16th January entry, Norfolk had been implicated in the 1569 Rising of the North and the Ridolfi Plot of 1571. In December 1571, Norfolk was charged with "having conspired and imagined to deprive the queen of her crown and dignity, and compassed to excite sedition, to cause great slaughter amongst the queen's lieges, to levy war and rebellion against the queen, to subvert the government, to change and alter the pure religion established in the kingdom, and to bring in strangers and aliens to invade the realm, and to carry on a bitter war against the queen." He was found guilty of high treason, but Queen Elizabeth was initially reluctant to execute him and only issued a death warrant after pressure from Parliament.

Norfolk went to his death on this day in 1572. He was attended by his friend and former tutor, martyrologist John Foxe, and Alexander Nowell, Dean of St Paul's. Even though Norfolk started his scaffold speech by saying that he would be brief, he gave an incredibly long scaffold speech, ignoring those who sought to interrupt him and put a stop to his speech. Although Norfolk spoke of how he would not complain of any injustice, he maintained his innocence and denied being a papist: "God is my judge, before whom I stand, I thank God I was never a papist since I knew what religion meant".

The sheriff finally interrupted his speech, and Norfolk embraced

Sir Henry Lee, who was present at his execution in his role as Master of the Armour, and then said, "I have, and always have had as true a heart to my prince as ever any subject hath had."

He knelt, asked the queen's forgiveness, got up again and embraced the Dean of St Paul's before shaking the hands of others present on the scaffold and asking them to pray for him. The executioner then asked Norfolk's forgiveness, which Norfolk gave to him along with his payment. Norfolk knelt once again and, with the Dean, prayed and read Psalm 51. After saying in Latin what translates to "Lord into thy hands I commend my spirit", he removed his gown, doublet and cap. After rearranging the straw on the scaffold and refusing a blindfold, Norfolk put his head on the block, and the executioner beheaded him with one stroke.

Norfolk's remains, head and body, were placed into a coffin and then carried to the Chapel of St Peter ad Vincula within the Tower confines and buried there by the Dean of St Paul's.

3 June

On 3rd June 1535, Thomas Cromwell, Vicar-General, issued orders regarding the royal supremacy.

But what was the royal supremacy?

During the Great Matter, Henry VIII's quest for an annulment of his marriage to Catherine of Aragon, a copy of William Tyndale's "The Obedience of a Christen Man" found its way into the king's hands. In this book, Tyndale wrote of how rulers were answerable directly to God and not to the pope. After reading this book, Henry VIII declared, "This book is for me and all kings to read", and it is his reading of this text that is credited with making the king believe that he could break with Rome and make himself head of the church in England, rather than being answerable to the pope.

The Act of Supremacy was passed in November 1534. It declared, "Albeit the Kynges Majestie justely and rightfully is & oweth to be supreme hede of the Churche of England and so is recognysed by the Clergy of the Realme in their convocacions." This Act came into force in February 1535. The authority of Rome was abandoned, and this was the start of the English Reformation.

On 3rd June 1535, Cromwell sent out royal orders to all bishops in England to preach in support of the royal supremacy and to make sure that their priests also preached every Sunday and feast day, renouncing the pope and supporting the royal supremacy. Cromwell's orders are no longer in existence, but we can tell what was said from the replies he received from bishops. Archbishop Thomas Cranmer replied, "concerning the diligent declaration of the King's title and stile of Supreme Head in Earth, immediately under God, of the Church of England. Will satisfy the King's command to the best of my power". Nicholas Shaxton, Bishop of Salisbury, wrote that he "Rejoices that it has pleased his Highness to write so earnestly to his bishops in this so earnest a cause. Prays Cromwell, whose wisdom, no doubt, stirred him to it, to persevere till the usurped power of that man of Rome be clean abolished", and the Bishop of Bangor wrote to the king saying that he'd received his letters "concerning the diligent setting forth and sincere preaching within the diocese of Bangor of your most just title of Supreme Head of the Church of England, and the abolition of the usurped power of the bishop of Rome, which I will do or cause to be done with all celerity." Many other bishops replied, assuring the king and Cromwell that they would obey. Schoolmasters were also to teach their students about the king's supremacy.

The clergy were also instructed to remove all references to the pope from mass books and other church books.

Of course, not everybody was on board with these changes, and men like Sir Thomas More, John Fisher, Bishop of Rochester, and the Carthusian monks of London Charterhouse lost their lives due to their opposition.

Although, as I said, this break with Rome was the start of the English Reformation, Henry VIII was not changing the faith of England. Henry VIII died as a Catholic. He was simply making himself head of the church and denying the pope's authority. This did allow those of the reformed faith, men like Cranmer and Cromwell, to bring in changes to reform the church. Still, England didn't become "Protestant" until Edward VI's reign and then during Elizabeth I's reign with her religious settlement.

4 June

On the afternoon of Wednesday 4th June 1561, the eve of Corpus Christi, the city of London was hit by a tremendous thunderstorm. According to contemporary accounts, there was "a marvellous great fiery lightning" and "a most terrible hideous crack of thunder, such as seldom hath been heard."

Contemporary accounts recorded that "a thunderbolt smote down certain great stones from the battlement of the steeple" of the Church of St Martin Ludgate, "which fell down upon the leads of the church, and brake the leads and boards, and a great chest in two pieces". The church was destroyed by fire.

Lightning also struck the steeple of St Paul's Cathedral. In "Everyday Life in Tudor London", Stephen Porter explains that this steeple was made from oak covered with lead and that it was topped with a ball containing relics, a cross and a weathercock, which was in the form of an eagle. The steeple dated back to 1462, when it replaced a steeple hit by lightning on Candlemas Eve in 1444. In 1506, the weathercock was replaced after the wind blew it down, and in 1553, the whole steeple was removed and repaired.

In "A Survey of the Cities of London and Westminster, Borough of Southwark, and Parts Adjacent" which was based on the work of 16th-century historian John Stow, is the following account:

> "In the year 1561, the 4th of June, betwixt the hours of three and four o'clock in the afternoon, the great spire of the steeple of St. Paul's Church was fired by Lightning. Which broke forth (as it seemed) two or three Yards beneath the Foot of the Cross; and from thence it burnt downwards from the Spire, to the Battlements, Stone-Work, and Bells, so furiously, that within the Space of four Hours the same Steeple, with the Roof of the Church, were consumed."

Contemporary accounts don't agree on what time the lightning struck the steeple, but the fire was recorded as breaking out around four o'clock in the afternoon, starting just below the ball. Holes had been left in the lead for scaffolding, so the fire caught the oak underneath, and within around 15 minutes, the cross and eagle fell onto the roof of the south transept, and the steeple was described as burning "downward, like a candle consuming". The melted lead of the steeple poured down on the roof like molten lava, and the cathedral bells melted. All the roofs of the cathedral caught fire, and the rafters were consumed. The streets below "seemed to be paved with lead". The air was full of sparks and debris.

As the steeple burned, a crowd gathered. There was talk of shooting the steeple down with artillery or men scaling the roof to attack it with axes to try and stop the fire from spreading. Still, things happened so fast that it was decided instead to concentrate on saving the bishop's palace, which joined onto the cathedral on the north side. If the palace had caught fire, the fire would also have spread to its adjoining properties. Five hundred people were involved in fetching water, and they managed to save the palace, but the steeple and all four cathedral roofs were destroyed. The interior of the cathedral survived except for the communion table.

It was soon rumoured that the fire had been started by a negligent plumber who had left a pan of hot coals in the steeple, but no plumber or workman had laboured in the cathedral for six months, and there were also rumours that it was caused by "some wicked practice of wild fire or gunpowder", but there was no evidence to support this. Others blamed the fire on popery, while others blamed the Puritans. James Pilkington, Bishop of Durham, preached at Paul's Cross that it was "a general warning for the whole realm and namely to the city of London of some greater plague to follow, if amendment of life in all states did not follow". It was seen as a sign from God.

It was recorded that Elizabeth I sent her mandate to the Lord Mayor of London, commanding him "to take a method for the immediate repair of the damage". In his 1902 book, "Old St Paul's Cathedral", William Benham explains that the queen gave the mayor 1000 marks from her own purse and provided him with warrants for 1000 loads of timber from her woods. The clergy and laymen of London were able to raise nearly £7,000, and within a month, there was a temporary roof of boards and lead. By the end of the year, the church's aisles were recorded as being "framed out of new timber, covered with lead, and fully furnished", and the cathedral had been completely reroofed by April 1566. However, the steeple was never rebuilt.

One hundred years after the cathedral had been reroofed, the whole of St Paul's Cathedral was destroyed in the September 1666 Great Fire of London. The present building was built between 1675 and 1710 and was designed by Sir Christopher Wren.

5 June

On 5th June 1604, Tudor physician and naturalist Thomas Moffet, or Muffet, physician and naturalist, died at Wilton in Wiltshire.

Moffet is known for his 1599 poem, "The Silkewormes and their Flies", dedicated to Mary Herbert, Countess of Pembroke, who he described as "the most renowned patroness and noble nurse of learning". Moffet describes himself as a country farmer and an apprentice in physic, and states that his poem is "for the great benefit and enriching of England".

"The Silkeworms and their flies" has been described as "the first Virgilian georgic poem in English. In it, Moffet describes the silkworms he saw when he visited Italy in 1580. Moffet also covers silk and its history, the silkworm's colour, what day of the week they were created, their virtues, their manner of dying, their eggs, how they feed, the causes of their sickness, and all sorts of other information on the silkworm, all in the form of a poem.

Here is one verse from the start of Book 2:

"This little breed? Nay, even the least of all,
The least? Nay greater than the greatest are:
For though show their substance be but small,
Yet with their worth what great ones may compare?
What eggs as these, are so much spherical
Of all that ever winged Natures bare?
As though they only had deserved to have,
The self same form which God to heavens gave."

His observation of the silkworms sparked an interest in insects, and he went on to write a book on the natural history of insects, which he dedicated to Queen Elizabeth I. It was published posthumously in Latin in 1634 and later translated into English.

His other works include a treatise on diet, and a biography of Sir Philip Sidney, along with medical texts.

Trivia: his biographer Victor Houliston states that it is thought that Moffat's daughter, Patience, was the little Miss Muffet of the famous nursery rhyme.

6 June

On 6th June 1522, Holy Roman Emperor Charles V and King Henry VIII, "with all their companies", set off from Greenwich Palace and marched towards London to make a grand entry into the city.

Charles had landed at Dover on 26th May 1522. The purpose of his visit was to ally with Henry VIII against Francis I, King of France, in what would be the Treaty of Windsor, which included a promise of marriage between Charles and Mary, Henry VIII's six-year-old daughter.

A 19th-century writer has described Charles's 1522 visit to England as "probably the most splendid royal visit ever paid to England", and there was certainly lots of pageantry.

Chronicler Edward Hall gives a detailed account of the entry of the emperor and king into London on this day in 1522 and the nine pageants that had been organised.

Hall writes of how a rich tent of cloth of gold had been put up a mile from St George's Bar, and this is where the two rulers changed into coats of cloth of gold and their companions into cloth of gold, tissue, silver, tinsel and velvet of all colours. The heralds arranged the retinues in order, pairing every Englishman with a visitor according to their degrees. They then processed to Deptford, where the mayor and aldermen greeted them, and an eloquent Latin oration from Sir Thomas More praised the two rulers and the peace and love between them.

At Southwark, the emperor and king were received by the clergy, and then at Marshalsea and the King's Bench, the Emperor requested a pardon for "a great number" of prisoners, which the King granted.

The city streets were decorated with cloths of gold, silver velvet and arras, and the people could watch the procession from behind railings.

Let me give you a brief rundown of the pageants in the streets of London that day:

- At the drawbridge at London Bridge, which had been decorated with Charles's arms, the giants Hercules and Samson held a great tablet on which was written in gold letters the names of all of Charles V's lands and dominions.
- In the middle of the bridge, there was an imitation building and towers and a pageant with Jason holding the Golden Fleece. There was a fiery dragon and fire-breathing bulls.
- At the conduit at Gracechurch Street was a bastille with two great gates and three great towers. The Hanseatic merchants had built it. A representation of the emperor sat under a cloth of estate, and in a tower, there was a representation of the king. Charlemagne was depicted giving the Sword of Justice to the emperor and the Sword of Triumphant Victory to the king. Before Charlemagne, sat the pope, to whom Charlemagne gave the crown of thorns and three nails.
- At Leadenhall was a pageant created by the Italian merchants. Here, in a "goodly pagiant wonderfull curiously wrought", John of Gaunt, Duke of Lancaster and son of Edward III, sat on a root and out of that root sprang many branches and on each branch were images of kings, queens or noble persons who were descended from the Duke. The tree culminated with images of the Emperor, Henry VIII and Catherine of Aragon.
- At the conduit at Cornhill were gateways, arches and towers decorated with the arms of the two rulers. The towers were full of musicians and between them was a palace where King Arthur sat under a rich cloth of estate and at his round table.
- At the little conduit at the Stocks was a pageant designed by author and printer John Rastell. It featured flowers, birds and beasts, and things of pleasure, plus "water full of fish". Around it, were the elements, planets and stars, and on top, the trinity and angels singing. "The Trinitie blessed the kyng & the Emperor, and under his feete was written, behold the lover of peace and concorde."
- At the great conduit in Cheapside was a pageant with four towers linked by galleries, all decorated with sumptuous fabrics like cloth of gold and decorated with the arms of the king and emperor. In the four towers were four fair ladies,

symbolising the Cardinal Virtues. Children, men and women sat in the galleries, all singing and playing instruments.

- At the Standard in Cheapside was a huge timber building with towers, arches and pillars supported by monsters and decorated with the arms of the two rulers. At the foot of this pageant sat King Alphonso of Spain, known as Alphonso the Wise, with a branch springing from his breast. Out of this branch sprang many kings, queens and princes who were all richly apparelled and "every one with a scutchion of armes shewing their marriages". On the highest branch sat the Emperor and King.

- The final pageant was at the little conduit at Cheapside and depicted the Assumption of the Virgin Mary, along with minstrels playing, angels singing, and apostles saying verses in Latin. The pageant also featured St George, St John the Baptist and English saints, including King Edmund, Edward the Confessor, Dunstan, Thomas Becket and Erkenwold, and Henry VI, whose canonization had not been completed.

At St Paul's, Henry VIII and Charles V were received by the Archbishop of Canterbury and 21 prelates. The two men made offerings at the high altar before riding to Blackfriars, where the emperor was lodged.

7 June

On 7th June 1536, there were celebrations for England's new queen, Jane Seymour, the third wife of King Henry VIII.

Jane had married Henry VIII on 30th May 1536, following the execution of his second wife, Queen Anne Boleyn. Jane's new status as Henry's queen consort was celebrated on this day in 1536 with a water pageant on the River Thames, from Greenwich Palace to Whitehall, or York Place.

Here is an account of the pageant by herald and chronicler Charles Wriothesley:

"Also, the 7th day of June, being Wednesday in Whitsun week, the King and the Queen went from Greenwich to York Place, at Westminster, by water, his lords going in barges before him, every lord in his own barge, and the King and the Queen in a barge together, following after the lords' barges, with his guard following him in a great barge; and as he passed by the ships in the Thames every ship shot guns, and at Radcliffe the Emperor's ambassador stood in a tent with a banner of the Emperor's arms set in the top of his tent and diverse banners about the same, he himself being in a rich gown of purple satin, with diverse gentlemen standing about him with gowns and coats of velvet; and when the Beach King's [the Master of Ceremonies?] barge came by him, he sent two boats of his servants to row about the King's barge, one of them were his trumpeters, and another with shalms and sackbuts, and so made a great reverence to the King and Queen as they came by him, and then he let shot a forty great guns, and as the King came against the Tower of London there was shot above four hundred pieces of ordinance, and all the tower walls towards the water side were set with great streamers and banners; and so the King passed through London Bridge, with his trumpets blowing before him, and shalms, sackbuts, and drummers playing also in barges going before him, which was a goodly sight to behold."

It doesn't sound as lavish a spectacle as Anne Boleyn's coronation river procession back in 1533, which featured a mechanical fire-breathing dragon, monsters and wild men, but it still must have been a wonderful sight. I wonder what the common people thought of it all – a queen executed just over two weeks previously, and now there are celebrations for a new queen.

8 June

On 8th June 1536, exactly three weeks after the execution of Queen Anne Boleyn, second wife of King Henry VIII, the sixth Parliament of Henry's reign met.

This parliament went on to pass the Second Act of Succession, removing Mary, the king's daughter by Catherine of Aragon, and Elizabeth, his daughter by Anne Boleyn, from the line of succession and declaring them bastards.

In the First Act of Succession, Mary had already been declared illegitimate on 23rd March 1534. That act had also declared the validity of Henry VIII's marriage to Anne Boleyn and recognised the rights of their issue, i.e. Elizabeth and any future children, to inherit the throne. However, following the fall and execution of Anne Boleyn in May 1536, Parliament needed to do something to change this legislation. The Second Act of Succession confirmed the annulment of Henry VIII's marriage to Anne Boleyn. It declared that "the issue of this marriage is also illegitimate", stating that "the succession to the throne be now therefore determined to the issue of the marriage with Queen Jane."

Parliament praised the king for his "most excellent goodness to enter into marriage again" with Jane Seymour, and the bill went on to praise the new queen:

> "[…] and [forasmuch as you] have chosen and taken a right noble, virtuous, and excellent lady, Queen Jane, to your true and lawful wife; who, for her convenient years, excellent beauty, and pureness of flesh and blood, is apt to conceive issue by your Highness; which marriage is so pure and sincere, without spot, doubt or impediment […]"

The passing of this Second Act of Succession meant that although the kind had three living children, he had no legitimate children or heirs, for his son, Henry Fitzroy, Duke of Richmond and Somerset, was also illegitimate, being the son of Henry VIII's mistress Elizabeth, or Bessie, Blount. This parliament was Fitzroy's last public appearance. He was recorded as being "consumptive and incurable" by imperial ambassador Eustace Chapuys on 8th July 1536, and he died on 22nd July 1536.

The pressure was now on Jane Seymour to produce a living son and heir as quickly as possible. Of course, she gave birth to a healthy son on 12th October 1537, a boy who became King Edward VI on the death of his father in 1547.

On the very same day that Parliament declared her illegitimacy,

Mary, the king's eldest daughter, wrote to her father from her home at Hunsdon. Letters and Papers has a record of her letter:

> "Begs his daily blessing. Though she understands, to her inestimable comfort, that he has forgiven all her offences and withdrawn his displeasure long time conceived against her, her joy will not be full till she is allowed to come to his presence. Begs pardon for her continual suit and rude writing, for nature will suffer her to do no otherwise. Hopes God will preserve him and the Queen, and send them a prince."

However, the king did not want anything to do with his daughter until she toed the line, obeyed him and submitted to him.

9 June

On 9th June 1549, at Whitsun services around England, the Book of Common Prayer was used for the first time. This was in the second year of King Edward VI's reign.

The Book of Common Prayer, or to give it its full title, "The book of the Common Prayer and administration of the Sacraments and other rites and ceremonies of the church", was the official liturgy of Edward VI's Protestant Church and was composed mainly by Thomas Cranmer, Archbishop of Canterbury. It was written in English, and it replaced the traditional Latin mass. It was revised in 1552.

Beth von Staats, author of "Thomas Cranmer in a Nutshell", calls the book a "literary masterpiece" and writes of how Cranmer's words became "profoundly embedded into the very cultural soul of the British people, the lyrical vernacular deeply imprinted into every English speaking person worldwide."

Cranmer's book was based on other works, such as Salisbury's Latin "Use of Sarum", the liturgy of the Reformed Church of Cologne, the work of Martin Luther and the English Great Bible. Still, he was writing his book in English and for the use of the English people, rather than just the clergy.

It comprised:
- A table and calendar for Psalms and lessons
- The order for matins and evensong throughout the year

- The introits, collects, epistles and gospels to be used at the celebration of the Lord's Supper and Holy Communion through the year, with proper psalms and lessons for diverse feasts and days
- Holy Communion
- The Litany and suffrages
- Services for Baptism, confirmation, matrimony, visitation of the sick, burial, purification of women
- A declaration of scripture with prayers for the 1st day of Lent
- And explanatory notes

The book used today in Anglican church services descends from Cranmer's book.

10 June

On 10th June 1584, Francis, Duke of Anjou and Alençon, died in Paris. It is thought that he died of malaria.

For a time, the duke was a suitor of Queen Elizabeth I and the queen even affectionately called him her "frog".

In the summer of 1579, the forty-five-year-old queen welcomed twenty-three-year-old Francis, or François, Duke of Anjou, to the English court. Francis was coming to woo the queen and put forward his suit for marriage. In an article on the History Extra website, Historian Anna Whitelock writes, "It was not an ideal match. Anjou was a 20-something tiny and pockmarked Catholic who was widely rumoured to be a transvestite. Nonetheless, Elizabeth had always longed to be wooed in person by one of her illustrious suitors, and for a time she seemed to be genuine in her affections and interest in Anjou". He wasn't exactly Robert Dudley, but Dudley had just married Lettice Devereux.

Anjou stayed at Greenwich with the royal court for ten days, flirting with the queen at every opportunity while being entertained with balls and banquets. The queen enjoyed his attentions, and Whitelock writes of how the queen would sneak out of the palace and visit the duke at the pavilion where he was staying with his ambassador, Simier. Unfortunately, although Elizabeth seemed happy with the duke's wooing and appeared to welcome the idea of marriage, there was opposition from her people, and pamphlets and ballads deriding the match began to circulate. Prominent courtier Philip Sidney petitioned the queen not to go ahead with the match. Elizabeth asked for the opinions of her council, but they left the decision to her. After weeks of procrastinating, Elizabeth decided to go ahead with marrying Anjou and sent a draft marriage treaty with Simier to France. However, she did say that she would only finally sign the treaty if her people agreed within two months.

In January 1580, Elizabeth informed Anjou that her people were against her marrying a Catholic. Anjou wasn't going to take no for an answer, though, and asked her to reconsider. Elizabeth taking her time to mull it over was a good strategy because there were fears of a Catholic invasion, so an alliance with France would help. In April 1581, a large French embassy came to England to negotiate terms for the marriage, staying six weeks and hoping to attend the marriage of Elizabeth and Anjou. Still, although Elizabeth was interested in an alliance with the French, she now didn't want that to include marriage. How could she marry a Catholic at a time when Jesuit priests arriving in England to convert people to catholicism were causing such concern for her government?

The French ambassador tried to push the queen, saying she needed to marry the duke because she had already slept with him, a rumour Elizabeth firmly denied. While Elizabeth argued the case for not marrying Anjou, pointing out the age gap, Anjou wooed her with love letters, rather hot and steamy letters too. He wrote of how he wanted to be "kissing and rekissing all that Your Beautiful Majesty can think of" and to be "in bed between the sheets of your beautiful arms". He travelled to England in October 1581, hoping to persuade her, and Elizabeth fell under his spell once more, visiting him every morning while he was still in bed to take him a cup of broth. On 22nd November 1581, the queen told the French ambassador to let Anjou's brother, the King of France, know that she would marry Anjou and then she kissed the duke and gave him a ring as a pledge. This public act upset members of her privy council and Elizabeth's ladies, who begged her not to marry a foreigner. Elizabeth had to do an about-turn and let the duke down gently. He left England in February 1582, leaving a seemingly grief-stricken Elizabeth, who even wrote a poem "On Monsieur's Departure":

> "I grieve and dare not show my discontent,
> I love and yet am forced to seem to hate,
> I do, yet dare not say I ever meant,
> I seem stark mute but inwardly to prate.
> I am and not, I freeze and yet am burned.
> Since from myself another self I turned.
> My care is like my shadow in the sun,
> Follows me flying, flies when I pursue it,
> Stands and lies by me, doth what I have done.
> His too familiar care doth make me rue it.
> No means I find to rid him from my breast,
> Till by the end of things it be supprest.
> Some gentler passion slide into my mind,
> For I am soft and made of melting snow;
> Or be more cruel, love, and so be kind.
> Let me or float or sink, be high or low.
> Or let me live with some more sweet content,
> Or die and so forget what love ere meant.

The queen and Anjou continued writing to each other, but any idea of marriage ended when Anjou died of a fever, probably malaria, on this day in 1584. When she was told of his death, she was "greatly grieved" and went into mourning, wearing black for six months and weeping "in public every day for three weeks."

Was Elizabeth ever serious about marrying this French duke, or did it suit her to procrastinate and keep her foreign policy options open? It's hard to know, but there seems to have been true affection, if not love, between the two.

Why did Elizabeth call Anjou her frog? We don't know. Possibly he had bandy legs, or it might be simply that he gave her a frog-shaped piece of jewellery. Elizabeth loved to give her friends and advisors nicknames – William Cecil was her spirit, Walsingham was her Moor, Dudley her eyes, Hatton her mouton. It was nothing to do with the slang term of abuse that used to be thrown at the French.

11 June

On 11th June 1509, just over seven weeks after becoming king, seventeen-year-old Henry VIII married twenty-three-year-old Catherine of Aragon (Catalina de Aragón), daughter of Isabella I of Castile and Ferdinand II of Aragon, in a private ceremony in the queen's closet at Greenwich Palace.

The wedding ceremony was a private and low-key affair as the king was in the middle of planning a lavish joint coronation for himself and Catherine, which was due to take place on 24th June, the Feast of St John and also Midsummer's Day, at Westminster Abbey. There were just two witnesses to the marriage ceremony: George Talbot, Earl of Shrewsbury and Henry VIII's Lord Steward, and William Thomas, groom of the privy chamber.

Catherine of Aragon was, of course, the first of six wives for Henry VIII, and Henry was her second husband. She'd previously been married to Henry's brother, Arthur, Prince of Wales, but he had died six months into their marriage in April 1502.

On the 23rd June 1503, a marriage treaty for Catherine to marry Prince Henry was signed, and the couple Henry became betrothed at a ceremony on the 25th June. It was planned that a proper marriage ceremony would take place on Henry's 15th birthday, the 28th June 1506, giving England and Spain the chance to get a papal dispensation to allow the couple to marry. In the summer of 1504, the pope showed that he was willing to grant the dispensation, but shortly after Isabella received it in November 1504, she died.

Isabella's death had a major impact on Catherine. Not only did it leave Catherine grief-stricken, but it made her a less attractive bride for Henry VII's son and heir, as Catherine's father was not the heir to Castile. Henry VII, therefore, discouraged his son from the union, and on the 27th June 1505, the day before the marriage was meant to be solemnized, Prince Henry repudiated the betrothal. Poor Catherine was left in an impossible position: her father did not want her to return to Spain, but Henry VII had cut off her allowance as she was no longer marriage material. Catherine had no choice but to remain in England, live in virtual poverty, and hope that things would turn out right. Things got better when her father appointed her as a Spanish ambassador, but she had to wait until her knight in shining armour came to rescue her in 1509 for things to be right again.

Of course, Henry VIII went on to have his marriage to Catherine annulled in 1533 after a six-year quest for an annulment. Catherine died in January 1536, just a few months before her successor, Anne Boleyn, was executed.

12 June

On Sunday 12th June 1530, King Henry VIII got a good telling off from Catherine of Aragon.

By this time, Henry was involved with Catherine's former maid of honour, Anne Boleyn, and was trying desperately to get his marriage to Catherine annulled. Although Henry continued to treat Catherine with respect and appeared with her in public as man and wife, king and queen, Anne was rising in prominence and was a real threat to Catherine. Six months earlier, Eustace Chapuys, the imperial ambassador, had described "a grand fête in this city, to which several ladies of the Court were invited" and how Anne Boleyn took precedence over all the other ladies, who included "queen Blanche and the two duchesses of Norfolk, the dowager and the young one)", and that she sat by the king "occupying the very place allotted to a crowned queen". Chapuys went on to report:

"After dinner there was dancing and carousing, so that it seemed as if nothing were wanting but the priest to give away the nuptial ring and pronounce the blessing. All the time, and whilst the carousal was going on, poor queen Katharine was seven miles away from this place holding her own fête of sorrow and weeping."

So what exactly did Catherine say to her husband on this day in 1530? According to Chapuys, Catherine exhorted her husband "to be again to her a good prince and husband, and to quit the evil life he was leading and the bad example he was setting."

Catherine went on to tell him that even if he did not respect her, "his true and lawful wife", that "he should at least respect God and his conscience", and that he should not ignore the brief issued by the pope. Catherine had applied to the pope for this brief "for to the effect that nobody shall, under pain of excommunication, judge, allege, counsel, procure, solicit, or otherwise speak "á complacentia o gratia," of this matter of the dissolution of matrimony between the King and Queen, unless it be as God and his conscience may dictate."

Unfortunately, Catherine's words had no effect on the king. Henry argued that the pope's brief, which was urging the king to practise restraint, "was of very little consequence" and that plenty of people were on his side. The king then "left the room abruptly without saying another word."

13 June

On 13th June 1587, actor William Knell was killed in a pub brawl in Thame, Oxfordshire.

Let me tell you more about William Knell and how he died.

His birthdate is unknown, and his early life is a mystery, although he was described after his death as being from St Mary Aldermanbury in London. But by 1585, he had come to the notice of Edmund Tilney, who Sir Francis Walsingham had commissioned to find actors for "The Queen's Men", a new company of actors which, as Knell's biographer Peter Thomson points out, was expected to "outshine all rival companies". Knell joined the company, whose patrons were the Earls of Sussex, Leicester and Warwick, i.e. Henry Radclyffe, Robert Dudley and Ambrose Dudley, and played heroic parts such as Henry V in "The Famous Victories of Henry V". Renowned Elizabethan actor Richard Tarlton played the clown in the same play. An account of the performance says, "Knell, then playing Henry the fifth, hit Tarlton a sound box indeed, which made the people laugh the more".

Thomson explains how the company were expected to tour England in the summer and early autumn months with what he describes as "a broadly protestant and insistently patriotic repertory", Walsingham's agenda. The tough schedule and less than adequate travelling conditions led to problems. Perhaps the stress of the situation led to Knell drawing his sword and attacking another actor, John Towne, in Thame on the evening of 13th June 1587. Towne fought back, sticking his sword through his attacker's neck. Knell soon died of his injuries. His resting place is not known.

A coroner's inquest ruled that Towne had acted in self-defence, saying, "William Knell continuing his attack as before, so maliciously and furiously, and Towne... to save his life drew his sword of iron (price five shillings) and held it in his right hand and thrust it into the neck of William Knell and made a mortal wound three inches deep and one inch wide."

Knell was survived by his wife, Rebecca Edwards, who married another actor, John Heminges, who worked with William Shakespeare, and had children with him.

There is a story that William Knell's death led to William Shakespeare becoming an actor and going to London. The idea being that the company were short of an actor after Knell's death, so Shakespeare took his place when they visited Stratford-upon-Avon. However, no evidence has been found to back up this story.

It is not clear whether he is the Willy of Edmund Spenser's poems "The tears of the muses":

> "Our pleasant Willy, ah is dead of late:
> With whom all joy and jolly merriment
> Is also deaded, and in dolour drent."

14 June

On 14th June 1571, Yorkshire nobleman and Catholic Sir Christopher Danby died.

Danby was a member of a well-known family in the Tudor period and one of quite a few Christopher Danbys. He is known for his Catholic beliefs, links with rebellions, and how he managed to escape punishment.

Let me give you some facts about this Tudor man.

- He was born in 1503 and became a ward of the crown on his father's death in 1518.
- He was married to Elizabeth Neville, daughter of Richard, 2nd Baron Latimer, and they had 14 children together – six sons and eight daughters.
- Danby was knighted in 1533.

- In 1536, in the early stages of the Pilgrimage of Grace, he was with the rebels at Pontefract Castle but managed to escape punishment for his involvement.
- He was a foreman of a grand jury trying the rebels of the rebellion.
- He served as commissioner for musters, a justice of the peace, high sheriff and member of Parliament.
- In Elizabeth I's reign, his Catholic faith caused him problems. He was brought before the Council of the North for questioning about a potential rebellion, but, again, he escaped being charged.
- He died a natural death on 14th June 1571 at 68.

15 June

On 15th June 1559, William Somer (Sommers), court fool to Henry VIII, Edward VI and Mary I, died in Shoreditch, London.

Nothing is known of Somer's early life, but it appears that he started serving as King Henry VIII's fool in June 1535. Just a month later, he got into trouble with the king. Eustace Chapuys, the Imperial ambassador, recorded that Henry VIII was so angry with Somer that he nearly killed him:

> "He the other day nearly murdered his own fool, a simple and innocent man, because he happened to speak well in his presence of the Queen and Princess [Catherine of Aragon and Mary], and called the concubine "ribaude" [whore] and her daughter "bastard." He has now been banished from Court, and has gone to the Grand Esquire, who has sheltered and hidden him."

The "Grand Esquire" refers to Sir Nicholas Carew, chief esquire of the king.

Fortunately for Somer, he managed to work his way back into the king's favour, and he often took part in disguisings and performances with a choir, although it is not known what his role was in this. After Henry VIII's death, he served Edward VI and Mary I. He attended Elizabeth I at her coronation in January 1559 but seems to have retired after that. He died on 15th June and was laid to rest at St Leonard's Church, Shoreditch, London.

Historian J. R. Mulryne wonders if the mention in Robert Armin's 1600 work "Foole upon Foole", of Somer tending to fall asleep suddenly points to Somer having some condition or illness, perhaps one that was progressive.

William Somer can be seen in the Family of Henry VIII painting which hangs at Hampton Court.

16 June

On 16th June 1487, the Battle of Stoke Field took place in a field to the southwest of East Stoke in Nottinghamshire.

It was fought between Henry VII's forces and the Yorkist forces of Lord Lovell and John de la Pole, Earl of Lincoln.

It is known as the last battle between the Houses of York and Lancaster in the civil war that we call the Wars of the Roses. Many people think that the civil war ended with the Battle of Bosworth on 22nd August 1485, when Henry Tudor's forces defeated those of Richard III, and Richard was killed, but that's not true. On the morning of 16th June 1487, the Yorkist forces of Francis, Lord Lovell; John de la Pole, Earl of Lincoln; and Thomas FitzGerald engaged in battle with those of Henry VII, under the command of the Earl of Oxford and Jasper Tudor, the king's uncle.

The Yorkists were looking to remove Henry VII from the throne and replace him with pretender Lambert Simnel, who they claimed was Edward, Earl of Warwick, son of George, Duke of Clarence. Although Warwick was imprisoned in the Tower of London at this time, Simnel was crowned King Edward VI in Dublin on 24th May 1487.

In early June, the Yorkist forces had some success against the Lancastrians, but the Battle of Stoke Field was a decisive Lancastrian victory. Although the Yorkist forces were swelled by 1500-2,000 German mercenaries led by Martin Schwarz, an expert commander, they were outnumbered when they met Henry VII's forces at Stoke Field. It is thought that Henry VII's forces numbered up to 15,000, while the rebels only had around 8,000.

The battle was over before three hours was up. The Yorkists lost around 4,000 men, among them Lincoln and Fitzgerald. Lovell is thought to have escaped and fled to Scotland, and Lambert Simnel, who was only about ten years old, was spared by Henry VII, who put him to work in his kitchens. Simnel later became a falconer. Simnel died a natural death sometime between 1525 and 1535.

17 June

On 17th June 1497, the Cornish Rebellion was ended by the Battle of Blackheath, also known as the Battle of Deptford Bridge, when Henry VII's forces were triumphant against the rebels.

A year earlier, King Henry VII had attempted to introduce new legislation regarding tin mining into the Cornish Stannary Parliament. However, he was met with opposition from the Cornish tin miners. The tin miners were even more unhappy when he suspended the Stannary Court. They lost the privileges the Stannaries had offered them since the early 1300s, so they were no longer exempt from civil jurisdiction or paying taxes.

In 1497, things got worse when heavy taxes were levied for the king to finance his campaign against Scotland and Perkin Warbeck. Cornish rebels led by Michael an Gof, a blacksmith, and Thomas Flamank, a lawyer, decided to march to London to air their grievances and call for the execution of John Morton, Archbishop of Canterbury and the king's Lord Chancellor.

As the rebels marched through Somerset, they were joined by James Tuchet, 7th Baron Audley. They then marched through Bristol, Salisbury and Winchester before moving into Kent, where they hoped to drum up support from the county that had risen under famous rebel Jack Cade. Unfortunately, they were unsuccessful in their mission.

By the time the rebels arrived at Blackheath, which is now a district of south-east London, on 16th June, Henry VII had diverted the army he'd sent north with Giles, Lord Daubeney, back south to meet the Cornish rebels. Daubeney's forces numbered an estimated 8,000, and the rebels had started with 15,000, but by the morning of 17th June, many had deserted, leaving the Cornish rebels with 9-10,000 men. The king's mustering brought the royal forces to about 25,000, so the Cornish forces were significantly outnumbered.

The Earls of Oxford, Essex and Suffolk attacked the rebels from the right and the rear, while Daubeney's forces attacked them at the front.

At Deptford Bridge, it looked like the Cornish archers would beat Daubenay's forces, but then Daubenay's spearmen were able to take the bridge. Without horses and artillery, the Cornish forces were no match for the king's. The rebels were finally forced to surrender after losing somewhere in the region of 1-2,000 men.

The royal forces captured about 1,500 rebels. Rebel leader, Michael an Gof, was able to escape the battlefield and flee to Greenwich but was apprehended there and taken to the Tower of London. An Gof and Flamank were hanged, drawn and quartered at Tyburn on 27th June 1497, and Baron Audley was beheaded on Tower Hill on 28th June 1497.

18 June

On 18th June 1546, twenty-five-year-old Anne Askew, estranged wife of Thomas Kyme, was found guilty of heresy at London's Guildhall along with Nicholas Shaxton (former Bishop of Salisbury), Nicholas White and John Hadlam.

Chronicler and Windsor Herald Charles Wriothesley recorded the results of the hearing:

"The 18th day of June, 1546, were arraigned at the Guild Certain Hall, for heresy, Doctor Nicholas Shaxton, sometime bishop of Salisburie; Nicholas White, of London, gentleman; Anne Kerne[Kyme], alias Anne Askew, gentlewoman, and wife of Thomas Kerne [Kyme], gentleman, of Lincolnshire; and John Hadlam, of Essex, tailor; and were this day first indicted of heresy and after arraigned on the same, and their confessed their heresies against the sacrament of the altar without any trial of a jury, and so had judgment to be brent[burnt]."

Martyrologist John Foxe shares Anne Askew's own account of her condemnation at Guildhall:

"They said to me there, that I was a heretic, and condemned by the law, if I would stand in my opinion. I answered, that I was no heretic, neither yet deserved I any death by the law of God. But, as concerning the faith which I uttered and wrote to the council, I would not, I said, deny it, because I knew it true. Then would they needs know, if I would deny the sacrament to be Christ's body and blood. I said, 'Yea: for the same Son of God that was born of the Virgin Mary, is now glorious in heaven, and will come again from thence at the latter day like as he went up. And as for that ye call your God, it is a piece of bread. For a more proof thereof, (mark it when you list,) let it but lie in the box three months, and it will be mouldy, and so turn to nothing that is good. Whereupon I am persuaded that it cannot be God.'

After that, they willed me to have a priest; and then I smiled. Then they asked me, if it were not good; I said, I would confess my faults unto God, for I was sure that he would hear with favour. And so we were condemned by a quest.

My belief which I wrote to the council was this: 'That the sacramental bread was left us to be received with thanksgiving, in remembrance of Christ's death, the only remedy of our soul's recovery; and that thereby we also receive the whole benefits and fruits of his most glorious passion.' Then would they needs know, whether the bread in the box were God or no: I said, 'God is a Spirit, and will be worshipped in spirit and truth.' Then they demanded, 'Will you plainly deny Christ to be in the sacrament?' I answered, that I believe faithfully the eternal Son of God not to dwell there; in witness whereof I recited again the history of Bel, Dan. xix., Acts vii. and xvii., and Matt. xxiv., concluding thus: 'I neither wish death, nor yet fear his might; God have the praise thereof with thanks."

According to Anne, Nicholas Shaxton visited her in her prison and counselled her "to recant as he had done. I said to him, that it had been good for him never to have been born." Anne was then put to the rack illegally at the Tower of London by Sir Richard Rich and Sir Thomas Wriothesley in the hope that she would give them the names of reformers at court, particularly ladies linked to Queen Catherine Parr. Anne described her racking:

> "Then they did put me on the rack, because I confessed no ladies or gentlewomen to be of my opinion, and thereon they kept me a long time; and because I lay still, and did not cry, my lord chancellor and Master Rich took pains to rack me with their own hands, till I was nigh dead.
>
> Then the lieutenant caused me to be loosed from the rack. Incontinently I swooned, and then they recovered me again. After that I sat two long hours reasoning with my lord chancellor upon the bare floor; where he, with many flattering words, persuaded me to leave my opinion. But my Lord God (I thank his everlasting goodness) gave me grace to persevere, and will do, I hope, to the very end."

Anne, Shaxton, White and Hadlam were all sentenced to be burnt, but Shaxton and White were saved by recanting their heretical beliefs. Anne and Hadlam were burnt at the stake on 16th July 1546 with reformers John Lascelles and John Hemley. Anne had been so badly racked that she had to be carried to the stake on a chair, and the stake had to have a seat to support her body. She died for her faith and deserves to be remembered.

19 June

On 19th June 1573, Jesuit priest and former rector of a Lincolnshire parish, Thomas Woodhouse, was hanged, drawn and quartered at Tyburn. Woodhouse was the first priest to be executed in Elizabeth I's reign. Woodhouse was beatified in December 1886 by Pope Leo XIII.

Woodhouse was first arrested on 14th May 1561 and taken to the Fleet Prison. While he was in prison, he was received into the Society of Jesus, the Roman Catholic order of religious men founded by St. Ignatius of Loyola and known as Jesuits.

On 19th November 1572, his twelfth year of imprisonment, Woodhouse wrote a letter to Elizabeth I's chief advisor, William Cecil, Lord Burghley. This letter is said to have led to his martyrdom.

In the letter, he denied Elizabeth I's status as supreme head of the church, saying that Jesus had given supreme authority to St Peter and, in him, to his successors, the Bishops of Rome. He advised Burghley to "humbly and unfeignedly even from the very bottom of your heart, acknowledge and confess your great iniquity and offence against Almighty God, especially in disobeying that supreme authority and power of the See Apostolic, so ordained and established by the King of kings and Lord of lords, Jesus Christ". He called Elizabeth "Lady Elizabeth", rather than queen, and told Burghley to persuade her to submit herself to the pope. He said that if Burghley did not follow his advice, then it would lead to "the great desolation and ruin of our beloved country and people, and to the utter subversion and perishing of you and yours for ever in hell; where is the gnawing worm, where is the unquenchable fire, where is weeping and gnashing of teeth."

On receipt of this letter, Burghley called Woodhouse for an interview. Woodhouse again refused to acknowledge Elizabeth as queen and kept referring to Burghley as "Mr Cecil". When Burghley asked why he did not call him Lord Burghley or use his title of treasurer, Woodhouse explained that Elizabeth "gave you those names and titles" and that she "had no authority to do so." Burghley called him a traitor.

In April 1573, Woodhouse was tried for high treason at London's Guildhall, found guilty and condemned to death.

In the 1914 book "Lives of the English Martyrs", Father John H. Pollen gives the following account of Woodhouse's execution:

"He was drawn in the usual way to the place of execution. Hearing him pray in Latin, some of the crowd wanted him to pray in English so that all might join with him. He answered that with the Catholics he would willingly, but as for the others he would neither pray with them nor have them pray with him or for him; though he would willingly pray for them. The Sheriff was impatient at what he called his obstinacy, and cried out, 'Away with him, executioner, strip him of his garments, put the rope about his neck and do it quickly.' Then he called to the martyr to ask pardon of God, the Queen, and the country, but Blessed Thomas answered, 'Nay, I on the part of God, demand of you and of the Queen, that ye ask pardon of God and of holy Mother Church, because contrary to the truth ye have resisted Christ the Lord, and the Pope, His Vicar upon earth.' These bold words drew shouts from the ever-fickle crowd of 'Hang him, hang him, this man is worse than Storey.' He was cut down alive, so that 'he went between two from the gallows to the fire, near which he was spoiled, and came perfectly to himself before the hangman began to bowel him; inasmuch as some have said he spoke when the hangman had his hand in his body seeking for his heart to pull it out.'"

And that was the end of Blessed Thomas Woodhouse.

20 June

On 20th June 1540, Queen Anne of Cleves, Henry VIII's fourth wife, complained to her advisor, Carl Harst, the Cleves ambassador, about her husband's interest in one of her maids of honour, a certain Catherine Howard.

Harst tried to reassure the worried queen that it was just a "light romance" and that Anne and the king would soon be off on their summer progress, but Harst had known of the king's interest in Catherine for months.

There were also rumours going around about the king wanting to divorce Anne. London merchant Richard Hilles recorded what he'd heard about the king, Anne and Catherine Howard in a letter to Heinrich Bullinger:

> "Before St. John Baptist's day [24th June] it was whispered the King intended to divorce his queen Anne, sister of the duke of Gelderland, whom he had married publicly at Epiphany after last Christmas. Courtiers first observed that he was much taken with another young lady, very small of stature, whom he now has, and whom he was seen crossing the Thames to visit, often in the day time and sometimes at night. The bishop. of Winchester provided feastings for them in his palace, but it was looked upon as a sign of adultery, not of divorce."

On 22nd June, Harst reported that Anne was much happier, which historian Retha Warnicke puts down to Catherine Howard having left court. However, the queen's happiness was to be very short-lived. On 24th June 1540, Anne reported to Harst that she was being sent away from court to Richmond Palace and that she'd be leaving the next day. It was said that she was being sent there to avoid the plague and that the king would join her, but there was no plague, and she never saw the king again as his wife.

On 7th July 1540, a convocation of clergy agreed that "the king and Anne of Cleves were no wise bound by the marriage solemnised between them", and messengers were then sent to Anne to get her agreement to the annulment of the marriage. Anne must have been upset, for she believed herself to be the true queen, but she also feared what would happen if she resisted the king's request. Anne wrote to the king confirming that she accepted the annulment and signed herself "Anne, the daughter of Cleves" rather than "Anne, the Queen". Henry must have been delighted and relieved with her submission. He wrote back to her, addressing her as his "right dear and right entirely beloved sister", thanking her and informing her that he intended to endow her with £4000 per year and houses at Richmond and "Blechinglegh" (Bletchingley).

Anne was rewarded handsomely for her acceptance of the situation. She also received jewels, plate, hangings, furniture, a house in Lewes, and the lease of Hever Castle, the former Boleyn family home.

On 9th July 1540, Anne's marriage to Henry VIII was declared null "by reason of a precontract between lady Anne and the marquis of Lorraine, that it was unwillingly entered into and never consummated, and that the King is at liberty to marry another woman, and likewise the lady Anne free to marry". Less than three weeks after that, on 28th July 1540, Henry VIII married Catherine Howard.

Of course, Catherine fell in 1541 when it was found that she hadn't been a virgin when she married the king and that she'd been having secret meetings at night with Thomas Culpeper. Anne hoped that the king would return to her, but he didn't, and in 1543 he married his sixth and final wife, Catherine Parr. Anne may have been unhappy with the end of her marriage, but she kept her head and maintained good relationships with the king and her stepchildren. Anne outlived the king and his other wives, dying in July 1557 at 41.

21 June

On 21st June 1553, letters patent were issued stating that King Edward VI's heir was Lady Jane Grey, eldest daughter of the king's cousin, Frances Brandon, Duchess of Suffolk.

Fifteen-year-old King Edward VI was dying, having been ill for a few months, and in the original draft of his "Devise for the Succession", he stipulated that the Crown would descend through the male heirs of Frances, Duchess of Suffolk, if Edward died childless. The problem was that there were no male heirs yet, so when Edward made a turn for the worse, he decided to change the document to read: "To the Lady Fraunceses heirs males, if she have any such issue before my death to the Lady Jane and her heirs males."

On 12th June 1553, the judges of the King's Bench were shown Edward's devise and ordered to turn it into a legal will. The judges refused, as they were worried that overturning the succession would be considered treason, but Edward explained the reasons behind his decision:

> "For indeed my sister Mary was the daughter of the king by Katherine the Spaniard, who before she was married to my worthy father had been espoused to Arthur, my father's elder brother, and was therefore for this reason alone divorced by my father. But it was the fate of Elizabeth, my other sister, to have Anne Boleyn for a mother; this woman was indeed not only cast off by my father because she was more inclined to couple with a number of courtiers rather than reverencing her husband, so mighty a king, but also paid the penalty with her head – a greater proof of her guilt. Thus in our judgement they will be undeservedly considered as being numbered among the heirs of the king our beloved father."

He also passed over the Stuart line (Mary, Queen of Scots), as his father, Henry VIII, had done in his will.

Edward's devise was drawn up by Sir Edward Montague, Chief

Justice of the Common Pleas, and John Gosnold, Solicitor General of the Court of Augmentations, and on this day in 1553, it was issued as "Letters Patent for the Limitation of the Crown", and Lady Jane Grey became Edward VI's legal heir.

Here's an extract from the devise:

"[...] the said lady Mary as also the said lady Elizabeth to all intents and purposes are and be clearly disabled to ask, claim, or challenge the said imperial crown, or any other of our honours, castles, manors, lordships, lands, tenements, and hereditaments as heir or heirs to us or to any other person or persons whosoever, aswell for the cause before rehearsed, as also for that the said lady Mary and lady Elizabeth be unto us but of the half blood, and therefore by the ancient laws, statutes, and customs of this realm be not inheritable unto us, although they were legitimate, as they be not indeed."

Instead, the crown was to be passed to, in order of succession:

- "the eldest SONNE OF THE BODYE OF THE SAID LADY FRAUNCIS [Frances Brandon, Duchess of Suffolk], LAWFULLY BEGOTTONE, beinge borne into the world in our lyfetyme [...]"
- The Lady Jane Grey and her heirs male.
- Lady Katherine Grey, Jane's sister, and her heirs male.
- Lady Mary Grey, Jane and Katherine's younger sister, and her heirs male.
- "the eldeste sonne of the bodie of the fourth daughter of the said lady Frauncis", and his heirs male. - This fourth daughter didn't actually exist at the time the "devise" was drawn up.
- The eldest son of Lady Margaret Clifford, daughter of Lady Eleanor Brandon, the younger sister of Frances Brandon.
- The eldest son of the eldest daughter of Lady Jane Grey "and to the heires males of the bodye of the same eldest sonne", and, failing that, "from sonne to sonne as well of the body of the second daughter of the said lady Jane".
- The eldest son of the eldest daughter of Lady Katherine Grey, "and for lacke of such heires that then the said imperiall crowne and all and singuler other the premisses shall remaine, come,

and be unto the eldeste sonne of the body of the seconde daughter of the said lady Katherine lawfully begotten" and so on.

- The eldest son of the eldest daughter of Lady Mary Grey, and, failing that, the sons of the second eldest daughter.
- The eldest son of the eldest daughter of the fourth daughter of Lady Frances, and so on.
- The eldest son of the eldest daughter of Lady Margaret Clifford, and so on.

So, the focus was on the Brandons and Greys.

When Edward VI died just two weeks later, on 6th July 1553, the throne passed to Lady Jane Grey because her mother, Frances, had not had a son. Jane was proclaimed queen on 10th July. Her reign, however, was cut short when, on 19th July 1553, Edward's half-sister Mary was proclaimed queen and Jane was taken prisoner. Lady Jane Grey was executed for treason on 12th February 1554.

22 June

On the night of 22nd June 1509, King Henry VIII rewarded twenty-six men for their loyal service to the crown by making them Knights of the Bath as part of the celebrations for his coronation.

The men were Robert Radcliffe, Baron Fitzwalter; Henry Scrope, 7th Baron Scrope of Bolton; Lord Fitzhugh; William Blount, 4th Baron Mountjoy; Henry Daubeney, 1st Earl of Bridgewater and 2nd Baron Daubeney; Thomas Brooke, 8th Baron Cobham; Henry Clifford, 1st Earl of Cumberland; Sir Maurice Berkeley, de jure 4th Baron Berkeley; Sir Thomas Knyvet; Andrew Windsor, 1st Baron Windsor; Sir Thomas Parr (father of Catherine Parr); Sir Thomas Boleyn (father of Anne Boleyn); Sir Richard Wentworth; Sir Henry Ughtred; Sir Francis Cheyney; Sir Henry Wyatt (father of poet and diplomat Sir Thomas Wyatt the Elder); Sir George Hastings, 1st Earl of Huntingdon; Sir Thomas Metham; Sir Thomas Bedingfield; Sir John Shelton (Thomas Boleyn's brother-in-law); Sir Giles Alington; Sir John Trevanion; Sir William Crowmer; Sir John Heydon (his mother was a Boleyn); Sir Goddard Oxenbridge; and Sir Henry Sacheverell or Sackveyle.

The men were dubbed Knights of the Bath at a special ceremony at the Tower of London.

As you will have noticed, two of Henry VIII's future fathers-in-law were made Knights of the Bath, and I just wanted to draw attention to Thomas Boleyn being featured here. It is often said that Thomas Boleyn only rose at court because of his two daughters' relationships with the king, but this honour was in 1509 when his daughters were little girls at home at Hever Castle.

Thomas began his court career under King Henry VII, and being made a Knight of the Bath was a reward for his loyal service to the previous king. In 1497, with his father, William Boleyn, Thomas had fought on the king's side against the rebels of the Cornish Rebellion at the Battle of Blackheath. In 1501, he was present at the wedding of Prince Arthur and Catherine of Aragon. In 1503, he was a member of the party of men who escorted Margaret Tudor, Henry VII's daughter, to Scotland to marry King James IV. He was appointed an esquire of the body before the king's death and kept that position when Henry VIII came to the throne in April 1509.

He served King Henry VIII as a diplomat, carrying out incredibly important embassies. By 1514, again before either of his daughters was linked to the king, he owned or had been granted the controlling interest in around twenty manors and had other grants and offices. He was a very important man, a skilled diplomat and a royal favourite, and he'd continue to be so, being granted more manors and important offices, until the falls of his son and daughter in the spring of 1536

23 June

At 4pm on Saturday 23rd June 1509, the eve of their joint coronation, King Henry VIII and his first wife, Catherine of Aragon, processed through the streets of London, from the Tower of London to Westminster in preparation for the coronation at Westminster Abbey.

Chronicler Edward Hall gives an account of their procession and how the king and queen were dressed that day. Here are his descriptions of the king and queen:

First the king:

"The features of his body, his goodly personage, his amiable visage, princely countenance, with the noble qualities of his royal estate, to every man known needeth no rehearsal, considering, that for lack of cunning, I cannot express the gifts of grace and of nature, that God hath endowed him with all: yet partly to describe his apparel, it is to be noted, his grace wore in his upperest apparel, a robe of crimson velvet, furred with ermines, his jacket or coat of raised gold, the placard embroidered with diamonds, rubies, emeralds, great pearls, and other rich stones, a great baudericke about his neck of great balasses (rubies). The trapper (trappings) of his horse, damask gold with a deep pursell of ermines..."

And the queen:

"Queen then by name Katheryne, sitting in her litter, borne by two white palfreys, the litter covered, and richly apparelled, and the palfreys trapped in white cloth of gold, her person apparelled in white satin embroidered, her hair hanging down to her Back, of a very great length, beautiful and goodly to behold, and on her head a coronal, set with many rich orient stones."

According to Hall, the streets were "hanged with tapestry, and cloth of arras", and also railed and barred, and some parts, like the south-side of Cheap and Cornhill, were hanged with cloth of gold.

As for the rest of the procession, Hall describes how the king's knights and esquires wore crimson velvet, while his gentlemen, "others of his chapel", officers and household servants wore scarlet. The barons of the Sink Ports bore the cloth of estate. Hall says if he tried to describe everything and everyone, he "should omit many things, and fail of the number, for they were very many", but goes on to say, "I dare well say, there was no lack or scarcity of cloth of tissue, cloth of gold, cloth of silver, broderie [embroidery?], or of goldsmith's works: but in more plenty and abundance, than hath been seen, or read of at any time before, and thereto many and a great number of chains of gold, and bauderickes, both massy and great."

The king's master of the horse, Sir Thomas Brandon, was described as "clothed in tissue, embroidered with roses of fine gold, and traverse hs body, a great baudericke of gold, great and massy, his horse trapped in gold, leading by a rein of silk, the king's spare horse, trapped bard wise, with harnesss embroidered with bullion gold, curiously wrought by goldsmiths..."

The queen's retinue of lords, knights, esquires and gentlemen were richly apparelled "richly apparelled in tissues, cloth of gold, of silver, tinsels, and velvets embroidered, fresh and goodly to behold", and the ladies were in "cloth of gold, cloth of silver, tinsels and velvet, with embroideries" and "every complement of the said chariots, and the draught harnessses, were powdered with ermines, mixed with cloth of gold"

Hall finishes his account by saying that the procession "with much joy and honour, came to Westminster where was high preparation made, as well for the said coronation, also for the solemn feast and jousts, therein to be had and done."

The king and queen were crowned the following day, 24th June 1509, at Westminster Abbey.

24 June

On 24th June 1532, the feast of St John the Baptist, Robert Dudley, Earl of Leicester and favourite of Elizabeth I, was born.

Robert Dudley, Earl of Leicester, was the fifth son of John Dudley, Duke of Northumberland, and his wife, Jane Guildford. Robert received a humanist education, and his tutors included the likes of John Dee, Thomas Wilson, Roger Ascham, and Robert's uncle, Sir Francis Jobson. He was brought up as a Protestant. He could write and speak Italian fluently, had knowledge of French and Latin, and had a keen interest in navigation, engineering and mathematics. He married Amy Robsart, his sweetheart, on the 4th June 1550 in the presence of King Edward VI.

In July 1553, on the death of Edward VI, Lady Jane Grey, wife of Robert's brother, Guildford Dudley, became queen, but her reign lasted just thirteen days because Mary I seized the throne. Guildford, Jane and Robert's father, John Dudley, were later executed. Robert was imprisoned and condemned to death but was fortunately released in autumn 1554. He served Mary I fighting in the Battle of St Quentin, in August 1557.

Robert became Elizabeth I's Master of the Horse shortly after her accession in November 1558 and was elected a Knight of the Garter in April 1559. It was rumoured that he and the queen, whom he'd known since childhood, were more than friends, and there was a scandal when Robert's wife, Amy, died in September 1560. There is still debate today over Elizabeth and Robert's relationship.

Elizabeth called Robert her "Eyes" and "Sweet Robin" and spoke of making him the "Protector of the Realm" when she believed she was dying from smallpox in October 1562. He went on to serve her as a privy councillor. In 1563, Elizabeth proposed that Robert should marry Mary, Queen of Scots, but this idea came to nothing.

Robert was granted Kenilworth Castle in Warwickshire in June 1563, and he famously improved it for the queen's visit in 1575, adding a gatehouse, luxury apartments and a beautiful garden. He also held a lavish celebration there that lasted over two weeks and is seen as a last-ditch attempt to win the queen's hand in marriage. It didn't work.

On his father's side, Robert was descended from Richard Beauchamp, Earl of Warwick, and so adopted the Bear and Ragged Staff heraldic device of the Earls of Warwick.

Robert had an illegitimate son, Robert Dudley, from his relationship with Lady Douglas Sheffield. This Robert Dudley (1574-1649) became a well-known explorer and cartographer, leading an expedition to the West Indies in 1594.

Robert secretly married Lettice Knollys, daughter of the queen's cousin, Catherine Carey, and Sir Francis Knollys, and widow of Walter Devereux, on 21st September 1578. The queen was furious when she found out and referred to Lettice as "the she-wolf". In 1581, Robert and Lettice had a son, Robert Dudley, Lord Denbigh, known as "the noble impe", but he died in 1584 and was buried in the Collegiate Church of St Mary in Warwick.

Robert Dudley founded Lord Leycester's Hospital in Warwick in 1571, and this beautiful Tudor building can still be seen in Warwick today. He was made commander of the English forces in the Netherlands in 1585. When the Spanish Armada threatened

England in 1588, Robert was in charge of mustering the English land forces as Lieutenant and Captain-General of the Queen's Armies and Companies. He was responsible for Elizabeth's famous visit to Tilbury, where she gave her famous Tilbury speech.

Robert supported the execution of Mary Queen of Scots in 1587 and financially supported Sir Francis Drake's circumnavigation of the world.

He was chancellor of the University of Oxford and a known patron of the Arts, being interested in theatre, literature and history. He had his own company of players and was the patron of the artist and miniaturist Nicholas Hilliard.

Robert Dudley, Earl of Leicester, died at Cornbury Park near Oxford on 4th September 1588 on his way to take the waters at Buxton for his health. Elizabeth I was distraught at the news of Robert's death and locked herself away for days. She kept the last letter he wrote to her shortly before his death, keeping it in a box beside her bed and writing "His Last Letter" on it

Robert Dudley was buried at the Collegiate Church of St Mary in Warwick and shares a tomb there with his wife, Lettice, who died in 1634. His brother, Ambrose Dudley, Earl of Warwick, is also buried there.

25 June

On 25th June 1533, thirty-seven-year-old Mary Tudor, sister of Henry VIII and wife of his friend Charles Brandon, Duke of Suffolk, died at her home of Westhorpe Hall in Suffolk. She was survived by Suffolk, her second husband, and their children: Frances, Eleanor and Henry, although Henry died in March 1534. Suffolk remarried three months later, marrying his fourteen-year-old ward, Katherine Willoughby.

It is not known what killed Mary, and theories include angina, tuberculosis and cancer. David Loades writes of how Mary was taken ill at Woodstock in 1518 and attended by royal physicians. Then in March 1520, the Duke of Suffolk wrote to Cardinal Wolsey apologising for his absence in the king's council and excusing himself by way of his wife's ill health:

> "Whereas I, of a certain space, have not given mine attendance upon your lordship in the king's council, according to my duty, I beseech your lordship to pardon me thereof. The cause why, hath been that the said French queen hath had, and yet hath, divers physicians with her, for her old disease in her side, and as yet cannot be perfectly restored to her health. And, albeit I have been two times at London, only to the intent to have waited upon your lordship, yet her grace, at either time, hath so sent for me, that 1 might not otherwise do but return home again. Nevertheless, her grace is now in such good amendment, that upon Tuesday or Wednesday next coming, I intend, by God's grace to wait upon your lordship. From Croydon the 16th day of March."

Mary also mentioned her illness in a letter to her brother, the king. Mary had, however, recovered in time to accompany the king and queen to the Field of Cloth of Gold in June 1520.

Then, in 1533, Mary was taken ill again. It is difficult to know whether it was a new illness or the same illness that had caused her problems back in 1520, which had previously troubled her. In her book, "Lives of the Princesses of England", Mary Anne Everett-Green writes how elaborate the funeral honours paid to May were. Mary's body was embalmed and then enclosed in a leaden coffin and taken to what Everett-Green describes as "the beautiful cloistered chapel adjoining the house", where a pall of richly embroidered blue velvet was draped over it and tapers burned around it for three weeks, while attendants kept watch over it. A mass was performed each day.

On Monday 20th July, mourners gathered at the chapel at Westhorpe, and a solemn dirge was sung. On Tuesday 21st July, Mary's eldest daughter, Frances, acted as chief mourner and attended mass, with family members, before the funeral. Six gentlemen carried Mary's coffin from the chapel to a "funeral-car" drawn by six horses. The cart and horses were all draped with black velvet, and the velvet on the horses was embroidered with the dowager queen's arms. A pall of cloth of gold of frize decorated with a cross and a representation of the queen in her state robes with a crown and sceptre was thrown over the coffin.

A hundred poor men in black and carrying a taper each led the procession, followed by the clergy of the chapel, knights, barons and gentlemen, then officers of the queen's household, Garter and Clarencieux kings at arms, the queen's chamberlain, all on horseback. Then came the cart, which was surrounded by a hundred torch-bearing yeomen, then the Lady Frances on horseback with the Marquess of Dorset on her right and Lord Clifford on her left. Behind them came ten ladies on horseback, each attended by a servant, and they were followed by two mourning chariots, the queen's ladies on foot, and yeomen and servants and anyone else who wanted to pay their respects.

The procession arrived at the Abbey of Bury St Edmunds at 2pm that day and was met by the parish priests. The coffin was moved to a hearse decorated with black sarcenet fringed with silk and gold and embroidered with the queen's arms and devices and her motto "La volonté de dieu me suffit". The church's pillars and aisle were draped with black cloth bearing the queen's arms. After the mourners had entered, a dirge was chanted by the clergy, and the French poursuivant, who was in attendance, cried out, "Pray for the soul of the right, high excellent princess, and right Christian queen, Mary, late French queen, and all Christian souls!"

After the ceremony, the mourners enjoyed a supper before mourners were chosen to keep watch around the hearse.

Two masses were celebrated the next morning, and after breakfast, there was a requiem mass. Mary Anne Everett Green describes how after the sermon and mass, Lady Frances and her sister retired, missing the burial, and she believes they were too overcome with grief to carry on. With them missing, the coffin was lowered into the burial site, and the head-officers of the queen's household broke their staves of office and threw them into the grave, as was traditional. There was then a dinner for everyone, and food, drink and alms were distributed to the poor of Bury St Edmunds.

Everett- Green also writes of how Mary's brother, King Henry VIII, ordered funeral services to be performed at Westminster and St Paul's

When the abbey was dissolved during the Dissolution of the

Monasteries, Mary's remains were moved to St Mary's Church, Bury St Edmunds. In the 18th century, Mary's resting place was disturbed, and locks of her hair were cut off and preserved in lockets, one of which can be seen in Bury St Edmund's Moyse's Hall Museum.

26 June

On 26th June 1596, soldier Sir John Wingfield was buried in the cathedral at Cadiz in southern Spain. Wingfield had been shot in the head in the attack on Cadiz on 21st June.

At Wingfield's funeral, according to contemporary historian John Stow, "the generalls threw their handkerchiefs wet from their eyes into the grave", and the famous poet John Donne, who was a member of the expedition and so had witnessed Wingfield's courage firsthand, composed an epigram as a tribute to Wingfield, "Farther then Wingefield, no man dares to go".

Let me give you some facts about this brave soldier:

- Sir John Wingfield was the son of landowner and courtier Richard Wingfield of Suffolk, and his wife, Mary, sister of Bess of Hardwick.
- It is thought that he served Richard Bertie, husband of the late Catherine Willoughby, Duchess of Suffolk, and that's how he met his wife, Susan, their daughter and widow of Reynold Grey, whom he married without Queen Elizabeth I's permission on 30th September 1581. The queen was angry, and Wingfield's aunt, Bess of Hardwick, Countess of Shrewsbury, tried to help by asking Sir Francis Walsingham to intercede with the queen.
- It is not known how Wingfield started his military career, but it may have been with the help of his brother-in-law, soldier Peregrine Bertie, who served as governor of Bergen op Zoom. The Wingfields named their son, born in 1586, after Peregrine. In September 1586, Wingfield fought at the Battle of Zutphen. He was wounded and knighted for his service by Robert Dudley, Earl of Leicester.
- Wingfield was back in London in February 1587 when he was part of the funeral procession for poet and soldier Sir Philip Sidney.

- He was abroad again in the summer of 1587, serving as captain of foot soldiers garrisoned at Bergen and as deputy governor for Peregrine. In July 1588, he was appointed governor of Geertruidenberg. However, it was a troubled garrison, and in March 1589, the unpaid troops mutinied and imprisoned Wingfield after a surprise attack by Maurice of Nassau, son of William of Orange. The garrison surrendered to the Spanish on 10th April 1589, and Wingfield and his wife were released. However, they were imprisoned by the Spanish and branded traitors by the Protestant Netherlands States, who believed Wingfield had communicated with Spain. The Wingfields were eventually released following the intercession of Thomas Bodley on behalf of the queen and Lord Burghley.
- It is not known exactly when Wingfield was released, but he was in London by July 1591, preparing to take a company of men to Normandy under Robert Devereux, Earl of Essex, to help King Henry IV fight the Catholic League and Spain. In France, he served as Elizabeth I's master of the ordnance and fought at the Battle of Rouen in October 1591, where he was shot but not injured, only his clothing damaged. He went on to be in charge of munitions at the storehouse in Dieppe.
- Wingfield was recalled to England in 1592 and received an honourary MA when the queen visited Oxford in September 1592. In 1593, he served as a member of Parliament for Lichfield. His biographer, Mary L Robertson, notes that Wingfield also served on committees aiming to help poor and injured soldiers and mariners.
- In June 1596, Wingfield served as camp-master and colonel of a regiment of men sailing on the Vanguard under his good friend, Robert Devereux, Earl of Essex. They sailed to Cadiz on the coast of southwestern Spain and attacked the Spanish fleet. Wingfield then led a force of 200 men in an attack on Cadiz itself, which was defended by around 500 Spanish cavalry. Wingfield and his men pretended to retreat, encouraging the Spaniards to move forward into an ambush of a much larger force of English soldiers. The English force was able to break through the city gates, but Wingfield suffered a

wound to his thigh, leaving him unable to walk. The Earl of Essex and a band of men carried on into Cadiz's plaza, and the injured Wingfield, intent on following his friend, captured a horse. As Cadiz surrendered to Essex and his force, Wingfield was shot in the head and killed instantly.

- Wingfield was buried at Cádiz Cathedral, La Iglesia de Santa Cruz, on 26th June 1596. John Stow recorded his funeral, writing that he was buried "with all the funeral solemnities of war, the drums and trumpets sounding dolefully, the shot bearing the notes of their pieces downward, the pikes trailed, his body was borne by six knights, the generals threw their handkerchiefs wet from their eyes into the grave, and at the instant the most part of all the shot great and small, aboard and ashore, were discharged."

- Wingfield's wife, Susan, who had already been living in a precarious financial situation and had had to sell her jewels and plate and borrow money, was granted an annuity of £100 by the queen in 1597.

27 June

On 27th June 1497, lawyer and member of Parliament Thomas Flamank and blacksmith Michael Joseph (known as Michael an Gof), two of the chief commanders of the Cornish rebels, were hanged, drawn and quartered at Tyburn in London.

As I explained in a previous entry (see 17th June), the two men had been involved in the Cornish Rebellion against Henry VII, which ended on 17th June 1497 at the Battle of Blackheath, or Battle of Deptford, when the Crown's forces defeated the rebels.

"The Chronicles of London" record that Flamank and Joseph were arraigned for treason at Westminster on 26th June 1497 and, on this day in history, 27th June 1497, drawn from the Tower of London, through the city, to Tyburn, and there hanged until they were dead. They were then "stricken down, and headed and after quartered." Chronicler Edward Hall gives a slightly different account, stating that they suffered a full traitor's death, i.e. being alive when they were taken down from the gallows to be disembowelled and quartered. Hall records that the king ordered Joseph and Flamank to be hanged, drawn and quartered as traitors, and "their quarters to be pitched on stakes, and set up in diverse places of Cornwall, that their sore punishments and terrible executions for their traitorous attempts and foolish hardy enterprises might be a warning for other hereafter to abstain from committing like crime and offence", but after he was told that this might provoke the Cornish into more action, he decided to have their body parts displayed in London, to avoid more trouble when he needed to focus on Scotland.

Baron Audley, who'd also been involved in the rebellion, was beheaded on Tower Hill the following day and his head displayed on London Bridge.

On Blackheath Common, there is a memorial plaque in memory of Flamank and Joseph, which was erected on 21st June 1997 by the London Cornish Association and the Cornish Gorsedd. It reads, in Cornish and English:

"In memory of Michael Joseph the Smith and Thomas Flamank, leaders of the Cornish Rebellion who marched to London. They were defeated here and suffered execution at Tyburn 27th June 1497.

They shall have a name perpetual and fame permanent and immortal."

28 June

On 28th June 1557, Philip Howard, 13th Earl of Arundel, was born at Arundel House, the Strand, London.

Philip ended up being condemned to death for treason and dying of alleged poisoning in 1589 when he was just 32, so let me tell you a bit more about him and what led him to that very sticky end.

- Philip was the only child of Thomas Howard, 4th Duke of Norfolk, and his first wife, Mary Fitzalan, second daughter and co-heir of Henry Fitzalan, 12th Earl of Arundel.
- When he was baptised in Whitehall Palace's Chapel Royal on 2nd July 1557, Mary I's husband, Philip of Spain, and Nicholas Heath, Archbishop of York, stood as his godfathers, and Elizabeth Howard, Dowager Duchess of

Norfolk, stood as his godmother. Sadly, his mother died less than a month after his birth.

- As a child, Philip was known by the courtesy title of Earl of Surrey.
- In 1569, when he was 12, Philip married twelve-year-old Anne Dacre, eldest daughter of Thomas Dacre, 4th Lord Dacre of Gilsland. The marriage was properly solemnised when the couple turned 14 in 1571.
- In 1572, Philip's father was executed for treason, and Philip lost his title of Earl of Surrey, although he was allowed to retain most of the family's property.
- In 1576, he graduated MA from St John's College, Cambridge, and then moved to the royal court of Elizabeth I, leaving his wife in the country while he resided in London in Howard House. He hosted the queen at his estates of Kenninghall and Mount Surrey on her progress in 1578, upsetting his maternal grandfather and aunt with his lavish spending on entertainment for the queen, which led to him being in debt and having to sell some of his and his wife's properties.
- His maternal grandfather, the Earl of Arundel, died in 1580, and Philip became Earl of Arundel. Philip became wealthy, owning Arundel Castle in Sussex, Arundel House in London, and other estates and properties.
- Philip and his wife had two children together, Elizabeth, born in 1583, who died in her teens, and Thomas Howard, 14th Earl of Arundel, born in 1585.
- Philip's wife, Anne, converted to Catholicism in the 1580s, during the Protestant reign of Queen Elizabeth I, and was open about her conversion. Philip, who had been brought up a Protestant, also began to favour the Catholic faith, although he hid this from the queen. However, the fact that he didn't condemn his wife's beliefs led him into trouble. In December 1583, he was interrogated about harbouring Thomas Heywood, a Jesuit priest, and placed under house arrest until the following April.
- In September 1584, at Arundel Castle, Philip officially converted, being received into the Catholic Church by William

Weston, a Jesuit priest. He still kept his faith hidden and began planning to go into exile abroad.

- In April 1585, after writing the queen a letter explaining his reason for leaving England - his religious conscience - but assuring the queen that he was still her loyal servant, Philip set sail from Littlehampton on the Sussex coast, leaving his pregnant wife and daughter behind. Unfortunately, he was apprehended in the English Channel when his ship was boarded, and he was escorted to the Tower of London.

- Philip was taken before the Star Chamber and accused of being a Roman Catholic, leaving the country without the queen's permission, and claiming the dukedom of Norfolk. In May 1586, he was fined £10,000.

- Nearly three years later, in April 1589, he was tried, attainted and condemned to death after another Catholic claimed, while being tortured, that during their time in the Tower, Philip had arranged a secret mass for the success of the Spanish Armada. However, the queen did not sign his death warrant, and he kept his head and remained in prison, where he worked on religious translations and treatises on virtue.

- In August 1595, after over ten years of imprisonment, Philip became ill. He asked the queen's permission to see Anne and their children, and the queen replied, "If he will but once attend the Protestant Service, he shall not only see his wife and children, but be restored to his honors and estates with every mark of my royal favor." Philip remained firm in his faith and refused.

- He died at the Tower of London on 15th October 1595, some sources state 19th, from dysentery or malnutrition, although it was rumoured that he had been poisoned by his cook, who allegedly poisoned the sauce of a roasted teal.

- On 22nd October 1595, Philip was laid to rest in the Chapel of St Peter ad Vincula at the Tower of London. In 1624, his widow and son arranged for his remains to be brought to the Countess's home at West Horsley in Surrey, where they were put in an iron coffin before being taken to the Fitzalan Chapel of Arundel Castle and buried in a vault. In 1971, his remains were moved once more, this time to Arundel Cathedral. His son, Thomas, was restored in blood as 14th Earl of Arundel in 1604.

- Philip was beatified in 1929 and then canonised as a Catholic martyr in 1970. In 1973, his resting place, Arundel Cathedral, was dedicated to "Our Lady and St Philip Howard".

29 June

On 29th June 1537, Henry Algernon Percy, 6th Earl of Northumberland, died at around the age of thirty-five. He was buried at Hackney Parish Church, and his will appointed the king as supervisor and Edward Fox, Bishop of Hereford, and Thomas Cromwell as executors.

Henry Percy was born around 1502 and was the eldest son of Henry Algernon Percy, 5th Earl of Northumberland, and his wife, Katherine Spencer. He was brought up in Cardinal Wolsey's household, and while he was there, he fell in love with Anne Boleyn after her return to the English court in late 1521. Anne was serving Queen Catherine of Aragon as one of her ladies. George Cavendish, Wolsey's gentleman-usher, recorded that when the cardinal and his servants were at court, Percy "would then resort for his pastime unto the queen's chamber, and there would fall in dalliance among the queen's ladies, being at the last more conversant with Mistress Anne Boleyn than with any other." It was then "that there grew such a secret love between them that, at length, they were ensured together, intending to marry."

Unfortunately for the two lovebirds, they were supposed to be marrying other people. Percy's father had already planned Percy's marriage to Mary Talbot, daughter of George Talbot, fourth Earl of Shrewsbury. Anne was meant to marry James Butler, son of Piers Butler of Ireland. Cavendish also states that King Henry VIII was "much offended" at the news of the couple's romance because of his own "secret affection" for Anne. Consequently, Wolsey and Percy's father put a stop to the relationship. Percy married Mary Talbot in 1524, but the marriage was far from happy. In 1532, Mary accused her husband of being pre-contracted to Anne Boleyn and Percy was examined by the Dyke of Norfolk and the Archbishops of York and Canterbury. He swore on the blessed sacrament in front of the duke, the archbishops and the king's canon lawyers that there was no truth to his wife's story. Percy had to deny the precontract's existence again in 1536 when Thomas Cromwell was looking for a way to get the marriage of Henry VIII and Anne Boleyn annulled.

Percy served Henry VIII as warden of the East and Middle Marches and was one of the peers appointed to judge George and Anne Boleyn at their trial on 15th May 1536. Percy collapsed after Anne's death sentence was pronounced. His illness prevented him from taking an active role in the Pilgrimage of Grace rebellion of late 1536. This may have been fortunate, since his brothers, Thomas and Ingram, were arrested for their involvement, and Thomas was executed. Ingram died in prison in the Tower of London.

Antiquary John Weever, in his book "Ancient Funerall Monuments", mentions the tomb of Henry Percy at Hackney and records that it had the following inscription: "Here lieth interred, Henry lord Percy, earl of Northumberland, knight of the most honourable order of the Garter, who died in this town the last of June 1537, the 29th of HEN VIII."

30 June

On 30th June 1559, King Henry II of France suffered a mortal head wound while jousting. He died on 10th July and was succeeded by his son, Francis II.

Henry was the second son of King Francis I and Queen Claude of France. In 1533, at 14, he'd married Catherine de' Medici, and in 1536, he became heir to the French throne following the death of his older brother, Francis, Duke of Brittany, after a game of tennis. Henry's father died in March 1547, and Henry became King Henry II.

During his 12-year reign, Henry persecuted the Huguenots (French Protestant), and warred with Austria. In 1558, following the marriage of his son, the Dauphin Francis to Mary, Queen of Scots, and the death of Queen Mary I of England, Henry proclaimed the couple the rightful King and Queen of England.

In 1559, the Peace of Cateau-Cambrésis ended the Italian Wars. The Italian Wars were a series of wars that had been rumbling on between the Houses of Valois and Habsburg since 1494 and had been resurrected by Henry II in 1551 as he tried to lay claim once more to Italy. Unfortunately for Henry, France had been soundly beaten in the most recent battles, so it was time to make peace. The terms of the peace treaty included the agreement of a marriage between Philip and Elisabeth of Valois, King Henry II of France's daughter. Emmanuel-Philibert of Savoy also married Margaret of France, Duchess of Berry, Henry II's sister. To celebrate the treaty and the marriage of his daughter, Henry II arranged a tournament at the Place Royale at the Hôtel des Tournelles. Henry was a keen sportsman and loved jousting, so he participated in the joust on 30th June 1559, wearing the colours of Diane de Poitiers. Sadly, he suffered a fatal injury while jousting against Gabriel Montgomery, Captain of the King's Scottish Guard. Splinters from Montgomery's lance entered his right eye. His physicians Ambroise Paré and Andreas Vesalius did their best to try and save the king, but he died eleven days later, on 10th July 1559.

In their article "The Death of Henry II, King of France (1519-1559). From Myth to Medical and Historical Fact", Marc Zanello, Philippe Charlier, Robert Corns, Bertrand Devaux, Patrick Berche, and Johan Pallud use contemporary accounts and modern medical knowledge to conclude, "Henry II was the victim of craniofacial trauma involving the right eye and that he died from periorbital cellulitis caused by a retained foreign body in the wound, complicated by a left interhemispheric empyema preceded by a traumatic interhemispheric haematoma". They go on to say, "It would appear that the royal court doctors advocated a wait-and-see strategy, with little actual input from Ambroise Paré or Andreas Vesalius, with a clearly regrettable outcome."

The French Reformed theologian and scholar, Theodore Beza, wrote of the king's death:

> "Tool of bad men, Henry, thy thirst for blood
> Fit retribution found,
> From thy pierced eyeball gushed a purple flood
> Which crimsoned all the ground."

Henry was buried in the royal mausoleum of the Basilica of St-Denis, just outside Paris.

Henry was succeeded by his fifteen-year-old son, Francis II, with Mary, Queen of Scots, as his consort. Francis only reigned for just over a year, dying in December 1560 from complications from an ear infection.

1 July

On 1st July 1535, Sir Thomas More, Henry VIII's former Lord Chancellor, was tried for high treason by a special commission of oyer and terminer. He was found guilty and was executed on 6th July 1535.

Sir Thomas More once famously said of King Henry VIII that "if my head would win him a castle in France, it should not fail to go", and I often wonder how serious he was. Was it said in jest, or did More know exactly what Henry VIII was capable of? It's impossible to know, but his closeness to the king cost him his life.

In 1531, More refused to sign the Oath of Supremacy declaring that Henry VIII was Supreme Head of the English Church because he believed that this position belonged to the pope. He offered to resign several times and Henry finally accepted his resignation in 1532. More then refused to swear his allegiance to the Act of Succession, although he accepted Parliament's right to declare Anne Boleyn as queen, because he could not accept the part of the Act which asserted Parliament's authority to legislate in religious matters. In More's opinion, only the pope had this right. Resignation and silence were not enough for the king and his followers. More's refusal to sign the oath, and his refusal to attend Anne Boleyn's coronation, led to him being arrested for treason on charges of "praemunire".

On many occasions, Thomas Cromwell tried to persuade More to sign the oath, but More's conscience would not allow him to back down on matters of faith, and he ended up going to trial.

Letters and Papers, Foreign and Domestic, Henry VIII, includes a record of the commission of oyer and terminer which tried Sir Thomas More, Henry VIII's former chancellor, for treason on 1st July 1535, including a list of those who sat in judgement on More:

Sir Thomas Audley, More's replacement as chancellor; Thomas Howard, 3rd Duke of Norfolk; Charles Brandon, Duke of Suffolk; Henry Clifford, Earl of Cumberland; Thomas Boleyn, Earl of Wiltshire; George Hastings, Earl of Huntingdon; Henry, Lord Montagu; George Boleyn, Lord Rochford; Andrew, Lord Windsor; Thomas Cromwell, secretary; Sir William Fitzwilliam; Sir William Paulet; Sir John Fitzjames; Sir John Baldwyn; Sir Richard Lister;

Sir John Port; Sir John Spelman; Sir Walter Luke; and Sir Anthony Fitzherbert."

How fickle the Tudor court could be.

But what was Sir Thomas More charged with? He was tried for high treason for denying the validity of the new Act of Succession. The indictment stated that More had traitorously attempted to deprive the king of the title of the Supreme Head of the Church, and that he had written to his fellow prisoner Bishop John Fisher, saying, "The Act of Parliament is like a sword with two-edges, for if a man answer one way it will confound his soul, and if he answer the other way it will confound his body". This is something that he'd repeated during interrogations. More had held on to the belief that if he did not voice his denial of the king's supremacy over the Church in England, then he could not be found guilty, but unfortunately, Cromwell produced Richard Rich to claim that he had heard More deny that the king was head of the Church. After hearing this, More spoke up and said that "no temporal man may be the head of the spirituality"

At his trial at Westminster, More pleaded "Not guilty", but he was found guilty under the Treason Act of 1534 and sentenced to a full traitor's death to be carried out at Tyburn, although this was commuted to beheading on Tower Hill.

More was beatified on 29th December 1886 by Pope Leo XIII and then canonised on 19th May 1935. In 2000, Pope John Paul II declared him "the heavenly Patron of Statesmen and Politicians". More and his friend, Bishop John Fisher, who was executed on 22nd June 1535, are remembered by Catholics with a feast day on 22nd June every year.

2 July

On 2nd July 1536, Thomas Cromwell, the king's right-hand man, was formally appointed Lord Privy Seal.

The previous holder of the office had been Thomas Boleyn, Earl of Wiltshire. Wiltshire had held the office since January 1530, but he was stripped of the office on 29th June 1536, just over a month after the executions of his children, Queen Anne Boleyn and George Boleyn, Lord Rochford.

The record of Cromwell's appointment in Letters & Papers, dated 1st July 28th year of Henry VIII's reign, reads:

"Th. Crumwell. Appointment as keeper of the Privy Seal, with fees of 20s. a day, or 365 pounds. a year; 90 pounds thereof out of the customs of Pole, 200 pounds small custom of London, 56 pounds 13s. 4d customs of Bristol, and the remaining 18 pounds 6s. 8d customs of Plymmouthe and Fowey, the office having been granted during pleasure to Thomas earl of Wiltshire and Ormond by patent. 23 Jan. 21 Hen. VIII. Westm."

But what is the privy seal, and what does it mean to be Lord Privy Seal?

Well, the privy seal is not to be confused with the Great Seal of State, which the Lord Chancellor held. The privy (or private) seal was the personal seal of the monarch, in this case, Henry VIII, which was used for authenticating documents. The Lord Privy Seal was the keeper of this seal and was one of the top officers of state, coming below the chancellor and treasurer.

The Encyclopaedia Britannica explains that the first privy seal was used by King John, who ruled from 1199 to 1216, but back then, it was kept by the clerks of the king's chamber. Then, in the reign of King Henry III, it was transferred to the Wardrobe, and in the reigns of Kings Edward I and Edward II, it was kept by the comptroller of the Wardrobe. In 1311, the seal was transferred to its own keeper, and the term Lord Privy Seal was first used in the 15th century when Richard Foxe, Bishop of Winchester, was its custodian. The monarch would produce writs of privy seal that would have his personal seal on them and authorise his chancellor to issue letters under the great seal. The Encyclopaedia also explains that the "privy seal was used for royal letters sent to foreign monarchs and to officers and subjects in England as well as those overseas."

As well as Thomas Boleyn and Thomas Cromwell, Tudor Lord Privy Seals included Cuthbert Tunstall, Bishop of London; Sir Nicholas Bacon; William Cecil, Lord Burghley; William Howard, 1st Baron Howard of Effingham; Sir Francis Walsingham, and Robert Cecil, Earl of Salisbury.

The office of Lord Privy Seal is still going today. The UK

government's website states, "The Lord Privy Seal is responsible for the organisation of government business in the House, providing assistance to all Lords and offering advice on procedure. The Lord Privy Seal also expresses the collective feelings of the House on formal occasions, such as motions of thanks or congratulations."

3 July

On 3rd July 1495, the pretender Perkin Warbeck landed at Deal in Kent with men and ships. In the ensuing battle, the Battle of Deal, with Kentish men who supported King Henry VII, around 150 of Warbeck's men were killed and over 160 captured. Warbeck managed to escape, fleeing to Ireland.

Warbeck claimed to be Richard of Shrewsbury, Duke of York, the younger of the Princes in the Tower. With Yorkist support and that of Margaret, Dowager Duchess of Burgundy, and Emperor Maximilian, he set about claiming the throne.

Here's an account of Warbeck's landing at Deal taken from Sir Frederick Madden's 19th-century work on Warbeck based on contemporary sources.

"It was in the course of the summer immediately following, that Perkin having received from Maximilian, Philip and Margaret, the aid of ships and men, made his first attempt on the coast of England, and on the 3rd July, 1495, landed a portion of his troops at Deal in Kent. The time had been well chosen (having probably been previously concerted with some secret agent in England) for Henry was then engaged on a progress towards the north, and did not return till the middle of October. Had the adventurer indeed at this period been joined by any persons of rank, or his cause espoused by the people, as he had vainly been led to hope, the issue might have been very different. Finding, however, that the forces he had landed were received as enemies, and either slain or captured, he immediately altered his course, and steered towards Ireland, where with the assistance of the Earl of Desmond, he laid siege to Waterford; but having been compelled to raise the siege by an army under the command of the Lord Deputy, and having lost three of his ships, he retreated with precipitation, and returned again to Flanders, re infecta."

A contemporary account is given in Edward Hall's chronicle. In it, Hall writes that while Henry VII was on his progress to Lancashire, "there to recreate his spirits and solace himself with his mother the Lady Margaret", Warbeck, who was in Flanders, "determined not to leave the hope and trust that he had conceived in his mad head to obtain the crown and realm of England". Warbeck gathered what Hall describes as "a great army of valiant Captains of all nations", which included Englishmen in exile, thieves, robbers and vagabonds, a "rabblement of knaves", and departed from Flanders in ships provided by his supporters. Hall writes that he didn't have a fixed place to land in mind, just "wheresoever the wind brought him", and the wind drove him on the coast of Kent, where he cast his anchors. He decided "to make exploration and enquiry whether the Kentishmen would take his part and follow him as their captain", as in the past they had shown themselves "not timorous or afraid of their own mind in troubleous seasons to move war against their princes."

In the meantime, Hall explains, the Kentishmen had heard "that this feigned duke was come, and had heard that he was but a painted image" and were considering what to do, whether to help him or support their kind. They considered "how small a profit" had been earned in previous rebellions and concluded that this pretender came "to spoil, destroy and waste the country" rather than "to conquer it for their wealth and commodity", and he was also bringing strangers and foreigners with him. So, the Kentish men decided not to support Warbeck and instead decided that they should lure his men off their ships "by fair promises and friendly words" and then fight them.

Warbeck was suspicious, so he decided to stay on board his ship until he was sure of their support, but he did allow his men to go ashore. They were surrounded and attacked by the Kentish men, "& at one stroke vanquished and driven back to their ships, & there were take prisoners an hundred and sixty persons". Hall states that the captured rebels were taken to London "railed in ropes like horses drawn in a cart", tried and executed, some in London and some in coastal towns.

Hall concludes his account of Warbeck's landing by saying, "Wherefore Perkyn failing of his purpose fled back into Flanders and there tarried, consulting with his friends until such time as he had better prepared for things to come more prudently then he had done before time."

Warbeck landed for a second time in England on 7ᵗʰ September 1497, landing at Whitesand Bay, near Land's End, in Cornwall. He challenged Henry VII's claim to the throne by raising a rebellion in Cornwall after being declared King Richard IV on Bodmin. However, the rebellion was squashed, and Warbeck was captured and imprisoned. He was hanged at Tyburn on 23ʳᵈ November 1499 after escaping twice from the Tower of London and being recaptured.

4 July

On 4ᵗʰ July 1533, thirty-year-old reformer and theologian John Frith, who hailed from Kent, was burnt at the stake at Smithfield for heresy. He had been charged with heresy because of his religious views, which included his belief that Christ's words about the sacrament, "This is my body", were not to be taken literally, and his belief that Purgatory did not exist. Frith was given a chance to recant, but he refused. He was burnt with Andrew Hewet, a young tailor's apprentice, who refused to recant his belief that the sacrament was not "really the body of Christ, born of the Virgin Mary".

Frith had been educated at Eton College and then King's College, Cambridge, before being called to Cardinal's College, Oxford, by Cardinal Thomas Wolsey. According to Fox, while he was there, he was imprisoned in "a prison of the college where salt-fish lay" for heresy but later released, fleeing to Antwerp, where reformer and Bible translator William Tyndale was based. While Frith was abroad, he worked on an English translation of Patrick Hamilton's "Divers Fruitful Gatherings of Scripture", "A revelation of Antichrist" with Martin de Keyser, which was a translation of Martin Luther's work, and the "Disputacion of Purgatorye", which was to get him into so much trouble later.

Frith returned to England in July 1531 and ended up in the stocks at Reading. Then Sir Thomas More issued a warrant for his arrest for heresy, and although he tried to hide and disguise himself and flee back to Antwerp, he was apprehended in Essex. While imprisoned, he produced more religious works that would be used against him. He also wrote "'The Articles wherefore John Frith dyed which he wrote in Newgate the 23 day of June the yeare of our lorde 1533".

Martyrologist John Foxe gives an account of Frith's life, examination and martyrdom in his book "The Acts and Monuments of the Christian Church". His account starts with the words:

> "Amongst all other chances lamentable,: there hath been none a great time which seemed unto me more grievous, than the lamentable death and cruel handling of John Frith, so learned and excellent a young man; which had so profited in all kind of learning and knowledge, that scarcely there was his equal amongst all his companions; and besides, withal, had such a godliness of life joined with his doctrine, that it was hard to judge in whether of them he was more commendable, being greatly praiseworthy in them both: but as touching his doctrine, by the grace of Christ we will speak hereafter."

Here's an extract about the executions of Frith and Hewet:

> "Wherefore on the fourth day of July, in the afternoon, he [Hewet] was carried into Smithfield with Frith, and there burned.
>
> The wind made his death somewhat the longer, which bare away the flame from him unto his fellow that was tied to his back … but God giving him strength, that even as though he had felt no pain in that long torment, he seemed rather to rejoice for his fellow, than to be careful for himself.
>
> When they were at the stake, one Doctor Cook, a parson in London, openly admonished all the people, that they should in no wise pray for them, no more than they would do for a dog; at which words Frith, smiling, desired the Lord to forgive him. These his words did not a little move the people unto anger, and not without good cause. Thus these two blessed martyrs committed their souls into the hands of God."

Chronicler Edward Hall also recorded their ends, although he gives 22nd July as their execution date. He describes Frith as being "very well learned" with "an excellent goodly wit" who had been imprisoned for "making of a book against Purgatory". He writes of how a tailor called William Holt, "which outwardly professed much honesty, but inwardly was a very spy and a very betrayer of as many men as he might bring in danger", obtained Frith's work from a friend of Frith and gave it to Sir Thomas More. Frith then underwent "diverse and sundry examinations and was taken before the consistory in St Paul's Church. He was condemned and delivered to the secular authorities to be burnt as a heretic.

Hall describes Andrew Hewet as "a very simple and utterly unlearned young man, a Taylor, which was also betrayed by the aforesaid Holt" and writes of how he was also accused in the Consistory "for holding opinion against the Sacrament."

Hall states that Frith and Hewet were both burnt at one stake at Smithfield.

Hall also mentions Doctor Cook:

> "one doctor Cook, which was person of Honey Lane,
> & one that was the Master of the Temple, willed the
> people to pray no more for them than they would pray
> for dogs, at which uncharitable words Frith smiled &
> prayed God to forgive them, and the people sore grudged
> at them for so saying."

Chronicler and Windsor herald Charles Wriothesley simply recorded:

> "This year, in July, on a Friday, one Frith, a serving
> man, a great clerk in the Greek and Latin tongue, was
> burnt in Smithfield, and a tailor of London with him,
> for heresy."

Frith's biographer, David Daniell, writes of how Frith's death "caused widespread grief in London and elsewhere in England, and also on the continent; he was mourned as a talented, modest, and good young man. His later influence was important, for the articles which he set out shortly before his execution differ little from those adopted by the reformed church in the prayer book of 1552."

5 July

On 5th July 1589, Joan Cunny (Cony), one of the notorious 'Essex Witches', was hanged at Chelmsford in Essex.

Joan Cunny was born around 1508 and was from Stisted in Essex. She was accused of killing her neighbours and causing a great storm. Cunny had told of how she had learnt witchcraft twenty years earlier from a woman who had told her to kneel in a circle and pray to Satan to conjure her familiar and spirits. She'd done that and had given these spirits her soul before taking the spirits home with her to feed them. Joan then used these spirits for evil acts.

The pre-trial examination of Joan Cunny, along with those of Joan Prentice and Joan Upney, was published in 1589 as "The Apprehension and Confession of Three Notorious Witches", a pamphlet that was sold because these women's crimes became so notorious. As historian Kate Cole has pointed out, this pamphlet was more a tabloid report full of gossip and tittle-tattle rather than a serious account.

This pamphlet said of Joan Cunny:

"Joan Cunny, living very lewdly, having two lewd daughters, no better than naughty packs, had two bastard children: being both boys, these two children were chief witnesses, and gave in great evidence against their Grandam and Mothers, the eldest being about 10 or 12 years of age.

Against this mother Cunny the elder boy gave in this evidence which she herself after confessed, that she was going to Braintree Market, came to one Harry Finch's house, to demand some drink, his wife being busy and a brewing, told her she had no pleasure to give her any. Then Joan Cunny went away discontented, and at night Finch's wife was grievously taken in her head, and the next day in her side, and so continued in most horrible pain for the space of a week and then died."

It was believed that Joan had used her witchcraft on Finch's wife.

Joan Cunny's daughters, Avice and Margaret, were also charged with witchcraft in 1589. Avice was sentenced to hang, like her mother, but pleaded pregnancy and so was hanged in 1590 after the birth of her baby. Margaret was found guilty of two counts of bewitchment and sentenced to a year of imprisonment and six appearances in the stocks. Avice and Margaret's illegitimate sons, Joan's grandsons, were among those who accused these women of witchcraft.

Joan Prentice, who allegedly had a ferret-shaped familiar named Satan who sucked her blood and allegedly killed a child, was also hanged on 5th July, as was Joan Upney of Dagenham, whose daughters were also accused of witchcraft. Upney was accused of two murders. Kate Cole explains that the women hanged on this day in 1589 for murder by witchcraft hadn't been working together and probably didn't know each other.

These three women were three of thirty-one Essex people (thirty women and one man) accused of witchcraft under the 1563 Witchcraft Act, full name: An Act Against Conjurations, Enchantments and Witchcrafts (5 Eliz. I c. 16). According to this act, anyone who did "use, practise, or exercise any Witchcraft, Enchantment, Charm, or Sorcery, whereby any person shall happen to be killed or destroyed" was to be put to death.

Trivia: Kate Cole has pointed out that English witches were prosecuted for murder and therefore hanged to death, hanging being the punishment for murder, whereas witches in Scotland were tried for heresy and therefore burnt at the stake.

6 July

On Tuesday 6th July 1535, Henry VIII's former friend and Lord Chancellor, Sir Thomas More, was beheaded on Tower Hill as a traitor.

More had been found guilty of high treason under the Treason Act of 1534 for denying the king's supremacy and refusing to take the Oath of Succession. The punishment for high treason was death, and he was lucky that his sentence was commuted from being hanged, drawn and quartered to beheading.

Chronicler Charles Wriothesley recorded his death as follows:

"This year also, the first day of July, being Thursday,
Sir Thomas More, knight, sometime Chancellor of
England, was arraigned at Westminster for high treason
and there condemned, and the Tuesday after, being the

6th of July, he was beheaded at the Tower Hill, and his body was buried within the chappel in the Tower of London, and his head was set on London Bridge. The effect of his death was for the same cause that the Bishop of Rochester died for."

Chronicler Edward Hall wrote:

"Also the vi. day of July was Sir Thomas More beheaded for the like treason before rehearsed, which as you have heard was for the denying of the king's Majesty's supremacy. This man was also counted learnèd, & as you have heard before he was lord Chancelor of England, and in that time a great persecutor of such as detested the supremacy of the bishop of Rome, which he himself so highly favored that he stood to it till he was brought to the Scaffold on the Tower hill where on a block his head was stricken from his shoulders and had no more harm.

I cannot tell whether I should call him a foolish wiseman, or a wisefoolishman, for undoubtedly he beside his learning, had a great wit, but it was so mingled with taunting and mocking, that it seemed to them that best knew him, that he thought nothing to be well spoken except he had ministered some mock in the communication insomuch as at his coming to the Tower, one of the officers demanded his upper garment for his fee, meaning his gown, and he answered, he should have it, and took him his cap, saying it was the uppermost garment that he had. Like-wise, even going to his death at the Tower gate, a poor woman called unto him and besought him to declare that he had certain evidences of hers in the time that he was in office (which after he was apprehended she could not come by) and that he would entreat she might have them again, or else she was undone. He answered, good woman have patience a little while, for the king is so good unto me that even within this half hour he will discharge me of all businesses, and help thee himself. Also when he went up the stair on the Scaffold, he desired one of the Sheriff's officers to give him his hand to help him up, and said, when I come down again, let me shift for my self aswell as I can. Also the hangman kneeled down to him asking him forgiveness of his death (as the manner is) to whom he said I forgive thee, but I promise thee that thou shalt never have honesty of the striking of my head, my neck is so short. Also even when he should lay down his head on the block, he having a great grey beard, striked out his beard and said to the hangman, I pray you let me lay my beard over the block lest ye should cut it, thus with a mock he ended his life."

A document in Letters and Papers gives the following information about More after his trial and about his execution:

"On his way to the Tower one of his daughters, named Margaret, pushed through the archers and guards, and held him in her embrace some time without being able to speak. Afterwards More, asking leave of the archers, bade her have patience, for it was God's will, and she had long known the secret of his heart. After going 10 or 12 steps she returned and embraced him again, to which he said nothing, except to bid her pray to God for his soul; and this without tears or change of colour. On the Tuesday following he was beheaded in the open space in front of the Tower. A little before his death he asked those present to pray to God for him and he would do the same for them [in the other world.] He then besought them earnestly to pray to God to give the King good counsel, protesting that he died his faithful servant, but God's first.

Such was the miserable end of More, who was formerly in great reputation, and much loved by the King, his master, and regarded by all as a good man, even to his death."

As Wriothesley says, his body was buried at the Chapel of St Peter ad Vincula, at the Tower of London, and his head put on a spike on London Bridge. Heads would eventually be thrown into the River Thames, but More's wasn't. E. E. Reynolds, in the book "Margaret

Roper: Eldest Daughter of St Thomas More", quotes Thomas Stapleton, an early biographer of Thomas More:

"[The head] by order of the king, was placed upon a stake on London Bridge, where it remained for nearly a month, until it had to be taken down to make room for other heads ... The head would have been thrown into the river had not Margaret Roper, who had been watching carefully and waiting for the opportunity, bribed the executioner, whose office it was to remove the heads, and obtained possession of the sacred relic. There was no possibility of mistake, for she, with the help of others, had kept careful watch, and, moreover, there were signs so certain that anyone who had known him in life would have been able now to identify the head."

Reynolds then explains:

"After the death of Margaret Roper, the head was in the keeping of her eldest daughter, Elizabeth, Lady Bray, and it was probably at her death in 1558 that it was placed in the Roper vault under the Chapel of St. Nicholas in St. Dunstan's, Canterbury.

It was seen there in 1835 when, by accident, the roof of the vault was broken; the head was enclosed in a leaden case with one side open; this stood in a niche protected by an iron grille. The vault was later sealed, but a tablet on the floor above bears the inscription:

"Beneath this floor is the vault of the Roper family in which is interred the head of Sir Thomas More of illustrious memory, sometime Lord Chancellor of England, beheaded on Tower hill 6th July 1535. Ecclesia Anglicana libera sit."

In the article "The scull [sic] of Sir Thomas More", in The Gentleman's Magazine of May 1837, there is the following quote about More's head being seen in the vault in the 18th century: "Dr. [then Mr.] Rawlinson informed Hearne, that when the vault was opened in 1715, to enter into one of the Roper's family, the box was seen enclosed in an iron grate."

7 July

On 7th July 1556, in the reign of Queen Mary I, Henry Peckham and John Danyell were hanged, drawn and quartered after being found guilty of treason for their involvement in the Dudley Conspiracy.

Merchant-tailor Henry Machyn recorded their executions in his diary:

> "The 7th day of July was hanged on the gallows on Tower Hill for treason against the queen, one master Harry Peckham, and the other master John Daneell, and after cut down and beheaded, and their heads carried unto London Bridge and there set up, and their bodies buried at All Hallows-Barking."

But who were these men, and what was the Dudley Conspiracy?

Henry Peckham was the son of Sir Edmund Peckham, a man who had served King Henry VIII in many different offices, who was instrumental in helping Mary I seize the throne in July 1553 and who was rewarded with a position on her privy council. Henry married Elizabeth Dacres, a niece of Sir Anthony Denny, in 1547, and it is thought that Elizabeth and her family had a role in converting Henry to Protestantism. However, he opposed the plan to put Lady Jane Grey on the throne in 1553 and supported Queen Mary I during Wyatt's Rebellion in 1554, helping defend Ludgate from the rebels. The queen rewarded his efforts with several manors, but historian David Loades notes Henry's discontent – Henry claimed that the queen had "given him but one hundred marks a yere and taken away four".

In 1555 Henry became involved with a group of men who included Sir Henry Dudley, a relative of both the late Henry Grey, Duke of Suffolk and father of Lady Jane Grey, and the late John Dudley, Duke of Northumberland, men who had been executed by Mary I. Dudley had become unhappy with Spanish interference in England, the result of Mary I's marriage to Philip of Spain, and the persecution of Protestants, so together with men including Sir Anthony Kingston, John Throckmorton, Christopher Ashton, Sir Henry Killigrew, and Richard Uvedale had hatched a plot, which would be supported by the French king, to lead an invasion of English exiles from France to remove Mary I from the throne and to replace her with her half-sister Elizabeth. To do this, they would steal £50,000 worth of silver bullion from the exchequer. The men met at Henry Peckham's rooms at Blackfriars, where they planned to store the silver bullion.

Unfortunately for the conspirators, the plot came to light in spring 1556 when Cardinal Reginald Pole got wind of it. Several plotters, including Henry Peckham, were arrested in March 1556 and sent to the Tower of London. On 7th May 1556, Peckham and fellow conspirator John Danyell were tried for treason at Guildhall. His brother Robert, a privy councillor, tried to help him, claiming that Peckham had joined the conspiracy only to spy on the plotters, but his intervention made no difference.

The plot was huge, and it took the Crown three months to arrest and interrogate alleged conspirators, including members of Mary I's half-sister Elizabeth's household and Exchequer officials. Thirty-six plotters were indicted, and ten were executed, including Peckham, Danyell, John Throckmorton, and Richard Uvedale. Sir Anthony Kingston died on his way to London for interrogation. However, Sir Henry Dudley, who was abroad when the plot was discovered, was safe in exile and died soon after his return to England in the mid-1560s, in the reign of Elizabeth I.

On 7th July 1556, three conspirators were scheduled to be executed, but William West, 1st Baron Delaware, was reprieved and later pardoned. The Venetian ambassador recorded:

> "Of the three individuals sentenced to death, only two were executed, but being of noble birth, it was granted them as an especial favour not to be put to death at Tyburn, but on Tower Hill, the place of execution for chief lords and gentlemen. By their dying speech delivered to the populace as usual, they seemed to make so Christian and Catholic an end, that neither greater faith, nor more true and certain knowledge of God, could have been desired in anyone, so that not only were the people greatly affected, but also many noblemen and persons of quality who had flocked thither; no one having been able from compassion to restrain their tears, whilst all, both good and bad, admitted that the execution was just and holy."

Mary I was distressed and furious. The French ambassador recorded, "She is utterly confounded by the faithlessness of those whom she most trusted, seeing that the greater part of these miserable creatures are kith and kin or favoured servants of the greatest men in the kingdom, even Lords of the Council." It showed just how disenchanted some of her subjects were with her marriage and religious policies.

8 July

On 8th July 1503, during the reign of King Henry VII, Thomas Boleyn, father of Anne Boleyn, left Collyweston in Northamptonshire to undertake an important job for the king.

Thomas had been appointed as a member of a large retinue headed by his father-in-law, Thomas Howard, Earl of Surrey, to escort Henry VII's daughter, thirteen-year-old Princess Margaret, on her journey to Edinburgh, Scotland. Margaret was travelling to Scotland to prepare for her marriage to thirty-year-old King James IV of Scotland.

Margaret and her escorts had left Richmond Palace to travel to Collyweston, home of her paternal grandmother, Lady Margaret Beaufort, on 27th June 1503. They were accompanied that far by King Henry VII. The party spent eleven days there before starting their journey north. The journey took just over three weeks, and stops included Grantham, York, Durham, Newcastle and Berwick. On 1st August, they arrived in Scotland, and Margaret and the Scottish king were married at the Palace of Holyroodhouse, in Edinburgh, by the Archbishops of York and Glasgow on 8th August 1503. Thomas Boleyn enjoyed five days of celebrations before leaving Edinburgh for home.

Here is John Leland's account of the journey:

> "The Year of the Incarnation of our Lord God, a Thousand Five hundreth and Three, the Twenty-seventh Day of June, was transported out of his Manor of Richmond, the right high, right mighty, and right excellent and most Christian Prince, Henry by the Grace of God, King of England and of France, Lord of Ireland, the Seventh of his Name, and in the 18th Year of his

reign, towards Coliweston, a Place of the right high and mighty Princess my Lady his Mother, accompanied of the right excellent Princess the said Margaret Queen of the Scots, his first begotten Daughter, And he being at Coliweston the 8th Day of the Month of July following, gave her Licence, and made her to be conveyed very nobly out of his said Realm; as more plainly shall be here following remembered, toward the right high and mighty and right excellent Prince James, by the Grace of God, King of Scots, in following the good Life, fraternal Dilection, and Intelligence of Marriage betwix him and the said Queen — The Holy Ghost, by his Grace, will maintain them in long Prosperity.

First, in the said Conveying, was ordained by the King, for Principal, the Earl of Surrey, Treasurer of England, very nobly arrayed, and all his Train. And also many Nobles, Lords, Knights, and Squires in his Company, together with my Lady his Wife, accompanied of many Ladies and Gentlewomen very nobly arrayed. Of the which it was a fair Sight, to the great Joy of all Nobless, there to be, to the End of the Performation of the said Marriage, and after the said Marriage made and accomplished, they returned."

In "The manuscripts of His Grace the Duke of Rutland: preserved at Belvoir Castle" is a "List of persons who accompanied the Queen into Scotland", and Thomas Boleyn's name can be found in the section "These be the names of them that were at the high feast with the Queen that be no knights". He's listed as "Master — Bolen, son and heir of Sir William Boleyn." To be a part of this retinue was an honour for Thomas Boleyn.

9 July

On 9th July 1553, the day after she had declared herself queen in front of her household at Kenninghall, Mary, daughter of the late King Henry VIII and his first wife, Catherine of Aragon, wrote an important letter to the privy council.

On 3rd July 1553, Mary was at Hunsdon when she received news that her half-brother, King Edward VI, was dying and that there was an "aristocratic conspiracy aimed at her destruction". She decided it was safer to make her way to her estates in East Anglia. The following day, she set off for Sawston Hall in Cambridgeshire, the home of Catholic Sir John Huddleston, a man she could trust, and arrived there on the 5th, staying one night. She set off again on the 6th and possibly spent that night at the home of John Bourchier, 2nd Earl of Bath, Hengrave Hall in Bury St Edmunds. On 7th July 1553, she reached Euston Hall, home of Lady Burgh, and it was there that she received news from London goldsmith Robert Reyns that the king had died on 6th July. She hurried on to Kenninghall and there, on 8th July, she gathered her household together, telling them of the king's death and that "the right to the crown of England had therefore descended to her by divine and by human law". Mary's household reacted by cheering, and then they "proclaimed their dearest princess Mary as queen of England."

On the same day that Mary proclaimed herself queen at Kenninghall, the late Edward VI's wishes for the succession, i.e. that Lady Jane Grey was his successor, were made to local magistrates.

On 9th July 1553, Mary put quill to parchment and wrote to her half-brother's privy council, stating her claim to the throne and demanding their allegiance. She wrote of how she had learned that Edward was dead, news that was "woeful unto our hearts", and moved on to talking about the crown and how they could not be ignorant of the fact that an act of Parliament and her father's last will had given her the right to be queen, and that her right and title should "be published and proclaimed accordingly". She commented that it "seemeth strange" that she had received no official news of the king's death from the council but that she had "great hope and trust and much assurance" in their loyalty and service and that they would "like noble men work the best". Mary did mention, however, that she was "not ignorant" of what was going on, "some evil", she called it, but that she was "ready to remit and fully pardon" them "to eschew blood-shed and vengeance". She concluded by writing:

> "Wherefore, my lords, we require you and charge you,
> for that our allegiance which you owe to God and us,
> that, for your honour and the surety of your persons, you

employ your selves and forthwith upon receipt hereof cause our right and title to the Crown and government of this realm to be proclaimed in our City of London and such other places as to your wisdoms shall seem good and as to this case appertaineth, not failing hereof, as our very trust is in you. And this letter signed with our hand shall be your sufficient warrant."

While Mary was writing this letter at Kenninghall on 9th July, Nicholas Ridley, Bishop of London, preached at St Paul's Cross in London, denouncing Mary and her half-sister, Elizabeth, as bastards. He did not get the support he was hoping for. The congregation there was described as being "sore annoyed with his words".

And on that very same day, John Dudley, Duke of Northumberland, who had led Edward VI's government in his final years, informed his daughter-in-law, Lady Jane Grey, of the king's death and told her that Edward had nominated her as his successor. Jane collapsed weeping and declared, "The crown is not my right and pleases me not. The Lady Mary is the rightful heir." Northumberland and Jane's parents, the Duke and Duchess of Suffolk, then explained Edward's wishes to the distressed Jane, and she accepted the crown as her duty. She later described this moment, saying:

"Declaring to them my insufficiency, I greatly bewailed myself for the death of so noble a prince, and at the same time, turned myself to God, humbly praying and beseeching him, that if what was given to me was rightly and lawfully mine, his divine Majesty would grant me such grace and spirit that I might govern it to his glory and service and to the advantage of this realm."

She took the crown, believing that it was God's plan for her. Of course, Jane's short reign would end on 19th July 1553 when Mary was officially proclaimed Queen Mary I. Jane was executed as a traitor in February 1554.

10 July

On 10th July 1584, Catholic conspirator Francis Throckmorton was executed at Tyburn for high treason after the Throckmorton Plot was discovered.

Let me tell you a bit more about Throckmorton and his plot.

Francis Throckmorton, or Throgmorton, was born in 1554 and was the son of Sir John Throckmorton of Feckenham, Worcestershire, a staunch Catholic, and his wife, Margaret Puttenham. Sir John had served Queen Mary I as vice-president of the council in the Marches of Wales, was knighted by Queen Elizabeth I, and made chief justice of Chester.

Francis was educated at Hart Hall, Oxford, and then at the Inner Temple, one of London's inns of the court. In the 1570s, he married Anne or Agnes Sutton, daughter of Edward Sutton, 4th Baron Dudley, and the couple had a son, John. In 1578, the Throckmorton family got into trouble when Francis's mother, Lady Throckmorton, was reported for celebrating the mass in the household of her brother-in-law. Francis was accused of "being present at exercises of religion contrary to present practices". As a result, he was placed in the custody of the dean of St Paul's, but this was only for a month as his Protestant cousins interceded on his behalf. Then, a year later, Francis's father was removed from his office as chief justice of Chester for allegedly showing undue partiality in a case. He died a year later.

Perhaps his family's treatment, combined with his faith, led to Francis's subsequent actions. He'd gone into exile in the Low Countries following his release, and it's there that he began talking with other discontented Catholics about "the altering of the state" in England and how a foreign invasion would help this. As soon as he was back in England in the early 1580s, he began plotting with other like-minded young Catholic men who supported the claim of Mary, Queen of Scots, to the throne of England.

His plotting soon came to the notice of Sir Francis Walsingham, Elizabeth I's famous spymaster, whose agent reported that Francis had dined with the French ambassador, who had sent money to Mary, so Walsingham ensured that Francis was watched. In November 1583, Francis was in the middle of writing a letter to the Scottish queen when he was arrested. He managed to destroy the letter by burning it and sent other treasonous correspondence to the Spanish ambassador, Bernardino Mendoza, via his maid. Still, his remaining papers were evidence of him plotting a foreign invasion with other Catholics. He was tortured by racking but would not confess or give any incriminating evidence against his friends, claiming that the government had forged the papers that were evidence against him. His biographer, Alison Plowden, writes that he was able to smuggle a message out to Mendoza written in cypher on the back of a playing card, assuring the ambassador that he would not betray his friends. However, he confessed all after a second racking.

Francis told of how the Duke of Guise, supported by the King of Spain, was preparing to invade England, release Mary, depose Elizabeth and replace her with Mary. Along with his brother, Thomas, and the Spanish ambassador, Francis's role was to organise a group of Catholic men to welcome the invasion at Guise's landing at Arundel in Sussex. Thomas was able to flee into exile before Walsingham could arrest him. Still, the Spanish ambassador, who was protected by diplomatic immunity, was expelled from England in January 1584, and Francis was tried for high treason. At his trial on 21st May 1584, he tried to retract his confession blaming the torture he'd suffered, stating that he would have said anything to stop his pain, but he was convicted of treason and sentenced to death.

He was executed at Tyburn on this day in history, 10th July 1584, going to his death "very stubbornly" and refusing to ask the queen's forgiveness for his actions.

11 July

By this day in Tudor history, 11th July 1533, Pope Clement VII had really had enough of King Henry VIII's behaviour.

Henry, who had been awarded the title "Fidei Defensor" (Defender of the Faith) by Pope Leo X in 1521 for defending the Catholic Church against the works of Martin Luther, had not only abandoned his first wife, Catherine of Aragon, without an annulment from the pope, but he had remarried AND been granted the title of Supreme

Head of the Church in England by Convocation. It was all too much for Pope Clement.

On 11th July 1533, Pope Clement declared that the king's marriage to Anne Boleyn was null and void, as was the annulment declared by Thomas Cranmer, Archbishop of Canterbury, in May 1533. The pope also restored Catherine of Aragon to her "royal state" and ordered the wayward king to abandon the newly crowned and pregnant Anne Boleyn and return to Catherine. If he didn't, Pope Clement would issue the bull of excommunication that he had drawn up.

Henry had until September to heed the pope's warning, otherwise, he'd be excommunicated from the Catholic Church, the most severe punishment the Church could inflict.

Did Henry VIII take any notice of the pope?

Of course not.

Henry had come to believe that as a king, he was only answerable to God and not to the pope, so he made no effort to obey. He did manage to escape excommunication temporarily, though. He was finally excommunicated on 17th December 1538 by Pope Paul III following his further misbehaviour, i.e. his break with Rome, his persecution of those who did not accept his supremacy, the dissolution of the monasteries, and his desecration of religious shrines, including that of Thomas Becket.

12 July

On 12th July 1553, in the month of three Tudor monarchs, Mary, half-sister of the late king, Edward VI, moved from her estate of Kenninghall to Framlingham Castle, where she began to rally support.

In his contemporary account of Mary's fight for the throne in 1553, Robert Wingfield lists some of the men who flocked to Mary's cause. These included Henry Radcliffe, Earl of Sussex; Thomas Lord Wentworth; Sir Henry Bedingfield; Edmund Rous, Thomas Brend, John Colby and John Jennings, who all carried out Mary's orders with speed and zeal, and who, with hard work, "turned an unskilled and disorganised mob into skilled and disciplined soldiers obedient to orders and eager to meet the enemy."

According to Wingfield, in the days that followed, Mary visited her troops and was described as their gentle and beloved mistress. Wingfield writes that the soldiers "offered her such reverence that I had serious doubts whether they could have given greater adoration to God if he had come down from Heaven." He also writes of Mary speaking to her forces with "exceptional kindness", a wonderfully relaxed approach, and states that she won everyone's affections.

On this day in Ipswich, Sir Thomas Cornwallis, Sheriff of Norfolk and Suffolk, recanted his previous day's proclamation regarding Queen Jane being the rightful queen and proclaimed Mary as queen instead. He also met Mary while she was on her way to Framlingham and "most humbly prostrated himself before her Highness", both to beg a pardon for his "misdeed" and "to offer his due fealty on behalf of Norfolk and Suffolk" by surrendering his white staff of office to her. Wingfield records how, at first, Mary "seemed to berate the man for being somewhat slow and stubborn and less mindful of his duty than he ought to have been despite the repeated requests of her letters", but, according to Wingfield, "soon the tender-hearted sovereign saw how utterly miserable he was at what he had done" and granted him mercy and made him one of her council.

Meanwhile, in the city of Norwich, in Norfolk, Mary was proclaimed queen.

Back in London, on Queen Jane's side of things, a muster was called on Tothill Fields, Westminster. According to "The Chronicle of Queen Jane and of Two Years of Queen Mary, and Especially of the Rebellion of Sir Thomas Wyat", Queen Jane's council decided that Jane's father, Henry Grey, Duke of Suffolk, should go "with certain other noblemen" to apprehend Mary and to bring her to London. However, that same night, Suffolk's mission was cancelled after Queen Jane "with weeping tears" implored her council to let her father stay at home with her. So, instead, her father-in-law, the Duke of Northumberland, was persuaded to go. This was a huge mistake, for Northumberland could have held Jane's council together and kept them loyal to her.

13 July

On 13th July 1553, during the short reign of Queen Jane, while the Duke of Northumberland was preparing to leave London with the Marquess of Northampton, Earl of Huntingdon and troops to apprehend Mary, members of the council were meeting with the imperial ambassadors.

According to the four imperial ambassadors in England at that time, in a dispatch sent to the emperor, John Russell, Earl of Bedford and Lord Privy Seal, the Earls of Arundel, Shrewsbury and Pembroke, Lord Cobham, Sir John Mason, and Sir William Petre requested an audience with the ambassadors. One of the aims of the meeting was, according to the ambassadors, "to ensure the Lady Mary's safety" following a meeting the previous day with Cobham and Mason in which the English councillors had informed the ambassadors that Jane was queen and that Mary was opposing it. The councillors said that the new queen's council did not want the ambassadors "to assist the Lady Mary or communicate with her to give her advice and support", and informed them that Mary was going to be brought to London, "not to offer any violence to her person if she gave them no reason to do so, but only to restore peace and order where they had been troubled." The councillors allegedly threatened the ambassadors with "barbarous laws" if they acted in any way to cause suspicion.

The meeting between the councillors and the ambassadors on 13th July seems to have gone well, with the ambassadors recording that "Unless their countenances belied them, the Council were pleased with our discourse, because of the statement of your Majesty's affection for England; and they answered that they intended to reciprocate and act as good neighbours should".

It is not known whether it was the meetings with the ambassadors or news that Mary was successfully rallying support in East Anglia, or a combination of factors which made some members of the council start to have second thoughts about their support for Queen Jane. Still, by 13th July 1553, councillors including William Herbert, Earl of Pembroke, and Henry Fitzalan, Earl of Arundel, were beginning to worry and began considering changing sides. And the Duke of Northumberland, the previous leader of the government and a strong leader, was not there to dispel their worries and unite the council. Jane really should have let her father go after Mary.

14 July

On 14th July 1551, in the reign of King Edward VI, fifteen-year-old Henry Brandon, 2nd Duke of Suffolk, and his fourteen-year-old brother, Charles, 3rd Duke of Suffolk, died of sweating sickness at Buckden in Huntingdonshire. They were the sons of the late Charles Brandon, 1st Duke of Suffolk, and his fourth wife Catherine Willoughby, Baroness Willoughby de Eresby and Duchess of Suffolk.

Sweating sickness, or the English Sweat, was a horrible disease which decimated towns and took thousands of lives in its five major epidemics in England in 1485, 1508, 1517, 1528 and 1551. It was an illness which killed quickly. Chronicler Edward Hall wrote of how it could kill within 2-3 hours, commenting, "some merry at dinner and dead at supper".

Henry and Charles Brandon had been studying at St John's College, Cambridge, when sweating sickness broke out in the town. Fearing for their lives, their mother, who had been staying in Kingston, a village just outside Cambridge, had the boys moved to the home of the Bishop of Lincoln in Buckden, Huntingdonshire.

While the boys were being moved to Buckden, the duchess became ill. By the time she had recovered enough to travel to Buckden, Henry had died, and Charles, who had succeeded his brother as Duke of Suffolk, was dying. Both boys died on the same day. The duchess must have been heartbroken.

The boys were buried privately at Buckden, and then a special requiem mass, known as "A Month's Mind", was celebrated on 22nd September 1551. John Strype writes that "it was performed with two standards, two banners, great and large, ten bannerols, with divers coats of arms; two helmets, two swords, two targets crowned, two coats of arms; two crests, and ten dozen of escutcheons crowned; with lamentation that so noble a stock was extinct in them."

15 July

On 15th July 1553, the royal ships guarding the eastern coast for Queen Jane swapped their allegiance to Queen Mary. Their crews had not been paid, and they received a visit from Sir Henry Jerningham asking them to support Mary instead of Queen Jane. It was an easy decision for these unpaid men.

In "The Navy of Edward VI and Mary I", C.S. Knighton explains that "Sir Henry Jerningham (d. 1572) had been in Mary's service since 1528 and had gone at once to join her at Kenninghall; he then mustered support for her cause in Suffolk [...] Jerningham heard of the ships in the Orwell from a drunken sailor late on the night of 14 July, and found them beached at Landguard Point early next morning."

Robert Wingfield of Brantham, who accompanied Jerningham, recorded the following:

"Very early the next day Jerningham, accompanied by Tyrrell and Glemham, rode up to inspect the ships thus brought to the haven by a lucky tide and wind, as they say. When they had reached the haven he ordered Richard Brooke, the squadron's commander, a diligent man and skilled in seamanship, to be called to him, and took him to Framlingham castle to bring news of this happy and unexpected arrival to the queen.

This happened on 15 July; next day Thomas, Lord Wentworth arrived, to avoid the appearance of breaking his pledge, clad in splendid armour and accompanied by a not inconsiderable military force, besides several gentlemen of the county who were wont to go in his company. I would like to record for this treatise the more notable men who led any of the military reinforcements for this loyal campaign. There was Sir Richard Cavendish, a veteran campaigner, with his two sons; Sir Henry Doyle, also with two sons; Robert Wingfield, son of the late Sir Anthony Wingfield K.G., with his two brothers Anthony and Henry; Lionel Tollemache, a man well-supplied with ancient lineage and wealth; Edward Withipoll, a man of diligence; John Southwell and Francis Nunn, both lawyers; Robert Wingfield of Brantham; John Colby, an experienced soldier, with his two brothers; Jennings, skilled in warfare, and others not less active whom I forget at the moment. That nobleman, most striking both in appearance and dress, came with a splendid force of both heavy and light horse and of infantry. There is no doubt that his arrival wonderfully strengthened the morale of the queen's army and much dispirited the enemy."

"The Chronicle of Queen Jane" records:

"About this time or thereabouts the 6 ships that were sent to lie before Yarmouth, that if she had fled to have taken her, was by force of weather driven into the haven, where about that quarters, one master Jerningham was raising power on queen Mary's behalf, and hearing thereof came thither. Whereupon the captains took a boat and went to their ships. Then the mariners asked master Jernyngham what he would have, and whether he would have their captains or no; and he said, "Yea, mary." Said they, "Ye shall have them, or else we shall throw them to the bottom of the sea." The captains, seeing this perplexity, said forthwith they would serve queen Mary gladly; and so came forth with their men, and conveyed certain great ordnance; of the which coming in of the ships the lady Mary and her company were wonderful joyous, and then afterward doubted smally the duke's puissance."

Just four days later, Mary was proclaimed queen, becoming Queen Mary I of England.

16 July

On 16th July 1557, forty-one-year-old Anne of Cleves, the fourth wife of King Henry VIII, died at her home, Chelsea Old Manor.

Anne had been ill for a few months, but by the 12th July, she was bedridden and drafting her will. Her biographer, Elizabeth Norton, writes of how her will "demonstrates her kindness and the fondness which she felt for her household", because she left money to her ladies, gentlemen, yeomen, grooms and the children of the house, listing every member of her household by name. She also asked her stepdaughter, Mary I, to make sure that the rents received from her lands at Michaelmas would be used to meet the expenses of her household. Anne also bequeathed jewellery to her family, a ring to Catherine Brandon, Duchess of Suffolk, another ring to the Countess of Arundel and jewels to her stepdaughters, Mary and Elizabeth. In recompense for these jewels, she asked Mary to ensure that her servants were rewarded for their long service to her, and she asked Elizabeth to take one of her maids into service.

On the same day she died, Anne's body was embalmed and placed in a coffin covered with a cloth bearing her arms. Tapers were lit around her coffin, and prayers were said daily.

On 3rd August, according to diarist Henry Machyn, her coffin was moved from Chelsea to Westminster in preparation for her burial the next day. Machyn records:

"The 3rd day of August my lady Anne of Cleve, sometime wife unto King Henry the 8th came from Chelsea to be [buried] unto Westminster, with all the children of Westminster and [many] [priests] and clerks, and then the grey [amice] of Paul's and 3 crosses, and the monks of Westminster; and my lord bishop of Lo[ndon] and my lord abbott of Westminster rode together, next the monks, and then the 2 [executors] Sir Edmond Peckham and Sir (Robert) Freston, cofferer to the queen of England; and then my lord admiral, my (lord) Darcy of Essex, and many knights and gentlemen; and afore her servants, and after her banner of arms; and then her gentlemen and her head officers; and then her chariot with 8 banners of arms of diverse armes, and 4 banners of images of white taffeta, wrought with fine gold and her arms; and so by saint James, and so to Charing Cross, with a 100 torches burning, her servants bearing them, and the 12 bed-men of Westminster had new black gowns; and they had 12 torches burning, and 4 white branches with arms; and then ladies and gentlewomen all in black, and horses; and 8 heralds of arms in black, and their horses; and arms [set] about the hearse behind and before; and 4 heralds bearing the 4 white banners; and at (the) church door all did alight and there did receive the good lady, my lord of London and my lord abbott in their mitres and copes, sensyng her, and their men did bear her with a canopy of black velvet, with 4 black staffs, and so brought into the hearse and there tarried dirge, and so there all night with light burning."

Then, on the 4th August, there was a requiem mass for Anne with a "godly sermon" by the Lord Abbot of Westminster. Her coffin was then taken to her tomb and her body interred with the cloth-of-gold laid over her. Then, her head officers broke their staves, and her ushers broke their rods and cast them into her tomb. After another mass, there was a dinner led by the chief mourner, Elizabeth, Marchioness of Winchester, the Lord Admiral and Lord Darcy.

Anne of Cleves is the only one of Henry VIII's wives to be buried at Westminster Abbey, and her tomb is on the south side of the High Altar. It is decorated with carvings of a crown and her initials, AC, skulls and crossed bones, and a lion's head.

17 July

On 17th July 1555, antiquary, bee-keeper, translator and poet Richard Carew was born at Antony House, Torpoint, in Cornwall. Carew was a member of the Elizabethan Society of Antiquaries, and his works included his "Survey of Cornwall", a county history.

But let me tell you a bit more about this multi-talented Tudor chap.

- Richard Carew was the eldest son of Thomas Carew and his wife, Elizabeth Edgcumbe.
- He inherited his father's estate when he was just eight years old.
- Carew was educated at Christ Church, Oxford, where he was friends with historian and antiquary William Camden and poet Philip Sidney. Then he studied law at the Middle Temple, one of the four inns of the court in London. He taught himself Greek, Italian, Spanish, German and French.
- He married Juliana Arundell in his home county of Cornwall in 1577, and they went on to have ten children together.
- At his Cornish estate, Antony House, Carew was a keen bee-keeper and fisherman, but he managed to mix leisure time at home in the country with public office. He served as a Justice of

the Peace, a burgess, bailiff, sheriff, deputy lieutenant, treasurer of the lieutenancy, and colonel of the regiment in Cornwall between 1581 and 1597.

- Carew was also an intellectual and produced translations of famous Italian, Spanish and French works. It is also thought that he wrote the anonymously published poem "A Herring's Tayle". He was very interested in language and etymology and wrote "The excellencie of the English tongue". His interest in the English language led to him becoming involved in a dispute over whether the English language should assimilate foreign words or be pure. Others involved in this dispute included William Shakespeare, Thomas Nashe, Edmund Spenser, and Verstegan. Historian S Mendyk explains that "Carew accepted Saxon as the 'natural language' of England (Jones, 220), but he was much more willing to recognize the contributions of foreign tongues and cultures than Verstegan was."
- In 1602, he published his two-volume county history, "Survey of Cornwall", dedicated to Sir Walter Ralegh.
- Following its publication, Carew's health began to go downhill, and he lost much of his sight. He died at his home, Antony House, in his study, on 6th November 1620. He was laid to rest in the crypt of the local parish church on 7th November. Only five of his ten children outlived him, and he bequeathed his estate to his wife and his second son, Richard.
- Carew has been referred to as "the prince of Cornish historians", and his Survey of Cornwall has been reprinted on several occasions, the most recent being in 1953.

18 July

On 18th July 1509, just under three months after Henry VIII had come to the throne, Edmund Dudley, administrator, President of the King's Council in the reign of Henry VII and speaker of the House of Commons, was convicted of treason after being blamed for the oppression of the reign of Henry VII, the new king's father.

Dudley, who was the father of John Dudley, later Duke of Northumberland, and grandfather of Robert Dudley, Earl of Leicester, was charged with conspiring to "hold, guide and govern the King and his Council" and ordering his men to assemble in London during the final days of Henry VII's life.

The record of his trial and conviction by commission of oyer and terminer gives us details of the full charges against him. It calls him a "false traitor" and states that on 22nd April 1509, "in the parish of St Swithin, in the ward of Candlewick-street", Dudley "falsely, feloniously, and traitorously conspired, imagined, and compassed how and in what manner he, with a great force of men and armed power, might hold, guide, and govern the King and his Council against the wishes of the King either by himself or others, according to the will and intention of the said Edmund, and falsely and traitorously, and totally deprive the King of his Royal liberty: and to make and move discords, divisions, and dissensions amongst the Magnates and Councillors of the King and his kingdom; and that if by him the said Edmund, or by others his adherents, the King and Council should refuse to be held, ruled, and governed in the before-mentioned manner, the completely to destroy the King and to depose, remove, and deprive him from and of his Royal authority."

It goes on to state that "in order to fulfil such wicked intention, the said Edmund Dudley, wrote or caused to be written divers letters to divers of the King's lieges, viz., one to Edward Sutton, Knight; another to Francis Cheyne, Knight, then Esquire; a third to Edward Darell, Knight; a fourth to Thomas Turbervyle; a fifth to Thomas Asshebournham, Esquire; a sixth to William Scott, Knight; a seventh to Henry Long; an eighth to Thomas Knyaston; and a ninth to John Mompesson, Esquire; requiring that they, with their servants and adherents, and all their power arrayed in a manner of war, should come together and speedily repair to him at London, and adhere to and follow his will. Furthermore, that the said Edmund, in order to carry into effect the said false and traitorous intention, on the said day, delivered the letters to Richard Page and Angell Messenger, [Ayngell' Messynger,] to deliver the same to the said Sir Edward Sutton and the others aforementioned, who delivered the same accordingly; by reason whereof a great multitude and power of people, arrayed in manner of war, came to London, the in parish and ward aforesaid, according to the tenor of the letters, against the allegiance of the said Edmund."

Although Dudley pleaded "not guilty" to the charges, the commission found him guilty and sentenced him to death. His colleague, Sir Richard Empson, who had also been one of King Henry VII's chief advisors, was also convicted of treason, and the two men were thrown into the Tower of London to await their deaths. They were beheaded on Tower Hill on 17th August 1509.

Historians have seen these men as scapegoats for Henry VII's unpopular regime and have attributed their falls "to Henry's desire to win popularity and signify his distancing himself from his father's draconian financial measures", but historian Derek Wilson, in his book "In the Lion's Court: Power, Ambition, and Sudden Death in the Reign of Henry VIII", writes of there being more to their falls than that:

> "The King certainly had these motives but they do not fully explain the significance which the fate of the two ministers held for some of those most closely involved. There was a very pointed message in the precise words of the indictment, to 'govern the king and his council against the wishes of the king' [....] The very first power Henry VIII had displayed was the power to destroy highly placed servants who failed to do his bidding. It was a power he would exercise frequently and to devastating effect in the years ahead."

It was a clear warning from the new king to those around him who might want to control or manipulate a young king.

Empson's biographer M. M. Condon comments, "Ruthless though he was, Empson acted by the king's command and was occasionally subject to his check", and Dudley's biographer, Steven Gunn, writes that Dudley was "made a convenient scapegoat for Henry VII's exactions" and that "Certainly he had exploited his position as the king's executive, but so to a less extreme degree had most of Henry's other councillors. There are many signs that the general shape of policy was the king's". They were doing the king's bidding.

19 July

On 19th July 1545, Henry VIII's flagship, the Mary Rose, sank right before his eyes in the Battle of the Solent between the English and French fleets.

The English fleet had moved out to attack the French fleet in the late afternoon of the 19th July as "a fitful wit sprang up", and something went wrong as the ship carried out a turning manoeuvre. The Mary Rose sank along with most of her crew, including Sir George Carew, her captain.

But why did a ship whose illustrious career had started in 1512 sink to the bottom of the Solent on that fateful day in 1545? Well, there is still speculation over this question today with the following reasons being put forward:

- A French hit caused her sinking – According to the French fleet, they hit her, and she sank after they lured the English ships within range of their main fleet.
- She heeled over in the wind, and water entered her gun ports – Van der Delft, the Imperial ambassador, told of how she sank, drowning just under 500 men, and how he "was told by a Fleming among the survivors that when she heeled over with the wind the water entered by the lowest row of gun ports which had been left open after firing."
- Human Error – According to Sir Peter Carew, brother of the Vice-Admiral of the Mary Rose, Sir George Carew, who died when the ship sank, his uncle Sir Gawain Carew had sailed past the Mary Rose as she began to heel and asked Sir George what was wrong. Sir George replied, "he had the sort of knaves whom he could not rule." It was also Sir George Carew's first naval command, so he was inexperienced.
- The Mary Rose had become unseaworthy – Some people believe that modifications over the years had added to the ship's weight and made her unseaworthy.
- Carew's crew may not have understood his orders, with some being from overseas.

Henry VIII's secretary of state, William Paget, ordered a salvage operation within days of the sinking, but operations in 1545, 1547 and 1549 only managed to raise some guns and rigging. Nearly 300 years later, on the 16th June 1836, a fisherman snagged his gear on the wreck, and John Deane, a diver exploring a nearby wreck, agreed to help the fisherman disentangle his gear in return for a half share of whatever the gear was caught up on. Dean found the Mary Rose and recovered several items between 1836 and 1840, including iron guns, bows, and timbers. The ship, though, was left lying in her watery grave.

In 1965, 420 years after the sinking, Alexander McKee decided to try and find the wreck of the Mary Rose. With the collaboration of Professor Harold E Edgerton and John Mills and their sonar systems, a sub-seabed anomaly was found in 1967 and confirmed in 1968 by a sonar survey. Dives were carried out in the area between 1968 and 1971, and divers found timbers and an iron gun. Then, on the 5th May 1971, Percy Ackland discovered three of the port frames of the Mary Rose.

In 1979, The Mary Rose Trust was formed, and an archaeological team led by Dr Margaret Rule CBE began to excavate the Mary Rose wreck. This culminated in the raising of the Mary Rose on 11th October 1982 by a team of Royal Engineers. The wreck was placed in a dry dock with a relative humidity of 95% and a temperature of 2-6ºC. A preservation programme then began in earnest.

On the 4th October 1983, just under a year after she was raised, the Mary Rose was put on public display in Portsmouth, and a museum was created to display some of the artefacts found in the wreck. In 2013, a new museum was opened after further conservation work was carried out.

It is a myth that the ship was named after Henry VIII's sister, Mary Tudor, Queen of France. There is no evidence that Mary was ever known as Mary Rose, and, as the Mary Rose Trust points out, "It's more likely the ship was named after the Virgin Mary, who was also known at the time as 'The Mystic Rose'".

20 July

On 20th July 1554, Philip of Spain arrived in England, at Southampton, in readiness for his marriage to Mary I.

Winchester Cathedral, the seat of Bishop Stephen Gardiner, had been chosen as the wedding venue due to the recent Wyatt's Rebellion in London, and Mary and her court set off from Richmond on 16th June.

When Philip landed at Southampton, he was met by a host of gentry and nobles, including the Earl of Arundel, who presented him with the Order of the Garter. There was, however, upset due to Philip bringing his Spanish household when an English household of 350 had been appointed for him.

Philip and Mary married at Winchester five days later in a ceremony performed by Bishop Gardiner.

21 July

On 21st July 1553, just days after he'd left London with an army to apprehend Mary, half-sister of the late king, Edward VI, John Dudley, Duke of Northumberland, was arrested near Cambridge.

Northumberland had reached Cambridge by 15th July and was on his way to Bury St Edmunds to confront Mary's men when he heard reports of the size of her army, which well outnumbered his own. He decided, therefore, to retreat to Cambridge. He didn't know that Queen Jane's council, without his strong leadership, had swapped sides and had decided to proclaim for Mary instead. On 19th July 1553, Mary was officially proclaimed Queen Mary I in London.

Northumberland reached Cambridge once more on 20th July 1553, and there heard the news of the privy council's betrayal and that Mary had been proclaimed queen in Jane's place. Martyrologist John Foxe shares the eye-witness account of Dr Edwin Sandys, vice-chancellor of Cambridge University, regarding what Northumberland did on hearing this bad news:

> "The duke that night retired to Cambridge, and sent for Dr. Sands to go with him to the market-place, to proclaim queen Mary. The duke cast up his cap with others, and so laughed, that the tears ran down his cheeks for grief. He told Dr. Sands, that queen Mary was a merciful woman, and that he doubted not thereof; declaring that he had sent unto her to know her pleasure,

and looked for a general pardon. Dr. Sands answered, "My life is not dear unto me, neither have I done or said any thing that urgeth my conscience. For that which I spake of the state, hath instructions warranted by the subscription of sixteen counsellors; neither can speech be treason, neither yet have I spoken further than the word of God and the laws of the realm do warrant me, come of me what God will. But be you assured, you shall never escape death; for if she would save you, those that now shall rule, will kill you."

Sandys says that the guard came that very same night and apprehended Northumberland. The next morning, the Earl of Arundel visited Northumberland, who "fell on his knees" and reminded the earl that he had "done nothing but by the consents of you and all the whole council". The earl replied that the queen had sent him to arrest him and arrest him he did.

On 25th July 1553, Northumberland; his sons, John, Ambrose and Henry; his brother, Sir Andrew Dudley; the Earl of Huntingdon; Lord Hastings; and several others were taken to the Tower of London, being greeted in London by a hostile crowd that threw stones at Northumberland and called him "traitor and heretic". More prisoners were brought to the Tower the next day, including the Marquess of Northampton and Robert Dudley, another of the duke's sons. Of course, his other son, Guildford, consort of the former Queen Jane, was already a prisoner there.

On 18th August 1553, Northumberland was found guilty of treason for his part in putting Lady Jane Grey on the throne. His execution was scheduled for 21st August. However, his execution was temporarily cancelled. Instead, the duke was taken to mass at the Chapel of St Peter ad Vincula at the Tower, where he recanted his Protestant faith. This was probably more an appeal for mercy and a way of trying to save his sons than a true recantation. It didn't save the duke, for he was beheaded on Tower Hill the following day, 22nd August 1553, and laid to rest next to his predecessor, Edward Seymour, Duke of Somerset. His son, Guildford, was executed in February 1554, on the same day that Lady Jane Grey was executed. John, Ambrose, Henry and Robert all survived the events of 1553, as did the Marquess of Northampton and the Earl of Huntingdon, and were later released.

22 July

On 22nd July 1576, in the reign of Queen Elizabeth I, playwright and pamphleteer Edward Sharpham was baptised at Colehanger, East Allington, in Devon. His birthdate is not known, but babies were usually baptised within a few days of birth. Sharpham is thought to have written the plays "The Fleire" and "Cupid's Whirligig".

Let me tell you a bit about this little-known Tudor chap.

- Edward Sharpham was the third child of Richard Sharpham and his wife, Mary Pomeroy.
- Sadly, Sharpham's father died when he was five years old and interestingly, his mother sued a man named Thomas Fortescue for killing her husband by witchcraft and using witchcraft to make her fall in love with him. In 1596, twenty-year-old Sharpham also sued Fortescue and a man named William Bastard of the Middle Temple, one of the inns of the court, for tampering with evidence related to his mother's lawsuit. Sharpham's mother ended up remarrying, but not Fortescue. She married Alexander Hext and had three children with him. After he died in 1588, she married Charles Barnaby.
- It is thought that Sharpham was educated at grammar school before being admitted to the Middle Temple in 1594.
- The 1597 "The Discoverie of the Knights of the Poste", a pamphlet about the criminals that could be encountered on the road between Exeter and London, is attributed to ES, and is thought to have been by the 21-year-old Edward Sharpham. Another piece of writing by ES is a commendatory poem to the comedy Volpone by Ben Jonson. Other works attributed more certainly to Sharpham include the 1607 "The Fleire", which was written for the Children of the Blackfriars, a boys' theatre company, and the 1607 "Cupid's Whirligig". "The Fleire" is a satire of King James I's court, and "Cupid's Whirligig" is a comedy set in London about a man who suspects his wife of being unfaithful. According to the play's synopsis, the man, Sir

Troublesome, comes up with plan upon plans to prove his wife is unfaithful, including the idea of castrating himself and seeing if his wife gets pregnant. Lady Troublesome comments in the play, "tis such a jealous fool, that if he catch but a Flea in her bed, he will be searching to see if it bee a male or a female, for fear a comes to Cuckold him". The play was performed by the Children of the King's Revels in the Whitefriars Theatre in 1607.

- In 1608, when he was 31 years old, Sharpham fell ill with the plague. He wrote his will on 22nd April 1608 and was buried on 23rd April 1608 at St Margaret's Church, Westminster.

Trivia: playwright Ben Jonson referred to Sharpham as "a rogue", along with playwright John Day and author Thomas Dekker.

23 July

On 23rd July 1543, or 24th according to some sources, Marie de Guise and her baby daughter, Mary, Queen of Scots, escaped from Linlithgow Palace, where they were being watched, and were subsequently taken to Stirling Castle. Cardinal Beaton helped them.

Why did they have to escape? What was going on?

Marie's husband, King James V of Scotland, had died on 14th December 1542, leaving the throne to his six-day-old daughter, Mary, who became Mary, Queen of Scots. Due to Mary's age, a regent was necessary. Two men vied for the position: Protestant James Hamilton, 2nd Earl of Arran, who was next in line to the throne after Mary, and Catholic Cardinal David Beaton, Archbishop of St Andrews, who claimed that James had appointed him regent in his will, which was unfortunately viewed as a forgery. Arran won and was appointed Governor and Protector of Scotland. Beaton was arrested, accused of inviting France to invade Scotland, and put under house arrest at his home at St Andrews.

In the summer of 1543, Arran negotiated an alliance with Henry VIII, which included the marriage of Henry's young son, Prince Edward, the future Edward VI, to Mary, Queen of Scots. The Treaty of Greenwich was signed on 1st July 1543, and it was decided that Mary would move to England at the age of ten to marry Edward. The treaty, which would see the union of the thrones of England and Scotland, was greeted with resistance by those in Scotland who favoured the Auld Alliance, i.e. Scotland's relationship with France. Beaton was able to take advantage of this, and on 20th July 1543, he and his supporters signed a bond, the Secret Bond or Band, agreeing to resist the terms of the treaty and to protect the young queen from England's plans. On 23rd July 1543, Beaton and his armed supporters mustered at Linlithgow, where Mary and her mother were residing, and it was agreed that Mary and Marie would be moved to Stirling Castle. On 27th July 1543, mother and child were escorted by an armed guard of 3,500 men to Stirling and Mary was crowned there on 9th September 1543.

In December 1543, the Scottish Parliament annulled the Treaty of Greenwich and renewed the country's Auld Alliance with France. This led to the Rough Wooing, a war between Scotland and England, which sought to force a marriage between Mary and Edward and weaken Scotland. The war was eventually brought to an end in 1550 by the Treaty of Boulogne.

Mary didn't marry Edward. Instead, in 1558, she married the Dauphin Francis, son and heir of King Henry II of France. Francis became King of France, and Mary his queen consort, in 1559 following the death of Henry VII, but Francis sadly died in December 1560, and Mary returned to Scotland in August 1561.

But what of Cardinal Beaton, who had helped Mary and Marie?

The cardinal was murdered at his home, at the castle of St Andrews, on 29th May 1546 by a group of lairds from Fife whose grievance against Beaton included the recent execution of Protestant preacher George Wishart.

Mary herself came to a sticky end when she was executed in February 1587 after being implicated in plots against Queen Elizabeth I.

24 July

On 24th July 1553, merchant and conspirator Richard Hesketh was born in Lancashire. Hesketh is known for the Hesketh Plot of 1593, when he urged Ferdinando Stanley, 5th Earl of Derby, to lead a rebellion to claim the throne of England.

Let me tell you a bit more about Richard Hesketh and his plot.

Richard Hesketh was the fourth son of landowner Gabriel Hesketh, from Aughton New Hall in Lancashire, and his first wife, Jane Halsall. Hesketh was apprenticed to a man called Hugh Fayreclough and became a freeman of the Clothworkers' Company in London in 1578 when he was 25. He was mentioned by John Dee in his diary in 1581 as a friend and agent in Antwerp who, while exporting cloth, also carried letters from Dee to his contacts in Antwerp and who searched for books for him.

Hesketh married widow Isabel Shaw in around 1586. In 1589, he was forced into exile for three years following his involvement in a riot near Preston, which caused the death of two men. While in exile in Prague, he joined the circle of alchemist Edward Kelley and was protected from trouble when Kelley fell from favour in 1591 by Jesuit Thomas Stephenson. A year later, he was working in intelligence for Sir William Stanley in Flanders, who was there fighting for Spain and supporting the claim of Henry Stanley, 4th Earl of Derby, to the throne of England. Hesketh returned to England in the summer of 1593, and in September 1593, he travelled to Lathom House, home of the Stanleys. Henry Stanley died that very day and his son, Ferdinando, became the 5th Earl of Derby. Ferdinando had a claim to the throne as his mother was Lady Margaret Clifford, granddaughter of Charles Brandon, Duke of Suffolk, and Mary Tudor, Queen of France, sister of King Henry VIII. Hesketh put forward the idea that Ferdinando should lead a revolt against Elizabeth I and claim the throne. Ferdinando had two meetings with Hesketh regarding Hesketh's plot. Still, when Hesketh joined him on his journey to the royal court at Windsor, Ferdinando took him as a prisoner and turned him over to the queen's privy council.

Hesketh was interrogated at Ditton House, near Windsor Castle, and on 15th October 1593, Hesketh confessed to the plot. On 24th November, he was tried for treason at St Albans, as London was affected by an outbreak of plague. His trial was presided over by Sir Thomas Egerton, attorney general. Hesketh was found guilty and executed on 29th November 1593, denying his Catholic faith.

On 5th April 1594, Ferdinando was suddenly taken ill, vomiting violently, his vomit being described as the colour of "soot or rusty iron". Ferdinando believed that he had been bewitched, and others claimed he had been poisoned. He took all kinds of medicines, including bezoar stone and unicorn's horn, but nothing worked. He died on 16th April 1594.

25 July

On 25th July 1602, thirteen-year-old actor Salomon Pavy was buried at the Church of St Mary Somerset, near Blackfriars Theatre.

It is thought that Salomon was abducted to serve as an actor in the Children of Paul's, for in 1601, when four men were accused of abducting another boy to serve as an actor, the name "Salmon Pavey, apprentice" was mentioned as a past abductee.

Salomon later joined the Children of the Queen's Revels at the Blackfriars Theatre and had parts in plays by Ben Jonson.

Ben Jonson composed an epitaph in his honour:
"Yet three filled Zodiacs had he been
The stages jewel;
And did act (what now we moan)
Old men so duly,
As, sooth, the Parcae thought him one,
He played so truly."

26 July

On 26th July 1538, George Talbot, 4th Earl of Shrewsbury and 4th Earl of Waterford, died at South Wingfield Manor, Derbyshire. He was buried at St Peter's Church, Sheffield.
- Shrewsbury was born in 1468 and was the son of John Talbot, 3rd Earl of Shrewsbury, and Katherine Stafford.
- He was the ward of William Baron Hastings, who arranged Shrewsbury's marriage to his daughter, Anne.
- He fought at the Battle of Stoke Field in 1487 and was made a Knight of the Garter afterwards.

- He served Henry VIII as chamberlain of the exchequer, a diplomat, and a lieutenant in France and on the Scottish borders.
- And in 1536, he played an important part in suppressing the Pilgrimage of Grace rebellion

27 July

On 27th July 1593, Roman Catholic priest and martyr Blessed William Davies was hanged, drawn and quartered at Beaumaris Castle on the Island of Anglesey.

But who was Davies, and why was he executed? Let me give you a few facts about this Welshman.

- We don't know Davies's precise birthdate, but it was probably around 1556.
- He came from Croes-yn-Eirias, a hamlet west of Colwyn Bay in North Wales.
- A "William Davies" studied at St Edmund's Hall, Oxford, from 1575 and graduated in 1578, but we don't know whether it was this William Davies.
- In April 1582, he entered the Jesuit seminary at Reims in France, where he was ordained as a priest by Cardinal Guise on the eve of Passion Sunday in April 1585. This was the same year that Elizabeth I's government brought in its act against Jesuits and seminary priests, making it treason for a Jesuit priest to be in England. Davies was then sent to England on a mission to convert people to the old ways, i.e. the Catholic faith.
- Davies returned to his home territory in North Wales, which came under English rule. There, he joined forces with local dignitary Robert ap Hugh, or Robert Pugh, resided at his house, Plas Penrhyn, and joined a local community of recusants. In 1586, Davies, Pugh and their fellow recusants were forced into hiding, finding refuge in caves in the cliffs of the Little Orme headland. It is not known what made them move, but their move coincided with the death of Sir Henry Sidney, Lord President of the Council in the Marches, who was alleged to have had Catholic sympathies. Following his death,

the council were commanded to take action against Catholic gatherings and those celebrating the Mass.

- While the recusants were hiding in the caves, they built a printing press, and it is believed that Davies and Pugh were among those involved in the printing of "Y Drych Christianogawl", or The Christian Mirror, an important early Welsh Catholic book and the first book to be printed on Welsh soil. The book dealt with the Catholic teaching on death, the day of judgement, hell and heaven. It was printed as a pocket book to be carried and hidden easily.
- Davies was arrested at Holyhead in March 1591 by Foulk Thomas. He was with four young men whom he was planning on escorting to Ireland for them to travel on to Valladolid in Spain to become seminary priests. They were also arrested.
- Davies was taken to Beaumaris Castle, where he was interrogated in the presence of Hugh Bellot, Bishop of Bangor. Davies eventually confessed to his missionary work but would not name names. He was put into solitary confinement in a dungeon in the castle for a month before being allowed to talk to fellow Catholics and celebrate Mass with them. He was also allowed visits from Protestants who wanted to debate with him.
- Robert Pugh, who had managed to avoid arrest, wanted to help Davies escape, but Davies wouldn't.
- Davies was found guilty of treason at the next Anglesey Assizes, but he was not sentenced as it was hoped that he could be persuaded to recant his Catholic faith. He was sent to Ludlow to be examined by the Council of the Marches. Still, he would not turn away from his faith, and he was imprisoned in Bewdley for a time before being sent back to Beaumaris, where he spent his last six months ministering to his fellow Catholic prisoners and praying.
- The summer assizes of 1593 sentenced him to die as a traitor.
- On this day in history, 27th July 1593, Davies was drawn to the gallows within Beaumaris Castle's walls. There, he prayed on his knees before climbing the scaffold and saying, "This island (Anglesey) was called in the old time the dark island, the which name it never better deserved than at this present.

But I beseech God that the blood which I am brought hither innocently to shed, may give a light unto it of that faith which it hath received above a thousand years agone." He then took the noose, kissed it, placed it around his neck and said, "Thy yoke, O Lord, is sweet and Thy burden light." Fortunately for him, Davies was hanged until he was dead rather than being cut down alive, and then he was disembowelled, beheaded and quartered. According to an article by Joseph Kelly, "The head was set on top of his prison cell, two of his quarters were hung in Beaumaris Castle, one in Conwy Castle, and the fourth at Caerwys".

- In 1909, a chapel was erected to his memory at Beaumaris, and he was beatified in November 1987 by Pope John Paul II as one of the 85 martyrs of England and Wales.

28 July

On 28th July 1540, at Oatlands Palace, in Surrey, King Henry VIII married his fifth wife, Catherine Howard, daughter of Edmund Howard and Joyce or Jocasta Culpeper, and niece of Thomas Howard, 3rd Duke of Norfolk. The groom was forty-nine years of age, and the bride was about seventeen, and the wedding was a low-key affair, with Henry's marriage to Anne of Cleves having only just been annulled. It was kept quiet for over a week, and Catherine did not appear in public as queen until 8th August.

The first mention chronicler Edward Hall makes of the new queen is an entry for 8th August:

> "The eight day of August was the Lady Katheryn Howard, niece to the duke of Norfolk, and daughter to the lord Edmund Howard, showed openly as Queen at Hampton Court, which dignity she enjoyed not long as after ye shall hear."

And chronicler and Windsor Herald Charles Wriothesley even dated the marriage to 8th August, writing:

> "This year, the eight day of Awgust, being Sunday, the King was married to Katherin Howarde, daughter of the late Edmund Howard deceased, and brother to the Duke

of Norfolk, at his manor of Hampton Court, and that day she dined in her great chamber under the cloth of estate, and was there proclaimed Queen of England."

The king's fifth marriage appeared happy at first, with Henry doting on his young bride and having a new lease of life. Catherine's biographer, Lacey Baldwin Smith, writes of how the king, who had previously felt "the weight of age close upon him", was suddenly "filled with fresh vitality". He started getting up early (between 5 and 6am) to go hunting and the French ambassador wrote of his "good spirits" and "good humour". Henry VIII was happy. He had high hopes for the future, but his hopes would be dashed just over 15 months later when he was made aware of Catherine's sexual history and then her secret assignations with Thomas Culpeper, a groom of his privy chamber. Henry was devastated. Catherine was executed for treason on 13th February 1542, after being found guilty by a bill of attainder.

While Henry VIII and Catherine Howard were getting married at Oatlands, Thomas Cromwell, Earl of Essex and Henry VIII's former right-hand man, was beheaded on Tower Hill. He had been found guilty by a bill of attainder of corruption, heresy and treason.

This Tudor statesman, who had served King Henry VIII faithfully for many years, had an awful end, his execution being botched by what was described as a "butcherly" executioner.

Henry VIII never spoke of any regret for the execution of his fifth wife. However, according to Charles de Marillac, the French ambassador, the king later regretted Cromwell's execution, blaming it all on his privy council, saying that "on the pretext of several trivial faults he [Cromwell] had committed, they had made several false accusations which had resulted in him killing the most faithful servant he had ever had."

29 July

On Sunday 29th July 1565, twenty-three-year-old Mary, Queen of Scots, married her second husband, nineteen-year-old Henry Stuart, Lord Darnley.

Mary, Queen of Scots, was queen regnant of Scotland and was the daughter of King James V of Scotland and Marie de Guise. Her paternal grandparents were King James IV and Margaret Tudor, Margaret being Henry VIII's sister and Henry VII's eldest daughter.

Mary had become Queen of Scotland after her father's death when she was just six days old.

The bridegroom, Lord Darnley, was the son of Matthew Stuart, 4th Earl of Lennox, and Margaret Douglas, daughter of Margaret Tudor, making Mary and Darnley related as half-cousins.

The banns for the marriage had been read in St Giles's Cathedral, High Kirk of Edinburgh, on Sunday 22nd July, and that afternoon, Darnley was made Duke of Albany. On Saturday 28th July, heralds proclaimed the forthcoming marriage of Mary and Darnley at the Market Cross in Edinburgh and proclaimed that Darnley would be made king following the wedding.

At 6am on Sunday 29th July, the couple got married in Mary's private chapel at Holyrood Palace (the Palace of Holyroodhouse), Edinburgh. The bride, who had been married before, to Francis II of France, and had been widowed following his death in 1560, wore her "deuil blanc" (her white, mourning attire). She was led to the altar by the Earls of Lennox and Atholl. The couple made their vows, and Darnley placed three rings on Mary's right hand. After prayers, Darnley left, leaving Mary to celebrate the nuptial mass without him. Historian John Guy writes that Darnley "wished to avoid the charge of 'idolatry'".

At midday on Monday 30th July, heralds proclaimed that Darnley was King of Scotland, with the couple's official title being "Henry and Marie, King and Queen of Scotland".

The marriage was not to be happy for very long. In March 1566, Darnley, with a gang of friends, murdered Mary's private secretary, David Rizzio, in front of a pregnant Mary. Darnley was jealous of Mary's friendship with Rizzio. Mary gave birth to Darnley's son, the future James VI of Scotland (James I of England), on 19th June 1566. Darnley's increasingly erratic behaviour and desire to be awarded the Crown Matrimonial (the right to co-reign with Mary) led to him becoming unpopular, and he became a real problem for Mary and the Scottish Lords. In February 1567, the problem was solved when Darnley was killed in an explosion at Kirk O'Field. It is thought that James Hepburn, Lord Bothwell, supplied the gunpowder, but he was acquitted of murder in April 1567. On the 24th April 1567, Bothwell kidnapped Mary (it is unclear whether this was planned by Mary and Bothwell) and allegedly raped her. They were married on the 15th May 1567.

30 July

On 30th July 1540, in the reign of King Henry VIII, Catholics Thomas Abell, Edward Powell and Richard Fetherston were hanged, drawn and quartered at Smithfield for refusing to acknowledge the royal supremacy. Thomas Abell had also been a staunch supporter of Queen Catherine of Aragon and had written a treatise against Henry VIII's plans to annul his marriage to Catherine.

Also, at Smithfield that day, religious reformers Robert Barnes, William Jerome and Thomas Garrard were burnt at the stake for heresy.

Edward Hall gives an account of that day:

"The thirty day of July, were drawn on hurdles out of the Tower to Smithfeld, Robert Barnes Doctor in Divinity, Thomas Garard, and William Jerome Bachelors in Divinity, Powell, Fetherston and Abell. The first three were drawn to the stake, there before set up, and were burned: and the latter three drawn to the Galowes, likewise there set up, and were hanged, headed, and quartered.

Here ye must note, that the first three, were men that professed the Gospel of Jesu Christ, and were Preachers thereof: But wherefore they were now thus cruelly executed, I knowe not, although I have searched to knowe the truth. But this I find in their attainder, for ye must understand, that after they had Preached at Saintt Mary Spittle, as before I have declared, Barnes for learning his lesson no better was committed to the Schoolehouse before prepared, which was the Tower, where he was kept, and never called to examination, till his rod that he should be beaten withall, was made, which was a sharp and great Fire in Smithfield: and for company sake was sent to the Skolehouse with him, the forenamed Garrard, and Jerome, which drank all of one cup.

And as I said before, thus much I find in their attainder, that they were detestable and abominable Heretics, and that they had taught many heresies, the number whereof was too great in the attainder to be recited, so that there is not one alleged, which I have often wondered at, that their heresies were so many, and not one there alleged, as special cause of their death. And indeed at their death, they asked the Sheriffs, wherefore they were condemned, who answered, they could not tell: but if I may say the truth, most men said it was for Preaching, against the Doctrine of Stephen Gardiner Bishop of Winchester, who chiefly procured this their death, God and he knoweth, but great pity it was, that such learned men should so be cast away, without examination, neither knowing what was laid to their charge, nor never called to answer.

The last three, which were Powell, Fetherston, and Abell, were put to death for Treason, and in their attainder, is special mention made of their offences, which was for the denying of the king's supremacy, and affirming that his Marriage with the Lady Katheryne was good: These with other were the treasons, that they were attainted of, and suffered death for."

Reformers and Catholics being executed on the same day - I wonder what the common people made of that! Edward Hall sounded rather confused in his account, trying to figure out why Robert Barnes, William Jerome and Thomas Garrard were attainted, and putting it down to Stephen Gardiner's involvement.

The stone walls of the Beauchamp Tower at the Tower of London are covered with Tudor graffiti, i.e. carvings in the stone done by prisoners there. One was done by Thomas Abell and is a play on his name. It has the word Thomas and then a bell underneath it with an A on it.

31 July

On 31st July 1553, Henry Grey, Duke of Suffolk, was, according to the contemporary chronicler Charles Wriothesley, "discharged out of the Tower by the Earle of Arundell and had the Quenes pardon."

But why was he in the Tower, and why was he pardoned? Let me tell you but first, let me tell you a bit about Henry Grey.

- Henry Grey was born in 1517 and was the eldest son of Thomas Grey, 2nd Marquess of Dorset, and his second wife, Margaret Wotton.
- In 1530, after his father's death, Grey's wardship was granted to Charles Brandon, Duke of Suffolk, Henry VIII's best friend and brother-in-law. Grey also became Marquess of Dorset on his father's death.
- In 1533, Suffolk arranged the marriage of his daughter, Frances Brandon, to Grey, and Grey was made a Knight of the Bath during the celebrations for Queen Anne Boleyn's coronation.
- Grey was chief mourner at the funeral of King Henry VIII in 1547 and acted as Lord High Constable at King Edward VI's coronation.
- He became a Knight of the Garter in 1547, following the accession of Edward VI.
- Also, in 1547, Thomas Seymour, Baron Seymour of Sudeley and brother of the Lord Protector, Edward Seymour, took on the wardship of the Greys' eldest daughter, Lady Jane Grey, promising to arrange a marriage between Jane and his nephew, the king. Seymour went on to marry the dowager queen, Catherine Parr, and Jane joined their household. However, scandal soon surrounded Seymour's behaviour with the king's half-sister, Elizabeth, and Seymour ended up on the scaffold.
- In 1551, following the fall of the Lord Protector and the rise of John Dudley, Grey was made Duke of Suffolk at the same time that Dudley was made Duke of Northumberland. Grey was one of those who convicted the former Lord Protector, and he was rewarded with some of Seymour's property.

- In May 1553, Grey's eldest daughter, Lady Jane Grey, married Northumberland's son, Lord Guildford Dudley, and the dying King Edward VI, Frances Grey's first cousin, chose Lady Jane Grey as his successor. Jane was proclaimed queen on 10th July 1553.
- Although Jane's council chose Grey to leave London to apprehend Edward's half-sister, Mary, who had proclaimed herself queen, Jane chose her father-in-law, Northumberland, to go instead. Without Northumberland's leadership, Jane's council betrayed her and proclaimed for Mary and Jane's reign ended on 19th July 1553, with her father being the one to inform her and to take down her cloth of estate.
- Jane, her husband Guildford, her father, her father-in-law, her brothers-in-law, and other supporters were imprisoned in the Tower of London, but Grey was released without charge on this day in history, 31st July 1553. According to contemporary Robert Wingfield, Grey's wife, Frances, Mary's first cousin, went to visit Mary at Beaulieu to intercede for her husband and "to obtain his liberty on parole". Wingfield records that Mary "freely conceded this, won over by cousinly affection, by her entreaties and by her own merciful nature". Frances may have tried to appeal for her daughter too, but Jane remained in the Tower. While Frances went to court with her cousin, the queen, Grey stayed at home at East Sheen.
- On 1st November 1553, Simon Renard, the Spanish ambassador, recorded that "The Duke of Suffolk is doing bad work in connexion with religion, and the Queen is angry with him for his manner of abusing her clemency and good nature". On 14th November, in his report on the condemnation of Lady Jane Grey, Renard mentioned that the queen was "truly irritated against the Duke of Suffolk". However, just three days later, Renard reported that Grey had recanted his Protestant faith and that Queen Mary I had "reinstated him by means of a general pardon."
- You'd think that Henry Grey would have stayed out of trouble for the sake of his imprisoned daughter, who'd been condemned to death, but, he became involved in Wyatt's Rebellion, a rebellion seeking to depose Mary and replace her with her half-

sister, Elizabeth. Unfortunately for Grey and his daughter, the rebellion failed, and Grey was arrested as he tried to flee the country in disguise. After she'd been merciful, his betrayal of the queen led to Mary finally signing the death warrants of his daughter, Jane, and her husband, Guildford. Jane and Guildford were executed on 12th February 1554, and Grey was found guilty of high treason on 17th February and condemned to death. He was executed by beheading on 23rd February 1554.

1 August

On 1st August 1556, a blind woman named Joan Waste was burnt in Derby for heresy after refusing to recant her Protestant faith.

Let me tell you a bit more about this Protestant martyr.

Martyrologist John Foxe writes of Joan, who he describes as a "poor honest godly woman", being about 22 years of age at her burning, so she was born in about 1534. She was the daughter of barber William Waste, who was also a ropemaker. Joan and her twin brother Roger were born in the parish of All Hallows in Derby, and Joan was blind from birth. Foxe recorded that from the age of 12-14, Joan had learnt to knit hosen and sleeves and was also able to help her father make ropes.

Following her parents' death, she lived with her brother, and in the Protestant reign of King Edward VI, she worshipped daily and became devout in her reformed faith. She saved up for a New Testament and got a man named John Hurt, who was in the Common Hall prison in Derby for debt, to read it to her, which he did, one chapter daily. If he could not read it one day, she would ask another man, a clerk of the local parish church, to read to her, or she'd pay someone. The result of this, John Foxe writes, was that "she was able not only to recite many chapters of the New Testament without book, but also could aptly impugn, by divers places of Scriptures, as well sin, as such abuses in religion, as then were too much in use in divers and sundry persons."

But then the Catholic Mary I came to the throne. Joan continued her biblical education and refused "to communicate in religion with those which taught contrary doctrine". Her religious zeal led to her being called before Ralph Banes, Bishop of Derby, and his chancellor, Dr Draicot. The main charge laid against her was that she viewed the bread and wine of the sacrament as just a representation of Christ's body and blood and did not believe that it was converted into his actual body and blood.

Joan defended herself by stating that she believed what the Holy Scriptures taught her, what diverse learned men had preached, and that they believed in all conscience that what they taught was true. She also stated that she would give up her life for her faith. The bishop, chancellor and their men argued with her, stating their beliefs on the sacrament, but Joan stood firm in her faith and refused to recant. They then sentenced her as a heretic and delivered her to the bailiffs of All Hallows.

After about five weeks, she was sentenced to be burnt for heresy and taken to the parish of All Saints.

On 1st August 1556, Joan was taken to the Church of All Saints and placed before the pulpit to hear Dr Draicot preach against her and her beliefs. He explained to the congregation that she was condemned for denying the blessing of the sacrament and that not only was she blind in the eyes, "but also blind in the eyes of her soul". He finished his sermon by saying that her body would shortly be burnt by fire, and her soul would be burnt by everlasting fire.

Here is how Foxe concludes his section on Joan:

> "And so with many terrible threats he made an end of his sermon, and commanded the bailiffs and those gentlemen to see her executed. And the sermon thus ended, eftsoons the blessed servant of God was carried away from the said church, to a place called the Windmill pit, near unto the said town, and holding the foresaid Roger Waste her brother by the hand she prepared herself, and desired the people to pray with her, and said such prayers as she before had learned, and cried upon Christ to have mercy upon her, as long as life served. In this mean season, the said Dr. Draicot went to his inn, for great sorrow of her death, and there laid him down, and slept, during all the time of her execution! And thus much of Joan Waste."

What a sad end to a courageous and faithful young woman!

2 August

On 2nd August 1581, in the reign of Queen Elizabeth I, Protestant Richard Atkins was burnt to death. However, he was not executed in England, but before St Peter's in Rome.

As Atkins was taken to St Peter's to meet his death, his back and breast were burnt by men holding torches. His right hand was then cut off, and his legs burnt first to prolong his suffering.

But how did this Englishman end up suffering this way in Rome?

In his 1582 book "The English Romayne Lyfe", published just a year after Atkins' execution, Anthony Munday recounts Atkins' alleged crimes in a chapter dedicated to him. He explains that Herefordshire man Atkins travelled to Rome and went straight to the English College there, the Catholic seminary, and told the priests that he had come "to rebuke the great misorder of your lives" and then went on to call the pope, the head of their church, the Antichrist. The College reported him to the Inquisition, who examined Atkins and then released him.

However, Atkins wasn't going to keep quiet regarding his feelings about the Catholic faith. Munday records that he met a priest carrying the sacrament in the street, and his conscience was "offended" when he saw people crouching and kneeling to it in worship. So, he tried to grab it, to throw it to the floor, but missed. He got away with that, but Munday goes on to write:

> "A few days after, he came to Saint Peter's Church, where diverse Gentlemen & others, were hearing Mass, and the Priest being at the elevation: he using no reverence, stepped amongst the people to the Altar, and threw down the Chalice with the Wine, striving likewise to have pulled the Cake out of the Priest's hands. For which, diverse rose up, and beat him with their fists, and one drew his Rapier, and would have slain him: so that in brief, he was carried to prison, where he was examined, wherefore he committed such a heinous offence: whereto he answered, that he came purposely for that intent, to rebuke the Pope's wickedness, and their Idolatry. Upon this, he was condemned to be burned: which sentence he said, he was right willing to suffer, and the rather, because the sum of his offence, pertained to the glory of God."

As Munday states, Atkins was imprisoned and refused to recant his beliefs. Munday records his death:

> "Within a while after, he was set upon an Ass, without any saddle, he being from the middle vpward naked,

having some English Priests with him, who talked to him, but he regarded them not, but spake to the people in so good language as he could, and told them they were in a wrong way, and therefore willed them for Christ's cause, to have regard to the saving of their souls.

All the way as he went, there were four that did nothing else, but thrust at his naked body with burning Torches: whereat he neither moved nor shrunk one jot, but with a cheerful countenance, laboured still to persuade the people, often bending his body to meet the Torches as they were thrust at him, & would take them in his own hand, and hold them burning still uppon his body, whereat the people not a little wondered. Thus he continued almost the space of half a mile, til he came before Saint Peters, where the place of Execution was. When he was come to the place of Execution, there they had made a devise, not to make the fire about him, but to burn his leggs first, which they did, he not dismaying any whit, but suffered all marvellous cheerfully, which moved the people to such a quandary, as was not in Rome many a day. Then they offered him a Cross, and willed him to embrace it, in token that he died a Christian: but he put it away with his hand, telling them, that they were evil men to trouble him with such paltry, when he was preparing him self to God, whom he beheld in Majesty and Mercy, ready to receive him into the eternal rest. They seeing him still in that mind, departed, saying: Let us go, and leave him to the devil, whom he serves. Thus ended this faithful Soldier and Martyr of Christ who is no doubt in glory with his Master, whereto God grant us all to come. Amen."

Atkins had not only been a heretic, but also attacked the Catholic church and its doctrines in the holy city of Rome. Not a wise move, but then this man believed he could save people's souls by pointing out the error of their ways.

3 August

On 3rd August 1562, Essex magnate and notorious rake John de Vere, 16th Earl of Oxford, died at Hedingham Castle, in Castle Hedingham, Essex.

Let me share with you a few facts about this Tudor rake.

- Oxford was born at Hedingham Castle, in Essex, in 1516 and was the eldest son of John de Vere, 15th Earl of Oxford, and his second wife, Elizabeth Trussell.
- Oxford's father, the 15th earl, had served Henry VIII as an esquire of the body, great chamberlain, and a royal councillor and had carried the crown at Anne Boleyn's coronation in 1533, as well as subsequently sitting on the jury trying her in 1536.
- Oxford was Lord Bulbeck until his father died in 1540, when he became the 16th Earl of Oxford. Unfortunately, he didn't follow in his father's footsteps as chamberlain as that title was granted to Thomas Cromwell.
- With his father, Oxford was present at the reception of Anne of Cleves in London in January 1540. He served in Henry VIII's French campaign in 1544 as captain of the rearguard and was a chief mourner at the king's funeral in 1547. He also served in that role at Edward VI's funeral in 1553.
- Oxford was knighted in the celebrations for Edward VI's coronation in 1547.
- Oxford married Dorothy Neville, daughter of Ralph Neville, 4th Earl of Westmorland, in 1536 in a ceremony attended by Henry VIII. The couple had a daughter, Katherine, in 1538, but Dorothy left Oxford in June 1546. When the Duke of Norfolk, who was related to her by marriage, tried to persuade her to return to her husband, Dorothy explained that "she wold never goe home agayne amongst such a bad companye as were about the Earle of Oxford at that tyme". She was referring to men like John Lucas, master of requests, who gambled with Oxford and even won the wardship of a young woman from Oxford via a game of dice. Oxford also had a mistress, and it was said that he made a bigamous marriage to a woman called Joan Jockey, who was subsequently attacked, her

nose cut, by Thomas Darcy and Edmund Sheffield, who were married to Oxford's sisters, Elizabeth and Anne. By the time of Dorothy's death in January 1548, Oxford was already involved with Dorothy Fosser, his daughter's servant, and even had banns of marriage read out in 1547 before Dorothy's death. However, in August 1548, he married Margery Golding and had a son with her, Edward de Vere, 17th Earl of Oxford, and a daughter, Mary.

- In 1552, Henry Neville, Dorothy's brother, attacked Oxford, striking him and drawing blood. It is not known what provoked the attack.
- In 1553, Oxford was one of those who signed Edward VI's letters patent in which the king named Lady Jane Grey as his heir, and he was said to have imprisoned a man named Clement Tusser in Hedingham Castle after Tusser had proclaimed Edward VI's half-sister, Mary, as queen. Tusser was able to get Oxford's servants on side, though, and Oxford did an about-turn and released Tusser and confined those in his household who were on Lady Jane Grey's side. He then organised his men and supported Mary with his force. He was rewarded for his support by being made great chamberlain after the office was taken off the Marquess of Northampton.
- In 1554, he opposed the marriage match of Mary I and Philip of Spain but avoided getting implicated in any plots against the queen.
- In 1555, as the local magnate, he helped oversee the burnings of heretics in Colchester and Manningtree.
- When Elizabeth I came to the throne, Oxford kept his office of chamberlain and served as Lord Lieutenant of Essex. He was on the jury that tried Thomas Wentworth, 2nd Baron Wentworth, for his part in losing Calais in 1558.
- In 1561, he entertained Queen Elizabeth I at his home.
- Like Earls of Oxford before him, Oxford maintained a company of players who performed in London and the provinces.
- He died on this day in Tudor history, 3rd August 1562. Although he had stated in his will that he wanted to be buried at Earl's Colne, it appears that he was buried at Castle Hedingham.

- Oxford's widow married Charles Tyrell but was buried with Oxford when she died in 1568. Oxford's son and heir, Edward, became the ward of Sir William Cecil, chief advisor to Elizabeth I.
- Oxford's daughter, Katherine, married Edward Windsor, 3rd Baron Windsor; his son, Edward, married Anne Cecil and then Elizabeth Trentham. His daughter Mary married Peregrine Bertie, Baron Willoughby, and then Sir Eustace Hart.

4 August

On 4th August 1549, the Battle of Woodbury Common, part of the Prayer Book Rebellion, took place on Woodbury Common, near the village of Woodbury in East Devon. The battle began at 4am and happened when the rebels, who had been defending Clyst St Mary, marched to Woodbury Mill where John Russell, 1st Earl of Bedford, and his Crown troops had camped for the night. The rebels were defeated.

Before I share an account of that day in 1549, let me just explain how and why this rebellion came about.

Edward VI's father, Henry VIII, had broken with Rome in the 1530s and had been declared the Supreme Head of the Church in England. Although Henry had died a Catholic, the break had brought religious changes to the country, and these had become more Protestant when his young son came to the throne.

In 1549, the Book of Common Prayer, composed mainly by Archbishop Thomas Cranmer and the official liturgy of Edward VI's Protestant Church, was introduced into England. It was in English and replaced the Catholic Mass that the English people were used to celebrating. This change wasn't embraced by all of the English people, and in the summer of 1549, there was trouble in the southwest of England, in Devon and Cornwall. The rebels called for the rebuilding of abbeys, the restoration of the Six Articles, the restoration of prayers for souls in purgatory, the policy of only the bread being given to the laity and the use of Latin for the mass.

In July 1549, the Cornish and Devonshire rebels laid siege to the city of Exeter. The siege lasted for 5-6 weeks. On 28th July, there was the Battle of Fenny Bridges, an inconclusive battle between the rebels and the Crown's forces led by John Russell, 1st Earl of Bedford, and then, on this day in 1549, there was the Battle of Woodbury Common.

In "The ancient history and description of the city of Exeter" (1765), John Hooker writes of the battle:

"Accordingly, about six days after, on Saturday 3rd August, he [Lord Russell] set out from Honiton, and marched in good order, towards Exeter, with about 1000 fighting men under his command; but leaving the direct high road, he came over the down towards Woodbury, and there pitched his camp that night at a windmill belonging to one Gregory Carie, Gent. When the rebels of St. Mary Clyst heard thereof, they forthwith assembled all their force, and marched forward until they came to the aforesaid mill, where they gave battle; and notwithstanding they fought most valiantly, at length they were defeated, and a great number of them slain."

5 August

On 5th August 1549, during the reign of King Edward VI, the Battle of Clyst St Mary took place at the village of Clyst St Mary, 3 miles east of Exeter in Devon. It was part of the Prayer Book Rebellion and took place the day after the Battle of Woodbury Common (see yesterday).

In the 18th-century book "The ancient history and description of the city of Exeter", John Hooker gives an account of the battle. He explains that the Crown's forces led by the Earl of Bedford and Sir William Francis reached Clyst at 9am and divided into three forces to enter the town by three different ways. The rebels had fortified the town and had also set up an ambush. Hooker explains:

"Now as the King's army was marching in good Order into the Town, one of the chief captains of these rebels, viz. Sir Thomas Pomeroie, Knightt. hid himself in a Furse-Brake; and seeing the army was past him, having a Trumpeter and Drummer with him, commanded the Trumpeter to sound, and the Drummer to beat a March. Lord Russell and his company, on hearing of this and supposing verily that there had been an ambush behind, to have entrapped and inclosed 'em, retired back with all the haste they could. Which those in the town perceiving, immediately followed them, until they came to the Waggons, which stood in the High Way, and which now by the retreat of the Army, instead of being in its rear, were nearest to the Town. These, being laden with Ammunition, Provisions, and Treasure, they took and brought back into the Town, out of which they took what they thought fit, destroyed the rest, and employed the Ordnance, Shot, etc. against Ld. Russell and his forces.

The army having recovered the hill did pause there for a while; and finding themselves to be deceived, marched back again towards the town; but before they came thither, his Lordship was inform'd that every house therein was fortified, and full of men; and that it was not possible to pass that way without great danger unless the town was set on fire. Upon this, order was given to set fire thereto, notwithstanding it belonged to his Lordship. Sir William Francis, who was at the head of the foremost division, leaving the road which he first march'd, took now one that was both deep and narrow; when the enemy, being upon the banks on each side of the road, with stones so beat him, that they struck his headpiece fast to his head, of which he died.

The army having, however, got into the town, set fire to every house they could come at. But the rebels, who now assembled themselves in the middle of it, stood upon their defence; when a very fierce, cruel, and bloody fight began, in which some were slain by the sword, some burnt in the houses, some shifting for themselves, were taken prisoners, and many, thinking to escape over the water, were drowned; so that there fell that day about a thousand of these obstinate and foolish men."

As Hooker describes, some were killed fighting, some burnt to death, and some drowned. It was a resounding victory for the Crown, who took around 900 prisoners and then massacred them later that day to stop them from escaping and rejoining the enemy. A dreadful day.

6 August

On 6th August 1549, the Battle of Clyst Heath took place. This was another battle in the Prayer Book Rebellion.

Upon hearing of the news of the massacre of the rebels the previous day, two thousand more rebels made their way to Clyst Heath, where John Russell, Earl of Bedford, and Lord William Grey were camped, and opened fire. The battle lasted all day, but the rebels were defeated.

John Hooker wrote of the battle:

"The Rebels which lay about Exeter, hearing of the many Defeats given to the Malcontents, their neighbours, assembled together as many men as they could raise, and in all haste came to Clyst-Heath; and on the Lower Side thereof, next the Highway, entrenched themselves, and fortified a place fast by a hedge, where they secretly planted their Ordnance in the Night, and put all Things in Readiness, being resolved to abide the Brunt. At Break of day, having therefore discharged their pieces against the Army encamped upon the Top of the Hill, the Lords and Captains, the sooner to end the Quarrel, determined to give the Onset, accordingly they divided themselves into three parts, every one having his proper place assigned him.

Lord Russell having no way open before him caused his pioneers to cut thro' the hedges of inclosed grounds; by which means he at length came upon the very Back of the Enemy; and they were so entrapped on every Side, that they could not any Way escape, but must either yield or Fight. The one they would not, and in the other they prevailed not; tho' indeed they fought most stoutly, nor would give out as long as life and limb lasted; so that few or none were left alive. Great was the slaughter and cruel was the fight; and such was the Valour of these men, that the Lord Grey declared, that he never, in all the wars that he had been, knew the like."

The Earl of Bedford then marched on to Exeter to relieve the city, which had been under siege for five weeks.

The final battle of the rebellion was the Battle of Sampford Courtenay on 17th August 1549. The rebels were defeated, and those who survived the battle fled to Launceston Castle, where they were captured and taken to the Tower of London.

7 August

On Sunday 7th August 1485, Henry Tudor (the future Henry VII), son of Lady Margaret Beaufort and the late Edmund Tudor, Earl of Richmond, "came unto Wales", landing at Mill Bay.

He had left Harfleur in France, where he had been in exile in Brittany, on 1st August 1485, sailing with a force of French mercenaries and English exiles. He intended to claim the throne of England from Richard III. Henry dropped anchor at Mill Bay, near Milford Haven, Wales.

Polydore Vergil recorded his return from exile:

"He loosed from the mouth of the Seyne with two thousand only of armed men and a few ships, the calends of August, and with a soft southern wind. The weather being very fair, he came unto Wales the 7th day after, a little before sunset, where, entering the haven called Milford, and forthwith going a land, he took first a place the name whereof is Dale, where he heard that certain companies of his adversaries had had their stations the winter by past to have kept him from landing."

Chronicler Robert Fabyan recorded that on disembarking at Mill Bay, Henry knelt on the beach and recited the psalm "Judge me, O God, and favour my cause". He then "kissed the ground meekly and reverently, made the sign of a cross upon him" and then "commanded such as were about him boldly in the name of God and Saint George to set forward."

Vergil states that "From thence departing in the break of day he went to Haverford, which is a town not ten miles from Dale, where he was received with great goodwill of all men, and the same he did with such celerity as that he was present and spoken of all at once."

Henry and his force then set off for London, marching through Wales and the Marches and gathering support on their journey. Although they were aiming for London, they encountered King Richard III and his forces in Leicestershire. On 22nd August 1485, the forces of Henry Tudor and King Richard III clashed at the Battle of Bosworth Field, near Market Bosworth. King Richard was killed during the battle, and Henry Tudor became King Henry VII. Henry ruled until his death in April 1509 and passed the throne on to his second son, who became King Henry VIII.

8 August

On 8th August 1553, fifteen-year-old King Edward VI was buried in a white marble vault beneath the altar of Henry VII's Lady Chapel in Westminster Abbey.

Edward had died on 6th July 1553, but the struggle for the throne between the heir he had appointed, Lady Jane Grey, and his half-sister, Mary, plus discussions between Mary I and her ministers over his funeral rites, had led to a delay in burial. It was finally decided that Edward would be buried with Protestant rites, the first use of the English Book of Common Prayer for a monarch's funeral. Thomas Cranmer, Archbishop of Canterbury performed the service.

Merchant-tailor Henry Machyn recorded the funeral procession in his diary:

> "The 8th day of August was buried the noble king Edward the vi, and 7th year of his reign; and at his burying was the greatest moan made for him of his death as ever was heard or seen, both of all sorts of people, weeping and lamenting; and first of all went a great company of children in their surplices, and clerks singing; and then his father's bedmen, and then 2

heralds and then a standard with a dragon, and then a great number of his servants in black, and then another standard with a white greyhound, and then after a great number of his officers and after them came more heralds, and then a standard with the head officers of his house; and then heralds, Norroy bore the helmet and the crest on horseback, and then his great banner of arms embroidered, and with diverse other banners, and then came riding master Clarenceux with his target, with his garter, and his sword, gorgeously and rich, and after Garter with his coat armour embroidered, and then more heralds of arms; and then came the chariot with great horses trapped with velvet to the ground, and every horse having a man on his back in black, and every one bearing a banner-roll of diverse kings arms, and with escutcheons on their horses, and then the chariot covered with cloth of gold, and on the chariot lay on a picture lying richly with a crown of gold, and a great collar, and his sceptre in his hand, lying in his robes and the garter about his leg, and a coat in embroidery of gold; about the corpse were borne four banners, a banner of the order, another of the red rose, another of queen Jane (Seymour), another of the queen's mother. After him went a goodly horse, covered with cloth of gold unto the ground, and the master of the horse, with a man of arms in armour, which was offered, both the man and the horse. There was set up a goodly hearse in Westminster abbey with banner rolls and pensells, and hung with velvet about."

Edward's half-sister, the Catholic Queen Mary I, did not attend and had requiem masses sung at the Tower of London for three days beginning on 8th August at Vespers.

Edward's grave was unmarked until 1966, but his coffin was seen in the 19th century, and it was labelled with a Latin inscription which, when translated, read:

"Edward the sixth by the Grace of God King of England, France and Ireland, Defender of the Faith and on earth under Christ supreme head of the churches of England and Ireland and he migrated from this life on the 6th day of July in the evening at the 8th hour in the year of our Lord 1553 and in the 7th year of his reign and in the 16th year of his age."

In 1966, a stone was placed in front of the altar of the chapel, marking his burial site and inscribed with the following memorial:

"IN MEMORY OF KING EDWARD VI BURIED IN THIS CHAPEL THIS STONE WAS PLACED HERE BY CHRIST'S HOSPITAL IN THANKSGIVING FOR THEIR FOUNDER 7 OCTOBER 1966."

9 August

On 9th August 1588, Queen Elizabeth I appeared before the troops gathered at Tilbury Fort in anticipation of a Spanish attack and gave her famous "Tilbury Speech".

There are no reliable eye-witness accounts of what Elizabeth was wearing that day, but tradition places her on a warhorse, wearing a gown of white velvet and a silver cuirass, and holding a silver truncheon in her hand. In her article, "The Myth of Elizabeth at Tilbury", Susan Fry points out that an analogy is being drawn between Elizabeth I and Britomart, the armed heroine of Edmund Spenser's "The Faerie Queene", the Virgin Knight of Chastity and Virtue.

The most famous rendition of Elizabeth I's speech that day is from a letter from Dr Leonel Sharp to the Duke of Buckingham in the early 17th century. Sharp was at Tilbury that day, but was writing from memory and, as Susan Frye notes, was using it to make a point in his letter - he feared the proposed Spanish marriage of Prince Charles. Here is his version of the speech:

"My loving people, We have been persuaded by some that are careful of our safety, to take heed how we commit our selves to armed multitudes, for fear of treachery; but I assure you I do not desire to live to distrust my faithful and loving people.

Let tyrants fear. I have always so behaved myself that, under God, I have placed my chiefest strength and safeguard in the loyal hearts and good-will of my subjects; and therefore I am come amongst you, as you see, at this time, not for my recreation and disport, but being resolved, in the midst and heat of the battle, to live and die amongst you all; to lay down for my God, and for my kingdom, and my people, my honour and my blood, even in the dust.

I know I have the body but of a weak and feeble woman; but I have the heart and stomach of a king, and of a king of England too, and think foul scorn that Parma or Spain, or any prince of Europe, should dare to invade the borders of my realm; to which rather than any dishonour shall grow by me, I myself will take up arms, I myself will be your general, judge, and rewarder of every one of your virtues in the field.

I know already, for your forwardness you have deserved rewards and crowns; and We do assure you in the word of a prince, they shall be duly paid you. In the mean time, my lieutenant general shall be in my stead, than whom never prince commanded a more noble or worthy subject; not doubting but by your obedience to my general, by your concord in the camp, and your valour in the field, we shall shortly have a famous victory over those enemies of my God, of my kingdom, and of my people."

However, the speech recorded in 1612 by William Leigh, in his sermon "Quene Elizabeth, Paraleld in Her Princely Vertues", where he describes Elizabeth appearing before her troops "with God in her heart, and a commanding staff in her hand", may be more accurate. Here it is:

"Come on now, my companions at arms, and fellow soldiers, in the field, now for the Lord, for your Queen, and for the Kingdom. For what are these proud Philistines, that they should revile the host of the living God?

I have been your Prince in peace, so will I be in war; neither will I bid you go and fight, but come and let us fight the battle of the Lord. The enemy perhaps may challenge my sex for that I am a woman, so may I likewise charge their mould for that they are but men, whose breath is in their nostrils, and if God do not charge England with the sins of England, little do I fear their force… Si deus nobiscum quis contra nos? (if God is with us, who can be against us?)"

It is corroborated by a very similar speech which appears beneath a late 16th or early 17th century painting of Elizabeth at Tilbury at St Faith's Church, Gaywood:

"Now for Queen & For the kingdom. I have been your Queen in Peace, in war, neither will I bid you go & Fight, but come & let us Fight the battle of the Lord. For what are these proud Philistines that they should Revile the host of the Living God. It may be they will challenge my sex, for that I am a woman, so may I charge their mould for that they are but men whose breath is in their nostrils and if God does not charge England with the sins of England, we shall not need to fear what Rome or Spain can do against us, whom is but an army of Flesh, where as with us in the Lord our God to Fight our battles & to help with us, it skills not Greatly if all the devils in hell be against us."

10 August

On 10th August 1512, the Battle of Saint-Mathieu, a naval battle in the War of the League of Cambrai, took place between the English and Franco-Breton fleets off the coast of Brest. England was allied with Spain and the Holy Roman Empire at this time.

As the Mary Rose Museum points out on their excellent website, it was the Mary Rose's first battle, and she was chosen as the English fleet's flagship by the English admiral, Sir Edward Howard. Howard, who was moored with the English fleet at Portsmouth on the south coast of England, had heard that the French fleet had gathered at Brest and set off to meet them. The two fleets met in Bertheaume Bay, near Brest, on 10th August, and the battle began.

The English fleet had twenty-five ships, and the French fleet had twenty-one.

The Mary Rose Museum states that:

> "It was the Mary Rose that, according to records, drew first blood, when she shot off the main mast of the French flagship Grand Louise, commanded by Admiral René de Clermont. Although the Grand Louise was able to escape, with the loss of 300 men, this marked the first time in the history of Naval warfare that ships with lidded gunports had engaged one another."

The battle lasted hours, but the English fleet had the victory in the end. However, its largest ship, the Regent, sank, as did France's the Marie La Cordelière. The two ships had been firing at each other at close quarters when a fire broke out on board La Cordelière. It soon reached the ship's powder magazines, and when that happened, the Regent and La Cordelière were blown up. Both captains were killed, along with around 1,500 men. Those killed included Sir Thomas Knyvet and Sir John Carew, who had been given joint command of the Regent. Edward Hall recorded this in his chronicle:

> "[...] but for all that the English men entered the Carick, which, seeing a varlet Gunner being desperate, put fire in the Gunpowder as other say, and set the whole ship of fire, the flame whereof, set fire in the Regent, and so these two noble ships which were so grappelled together that they could not part, were consumed by fire [...] The captain of this Carick was Sir Piers Morgan and with him 900 men slain and died: and with Sir Thomas Knyvet and Sir John Carew were 700 men drowned and burnt, and that night all the Englishmen lay in Berthhaume Bay, for the French fleet was sparkeled as you have heard."

Cardinal Thomas Wolsey wrote of the battle in a letter to Richard Fox, Bishop of Winchester:

> "Gives an account of a severe sea fight near Brest on Tuesday fortnight, where the Regent captured the great carrick of Brest; but both, fouling, were burnt, and most part of the crew in them. Sir Thomas Knyvet

and Sir John Carew slain. Begs he will keep the news secret.

P.S.—The French fleet has fled to Brest. Sir Edward [Howard] has vowed "that he will never see the King in the face till he hath revenged the death of the noble and valiant knight Sir Thomas Knyvet.""

According to Edward Hall, when Henry VIII heard of the loss of the Regent, he ordered another ship to be made, the Henry Grace à Dieu.

11 August

On 11th August 1581, Sir Maurice Berkeley, gentleman usher of Henry VIII's privy chamber, died. Berkeley served Edward VI as a gentleman of the privy chamber and was the man who arrested the rebel Thomas Wyatt the Younger in Mary I's reign.

But let me give you a few more facts about this lesser-known Tudor man.

- Sir Maurice Berkeley was the son of landowner Richard Berkeley of Stoke, and his wife, Elizabeth Coningsby. His birthdate is not known, but it was sometime before 1514.
- Little is known of his early life except that he was trained in the law in the office of the prothonotary of the common pleas.
- In 1535, his stepfather, Sir John Fitzjames, chief justice of the court of the king's bench, recommended Berkeley to Thomas Cromwell for the position of clerk to the assize. Cromwell did not appoint him to that position. Still, by 1537, he'd appointed Berkeley in his household, and Berkeley became a favourite of Cromwell, being rewarded with leases and offices in the lands of Glastonbury Abbey.
- In 1536, a Mr Bark was listed as jousting at Lord William Howard's wedding celebrations, and it is thought that this was Berkeley.
- By 1539, Berkeley was serving as a gentleman usher of the privy chamber.
- Berkeley survived Cromwell's fall in 1540, continuing to serve the king as a gentleman usher.

- In 1541, he was rewarded with the site and much of the land of Bruton Priory, which became his seat.
- At some point, Berkeley married Catherine, daughter of William Blount, 4th Baron Mountjoy, and widow of John Champernowne. The couple had three sons and five daughters.
- In 1543, he was rewarded for his service to the king by being granted a licence to hold a prebend at Ripon even though he was not a man of the church and he was married. In 1543, he was also listed as serving in Queen Catherine Parr's household.
- In 1544, he served in Henry VIII's French campaign and was knighted in France.
- In 1545, he was appointed a chief banner-bearer of England, a post previously held by his brother.
- Other offices in Henry VIII's reign included Keeper of Northwood Park, Constable of Berkeley Castle, Chief Steward of the lands of Bath Abbey, and commissioner of the musters in Somerset.
- When Henry VIII died in January 1547, he left Berkeley £133 6s. 8d. in his will.
- Berkeley jousted in the celebratory jousts for the coronation of King Edward VI and continued in his royal service, being appointed as a gentleman of the privy chamber in 1550. He benefited from the fall of Lord Protector Somerset by being given some grants.
- He served as a member of Parliament on four occasions between 1547 and 1572, for the constituency of Somerset three times and for Bletchingley once.
- In 1553, Berkeley signed Edward VI's devise for the succession, in which Edward chose Lady Jane Grey as his heir, but he kept out of subsequent events. He benefited from Mary I's general pardon but did lose his office as banner bearer. He proved his loyalty to the new queen by arresting rebel leader Thomas Wyatt the Younger in 1554. However, he did not sit in any of the parliaments of her reign.
- Berkeley was back in favour following the accession of Queen Elizabeth I, and in 1562 he married Elizabeth Sands, daughter of Anthony Sands and a woman who served as one of the

queen's gentlewomen. They went on to have two sons and a daughter.

- Berkeley served as sheriff for Somerset and Dorset from 1567-8.
- He built Berkeley House in Clerkenwell, London, shortly before his death.
- He died on this day in Tudor history, 11th August 1581.

12 August

On 12th August 1570, Lady Ursula Stafford, only daughter of the late Margaret Pole, Countess of Salisbury, died.

Here are some facts about this interesting Tudor lady:

- Ursula was born around 1504 and was the only daughter of Sir Richard Pole and his wife, Margaret Pole, Countess of Salisbury. Ursula's maternal grandparents were George, Duke of Clarence, brother of Kings Edward IV and Richard III, and his wife, Isabella Neville, so Ursula had Plantagenet blood.
- Ursula's father died in 1505 when Ursula was just a baby.
- Ursula is first recorded in the court records in 1513 when she was about nine, and King Henry VIII granted his "dear and wellbeloved cousin" gowns, kirtles and fabric.
- In October 1518, when she was about 14, she married Henry Stafford, son and heir of Edward Stafford, 3rd Duke of Buckingham, and went to live in the duke's household. They went on to have around 14 children together, the first being born in 1520.
- In 1521, Ursula's father-in-law was executed as a traitor, and although Henry and Ursula were granted some of his lands, the most valuable ones were taken and given to others.
- Their daughter, Margaret, was placed with her grandmother, the Countess of Salisbury, and their daughter, Dorothy, with Princess Elizabeth to help the Staffords' financial situation.
- In 1538, Ursula's mother and brothers, Henry, 1st Baron Montagu, and Geoffrey, were accused of treason and arrested. It was said that they had been corresponding with Ursula's other brother, Cardinal Reginald Pole. He had famously fallen out with King Henry VIII after speaking out against the annulment

of his first marriage. Montagu and the countess were executed, and Geoffrey was pardoned after he tried to commit suicide twice during his imprisonment in the Tower. The countess's execution was particularly unsavoury. She was a frail sixty-seven-year-old and had done nothing. Ursula was lucky to survive her family's fall.

- Ursula went on to have close relationships with Montagu's daughter, Katherine, Countess of Huntingdon, her niece, and also, after his return to England in Mary I's reign, her brother, Reginald, who became Archbishop of Canterbury.
- Her husband died in 1563, and their son, Henry, became 2nd Baron Stafford, but only for two years as he died in 1565. His younger brother, Edward, inherited the title, becoming 3rd Baron Stafford.
- Ursula died on 12th August 1570 at about sixty-six years of age.

13 August

On 13th August 1579, Roman Catholics Friar Conn (or Connatius) O'Rourke and Patrick O'Healy, Bishop of Mayo, were hanged just outside Kilmallock, County Limerick.

O'Rourke and O'Healy were from the County Leitrim area and had joined the Franciscan Order before travelling to the Continent to train as priests. O'Healey, born around 1545, had studied theology and philosophy in Spain and trained as a priest there. In 1575, he travelled to Rome on behalf of Sir James Fitzmaurice, who was planning a military expedition to Ireland to defend the Catholic faith there. In 1576, while he was in Rome, Pope Gregory XIII made O'Healey Bishop of Mayo.

In the winter of 1577/8, O'Healey and Fitzmaurice set sail from Portugal for Ireland but had to abandon the journey due to storms. Fitzmaurice decided to travel to Spain. O'Healey went to Paris, where he helped educate young priests of the Franciscan Order and participated in public disputations at the Sorbonne, impressing everyone with his knowledge and command of theology and philosophy. In Paris, he met Conn O'Rourke, who had been born around 1550.

In the summer of 1579, O'Healey and O'Rourke, dressed as sailors, took a boat from Brittany to Ireland, landing at Smerwick Harbour in County Kerry. They travelled through Kerry and Limerick to Askeaton, home of Gerald Fitzgerald, 14th Earl of Desmond, cousin of Fitzmaurice and a powerful man. They hoped that he would help them, seeing as he had no love for Elizabeth I and had even been imprisoned in the Tower of London for a time. The earl was absent, and the countess feared that his involvement in rebellion would lead to his execution and the loss of his lands and property in Ireland. Still, she kept this to herself and offered hospitality to the bishop and priest.

After spending three days with the countess, O'Healey and O'Rourke set off, planning to travel through Limerick to Mayo, the bishop's diocese. However, while they were on the road, the countess, who was keen to prove her loyalty to Queen Elizabeth, sent word to the Mayor of Limerick of these travellers. The mayor's men apprehended O'Healey and O'Rourke, and they were imprisoned in Limerick jail.

While the two were imprisoned, on 18th July 1579, Fitzmaurice landed at Smerwick with several hundred soldiers and called on the Irish people to join him in rebellion. While the English set about sending soldiers to put down his rebellion, Sir William Drury, Lord President of Munster, travelled to Limerick to question O'Healey. Dury questioned the bishop about Fitzmaurice, the pope and King of Spain, and their plans for invasion, believing that O'Healey and O'Rourke had been sent ahead by Fitzmaurice and had information. O'Healey refused to talk even when nails were hammered into his fingers, his hands and feet were broken, and then his fingers were torn from his hands. Drury then used martial law to condemn the two men for treason without a trial, ordering them to be hanged.

O'Rourke and O'Healey were then bound with rope and taken to Kilmallock. As the men were taken to the trees that would act as their gallows, they recited the litany and absolved each other. After encouraging O'Rourke to be strong in the face of death, Bishop O'Healey addressed the crowd, calling on them to be steadfast in their faith and their obedience to the pope. He then asked for their prayers. The two men were hanged to death, and their bodies were left there for about a week, being used as target practice by soldiers, before being laid to rest.

Less than two months later, on 3rd October, Sir William Drury died, something that the people of Ireland saw as retribution for his treatment of these two faithful men.

Pope John Paul II beatified the two men in September 1992.

14 August

On 14th August 1473, in the reign of King Edward IV, Isabelle Neville, Duchess of Clarence and daughter of Richard Neville, Earl of Warwick and a man known as the Kingmaker, gave birth to a daughter by her husband, George, Duke of Clarence, brother of King Edward IV.

Isabelle gave birth at Farley Hungerford Castle, near Bath in Somerset. George and Isabelle called their little girl Margaret, and she would go on to be known as Margaret Pole, Countess of Salisbury. Isabelle died in December 1476, when her daughter was just three years old, and the Duke of Clarence died in February 1478 while imprisoned in the Tower of London. It was rumoured that he was drowned in a barrel of Malmsey wine.

Margaret was brought up with her brother, Edward, Earl of Warwick, first at Sheriff Hutton Castle. Then, after King Henry VII came to the throne in 1485, Margaret's brother was imprisoned in the Tower of London while Margaret was brought up at court. After the Perkin Warbeck Plot of 1499, Edward was attainted and executed. By this time, Margaret had been married off to Sir Richard Pole, a man loyal to King Henry VII. Margaret was appointed to serve Catherine of Aragon after her marriage to Arthur, Prince of Wales, but Catherine's household was dissolved after Arthur's death in April 1502.

Margaret had five children before she was widowed in 1505. One of her children was Reginald Pole, who became a cardinal and then, in the reign of Queen Mary I, Archbishop of Canterbury.

At the beginning of King Henry VIII's reign, Margaret was favoured. The king allowed her to become the 8th Countess of Salisbury, in her own right, and she was Princess Mary's godmother and governess. However, things changed when her son, Reginald, spoke out against the king's annulment of his marriage to Catherine of Aragon. Things got even worse when Reginald published his treatise

"Pro ecclesiasticae unitatis defensione", in which he denounced Henry VIII's policies. This brazen insult to the king made Henry want to wreak his revenge on the Pole family, and the situation was not helped by Margaret's Plantagenet blood, which Henry VIII also saw as a threat.

In November 1538, various members of the Pole family were arrested for treason and taken to the Tower of London. In January 1539, many of them were executed. Even though the countess was elderly (for Tudor times), being 65 years of age in 1538, she was questioned and taken to Cowdray House near Midhurst. In May 1539, a Bill of Attainder was issued against her by Thomas Cromwell. A tunic displaying the Five Wounds, which was used as a symbol in the Northern rebellions, was used as evidence against her, having allegedly been found in her belongings. She was stripped of her titles and imprisoned in the Tower of London.

After two years of imprisonment as a traitor in the Tower, the now frail 67-year-old Plantagenet heiress was executed. As a woman of noble birth, Margaret Pole was given a private execution within the Tower walls on 27th May 1541.

There are two accounts of her execution. One says that she was executed by an inexperienced axeman who missed her neck the first time, gashing her shoulder, and that it took a further ten blows to finish her off. The second account tells of how she managed to escape from the block and that she was hewn down by the executioner as she ran. This second account concurs with the first in that it says that eleven blows were required. Whichever account you believe, this lady had a truly awful end.

On the 29th December 1886, Pope Leo XIII beatified Margaret, making her Blessed Margaret Pole, a Catholic martyr. Her feast day is the 28th May, which some sources give as her execution date.

A ballad said to have been based on words found carved into her cell wall goes:
"For traitors on the block should die;
I am no traitor, no, not I!
My faithfulness stands fast and so,
Towards the block I shall not go!

Nor make one step, as you shall see;
Christ in Thy Mercy, save Thou me!"

15 August

On 15th August 1603, just under five months after the
death of Queen Elizabeth I and accession of King James I, Lady Mary
Scudamore (née Shelton), a member of Elizabeth I's Privy Chamber
and one of her favourite sleeping companions, was buried at Holme
Lacy in Herefordshire.

Mary was in her early fifties when she died, having been
born c.1550/1551 to Sir John Shelton of Shelton Hall, Norfolk,
and Margaret Parker. Mary was second cousin to Queen Elizabeth I.
Mary's paternal grandmother was Lady Anne Shelton (née Boleyn),
sister of Thomas Boleyn, Elizabeth's maternal grandfather. In 1568,
Mary began serving her relative, the queen, as a gentlewoman of the
queen's privy chamber. In 1571, she was promoted to chamberer.

Mary met Catholic Sir John Scudamore, a widower with five
children, at court. He was close to Sir James Croft, Comptroller of
the Household, having been his ward in his youth, and Croft helped
him rise at court and become a gentleman usher to the queen. Mary
and John asked Croft to find out if the queen would approve of their
marriage match and when it was made clear that she would not, they
were married secretly by a Catholic priest in 1574.

The queen was furious at their deception. In a letter written to
Elizabeth I, Mary, Queen of Scots, mentioned a story she'd heard
concerning Elizabeth's reaction to news of the Scudamores' marriage.
She wrote of Lady Talbot refusing to be in service to the queen "because
she should be in fear, that when you was in wrath, you would do to
her as you did to her cousin Skedmur, one of whose fingers you broke,
and made those of the court believe that it was broken by a chandelier
falling down from above."

Mary, Queen of Scots, also accused Elizabeth of attacking another
lady waiting on her at the table, saying Elizabeth "gave her a great blow
with a knife upon the hand."

Another letter, written by Eleanor Bridges, one of the queen's maids
of honour, stated, "The Queen has used Mary Shelton very ill for her

marriage. She hath telt liberall bothe with bloes and yevell wordes, and hath not yet graunted her consent."

The Scudamores were eventually forgiven and continued in their rise at court, with Mary being one of Elizabeth's closest confidantes at the end of her reign.

Mary became ill in 1602 and had to retire to her home at Holme Lacey. However, she was able to attend the queen's funeral. Mary died sometime in the summer of 1603 and was buried on this day in 1603

16 August

On 16th August 1599, soldier and Lord President of Munster in Ireland, Sir Thomas Norris, died at his home, Mallow Castle, in Cork, due to an injury he'd sustained in a skirmish with Irish troops on 30th May 1599.

His brother, Sir Henry Norris, died just five days later, on 21st August 1599, following complications from his leg being amputated after being injured in a skirmish with Irish troops in June 1599.

These two men were the sons of Henry Norris, 1st Baron Norris, and his wife, Margery Williams, and the grandsons of the Henry Norris, who was groom of the stool to Henry VIII and who was executed in May 1536 in the fall of Anne Boleyn.

Thomas and Henry were not the only sons that Baron Norris and his wife lost in service to the crown. They had lost their eldest son, Sir John Norris, while he served as Lord President of Munster in September 1597; their son, William, in 1579, also in Ireland; and another son, Maximilian, who died campaigning in Brittany in 1593. Five sons lost serving as soldiers for Elizabeth I.

The Norrises had a long-standing connection with Queen Elizabeth I. Baron Norris had been appointed by Mary I to guard Elizabeth during her house arrest at Woodstock in 1554. Elizabeth became close to the baron and his wife. After becoming queen, Elizabeth made several visits to their home at Rycote in Oxfordshire, and she affectionately called Margery her "own dear crow". Elizabeth also rewarded Norris with several titles and offices, including a knighthood and a barony. She also made him Lord Lieutenant of Oxfordshire.

After the Norrises lost their son, John, in 1597, Elizabeth wrote them a letter of condolence, and she did the same in 1599 following the deaths of Thomas and Henry. The letter still survives in the Bodleian Library Collection. Here is what she wrote:

"Your most Lovinge and Afectionate Soveraigne.

Elizabeth R.

Right Trustie and right welbeloved, And right deare and welbeloved we greet you well. The bitter accidentes befallen you which is the Cause of our writinge, beinge that which toucheth you bothe with equall smarte, And our desire that all the Comforte which we wishe to you, may reatch to each of you together with our lettres. Lothe we were to have written att all, because in such accidentes (for the most parte) the offeringe of Comforte, is but the presentinge of freshe occasion of sorrowe. But yet beinge well perswaded of your Constant resolution, grownded as well on the experience of other like mishapes (which yours have seene) as also Cheefely upon your religious obedience to the worke of his hande whose strokes ar avoidable we could not forbeare to doe our parte. Partely because we conceave that we shall therin propose our selves for an example to you, our losse in politicke respecte (Consideringe their great merritt) beinge no lesse then yours in naturall Consideration. And partly by givinge you assuraunce that whatsoever from us may minister Comforte by demonstratinge towardes you the valeue we made of The departed, shall not faile to be ymployed to your best Contentmentes. Assuringe you that for this harde happ of yours we will give order that assone as possible he may leave his Charge in good sorte, he shalbe with you to yeald you all duety and service he may because we knowe it wold be some stay to your sorrowes, to have hym in your ey who nowe is in forraine partes and that your hard hap shall rather serve us for matter to increase our care of you then any waye to abate it. geven under our Signett att our Honor of Hampton Corte the 6th of September 1599 in the 41th yeare of our Raigne."

When Elizabeth is talking about giving orders that "he may leave his charge" and saying that having him in their eye will "be some stay to your sorrows", she is talking about the Norrises' last surviving son, Sir Edward Norris, who, like his brothers, was a distinguished soldier, and who'd been appointed Governor of Ostend in 1590. He died a natural death in October 1603.

17 August

On 17th August 1517, Italian humanist scholar, cleric and poet Andreas Ammonius (also known as Andrea Ammonio and Andrea della Rena) died in London from sweating sickness. He was laid to rest at St Stephen's, Westminster.

Ammonius served Henry VIII as Latin Secretary and received various church offices, including the canonry and prebendary of St Stephen's, Westminster. He also served the papacy as sub-collector of taxes in England.

But let me give you a few more facts about this man.

- Ammonius was born in 1476 in Lucca, Tuscany, and was the son of Francesco della Rena and Elizabetta Vanni.
- He was from a family of silk weavers, but was educated for a career in the church, studying at the University of Bologna. While in Bologna, in 1495, his tutor Oliviero da Montegallo, a professor of logic, entrusted him with a revision of Stephanus de Flandria's "Logica".
- He spent time in Rome, where he met Silvestro Gigli, Henry VII's ambassador, and by 1506 he'd arrived in England.
- In 1509, he was working as a secretary to William Blount, Lord Mountjoy, who was close to the humanist scholar Erasmus, whom Ammonius met on several occasions. Ammonius became great friends with Erasmus, exchanging letters, jokes, poems and compliments, and Erasmus referred to him as the "dearest of mortals". Ammonius also became close to Thomas More, Thomas Linacre, John Colet, Cuthbert Tunstall and Richard Pace.

- Between 1503 and 1511, Ammonius wrote poetry in Latin, which was printed in Paris, and we know that he also wrote work on Henry VIII's campaigns in France and the Battle of Flodden, which have unfortunately not survived.
- In July 1511, Ammonius was appointed as Henry VIII's Latin secretary, and in 1512, he became canon and prebend of St Stephen's, Westminster. In 1513 and 1517, he added benefices in Salisbury and Bath and Wells to the list.
- In 1513, he accompanied Henry VIII on his campaign in France and in April 1514, he became an English citizen.
- In 1515, Ammonius was appointed sub-collector of papal taxes in England by Pope Leo X, then collector in June 1517 after his rival Polydore Vergil was imprisoned and his other rival, Cardinal Castellesi, was linked to a conspiracy.
- Ammonius died during the night of 17th/18th August 1517, in the third sweating sickness epidemic to hit England. Chronicler Edward Hall recorded it, writing: "sudainly there came a plague of sickness called the Swetying Sickness that turned all his [the King's] purpose. This malady was so cruell that it killed some within three houres. Some within two houres, some merry at dinner and dedde at supper. Many died in the Kynges courte, the lorde Clinton, the lorde Gray of Wilton, and many Knightes, gentelmen and officiers. For this plague Mighelmas Terme was adiorned [...]" Many of Cardinal Wolsey's household died, and it was recorded that "upwards of 400 students had died in less than a week" in Oxford. Thomas More wrote to Erasmus, saying, "Multitudes are dying around us. Almost everyone in Oxford, Cambridge and London has been ill lately." More also wrote that it was safer to be on a battlefield than in London at that time.

18 August

On 18th August 1553, less than a month after his daughter-in-law, Lady Jane Grey or Queen Jane, had been overthrown by Queen Mary I, John Dudley, Duke of Northumberland, was tried for treason at Westminster Hall in London.

Northumberland had been arrested in Cambridge on 21st July 1553 after Mary had been officially proclaimed the rightful queen in London. Queen Jane had ruled for just thirteen days, and while Northumberland had been travelling with a force to apprehend Mary, Jane's remaining council had betrayed her and proclaimed for Mary. Northumberland had been taken to the Tower of London on 25th July 1553 to await trial.

On 18th August, Northumberland was taken to Westminster for his trial. Merchant-tailor and diarist Henry Machyn recorded:

> "The 18 day of August was arraigned at Westminster hall the Marquess of Northampton, and the duke, and the Earl of Warwick, and so they were condemned to be had to the place that they came from, and from thence to be drawn through London unto Tyburn, and there to be hanged, and then to be cut down, and their bowels to be burnt, and their heads to be set on London bridge and other places."

Another contemporary source, "The Chronicle of Queen Jane", gives the following record of Northumberland's trial:

> "The 18. of August, John Dudley, duke of Northumberland, William Parre, marquesse of Northampton, and John earle of Warwicke, sonne and heire to the duke, were arraigned at Westminster-hall, before Thomas duke of Norfolke, high steward of England, where the duke of Northumberland, with great reverence towards the judges, protested his faith and alleageance to the queene, whom hee confessed grievously to have offended, and said that he meant not anything in defence of his fact, but requested to understand the opinion of the court in two poynts: first, whether a man doing any act by authority of the prince's councell, and by warrant of the great seale of England, and doing nothing without the same, might be charged with treason for any thing which hee might doe by warrant thereof? Secondly, whether any such persons as were equally culpable in that crime, and those by whose letters and commaundements hee was directed in all his

doinges, might be his judges, or passe upon his tryall as his peeres?

Whereunto was answered, that as concerning the first, the great seale (which hee layd for his warrant) was not the seale of the lawfull queene of the realme, nor passed by authority, but the seale of an usurper, and therefore could be no warrant to him. As to the second, it was alleged, that if any were as deepely to be touched in the case as himselfe, yet so long as no attainder were of record against them, they were neverthelesse persons able in law to passe upon any tryall, and not to be chalenged therefor, but at the prince's pleasure. After which answer, the duke used few words, but confessed the indictment; by whose example the other prisoners arraigned with him did the like, and thereupon had judgement.

And when the judgement was geven, it is saide the duke shoulde saie, "I beseche you, my lordes all, to be humble suters to the quenes majestie, to graunt me iiij. requestes, which are theis: firste, that I may have that deathe which noblemen have had in tymes past, and not the other; secondarylie, that her majestie wilbe gratyous to my chillder, which may hereafter do hir grace gode service, concydering that they went by my commaundement who am their father, and not of their owne free willes; thirdely, that I may have appoynted to me some learned man for the instruction and quieting of my concyence; and iiij th, that she will sende ij. of the counsayle to comon with me, to whom I will declare suche mattyers as shalbe expedyent for hir and the comonwealthe. And thus I beseche you all to pray for me.""

So, during his trial, Northumberland was pointing out that it could not be treason to act in accordance with his king's wishes and under his warrant and seal, and that he was being judged by those who also originally acted as he did, in accordance with Edward VI's wishes. Of course, this didn't get him anywhere, and he was still found guilty and condemned to death.

The sentence of a full traitor's death was commuted to beheading, though, so thankfully, he got a more merciful end. Northumberland was beheaded on 22nd August 1553.

As for those tried with him on this day in 1553 - the Marquess of Northampton and John Dudley, Earl of Warwick, Northumberland's eldest surviving son - they were later released. However, John died shortly after his release in October 1554.

19 August

On 19th August 1551, Princess Mary, the future Mary I, wrote to her half-brother, King Edward VI. Her letter was in response to Robert Rochester, Comptroller of the Royal Household, and two of Mary's household officers, Edward Waldegrave and Sir Francis Engelfield, being called before the king's privy council on 14th August 1551. They were ordered to go to Mary's household at Copt Hall in Essex and to tell her chaplains that the saying of Mass in her household was forbidden and that no member of her household was to hear it. The men went to Copt Hall but did not do as they were instructed and instead brought back a letter from Mary to the king with them.

The editor of "Original Letters, Illustrative of English History...", Henry Ellis, writes that this letter "is probably the best specimen which we have in our power to give of her talent at writing: and, with the singular Paper which follows it by way of comment, will show her to have been a woman of more intellect than the world has usually supposed."

Here's Mary's letter:

"My duty most humbly remembered unto your Majesty. It may please the same to be advertised that I have by my servants received your most honorable Letter, the contents wherof do not a little trouble me, and so much the more for that any of my servants should move or attempt me in matters touching my soul, which I think the meanest subject within your Realm could evil bear at their servants hand; having for my part utterly refused heretofor to talk with them in such matters, and of all other persons least regarded them therein;

to whom I have declared what I think as she which trusted that your Majesty would have suffered me your poor humble sister and beadeswoman to have used the accustomed Mass, which the King your father and mine with all his predecessors evermore used; wherein also I have been brought up from my youth, and thereunto my conscience doth not only bind me, which by no means will suffer me to think one thing and do another, but also the promise made to the Emperor by your Majesty's Counsell was an assurance to me that in so doing I should not offend the Laws, although they seem now to qualify and deny the thing.

And at my last waiting upon your Majesty I was so bold to declare my mind and conscience to the same, and desired your Highness, rather then you should constrain me to leave the Mass, to take my life, whereunto your Majesty made me a very gentle answer.

And now I beseech your Highness to give me leave to write what I think touching your Majesty's Letters. In deed they be signed with your own hand, and nevertheless in my opinion not your Majesty's in effect, because it is well known (as heretofore I have declared in the presence of your Highness) that although, Our Lord be praised, your Majesty hath far more knowledge and greater guisles than others of your years, yet it is not possible that your Highness can at these years be a judge in matters of Religion. And therefore I take it that the matter in your Letter proceedeth from such as do wish those things to take place, which be most agreeable to themselves: by whose doings (your Majesty not offended) I intend not to rule my Conscience.

And thus, without molesting your Highness any further, I humbly beseech the same ever, for Gods sake, to bear with me as you have done, and not to think that by my doings or example any inconvenience might grow to your Majesty or your Realm; for I use it not after any such sort; putting no-doubt but in time to come, whether I live or die, your Majesty shall perceive mine intent is grounded upon a true love towards you, whose royal estate I beseech Almighty God long to continue, which is and shall be my daily prayer, according to my duty.

And after pardon craved of your Majesty for these rude and bold Letters, if neither at my humble suite, nor for regard of the promise made to the Emperor, your Highness will suffer and bear with me, as yon have done, till your Majesty may be a Judge herein yourself, and right understand their proceedings, (of which your goodness yet I dispair not,) otherwise, rather than to offend God and my conscience I offer my body at your will, and death shall be more welcome than life with a troubled conscience.

Most humbly beseeching your Majesty to pardon my slowness in answering your Letters, for my old disease would, not suffer me to write any sooner. And thus I pray Almighty God to keep your Majesty in all virtue and honour, with good health and long life to his pleasure. From my poor house at Copped Hall the 19 of August.

Your Majesty's most humble sister
MARY."

It is a beautifully written letter, and Mary points out that promises had been made to Emperor Charles V that Mary could continue to worship in the way she wanted in private. She states that she is willing to die for her faith rather than suffer a troubled conscience from compromising her faith. She shows courage, fortitude and a great deal of stubbornness!

But then Edward was stubborn too. Ellis explains that on 23rd August, following receipt of Mary's letter, the same men were "directed to execute the charge they had received on the 14th" but that they declined to proceed with their charge, "Rochester and Walgrave voluntarily offering rather to endure imprisonment". On 28th August 1551, Lord Chancellor Richard Rich, Sir Anthony Wingfield and Sir William Petre visited Mary at Copthall. The purpose of their visit was to deliver the king's order that Mary and her household desist from celebrating the Catholic mass, and also to inform Mary that Wingfield should replace Robert Rochester, whom Edward's council had removed, as Mary's comptroller.

Mary was furious with the men. She replied that she was her brother's "most humble and obedient subject" but that "she would lay her head on a block" before using "any other service than was used at the death of the late king, her father". Mary rebuked the men for trying to appoint her servants, telling them that she would appoint her own. She continued, saying, "I am sickly, and yet I will not die willingly, but will do the best I can to preserve my life: but if I shall chance to die, I will protest openly, that you of the council be the causes of my death. You give me fair words, but your deeds be always ill towards me." Mary refused to obey them, and they were forced to leave, having failed their mission.

Edward and Mary loved each other as siblings, but Edward would not have his sister defy his laws, and Mary would not have her brother tell her how to worship.

20 August

On 20ᵗʰ August 1589, twenty-three-year-old King James VI of Scotland married fourteen-year-old Anne of Denmark by proxy at Kronborg Castle, Helsingør, Denmark. James was represented by his ambassador at the Danish court, George Keith, 5ᵗʰ Earl Marischal.

James was the son of Mary, Queen of Scots, and her second husband, Henry Stuart, Lord Darnley. He'd become King of Scotland when he was just one year old after his mother had been forced to abdicate in June 1567 following her marriage to James Hepburn, Earl of Bothwell, a man who had been implicated in the murder of Lord Darnley a few months earlier.

Anne of Denmark was the second daughter of the late King Frederick II of Denmark, and his wife, Queen Sophia, and sister of King Christian IV of Denmark.

After praying and meditating for three days over portraits of Anne and another prospective bride, thirty-year-old Catherine of Navarre, James chose Anne as his bride. Anne was keen on marrying James, and it was recorded that she was "so far in love with the King's Majesty as it were death to her to have it broken off and hath made good proof divers ways of her affection which his Majestie is apt enough to requite", and she set about embroidering shirts for him.

In June 1589, a Scottish embassy travelled to Denmark to finalise the marriage negotiations, which saw Denmark giving up on the idea of Scotland returning the isles of Orkney and Shetland and agreeing to a dowry of 75,000 rixdollars, or £150,000 Scots pounds.

On this day in Tudor history, 20th August 1589, the proxy wedding took place in Kronborg Castle's great hall. Anne's fleet of ships set sail for Scotland on 5th September, but it wasn't plain sailing. A cannon saluting Anne on her departure blew up, killing two gunners, and then a cannon on Anne's ship exploded, killing another gunner. Then, there were awful storms on the voyage, which delayed them as they had to seek refuge in the Norwegian fjords. Anne then travelled by land to Oslo. Impatient at waiting for his new bride, James set off for Norway, arriving on 19th November. On 23rd November 1589, James and Anne married in person at the Old Bishop's Palace in Oslo, with James's chaplain, David Lindsay, conducting the ceremony in French, which Anna had learned so that she and James had a common language.

Although the marriage started well, it didn't stay happy. Both of them were the subject of scandalous romantic rumours. There were also disagreements over the bringing up of their children, religion, Anne's household, James's drinking, and their different lifestyles.

Anne had several pregnancies that ended in miscarriage, and out of the seven children who survived birth, three of them died young. Their eldest son, Henry, died aged 18, and James was succeeded by their second son, Charles, as Charles I.

What was a proxy wedding?

A proxy wedding was a ceremony where either the bride or groom, or even both, were represented by a proxy, i.e. someone who stood in for the person. The wedding was normal, and the proxy made vows on behalf of the person they represented. It was legal and binding, rather than just a practice ceremony or dress rehearsal for the big day. In this case, James was represented by a proxy, George Keith, who made vows on his behalf, but Anne was there in person.

Proxy marriages weren't commonplace for normal citizens, as

there was no need. Still, they were quite common from the Middle Ages onwards for diplomatic unions between the ruling houses of Europe. Peace treaties between countries or empires often comprised a marriage agreement. However, travelling time or situations could make it difficult for the couple to get together quickly to solidify the agreement. Rulers didn't want to risk an advantageous match or peace being compromised by having to postpone the actual wedding for a few months.

21 August

On 21st August 1568, antiquary, translator and cartographer Humphrey Llwyd died from a fever.

Here are some facts about this Welshman, a man who deserves to be remembered because he produced the first-ever printed map of Wales.

- Llwyd was born in Denbigh in North Wales around 1527 and was the only child of Robert Llwyd, Clerk of Works at Denbigh Castle, and his wife, Joan Piggott.
- He studied at Oxford, obtaining a BA from one of the colleges and then an MA from Brasenose College.
- In 1553, he entered the service of Henry Fitzalan, 12th Earl of Arundel, who was chancellor of Oxford University and a leading magnate in the reign of Mary I.
- In 1559, after Elizabeth I's accession, Llwyd stood as a member of Parliament for East Grinstead.
- He appears to have helped the Earl of Arundel with his legal and political activities, his properties, and collecting books for his library. Llwyd also collected books for himself.
- Llwyd married Barbara Lumley, the sister of John, Lord Lumley, who was the Earl of Arundel's son-in-law. They went on to have six children.
- By 1563, he was back in Denbigh. He served as an alderman and as an MP for the area. It is said that he was active in promoting the Welsh translation of the Book of Common Prayer.

- He travelled to the Continent with Arundel in 1566-7, where he met mapmaker Abraham Ortelius, a man he learnt from working with.
- On his return to Wales in 1567, Llwyd received a stipend from the Crown to create a map of Wales, the first to be printed. It was published in Ortelius's "Theatrum Orbis Terrarum". Sadly, Llwyd died before it was published.
- He became ill with a fever in London in the summer of 1568 and then died on this day in 1568 in Denbigh, although Ortelius recorded his death as 31st August.
- Llwyd was buried in the north aisle of St Marcella's Church in Denbigh, where a memorial describes him as "a famous worthy wight".
- Llwyd's other works included an almanack, an English translation of an early Welsh Chronicle, a historical and geographical description of Britain, in which he used the words British Empire, and a map of England and Wales. He also helped popularise the myth of Prince Madoc's discovery of America.
- An exhibition in January 2019 at the National Library of Wales celebrated his life and works, calling Llwyd the "Inventor of Britain". The website explained that he is thought of by many as "the Inventor of Britain, having been credited with inventing the term British Empire" and that he "played a major part in creating the concept of Wales as a nation." He has also been described as "one of the most important of Welsh humanists and a key figure in the history of the Renaissance in Wales".

22 August

On 22nd August 1553, John Dudley, Duke of Northumberland, was beheaded on Tower Hill for his part in putting his daughter-in-law, Lady Jane Grey, on the throne. Northumberland's friends, Sir John Gates and Sir Thomas Palmer, were also executed on this day in 1553 for supporting Northumberland.

In his excellent book on the Dudley family, "The Uncrowned Kings of England: The Black Legend of the Dudleys", historian Derek

Wilson writes of how John Dudley became a scapegoat and that "he and he alone was to be branded as guilty, not only for the Jane Grey plot, but for all the ills that had beset the realm since 1549". He says, "Gardiner, Bonner, Howard and other religious conservatives concocted the official story that Northumberland had seduced the boy king into heresy". Apparently, Edward VI had had no mind of his own, and everything was down to Northumberland. But then, Edward had been Mary I's half-brother, and it suited Mary to blame the duke instead.

Northumberland had been found guilty of treason in a trial at Westminster Hall on 18th August 1553 and condemned to die on 21st August at 8am. Diarist and merchant-tailor Henry Machyn records that the scaffold was made ready, but the execution was suddenly cancelled:

> "The 21st of August was, by 8 of the cloke in the morning, on the Tower Hill about 991 men and women for to have [seen] the execution of the duke of Northumberland, for the scaffold was made ready, and sand and straw was brought, and all the men that belong to the Tower, as Hogston, Shordyche, Bow, Ratclyff, Lymhouse, Sant Kateryns, and the waiters of the Tower, and the guard, and sheriff's officers, and every man stand in order with their halberds, and lanes made, and the hangman was there, and suddenly they were commanded to depart.
>
> And the same time after was sent for my lord mayor and the aldermen and chiefest of the crafts in London, and diverse of the council, and there was said mass afore the Duke and the rest of the prisoners."

So instead of the scheduled execution on Tower Hill, the duke and others were taken to the Chapel of St Peter ad Vincula in the Tower grounds for mass. At this service, Northumberland, who was a Protestant, took Catholic communion and addressed the congregation, saying:

> "Truly, I profess here before you all that I have received the sacrament according to the true Catholic

faith; and the plagues that is upon the realm and upon us now is that we have erred from the bottom of my heart."

Northumberland was recanting his Protestant faith, which has often been seen as weakness and evidence of his fickle faith. However, it is more likely to have been an appeal for mercy and an attempt to save his family from retribution. Derek Wilson points out that "if Dudley is to be accused of cynicism and cowardice for changing his coat others must stand in the dock with him", citing the examples of William Cecil, Thomas Cranmer, the Marquess of Northampton and even Princess Elizabeth, the future Elizabeth I.

The following morning, the 22nd August, Northumberland was led out of the Tower of London and up on to Tower Hill. There is an account of the executions of Northumberland, Gates and Palmer in "The chronicle of Queen Jane". Here is the part about Northumberland:

> "And when he came upon the scaffold, first, he put off his gown of crane-colored damask, and then he leaned upon the rail towarde the east, and said to the people, almost in every point as he had said in the chapel, a saving that when he came to the confession of his belief he said, 'I trust, my lord the bishop here will bear me witnes hereof.' At the last, he put off his jerkin and doublet, and then said his prayers; after which time the hangman reached to him a kerchief, which he did knit himself about his eyes, and then laid him down, and so was beheaded."

The life of the man who had once ruled England, albeit as head of Edward VI's government rather than king, was over. He was buried in the Chapel of St Peter ad Vincula and is thought to lie under the chancel floor next to Edward Seymour, Duke of Somerset, and between Queens Anne Boleyn and Catherine Howard. In 1876, during renovation work on the Chapel, the Victorian workers unearthed his remains, which Dr Mouat described as belonging "to a large man, about six feet in height; and aged about 50 years."

23 August

On 23rd August 1553, Stephen Gardiner, Bishop of Winchester, was made Lord Chancellor by Mary I, who had been proclaimed queen on 19th July 1553.

Catholic Gardiner had risen to prominence in Henry VIII's reign following his service to Cardinal Wolsey. He served Henry VIII as a diplomat, Bishop of Winchester, and advisor. He also helped prepare the "Six Articles".

Gardiner was imprisoned in Edward VI's reign, first in the Fleet and then in the Tower of London, after he opposed the religious reforms. He was also deprived of his bishopric. However, his fortunes changed when Edward's half-sister, Mary, came to the throne. He was released from prison and became Bishop of Winchester once more.

Gardiner crowned Mary at her coronation in October 1553 and presided over her wedding to Philip of Spain in July 1554, a marriage he had helped negotiate. He helped his queen restore England to the Church of Rome.

"Wily Winchester", as martyrologist John Foxe called him, only served as Lord Chancellor for two years as he died on 12th November 1555.

24 August

On 24th August 1507, Cecily of York, Viscountess Welles, died at Hatfield. She was buried at "the friars", but it is not known what religious house the record was referring to.

Here are some facts about this Plantagenet princess:

- Cecily was born at Westminster Palace in London on 20th March 1469 and was the third daughter of King Edward IV and Elizabeth Woodville and the sister of Elizabeth of York and the Princes in the Tower. It is believed that Cecily was named after her paternal grandmother, Cecily Neville, Duchess of York.
- In October 1474, when she was five, Cecily was betrothed to Prince James, son of King James III of Scotland, as part of a peace treaty between England and Scotland. However, relations

broke down between the two countries after James supported English raids and Edward supported the claim to the Scottish throne of Alexander Stuart, Duke of Albany, James's exiled brother. In June 1482, it was decided that if Albany could annul his marriage, then Cecily would marry him. It didn't happen, and then, in October 1482, the betrothal between Cecily and Prince James was broken off.

- Cecily's father died suddenly on 9th April 1483, when Cecily was 14, leaving the throne to Cecily's brother, Edward, who became Edward V. However, their uncle, Richard, Duke of Gloucester, took the throne as King Richard III and Edward and his brother, Richard, disappeared. Their fate is unknown.

- Cecily's mother, the dowager queen, had taken Cecily and her sisters into sanctuary at Westminster Abbey, and they remained there until March 1484. Richard III promised Elizabeth Woodville that he would ensure that his nieces would have good marriage matches and that he'd give each of them 200 marks per annum in land. Cecily was married off to Ralph Scrope, brother of Thomas Scrope, 6th Baron Scrope of Masham.

- In 1486, following the accession of King Henry VII, who was married to Cecily's sister, Elizabeth of York, Cecily's marriage to Scrope was annulled. She married John Welles, 1st Viscount Welles, maternal half-brother of Lady Margaret Beaufort and half-uncle of King Henry VII. The couple had two daughters, Elizabeth and Anne, who died young.

- In September 1486, Cecily carried her nephew, Prince Arthur Tudor, to the font at his christening at Winchester. In November 1487, she carried her sister Elizabeth of York's train at her coronation at Westminster Abbey.

- In February 1499, Viscount Welles died, and Cecily was left a life interest in his lands. However, she lost these when she married Thomas Kyme of Friskney, Lincolnshire, without Henry VII's permission. The king's mother, Lady Margaret Beaufort, ended up sheltering the couple and was able to intercede with the king on their behalf. Some of Cecily's lands were restored to her on the condition that the king could keep hold of some.

- Cecily died on this day in Tudor history, 24th August 1507, at the age of just 38.

25 August

On 25th August 1549, Robert Kett, leader of the rebels in Kett's Rebellion, launched an attack on the south side of Norwich.

Kett's Rebellion started in East Anglia in July 1549, in the reign of King Edward VI, while Edward Seymour, Earl of Hertford and the king's uncle, was head of the government as Lord Protector.

In the 1540s, more and more common land was being 'enclosed', i.e. fenced off, by local landowners for grazing their sheep. This meant that villagers and small farmers didn't have as much land to graze their sheep, and many faced real hardship. Edward Seymour, Lord Protector, was concerned about the greed of landowners and the impact it had on smaller farmers. He set up an enclosure commission to investigate and report illegal enclosures of common land. Only one commission went ahead, but Somerset's measures were enough to make the common people believe that the government was on their side, and they started tearing down the hedges and fences that enclosed the common land.

In Norfolk, Robert Kett, a landowner from Wymondham who had enclosed local common land for his own use, listened to the rebels who came on to his land. He was moved by their plight and helped them remove the fences and hedges and decided to become their spokesman and leader. On 8th July 1549, the protesters marched on the city of Norwich, picking up supporters on the way. By the time they set up camp at Mousehold Heath, near Norwich, it is said that they numbered around 16,000.

The rebels drew up a list of 29 demands and grievances and sent them to Protector Somerset. On 21st July, the rebels received an answer from the king's council. The message declared them rebels and offered them a pardon, which they rejected.

On 22nd July, the rebels attacked Norwich and took the city. Once in the city, they set up their own local government and began trying cases brought against landowners by commoners. Landowners who were found guilty of enclosing common land illegally were imprisoned. Some of these cases were heard under the Oak of Reformation, an oak tree on Mousehold Heath.

The Marquess of Northampton was sent to win back Norwich from the rebels but was defeated by the rebel forces. John Dudley, Earl of Warwick, was then sent with a large army. Warwick set about fortifying the city gates, setting guards around the city and destroying White Friars Bridge to prevent the rebels from entering the city. But on this day in history, 25th August, Kett attacked the city's southern side, setting fire to several warehouses.

On 26th August, Warwick received 1,000 mercenaries as reinforcements to fight the rebels, and on 27th August, the Battle of Dussindale took place. The rebels were defeated, and the rebellion was brought to an end.

History teachers Mr Worn and Miss Cust point out to students on their blog Tudor Rebellions that Kett's Rebellion was not just caused by illegal enclosure of common land. Other causes included bad local government and religion. Miss Cust writes that "7 articles in Kett's manifesto contain more protestant demands – that priests should preach and teach more, that priests live with aristocrats rather than with their flocks, and that they are grasping over tithes. They demanded that parishioners should choose new priests if their existing priest was not good enough."

26 August

On 26th August 1555, Queen Mary I and her husband, Philip of Spain, departed from Whitehall in preparation for Philip's return to the Low Countries.

This was just a month after the daily processions and prayers for Mary's safe delivery of the child she thought she was carrying had been cancelled, and just over three weeks since she'd come out of confinement at Hampton Court Palace and the royal court had moved to Oatlands. There was no baby. The months of praying and waiting had come to nothing. Although Mary's body had swelled, and her breasts had enlarged and produced milk, she just wasn't pregnant. It must have been such a blow to her and Philip.

On 19th August 1555, the Venetian ambassador, Giovanni Michieli, recorded, "Last week their Majesties returned to Hampton Court, the Lady Elizabeth remaining at the seat to which she went; and now the Queen shows herself and converses with everybody as usual, her health being so good as perhaps never to have been better, to the universal surprise of all who see her, but of delivery or pregnancy small signs are visible externally, and no one talks or thinks of them any longer."

With the months of waiting having ended, Philip arranged to leave for the Low Countries, where he was needed. He was, however, worried about breaking the news to his already devastated wife, writing to one of his chief advisors: "Let me know what line I am to take with the Queen about leaving her and about religion. I see I must say something, but God help me!"

On 26th August 1555, the king and queen rode through London. Merchant-tailor and diarist Henry Machyn recorded:

> "The 26 day of August came from Westminster, riding through London unto Towers-wharf, the King and the Queen, and there they took their barge unto Greenwich, and landed at the long bridge, and received by my lord chancellor, and my Lord of Ely, and my lord Viscount Montagu, master comptroller, master Southwell, and diverse more, and the guard, and diverse holding torches burning, and up to the Friars, and there their graces made their prayers, and at her grace's landing received 9 or 10 supplications, and so back again to the court with a 100 torches burning."

The Venetian ambassador wrote of them leaving Hampton Court instead, recording:

> "Their Majesties came hither from Hampton Court yesterday morning, remaining merely to dine, and then went to Greenwich, where the Queen will remain during the whole time of the King's stay beyond sea. On departing hence, his Majesty had determined, when passing through London, to show himself in public to

the people on horseback, leaving the Queen to follow him at leisure by water as usual, but her Majesty chose to give the City the satisfaction of seeing her likewise in his company, she having made the determination when in the very act of embarking; so having herself carried in an open litter, she went, accompanied not only by the English and Spanish nobility now at the court, but also by the Cardinal Legate and the ambassadors, the Lord Mayor and all the aldermen having met her at Temple Bar coming with the royal insignia and all the other solemnities, as customary when the Queen appears in public. It is not to be told what a vast crowd of people there was all along the road, which is a very long one, nor yet the joy they demonstrated at seeing their Majesties, which was really great, and the more as the London populace were firmly convinced that the Queen was dead; so when they knew of her appearance, they all ran from one place to another, as to an unexpected sight, and one which was well nigh new, as if they were crazy, to ascertain thoroughly if it was her, and on recognising and seeing her in better plight than ever, they by shouts and salutations, and every other demonstration, then gave yet greater signs of their joy, inasmuch as to their great comfort and that of her Majesty they saw her come with the King on one side of her and Cardinal Pole on the other, both of whom are universally popular by reason of the reported kindness of their nature, and of which daily proof is afforded by facts, so that the determination to make this display, most especially at the present moment, has been very useful."

It was important to Mary that she show her people that she was alive and well. However, despite the joy of her people, Mary was depressed at the thought of Philip leaving her. The Venetian ambassador noted: "In the meanwhile, as may be imagined with regard to a person extraordinarily in love, the Queen remains disconsolate, though she conceals it as much as she can, and from what I hear mourns the more when alone and supposing herself invisible to any of her attendants."

The Venetian ambassador explained that Philip planned to stay at Greenwich until his fleet was ready and waiting at Dover. On 29th August, Philip left for Dover, accompanied by a party of English nobles and soldiers. He reached Sittingbourne on that day, "where he was received with great demonstrations of honour, having been met three miles in advance by the Lord Warden, Captain of the Cinque Ports, and Lord Lieutenant (Governator) of Kent, with a company of gentlemen of the county, in number 200, all on foot, clad in one livery; and on entering the town they found tables prepared in the streets as a mark of rejoicing, everybody being boarded and lodged gratis." Then, he travelled to Canterbury, where he stopped to wait for news from his admiral on the arrival of the Flemish ships that were due to act as his escort on his crossing to Dover.

The Venetian ambassador records how the queen acted on Philip's departure:

> "Much to my pleasure I accompanied Cardinal Pole and the other noblemen on the day when they went with the King to his barge, to see him take leave of the Queen, who on that occasion really expressed very well the sorrow becoming a wife, and a wife such as she is, invested with the regal habit and dignity, for without displaying much extrinsic disquietude, though evidently deeply grieved internally, she chose to come with him through all the chambers and galleries (sale) to the head of the stairs, constraining herself the whole way to avoid, in sight of such a crowd, any demonstration unbecoming her gravity, though she could not but be moved when the Spanish noblemen kissed her hand, and yet more, when she saw the ladies in tears take leave of the King, who, according to the custom of the country, kissed them one by one. On returning, however, to her apartments, placing herself at a window which looks on the river, not supposing herself any longer seen or observed by any one, it was perceived that she gave free vent to her grief by a flood of tears, nor did she once quit the window

until she had not only seen the King embark and depart, but remained looking after him as long as he was in sight; and the King on his part mounted aloft on the barge in the open air, in order to be better seen when the barge approached in sight of the window, and moreover, waived his bonnet from the distance to salute her, demonstrating great affection. Now whilst his Majesty is at Canterbury, not only every day, but every hour, expresses are on the road from the King to the Queen, and in like manner from hence to his Majesty, the gentlemen-in-waiting being always booted and spurred ready for a start."

While Philip was away, Mary had arranged for her Archbishop of Canterbury and good friend, Cardinal Reginald Pole, to lodge with her "that he may comfort her and keep her company, Her Majesty delighting greatly in the sight and presence of him". And Pole wrote to Philip of how Mary was spending her days, passing "the forenoon in prayer after the manner of Mary, and in the afternoon admirable personates Martha, by transacting business."

Sadly, Philip was away for over 18 months, only arriving back in England on 20th March 1557, being greeted by a gun salute, bells ringing out, banquets, dances and masques. He hadn't returned for his queen, though, he'd returned because he needed money and English support for a campaign against France. War was what he was after. This wasn't what Mary's council wanted. Still, they were dragged into supporting Spain, which was a disaster for England, leading to the loss of Calais in January 1558, a territory England had held since the mid 14th century.

27 August

On 27th August 1557, St Quentin was stormed by English and Imperial forces. Admiral de Coligny and his French troops, numbering only a thousand, were overcome by around 60,000 soldiers, and St Quentin fell. Henry Dudley, the youngest son of the late John Dudley, Duke of Northumberland, was killed by a cannonball during the storming.

News of the victory reached England on the 3rd September, with Henry Machyn recording,

> "the same day at night came commandment that every church in London, and other country and shire, to sing and make bonfires for the winning of Saint Quentin; and there was slain my lord Harry Dudley the younger son of the duke of Northumberland that was headed, with many more, at the winning of it."

Chronicler Charles Wriothesley simply wrote,

> "This month the king laid siege to the town of St Quentins by the water of Somme, and on Friday the 27th of August the town was won by the king with the help of Englishmen."

Juan de Piñedo wrote to Francisco de Vargas saying,

> "The news are that between three and four this afternoon our troops fought their way into St. Quentin. Both sides fought most choicely, and the English best of all. I will give you further details by the earliest opportunity. For the moment there is no more to say, because blows are still being exchanged inside the town, although they say that the Admiral of France has already been taken prisoner. Our Lord will give Philip the victory, because he has behaved like a true Christian throughout."

The Venetian ambassador went into a bit more detail in a dispatch written to the Doge and Senate on 27th August:

> "The besiegers at St. Quentin, with their pioneers and batteries, made such a breach that they thought at length they might give the assault, having simultaneously digged some mines underneath the platform, with the intention of exploding them at the moment of the assault when the defenders would be on it. This scheme having been communicated to the Duke de Nevers by his spies in the enemy's army, and the Duke imparting it to the Admiral, the latter, when the assault was made, instead of allowing his troops to show themselves on the platform, made them remain on the trench, and to prevent the

enemy from mounting the breach, he placed a good number of harquebusiers in the casemates, and other artillery on the flanks fronting the fosse, and when, on St. Bartholomew's day [24th August] the enemy gave the assault in several quarters, according to their project, and not seeing anyone appear for the defence, they commenced mounting the breach; but as the harquebusiers in the casemates and the artillerymen on the flanks did their duty, a constant fire being also kept up by the town, the defence was such that after six hours toil the besiegers were compelled to retire with the loss of about 1,000 men, and on their retreat the garrison sallied forth and killed a few others who were more slow to escape. This news was brought to the King yesterday, and has confirmed and increased the hopes of his Majesty and of everybody else, that the town will be kept; and although it is heard that they are again about to make another more formidable assault, it is nevertheless hoped that through the heart taken by the besieged owing to this feat they will maintain it manfully."

Although St Quentin had been a victory for Spain, aided by English troops, Mary I's husband, Philip of Spain, just didn't have the finances or troops to take things further and march on Paris. France was able to plan her revenge, which she did when she took Calais from the English in January 1558.

28 August

On 28th August 1588, an ailing Robert Dudley, Earl of Leicester, wrote his final letter to his queen and childhood friend, Elizabeth I. He wrote it from the home of Lady Norreys at Rycote, where he was staying on his way to Buxton, in Derbyshire, to take the waters there. It read:

"I most humbly beseech your Majesty to pardon your poor old servant to be thus bold in sending to know how my gracious lady doth, and what ease of her late pains she finds, being the chiefest thing in this world I do pray for, for her to have good health and long life. For my own poor case, I continue still your medicine and find that (it) amends much better than with any other thing that hath been given me. Thus hoping to find perfect cure at the bath, with the continuance of my wonted prayer for your Majesty's most happy preservation, I humbly kiss your foot. From your old lodging at Rycote, this Thursday morning, ready to take on my Journey, by your Majesty's most faithful and obedient servant,

R. Leicester"

He added a postscript:

"Even as I had writ thus much, I received Your Majesty's token by Young Tracey."

Leicester died at his lodge at Cornbury, near Woodstock in Oxfordshire, while still on his way to Buxton on 4th September 1588.

Elizabeth I was devastated by his death, locking herself away in her chambers at St James's Palace. Sir Francis Walsingham wrote that he could not do any state business with the queen by "reason that she will not suffer anybody to access unto her, being very much grieved with the death of the Lord Steward". She stayed in her chambers for days and only came out when her doors were broken down on the orders of William Cecil. When the queen received a letter from the Earls of Derby and Shrewsbury offering their congratulations on the victory over the Armada and their condolences on Dudley's death, she replied:

"We desire rather to forbear the remembrance thereof as a thing whereof we can admit no comfort, otherwise by submitting our will to God's inevitable appointment. Who notwithstanding his goodness by the former prosperous news hath nevertheless been pleased to keep us in exercise by the loss of a personage so dear unto us."

At her death in March 1603, Leicester's letter was found in the special treasure or keepsake box Elizabeth kept at her bedside. It had been marked by Elizabeth "His Last Letter".

I can imagine Elizabeth taking that letter out of the box regularly and reading and re-reading it. I believe that her keeping the letter and her reaction to receiving news of his death show how much

Elizabeth loved Robert Dudley. She chose to be married to England, but her heart belonged to him.

29 August

On 29th August 1538, Geoffrey Pole, fourth son of the late Sir Richard Pole and Margaret Pole, Countess of Salisbury, was arrested on suspicion of being in contact with his brother, Cardinal Reginald Pole, who had denounced King Henry VIII and his policies in his treatise, "Pro ecclesiasticae unitatis defensione". He was taken to the Tower of London.

Geoffrey, a staunch supporter of Catherine of Aragon and Princess Mary, had previously been banished from court following his brother's promotion to cardinal.

On 26th October 1538, nearly two months after his arrest, Geoffrey was interrogated regarding letters he and his family had received from Reginald and words Geoffrey had uttered showing his support for the cardinal. As a result of information gleaned from Geoffrey in seven separate rounds of interrogations, on 4th November 1538, Geoffrey's brother, Henry Pole, 1st Baron Montagu, was arrested for treason along with his brother-in-law, Sir Edward Neville, and Henry Courtenay, Marquess of Exeter, and his family (wife Gertrude Blount and son Edward Courtenay). They were accused of conspiring against the king, seeking to deprive the king of his title of supreme head of the church, and plotting with Cardinal Reginald Pole. Pole's mother, the Countess of Salisbury, was arrested on 12th November by William Fitzwilliam, Earl of Southampton, and Thomas Goodrich, Bishop of Ely and imprisoned in the Tower of London.

On 9th December 1538, Sir Edward Neville was beheaded. On 2nd January 1539, Geoffrey was pardoned due to his mental state and several suicide attempts and his testimony against his family, given when, according to his wife Constance, he was in a frenzy. His most recent suicide attempt had been over Christmas 1538, when he was said to have tried to suffocate himself with a cushion.

Montagu and Exeter were beheaded on 9th January 1539, and Geoffrey's mother, Margaret, was executed on the 27th May 1541. Exeter's wife was released in 1540, and his son in 1553. Cardinal Pole managed to escape the wrath of Henry VIII, being abroad at the time. He was attainted for treason in 1539 'in absentia', but this was reversed by Mary I in 1554, and he ended up serving her as her Archbishop of Canterbury, dying on the same day as his queen, 17th November 1558.

Geoffrey fled into exile in Flanders following the execution of his mother. He also travelled to Rome to see his brother and obtain absolution for his part in his family's fall. The pope absolved him, and then he was sent back to Flanders. He stayed on the Continent until Mary I's accession, and he died a few days before the queen and his brother in 1558. His wife and 11 children survived him.

Trivia: in the autumn of 1532, when Henry VIII visited Calais with his sweetheart Anne Boleyn to obtain Francis I's blessing for their marriage, Geoffrey went to Calais in disguise. He hid himself in his brother Montagu's apartments and then, at night, went information gathering. He took the information back to England to report to Catherine of Aragon.

30 August

On 30th August 1525, the Treaty of the More was agreed between Henry VIII of England and Louise of Savoy, who was acting as regent for her son, Francis I of France, while imperial forces imprisoned him.

Francis I had been captured at the Battle of Pavia six months previously when the French were defeated and many of his chief nobles killed or imprisoned with him. During the battle against Emperor Charles V, Francis had fallen from his horse and had been forced to surrender. He was imprisoned first in Italy and then in Madrid, Spain.

The Treaty of the More, so-called because negotiations took place at "The More", Cardinal Thomas Wolsey's Hertfordshire property, was an about-turn for Wolsey, who had previously been pro-Empire. However, England was concerned about Scotland renewing its Auld Alliance with France, so it wanted to get the French on side.

By the treaty negotiated by Wolsey, Henry VIII agreed to help secure King Francis I's release and give up claims to several French territories. In return, Louise, who was represented by her ambassadors, Jean Brinon, Lord of Villaines, and John Joachim de Vaulx, agreed that France would award England with a pension of £20,000 per year and settle what was owed to Henry VIII's sister, Mary Tudor, Dowager Queen of France.

The following day, Louise wrote to her ambassadors, ordering them to thank Cardinal Wolsey for his "wise discourse, and the affection he shows to France" and beg him "to continue his efforts for the preservation of friendship between England and her son". However, it appears she then received word from her ambassadors regarding the negotiations. She wrote another letter regarding the final settlement and wondering that Wolsey had the "conscience" to demand what he did and suggesting that the "declaration desired by Wolsey about the comprehension of Scotland ought not to be so strict" and ordering the ambassadors that whatever was negotiated they "must see that the honor of France be saved." She then sent them the required "amended power".

Three years earlier, Emperor Charles V had been contracted to marry his cousin, Henry VIII's daughter, Mary. However, the agreement between England and France allowed Charles to put that aside and, instead, marry Isabella of Portugal. Poor Mary would not marry until 1554, when she married Charles's son, Philip of Spain.

King Francis I was eventually released in the spring of 1526 following the 14th January Treaty of Madrid, by which France had to make huge concessions to the emperor, with Francis surrendering lands in Italy, Flanders, Artois, and Tournai. However, when Francis set foot on French soil, he repudiated the treaty, refusing to ratify it and claiming it had been agreed under duress. Instead, he negotiated the League of Cognac, an alliance between France, Pope Clement VII, Venice, England, Milan and Florence against the Empire.

31 August

On 31st August 1545, a contagious disease known as the 'Bloody flux' hit the port of Portsmouth.

The previous year, King Henry VIII had come to terms with Charles V, Holy Roman Emperor, over a war with their joint enemy, France. However, he was soon left high and dry when Charles betrayed him and came to an agreement with France. The ageing Henry VIII was intent on war, though, and set about gathering troops and ships at the port of Portsmouth on the south coast of England. France was also intent on invading England.

On 19th July 1545, Henry VIII's ships, Henry Grace à Dieu and the Mary Rose, sailed out into the Solent off Portsmouth, leading the English fleet against the French, who had advanced on them. Sadly, Henry VIII's favourite flagship, the Mary Rose, sank, taking most of her crew with her.

This wasn't the only bad news for the English fleet. On 1st August 1545, Lord Lisle wrote to the Duke of Suffolk from on board The Harry, informing him of the bad news that disease had hit the ships that were making their way to Portsmouth to cross to Boulogne, which the French were now threatening. Lisle wrote, "there is a great disease fallen amongst the soldiers and mariners almost in every ship", explaining that the men had "swelling in their heads and faces and in their legs" and that many of them had "the bloody flux".

On 15th August, Thomas, Lord Poynings, governor of Boulogne, wrote to Henry VIII from Boulogne, saying, "am somewhat diseased with the bloody flux, and forced to keep my bed these three days; and, albeit I mistrust not but to recover", so the disease had obviously taken hold there too. Poynings died just three days later. By the end of the month, there was an epidemic in Portsmouth, and it killed many of the men serving on ships stationed in the port.

But what was bloody flux?

It was what we'd call dysentery today. It was a real killer in the medieval and Tudor periods and is still killing people in the developing world today. Symptoms include fever, stomach cramps, dehydration and severe diarrhoea. In severe cases, the sufferer would pass bloody stools, hence the name. It is an infection spread through contaminated food or water, such as water contaminated by faecal matter, or person-to-person due to poor hygiene. It's little wonder that soldiers and sailors suffered when they were in close contact and didn't have access to good hygiene and toileting.

Parasites or bacteria can cause dysentery, and today, treatment for it depends on which type of dysentery it is. It can include drinking plenty of water or special hydration drinks and medicine to kill parasites. Back in the Tudor period, treatment for the bloody flux would include blood-letting.

As well as the soldiers and sailors of Portsmouth, famous victims of dysentery include Cardinal Thomas Wolsey, who died of it at Leicester Abbey in 1530 while travelling to London to face charges of treason; Erasmus, the famous Humanist scholar, who died from dysentery in Basel in 1536; Sir Francis Drake, the Elizabethan explorer, who died of it in Panama in 1596, and King James I, who died during a severe attack of dysentery in 1626 after having been weakened by several other health issues.

Fulminant amoebic dysentery today has a 55-88% mortality rate, and between 40,000 and 100,000 people die of it each year. It's still having an impact on our world.

1 September

On 1st September 1566, Edward Alleyn, actor, theatre entrepreneur and founder of Dulwich College and Alleyn's School, was born in the parish of St Botolph without Bishopsgate, London, and baptised the following day.

Alleyn was a major figure in the Elizabethan theatre, being a member of the Earl of Worcester's Players, Lord Strange's Men and then leading the Admiral's Men. In the 1590s, he played title roles in "Doctor Faustus", "Tamburlaine", and "The Jew of Malta" by Christopher Marlowe. His career's business side saw him partner with Philip Henslowe and become part-owner of the Rose Theatre, the Paris Garden and the Fortune Theatre.

Let me share with you a few more facts about this Tudor man.

- Edward Alleyn was one of five sons born to Edward Alleyn of Willen in Buckinghamshire, and his wife, Margaret Townley.
- His father had moved to London by 1566 and had owned an inn in Bishopsgate before moving on to the royal court, where, in 1567, he was working as a porter to Queen Elizabeth. He was also head of Bethlehem Hospital (Bedlam).
- Alleyn's father died in 1570, and his mother married Richard Christopher and then John Browne.
- Alleyn was performing with the Earl of Worcester's men by 1583, when he was 17, following in his brother John's footsteps.
- In 1589, his brother John was the manager and leader of the Admiral's Men.
- By the early 1590s, Edward Alleyn was a member of Lord Strange's Men and performed at Philip Henslowe's Rose Theatre. He married Joan Woodward, Henslowe's stepdaughter, in October 1592. The marriage was successful and loving, with Alleyn referring to her as his "mouse". He also went into a business partnership with Henslowe, running the Rose Theatre together.
- By 1594, Alleyn was the leader of the Admiral's Men, a troupe of actors which competed with Shakespeare's Lord Chamberlain's Men.

- Alleyn received much praise for his acting from the likes of Ben Jonson.
- Alleyn retired from the stage in 1597 and focused on business and trying to gain court positions. One he wanted was master of the bears, bulls and mastiff dogs, but the new king, James I, granted it to his friend Sir William Stewart. Fortunately for Alleyn and Henslowe, Stewart allowed them to purchase the patent for the position in 1604, and the two men held the office jointly until Henslowe died in 1616. Alleyn then shared it with Henslowe's son-in-law. In this position, Alleyn baited a lion before King James I at the Tower of London.
- In 1604, Alleyn was back acting, playing a role in a play for King James's formal entry into London.
- In the late 1590s, Alleyn and Henslowe started work on a project to build a new playhouse in St Giles Cripplegate. Construction began in 1600, and the men had the support of Lord Admiral Charles Howard against opposition from local justices of the peace. The new playhouse, the Fortune, opened in summer 1600, hosting the Admiral's Men troupe and featuring comedies and plays written by the likes of Thomas Dekker. It operated until it burnt down in December 1621. Alleyn immediately set about building a replacement.
- In 1607 and 1608, Alleyn worked as a vestryman and auditor of token books for his local church.
- In June 1623, Alleyn's wife, Joan, died childless. Alleyn had her laid to rest in the chapel of a hospital he had endowed in 1619, a hospital which became Dulwich College. Alleyn remarried in December 1623, taking John Donne's daughter, Constance, as his second wife. The marriage was also childless.
- Alleyn became ill in 1626 and made his will on 13th November. He died on 25th November 1626, aged 60, and was buried on 27th November in Dulwich College's chapel. In his will, he left instructions and provision for building 10 almshouses.

2 September

On 2nd September 1534, Gerald Fitzgerald, 9th Earl of Kildare and Lord Deputy of Ireland, died in the Tower of London at around 47. An already ill Kildare had been arrested on 29th June 1534, accused of corruption and causing rebellion in Ireland.

By his death, he was one of the ten wealthiest Tudor magnates with a yearly income of over 2,000 Irish pounds.

But who was Kildare, and how did he come to this sad end?

- Kildare was born in 1487 and was the only son of Gerald Fitzgerald, 8th Earl of Kildare, Lord Deputy of Ireland, and his wife, Alison Eustace.
- It is thought that he went to the English royal court when he was about seven or eight following his father's arrest, as surety for his father's loyalty. He was educated there.
- In 1502, when he was about 15, Gerald played Man of Arms at the funeral of Arthur Tudor, Prince of Wales, eldest son of Henry VII, riding Arthur's courser and wearing the prince's armour.
- In July 1503, he married Elizabeth Zouche, daughter of Sir John Zouche of Codnor, Derbyshire, and a cousin of King Henry VII. In August 1503, he returned to Ireland with his father and his new wife. The couple had two children, Thomas and Alice.
- In 1504, Gerald was appointed Lord High Treasurer of Ireland, and in 1505 he fought at the Battle of Knockdoe, serving under his father. He fought well but made the mistake of committing the reserve he commanded too soon.
- In 1513, his father died, and Gerald became Earl of Kildare. Henry VIII also appointed him Lord Deputy of Ireland.
- Kildare first faced accusations regarding his work in Ireland in 1515, when he was accused of acting without the council's consent and imposing unlawful levies on the king's subjects. However, he kept the king's favour, receiving grants and a licence to found and endow a college at Maynooth.
- Kildare's wife died in October 1517.

- In 1519, Kildare made another visit to the court at London. While there, he clashed with Cardinal Wolsey and was accused of maladministration. In May 1520, he was ordered not to leave London, but in June 1520, he was able to accompany the king to the Field of Cloth of Gold. He was imprisoned temporarily but released in November of the same year. However, he was in trouble again in the spring of 1521 and ordered to appear before the Star Chamber. He was soon exonerated and married Elizabeth, daughter of Thomas Grey, Marquess of Dorset, in 1522. They went on to have six children together, including Elizabeth, Countess of Lincoln, the "Fair Geraldine" of Henry Howard, Earl of Surrey's sonnet.
- Kildare returned to Ireland with his bride in 1523, where he clashed with Piers Butler, Earl of Ormond, who'd been acting as governor while he was away. A commissioner had to be sent to settle the feud, but Kildare was reinstated as Lord Deputy. However, they clashed again in 1526, and both men were called to court. Kildare had aroused the king's suspicions over his seeming inability to arrest his relative, James Fitzgerald, Earl of Desmond. Kildare travelled to London with his daughter Alice, taking her so that she'd be able to return to Ireland and report back if he was apprehended. He left his brother, Thomas, as vice-deputy, but Henry VIII replaced him with Lord Delvin while Kildare was kept under house arrest at the Duke of Norfolk's residence at Newington. He was granted a general pardon in 1530 and was allowed to return home in August 1530 with Sir William Skeffington as deputy.
- Kildare and Skeffington worked well together at first, restoring order, but had fallen out by July 1531. By this time, Kildare was once more feuding with Butler, who was now Earl of Ossory. Ossory's son, Lord Butler, and Kildare were summoned to England, and Henry VIII reappointed Kildare as Deputy and Butler as treasurer.
- In 1532, Kildare was shot while besieging Birr Castle. He was described as "shot into the bodye with a hand gone and ney slayne, but he was neuer holl againe, the mor pittie".

- By 1533, Henry VIII's chief advisor, Thomas Cromwell, had received more complaints about Kildare. In that September, he was summoned to court to face accusations regarding "excess of his illegality and his injustice on them". He sent his wife first, pleading his injury, but the king wanted Kildare himself. In February 1534, at a council meeting at Drogheda, Kildare appointed his son, Thomas Fitzgerald, who would become known as Silken Thomas, as his deputy and set off for London.
- Thomas heard rumours that his father had been executed and publicly renounced his allegiance to the king at St Mary's Abbey in Dublin in June 1534 and asserted his allegiance to the pope. He then launched a rebellion against King Henry VIII. Chronicler Edward Hall records that "he took all the king's ordinance, and sent ambassadors to the Emperor to have entreated to him to take part with him. Also he slew the Bishop of Dublin and burnt and robbed all such as would not obey him." Sadly, Thomas's actions led to his father's arrest on 29th June 1534 and his imprisonment in the Tower of London.
- His injury from being shot had led to Kildare partially losing the use of his limbs and being unable to speak. He was nursed in the Tower by his wife, dying there on this day in Tudor history, 2nd September 1534. He was buried in the Chapel of St Peter ad Vincula at the Tower.
- Kildare was posthumously attainted for treason in 1536, and on 3rd February 1537, his heir, Silken Thomas, and Kildare's five brothers were executed as traitors at Tyburn. Gerald, his eldest son by his second wife, was restored to the earldom of Kildare by Mary I in 1554.

3 September

On 3rd September 1592, writer and playwright Robert Greene died in Dowgate, London.

He died from a fever and was said to have been buried in a churchyard near Bedlam. Greene was a prolific writer, writing autobiographical works, plays and romances, but is best known for the pamphlet "Greene's Groats-worth of Wit bought with a Million of Repentance", which he was said to have written on his deathbed.

This pamphlet is the first known contemporary reference to William Shakespeare as a playwright. The Folger Shakespeare Library "Shakespeare documented" website describes the work as "a tale of two brothers, Roberto and Luciano". It goes on to explain that in the tale, Roberto tries to steal Luciano's wealth but fails and is forced to make a living from being a playwright, while his brother ends up spending his money on women and ends up working as a pimp. At first, Roberto is successful with his writing but squanders what he earns and is left on his deathbed with a single groat. At the end of the story, the reader learns that Roberto is Robert Greene, who then uses the work to repent of his sins and to write a letter of warning to three unnamed playwrights. As the Folger website notes, these three "bear strong resemblances to Thomas Nashe, Christopher Marlowe, and George Peele", other well-known 16th-century playwrights. Greene warns them to beware of other actors who are also playwrights, including one who he describes as "an upstart crow, beautified with our feathers, that with his Tiger's heart wrapped in a player's hide, supposes he is well able to bombast out a blank verse as the best of you: and being an absolute Johannes fac totum is in his own conceit the onely Shake-scene in a country. O that I might entreat your rare wits to be employed in more profitable courses: & let those Apes imitate your past excellence, and never more acquaint them with your admired inventions. "

It appears to be an attack on the uneducated upstart Shakespeare. The Folger website points out that "Tygers hart wrapt in a Players hyde" is a play on a line from Shakespeare's Henry VI Part 3: "O tiger's heart wrapped in a woman's hide", that "johannes fac totum", or Johnny-do-all means the same as Jack of all trades and is a dig at Shakespeare's arrogance and pride, and perhaps even accusing him of plagiarism, and that the attack is all to do with the lowly Shakespeare's mastery of blank verse, something that the university-educated Nashe, Marlowe and Peele all used.

Although the pamphlet was printed in 1592 as being written by Robert Greene, "Written before his death and published at his dyeing request", there is now controversy over authorship. Scholars believe it was written by Greene's fellow authors and dramatists, Henry Chettle or Thomas Nashe.

4 September

On 4th September 1539, William, Duke of Cleves, signed the marriage treaty promising his sister, Anne of Cleves, in marriage to King Henry VIII. The duke then sent the treaty to England, where it was ratified and concluded by early October, being signed by the king's commissioners on 4th October 1539.

In her book, "The Marrying of Anne of Cleves: Royal Protocol in Tudor England", historian Retha Warnicke gives details of the marriage treaty, including the financial settlement. The Duke of Cleves promised a dowry of 100,000 gold florins for Anne. This was to be split into a wedding day payment of 40,000 and the remainder paid within a year of the marriage. Warnicke notes, "In related documents Henry waived this sum, which her brother could ill afford". The king also promised a dower (a widow's share of her husband's estate) of 20,000 gold florins. A copy of the treaty can be found in Letters and Papers, and here are the other provisions:

- The duke would "within two months, if he can obtain safe conduct, convey, at his own expense, the lady Anne his sister honourably to Calais" where the king would "receive her, by his commissioners, and traduct her thence as soon as possible into his realm and there marry her publicly." If safe-conduct could not be obtained, the duke would "send her, as soon as possible, to some sea-port and transport her thence to England with a suitable convoy of ships at his expense."
- If Henry VIII died and Anne had no surviving children and wanted to return to Cleves, she would be given "a pension of 15,000 florins, payable half-yearly, for life, and her own dress and jewels; and it shall be at the choice of the King's heirs to pay the pension or redeem it with 150,000 florins."
- If her brother, the duke, died "without lawful issue" and his duchy was inherited by Anne's sister, Sibilla, wife of the Duke of Saxony, and she then died without lawful issue, the succession would go to Anne.

- If the succession went to the Duke of Saxony, he would pay a sum of 160,000 florins within four years to Anne and her other sister, Amelia, or their heirs. If either sister died without issue, her share would go to the surviving sister or her children.
- If Saxony inherited, Anne would also inherit three castles, in Cleves, Juliers and Berg.
- Anne's brother was also to keep Henry VIII "informed by letter of his proceedings for the transportation of the lady Anne, so that the King may thereby time his preparations for her reception."
- The king and the dukes of Saxony and Cleves were to confirm the treaty by "letters patent under their hands and seals to be mutually delivered within six weeks from the date of the treaty".

Of course, all these negotiations were for nothing. Although the couple married on 6th January 1540, Henry VIII claimed it was never consummated, saying, "he could never in her company be provoked and stirred to know her carnally". On 9th July 1540, Convocation ruled that the marriage was null and void "by reason of a precontract between lady Anne and the marquis of Lorraine, that it was unwillingly entered into and never consummated". Anne agreed to the annulment of the marriage, becoming the king's beloved sister, and on 28th July 1540, Henry married wife number 5, Anne's former maid of honour, Catherine Howard.

5 September

On 5th September 1569, Edmund Bonner, Bishop of London and a man nicknamed "Bloody Bonner", died in Marshalsea Prison.

Let me tell you more about this bishop who got his nickname from being in charge of burning reformers in London.

Edmund Bonner was born around 1500, in the reign of King Henry VII, probably in Hanley in Worcestershire. His parents were sawyer Edmund Bonner and Elizabeth Frodsham, although it was rumoured that his birth father was George Savage, rector of Davenham in Cheshire.

He was educated at Broadgates Hall, now Pembroke College, Oxford, where he studied civil and canon law. In 1526, he received a doctorate in civil law and was admitted to London's College of Advocates.

In 1527, he undertook a diplomatic mission to the Netherlands, and by 1529 he was serving Cardinal Thomas Wolsey as a chaplain. In August 1529, he went to France on a mission for King Henry VIII. Following Cardinal Wolsey's fall in 1530, he served Thomas Cromwell. In January 1532, he was sent to Rome by the king, and in 1536, he was sent to negotiate with the Protestants of Denmark and northern Germany. Two years later, the king sent Bonner to negotiate with the Holy Roman Emperor regarding a general council and then he was sent to King Francis I's court in France, where he served until early 1540. He served as an ambassador to the emperor in Spain and Germany in 1542 and 1543.

Bonner was elected Bishop of Hereford in 1538, then in 1539, he was elected as Bishop of London following the death of John Stokesley.

In Edward VI's reign, Bonner opposed the religious changes that Edward Seymour, Duke of Somerset and Lord Protector, and Archbishop Thomas Cranmer implemented. In 1549, he was committed to Marshalsea Prison and deprived of his bishopric after he had neglected to enforce the Act of Uniformity and Book of Common Prayer. He had also preached in support of the miracle of the eucharist and had not followed orders to preach in support of the king's authority.

The accession of the Catholic queen, Mary I, in July 1553 led to Bonner's release and restoration as Bishop of London. Bonner set about restoring the old faith in London, and in 1555, he began his persecution of people he deemed heretics, for which he became known as "Bloody Bonner". Historian Kenneth Carleton notes, "Of 282 burnings recorded in episcopal registers for the period, 232 took place in the dioceses of London, Canterbury, Norwich, and Chichester; half the burnings in these four dioceses took place in Bonner's see of London." In 1556, he was involved in the degradation of Archbishop Cranmer.

Mary I died on 17th November 1558 and her Protestant half-sister, Elizabeth, became queen. Bonner refused the oath of supremacy in May 1559 and was deprived of his bishopric. In 1560, he was imprisoned once more in Marshalsea Prison. In 1564, he again refused the oath, a capital offence, but he escaped death when he argued that the consecration of Bishop Horne, who had tendered the oath, was not legal. He spent the rest of his life in prison and died in the Marshalsea on this day in 1569.

His written works include "Responsum et Exhortatio in laudem Sacerdotii" (1553); "Homelies sette forth by Eddmune Byshop of London, ... to be read within his diocese of London of all Parsons, vycars and curates, unto their parishioners upon Sondayes and holy days" (1555); and "A Profitable and Necessary Doctrine with Certain Homilies Adjoined Thereto" (1555).

The work of martyrologist John Foxe emphasised Bonner's role in the Marian persecutions. Kenneth Carleton concludes, "He seems to have become more violent as he grew older, perhaps as a result of his harsh confinement in the early 1550s; even so, it is possible that some of his reported excesses of behaviour were intended to frighten heretics into recantation and so to save them from the flames. Although clearly a difficult personality, it is none the less unfortunate that his reputation for cruelty has come to overshadow many years of valued service to both church and state."

Bonner was buried at St George's, Southwark, but it is thought that his remains were later moved to Copford, near Colchester, a manor held by Bonner as Bishop of London.

6 September

On 6th September 1615, in the reign of King James I, physician, clergyman and inventor of modern shorthand, Timothy Bright, was buried at St Mary's Church, Shrewsbury.

Although his funeral took place in the Stuart period, Bright is known for two works published in the reign of Queen Elizabeth I: his "A Treatise of Melancholie" (1586) and his "Characterie: an Arte of Shorte, Swifte, and Secrete Writing by Character" (1588). In his second work, Bright invented shorthand, the abbreviated symbolic writing method used the world over by secretaries and others needing to take detailed notes quickly.

Let me give you a few facts about the inventor of modern shorthand.

- He was born around 1551, in the reign of King Edward VI, probably in Sheffield in Yorkshire.
- He was educated at Trinity College, Cambridge, before moving to Paris to continue his medical studies.
- He took refuge in the home of Sir Francis Walsingham in August 1572, along with poet Sir Philip Sidney, during the St Bartholomew's Day massacre of the Huguenots.
- He was awarded his MD in 1579 and worked as a physician in Cambridge and Ipswich.
- Between 1586 and 1590, he was a physician at St Bartholomew's Hospital (Barts) and wrote his treatise on melancholy.
- He took holy orders after giving up medicine.
- His 1588 work on shorthand, "Characterie", was dedicated to Queen Elizabeth I. Eight copies of the work still survive today, but only four are complete. One can be found in the Bodleian Library in Oxford.
- In his dedication to the queen, Bright explained: "Cicero did account it worthy his labour, and no less profitable to the Roman common weale (Most gracious Soveraigne) to invent a speedy kind of writing by Character, as Plutarch reporteth in the life of Cato the younger. This invention was increased afterwards by Seneca; that the number of characters grew to 7000. Whether through injury of time, or that men gave it over for tediousness of learning, nothing remaineth extant of Cicero's invention at this day. Upon consideration of the great use of such a kind of writing I have invented the like: of few Characters, short and easy, every Character answering a word: My Invention mere English, without precept or imitation of any. The uses are diverse: Short that a swift hande may therewith write orations, or public actions of speech, uttered as becometh the gravity of such actions, verbatim. Secret as no kind of writing like. And herein (besides other properties) excelling the writing by letters and Alphabet, in that, Nations of strange languages, may hereby communicate their meaning together in writing, though of sundry tongues." The Encylopaedia Britannica explains that Bright's system consisted of "straight lines, circles and half circles".

- Bright also produced other works, including "An Abridgment of John Foxe's "Booke of Acts and Monumentes of the Church", which he dedicated to Sir Francis Walsingham, "Hygieina, on preserving health", and "Therapeutica, on restoring health".
- Elizabeth I appointed him as rector of Methley in Yorkshire, and he held this living, and that of Barrick-in-Elmet, until his death.
- He made his will on 9th August 1615
- He was survived by his wife, Margaret, two sons, Timothy and Titus, and a daughter, Elizabeth.

7 September

On 7th September 1533, just over two months after the death of his previous wife, Mary Tudor, Queen of France, forty-nine-year-old Charles Brandon, Duke of Suffolk, married his ward, fourteen-year-old Catherine Willoughby.

A 49-year-old man marrying a teenager might sound rather distasteful to us today, but it wasn't abnormal in Tudor times, and it was seen as good for the bride in that her husband was well-advanced in his career and could provide well for her. It was also highly probable that he wouldn't be long for this world, and as a widow, she'd have more freedom in who she could choose for her next husband. She'd also be in a good position financially when she could make that choice. It was a win-win situation as the groom got a young wife who was more likely to be fertile than a woman his age, to give him an heir and a spare if he didn't already have one.

Let me share a few facts about this Tudor couple.

- Catherine was the daughter and only child of William Willoughby, 11th Baron Willoughby de Eresby, and Lady Maria de Salinas, lady-in-waiting to Catherine of Aragon, and a woman who'd travelled to be with Catherine of Aragon during her final hours. Catherine was born on 22nd March 1591.
- Catherine's father died in 1526, and in February 1529, her wardship was purchased by Charles Brandon, Duke of Suffolk, who was married to Henry VIII's sister, Mary Tudor, Queen of France.

- Catherine was initially seen as a potential bride for Suffolk's son, Henry Brandon, 1st Earl of Lincoln, who was ten in 1533. Still, it may have been clear that he was ill and not likely to survive and Suffolk was desperate to keep control of the Willoughby estates. Lincoln did indeed die young, dying in 1534.
- After Mary Tudor's death on 25th June 1533, Catherine played chief mourner at her funeral.
- Stephen Gunn points out that "Mary's death necessitated a financial reckoning with the crown, one which cost the duke all his Oxfordshire and Berkshire estates and Suffolk Place in Southwark", so Suffolk needed Catherine's estates.
- The couple married on this day in 1533, and Suffolk fought Catherine's uncle, Sir Christopher Willoughby, for her father's lands, a fight concluded in Suffolk's favour by 1536.
- Even though there were over 30 years between them, the Willoughby-Brandon marriage was successful, and Catherine gave Suffolk two sons, Henry and Charles.
- Catherine attended the funeral of Catherine of Aragon in 1536. In the autumn of 1536, Suffolk was one of those involved in putting down the Pilgrimage of Grace rebellion in the North of England.
- Suffolk spent much of his final years at home in Lincolnshire, but he did serve on the privy council and was active in Henry VIII's campaigns against Scotland and France in the early 1540s. In 1541, he played host at Grimsthorpe to the king and his fifth wife Catherine Howard on their northern progress.
- In 1544, just a year before his death, he commanded troops in France.
- Suffolk died on 22nd August 1545 at Guildford at around 61 years of age. It is not known what caused his death, and he was just about to lead troops in Boulogne. He was buried in St George's Chapel, Windsor.
- Suffolk appears to have been a conservative in terms of religion, requesting dirges in his will. Still, his young wife was a zealous reformer and acted as patron to up-and-coming reformers, employing Bible translator Miles Coverdale as tutor to her sons.

- The couple's eldest son, Henry, became 2nd Duke of Suffolk on his father's death and was sent to court to be educated with Prince Edward, the future Edward VI.
- A sweating sickness epidemic struck in July 1551, and the boys left their studies at Cambridge and travelled to Buckden to try and escape the illness. The boys sadly died on 14th July. Henry died first, leaving the dukedom to Charles, who survived him by only 30 minutes or so.
- Catherine and her friend, Queen Catherine Parr, were lucky to escape being caught up in the execution of Protestant Anne Askew in 1546, and Catherine was not backwards regarding her feelings about Catholic conservative Stephen Gardiner, Bishop of Winchester, allegedly calling her dog Gardiner so that she could call him to heel in the bishop's presence.
- In 1552, Catherine married her gentleman usher, Richard Bertie, and had two children with him: Susan and Peregrine.
- Catherine died on 19th September 1580 at the age of 61. She was buried in Spilsby Church, Lincolnshire.

8 September

On 8th September 1601, John Shakespeare, father of playwright William Shakespeare, was buried at Holy Trinity Church in Stratford-upon-Avon.

John's birthdate is unknown, but it was around 1530/1531. He appears to have been the son of husbandman or tenant farmer Richard Shakespeare who had settled in the Snitterfield area, near Stratford-upon-Avon, by 1529. By the time of his marriage to Mary Arden, between 1556 and 1558, John was a glover and whittawer, i.e. someone working with light-coloured leather, working out of his home in Henley Street, Stratford. Mary was the daughter of Robert Arden, from whom John's father rented property. Her family were prosperous and important. Robert died in 1556. He left Mary property which included his estate in Wilmcote.

John and Mary had their first child, a daughter, Joan, in 1558, but she didn't survive infancy. She was followed in 1562 by Margaret, who only lived for a few months, and then by William in April 1564, who luckily survived the plague that hit the town that summer. There were five more children after William, although Anne, born in 1571, didn't survive childhood.

In 1557, John was working as an ale-taster for Stratford, but by the time of William's birth in April 1564, he had risen to be a burgess of Stratford, and a year later, he became alderman. In 1568, he was made high bailiff, or mayor. In 1571, he was made chief alderman and deputy bailiff.

In the late 1560s, John applied for a coat of arms, believing his ancestors to have been "advanced and rewarded" by King Henry VII, but the application was subsequently withdrawn. Arms were, however, granted in 1596. The position of alderman gave John the right to have his children educated for free at the local grammar school, and it appears William attended.

John's luck ran out in the 1570s when he was prosecuted for usury, the action or practice of lending money at unreasonably high rates of interest, and illegal wool trading. He ended up in debt, which led to him mortgaging some of his wife's properties and losing them in 1580 when he could not keep up with the repayments. In 1586, he was replaced as an alderman due to his poor attendance at meetings.

Outwardly, John was a conforming Protestant, acting in accordance with Elizabeth I's religious legislation and having wall paintings whitewashed over in the Guild Chapel in Stratford due to them being viewed as superstitious and idolatrous. However, his wife Mary was from a Catholic family, and John may well have been a Catholic or, at least, had Catholic sympathies.

As bailiff, John would have attended performances by players such as the Queen's Players, Worcester's Men, Leicester's Men, Warwick's Men, and others. It seems likely that his son William accompanied him. They may have also attended the entertainment at the Earl of Leicester's home, Kenilworth Castle, when the queen visited in 1575.

It is not known when John died, but he was buried on this day in history, 8th September 1601, at Holy Trinity Church, the church that is also the resting place of William Shakespeare.

Trivia: his whitewashing of the wall paintings in the Guild Chapel of the Holy Cross, for which he paid two shillings for "defasyng ymages in ye chapel", wasn't a brilliant job as by the 19th century, they were beginning to show through. A restoration project in 2016 uncovered more of the wall paintings, and they are interesting to see if you can visit the chapel.

9 September

On 9th September 1543, the 30th anniversary of the Battle of Flodden, which saw the death of her grandfather, King James IV, the infant Mary, Queen of Scots, was crowned queen at the Chapel Royal of Stirling Castle in a ceremony which was shortened due to her age.

Mary was born on 8th December 1542 and was the daughter of King James V, King of Scotland, and his French wife, Marie de Guise. She was just six days old when she became queen on her father's death on 14th December 1542 following the Scots' defeat by the English at the Battle of Solway Moss.

Ralph Sadler and Henry Ray were underwhelmed by Mary's coronation, writing that the little girl was crowned with "such solemnity as they do use in this country, which is not very costly". James Hamilton, 2nd Earl of Arran, who was regent, carried the crown, which was held over Mary's little head at her coronation by Cardinal Beaton. Matthew Stewart, Earl of Lennox and Mary's future father-in-law, carried the sceptre, and Archibald Campbell, Earl of Argyll, Arran's brother-in-law and the most powerful Scottish lord, bore the sword of state.

Cardinal David Beaton, Archbishop of St Andrews, blessed the infant Mary and anointed her with holy oil. Her biographer John Guy notes that Mary howled while he did this, continuing to do so while her bishops and peers knelt one by one to take their oath of allegiance to her.

Although Mary was far too young to know about them, never mind join in, banquets, masques, and dancing were all part of the entertainment to celebrate her coronation.

Mary was just nine months old when she was crowned at Stirling, but she was already promised in marriage to Henry VIII's son, Prince Edward, the future Edward VI, who was five years of age. Their marriage had been one of the terms of the 1st July 1543 Treaties of Greenwich between England and Scotland. The treaties had been ratified by the regent, the Earl of Arran, on 25th August 1543, but in December 1543, the Scottish Parliament rejected them. Their rejection led to Henry VIII launching a campaign against Scotland to force the marriage. This war was known as the Rough Wooing and continued until 1550, in Edward VI's reign, when it was ended by the Treaty of Boulogne.

Mary didn't marry Edward. Instead, at the age of five, she set off for a new life in France and to prepare for her marriage to the dauphin, François, or Francis, son of King Henry II of France, whom she married in April 1558, becoming Queen of France.

10 September

On Saturday, 10th September 1547, the Battle of Pinkie Cleugh, also known as the Battle of Pinkie, took place near Musselburgh, Scotland, on the banks of the River Esk. The English forces, led by Edward Seymour, Duke of Somerset, defeated the Scots, killing thousands.

The battle was part of the "War of the Rough Wooing", so-called because it started when Henry VIII tried to force Scotland to stick to the terms of the 1543 Treaties of Greenwich, which included a marriage between his son Edward, the future Edward VI, and the infant Mary, Queen of Scots. Eight years of conflict between the two kingdoms began in December 1543. They continued into Edward VI's reign, with Edward Seymour, Duke of Somerset and Lord Protector, continuing Henry VIII's policy of a forcible alliance with the Scots.

The Battle of Pinkie Cleugh is regarded as the last pitched battle between England and Scotland, i.e. a battle where both sides chose to fight at a scheduled time and location. The English forces, led by Somerset, defeated the Scots, led by the Earl of Arran. Between 6,000 and 15,000 Scots were killed at the battle, compared to 500-600 Englishmen.

William Patten, who accompanied Somerset and his troops to Scotland as judge of the Marshalcy, wrote a detailed eyewitness account of the battle in his pamphlet "The expedicion into Scotlande of the most woorthely fortunate prince Edward, duke of Soomerset", along with a plan of the battlefield.

He manages to conjure in our imaginations just how difficult a situation this battle was for all concerned, writing:

> "Herewith waxed it very hot, on both sides, with pitiful cries, horrible roar, and terrible thundering of guns besides. The day darkened above head, with smoke of shot. The sight and appearance of the enemy, even at hand, before. The danger of death on every side else. The bullets, pellets, and arrows flying everywhere so thick and so uncertainly lighting, that nowhere was there any surety of safety. Every man stricken with a dreadful fear, not so much, perchance of death, as of hurt; which things, though they were but certain to some, were yet doubted of all. Assured cruelty at the enemy's hands, without hope of mercy. Death to fly, and danger to fight.
>
> The whole face of the field, on both sides, upon this point of joining, both to the eye and the ear, so heavy, so deadly, lamentable, outrageous, terribly confused, and so quite against the quiet nature of man..."

According to Patten, the battle started well for the Scots with them wounding many of the English cavalry:

> "The Scots again caught courage afresh, ran sharply forward upon them, and, without any mercy, slew every man of our men that abode furthest in press; a six more, of Boulogners and others, than I have here named: in all, to the number of twenty-six, and the most part gentlemen."

He tells of how Lord Grey suffered a pike wound through the mouth, and Lord Edward's horse was fatally wounded.

But then the English archers "pricked them sharply with arrows" and the Scots were shot at by the artillery "with great puissance and vehemency". Then, according to Patten, the Scots saw the English footmen, who were nearly upon them and had been hidden before by the cavalry and the dust the horses had raised.

Patten records,

> "Their Governor... like a doughty captain, took hastily his horse that he might run foremost away... The Earl of Angus and other chief captains did quickly

follow, as their Governor led, and with the foremost, their Irishmen. Therewith then turned all the whole rout, cast down their weapons, ran out of their wards, off with their jacks and with all that ever they might, betook them to the race that their Governor began..."

The English men pursued them "and spared indeed but few".

Patten describes how the ground was thick with pikes, swords, bucklers, daggers and other weapons that the Scots abandoned as they fled the battlefield. He continues with his account:

"Soon after this notable strewing of their footmen's weapons, began a pitiful sight of the dead corpses lying dispersed abroad. Some, with their legs off; some but hamstrung, and left lying half dead: others, with the arms cut off; diverse, their necks half asunder; many, their heads cloven; of sundry, the brains smashed out; some others again, their heads quite off: with a thousand other kinds of killing.

After that, and further in chase, all, for the most part, killed either in the head or in the neck; for our horsemen could not well reach them lower with their swords.

And thus with blood and slaughter of the enemy, this chase was continued five miles in length westward, from the place of their standing, which was in the fallow fields of Inveresk, unto Edinburgh Park, and well nigh to the gates of the town itself, and unto Leith; and in breadth nigh three miles, from the Frith sands, towards Dalkeith southward. In all which space, the dead bodies lay as thick as a man may note cattle grazing in a full replenished pasture. The river ran all red with blood: so that in the same chase were counted, as well by some of our men that somewhat diligently did mark it, as by some of them taken prisoners, that very much did lament it, to have been slain above thirteen thousand. In all this compass of ground, what with weapons, arms, hands, legs, heads, blood, and dead bodies, their flight might have been easily tracked to each of their three refuges.

And for the smallness of our number, and the shortness of the time, which was scant five hours, from one to well nigh six, the mortality was so great, as it was thought, the like aforetime had not been seen."

Patten also notes that the English were more merciful:

"And yet, notwithstanding all these our just causes and quarrels to kill them, we showed more grace, and took more to mercy, than the case on our side, for the causes aforesaid, did well deserve or require."

It may have been a victory for the English forces this time, but Scotland still refused to recognise the Treaties of Greenwich. The War of the Rough Wooing was finally brought to an end by the Treaty of Boulogne in March 1550.

11 September

On 11th September 1581, Barnaby Fitzpatrick, 2nd Baron of Upper Ossory, died in Dublin at the home of surgeon William Kelly.

In his youth, Fitzpatrick had been friends with Prince Edward (Edward VI) and had been educated with him. He served Edward as a gentleman of the privy chamber when Edward became king.

Let me give you a few more facts about Barnaby.

- Barnaby was born around 1535 and was the oldest son of the chieftain and landowner Barnaby or Brian Fitzpatrick, 1st Baron of Upper Ossory, and Margaret Butler, daughter of Piers Butler, 8th Earl of Ormond.

- In 1541, in the reign of King Henry VIII, Barnaby's father gave up the Gaelic title "MacGiolla Phádraig", meaning Son of the Devotee of St Patrick, anglicising it to Fitzpatrick. He also gave up his claim to the kingdom of Ossory, being created 1st Baron of Upper Ossory instead. This was part of the surrender and regrant, in which Henry VIII sought to extend and secure his control of Ireland.

- In 1543, to show his loyalty to King Henry VIII, the baron sent Barnaby to the royal court in London to be educated. Barnaby shared lessons with his maternal cousin, Thomas Butler, 10th Earl of Ormond, and Henry VIII's son, the future Edward VI, who was about two years his junior. Barnaby became good friends with the prince, serving as one of his nine henchmen.

- Barnaby was once thought to have been Edward's whipping boy, meaning that he took the punishment for the prince's wrongdoings, but modern historians challenge this idea.
- In August 1551, Barnaby was sworn in as a gentleman of King Edward VI's privy chamber. In autumn 1551, Edward VI sent him to France to finish his education and learn about European politics and warfare. He impressed Edward VI's secretary, Sir William Cecil, and King Henry II of France, who made him a gentleman of his chamber. While he was away, Barnaby exchanged letters with his good friend, King Edward.
- In 1552, Barnaby's father became ill, and Barnaby left France for Ireland, visiting the English court to catch up with his friend on the way.
- His good friend, the king, died in July 1553 and Mary I became queen. Although, like Edward, Barnaby was a staunch Protestant, he did help to put down Wyatt's Rebellion in early 1554 but did get involved in a fight involving a priest. "The Chronicle of Queen Jane and of Two Years of Queen Mary" records "the Erle of Ormonde, Sir Courteney Knight, and Mr. Barnaby fell out in the night with a certayn priest in the streate, whose parte a gentyllman comyng by chance took, and so they fell by the eares; so that Barnabye was hurte. The morrowe they were ledd by the ii sheryves to the counter in the Pultry, where they remained [blank] daies". He then returned to Ireland.
- The queen called him to court in 1555, but he didn't go as he was in charge of things in Ireland while his father was ill. He was at the Siege of Leith in 1560.
- When he was about 25, in 1560, Barnaby married his cousin, Joan Eustace, daughter of Rowland Eustace, Viscount Baltinglass, and the couple had a daughter, Margaret.
- He was knighted by his friend Sir Henry Sidney, Lord Deputy of Ireland, after supporting him against Shane O'Neill in 1566.

- In 1568, he sat in the Irish Parliament, and in 1569, he was made sheriff of Leix-Offaly.
- In the 1570s, he feuded with Thomas Butler, 10th Earl of Ormond, and accused him of being involved in the kidnapping of his wife and daughter in 1573. He used Piers Grace, a notorious criminal, to steal back his daughter, and his wife was later returned unharmed. Butler's involvement could not be proved, but that didn't stop Barnaby and his brothers from spoiling the earl's lands as revenge. For his part, Butler accused Barnaby of being disloyal, and Barnaby was summoned before the council in Dublin but acquitted.
- In 1575, he succeeded his father as Baron of Upper Ossory, and in 1578, he caught and murdered rebel Rory O'More. However, he soon faced fresh accusations of being involved with rebels and was summoned to appear before the privy council in May 1580. Although he appealed to his good friend, Robert Dudley, Earl of Leicester, he and his wife were imprisoned in January 1581 in Dublin Castle due to his brothers' links with rebels and his father-in-law being involved in a rebellion. Despite the lack of evidence against him and the intercession of men like Sir Henry Wallop, who said of Barnaby "as sound a man to her majesty as any of his nation", he was not released.
- Barnaby fell ill during his imprisonment and died on this day in 1581 at the home of surgeon William Kelly while being treated. His friend Sir Henry Sidney wrote, "the most sufficient man in counsel and action for the war that ever I found of that country birth; great pity it was of his death."
- Barnaby was survived by his wife, Joan, and his daughter Margaret, who married James Butler, 2nd Baron Dunboyne. His brother, Florence Fitzpatrick, inherited his title, becoming 3rd Baron of Upper Ossory.

12 September

On 12th September 1573, the Protestant reformer and leading politician in the reign of Mary, Queen of Scots, Archibald Campbell,

5th Earl of Argyll, died suddenly at Barbreck. He had married six weeks earlier and showed no signs of illness before retiring to bed. He was laid to rest in the family mausoleum at Kilmun Church on the Holy Loch.

Argyll was the third most important noble in Scotland, holding the offices of justice-general, master of the royal household and chancellor. He was also the most important highland chief and an important landowner, holding land in the west highlands and Scottish islands. His biographer, Jane E. A. Dawson, said he was "the most powerful magnate in the British Isles".

Let me give you some more facts about this important Scot.

- Archibald Campbell, 5th Earl of Argyll, was born in around 1538. He was the eldest son of Archibald Campbell, 4th Earl of Argyll, and his first wife, Lady Helen Hamilton, daughter of James Hamilton, 2nd Earl of Arran and regent of Scotland for Mary, Queen of Scots.
- In his childhood, Archibald was fostered by Colin Campbell of Ardkinglas and his wife, Matilda. In his youth, he was known as Lord Lorne, the courtesy title given to the heir of the Earl of Argyll.
- In 1554, he married Lady Jean Stewart, illegitimate daughter of King James V by Elizabeth Beaton, making him the brother-in-law of Mary, Queen of Scots. Jean had been brought up in the household of Marie de Guise, James V's wife. The marriage brought him into the queen's close royal circle. Archibald and Jean's marriage was childless and unhappy. The couple separated in 1567 and divorced in June 1573. Archibald did have several illegitimate children, though.
- In 1555, he led a military expedition to Ireland.
- His father had been converted to Protestantism and employed reformers in his household, such as John Carswell, who, in turn, influenced Archibald. Archibald later acted as a patron of Carswell, who translated the liturgy of the Protestant kirk, the Book of Common Order, into Gaelic. Archibald was also influenced by hearing John Knox preach in the winter of 1555/6. As a result, he and his father supported ecclesiastical reform. When his father was dying, he told Archibald "to study

to set forward the public and true preaching of the Evangel of Jesus Christ and to suppress all superstition and idolatry".

- His father died in November 1558, and Archibald became Earl of Argyll.
- Argyll was a founding member of the Lords of the Congregation, a group of Scottish lords who favoured the reformation of the church according to Protestant principles and an alliance with England. The Lords of the Congregation rose against Marie de Guise, with Argyll providing the majority of soldiers for the cause. In July 1559, they took Edinburgh, although the castle held out against them. They then withdrew under the Articles of Leith. Argyll and Lord James Stewart, later Earl of Moray, negotiated the Treaty of Berwick in 1560 with William Cecil, Elizabeth I's chief advisor, to secure English help against Marie de Guise in exchange for Argyll helping the English with Ulster in Ireland.
- Marie died in June 1560. On her deathbed, she reconciled with the Lords of the Congregation, leading to the Treaty of Edinburgh between England and Scotland. This allowed Argyll, Lord James and William Maitland of Lethington to steer Parliament into passing acts against papal authority and Catholic worship in Scotland and establishing a new Protestant kirk.
- Mary, Queen of Scots, returned to Scotland in 1561 following the death of her husband, King Francis II of France. She chose Argyll, Lord James and Maitland as her chief advisors, although she continued celebrating mass privately.
- Argyll and Moray opposed the marriage of Mary and Lord Darnley, and the Protestant lords rose in rebellion against their queen. They failed, and all but Argyll, who had substantial lands to retreat to, were forced into exile. He felt betrayed by England's lack of support and stopped helping Elizabeth I in Ireland, causing problems for her with Ulster.
- He was able to climb back in favour with Mary in 1566 and was named one of the regency council for her son, the future James VI if Mary died while giving birth to him.

- He was present when the queen visited her husband, Lord Darnley, on the night before his murder in February 1567. He presided over the Earl of Bothwell's trial for the murder, in which Bothwell was acquitted.
- However, he was unhappy with Mary's marriage to Bothwell and joined those lords who rebelled against her and fought her and Bothwell at Carberry Hill, where Mary was captured and imprisoned. He didn't go as far as supporting her subsequent forced abdication, though, and so left the Lords of the Confederate.
- When Mary escaped from Lochleven Castle, he led her troops as lieutenant-general at the Battle of Langside in May 1568, but Mary's forces were defeated. It is unclear whether Argyll was taken ill at the beginning of the battle or whether that was just a rumour. Mary fled the battlefield and eventually fled to England, where she was imprisoned. Argyll eventually reconciled with the Earl of Lennox, who was acting as regent for Mary's son, King James VI, and persuaded others who had supported Mary to reconcile and support the new king. He worked closely with James Douglas, 4th Earl of Morton, the regent from 1572, and was made lord chancellor in January 1573.
- At the beginning of August 1573, Argyll married Jean or Janet Cunningham, daughter of the Earl of Glencairn. Sadly, Argyll died suddenly at Barbreck while travelling through Argyll on 12th September 1573. He'd been perfectly fine when he'd gone to bed the night before but was found dead that morning. His cause of death was given as the "stone", which was used for internal disorders. His half-brother, Colin, succeeded him as Earl of Argyll.
- Argyll's wife was pregnant at his death and gave birth to a stillborn son in June 1574.
- Argyll was buried at Kilmun Parish Church, the traditional burial place of Clan Campbell.

13 September

On 13th September 1503, poet and antiquary John Leland was born.

Leland is known for his Latin poems and his antiquarian writings, which included a defence of the history of King Arthur, which he presented to Henry VIII; "The laboryouse journey & serche of Johan Leylande for Englandes antiquitees", which he also presented to the king; his biographical dictionary of British authors, a collection of excerpts from British classical and medieval texts; and his "Itineraries", which recorded his travels around England and Wales.

Let me tell you a bit more about this Tudor poet.

- We know he was born on 13th September in London due to his poetry, but the precise year is not known. It must have been around 1503.
- He had an older brother called John. It wasn't unusual in Tudor times to name sons the same because infant mortality was high. "John" was obviously an important family name.
- Leland and his brother were orphaned as children and brought up by Thomas Myles. Myles sent him to be educated at St Paul's School, a school founded in 1509 by John Colet. Scholar William Lily was his headmaster and it was at St Paul's that Leland met William Paget, Anthony Denny, Thomas Wriothesley and Edward North. All of them would act as his patrons later.
- After St Paul's, Leland studied for his BA at Christ's College, Cambridge, and was imprisoned for a time after being linked to a knight who was in contact with pretender Richard de la Pole, who was in France.
- Following his release and graduation, he entered the service of Thomas Howard, 2nd Duke of Norfolk, working as a tutor to his sixth son, Lord Thomas Howard.
- In 1524, the duke died, and King Henry VIII sent Leland to Oxford, where he was unhappy with the conservative teaching.
- By 1528, he was in Paris working on his poetry and mixing with scholars like Jacques Lefèvre d'Etaples, Guillaume Budé and François du Bois, principal at the Collège de Tournai. He

- also corresponded with important men back in England, such as Cardinal Wolsey.
- Leland returned to England in 1529 and was made a royal chaplain.
- In 1533, he and Nicholas Udall wrote verses for pageants for Queen Anne Boleyn's coronation procession.
- In 1533, the pope granted him a dispensation to hold up to four benefices so long as he took orders to become subdeacon within two years and priest within seven.
- According to Leland, it was also in 1533, prior to the dissolution of the monasteries, that Henry VIII appointed him "to peruse and dylygentlye to searche all the lybraryes of monasteryes and collegies" of the realm and list the books, which he did in his "Collectanea". He was able to save some books for the royal libraries at Greenwich, Hampton Court and Westminster, and others for himself.
- At New Year 1534, Leland gave the king two books of stories, and the king gave him a gilt vessel.
- In 1535, he became the prebendary of Wilton Abbey.
- In the late 1530s, he became interested in English and Welsh topography, spending six years travelling around and recording his travels in notebooks. These notes were used for his work "The Itinerary".
- In the 1530s, he also wrote a tract defending the Arthurian tradition, followed in the 1540s by a longer work.
- In the 1540s, he was the rector of Great Haseley in Oxfordshire and canon and prebendary of King Henry VIII College, Oxford.
- In 1543 or 1544, Leland gave the king his work "The laboryouse journey & serche of Johan Leylande for Englandes antiquitees", probably as a New Year's gift. This was later published by Leland's friend, John Bale, in 1549. The work was a record of Leland's travels around the kingdom to preserve books.
- In 1546, the king sent him to France to bring back trees, seeds and grafts.
- In around 1547, the year of Henry VIII's death and Edward VI's accession, Leland had a breakdown and fell into madness. In 1551, his brother John was granted custody of Leland and his property.

He died on 18th April 1552 and was buried in his brother's parish, St Michael-le-Querne. King Edward VI granted custody of Leland's papers to Sir John Cheke, but the collection was broken up and dispersed following Cheke's departure into exile and subsequent death. John Dee obtained several medieval manuscripts from Leland's collection at a sale of his papers in May 1556. William Burton, a Leicestershire historian, ended up with some of Leland's works and passed them on to the Bodleian Library

- His poetical works include a Latin elegy of Sir Thomas Wyatt the Elder; a lamentation commemorating the death of Sir Henry Dudley at Boulogne; a poem inspired by Edward VI's birth in 1537; three poems on Henry VIII's victories in France, and a long poem describing a river trip from Oxford to Greenwich on the Thames, in which he gave interesting topographical and historical information.
- His antiquarian work was used as primary sources for historians and antiquaries like William Harrison, William Camden, John Stow, William Dugdale, John Aubrey and Robert Plot. And his works are still used by historians today.

14 September

On 14th September 1538, in the reign of King Henry VIII, Dr John London destroyed the Shrine of Our Lady of Caversham, near Reading, on the king's orders. It was a shrine that had stood since 1106.

These shrines were holy places housing relics of a saint, or icons or statues of a saint, such as the Virgin Mary. People could visit these shrines on pilgrimage to worship, venerate, give thanks or pray for saintly intercession and miracles. Catherine of Aragon, Henry VIII's first wife, was said to have been a regular pilgrim to the Shrine of Our Lady of Caversham. On 17th July 1532, she travelled there to pray for the Virgin Mary's help in her situation due to her husband wanting an annulment of their marriage.

But fast-forward six years, and Henry VIII was destroying it. London reported to Thomas Cromwell on 17th September:

> "Has pulled down the image of Our Lady at Caversham, whereunto was great pilgrimage. It is plated over with silver. Has put it in a chest fast locked and nailed up, and will send it by next barge to London. Has pulled down the place she stood in with the lights, shrouds, crutches, images of wax etc. about the chapel, and defaced the same thoroughly.
>
> This chapel belonged to Notley Abbey and there was always a canon of that monastery warden of Caversham, who sang in chapel and had the offerings. He was accustomed to show many pretty relics, among others the holy dagger that killed King Henry, and the holy knife that killed St. Edward. All these with the coats of this image, her cap and hair, my servant will bring your Lordship next week. Has sent the canon home to Notley and made fast the doors of the chapel, the lead of which, if desired, he will make sure for the King: otherwise it will be stolen by night,—as happened at the Friars, where they took the clappers of the bells, and but for the aid of Mr. Fachell and the mayor they would have made no little spoil."

He wrote another report to Thomas Wriothesley mentioning a "great relic", which was "an angel with one wing that brought to Caversham the spear's head that pierced our Saviour's side upon the Cross".

The Shrine of Our Lady of Caversham wasn't the only shrine destroyed in Henry VIII's reign as part of the Dissolution of the Monasteries. The Shrine of Our Lady of Walsingham was destroyed that same year, and that was a shrine that Henry VIII had walked to barefoot for a mile to give thanks for the birth of his son, Henry, Duke of Cornwall, in 1511. The shrine of St Thomas Becket at Canterbury was also destroyed in 1538. When Pope Paul III announced Henry VIII's excommunication in December 1538, he stated that one of the reasons for the excommunication was "still further excesses, having dug up and burned the bones of St, Thomas of

Canterbury and scattered the ashes to the winds, (after calling the saint to judgment, condemning him as contumacious, and proclaiming him a traitor), and spoiled his shrine."

It seems so sad that shrines that had stood for centuries, places of real spiritual significance and help for the common people, were destroyed under the guise of ridding England of superstition, but really for adding wealth to the royal coffers.

15 September

On 15th September 1500, in the reign of King Henry VII, John Morton, Archbishop of Canterbury, cardinal and Henry's Lord Chancellor, died at Knole, the Archbishop's country residence, from the plague. He was buried in the crypt at Canterbury Cathedral.

He has gone down in history for his unpopular taxation rationale Morton's Fork, which meant that everyone was liable to taxes no matter their status and situation. He said, "If the subject is seen to live frugally, tell him because he is clearly a money saver of great ability, he can afford to give generously to the King. If, however, the subject lives a life of great extravagance, tell him he, too, can afford to give largely, the proof of his opulence being evident in his expenditure"- so the poor man was living frugally and saving his money, so could afford taxes, and the rich man with all his money could also afford taxes. There was no way out.

However, even though it's referred to as Morton's Fork, and that term now means "a false dilemma", author Nathen Amin points out that this policy of taxation was not Morton's. It did not even originate in Henry VII's reign, and was used in Edward IV's reign.

So Morton's Fork has little to do with Morton, even though Henry VII's financial policies had become very unpopular by the end of his reign.

Here are some facts about John Morton.
- He was born around 1420 in Dorset.
- It is thought that he was educated at Balliol College, Oxford.
- He practised law as well as being a clergyman.
- He served Henry VI as Keeper of the Privy Seal and was a lawyer in his government.

- He changed sides from the Lancastrians to the Yorkists after the death of King Henry VI and was pardoned for his past actions, such as being responsible for drafting the Bill of Attainder against Richard, Duke of York, by Edward IV.
- He served Edward IV as Master of the Rolls and had many church offices during his reign, including Archdeacon of Winchester, Berkshire, Norfolk and Leicester.
- He also served Edward IV as a diplomat.
- In 1478, he was appointed Bishop of Ely.
- He was not a supporter of King Richard III and spent some time imprisoned in Brecknock Castle.
- In 1486, after the accession of King Henry VII, he was made Archbishop of Canterbury and then, in 1487, Lord Chancellor.
- In 1493, Pope Alexander VI made him a cardinal.
- Thomas More, Henry VIII's Lord Chancellor, served in Morton's household as a page, and More used Morton as one of his sources for his work "History of King Richard III".
- Morton was the builder of the Old Palace of Hatfield, the palace used by Elizabeth I as her main residence before she became queen. He used it as the Bishop of Ely's residence.
- Morton, Edmund Dudley and Richard Empson are known for their work in restoring the Crown's wealth via taxation. Of course, Henry VIII had Empson and Dudley executed in 1510, but Morton was already dead.

16 September

On 16th September 1519, scholar, humanist, theologian, Dean of St Paul's and founder of St Paul's School, John Colet, died after suffering three attacks of sweating sickness between 1517 and 1519. He was buried in St Paul's Cathedral. Colet's work influenced humanists such as Erasmus.

Let me give you a few more facts about this Tudor scholar.

- John Colet was born in January 1467, probably in London, and was the son of mercer Sir Henry Colet, who served as mayor of London twice, and his wife, Christian Knyvet. John was one of at least twenty children born to the couple. The humanist scholar Erasmus wrote of John as the eldest son and the only surviving child of the couple's eleven sons and eleven daughters.

- Colet was educated at either the school of St Antholin's Hospital or St Thomas of Acon, before moving on to Oxford and Cambridge.
- By the time he was ordained as a deacon in December 1497, he held a doctorate in theology.
- In the mid-1480s, he held the rectorship of Dennington in Suffolk and Hilberworth in Norfolk, and in the 1490s, he became rector of Thurning, in Huntingdonshire, canon of York, prebendary of Botevant, canon of St Martin's-le-Grand and prebendary of Goodeaster.
- Colet was ordained as a priest in March 1498 and went on to hold the living of Stepney and to become canon of Salisbury, prebendary of Durnford, rector of Lambourn, treasurer of Chichester, and dean of St Paul's.
- He spent some of the 1490s travelling in France and Italy, visiting Paris, Orléans, Rome, and probably Florence to continue his studies. He was in Oxford by the late 1490s and is believed to have lectured on the epistles of St Paul. During this time, he corresponded regularly with Erasmus, and twenty-three of their letters survive. The two men also met. Erasmus certainly served as a mentor to Colet.
- Colet's father died in October 1505, making Colet a wealthy man. He used the wealth to refound St Paul's School, with the intention "specially to incresse knowledge, and worshipping of god and oure lorde Christ Jesu, and good Cristen lyff and maners in the Children". The first high master appointed to the school was William Lily. Erasmus did not teach at the school but did advise on appointments and wrote works that were used at the school.
- Colet was known for his serious and dramatic preaching. He preached Good Friday sermons at court between 1510 and 1517, with his sermon in 1513 condemning war and declaring that it was contrary to Christianity. He also preached to the

Convocation of Canterbury, and in 1515 he preached when Thomas Wolsey was made cardinal.

- It is thought that Wolsey influenced Colet's appointment to the king's council.
- In 1517, Colet, who already had a liver condition, caught sweating sickness for the first time and went on to have two further attacks, which weakened him and exacerbated the problems he had with his liver. He made his will on 22nd August 1519, leaving instructions to be buried at St Paul's Cathedral. He died on this day in history, 16th September 1519. His mother, Christian, survived him.
- Colet's works include his convocation sermon, commentaries on St Paul's epistle to the Romans, commentaries on 1 Corinthians and 1 Peter, responses to other works such as the Celestial Hierarchy of the Pseudo-Dionysius, and an unfinished commentary on the creation story in Genesis.
- His biographer J. B. Trapp writes of how the more learned Erasmus may have tried to steer him, but "Colet remained profoundly his own man as he attempted to arrive at holiness through a true perception of scripture."
- John Colet is still remembered today by St Paul's with a special John Colet Day and John Colet Day service.

17 September

On 17th September 1563, in the reign of Queen Elizabeth I, courtier and soldier Henry Manners, 2nd Earl of Rutland, died during a plague outbreak in London. He was buried at St Mary's Parish Church, Bottesford, in Leicestershire, where he has a beautiful alabaster monument. The Bottesford Living History website describes how his and his first wife Margaret's tomb "is a reflection of the religious changes and turmoil of the period". It goes on to say, "The Earl and his Lady show their confusion at all this religious change and are shown lying not on the traditional altar tomb, but underneath the Protestant table, holding The Book of Common Prayer, in an attempt at compromise and to show their loyalty to the new Elizabethan settlement."

Manners was the son of Thomas Manners, 1st Earl of Rutland, and his wife, Eleanor Paston, who served four of Henry VIII's wives as a lady-in-waiting: Anne Boleyn, Jane Seymour, Anne of Cleves and Catherine Howard. The family seat was Beaver Castle In Leicester, home to the Dukes and Earls of Rutland since the 11th century. It is still home to the Manners family today.

In 1536, Manners married Margaret Neville, daughter of Ralph Neville, 4th Earl of Westmorland. The couple had three children: Edward Manners, 3rd Earl of Rutland; John Manners, 4th Earl of Rutland; and Elizabeth Manners. In 1559, Margaret died, and Manners went on to marry Bridget, daughter of John Hussey, 1st Baron Hussey of Sleaford, and a widow.

Manners became Earl of Rutland on his father's death in 1543 and was knighted by King Henry VIII in 1544. In 1547, he acted as a mourner at Henry VIII's funeral.

Manners served King Edward VI as Warden of the East and Middle Marches on the Scottish borders, joint Lord Lieutenant of Lincolnshire and Nottinghamshire, and Lord Lieutenant of Nottinghamshire. He was imprisoned in the Fleet when Mary I came to the throne for his support of John Dudley, Duke of Northumberland, who had followed Edward VI's devise for the succession and helped put Lady Jane Grey onto the throne. Manners was released into house arrest and then fortunately pardoned. He served Mary I as Captain-General of Horsemen and Lieutenant and Captain-General in Calais.

On Elizabeth I's accession, he was made a Knight of the Garter and served her as Lord Lieutenant of Nottinghamshire and Rutland and President of the Council of the North.

London was badly hit with plague in the summer and autumn of 1563, with at least 20,136 people dying in the city and surrounding parishes. About 24% of London's citizens died in this outbreak. The plague finally subsided in January 1564.

18 September

On 18th September 1544, Henry VIII rode triumphantly through the streets of Boulogne after the French surrendered.

This was the first Siege of Boulogne to take place that year, and this first one was part of England's invasion of France supported by their ally, the Holy Roman Emperor. A force led by Charles Brandon, Duke of Suffolk, had laid siege to the town on 19th July. The king had sailed from Dover to Calais on the 14th July and made his way to Boulogne, setting up camp there on 26th July. Chronicler Edward Hall writes of how Boulogne was "sore assaulted and so besieged with such abundance of great ordinance that never was there a more valianter assault made". He described how the English force undermined the castle, the tower and walls" and that Boulogne "was so beaten with ordinance that there was not left one house whole therein".

On 13th September, when it became clear that the French couldn't keep hold of the town, the French troops sent two of their chief captains out to tell the English force that the chief captain of the town was content to deliver the town into the hands of King Henry VIII so that they could then leave it safely. The king agreed to their surrender. The following day, the Duke of Suffolk rode into Boulogne and was given the keys to the town. The French then left, and Hall estimates that 4454 people left the town, not counting the sick, injured or old people. The grand captain of Boulogne was last to leave, and when he did, he approached the king on horseback, got off his horse and talked to the king. The king then took him by the hand, and the captain knelt, kissed the king's hand, then got back on his horse and departed.

On 18th September 1544, this day in Tudor history, King Henry VIII entered Boulogne. Hall writes that he had a naked sword carried before him and trumpeters standing on the walls sounded their trumpets as he entered. The Duke of Suffolk, who was already in the town, met him and delivered the town keys into the king's hands. The king then retired to his lodgings in the southern part of the town. According to Hall, a couple of days later, the king rode around Boulogne and commanded that the church, Our Lady of Boulogne, should be "defaced and plucked down" and a mount constructed "for the great force and strength of the town".

On 20th September, according to Charles Wriothesley, there was a procession at St Paul's, a Te Deum sung to give thanks for the king's victory over the French, and fires lit in London and around England in celebration.

On the same day that Henry VIII entered Boulogne triumphantly,

King Francis I of France signed a treaty of perpetual peace with Emperor Charles V, who was supposed to be Henry's ally. The French attacked Boulogne in October 1544, looting and killing people, but the English force drove them off. England kept hold of the town until it was returned to the French in 1550, in Edward VI's reign, as part of the Treaty of Boulogne, which ended the War of the Rough Wooing between England and France's ally, Scotland. Of course, England lost its last remaining stronghold on the Continent in Mary I's reign when the French conquered Calais in January 1558.

19 September

On 19th September 1560, explorer, navigator and privateer Thomas Cavendish was baptised at St Martin's Church, Trimley St Martin in Suffolk.

Cavendish is known for his imitation of Sir Francis Drake's circumnavigation of the globe, which he undertook in 1586, and for being the first Englishman to explore the island of St Helena, in the mid-Atlantic.

Let me give you a bit more information about this explorer.

- Thomas Cavendish was the son of William Cavendish of Grimston Hall, Trimley St Martin, and his wife, Mary Wentworth. Cavendish's father died in 1572, and Thomas Wentworth, 2nd Baron Wentworth, became his legal guardian.
- Cavendish was educated at Corpus Christi College, Cambridge, and then entered Gray's Inn, one of London's inns of the court.
- He got a reputation for being a spendthrift and, in the early 1580s, was taken to court for non-payment of debts.
- In the 1580s, Sir Walter Ralegh acted as his patron and at Durham House, Ralegh's London home, Cavendish was taught navigation by men such as Thomas Harriot.
- In 1585, Cavendish was made high marshal under Richard Grenville for an expedition to Virginia. His steward, Henry Seckford, either bought or fitted out the Elizabeth, a pinnace, which joined the fleet setting out from Plymouth on 9th April 1585. A storm scattered the fleet, but even though he was a novice navigator, Cavendish was able to rendezvous

with Grenville in Puerto Rica, as arranged just eight days later. There, Cavendish became friends with Ralph Lane, who was due to become governor of Virginia. Lane wrote of Cavendish, saying, "'Yt ys not possible for men to beehave themselves more fayethfully and more industryously in an Accion especially Master Candysshe our High Marshall".

- After returning to England with Grenville, Cavendish set about preparing for another voyage, ordering a galleon and a pinnace, Desire and the Hugh Gallant, supported by men including merchant John Foxe, Sir Walter Ralegh, Sir Francis Walsingham. Lord Hundson, Sir George Carey, admiralty judge Julius Caesar, and the Earl of Cumberland. Cavendish also collected charts and employed men who'd served under Sir Francis Drake and a mathematician and Portuguese pilots. The fleet set sail from Plymouth on 21st July 1586 with three ships and 123 men aiming to open up trade with the East, break the Spanish monopoly there, find locations for new colonies in South America, and raid Spanish ports and ships.

- Cavendish reached Brazil by 21st October and then entered the Strait of Magellan by early January 1587, clearing it by 24th February. The master of the Hugh Gallant was killed in an attack by Spaniards and several others, but the English fleet was also able to loot and burn Spanish vessels and towns and capture ships off the coast of South America. Cavendish went on to explore the Philippines and the Chinese coast before returning to England in September 1588, exploring the island of St Helena on the way. He took back with him a Great Map of China. His circumnavigation had been quicker than Drake's, taking two years and 49 days.

- In November 1588, he received Queen Elizabeth I on board the Desire but was not knighted. He passed on vital information gleaned on his travels to Sir Francis Walsingham, who, in return, ordered his physician to treat Cavendish, who was ill.

- His return was marred by Judge Julius Caesar threatening court action in 1589 over Cavendish's delay in paying him his profit and the subsequent impounding of the Desire, which Cavendish had just refurbished. Her pilot was also accused of piracy, and the bond of £2,000, which Cavendish had paid to the high court of admiralty to ensure that she would only attack Spanish vessels on the voyage, was forfeited. This delayed Cavendish's plans to return to the Far East.

- In 1591, the queen commissioned Cavendish for a voyage to the East, which he undertook with navigator John Davis, who wasn't keen on the idea. Their departure was delayed by setbacks, for example, the arrest and imprisonment of one of Cavendish's experienced crewmen. They finally set off on 26th August, sailing directly to Brazil. There were disagreements between Cavendish, his cousin John Cocke, and Davis, and the crews of their ships, with Davis requesting permission for his ship, the Daintie, to return to England laden with sugar. The loss of this ship from the fleet meant Cavendish had to build a replacement pinnace. He accused Davis of treachery, while Davis's supercargo accused Cavendish of negligence.

- Storms caused damage to the fleet, and Cavendish's newly built pinnace, the Crow, was completely lost. The Daintie headed home while Cavendish rendezvoused with the rest of his fleet at Port Desire. The fleet suffered further damage in storms just before they entered the Strait of Magellan in April 1592 and then the arrival of winter, combined with the fleet's lack of supplies, led to 40 men dying each week. Although Davies disagreed, Cavendish decided they should head for the Philippines. However, they were again beset by storms and driven back to the Port of Desire. Davis set about refitting the Desire to attempt to sail through the Strait of Magellan again while Cavendish headed for Santos. Shortage of food and a disgruntled crew led to delays in Cavendish's plans to return to the Strait and then to St Helena. Cavendish never made it home, dying a broken man in May or June 1592. Cavendish attacked John Davis in his will, calling him a villain and blaming him for their failed mission.

- Although he died on a failed mission, Thomas Cavendish had completed a successful circumnavigation; he'd taken home a map of China; he'd tried to establish new trade in Brazil, around the River Plate and in the Far East; and he had shown himself to be a good navigator and a man able to get backing and support for his missions.

20 September

On 20th September 1586, Anthony Babington, John Ballard, John Savage, Chidiock Tichborne and three other conspirators were executed near St Giles-in-the-Fields in London.

They were hanged, drawn and quartered for plotting to assassinate Queen Elizabeth I in the famous Babington Plot in support of Mary, Queen of Scots. A further seven were executed the following day.

But what was the Babington Plot?

The man who gave his name to the plot was Anthony Babington, a Derbyshire man who'd been brought up as a Catholic. As a boy, he had served as a page in the household of the Earl of Shrewsbury, who was acting as gaoler to Mary, Queen of Scots, at the time, and he appears to have become devoted to the Scottish queen from that point. In 1580, while in Paris, he met Mary's ambassador to France, James Beaton, Archbishop of Glasgow, and Thomas Morgan, who acted as a confidant and spy for Mary. On his return to England a few years later, Babington carried letters from Morgan to Mary.

In May 1586, twenty-five-year-old Babington received a visit from Catholic priest John Ballard. The latter had met with the Spanish ambassador Bernardino de Mendoza in Paris and was able to tell Babington that the pope had appointed the Catholic Dukes of Guise and Mayenne to lead an invasion of England to depose Queen Elizabeth I. When Babington pointed out that the dukes were unlikely to be successful, Ballard told him that a man named John Savage would assassinate the queen. Savage was put in touch with Babington, who was able to rally fellow Catholic young men to the cause. These men included Thomas Salisbury, Chidiock Tichborne, Edward Abington, Charles Tilney, Edward Windsor, Robert Barnewell, Edward Jones, Henry Donne, Jerome Bellamy, Robert Gage, John Travers, John Charnock, and Gilbert Gifford.

The conspirators met to discuss the plot on 7th June 1586. On 6th July, Babington wrote to Mary, Queen of Scots, in code, telling her that he, with ten gentlemen and 100 followers, would release Mary from her prison and dispatch the usurper, Elizabeth. He wrote that six men, his "private friends", would be in charge of "that tragical execution". Mary replied on 17th July, including the phrase "set the six gentlemen to work", thus supporting Elizabeth's assassination. Of course, she did not know that her letters were being intercepted and the code broken by Elizabeth I's spymaster, Sir Francis Walsingham and his agents. Babington was unaware that a man he'd confided in, named Robert Poley was, in fact, one of Walsingham's agents, as was Gilbert Gifford, who received the letters and passed them on to Thomas Phelippes, Walsingham's code-breaker. Copies of the letters were made before they were passed on.

On 4th August 1586, Babington was arrested. He'd fled and hidden at the family home of Jerome Bellamy when realising he was dining with one of Walsingham's agents who had orders to arrest him. He was soon apprehended. The city of London celebrated the uncovering of the plot against their queen with the ringing of bells, the burning of bonfires and the singing of psalms.

Babington and his fellow conspirators were interrogated, and all of them confessed. It is thought that John Ballard was tortured for information. Babington, Ballard, Tichborne, Salisbury, Donne, Barnewell and Savage were the first group tried and were arraigned on 13th and 14th September, with the remaining seven – Abington, Tilney, Bellamy, Charnock, Jones, Gage and Travers – being tried on 15th. All of the men were found guilty of high treason.

On this day in history, 20th September 1586, Babington and six of his fellow conspirators were executed near St Giles-in-the-Fields, where their plotting had taken place. They suffered full traitors' death, i.e. they were hanged, drawn and quartered. William Camden recorded their executions in his Annales of Elizabeth I's reign, writing:

> "The 20th of the same month, a gallows and a scaffold being set up for the purpose in St. Giles his fieldes where they were wont to meet, the first 7 were hanged thereon, cut down, their privities cut off, bowelled alive and seeing, and quartered, not without some note of cruelty. Ballard the Arch-plotter of this treason craved pardon of God and of the Queen with a condition if he had sinned against her. Babington (who undauntedly

beheld Ballard's execution, while the rest turning away their faces, fell to prayers upon their knees) ingenuously acknowledged his offences; being taken down from the gallows, and ready to be cut up, he cried aloud in Latin sundry times, Parce mihi Domine Iesu, that is, Spare me Lord Jesus. Savage brake the rope and fell down from the gallows, and was presently seized on by the executioner, his privities cut off, and he bowelled alive.

Barnwell extenuated his crime under colour of Religion and Conscience. Tichburne with all humility acknowledged his fault, and moved great pity among the multitude towards him. As in like manner did Tilney, a man of a modest spirit and goodly personage. Abbington, being a man of a turbulent spirit, cast forth threats and terrors of blood to be spilt ere long in England. The next day the other seven were drawn to the same place, and suffered the same kind of death; but more favourably by the Queen's commandment, who detested the former cruelty; for they all hung till they were quite dead before they were cut down and bowelled. Salisbury was the first, who being very penitent, warned the Catholics not to attempt to restore Religion by force and arms. In like manner did Donn, who followed him. Jones protested that he had dissuaded Salisburie from the attempt, and had utterly condemned Babington's proud and head-strong mind, and the purpose of invasion. Charnock and Travers, having their minds wholly fixed on prayer, commended themselves to God and the Saints. Gage extolling the Queen's great bounty to his father, detested his own perfidious ingratitude towards his Princess to whom he was so deeply bound. Jerome Bellamy, who had hidden Babington after he was openly proclaimed traitor (whose brother being guilty of the same crime, strangled himself in prison), with confusion and silence closed up the number."

Of course, this plot was Mary Queen of Scots' undoing, for Walsingham now had proof that she was plotting against Elizabeth I.

Mary was tried in October 1586 and convicted of treason. She was executed on 8th February 1587 at Fotheringhay.

21 September

On 21st September 1557, Henry Pendleton, theologian, chaplain and friend of Bishop Bonner, was buried at St Stephen Walbrook, London.

In Henry VIII's reign, Pendelton was against the reformed faith, which became known as Protestantism, then he supported it in Edward VI's reign, and then he converted back to Catholicism in Mary I's reign. We might call him a pragmatist or a survivor, but it seems strange for someone who was a theologian.

Let me share some facts about Henry Pendleton.

- Pendleton's birthdate is not known. He came from a Lancashire family and studied at Brasenose College, Oxford. He attained his BA in 1542, his Masters in 1544, and went on to get a degree and doctorate in theology in 1552. He was a fellow at Brasenose from 1542 to 1554, vice-principal from 1551 to 1552, and senior bursar there from 1553 to 1554.

- In Henry VIII's reign, he preached against Lutheranism but embraced it in Edward VI's reign. Edward, Earl of Derby, appointed him as an itinerant preacher with four others, including Laurence Saunders and John Bradford, "to preach the doctrines of the Reformation in the ignorant and popish parts of the country". In 1552, Pendleton became vicar of Blymhill in Staffordshire.

- The Catholic Mary I came to the throne in July 1553, and martyrologist John Foxe, in his chapter of Laurence Saunders, writes of how Pendleton and Saunders met and discussed "what was best for them to do in so dangerous a season". Foxe explains that Saunders was "so fearful and feeble-spirited, that he showed himself, in appearance, like either to fall quite from God and his word, which he had taught, or at least to betake him to his heels, and to fly the land, rather than to stick to his profession, and abide by his tackle". Pendleton, however, was "bold in courage" and comforted Saunders and admonished him, telling him that he could not "forsake cowardly his flock when he had most need to defend them from the wolf; neither, having put his hand to God's plough, to start now aside and give it over; nor yet, (that is worst of all,) having once forsaken antichrist, to fall either himself, or suffer others, by his example, to return to their vomit again." He even said, "I will see the uttermost drop of this grease of mine molten away, and the last gobbet of this pampered flesh consumed to ashes, before I will forsake God and his truth." Strong words, yet, as Foxe tells, when the two men arrived in London, it was Saunders who stood firm "mightily beating down antichrist, and lustily preaching Christ his Master", while "Pendleton the Proud", as Foxe calls him, "changed his tippet, and played the apostate, preaching, instead of sound doctrine, nothing almost but errors and lies, advancing antichrist, and overthrowing poor Christ with all his main" becoming "a sworn enemy of God". Pendleton returned to Catholicism, while Saunders stayed true to his faith and was burnt as a heretic in February 1555. I wonder how Pendleton felt on hearing about his friend's execution, particularly as he then reaped the reward for his turn to Catholicism, being made prebendary of Reculverland, canon of St Paul's, vicar of Todenham in Gloucestershire, canon of Lichfield, vicar of St Martin Outwich in London and then receiving the living of St Stephen's, Walbrook.

- Pendleton was appointed as chaplain to Edmund Bonner, Bishop of London, a man known as Bloody Bonner for his part in the persecutions of heretics in Mary I's reign. While serving Bonner, Pendleton participated in disputations with Protestants who had been arrested, men like his fellow preacher John Bradford, whom he visited in prison. According to John Foxe, Bradford reminded Pendleton of how the latter had once set forth the reformed faith "earnestly", just like he did, and wanted to know what had moved his conscience to alter his faith. Pendleton asked him why he was imprisoned, and Bradford explained that it was due to his beliefs about the sacrament and that he denied that men were receiving Christ's body. Foxe writes, "Here Master Pendleton, half amazed, began to excuse himself, if it would have been, as though he had not denied fully transubstantiation indeed" and the two went on to debate this. Bradford was burnt at the stake as a heretic in July 1555.

- Pendleton was famous for his preaching in Mary I's reign, preaching to what was said to be 20,000 people on Easter Monday, 1557. However, not everyone enjoyed his preaching. In his "Ecclesiastical Memorials", John Strype records that when Pendleton preached at St Paul's Cross on 10th June 1554, "a gun was shot off, and the bullet went over him, and hit the wall". Strype adds that the shooter was not found and that it was not clear whether it was done by someone "out of detestation of Pendleton's doctrine, or his person", seeing as he had been a "zealous professor of religion in King Edward's days, which he basely renounced under Queen Mary".

- Pendleton contributed two homilies to Bishop Bonner's 1555 "Book of Homilies".

- Pendleton died sometime in September 1557, and according to John Foxe, "at his death full sore repented that ever he had yielded to the doctrine of the Papists". However, his biographer, L. E. C. Wooding, notes, "references to a work now lost, entitled A declaration of Hen. Pendleton DD in his sickness, of his faith in all points, as the Catholic church teachest, against sclanderous reports against him (London, 1557), suggest that this was a matter of some debate". Did he change his faith once more at his death? We don't know, but perhaps so. He'd seen his friends and fellow preachers, Saunders and Bradford, go courageously to their deaths strong in their Protestant faith.

- Pendleton was buried in his church, St Stephen's Walbrook, on this day in 1557.

- Minister Robert Halley, in his 19th-century book, "Lancashire, its Puritanism and Non-conformity", describes Henry Pendleton as "an able man, handsome, athletic, possessed of a fine clear voice, mighty in the management of ready speech and powerful utterance" and writes of how "his preaching was in popularity and influence second only to that of John Bradford."

22 September

On 22nd September 1560, Amy Dudley (née Robsart), wife of Robert Dudley, Earl of Leicester, was buried in the chancel of the University Church of St Mary the Virgin, Oxford.

Amy had been found dead at the foot of the stairs of her home at Cumnor in Oxfordshire on 8th September 1560. At the subsequent inquest into her death, the coroner had ruled it death by misfortune, stating that Amy had fallen down the stairs by accident.

Following the inquest, Amy's remains were embalmed and placed in a coffin and then taken to Gloucester College, Oxford, which was hanged with black cloth and Leicester's arms. The church was then prepared, also being hung with black cloth and "garnished with scutcheons", that is to say, Leicester's arms, and a hearse was made in the middle aisle. The Dugdale Manuscript in the Ashmolean Collection records that the hearse was covered with black cloth and decorated with "scutcheons of arms" wrought in metal and a valance of black sarsenet "written with letters of gold and fringed with a fringe of black silk. Rails surrounding the hearse were covered with black cloth and garnished with more scutcheons, and the quire was hanged and decorated similarly.

On this day in 1560, Amy's coffin was processed from Gloucester Hall to the church's west door. The manuscript states that two conductors with black staves led the way, followed by 80 poor men and women. Then came the university and officers followed by the choir singing, then several royal heralds with banners of arms, and John Appleyard, Amy's half-brother, and then Amy's coffin, carried by "8 tall yeomen" and 4 assistants, two on each side of the coffin dressed in long gowns and hoods. A hooded and gowned gentleman carried a bannerol on each corner of the coffin.

Behind the coffin walked the chief mourner, Lady Margery Norris, her train being carried by Mrs Butler, assisted by Sir Richard Blount. Then came six ladies from Cumnor, walking in pairs: Mrs Wayneman and Lady Pollard, Mrs Doylly and Mrs Butler, the Elder, and Mrs Blount and Mrs Mutlowe. They were followed by three yeomen, other gentlewomen, more yeomen, and the mayor of Oxford and his men.

The procession took Amy's coffin into the church and placed it on the hearse, surrounded by gentlemen holding the bannerols and the mourners, and then the funeral service began. It opened with prayers, followed by the Ten Commandments, the epistle and gospel, and the offering. Then it was time for the sermon, which was preached by Dr Francis Babington, Doctor of Divinity and Master of Baliol College.

This lavish funeral cost Amy's widower, Robert Dudley, Earl of Leicester, over £2,000, and he didn't even attend, but widows and widowers did not usually attend their spouse's funeral.

Unfortunately, Amy's resting place has been lost over the centuries, but she is remembered now by a memorial tile reading: "In a vault of brick at the upper end of this quire, was buried Amy Robsart, wife of Lord Robert Dudley, Knight of the Garter, on Sunday 22nd September AD.1560"

23 September

On 23rd September 1605, in the reign of King James I, Tudor pamphleteer William Averell was buried at St Peter upon Cornhill.

His works included the 1581 romantic "An excellent historie, both pithy and pleasant, on the life and death of Charles and Julia, two Brittish, or rather Welsh lovers", the 1583 Protestant "A wonderfull and straunge newes, which happened in the county of Suffolke, and Essex, the first of February, being Friday, where in rayned wheat, the space of vi or vii miles compass", the 1584 collection of moral narratives "A Dyall for Dainty Darlings" and the 1588 "A Mervalious Combat of Contrarieties".

Before I tell you about a couple of his works, let me tell you about William Averell.

- Averell was baptised on 12th February 1556, in the reign of Queen Mary I, in the parish of St Peter upon Cornhill, London, and was the son of joiner John Averell and his wife, Margaret or Margareta.

- Nothing is known of his early life, but Averell became a member of the Worshipful Company of Merchant Taylors and the Worshipful Company of Vintners and worked as a parish clerk and schoolmaster in the parish of his birth.

- He married Gillian Goodale, a baker's daughter, in November 1578. Gillian was pregnant at the time of the wedding as she gave birth to their daughter, Anne, in February 1579. The couple went on to have another 16 children, but Gillian died after the birth of the last one.
- Averell remarried at some point and had a daughter, Elizabeth, born in November 1597.
- His first published work was his 1581 romantic work about the Welsh star-crossed lovers, Charles and Julia. Its full title was "An excellent historie bothe pithy and pleasant, discoursing on the life and death of Charles and Iulia, two Brittish, or rather Welshe louers No lesse delightfull for varietie, then tragicall in their miserie, not hurtfull to youthe, nor vnprofitable to age, but commodious to bothe". This work was dedicated to mercer and brewer Henry Campyon. The dedication read, "To the worshipful and his most approved friend, Maister Henry Campyon: W. A. wisheth health and wealth of body, quietness and contentation of mind, in this life fulness of felicitie, and in the life eternal true tranquillity." Rather than being based in Italy, like Romeo and Juliet, this work was set in Britain in the time of the legendary Brutus of Troy, who was known as the first king of Britain.
- Averell's next work was "A wonderfull and straunge newes, which happened in the county of Suffolke, and Essex, the first of February, being Friday, where in rayned wheat, the space of vi or vii miles compass, a notable example to put us in remembrance of the judgments of God, and a preparative sent to move us to a speedy repentance". Averell didn't see the shower himself but cited accounts from witnesses who saw the grain fall "in a drizzling snow". They described it as "a softer substance, greener colour without, whiter within, and of a mealier taste than common wheat." Averell saw it as presaging the end of the world.
- His 1584 "A Dyall for Dainty Darlings" was a collection of three moral narratives dedicated to William Wrathe, warden of the Mercers' Company. They were on divine punishment for sin and the reward for virtue.

- In 1588, the same year as the Spanish Armada's attempted invasion, Averell published his work "A mervailous combat of contrarieties Malignantlie striving in the members of mans bodie, allegoricallie representing unto us the envied state of our florishing common wealth: wherin dialogue-wise by the way, are touched the extreame vices of this present time. With an earnest and vehement exhortation to all true English harts, couragiously to be readie prepared against the enemie". It was dedicated to Sir George Bonde, Lord Mayor of London. Averell's biographer, William E. Burns, describes this work as beginning with "a dialogue between the parts of the body in which the tongue, urging a revolt of the body against the belly and back on the grounds of their greed and pride, was eventually unmasked as a traitor" and concluding with "an exhortation for loyalty to the queen". Burns explains that it contained attacks on Jesuits and Catholics and that it was used as a source for William Shakespeare's parable of the revolt of the members against the belly in his play "Coriolanus". In 1590, it was published with the three narratives of "A Dyall for Dainty Darlings" as "Four Notable Histories", dedicated to Hugh Ofly, a Marian exile and London alderman.
- Averell's date of death is not recorded, but he was buried on 23rd September 1605.

24 September

On 24th September 1589, Roman Catholic priest William Spenser and layman Robert Hardesty were executed in York. Spenser was executed for being a priest and Hardesty for sheltering Spenser.

In his book "Acts of English martyrs", John Hungerford Pollen writes that William Spenser was born in Gisburn in Yorkshire and was educated at Trinity College, Oxford, supported by his uncle William Horn. He was a scholar and fellow and graduated MA in 1580. Pollen states that he met Spenser at Oxford, writing,

"There I knew him for about eight years, always leading a most upright life, but suffering much at the hands of the heretics even before he left the university, because he was looked on as leaning somewhat towards the Catholic faith. They brought many charges against him, and he would argue against them, but never recklessly. From the time he was a boy his zeal for souls was marvellous, and he never neglected the first rudiments of faith taught him by his uncles, but acted up to them with zeal and constancy to the time of his death."

In 1582, Spenser was a member of a group of men who travelled to the Jesuit College at Reims to study "cases of conscience, Holy Scripture, and controversy" and to get ready to travel back to England to 'harvest' souls for the Catholic faith. After two years in Reims, he was ordained as a priest and returned to England. Pollen writes of how Spenser worked so "earnestly in order to help souls" that he voluntarily made himself a prisoner at York Prison so that he could save the prisoners there.

While on a journey, Spenser was recognised as "some Papist or seminary priest" and apprehended by a justice out hunting. He was condemned under the Elizabethan "Act against Jesuits, seminary priests, and such other like disobedient persons" for being a priest. Pollen writes, "he answered at the bar with intrepidity, and met his death with joy".

In his work "Examination of Fox's Calendar of Protestant Saints, Martyrs", William Eusebius Andrews writes that Spenser was sent on a mission to England in 1584 but that "The particulars of his labours and sufferings are not known, only that he was apprehended, tried and condemned for receiving holy orders beyond the seas, by authority derived from the bishop of Rome, and coming over to England, and there exercising his priestly functions." He says, "He received the sentence of death with an undaunted courage, and suffered with great constancy, being hanged, drawn and quartered at York, the 24th of September, 1589."

He adds that Robert Hardesty, "a layman of great probity and piety", was hanged with him "for having harboured and relieved the confessor of Christ, knowing him to be a priest."

Spenser and Hardesty were beatified in 1987 by Pope John Paul II as two of the Eighty-five Martyrs of England and Wales who were killed between 1584 and 1679.

25 September

On 25th September 1534, Pope Clement VII, born Giulio di Giuliano de' Medici, died in Rome.

He'd been pope since he was elected in 1523, having served as the chief advisor to the two previous popes, his cousin Pope Leo X and Pope Adrian VI. Pope Clement VII was pope at rather an interesting time – the Protestant Reformation sparked by Martin Luther was spreading through Europe, Henry VIII was seeking an annulment of his marriage to Catherine of Aragon, Emperor Charles V and Francis I of France both wanted the pope's support on their very different sides, Suleiman the Magnificent was causing trouble in Eastern Europe, and the church was having financial problems.

Then, in 1527, there was the Sack of Rome, a massacre and pillage carried out by the mutinous troops of Emperor Charles V and those associated with Cardinal Pompeo Colonna, an enemy of Clement. The pope was captured and imprisoned at the Castel Sant'Angelo, and the Vatican was plundered. Clement stayed holed up in the castle for seven months before escaping, allegedly dressed as a gardener.

Pope Clement VII was a scholar, expanding the Vatican Library and being friends with humanist men like Erasmus. He was a patron of the Arts, commissioning Michelangelo to paint the scene that turned out to be the Last Judgement in the Sistine Chapel. As a cardinal, he had commissioned Raphael to paint the "Transfiguration" altarpiece for his cathedral at Narbonne, in France. He also ordered the restoration and refurbishment of churches and buildings in Rome. He was also a patron of science. He personally approved Copernicus's theory that the Earth revolves around the Sun. He was also a patron of Machiavelli and opposed the Spanish Inquisition's treatment of the Jews. He was an interesting man.

And his death is rather interesting too!

It was said that he died from eating death cap mushrooms or from fumes from poisoned candles in his room, but it is unknown whether these rumours were based on any truth. In "Diseases and causes of death among the Popes", Louise Cilliers and F. P. Retief put his death down to natural causes, specifically a major anxiety neurosis. Pope Clement VII was laid to rest in the Basilica of Santa Maria sopra Minerva in Rome.

Ninety per cent of deaths related to mushroom poisoning worldwide are due to the death cap mushroom. These mushrooms can easily be mistaken for edible mushrooms and are even said to be quite tasty. As little as half a death cap mushroom contains enough toxin to kill an adult, but symptoms take some time to manifest – 6-24 hours after eating - so you don't find out you've eaten one for some time. Symptoms of death cap mushroom poisoning include abdominal pain, diarrhoea, nausea, vomiting, jaundice, delirium, seizures, coma, kidney failure, intracranial pressure and bleeding, and cardiac arrest. Death tends to happen between 6 and 16 days of eating the mushroom.

26 September

On 26th September 1588, Sir Amias (Amyas) Paulet, administrator, diplomat, Governor of Jersey and gaoler of Mary, Queen of Scots, died. He was buried in St Martin-in-the-Fields, Westminster.

Paulet served Elizabeth I as her resident ambassador in France and a privy councillor and was present at the execution of Mary, Queen of Scots. When he was acting as Mary's gaoler, Elizabeth I had suggested that it would be easier if Paulet quietly murdered her. Let me tell you a bit more about that.

Mary, Queen of Scots, had been tried for treason in October 1586, found guilty and condemned to death, but Queen Elizabeth I could not come to terms with executing a fellow anointed queen. Parliament petitioned her, but Elizabeth just kept delaying.

As John Guy points out in his excellent book on Mary, Elizabeth wanted a private citizen to act under the Bond of Association and assassinate Mary, rather than her having to commit regicide.

But what was this Bond of Association?

Sir Francis Walsingham and William Cecil drafted this bond in October 1584 to protect Queen Elizabeth I. It followed the assassination of William of Orange in 1584 and the Throckmorton Plot of 1583, a plot to assassinate Elizabeth and replace her with Mary.

As "The Encyclopedia of Tudor England" explains, "the first clause of the bond pledged all who signed it to obey the queen's commands and to stand ready to resist, pursue, and destroy any persons who sought her life."

Signatories also agreed that any attempt on Elizabeth's life would bar that person from the succession. They also had to agree to kill that person by any means available - "to prosecute such person or persons to the death... and to take the uttermost revenge on them... by any possible means... for their utter overthrow and extirpation." The bond was also interpreted to include "not only those directly involved in murder attempt" but also "any that have, may or shall pretend title to come to this crown by the untimely death of her Majesty so wickedly procured.". It was also taken to include the heirs of anyone benefitting from the assassination. So, if there was a plot to kill Elizabeth and replace her with Mary, signatories could kill both Mary and her son, King James VI of Scotland.

A sacred oath sealed the bond, and every member of Elizabeth's council signed it except William Davison. The bond was sent out around England, and local officials devised signing ceremonies. Thousands of people signed it, including Mary, Queen of Scots.

In 1585, the Act for the Queen's Safety was passed by Parliament. It declared that anyone supporting a claimant to the throne who sought to advance their claim by the assassination of the queen was guilty of treason. It authorised loyal subjects to pursue and kill both those who had attempted the murder and the claimant on whose behalf they acted. However, it did not empower those loyal subjects to seek out and kill the claimant's heirs. So, in the case of plots seeking to replace Elizabeth with Mary, only the plotters and Mary would suffer, and James VI would be safe unless he were involved in the plot. A special commission would investigate the deed and determine the guilty party's identity.

A special commission did indeed investigate the 1586 Babington Plot, and the plotters were caught and executed. Mary was, of course, the claimant in question and evidence was provided proving that she had also given her consent and support for the plot. Hence she was found guilty and sentenced to death.

Elizabeth wanted one of her loyal subjects to kill Mary under the terms of the act and bond; after all, her councillors had signed the Bond, and they had taken that sacred oath to hunt down and kill someone like Mary. However, her chief advisor, William Cecil, Baron Burghley, wanted Elizabeth to sign the death warrant and execute Mary like any other traitor. He attempted to scare the queen into action with rumours of threats to her life. Elizabeth called her secretary William Davison, instructing him to bring her Mary's death warrant. She then signed it. Elizabeth claimed later that she told Davison not to do anything with it, but it was sent to Fortheringhay and Mary was executed.

Historian John Guy believes that Elizabeth didn't intend for the warrant to be used. This is why she also told Davison to get Walsingham to write a letter to Sir Amias Paulet, Mary's gaoler, asking him to do away with Mary without a death warrant. She expected Paulet, as one of the first signatories of the Bond of Association, to do what he had pledged to do and to have Mary killed. Unfortunately for Elizabeth, Paulet was shocked. He wrote, "God forbid that I should make so foul a shipwreck of my conscience." When it came down to it, he couldn't do it. Even if the Queen of England wanted it done, killing a queen was just too big a risk.

Elizabeth sent for Davison again, telling him how she'd dreamt of Mary's death. She was making it known that she wanted Mary assassinated.

Guy points out that Elizabeth "had skilfully contrived things so that she would win whatever happened. If Mary was killed under the Bond of Association, Elizabeth could disclaim responsibility. If Cecil covertly sealed the warrant and sent it to Fotheringhay behind her back, she could claim she had been the victim of a court conspiracy."

The warrant arrived at Fotheringhay on 7th February 1587, and it was Sir Amias Paulet who then set about arranging Mary's execution. Then Paulet, his assistant Sir Drue Drury, and the Earls of Shrewsbury and Kent barged into Mary's room. Paulet tore down her cloth of state, and then he read out the warrant. She was executed by beheading the following day.

27 September

On 27th September 1442, in the reign of King Henry VI, John de la Pole, 2nd Duke of Suffolk, was born.

Let me give you some facts about him.

- He was the son of William de la Pole, 1st Duke of Suffolk, and his wife, Alice Chaucer.

- In 1449, when he was just a small boy, John married his distant cousin, Margaret Beaufort, who was, of course, the future mother of King Henry VII.

- John's father, William, was for a time the main power behind King Henry VI but was brought down by his enemies and impeached by the Commons. Henry VI intervened, sending the duke into exile, but his ship was intercepted, and he was given a mock trial and beheaded. John inherited his title, but the Crown took his father's offices, and John became a ward of the Crown.

- In 1453, John's marriage to Margaret Beaufort was annulled by King Henry VI, who made Margaret a ward of his half-brother, Edmund Tudor. Margaret married Edmund in 1455.

- In 1458, John married Elizabeth, daughter of Richard of York and Cecily Neville, and sister of the future Edward IV and Richard III. This allied John with the Yorkists, and he ended up being degraded from Duke of Suffolk to Earl of Suffolk in 1459 when the Duke of York was attainted and driven into exile.

- John fought on the Yorkist side at the Battles of St Albans and Towton in 1461 and acted as steward of England at his brother-in-law Edward IV's coronation.

- In 1463, a few months before he reached maturity, he came into his lands, and in 1465, he was granted an annuity by the king. In 1467, his eldest son, John, was made Earl of Lincoln.

- John fought on Edward IV's side at the Battles of Barnet and Tewkesbury in 1471. His rewards included being made high steward of Oxford University, a Knight of the Garter, and Lieutenant of Ireland.

- In 1475, he served Edward IV in France. In 1476, his mother, Alice, died, and he took possession of some of her dower estates.
- King Edward IV died suddenly in 1483, and John carried the royal sceptre at Richard III's coronation after Edward V had been ruled illegitimate. Following Richard's son's death, John's son, the Earl of Lincoln, was made President of the Council of the North in his place and may even have been considered Richard's heir. However, John lost his office of Constable of Wallingford to Francis, Viscount Lovell.
- In 1485, Henry Tudor, son of Lady Margaret Beaufort, returned from exile and fought King Richard III at the Battle of Bosworth. John didn't fight in the battle, but his son, Lincoln, fought on Richard III's side. Richard was killed, and Henry became King Henry VII. John and his son did not suffer for their links with Richard, and John was even reappointed as Constable of Wallingford in place of Lovell, who was attainted after Bosworth. John acted as a trier at the new king's first parliament, but in 1487, his son, Lincoln, rebelled against Henry VII, supporting pretender Lambert Simnel who claimed to be Edward, Earl of Warwick. Lincoln was subsequently killed at the Battle of Stoke Field. Fortunately for John, he managed to keep the king's trust, acting as trier at the next parliament and mustering for the king's expedition to Brittany. He did lose his Wallingford office, though.
- John died in May 1492 and was buried in the college he'd founded at Wingfield in Suffolk

28 September

On 28th September 1599, Elizabeth I's favourite, Robert Devereux, 2nd Earl of Essex, strode into the queen's bedchamber unannounced and saw her without her makeup or wig, without her "mask of youth".

Essex had been confirmed as Lord Lieutenant of Ireland on 30th December 1598 and had left England on 27th March 1599, arriving in Dublin on 14th April. His campaign against the Irish was unsuccessful. Essex had assumed he'd be able to defeat the Earl of Tyrone and his men quickly, but as things dragged on, he became disillusioned with the situation. Exhaustion, disillusionment and a fear that his enemies at court were undermining him and influencing the queen against him led to him giving up on the Irish situation, making a truce with the Irish rebel leader (against the queen's wishes) and returning to England without the queen's permission. This amounted to desertion and disobedience, something which Elizabeth I could not and would not tolerate

Devereux rushed back to court at Nonsuch Palace to explain but made things worse when he strode into the queen's bedchamber unannounced while she was getting ready. A contemporary account cited in Thomas Birch's 18th-century work "Memoirs of the Reign of Queen Elizabeth" tells us that:

> "His lordship lighted at the court gate about ten in the morning, and made all haste up to the presence and so to the privy-chamber, and did not stop till he came to the queen's bed-chamber, where he found her majesty newly up, and the hair about her face. He kneel'd to her, and kiss'd her hands, and had private speech with her, which seemed to give him great contentment; for coming from her to go to shift himself in his chamber, he was very pleasant, and thanked God, that tho he had suffered much trouble and storms abroad, he found a sweet calm at home."

However,

> "it was much wonder'd at in the court, that he went so boldly to her majesty's presence, she not being ready, and he so full of dirt and mire, that his very face was full of it."

Essex had two further meetings with the queen, and in the final one, Elizabeth pressed him to explain himself. Essex's biographer Paul E. J. Hammer writes that this was the last time the queen saw her favourite. The next day, 29th September, Essex was interrogated before the queen's council for around 5 hours. The council concluded that his truce with the Irish rebels was indefensible and that his return to England was desertion of duty. Essex was then put under house arrest at York House.

In June 1600, Essex appeared before a special court and was

punished by being deprived of his public office and confined to his home. However, in August, he was granted his freedom, although his sweet wines monopoly, his one source of income, was not renewed.

He may well have wormed his way back into the queen's affections if he had apologised and appealed to the queen for mercy; after all, she had a soft spot for him and was used to his impulsive behaviour. However, Essex made the fatal mistake of trying to enlist the support of the Scottish king, James VI, against Cecil's faction at court and planning a coup for March 1601 to seize control of the court, the Tower of London and the City, and then to remove his enemies from power. When, on the 7th February, Essex received a message from the queen that he was to present himself before her council, he decided to move things forward. He summoned three hundred followers, telling them that Cecil and Raleigh were planning to assassinate him and that the rising should take place the next day instead of in March.

On the 8th February 1601, Essex, his supporters and two hundred soldiers gathered at Essex House. Essex then marched into the city crying, "For the Queen! For the Queen! The crown of England is sold to the Spaniard! A plot is laid for my life!" but London's citizens remained indoors instead of joining him on his march. As his supporters deserted him, Essex was forced to give up and return home, where he surrendered after Lord Admiral Nottingham threatened to blow up his house if he did not give himself up.

Essex was tried for high treason on 19th February 1601 and condemned to death. He was executed on 25th February 1601 on Tower Green.

29 September

On 29th September 1528, the papal legate, Cardinal Lorenzo Campeggio, landed at Dover on the Kent coast. In early 1528, Cardinal Thomas Wolsey, Henry VIII's right-hand man, had written to Pope Clement VII outlining Henry VIII's demand that the case for an annulment of his marriage to Catherine of Aragon be decided in England by Wolsey and a visiting papal legate, who would act with the full authority of the Pope. On 13th April 1528, a papal bull had empowered Cardinal Wolsey as the pope's viceregent "to take cognisance of all matters concerning the King's divorce", and Campeggio had been made papal legate in June 1528 in preparation for hearing the divorce case.

On the 8th December 1528, Cardinal Campeggio arrived in London, but, as historian Eric Ives explains, his "powers were not complete", necessitating "further wearisome and unsatisfactory negotiation" with the papacy. This lack of authority was a papal stalling tactic.

Things were made worse for Henry VIII and Wolsey when Catherine of Aragon produced Pope Julius II's dispensation for her to marry Henry. This put a spanner in the works and caused delays with the case. In the meantime, Campeggio met with Catherine and advised her to join a convent, which would allow the marriage to be annulled easily. However, Catherine believed that she was Henry's true wife and queen and would not agree to take the veil.

Henry VIII and Wolsey then played dirty, threatening Catherine with separation from her daughter, Mary, if she would not obey the king. Instead of submitting to the king, Catherine decided to fight back.

Campeggio could only stall for so long, and formal proceedings finally began on the 31st May 1529 at the Legatine Court at Blackfriars.

On 16th June 1529, at Baynard's Castle, Catherine met with William Warham, Archbishop of Canterbury; Cuthbert Tunstall, Bishop of Durham; Nicholas West, Bishop of Ely; John Clerk, Bishop of Bath and Wells; John Fisher, Bishop of Rochester; Henry Standish, Bishop of St Asaph; Jorge de Athequa, Bishop of Llandaff; her almoner, Robert Shorton; and John Talcarne. In their presence, she wrote a formal appeal to the pope against the authority of the legatine court, requesting that the case be heard in Rome.

Two days later, Catherine and her husband, Henry VIII, were summoned to appear before the court. The king sent proxies, Richard Sampson, dean of the Chapel Royal, and Dr John Bell, but Catherine chose to appear at the court in person, accompanied by her ladies-in-waiting and the bishops who were to act as her counsel for the proceedings. Henry Ansanger Kelly explains that Catherine "read a protest, the essence of which was that her appearance there and anything that she should say were not to be taken as an indication of approval of the legates as competent judges in the case, nor to derogate from any allegations, protestations, provocations, appeals, complaints, supplications, recusations, and reclamations made to the pope". She made the point that the judges were far from impartial, being closely associated with the king, and stated that the court proceedings should not be taking place while the case was still pending in Rome. She instructed that her protest be recorded, and the judges stated that her protestation would be answered in proceedings on 21st June.

On 21st June, both Catherine and Henry appeared at the court. Rather than simply confirming her attendance, Catherine sank to her knees in front of her husband and gave the speech of her life. She reminded the king that she'd been his true wife for 20 years and a true maid at their marriage. She concluded by committing her cause to God. Catherine then rose to her feet, curtseyed to the king and walked out of the court, ignoring those who tried to make her return to her seat and saying, "On, on, it makes no matter, for it is no impartial court for me, therefore I will not tarry. Go on."

Catherine had stolen the show, and her speech was hard to follow. Henry VIII addressed the court, speaking of his love for Catherine and his troubled conscience regarding the fact that he had acted contrary to God's law in marrying his brother's widow.

Over the next month, Henry VIII tried to prove that Catherine had consummated her marriage to his brother, Arthur. Still, Catherine had already signed protestations of her virginity, and Bishop John Fisher shocked the court in his defence of Catherine's virtue, quoting from the Book of Matthew and saying, "Quos Deus conjunxit, homo non separet. 'What therefore God has joined together, let not man put asunder.' And, for as much as this marriage was made and joined by God to a good intent, I say that I know the truth; which is that it cannot be broken or loosed by the power of man."

He then said that he was so convinced of Catherine's cause that he would lay down his life for it.

Henry VIII then sent Wolsey and Campeggio to see Catherine and to try and bully her into submission, but this failed miserably. In desperation, Campeggio tried another stalling tactic. In July 1529, he announced that the court would adjourn until October for a summer recess since it was "reaping and harvesting" time in Rome when courts did not sit. Henry VIII was furious, but the Legatine Court was suspended, never to sit again because news reached England that Catherine's appeal to Rome had been successful. It was a huge blow for Henry, who had expected the court to pass sentence and rule in his favour.

Henry VIII's marriage to Catherine of Aragon was not annulled until nearly four years later, in May 1533, when Archbishop Thomas Cranmer and his court ruled that Henry and Catherine had never been legally married and that the king's marriage to Anne Boleyn, which had taken place in secret on the 25th January 1533, was valid. A pregnant Anne Boleyn was crowned Queen of England just days later.

30 September

On 30th September 1544, fifty-three-year-old King Henry VIII returned to England after his third invasion of France and his victory in Boulogne. The French forces surrendered on 13th September after a siege that had lasted from 19th July.

This French campaign had been provoked by France helping Scotland against England, and the English king had allied with Emperor Charles V against France.

From the 18th September entry, you will know that Henry VIII had ridden triumphantly through the streets of Boulogne after the French surrendered before being given the keys to the town by Charles Brandon, Duke of Suffolk. Chronicler Edward Hall writes, "When the king had set all things there in such order, as to his wisdom was thought best, he returned into England, to the great rejoicing of all his loving subjects."

It hadn't quite been Agincourt, but Henry VIII was triumphant.

1 October

On 1st October 1500, John Alcock, Bishop of Ely, died at Wisbech Castle.

Alcock wasn't just a bishop; he was a scholar, a royal tutor and an administrator.

Let me tell you a bit more about this man.

- John Alcock was born in 1430 in Beverley, Yorkshire, and was the son of William Alcock, who came from Hull.
- Alcock received a grammar school education at the school attached to Beverley Minster before studying at Cambridge University. He'd attained a doctorate in civil law by 1459 and worked in church administration in London.
- In the late 1460s, he was admitted to the prebends of Browneswood, St Paul's, and then North Alton in Salisbury Cathedral.
- In 1469 and 1470, he was a member of panels hearing debt cases.
- In April 1471, Alcock was in favour with King Edward IV, who had just returned from exile to reclaim the throne, and was appointed dean of the royal free chapel of St Stephen, Westminster, and, in the same month, was appointed keeper of the rolls of chancery.
- In 1471, Alcock was appointed as administrator of King Edward IV's eldest son, Prince Edward's lands and properties in Wales, Cornwall and Cheshire. The prince was just a baby.
- He was made Bishop of Rochester in 1472 and was responsible for keeping the great seal from September 1472 to June 1473.
- In 1473, Alcock was appointed as three-year-old Prince Edward's tutor and president of the prince's council at Ludlow.
- While the king was campaigning in France in 1475, with his chancellor, the Bishop of Lincoln, Alcock served as chancellor in England.
- In 1476, Alcock became Bishop of Worcester.
- In 1483, following Edward IV's death and the accession of the boy-king, Edward V, Alcock's pupil, the new king's uncle, Richard, Duke of Gloucester, took the throne as Richard III,

claiming that Edward and his siblings were illegitimate. It is not known what Alcock thought of the events of 1483.

- In October 1485, following Henry Tudor's accession to the throne as Henry VII, after the Battle of Bosworth, Alcock was appointed as chancellor and preached the sermon opening the king's first parliament in November 1485.
- In March 1486, John Morton, Archbishop of Canterbury, was made Lord Chancellor following his return from exile, but Alcock still served as a trusted advisor and councillor.
- In the summer of 1486, he was the leader of a delegation that negotiated a truce with Scotland. In September 1486, he christened Prince Arthur, eldest son of Henry VII and Elizabeth of York, at Winchester. He was made Bishop of Ely the following month.
- As well as being a clergyman and royal administrator, Alcock was involved in endowments and building projects. For example, he founded a chantry and school in the grounds of Holy Trinity, Hull, where his father had been laid to rest; he rebuilt a church at Little Malvern Priory, and he built a great hall at the bishop's palace in Ely and a chantry chapel in the cathedral.
- Alcock was also a scholar and wrote several religious texts.
- Alcock died on this day in 1500 and was buried at Ely Cathedral, in the beautiful chantry chapel he'd had built.

2 October

On 2nd October 1528, reformer and Bible translator William Tyndale's book "The Obedience of a Christen man, and how Christen rulers ought to govern, wherein also (if thou mark diligently) thou shalt find eyes to perceive the crafty convience of all jugglers", more commonly known as "The Obedience of a Christian Man", was published in Antwerp. It is an important book in the story of Anne Boleyn and King Henry VIII because it is thought that this book helped the king realise that rulers were accountable only to God, and not to the pope.

17th-century historian John Strype and George Wyatt, grandson of poet and diplomat Thomas Wyatt the Elder, tell the same story about how this heretical book found its way into the hands of King Henry VIII. According to them, in around 1529, Anne Boleyn lent Tyndale's book to Anne Gainsford, one of her ladies. Anne Gainsford's suitor, George Zouch, "plucked" it from his sweetheart, and it got confiscated from him by Dr Richard Sampson, Dean of the Chapel Royal, who saw Zouch reading it in the chapel.

Sampson, along with other clergymen, had been commanded by Cardinal Thomas Wolsey to keep an eye out for heretical books, so he took the book straight to Wolsey. In the meantime, Anne Boleyn had asked her lady if she could have the book back. Her lady was distraught that she could not give the book back to her mistress, but Anne was not angry or upset; she simply commented, "Well, it shall be the dearest Book that ever the Dean or Cardinal took away." Anne then went to her sweetheart, the king, to ask him to intervene with Wolsey to get the book returned. When the book was returned to her, Anne took it to the king and "besought his Grace most tenderly to read it." Wyatt writes of how she had marked matters "worthy of the King's knowledge" with her fingernail, and Strype describes how the king was "delighted" with the book and remarked that "This Book is for me and all Kings to read."

Strype continues:

> "And in a little Time the King by the Help of this virtuous Lady, by the Means aforefaid, had his Eyes opened to the Truth, to search the Truth, to advance God's Religion and Glory, to abhor the Pope's Doctrine, his Lies, his Pomp and Pride, to deliver his Subjects out of the Egyptian Darkness, the Babylonian Bonds, that the Pope had brought him and his Subjects under. And so contemning the Threats of all the World, the Power of Princes, Rebellions of his Subjects at Home, and the raging of so many and mighty Potentates abroad; set forward a Reformation in Religion, beginning with the Triple Crowned Head at first, and so came down to the Members, Bishops, Abbots, Priors, and such like."

Tyndale's "Obedience of a Christian Man" was instrumental in helping Henry VIII see how he could have his marriage to Catherine of Aragon annulled while limiting the papacy's power in England. The steps Henry VIII took after reading "Obedience" sparked the English Reformation.

However, Tyndale's message regarding how "God has appointed the kings, princes, and other secular leaders as his representatives on earth" – and kings, therefore, being the highest authority in the land – and his challenge of the pope's "temporal authority over king and emperor" were just a small part of the book. Other subjects included:

- The supremacy of God's word over everything else.
- The importance of God's word being made available to the laity in English.
- The importance of teaching scripture rather than focusing on ecclesiastical law.
- Instructions for how to live and what "obedience" means in daily life.
- The abuses of the Church.

Although Tyndale's book was so helpful to the king, he ended up being executed as a heretic in October 1536, after incurring the wrath of Henry VIII with the publication of another book, "The Practyse of Prelates", in which he opposed Henry VIII's planned annulment from Catherine of Aragon. So, one of his books helped the king, and another was Tyndale's undoing.

3 October

On 3rd October 1536, imperial ambassador Eustace Chapuys wrote to Emperor Charles V informing him that Jane Seymour's coronation was being postponed:

> "The Queen's coronation which was to have taken place at the end of this month is put off till next summer, and some doubt it will not take place at all. There is no appearance that she will have children. The delay of the coronation will do no harm except that the coming of the Princess to Court is put off till it takes place, and if it be delayed neither her affairs nor those of your Majesty will be the better for it."

But Jane's coronation wasn't just postponed; it never took place. Jane Seymour had become King Henry VIII's third wife on

30th May 1536, just eleven days after the execution of her predecessor, Anne Boleyn. Henry had high hopes for his third marriage. His previous wives had only been able to provide him with two daughters and a son who lived for less than two months, and he desperately needed a legitimate Prince of Wales. Jane's mother had had ten children, six of whom had survived childhood, three of whom were sons, so perhaps Henry saw Jane as a good bet for producing a son. He certainly did everything he could to get rid of Anne quickly and replace her with Jane.

But why didn't he rush to make a public display of his new wife and queen with a coronation?

Anne Boleyn had been crowned queen in a lavish coronation worthy of a reigning monarch on 1st June 1533, less than five months after her marriage and just days after that marriage had been ruled valid. Chapuys was under the impression that Jane would receive similar treatment. On the very day of Anne's execution, 19th May 1536, Chapuys wrote that Jane's coronation was "to be celebrated with great solemnity and pomp, the King intending, as I am told, to perform wonders, for he has already ordered a large ship to be built, like the Bucentaur of Venice, to bring the lady from Greenwich to this city, and commanded other things for the occasion." And we know that the king ordered work on Westminster Palace in preparation for Jane's coronation, which included building a high walkway from the palace into Westminster Abbey. However, the work on the palace was halted at the end of the summer of 1536. Chapuys, in a letter dated 1st July, recorded that the coronation had been postponed until after Michaelmas, that feast day being 29th September. John Hussee had written to Lady Lisle in Calais that the coronation was not due until after Hallowtide. However, he later wrote that it was expected to take place on St Edward's Day, 13th October, unless the plague delayed it. Henry, Lord Montagu, recorded in a letter dated 15th September that Jane's coronation was expected to be on "the Sunday before Allhallow Day".

In January 1537, following the Pilgrimage of Grace rebellion, rebel leader Robert Aske wrote of how the king had promised to have Jane crowned in York. However, no preparations were made, and it seems to have been just one of the empty promises the king made the rebels.

Chapuys speculated on the cause of the postponement, commenting that "Suspicious persons think it is to see if she shall be with child" and adding "and, if not, and there is danger of her being barren, occasion may be found to take another. I am told on good authority that this King will not have the prize of those who do not repent in marriage; for within eight days after publication of his marriage, having twice met two beautiful young ladies, he said and showed himself somewhat sorry that he had not seen them before he was married." Was the king already tiring of Jane?

The Milanese Ambassador had predicted that Anne Boleyn's coronation cost the city of London around 200,000 ducats or £46,000 and that the king also paid around half that amount himself. But then Anne Boleyn had been pregnant. Did Henry VIII want to spend all that money on a new queen who wasn't showing any signs of being pregnant yet?

It wasn't until February 1537 that Jane showed signs of being pregnant, much to the king's delight, and perhaps the king decided to wait until after the birth of their child for Jane's coronation. Of course, Jane died just 12 days after giving birth to the couple's son, Edward, so the king never had to go to the expense of getting her crowned. Henry VIII married another three times but never crowned those queens.

4 October

On 4th October 1507, Sir Francis Bigod was born at Seaton, Hinderwell, Yorkshire.

Bigod led an uprising in Beverley, Yorkshire, in January 1537, which became known as Bigod's Rebellion, but who was Bigod, what was his rebellion about and what happened to him?

- Francis Bigod was the eldest son of Sir John Bigod and Joan Strangeways and was descended from the Bigods who had been Earls of Norfolk up until the 14th century and the Lords Maulay of Mulgrave Castle in Yorkshire.
- His father died in 1513 or 1514, and his paternal grandfather died in 1515, leaving Francis as his heir. Francis, who was seven

then, became a ward of Cardinal Thomas Wolsey and was educated at Oxford.

- At the age of 21, he married Katherine Conyers, daughter of William Conyers, 1st Baron Conyers, and the couple went on to have a son, Ralph, and a daughter, Dorothy. Bigod was knighted in late 1529.
- Bigod was a reformer. Churchman and historian John Bale described him as "a lover of evangelical truth", and Bigod corresponded with reformers, including Thomas Garrett, and even considered entering the church.
- He served as a Justice of the Peace from 1532 and as a member of Parliament in 1529 and 1536. In 1535, he served Thomas Cromwell and King Henry VIII in the survey of church wealth known as the valor ecclesiasticus, which led to the dissolution of the monasteries. He also enforced the royal supremacy and punished those who didn't respond favourably. Bigod, however, supported the reform of the monasteries rather than their dissolution.
- Bigod, as a reformer, initially opposed the Catholic Pilgrimage of Grace Rebellion of autumn 1536 and fled from his home Mulgrave Castle by sea. When he landed at Hartlepool, he narrowly avoided being lynched by the rebels but was captured when he returned to Mulgrave. It was sometime soon after that he realised that he had grievances in common with the rebels, such as his opposition to the king's intervention in religion. The Pilgrimage of Grace rebellion ended in late 1536 after the king made promises to the rebels. Bigod was sceptical and launched his own rebellion in January 1537 with the support of his tenant John Hallam. Bigod sent out the rebels' articles around the north and even spoke from a hilltop, trying to rally support from former rebels, but his plans to seize Scarborough and Hull failed. On 19th January, a dawn raid at Beverley in Yorkshire saw the capture of 62 of his men. On 10th February, Bigod, who'd escaped the raid, was captured in Cumberland and taken to Carlisle Castle, where he was imprisoned.
- Sir Francis Bigod was hanged at Tyburn on 2nd June 1537 and buried at London's Greyfriars.

- Unfortunately, even though Bigod's Rebellion had been condemned by former Pilgrimage of Grace rebels like Robert Aske, it led to their undoing. Aske, Lord Darcy, Lord Hussey, Sir Thomas Percy and Sir Robert Constable were all convicted of treason and executed, along with several others.

5 October

On 5th October 1518, two-year-old Princess Mary, daughter of Henry VIII and Catherine of Aragon, became betrothed to François, the Dauphin of France, who was just a few months old, in a ceremony in Queen Catherine of Aragon's chamber at Greenwich Palace.

According to the notarial attestation by Robert Toneys and John Barett, after an oration *de laudibus matrimonii* by Dr Cuthbert Tunstall, Admiral Bonivet, who was standing in for the Dauphin at the ceremony, took little Princess Mary's hand "and espoused her in the name of the Dauphin of France; and the King and Queen espoused the Dauphin, in the person of Lord Bonivet, to the Princess." Bonivet then placed a ring on the fourth finger of Mary's right hand, with the assistance of Cardinal Wolsey. King Henry VIII and Bonivet then signed oaths.

After the ceremony, the king went to the high altar of his chapel at Greenwich and took an oath to the treaty that had been agreed upon the day before. The French ambassadors also swore to this oath on behalf of King Francis I. The treaty they agreed to, which this betrothal was part of, was the Treaty of London, Cardinal Wolsey's treaty of "Universal" peace. The treaty also stated that Tournai, which Henry VIII had conquered in 1513, was to be restored to France, with Francis I agreeing to pay 600,000 crowns for the city and 400,000 crowns for the castle which had been built there. There was also further payment due from Francis on behalf of the citizens of Tournai, "for their liberties and franchises"

Chronicler Edward Hall recorded, "Upon these agreements to be performed, it was concluded that the city of Tournai should be delivered to the French king. The Frenchmen the sooner to come to their purpose, made a pretence of marriage to be had between the Dauphin, son & heir to the French king & the lady Mary the king's daughter, which was agreed upon this condition, that if they both consented at lawful age, then to be firm & stable, or else not for they were both very young."

As Hall points out, it was decided that the betrothal would only be binding if Mary and François consented to it when they were older. The betrothal was broken off in 1521 when Mary was instead contracted to marry her cousin, Charles V, Holy Roman Emperor. Of course, that didn't go ahead either, and Mary didn't marry until 1554, when she married Charles V's son, Philip of Spain.

6 October

On 6th October 1510, John Caius was born in Norwich.

Caius was a theological scholar and founder of Gonville and Caius College, Cambridge. He also served as royal physician to Edward VI, Mary I and Elizabeth I and wrote a book on sweating sickness.

Let me tell you a bit more about this Tudor man.

- John was the son of Robert Caius and his wife, Alice Wode.
- He was educated at Norwich School and then at what was known as Gonville Hall, Cambridge, where he studied theology, being influenced by the works of the famous Humanist, Erasmus. He was gifted at languages. He studied Hebrew and translated Greek works into Latin.
- In 1533, John became principal of Physwick's Hall and then fellow of Gonville Hall.
- It is not clear when he became interested in medicine, but in 1539 he set off for Italy, where he studied medicine at Padua, where he would have learned the principles of the Greek physician Galen. At Padua, John shared a house with the famous 16th-century Flemish anatomist, physician and author Andreas Vesalius, who was teaching anatomy at Padua.
- Caius graduated in May 1541 and lectured on Aristotle's logic at Padua before moving to Pisa to study and then travelling around the important libraries of Italy, looking at Greek manuscripts on medicine and philosophy.
- Caius published a collection of Galenic texts in Greek at Basel in 1544, along with his own work "De methodo medendi",

based on what he'd been taught at Padua by his professor, Johannes Baptista Montanus. He then returned home to England.

- In 1546, he was appointed by King Henry VIII to start a series of anatomical demonstrations for the London Barber Surgeons, which he did for 20 years, and in 1547 he became a fellow of the London College of Physicians.
- In the reigns of Mary I and Elizabeth I, Caius served as president of the College of Physicians on several occasions. He made a living from working as a physician in London and at court, attending Edward VI, Mary I and Elizabeth I.
- His financial support of the College of Physicians led to the refurbishment of the tomb of its founder Thomas Linacre at St Paul's. He also used his wealth to enlarge, convert and refound Gonville Hall as Gonville and Caius College in 1557. He became master of the college in 1559.
- Caius was a religious conservative and hoarded religious relics at his college. In 1572, his room was ransacked, and his collection was burnt and smashed. Caius retired to London and died at his house near St Bartholomew's Hospital on 29th July 1573. He left his library and property to the college he'd founded, with instructions for a tomb to be built for him in the college chapel. His tomb is still there today, with its Latin inscriptions which translate to 'virtue lives beyond the grave' and 'I was Caius'.
- His works include a history of Cambridge University, translations of Galen's works, and works on the Greek and Latin languages. Caius was also interested in zoology and was a keen naturalist. He wrote a book on British dogs and also rare plants and animals. Caius also wrote a book on sweating sickness, noting that the illness was not entirely new but that it: "hath been before seen among the Greeks in the siege of Troy. In the emperor Octavius' wars at Cantabria, called now Biscay, in Hispain: and in the Turks, at the Rhodes." He also listed its main symptoms and wrote of how "he would have named the disease "Ephemera of Englande", an ephemera being "a fever of one natural day", rather than simply "sweating sickness",

because this disease only affected people for up to twenty-four hours and was "no sweat only" but a fever".

7 October

On 7th October 1577, author, poet, courtier and soldier George Gascoigne died in Stamford, Lincolnshire. He was buried in Stamford at St Mary's Parish Church. He was in his early forties.

As well as being a soldier, a mercenary who fought in the Low Countries in the early 1570s, Gascoigne was a gifted poet. He is listed as one of the most important Tudor poets, along with Sir Thomas Wyatt the Elder, Henry Howard, Earl of Surrey, and Philip Sidney. His works include "A Discourse of the Adventures of Master FJ", "The Supposes", "A Hundredth Sundry Flowres..." and "The Posies of George Gascoigne, Esquire".

Gascoigne was hired in 1575 by Robert Dudley, Earl of Leicester, to provide the entertainment for Elizabeth I's visit to Kenilworth Castle. Gascoigne recorded these in a book published in 1576: "The Princely pleasures, at the Court at Kenilworth. That is to say. The Copies of all such Verses, Proses, or Poetical inventions, and other devices of pleasure, as were there devised, and presented by sundry Gentlemen, before the QUENES MAIESTIE: In the yeare 1575".

Gascoigne wrote a masque to be performed for the queen at Kenilworth. It was called "Zabeta" (a play on the name "Elizabeth"). Historian Susan Doran points out in her book "Monarchy and Matrimony: The Courtships of Elizabeth I" that in the story, Zabeta "had been lost to Diana (the goddess of Chastity) for 'neere seventeene years past' (the number of years since Elizabeth's accession) and during this time had resisted the entreaties of Juno (the goddess of marriage) that she marry. Juno found Zabeta, who was then restored to Diana, and a debate ensued about whether the nymph should continue in her chastity. The masque ended with the goddess Iris extolling the virtues of marriage in a direct appeal to the queen."

It wasn't at all subtle. It was a marriage proposal from Robert Dudley.

Unfortunately, the masque was cancelled due to inclement weather, so Gascoigne ended up running alongside the queen as she was leaving the castle, telling her the story of his masque. Susan Doran writes of how Gascoigne told Elizabeth about the virgin nymph Zabeta who had rejected all her suitors and turned them into the trees and rocks that the queen could see around her, and how she had turned one of them, Deep Desire, into a holly bush with "prickes to prove the restless prickes of his private thoughts." As Elizabeth went past the holly bush, Deep Desire spoke to her, telling of his love for Zabeta and pleading with the queen to stay at Kenilworth:

"Live here, good Queen, live here;
You are amongst your friends.
Their comfort comes when you approach,
And when you part it ends."

Deep Desire was Leicester, and Doran says that the pricks of the holly bush symbolised his undiminished sexual desires.

This shortened performance was not successful in changing Elizabeth's mind about marriage, but I wonder how she would have felt if she'd seen the full masque.

8 October

On 8th October 1536, while the Pilgrimage of Grace rebellion was getting underway in Lincolnshire and spreading to Yorkshire, Henry VIII wasn't only issuing orders regarding the rebels, whom he regarded as "crafty persons" and "false traitors", he was also issuing orders regarding his eldest daughter.

Twenty-year-old Mary, the future Mary I, was the king's daughter by Catherine of Aragon. Henry VIII had had a troubled relationship with Mary following his banishment of her mother from court, the annulment of the marriage, his subsequent marriage to Anne Boleyn, and Parliament's declaration that Mary was illegitimate. Mary had had an awful few years, being prohibited from seeing her mother, going from being her father's "pearl" to being at best neglected and at worst treated cruelly, and then losing her mother in January 1536. It is little wonder that her health had suffered.

Things had looked up for Mary when Anne Boleyn was executed for high treason in May 1536. A week after her stepmother's beheading, Mary wrote to Thomas Cromwell, hoping her father's chief advisor would intercede with the king on her behalf. She wanted permission to write to the king and hoped that her relationship with her father could be mended now that Anne Boleyn, the person she held responsible for her ill-treatment, was out of the way. Sadly for Mary, although Anne Boleyn may have supported and even encouraged the king's actions towards his first daughter, the king was ultimately responsible for what had happened to the girl. He saw her as defiant and disobedient and needing punishment. The king wasn't interested in mending his relationship with Mary, treating her well or welcoming her back at court until she toed the line and submitted to him.

On 15th June 1536, he sent members of his council to Mary's home to try and bully her into accepting him as supreme head of the Church in England and acknowledging that she was not the legitimate heir to the throne. The visitors were so aggressive and threatening that Eustace Chapuys, the imperial ambassador and Mary's good friend, was worried about Mary's health and safety. So worried was the ambassador that he encouraged her to make the "sacrifice" and submit to her father, assuring her that it was the emperor's "advice and wish" and that "God looked more into the intentions than into the deeds of men". Mary went ahead and signed the submission to her father without reading it.

Mary's submission predictably led to a reconciliation with her father. Still, Chapuys recorded that signing the submission cost Mary dearly, "the Princess fell suddenly into a state of despondency and sorrow".

And that wasn't the end of the pressure on Mary. On this day in 1536, Chapuys recorded how the king was "compelling" Mary to write two letters, one to the pope and another to Mary of Hungary, the emperor's sister. Chapuys explains that in the letter to the pope, Mary was "to acknowledge the invalidity of her mother's marriage" and to state that she had "consented willingly, and not under compulsion, to do what the King wished". He requested that she add that she hoped that "the Pope will forbear meddling with English affairs, as the King is in the right." She was to explain the same thing to Mary of Hungary, asking her to pass that on to the emperor, saying that "she has freely renounced her right" and "she is well satisfied with what she has done". Chapuys wanted to explain the situation and to make sure that the pope and emperor knew that Mary had been compelled by

King Henry VIII to both submit and write these letters. He wanted to clarify that there was no "poison beneath what she does".

Eustace Chapuys was a good friend to the princess, and it's good that she had someone she could rely on for support and advice at a time like this.

9 October

On 9th October 1547, Miguel de Cervantes, author of the famous classic "Don Quixote", was baptised in Alcalá de Henares, Spain. His actual birthdate is unknown.

This event didn't happen in Tudor England, but it did happen in the Tudor period, and Cervantes is known worldwide. Let me share some facts about this man and his famous book.

- Cervantes' father, Rodrigo de Cervantes, was a barber surgeon from Cordoba, and it is thought that he and his wife, Leonor de Cortinas, had Jewish origins.
- We don't know what Cervantes looked like. The famous portrait said to be him has not been authenticated, unfortunately.
- When Cervantes was six, his father was imprisoned for a few months for debt, during which time Cervantes' mother supported the family.
- The Cervantes family spent time in Seville before moving to Madrid in 1566.
- Cervantes moved to Rome and then Naples after he was arrested and charged with wounding another man in a duel in Madrid in 1569.
- Although he was suffering from malaria at the time, Cervantes served in the fleet Don John of Austria at the Battle of Lepanto in 1571. Although the Ottoman fleet was defeated, Cervantes suffered injuries to his chest and left arm. In his later poetic work "Journey to Parnassus", or "Viaje del Parnaso", Cervantes wrote of his arm injury, saying that he "lost the movement of the left hand for the glory of the right".
- In September 1575, the ship on which Cervantes and his brother Rodrigo were serving was captured by Ottoman corsairs and the two men were held for ransom. Cervantes' family could not

afford both ransoms and only paid for Rodrigo. Cervantes was finally set free in 1580 when the Trinitarian Order ransomed him, and he was able to return home to Spain.

- In November 1584, Cervantes' illegitimate daughter, Isabel, was born. Her mother, Ana Franca, was the wife of an inn keeper in Madrid.
- A month later, in December 1584, thirty-seven-year-old Cervantes married Catalina de Salazar y Palacios, who was between 15 and 18 years of age.
- By 1592, Cervantes was a tax collector and spent time in prison for "irregularities".
- In 1613, Cervantes joined the Secular Franciscan Order, an order concerned with helping lay people learn the teachings of St Francis of Assisi, with a particular focus on charity.
- Cervantes died on 22nd or 23rd April 1616 and was laid to rest in Madrid's Convent of the Barefoot Trinitarians.
- His remains were lost during work at the convent in 1673 but were found and reburied in 2015.
- Cervantes' most famous work, "The Ingenious Gentleman Don Quixote of La Mancha", was published in two volumes in 1605 and 1615 and is known as "the first modern novel".
- The Encyclopaedia Britannica says of "Don Quixote": "Originally conceived as a parody of the chivalric romances that had long been in literary vogue, it describes realistically what befalls an aging knight who, his head bemused by reading such romances, sets out on his old horse Rocinante, with his pragmatic squire, Sancho Panza, to seek adventure. Widely and immediately translated (first English translation 1612), the novel was a great and continuing success and is considered a prototype of the modern novel."
- Don Quixote has been translated into more than 60 languages.
- Cervantes' other works include plays, of which only two survive, poems and sonnets, a collection of short stories "Novelas ejemplares", the pastoral romance "La Galatea", and the romance "Los trabajos de Persiles y Sigismunda".

- If you visit Madrid, you can visit Cervantes' resting place in the Church of San Ildefonso in the Convent of the Barefoot Trinitarians.

10 October

On 10th October 1588, Robert Dudley, Earl of Leicester, was buried in the Beauchamp Chapel of the Collegiate Church of St Mary, Warwick, according to his instructions.

Leicester had died on 4th September 1588 at his lodge at Cornbury, near Woodstock in Oxfordshire. He was on his way to take the waters at Buxton for his health. He had been suffering from a recurring stomach ailment.

The Beauchamp Chapel was the traditional burial place for the Earls of Warwick and was built in the 15th century as the resting place of Richard Beauchamp, 13th Earl of Warwick. The chapel was the resting place of Leicester's son, Robert Dudley, Baron Denbigh, the "noble impe", who died when he was three years old. Leicester's brother, Ambrose Dudley, Earl of Warwick, was laid to rest there in 1590. Leicester's wife, Lettice, was buried with Leicester following her death in 1634, and their tomb is topped with effigies of the couple praying and wearing their earl and countess's coronets. The Latin inscription above their tomb translated into English reads:

"Sacred to the God of the living. In certain hope of rising again in Christ, here is placed the most famous Robert Dudley, fifth son of John, Duke of Northumberland, Earl of Warwick, Viscount Lisle, etc., Earl of Leicester, Baron Denbigh; Knight of both the orders of St. George and St. Michael; Master of the Horse of Queen Elizabeth (with whom he was distinguished with exceptional favour); thereafter Steward of the Royal Household; Privy Councillor; High Justiciar of the Forests, Parks, Chases, etc. on this side of Trent: Lieutenant and Captain-general of the English army sent into the Netherlands by the said Queen Elizabeth, from 1585 to 1587; Governor-general and Commander of the United Provinces of the Netherlands; and Lieutenant of the Kingdom of England against the Spaniard Philip II, when he was invading England in 1588 with a numerous fleet and army.

He gave back his soul to God his saviour in the year of salvation 1588, on the fourth day of September. His most sorrowful wife, Lettice, daughter of Francis Knollys, Knight of the Order of St. George and the Queen's Treasurer, placed [this monument] to her best and dearest husband on account of her love and faith as his wife."

Leicester's funeral at Warwick on this day in 1588 was well attended, with the mourners being led by his widow, Lettice; his stepson, Robert Devereux, Earl of Essex; Leicester's brother-in-law, George Hastings, Earl of Huntingdon; and his nephew, Sir Robert Sidney. Other mourners included Robert Rich, husband of Leicester's stepdaughter, Penelope Devereux, members of the Knollys and Blount families, and Leicester's chaplains and his secretary. The sermon was preached by John Piers, Bishop of Salisbury.

11 October

On 11th October 1532, just before dawn, King Henry VIII and his sweetheart, Anne Boleyn, the newly created Marquess of Pembroke, set sail from Dover on the Kent coast aboard the king's ship, The Swallow.

They were headed for Calais, an English territory at the time. The purpose of their trip was to meet with King Francis I of France and gain his support for their relationship and their quest for the annulment of Henry VIII's marriage to Catherine of Aragon.

They landed at Calais at 10 o'clock the same morning. Wynkyn de Worde recorded the visit in his contemporary pamphlet "The Maner of the tryumphe of Caleys and Bulleyn", writing that the couple were "received with procession and with the mayor and the lord deputy and all the spears (knights) and the soldiers in array with a great peal of guns". Chronicler Edward Hall writes that Henry and Anne went to hear mass at the Church of St Nicholas before retiring to their lodgings at The Exchequer.

The couple stayed together there until 21st October when Henry left Anne to meet Francis I and spend time with him at the French court in Boulogne. After a few days with the French king, Henry brought Francis back to Calais to meet Anne, who made a dramatic entrance at a lavish masque held by the king in Francis's honour on 27th October.

The trip was a success. Francis I was sympathetic to Henry and Anne's plight and offered to give Henry French protection against Charles V, the Holy Roman Emperor and Catherine of Aragon's nephew. Francis was also displeased with the way the pope was handling the situation. In a letter to the Bishop of Auxerre, with instructions for him to talk to the pope, Francis wrote, "every one knows that it has not been usual to compel kings to come to Rome. Both the Kings desire to inform the Pope more fully of their causes of complaint, so that he may remedy them for the future".

Henry VIII and Francis I made their farewells on 29th October 1532, and Henry and Anne intended to leave for England immediately. However, storms and fog delayed their departure, and the couple didn't land at Dover until early on 14th November 1532, St Erkenwald's Day. Edward Hall writes of how Henry and Anne "maried priuily" on that day, keeping it a secret even when they arrived back in London on 24th November. On their return to London, the couple began co-habiting, and it wasn't long before Anne was pregnant. The couple had another secret ceremony at Whitehall on St Paul's Day, 25th January 1533, and their first child, a daughter, the future Elizabeth I, was born on 7th September 1533.

12 October

On 12th October 1555, Lewis Owen, member of Parliament and administrator in Wales, was assassinated on Dugoed Mawddwy, a mountain pass. He had become unpopular after supporting new legislation in Wales, and his assassination is viewed as revenge for his campaign, with John Wyn ap Meredydd of Gwydir, against outlaws. It had resulted in around eighty hangings.

Let me give you some facts about this Tudor Welshman.

- Lewis Owen, or Lewis ap Owen, was the son of Owen ap Hywel ap Llywelyn of Llwyn, Dolgelley, and his wife Gwenhwyfar. His birthdate is not known, but he was born by 1522.
- Owen's family were descended from Gwrgan ab Ithel, Prince of Powis.
- Nothing is known of Owen's early life and upbringing, but he served Henry VIII at the end of his reign as deputy chamberlain of North Wales, a baron of the exchequer at Caernarvon, as well as sheriff of Merioneth, a post he held on several occasions, and also as a member of Parliament.
- Owen was married twice. His first wife was Margaret, daughter of John Puleston, Constable of Caernarfon Castle and a burgess, under whom Owen served as sheriff. They had a large family, and his biographer Peter Roberts notes that "several of the later gentry families of the county … were to trace their descent from 'Baron' Owen and his first wife."
- He acquired lands, leases, monastic lands and fishing rights in the reign of Edward VI.
- While serving as sheriff of Merioneth in Mary I's reign, Owen came to his sad and violent end. Owen was intent on ridding the area of thieves and outlaws, particularly the Red Bandits of Mawddwy, a band of red-haired robbers and highwaymen. Robert Vaughn, a descendant of Owen, in his 17th-century Book of North Wales, recorded that these outlaws "never tired of robbing, burning of houses, and murthering of people, in soe much that being very numerous, they did often drive great droves of cattell somtymes to the number of a hundred or more from one countrey to another at middle day, as in tyme of warre, without feare, shame, pittie, or punishment, to the utter undoing of the poorer sort." Owen was determined to eradicate them, and in this, he was assisted by John Wyn ap Meredydd. The two men managed to execute about 80 of the bandits before the bandits attacked Owen while he was on his way home to Dolgellau from attending the Michaelmas assizes for Montgomeryshire and negotiating a marriage for his son, John. The bandits assassinated Owen at a spot known as "Llidiart-y-

barwn", or The Baron's Gateway. Elegies were composed about his tragic death.

13 October

On 13th October 1553, Queen Mary I wrote to the imperial ambassador, Simon Renard:

> "Sir: If it were not too much trouble for you, and if you were to find it convenient to do so without the knowledge of your colleagues, I would willingly speak to you in private this evening, as you four are to come to-morrow. Nevertheless, I remit my request to your prudence and discretion. Written in haste, as it well appears, this morning, 13 October. Your good friend, Mary."

It's an interesting letter because Mary wanted to speak to Renard secretly, without the knowledge of his colleagues. Why? What was going on?

In her biography of Mary I, historian Anna Whitelock explains how Renard had "an unprecedented role as secret counsellor and confidant" to the new queen and that he built on Mary's close relationship with her cousin, Emperor Charles V, whom Mary trusted and whom she addressed in letters as "her very dear and well beloved good brother". It appears that Mary trusted the emperor and his ambassadors more than her own council and advisors. On 23rd September 1553, the imperial ambassadors wrote to the emperor saying, "She could not trust her Council too much, well knowing the particular character of its members" and describing how they had visited the queen secretly, passing "through the park and a garden, unperceived by anybody, except for two of her servants and Dame Clarentius (Clarence), whom she trusts".

Anna Whitelock describes how Mary encouraged Renard to come to her in disguise after dark and notes how unusual it was for a monarch to consult a foreign ambassador in secret about affairs of the kingdom.

But it's not surprising that Mary had a good relationship with Charles V and his ambassadors. They had been her support in dark times, such as when her father put pressure on her to accept his supremacy and her illegitimacy back in 1536, and when she felt threatened during Edward VI's reign, in 1550, when she was in trouble for celebrating the mass. It had been the emperor and his ambassadors who'd come up with a plan for her to flee England by sea. Mary got cold feet and didn't go ahead with the escape plan, but the emperor had fully supported her and protected her. Charles had always had her back, and imperial ambassador, Eustace Chapuys, had been a good friend and perhaps even a father figure to Mary.

And now here she was, queen in her own right, but she knew how fickle men could be. She'd seen privy councillors betray Lady Jane Grey and change sides to Mary just a few months ago. She was also thinking of marriage, and it was the emperor she turned to for help, as the man she trusted. She wanted to make a match that he'd agree with, and it was marriage that she was discussing with his ambassadors secretly, knowing that her English councillors might not be supportive of her ideas. Her plans to marry the emperor's son, Philip of Spain, were met with opposition from some and even led to Wyatt's Rebellion in early 1554. There was concern that England might become just another of Philip's territories and that he'd involve England in his war and use the treasury to fund his campaigns. Many preferred the idea of an English consort for Mary, but Mary trusted the emperor and put her foot down. She was able to rally support against Wyatt's Rebellion and marry her choice of man. She was a determined lady.

14 October

On 14th October 1565, diplomat and poet Sir Thomas Chaloner the Elder died at his home in Clerkenwell, London. He was just forty-four years old. He'd served four Tudor monarchs as a diplomat and wrote English and Latin works.

Let me give you a few facts about Chaloner.

- Sir Thomas Chaloner was born in London in 1521 and was the eldest son of mercer and administrator Roger Chaloner and his first wife, Margaret Middleton.

- Chaloner was educated at Cambridge University before joining the service of Thomas Cromwell, the king's chief advisor, before or in 1538.
- In 1540, at 19, Chaloner accompanied ambassador Sir Henry Knyvet to the Regensburg imperial diet as his secretary and then accompanied Emperor Charles V on his campaign against the Moors in Algiers in 1541. Storms saw Chaloner being shipwrecked off the coast of Algeria, and Chaloner was only saved from drowning by holding onto a rope thrown from a galley with his teeth.
- In September 1547, in Edward VI's reign, Chaloner was knighted by Lord Protector Somerset after fighting against the Scots at the Battle of Pinkie.
- In 1550, Chaloner married Joan Cotton, widow of Sir Thomas Leigh, but she died in January 1557, and they didn't have any surviving children.
- In the reigns of Edward VI and Mary I, Chaloner served as an MP and Justice of the Peace.
- In January 1549, he was one of those appointed to search the home of Lord Admiral Thomas Seymour, who'd been arrested for treason.
- In 1549, along with several others, including his friend William Cecil, Chaloner testified in the deprivation trials of Edmund Bonner, Bishop of London, and Stephen Gardiner, Bishop of Winchester.
- In April 1553, Chaloner was sent to France to serve as special ambassador, but after the king's death in July 1553 and the accession of Mary I, he was recalled. He had avoided being caught up in the Lady Jane Grey versus Mary I struggle of July 1553 but was still named in the general pardon given by Mary.
- In 1556, he served Mary I in Scotland, negotiating with Marie de Guise, the dowager queen, and also served Mary I in her campaign in France.
- During the reign of Elizabeth I, Chaloner acted as the English ambassador to Ferdinand I, Holy Roman Emperor, in 1558,

and then ambassador to Philip II in the Low Countries and then Spain between 1559 and 1561.

- In Spain, he suffered from health problems including malaria, rheumatism, stomach trouble and kidney stones. Due to his failing health, he was recalled in late 1563 but didn't leave Spain for England until May 1565.
- In September 1565, he married Audrey or Ethelreda Frodsham.
- Chaloner died on 14th October 1565, having named his stepson, Audrey's son, Thomas, as his heir. Thomas became known as Sir Thomas Chaloner the Younger.
- Chaloner's works include translations of Erasmus's "Praise of Folly", Gilbert Cousin's "Office of Servants", Sir John Cheke's "An Homilie of Saint John Crysostome", Ovid's "Helen to Paris", and part of Boethius's "Consolations of Philosophy". His Latin works include a ten-book-long didactic epic. He also contributed a poem on Richard II for William Baldwin's "Mirror for Magistrates".
- Chaloner also wrote an "Elegy on the Death of Lady Jane Grey" in Latin. Although he was away in France in 1553, historian J Stephan Edwards notes that he was good friends with many who knew the young queen, including John Cheke and William Cecil.

15 October

On 15th October 1584, schoolteacher and Welsh-language poet Richard Gwyn was hanged, drawn and quartered for high treason at Wrexham in Wales due to his Catholic faith.

Let me tell you a bit more about this Tudor Welshman.

- Richard Gwyn was born around 1537 in Llanidloes, Montgomeryshire. His surname translates to White, so he's often referred to as Richard White.
- He was educated at Oxford and then Cambridge, where his studies were cut short due to his mentor and patron, the master Dr George Bullock, being deprived of his office. Gwyn returned to Wales and worked as a teacher for 16 years in the Overton and Wrexham areas of North Wales.

- He married Catherine from Overton, and they went on to have six children, although only three of them outlived their father.
- The Bishop of Chester and his officers began to put pressure on Gwyn when it was noticed that he was abstaining from Protestant communion. Gwyn gave in to the pressure at first, but one day, as he came out of church, he was attacked by crows and kites, which persecuted him all the way home. He decided then to embrace the Catholic faith wholeheartedly.
- In 1578, Gwyn's Catholic faith, his refusal to attend Protestant services and his support of missionary priests led him to go into hiding. He was arrested in early 1579 by the Vicar of Wrexham but managed to escape. He was arrested again in 1580 after mercer David Edwards tried to apprehend him, attacking him with a knife. It is said that Gwyn used his staff to hit Edwards on the head but was worried when he thought he'd killed him and so hung around until Edwards came round. Edwards got up and pursued Gwyn, who was captured when some workers cutting hay in a nearby field joined the chase and surrounded Gwyn. He was then taken to Ruthin gaol. A few months later, he refused the deal of a pardon if he would go to church.
- In May 1581, Gwyn was taken to the church at Wrexham in shackles and chains to listen to the sermon. However, according to one account, "so stirred his legs that with the noise of his irons the preacher's voice could not be heard". Afterwards, he was put in the stocks and taunted by the local Protestant clergy. One of them claimed to have the keys to heaven, to which Gwyn replied, "There is this difference, namely, that whereas Peter received the keys to the Kingdom of Heaven, the keys you received were obviously those of the beer cellar."
- In 1582, he was forced to listen to another Protestant sermon, but he and other Catholic prisoners heckled the preacher so much that the sermon was cut short.
- In the autumn sessions of 1584 in Wrexham, on 9th October, in a court presided over by Sir George Bromley, Chief Justice of Chester, Gwyn was tried for high treason. The charges included making rhymes against married priests, calling the Bible a babble, and defending the pope's authority. He was

tried with John Hughes and Robert Morris. Gwyn and Hughes were found guilty, and Morris was acquitted. Hughes was then reprieved, but Gwyn was sentenced to death. On hearing his sentence, he said, "What is all this? Is it any more than one death?" Gwyn's wife was also brought before the court and warned not to follow her husband's example. With her baby in her arms, she replied, "If you lack blood, you may take my life as well as my husband's; and if you will give the witnesses a little bribe, you may call them; they will bear evidence against me as well as they did against him." She was imprisoned temporarily.

- On 13th October, Gwyn was offered his life in return for acknowledging the queen's supremacy, but he refused.
- On 15th October 1584, Gwyn was led out of gaol for his execution, comforting those he passed who were weeping, telling them, "Weep not for me, for I do but pay the rent before the rent day". He then gave silver to the poor at the prison door, and gave his wife money and his beads, blessing the baby in her arms. He was drawn on a sled to the place of execution, the beast market in Wrexham, praying the rosary all the way. The heavens opened as he started his journey, with the rain not stopping until he had died. When he arrived at the gallows, he spoke to those gathered, saying, "God is merciful to us, behold the elements shed tears for our sins." After climbing the ladder, he said to the crowd, "I have been a jesting fellow, and if I have offended any that way, or by my songs, I beseech them for God's sake to forgive me." The executioner, who was also Gwyn's gaoler and who had been kind to him during his time in prison, tried to put an end to Gwyn's suffering by pulling on his legs while he was hanging, but it didn't work, and he had to suffer the full traitor's death while still conscious. His last words in Welsh translate to "Jesus, have mercy on me." His head and one of the quarters of his body were displayed at Denbigh Castle, and the other three parts were sent to Wrexham, Ruthin and Holt.
- Gwyn's works include a series of five carols defending the Catholic faith, written in his final years, and a funeral ode.

- Gwyn, who is considered the first Welsh Elizabethan martyr, was beatified in 1929 and canonised in 1970 by Pope Paul VI as one of the Forty Martyrs of England and Wales.
- According to one story, Bromley, the judge who sentenced him to death, became an idiot; the clerk who read out his indictment went blind; the deputy justice died soon after; Edwards, who helped capture him, died an awful death; and the court crier was struck dumb and became a fool.

16 October

On 16th October 1532, while King Henry VIII and his sweetheart, Anne Boleyn, Marquess of Pembroke, were lodged in Calais, Anne's uncle, Thomas Howard, 3rd Duke of Norfolk, and a group of nobles and gentlemen met with their French counterparts just outside of Calais. Wynkyn de Worde records this meeting in his contemporary pamphlet "The Maner of the tryumphe of Caleys and Bulleyn", writing:

"And on the xvi. day of October my lord of Norfolk accompanied with my lord of Derby and a great number of gentlemen besides, met with the great master of France vi miles from Calais at the English Pale, the said great master having two great lords in his company of their order and a hundred gentlemen attending upon them. And there my lord of Norfolk and the great master devised the place where the two kings should meet, which was at Sandingfield. And that done, they went both to Calais with their companies. And the said great master with diverse other strangers dined that day with the king."

Chronicler Edward Hall gives a slightly different account and dates the meeting to 15th October, writing:

"Suddenly came a messenger and reported that the Great Master of France, and the Archbishop of Rouen, with diverse noblemen of France, were come to Sandingfield, intending to come to Calais, to salute the king, from the king their master. He being thereof advertised, sent in great haste the xv day of October, the Duke of Norfolk, the Marquess of Exeter, the Earls of Oxford, Derby and Rutland, the Lord Sandys and the Lord Fitzwater, with 300 gentlemen, which honourably received the French lords at the English Pale, and so brought them to the king's presence in Calais, which stood under a rich cloth of estate of such value that they much mused of the riches. The king (as he that knew all honour and nurture) received the French lords very lovingly and amiably, and with them took a day and place of meeting. These lords were highly feasted and after dinner departed to Boulogne."

Whatever the date of this meeting, its purpose was to arrange a meeting between the two kings, King Henry VIII and King Francis I. Sandingfield was chosen as the meeting place. It was convenient because it was in the English Pale, between Calais, the English territory where Henry VIII was staying, and Boulogne, where Francis I was with the French court. You may not have heard of Sandingfield because it's now called Saint-Inglevert.

The two kings met at Sandingfield on 21st October 1532, and Francis then took the English king back to Boulogne, where they remained until 25th October, when they and their parties travelled to Calais for Henry VIII to play host.

17 October

On 17th October 1560, spy and Protestant martyr Walter Marsh was baptised at St Stephen's Church, Coleman Street, London.

Marsh came to a sticky end, being burnt to death in Rome's Campo dei Fiori after having his tongue cut out and one hand cut off. He had been accused of being paid by Queen Elizabeth I to spy on Catholics and of showing contempt for the Eucharist.

Walter Marsh was the son of MP and mercer John Marsh and his wife Alice Gresham, a cousin of the well-known merchant and financier Sir Thomas Gresham. Marsh was baptised on this day in 1560, and babies were usually baptised within a few days of birth.

Marsh was educated at the Merchant Taylors' School before going on to St John's College, Cambridge, where he graduated BA and MA. While he was at St John's, he wrote verses against idolatry. Marsh was ordained as an Anglican priest in 1586 and had risen to the position of Archdeacon of Derby by 1588. Still, he lost his archdeaconry after the position was contested by another clergyman, John Walton. By 1590, Marsh had given up all of his benefices.

In 1591, Catholic recusant Sir Thomas Tresham, who was under house arrest in London, recorded that Marsh had visited him. Marsh had cut off his beard and told Tresham that he would leave his ministry in England and travel to the English College at Douai, the Catholic seminary known for supplying missionary priests to England. These priests would enter England covertly and then try to bring the English people back to what they saw as the true faith. Tresham was suspicious of Marsh's motives, believing him to be a spy, and reported him.

Marsh did go to Douai, arriving in September 1591. However, just a few months after he had registered at the seminary, he travelled back to England via Flushing in the Low Countries, where he met with Sir Robert Sidney, who was governor there. Marsh offered to "discover matters which do greatly concern her Majesty". Marsh's father was an information gatherer or an intelligence agent for William Cecil, Lord Burghley, in England and on the Continent, so Marsh seems to have followed in his father's footsteps.

Marsh was admitted to the English College in Rome in March 1593 but left due to illness. He rejoined it later but was then burnt to death for committing sacrilege in Rome.

What happened?

There had been a procession in Rome on 15th June 1595, and Marsh had knocked the monstrance containing the Eucharist from the hands of a priest in the procession, shouting that it was an idol. On 20th June 1595, his tongue was cut out before he was escorted to the Campo dei Fiori to be executed.

His death is recorded in the Cecil Papers in a paper of news headed "Rome, 24 June 1595". It tells of how he was carried naked on a cart through the main streets of Rome, being tortured all the way by being scorched with torches. Then, his right hand was cut off at the place where he'd committed his offence of sacrilege. Finally, he was taken to the Campo dei Fiori, where he was burnt alive, all the time refusing to be converted although many powerful theologians tried to persuade him to. The paper goes on to say, "Under torture he confessed to being sent by the Queen of England to assassinate Cardinal Allen, who getting notice of it, sent him to the prison of the Holy Office; where he denied it and was released."

Father Robert Persons, the well-known English Jesuit priest who undertook religious missions to England with men like Edward Campion, wrote of Marsh in his memoirs:

"One Walter Marsh, having been an unquiet scholar in the College of Rome, and going away into England and returning suspiciously again, was put in the said Inquisition by the Cardinal Allen his means, but after his death being gotten forth by his suit (as is thought) of the Bishop of Cassano, and lodged in his own house, was burned openly in Rome for violence offered to the Blessed Sacrament the year 1595."

As we can see from Persons' record, Marsh was already in trouble in Rome before his outburst. He'd been interrogated by the Inquisition and had done penance for his acts against English Catholics and for being a spy for Elizabeth I and her government. His actions on 15th June were the last straw.

Former Catholic priest Richard Sheldon mentioned Marsh's death in his book regarding his conversion to the Protestant faith, going so far as to link his conversion to being in Rome when Marsh was executed:

"...but most of all I was filled with such foreapprehensions, and presages being in Rome upon the same day and hour when that glorious and renowned Christian Marsh suffered the cutting off of his right hand, the gagging of his mouth by the Counsel of the Ignatian Cowlin, who boasteth himself thereof in England, after that the pulling, tearing and burning of his flesh with hot glowing pincers for many hours together, through many streets of the city of Rome, and lastly death itself by fire, with such admirable patience and constancy, that the Romans themselves did greatly admire him therefore. His act, for which he was so tormented, was because he had thrown down their sacrament, as it was publicly carried through the streets of Rome in public procession to be adored, worshipped and invocated as God himself (an idolatrous superstition lately crept into the church contrary to the custom and practice of all ancient churches whatsoever.)"

What an awful end!

18 October

On 18th October 1555, Elizabeth, daughter of Henry VIII and Anne Boleyn, finally received permission from her half-sister, Queen Mary I, to leave court and travel to her own estate at Hatfield rather than return to house arrest in Woodstock, where she'd been confined previously

Elizabeth, the future Queen Elizabeth I, had been treated with suspicion by Mary and her council since Wyatt's Revolt in early 1554. Historian David Starkey says the revolt "led to the most dangerous and difficult time of her life when she feared imminent execution or murder. She even expressed a preference as to how she should die: like her mother, by the sword, rather than by the axe."

Elizabeth had been arrested and taken to the Tower of London in March 1554 following the revolt's failure. She was imprisoned in the royal apartments of the Tower's royal palace, the same apartments where her mother had spent her last days in May 1536. Several times, she was interrogated by members of Mary's council but never implicated herself and kept affirming her innocence. When rebel Thomas Wyatt the Younger went to the block in April 1554, he exonerated her in his execution speech:

"And whereas it is said and whistled abroad that I should accuse my lady Elizabeth's grace and my lord Courtenay; it is not so, good people. For I assure you neither they nor any other now in yonder hold or durance was privy of my rising or commotion before I began. As I have declared no less to the queen's council. And this is most true."

Elizabeth was released from the Tower on 19th May 1554, the anniversary of her mother's execution, but she was not a free woman. She was escorted to the Palace of Woodstock in Oxfordshire and kept under house arrest.

In April 1555, Elizabeth was summoned to court to attend the queen, who was expected to give birth soon. The baby never came; it was a false alarm. The sisters were able to reconcile, and it was Elizabeth who was at Mary's side as she tried to keep up the pretence of her pregnancy and when her husband, Philip of Spain, deserted her to take up the reins of his abdicated father, Charles V.

Finally, on this day in history, 18th October 1555, after over 18 months of being watched by her sister and her council, Elizabeth was granted permission to go to Hatfield. Hatfield was her own estate, and she'd spent most of her childhood there. There, Elizabeth could be her own woman and surround herself with people she loved and trusted. Thomas Parry joined her, as did her former governess, Kat Ashley, as soon as she was released from house arrest. We can only imagine Elizabeth's relief and happiness. Since March 1554, she had lived under the shadow of the axe, fearing that she would be executed as a traitor or assassinated, it had been a stressful and frightening time, but it was over.

19 October

On this day in history, an event took place in Spain that was not only important in Spanish history but also had an impact on Europe and links with the Tudors.

On 19th October 1469, in the Palacio de los Vivero in Valladolid, in what is now Castile and Leon, a couple who would become the famous Reyes Catolicos got married.

The bride was eighteen-year-old Isabella, daughter of John II of Castile and Isabella of Portugal. The groom was seventeen-year-old Ferdinand, son of John II of Aragon and Juana Enriquez. The couple were second cousins, both being descended from John I of Castile.

Isabella wasn't supposed to marry Ferdinand. Her half-brother, Henry IV of Castile, had negotiated several matches for her even after he had named her heir presumptive and promised he wouldn't force her to marry against her wishes. Most recently, in 1468, Henry had been arranging a match between Isabella and his brother-in-law Alfonso V of Portugal and then Charles, Duke of Berry, brother of King Louis XI of France. Isabella was against the idea, preferring Ferdinand, to whom she'd been betrothed when she was six years old. Isabella corresponded with John II of Aragon and secretly promised to marry Ferdinand. Cardinal Rodrigo de Borgia, the future Pope Alexander VI, helped the couple obtain a dispensation from the Pope to cover the fact that they were related within the prohibited degrees of consanguinity. Then Isabella left court, pretending that she was going to visit her brother's tomb in Ávila. Instead, she met up with Ferdinand, who had disguised himself as a servant. They married on this day in 1469.

Isabella became Queen Isabella I of Castile in 1474, following the death of her half-brother, and Ferdinand became King Ferdinand II of Aragon in 1479, following his father's death. Their marriage was important, for it united the powerful kingdoms of Aragon and Castile, a vast territory that comprised most of modern-day Spain.

They didn't have things easy, though. Isabella had to deal with plots against her and war over the succession, but she remained queen and reigned until her death in November 1504. Ferdinand remarried in 1506, taking Germaine de Foix, niece of King Louis XII of France, as his wife. He died in January 1516.

Here are a few more facts about this powerful European couple:
- They had seven children, five of whom survived childhood. They included Joan of Castile, also known as Juana la Loca or Joanna the Mad, and Catherine of Aragon, who married Arthur Tudor, eldest son of King Henry VII, and then Henry VIII. All five of their surviving children married heirs of European kingdoms.
- Their grandchildren included Holy Roman Emperors Charles V and Ferdinand I, and Queen Mary I of England. Charles V ruled a vast empire, inheriting the rule of the European Holy Roman Empire from his grandfather Maximilian I, the Netherlands from his father, Philip the Handsome, and Spain from his mother, Juana.
- Ferdinand and Isabella are known for completing the Reconquista, which saw the forced conversion of Jews and Muslims in Spain and the expulsion of others. In 1492,

they conquered Granada, the last Muslim Nasrid kingdom in mainland Spain. Recently, the Spanish government offered Spanish citizenship to Jews whose families were expelled in the 15th century when they were given a choice to covert, leave or die. Somewhere between 40,000 and 100,000 Jews are thought to have been expelled.

- They founded the Spanish Inquisition, or the Tribunal of the Holy Office of the Inquisition, to give it its full name, in 1478. It sought to identify heretics and regulate the faith of those converted from Judaism and Islam in their kingdoms.
- Pope Alexander VI gave Ferdinand and Isabella the title "Los Reyes Catolicos", the Catholic Monarchs, for their work against the Jews and Muslims.
- They sponsored the 1492 voyage of Christopher Columbus, or Cristóbal Colón as he's known in Spain, which saw him discovering the New World and claiming it for Spain.
- The couple restored finances and made government and administrative reforms in their kingdoms.
- The couple's resting place is the Capilla Real in Granada, and their beautiful tomb can be visited today.

20 October

On 20th October 1557, or possibly 21st, courtier Mary Arundell died at Bath Place in London.

Mary is an interesting Tudor lady. She served at least two of Henry VIII's wives, and was a countess twice over, having been married to the Earl of Sussex and the Earl of Arundel.

Let me tell you a bit more about Mary.

- Mary's birthdate is not known, but she was the only child of Sir John Arundell of Lanherne in Cornwall, and his second wife, Katherine Grenville. Her father had been made a Knight of the Bath in Henry VII's reign and had served the king fighting against the Cornish rebels in 1497 and then his son, King Henry VII, in France, at the siege of Therouanne in 1513.
- Mary made her debut at Henry VIII's court in 1536, when she served the king's new wife, Jane Seymour, as a maid of honour.

She also served Anne of Cleves before moving into the service of Henry VIII's eldest daughter, Mary.

- In January 1537, Mary married Robert Radcliffe, 1st Earl of Sussex, becoming a stepmother to his children from his previous two wives. With Sussex, Mary had two sons, one born in 1538, who died in infancy, and another, John, born in 1539.
- Sussex died in 1542, and in 1545, Mary went on to marry Henry Fitzalan, Earl of Arundel, as his second wife. They did not have any children.
- While they were married, Mary's husband, Arundel, served Henry VIII as Lord Chamberlain and a privy councillor. He was high constable at Edward VI's coronation, as he was at the coronations of Mary I and Elizabeth I. He was arrested after the fall of Edward Seymour, Lord Protector, but only spent a year in the Tower. In July 1553, following the accession of Lady Jane Grey, Arundel and his fellow councillor, William Herbert, Earl of Pembroke, were responsible for turning the royal council against Jane and proclaiming for Mary. He was also the man sent by Mary I to arrest Jane's father-in-law, John Dudley, Duke of Northumberland. He became a firm favourite of Queen Mary, but did not enjoy the same favour in Elizabeth's reign. He did not remarry, and died in 1580.
- In the past, Mary Arundell has been confused with her stepdaughter, Arundel's daughter, Mary, who married Thomas Howard, 4th Duke of Norfolk, and is known for her classical learning and translations of works. She has also been confused with Margaret Acland, Lady Arundell. And although a drawing of "Lady Ratcliffe" by Hans Holbein the Younger is often said to be her, there were several Lady Ratcliffes so we don't know the sitter's true identity.
- Mary died on 20th or 21st October 1557 and was laid to rest at St Clement Danes Church. However, at some point she was moved to the Fitzalan Chapel at Arundel Castle.
- Mary was outlived by her second husband, the Earl of Arundel, and her only son, John, who had been knighted in 1547, following Edward VI's accession, and went on to serve as a

Member of Parliament in Elizabeth I's reign. He never married and died childless in 1568.

21 October

On Monday 21st October 1532, according to Edward Hall's Chronicle and Wynkyn de Worde's "The Manner of the triumph of Calais and Boulogne", Henry VIII left Anne Boleyn behind in Calais to spend four days with Francis I, King of France, "his beloved brother", at the French court in Boulogne.

Hall describes how Henry was "accompanied with the Dukes of Norfolk and Suffolk, and with the Marquesses of Dorset and Exeter, the Earls of Arundel, Oxford, Surrey, Essex, Derby, Rutland, Huntingdon, and Sussex, and diverse Viscounts, Barons, Knights of the Garter, and Gentlemen, freshly apparelled, and richly trimmed".

Wynkyn de Worde adds that seven score men were accompanying the king, all dressed in velvet coats.

The two kings met at Sandingfield, as arranged. Hall describes how Henry VIII was wearing a "coat of great richs, in braids of gold laid loose on Russet Velvet, and set with trefoils, full of pearl and stone", while Francis I wore "a coat of crimson velvet, all to cut, lined with slender cloth of gold plucked out through the cuts." The kings embraced, and, after drinking each other's health, they processed on to Boulogne.

When the kings had got within a mile of Boulogne, they were met by Francis I's three sons (the Dauphin, the Duke of Orléans and the Duke of Angoulême), along with the Admiral of France and three cardinals (Wynkyn de Worde says four). Francis I said to his sons, "My children, I am your father, but to this Prince here you are as much bound, as to me your natural father, for he redeemed me and you from captivity: wherefore on my blessing I charge you to be to him loving always." Henry VIII then embraced the three princes.

As the party arrived at Calais, there was "a great shot of Artillery", which could be heard twenty miles away.

When Henry and Anne's trip to Calais had first been planned, Anne had wanted to attend the meeting at the French court in Boulogne as Henry's consort. She had hoped that she would be treated as Queen and at least meet Francis's sister, Marguerite of Angoulême, if Francis' wife, Eleanor, a niece of Catherine of Aragon, would not attend. However, Francis I did not want his sister to be compromised in any way by meeting a woman who was seen as the King of England's mistress, so he suggested the attendance of the Duchess of Vendôme, a woman of "regrettable reputation and light morals who therefore had no dignity left to preserve." When Anne heard this news, she decided to stay behind in Calais and meet with Francis I when he travelled back with Henry on 25th October.

22 October

On 22nd October 1577, Henry Parker, 11th Baron Morley and Roman Catholic exile, died in Paris. Morley had fled abroad after refusing to subscribe to Elizabeth I's "Act of Uniformity" and after being implicated in the 1569 Rising of the North.

Let me give you some facts about this lesser-known Tudor man.

- His birthdate is unknown but is around 1531/2. He was the eldest son of Sir Henry Parker and his first wife, Grace Newport.
- He was the grandson of Henry Parker, 10th Baron Morley, a man who had grown up in the household of Lady Margaret Beaufort and who was known for his literary translations.
- He was also the nephew of Jane Boleyn, Lady Rochford, wife of George Boleyn and sister-in-law of Queen Anne Boleyn.
- He was educated at Gonville Hall, Cambridge
- In October 1553, Morley was made a Knight of the Bath in the celebrations surrounding Queen Mary I's coronation.
- In November 1556, on the death of his grandfather, he became Baron Morley and attended his first parliament in December 1557. In 1560, he was made Lord Lieutenant of Hertfordshire.
- He was married to Elizabeth Stanley, daughter of Edward Stanley, 3rd Earl of Derby and Lady Dorothy Howard, and granddaughter of Thomas Howard, 2nd Duke of Norfolk.
- In 1561, he played host to Queen Elizabeth I for two days at his home, Allington Morley, in Great Hallingbury, Essex.

- In a letter to Philip of Spain that same year, the Spanish ambassador described him as "one of the best and most Catholic gentlemen of this kingdom and much attached to your Majesty's service".
- In 1569, he refused to subscribe to Elizabeth I's Act of Uniformity, passed by Parliament in 1559 and part of Elizabeth's Religious Settlement. His biographer, James Carley, writes that he refused it "on the plea of being a nobleman".
- In the same year, he was implicated in the Rising of the North, a rebellion led by Charles Neville, 6th Earl of Westmorland, and Thomas Percy, 7th Earl of Northumberland. These lords sought to depose Queen Elizabeth I, replace her with Mary, Queen of Scots (who would marry the Duke of Norfolk), and restore the Catholic faith as the faith of England.
- The rebellion failed, and due to being implicated in it, in early June 1570, Morley fled to the Continent, settling in Bruges at first.
- In August 1570, he wrote to the queen begging for her pardon and explaining why he had left England without her permission due to a scruple of conscience.
- Although Elizabeth commanded him to return, he spent the rest of his life on the Continent. He spent time in Bruges, Madrid, Lisbon, Paris, Venice, Antwerp, and Maastricht.
- In 1572, his estate was taken by the Crown.
- In March 1574, he and his brother, Edmund, were received by Philip of Spain in Madrid and given 600 ducats as a gift.
- On Palm Sunday 1574, his wife Elizabeth was arrested at her London home while she heard mass. Their eldest son, Edward, had been arrested and imprisoned in the Fleet in 1573.
- In September 1575, Elizabeth and the couple's daughter and youngest son arrived in Antwerp, and in 1576, they were with Morley in Maastricht.
- Morley died in Paris on this day in 1577, and his eldest son, Edward, became 12th Baron Morley. In 1578, Morley's estate was restored to Edward.

23 October

On 23rd October 1570, John Hopkins, poet, psalmodist and Church of England clergyman, was buried at Great Waldingfield in Suffolk.

Churchman and historian John Bale described Hopkins as "not the least significant of British poets of our time". Hopkins' psalms were included in the 1562 "The whole booke of Psalmes, collected into Englysh metre by T. Sternhold, J. Hopkins & others".

Here are some facts about Hopkins.

- He was born in Wednesbury, Staffordshire, in around 1520/1.
- It is thought that he studied at Oxford before moving to London.
- In December 1549, Printer Edward Whitchurch published "All such Psalmes of David as Thomas Sternehold late grome of the kinges majesties robes, didde in his life time draw into English metre" to which were added psalms by John Hopkins. Hopkins explained that these were added, "especially to fill up a place ... that the book may rise to his just volume".
- In the 1550s, it is thought that he worked as a schoolmaster as one of his contemporaries described him as "Maister John Hopkins, that worthy Schoolemaister".
- He was ordained and became rector of Great Waldingfield in Suffolk in 1561.
- By 1562, he had composed 54 new versions of psalms.
- In 1562, printer John Day published "The whole booke of Psalmes, collected into Englysh metre by T. Starnhold, J. Hopkins & others".
- He had a wife, Anne, a son John, and daughters, Martha and Sara.
- It is not known exactly when Hopkins died, but he made his will on 10th October 1570 and was buried on 23rd October 1570.
- In his will, he bequeathed "ten lambs to Martha 'to be delivered to her when her mother shall see good", so he had a flock of sheep and his flock of parishioners.
- As well as describing Hopkins as "not the least significant of British poets of our time" in 1559, churchman and historian

John Bale also described his "elegant, harmonious arrangement of words in English measures".

- His biographer Rivkah Zim notes, "From 1562 until the 1690s the Elizabethan metrical psalms were the best-known English verses because every English man, woman, and child sang them in church" and adds that "Hopkins was the author of the largest number, 61 out of 150 psalms."

24 October

On 24th October 1590, John White, the governor of the Roanoke Colony, returned to England after failing to find the lost colonists, including his daughter, Ellinor (Elenora), his son-in-law, Ananias Dare, and his granddaughter, Virginia Dare.

Virginia was the first child born to English settlers in the New World, and she was born in the Roanoke Colony, in what is now North Carolina, in August 1587, just days after the arrival of the colonists. Her grandfather, governor John White, had to return to England for supplies at the end of that year, but events such as the Spanish Armada conspired against him, and he couldn't return until three years later, in August 1590. When he arrived at the colony, all 115 people he'd left behind had disappeared. All that was left was the word "Croatoan" carved onto a post.

In 1587, when he was about to leave, White had instructed the colonists of Roanoke to leave a message, carving their new location on a tree or post for him to find or carving the Maltese Cross symbol if they were attacked. So, did the word Croatoan mean they had moved to Croatoan, now Cape Hatteras, which was 50 miles south of the colony, or were they referring to the Croatoan Indians?

Bad weather and events conspired against White once more. He was forced to return to England in October 1590 before he could search for his family and the other colonists and solve the mystery of this lost colony.

The lost colony is still a mystery, with archaeological digs in the Hatteras area finding 16th and 17th-century artefacts, but nothing definitive. But then, in 2012, a watercolour map thought to have been worked on by John White from the British Library collection was examined. On the map, 50 miles from the Roanoke Colony, was a patch that careful examination of the map found to be covering a blue and red star, which they thought might symbolise a fort. It's unknown why this location was covered up with a patch, but archaeology in this area found artefacts like guns, a nail, and English pottery that were not sent to the Americas after 1624. Again, nothing definitive, but the artefacts, combined with legends regarding a pale-skinned and blue-eyed native in the area, have led to the theory that the colonists may have split up and been assimilated by neighbouring tribes, some relocating to the spot marked with the star and others to Hatteras, or Croatoan, as it was known.

In 2020, there were news articles about more archaeological finds in what is now Bertie County, North Carolina, with English pottery pieces dating back to the 1580s being found there. The excavation area comprises 72 digs, each covering an area of 1.24 square metres. Phil Evans, president of the First Colony Foundation, said that the finds in the area suggest that about a dozen people from at least one Roanoke family lived there, possibly with their servants.

Other theories include the colonists being killed in an attack, dying of disease or dying due to extreme weather.

25 October

25th October is a feast day celebrated in medieval and Tudor times - the feast of Saints Crispin and Crispinian, martyrs of the Early Church. These men were brothers, perhaps twins, from a noble Roman family. It is said that they travelled to Soissons in France, fleeing persecution and that on their travels, they supported themselves as cobblers while converting people to the Christian faith.

The brothers were apprehended and tortured, millstones were tied around their necks, and they were thrown into a river on the orders of the Roman Governor Rictius Varus. They survived their ordeal only to be beheaded on 25th October 285 or 286 during the reign of Diocletian. A church was built in their honour in Soissons in the 6th century.

According to an old local legend recounted by Thomas Delaney in 1598, the brothers were sons of a British prince whom Emperor

Carausius executed. Their widowed mother, fearing for her sons' safety, made them flee their home in Canterbury, Kent. They set off in disguise along the Roman road to London and stopped at Faversham, where they noticed a shoemaker's premises. The workers there were so happy in their work that the brothers decided to settle there and work as apprentices. They eventually opened their own shoemaker's shop in Faversham, where they lived for the rest of their lives, making shoes. In Faversham, there is a plaque on the Swan pub which reads, "Near to this house dwelt Saints Crispin and Crispianus, the patron saints of bootmakers. The well to which the pump is connected is St Crispin's Well". This is only a legend, and it's not quite as dramatic as the other story, but interesting nevertheless.

In the 15th century, following the victory of England over France at the Battle of Agincourt, on the Feast of St Crispin and Crispinian, 25th October 1415, the day also became a celebration of the victory. Celebrations included bonfires, revelry and the crowning of a King Crispin.

In his play "Henry V", Elizabethan actor and playwright William Shakespeare included a special St Crispin's Day speech on the eve of the Battle of Agincourt. In this speech, the English king, Henry V, roused his men, who were vastly outnumbered by their French counterparts, to fight, pointing out, "The fewer men, the greater share of honour", and saying the famous words "We few, we happy few, we band of brothers."

As well as being the patron saints of cobblers, St Crispin and St Crispinian are the patron saints of saddlers and tanners.

26 October

On 26th October 1536, the rebels of the Pilgrimage of Grace halted at Scawsby Leys near Doncaster. There, they met crown troops captained by Thomas Howard, 3rd Duke of Norfolk. The rebels were said to number around 30,000, and Norfolk's army was only a fifth of the size, but the rebel leader, lawyer Robert Aske, chose to negotiate rather than fight.

A deal was eventually struck. Norfolk and others were able to report to the king on 28th October that

> "The lords and gentlemen who went from us yesterday to the commons at Pomfret have returned. They have declared your pardon and despatched them all to their houses."

Chronicler Edward Hall recorded:

> "Then, by the great wisdom and policy of the said captains, a communication was had, and a pardon of the kings Majesty obtained, for all the Captains and chief doers of this insurrection, and they promised that such things as they found themselves agreed with all they should gently be heard, and their reasonable petitions granted and that their articles should be presented to the kings Majesty, that by his highness authority, and wisdom of his Council, all things should be brought to good order and conclusion: and with this order every man quietly departed, and those which before were bent as hot as fire to fight, being letted thereof by God, went now peaceably to their houses, and were as cold as water."

Charles Wriothesley wrote of how the rebels had planned to fight the king's forces on the eve of the feast of St Simon and St Jude, 27th October, but "there fell such rain the night before they should have foughten, that they were so wet and their artillery that they could not draw their bows nor shoot", so, instead "at the request of the Duke of Norfolk, they desired him to sue to the king for their pardon [...]".

Norfolk gave promises from Henry VIII that the rebels' demands would be met and that they would be pardoned. Robert Aske then dismissed his troops. A royal proclamation was made to the rebels in early December 1536, offering them a pardon and saying that a parliament would be held in York. Unfortunately, Henry VIII later broke his promises to the rebels.

27 October

On 27th October 1561, Mary Herbert (née Sidney), Countess of Pembroke, writer and literary patron, was born at Tickenhall, near

Bewdley in Worcestershire. She was the third daughter of Sir Henry Sidney and his wife, Mary Dudley, daughter of John Dudley, Duke of Northumberland, and she was the sister of the poets Sir Philip Sidney and Robert Sidney, Earl of Leicester.

Mary's parents were loyal servants of the Crown. Edward VI had died in Mary's father's arms, and Mary's mother had nursed Elizabeth I through smallpox and been badly disfigured due to contracting the disease. Mary was also the niece of Robert Dudley, Earl of Leicester, Elizabeth I's favourite, and Ambrose Dudley, Earl of Warwick.

Mary was educated to a high level and was fluent in French, Italian and Latin. She made her debut at court in 1575, at the age of thirteen, and was present at Kenilworth Castle when her uncle, the Earl of Leicester, played host to the queen between 9th and 27th July 1575. Leicester arranged Mary's marriage to Henry Herbert, 2nd Earl of Pembroke. The couple married on 21st April 1577. Pembroke, who was over twenty years older than Mary, had lost his second wife in May 1576 and was childless. Mary and Pembroke had at least four children: William Herbert, 3rd Earl of Pembroke; Katherine; Anne; and Philip Herbert, 1st Earl of Montgomery and 4th Earl of Pembroke. Mary's biographer, Margaret Patterson Hannay, states that Mary also had at least one stillbirth or a child who died in infancy.

The Pembrokes divided their time between their estate at Wilton, near Salisbury, and Baynards Castle, London. Mary's brother, the famous poet Sir Philip Sidney, wrote the 1593 "The Countess of Pembroke's Arcadia" at Wilton, and Margaret Patterson Hannay writes that "Sidney seems to have entrusted several of his manuscripts to his sister, including those of Certain Sonnets, Astrophil and Stella, and the Lady of May, which she later had printed in the 1598 edition of the Arcadia, which served almost as Sidney's collected secular works."

Philip and Mary were obviously close.

In 1586, Mary lost her parents and her brother, Philip, and spent two years in mourning at Wilton, returning to London in November 1588 for the celebrations of Accession Day and the victory over the Spanish Armada. Patterson Hannay writes, "Mary Herbert honoured her brother's memory by serving as a literary patron to those who honoured him, by supervising the 1593 and 1598 editions of his Arcadia, by translating works that he would have approved, by completing the metric paraphrase of the Psalms that he had begun, and by writing poems to praise him. These efforts on his behalf also permitted her to achieve a literary career herself, despite cultural injunctions to female silence."

Mary acted as patron to several poets, supported by her husband, Pembroke, and was "the first non-royal woman in England to receive a significant number of dedications". Her family wrote poetry, as did members of her household. Mary was also known for her support of religious education and her beauty.

Mary's known works include:
- Her Psalmes, eighteen manuscripts of which still survive today.
- Her poems "To the Angell Spirit of the most Excellent Sir Philip Sidney" and "Even now that care".
- Two translations from French: "A Discourse of Life and Death" (originally by Philippe de Mornay) and "Antonius" (originally by Robert Garnier), written in 1590 and published together in 1592.
- "A dialogue between two shepherds, Thenot and Piers, in praise of Astrea, a pastoral dialogue in praise of the queen" written in 1599 and published in 1602.
- "The elegy for Philip Sidney".
- "A Dolefull Lay of Clorinda".
- A translation of Petrarch's "Trionfo della Morte".

In 2010, June and Paul Schlueter discovered five unpublished poems by Mary in a manuscript of English poems in the Landesbibliothek und Murhardsche Bibliothek in Kassel, Germany. These included "The Countess of Pembroke's mediation & sonnet", "Of the River Bankes between Meziers & Liege", and "Upon the death of the Countesse of Rutland daughter to Sir. Philip Sydney".

Mary's husband died in January 1601, and although he left her well-provided, his death did lead to a reduction in her literary patronage. However, Mary lived life to the full. Patterson Hannay describes how

"She subsequently helped to arrange the marriages of her children, continued her literary patronage on a much reduced scale, travelled on the continent, brought lawsuits against jewel thieves, pirates, and murderers, and built a country home, Houghton House, in

Bedfordshire. King James visited her there in July 1621 [...] she conducted a literary salon, wrote, danced, played cards, took tobacco, shot pistols, and carried on a flirtation with her handsome and learned doctor, Matthew Lister."

She was a busy lady! We also know from her correspondence that she continued writing, although these later works have not survived.

Mary died of smallpox on 25th September 1621 at her London residence in Aldersgate Street. She was fifty-nine years of age. She was laid to rest next to her husband at Salisbury Cathedral following a lavish funeral at St Paul's Cathedral. Her epitaph reads:

"Underneath this sable hearse,
Lies the subject of all verse,
Sidney's sister, Pembroke's mother.
Death, ere thou hast slain another
Fair and learned and good as she,
Time shall throw a dart at thee."

Patterson Hannay writes of how Mary is no longer in her brother Philip Sidney's shadow and is "currently recognized as one of the first significant women writers in English." John Donne praised her, and her work was either praised or borrowed from by famous writers including Gabriel Harvey, William Shakespeare, Edmund Spenser, and Mary Wroth. She deserves to be remembered, and her works read.

Trivia: the Mary Sidney Society puts forward the idea that Mary wrote the works attributed to William Shakespeare.

28 October

Monday 28th October 1532, the Feast of St Simon and St Jude, was the last full day of Henry VIII and Anne Boleyn's time with King Francis I of France in Calais.

On that day, King Henry VIII held a Chapter of the Order of the Garter in the presence of King Francis I, who was described as wearing the blue mantle of the order. At this meeting, two new knights were elected to the Order: Frenchmen Anne, duc de Montmorency, Grand Master of France, and Philippe de Chabot, Admiral of France. Chronicler Edward Hall writes of how their collars and garters were delivered to them, "for the which they rendered to the king great thanks".

Francis I had elected two English noblemen, Thomas Howard, 3rd Duke of Norfolk, and Charles Brandon, Duke of Suffolk, to the Order of Saint Michel on 25th October, so Henry VIII reciprocated on this day.

Then there was entertainment, including bear baiting and a wrestling match, which saw the English Cornish wrestlers provided by Sir William Godolphin beat the French side. "The Manner of the triumphe of Calais and Boulogne", a contemporary pamphlet, recorded this match:

> "And that day, there was a great wrestling between English men and French men before both the kings. The French king had none but priests that wrestled, which were big men and strong, they were brethren but they had most falls."

Sir William Godolphin had written to Thomas Cromwell in June 1532, stating that he had "had a match of wrestling to discover the best. If the King wishes me to serve him in this journey, I will bring him six or eight than whom there are no better". He was right!

In 1532, Henry VIII refrained from challenging the French king to a wrestling match, something he had done at the 1520 Field of Cloth of Gold when Francis I had beaten him. He didn't want a repeat of that humiliation.

29 October

On 29th October 1532, according to Wynkyn de Worde, King Henry VIII bid farewell to his "loving brother", King Francis I.

Wynkyn de Worde wrote, "And upon the 29 day of October the french king departed from Calais to Paris ward and our king brought him as far as Morgison which is from Calais 7 mile and so came to Calais again."

Chronicler Edward Hall dates the farewell to 30th October and writes:

> "The morrow after being the thirty day of October, the two kings departed out of Calais, and came near to

Sandingfield, and there alighted in a fair green place, where was a table set, and there the Englishmen served the Frenchmen of wine, hypocras, fruit, and spice abundantly. When the two kings had communed a little, they mounted on their horses, and at the very entering of the French ground, they took hands, and with Princely countenance, loving behaviour, and hearty words, each embraced other and so depart there departed."

The two kings had spent four days together in English-held Calais and four days together at the French court in Boulogne, but now it was time for these 'beloved brothers' to part and get on with ruling their kingdoms.

30 October

On 30th October 1600, Queen Elizabeth I refused to renew Robert Devereux, 2nd Earl of Essex's monopoly on sweet wines, saying that "an unruly horse must be abated of his provender, that he may be the easier and better managed."

But Essex was her favourite, wasn't he? Why would she leave him on the brink of bankruptcy, and why did she view him as unruly?

If you remember, from the 28th September entry, Essex had been in trouble for abandoning his post as Lord Lieutenant of Ireland and returning to England without the queen's permission, on top of making a truce with the Irish rebel leader, again without the queen's permission. He'd tried to explain himself to the queen, striding into her bedchamber unannounced and before the queen was properly dressed, on 28th September 1599. However, her council still interrogated him and then put him under house arrest for his actions in Ireland and desertion of his duty. In June 1600, Essex appeared before a special court, charged with insubordination during his time in Ireland. He was punished by being deprived of his public office and confined to his home.

Then, when he applied for the renewal of his monopoly on sweet wines, Elizabeth refused. Essex had held this royal monopoly since his stepfather Robert Dudley, Earl of Leicester's death in 1588 when the queen had transferred it to him. It was worth a lot of money and was one of his main sources of income. The loss of this monopoly would ruin him, showing just how much he'd fallen out of favour with the queen. She was cutting off his provender, and income to control him better. This backfired, though. Rather than Essex falling into line, this made him even more convinced that the queen was being turned against him by Robert Cecil, Elizabeth I's secretary of state, and his faction, which included the Earl of Nottingham, Lord Buckhurst, Lord Cobham and Sir Walter Ralegh. It couldn't be that the queen was fed up of his rebellion, disobedience and defiance, it had to be his enemies manipulating her, of course.

Essex was now a desperate man and that December he wrote to King James VI of Scotland, with whom he had corresponded for several years, hoping that he'd continue in royal favour once James became king of England. He appealed to James for help against his enemies, telling him there was a plot to divert the succession from the Scots king to the Spanish Infanta Isabella. Historian Susan Doran points out in her book, "Elizabeth I and Her Circle", that Essex was correct in viewing Cecil and the others as his enemies as they were very much concerned about a situation where James was king and Essex, his chief minister. However, although they were intent on bringing Essex down, they were not plotting a Spanish succession.

The Cecil faction did not have to bring Essex down, though. He did that by planning a coup to seize control of the court, Tower of London and city of London, and remove his enemies from power. Unfortunately for Essex, his coup in February 1601, known as Essex's Rebellion, failed. He could not get the citizens of London's support, and he was forced to surrender to Lord Admiral Nottingham. This one-time favourite of Queen Elizabeth I ended up on the scaffold on Tower Green as a traitor, being beheaded on 25th February 1601. He'd been reckless and arrogant and had taken the queen's affection for him for granted.

31 October

On 31st October 1537, Lord Thomas Howard, second son of Thomas Howard, 2nd Duke of Norfolk, and his second wife, Agnes Tilney, died while imprisoned in the Tower of London. He was about twenty-five years of age at his death. How had the Duke of Norfolk's son come to this rather sorry end? Well, he'd fall in love with the wrong woman. Let me tell you more about Lord Thomas Howard and the love affair that led to his undoing.

- Lord Thomas Howard was born around 1512 and was the younger half-brother of Thomas Howard, 3rd Duke of Norfolk.
- Antiquary John Leland is thought to have been his tutor or companion.
- Lord Thomas Howard made his debut at court in 1533 when he was about 21, the year that Henry VIII married Howard's niece, Anne Boleyn. He was appointed as one of the canopy bearers for the christening of Anne's daughter, the future Elizabeth I, in September 1533.
- At the royal court, he met and fell in love with Lady Margaret Douglas, daughter of Margaret Tudor, Dowager Queen of Scotland, and her second husband, Archibald Douglas, 6th Earl of Angus. Lady Margaret Douglas was also King Henry VIII's niece. In early 1536, Margaret and Thomas agreed to marry, but they had not sought the king's blessing for their relationship. When their relationship was discovered in July 1536, the king was furious. With the king's daughters both being illegitimate by this point, Margaret had a claim to the throne, and she was an important lady.
- Margaret and Thomas were thrown in the Tower of London for their disobedience. On 18th July 1536, an act of attainder was passed against Thomas, accusing the young man of having been "led and seduced by the Devil not having God afore his eyes, not regarding his duty of Allegiance that he oweth to have borne to the King our and his most dread Sovereign Lorde" and going on to say that "it is vehemently suspected and presumed maliciously and traiterously minding and imagining to put division in this Realm. And to interrupt impedity and let the said Succession of the Crown contrary to the limitation thereof mentioned in the said act". The act also sentenced him to death.
- Margaret fell ill while imprisoned in the Tower and was moved to Syon Abbey and eventually released on 29th October 1537. However, two days after her release, her former fiancé, Thomas,

died. It was a natural death rather than the death he'd been sentenced to. Although it was rumoured that he'd been poisoned, it appears he just became ill due to the conditions of his imprisonment.

- The day after Thomas's death, Edward Seymour, Earl of Hertford, wrote to Thomas Cromwell, the king's master secretary, saying that he had told the king of Lord Thomas's death along with a request from Thomas's mother, Agnes, to have her son's remains for burial. Hertford stated, "His Grace is content she shall have him, so that she bury him without pomp." Chronicler Charles Wriothesley records "his body was carried to Thetford, and there buried", referring to Thetford Abbey in Norfolk.

Trivia: The British Library's Devonshire Manuscript, a miscellany of early-modern Tudor courtly verse written by a circle which included Thomas Wyatt and Henry Howard, also contained several poems linked to the lovers, Lord Thomas Howard and Lady Margaret Douglas.

More Trivia: Lady Margaret Douglas fell in love with another Howard man, Thomas's half-nephew, Charles, in 1540 and ended up being confined to Syon and then Kenninghall for her behaviour. She married Matthew Stewart, Earl of Lennox, in 1544.

1 November

On 1st November 1527, the Feast of All Saints, William Brooke, 10th Baron Cobham, courtier and diplomat, was born.

Cobham was a close friend of William Cecil, Baron Burghley and Elizabeth's I's chief advisor, so Cobham became powerful in Elizabeth's reign. He served as Lord Warden of the Cinque Ports, privy councillor and Lord Chamberlain and escaped treason charges twice, thanks to his friends and patrons.

Let me tell you a bit more about this Tudor man.

- William was born in 1527 and was the eldest surviving son of George Brooke, 9th Baron Cobham, and his wife, Anne Bray.
- Although he was officially enrolled at Queen's College, Cambridge, in the early 1540s, it appears that William was in Padua and Venice, where he was supposed to be studying civil law. However, as his biographer Julian Lock points out, he was licensed to carry arms and might have been more interested in being a soldier.
- When he was eight years old, he was contracted to marry Dorothy Neville, daughter of George Neville, 3rd Baron Abergavenny, and the couple married in 1545. The marriage was unhappy, but they had a daughter, Frances, together before separating in around 1553. Dorothy died in 1559.
- In the late 1540s, William served as a soldier at the garrisons in Boulogne, then Calais, and he was knighted in December 1548.
- In 1549, he had his first diplomacy experience, accompanying Sir William Paget on an embassy to Brussels.
- He served King Edward VI as an esquire of the body, and in 1550 the leader of Edward's government, John Dudley, Duke of Northumberland, appointed William to the privy council. In 1551, he accompanied William Parr, Marquess of Northampton, his brother-in-law, on an embassy to France.
- In 1553, William avoided being caught up in the Lady Jane Grey succession crisis by abandoning Northumberland, but he was sympathetic to the rebel cause in the early 1554 Wyatt's Rebellion. The rebels besieged his father's home, Cooling Castle, in January 1554. William's father, who was Wyatt's uncle,

claimed he had fought valiantly against the rebels for seven hours before surrendering to them. However, his resistance is more likely to have been a pretence, and he and his sons joined the rebels willingly. William and his brother, George, escaped being tried as traitors thanks to the intervention of William's brother-in-law, Henry Nevill, 6th Baron Bergavenny.

- William's father died in September 1558, and William inherited the title of Baron Cobham. Then, in November 1558, Elizabeth I came to the throne, and William was made a special ambassador to take the news of Mary I's death to her husband, Philip II of Spain.

- In December 1558, thanks to his friendship with William Cecil, William was made Lord Warden of the Cinque Ports and Constable of Dover Castle. Then, in 1559, he was made Lord Lieutenant and Vice Admiral of Kent. He also served as a justice of the peace for the county.

- In 1560, William married Frances Newton, daughter of Sir John Newton and Margaret Poyntz, and a woman who was serving Elizabeth I in her privy chamber. The marriage was happy, and the couple went on to have seven children, four sons and three daughters.

- In 1571, William seized letters from Roberto di Ridolfi, known for the Ridolfi Plot against Elizabeth I. Still, according to William, his brother, Thomas, persuaded him not to turn them over to the privy council for fear that he and their friend, the Duke of Norfolk, would get into trouble. The fact that William didn't get into big trouble suggests that William was acting under instructions from Burghley and letting the plot play out or that Burghley realised that William was not involved in the plot. His punishment was seven months of house arrest in the custody of Burghley.

- In 1578, he was back working for the government, accompanying Sir Francis Walsingham on an embassy to the Netherlands.

- Although William was friends with Catholics like the Duke of Norfolk and the Earl of Arundel, and his wife, Frances, was a Catholic, Calvinist works were dedicated to him, and his chaplain was Protestant. He was also given the job of helping John Whitgift, Archbishop of Canterbury, investigate the Marprelate Tracts in 1588.

- In 1585, William was installed as a Knight of the Garter, and by early 1586 he was serving on Elizabeth I's privy council.
- In 1588, he wasn't involved in the Spanish Armada in his office at Dover because he was on a diplomatic mission to the Duke of Parma.
- In 1589, William's daughter, Elizabeth, married Robert Cecil, bringing William even closer to the Cecils.
- In 1592, William's wife died at their home, Cobham Hall.
- In 1596, William was made Lord Chamberlain following the death of Baron Hunsdon, but in the winter of 1596/7, his health began to suffer. He died on 6th March 1597, just over a month after his daughter, Elizabeth, and was buried at St Mary Magdelene Church, Cobham. In his will, he left money for the dissolved Cobham Chantry to become Cobham College almshouse. His eldest son, Maximilian, had died in 1583, so his second son, Henry, inherited his title, becoming 11th Baron Cobham.

2 November

On this day in history, 2nd November 1470, the Feast of All Souls, King Edward V was born at Westminster Abbey, London. Little Edward was King of England for just two months.

Edward wasn't a Tudor king, but his uncle, Richard III, taking the throne from him, is linked to the Tudors in that Henry Tudor decided to return from exile to challenge the throne of the man he viewed as an "odious tyrant" and usurper. Henry's forces beat those of Richard at the Battle of Bosworth. Richard was killed, and Henry became King Henry VII, the first Tudor king.

Let me tell you a bit more about Edward V's short life.

- Edward was the eldest son of King Edward IV and his wife, Elizabeth Woodville.
- He was born at Cheyneygates, the Abbot of Westminster Abbey's house, while his mother was in sanctuary tduring his

father's exile and Henry VI's restoration. He was baptised in the abbey with the abbot, prior, and Elizabeth, Lady Scrope, standing as his godparents.

- His father was restored to the throne after the Battles of Barnet and Tewkesbury in 1471, and on 26th June 1471, little Edward was made Prince of Wales and Earl of Chester.
- John Alcock, Bishop of Rochester, was appointed as his tutor and president of his council, and his maternal uncle, Anthony Woodville, Earl Rivers, was made his governor.
- Edward was knighted in April 1475, made a Knight of the Garter in May 1475, and made keeper of the realm in June 1475 while his father was in France.
- Potential brides for the Prince of Wales included the Spanish Infanta Isabella, the daughter of the Duke of Milan, and Anne of Brittany. In 1481, Edward IV and François, Duke of Brittany, ratified a marriage treaty between Edward and Anne of Brittany.
- The prince's council, led by Edward as president of the Council of Wales and the Marches, was set up in Ludlow, and Edward was at Ludlow Castle when news of his father's death on 9th April 1483 reached him. Edward was on his way to London to prepare for his coronation when his uncle, Richard, Duke of Gloucester, stopped the party at Stony Stratford. Gloucester arrested Edward's half-brother, Richard Grey, and his maternal uncle, Earl Rivers, and took custody of the prince. On hearing what had happened to Edward, Elizabeth Woodville went into sanctuary at Westminster once more with her daughters and her other son, Richard, Duke of York.
- After arriving in London in May 1483, Gloucester was made protector for Edward and Edward went to the Tower to prepare for his coronation. He was joined there in June 1483 by his brother Richard after Cardinal Bourchier persuaded Elizabeth Woodville to surrender the prince.
- Later that month, Dr Ralph Shaw preached at St Paul's Cross, declaring that Edward IV had already been precontracted to marry Lady Eleanor Butler when he married Elizabeth Woodville, making that marriage invalid and their children illegitimate.

Rivers and Grey were executed, and Gloucester then took the throne as King Richard III. The princes were last seen in public at the Tower in June 1483.

- The fate of Edward and his brother, Richard, who have gone down in history as the Princes in the Tower, is unknown and is still causing controversy today. Some believe that they were murdered on the orders of King Richard III, while others point the finger at other suspects, and still others believe that one or both of them may have been able to escape or go into exile. An excellent read on the survival theory is "The Survival of the Princes in the Tower" by Matthew Lewis.
- Henry VII, during his reign, had to deal with Pretender Perkin Warbeck, who claimed to be Edward V's brother, Richard, Duke of York. Warbeck's invasion and rebellion failed, and he was imprisoned and later executed.

3 November

On 3rd November 1534, Parliament passed the First Act of Supremacy.

This act confirmed the status of King Henry VIII, and his successors, as the supreme head of the church in England and made it treasonable to support the authority of the pope in England.

Here is the wording of the act from the Statutes of the Realm:

"Albeit, the King's Majesty justly and rightfully is and oweth to be the supreme head of the Church of England, and so is recognised by the clergy of this realm in their Convocations; yet nevertheless for corroboration and confirmation thereof, and for increase of virtue in Christ's religion within this realm of England, and to repress and extirp all errors, heresies and other enormities and abuses heretofore used in the same, Be it enacted by authority of this present Parliament that the King our sovereign lord, his heirs and successors kings of this realm, shall be taken, accepted and reputed the only supreme head in earth of the Church of England called Anglicana Ecclesia, and shall have and enjoy annexed and united to the imperial crown of this realm as well the title and style thereof, as all honours, dignities, preeminences, jurisdictions, privileges, authorities, immunities, profits and commodities, to the said dignity of supreme head of the same Church belonging and appertaining. And that our said sovereign lord, his heirs and successors kings of this realm, shall have full power and authority from time to time to visit, repress, redress, reform, order, correct, restrain and amend all such errors, heresies, abuses, offences, contempts and enormities, whatsoever they be, which by any manner spiritual authority or jurisdiction ought or may lawfully be reformed, repressed, ordered, redressed corrected, restrained or amended, most to the pleasure of Almighty God, the increase of virtue in Christ's religion, and for the conservation of the peace, unity and tranquillity of this realm: any usage, custom, foreign laws, foreign authority, prescription or any other thing or things to the contrary hereof notwithstanding."

Notice from the wording that Parliament wasn't making the king supreme head, it recognised that the king was "justly and rightfully" supreme head, so it was stating that it was an established fact.

This act of Parliament paved the way for the English Reformation and the subsequent dissolution of the monasteries. The king was now the highest authority in the land, under God, and support for the papacy or the pope's authority was deemed treason.

On 15th January 1535, in front of his privy chamber, Henry VIII proclaimed that he was now Supreme Head of the Church of England, and the act came into force in February 1535.

As part of the legislation, any person taking public or church office in England was required to swear the Oath of Supremacy, thus recognising Henry VIII as supreme head. The text of the oath read:

"I (name) do utterly testifie and declare in my Conscience, that the Kings Highnesse is the onely Supreame Governour of this Realme, and all other his Highnesse Dominions and Countries, as well in all Spirituall or Ecclesiasticall things or causes, as Temporall: And that no forraine Prince, Person, Prelate, State or

Potentate, hath or ought to have any Jurisdiction, Power, Superiorities, Preeminence or Authority Ecclesiasticall or Spirituall within this Realme. And therefore, I do utterly renounce and forsake all Jurisdictions, Powers, Superiorities, or Authorities; and do promise that from henchforth I shall beare faith and true Allegiance to the Kings Highnesse, his Heires and lawfull Successors: and to my power shall assist and defend all Jurisdictions, Privileges, Preheminences and Authorities granted or belonging to the Kings Highnesse, his Heires and Successors or united and annexed to the Imperial Crowne of the Realme: so helpe me God: and by the Contents of this Booke."

The Treason Act of 1534 made it treason to disavow the Act of Supremacy, the punishment being death.

Famous examples of those who refused to recognise the king's supremacy include the Carthusian monks of London Charterhouse and the king's former Lord Chancellor, Sir Thomas More.

Trivia: it was George Boleyn, Anne Boleyn's brother, who'd been sent to Convocation in 1531 to put forward the arguments for the king's supremacy. Although Convocation baulked at the idea initially, they recognised the king as supreme head "as far as the law of Christ allows". Then, the Reformation Parliament, as it is known, cemented this in 1534.

4 November

On 4th November 1530, Henry Percy, 6th Earl of Northumberland, and Walter Walsh, a groom of King Henry VIII's privy chamber, arrived at Cawood Castle, Cardinal Thomas Wolsey's seat as Archbishop of York, to arrest the cardinal for high treason.

Wolsey had been a royal favourite, serving King Henry VIII as Lord Chancellor. However, he had been unable to get the king an annulment of his marriage to Catherine of Aragon. As the late historian Eric Ives pointed out, Wolsey "lost Henry's confidence from late August 1529 onwards by miscalculating the king's mood and by mishandling the Treaty of Cambrai, in which Francis I totally deceived him and caused him, in turn, to mislead his master". He was charged with praemunire in 1529, but was pardoned and restored in February 1530. He then managed to dig his own grave by working towards what Eric Ives describes as "a rapprochement with Katherine, Charles V and Rome", something which led to the pope ordering Henry VIII to leave Anne Boleyn and return to Catherine. Anne and the king were furious with the situation. Henry VIII believed that Wolsey had "intrigued against them, both in and out of his kingdom" and entered into "presumptuous sinister practices made to the court of Rome for reducing him to his former estates and dignity". It was treason.

On 1st November 1530, Walter Walsh was sent to Yorkshire with a warrant for Wolsey's arrest, and he accompanied Henry Percy, Earl of Northumberland, who had once served in the cardinal's household, to Cawood on 4th November.

Edward Hall records Wolsey's arrest in his chronicle:

> "When the earl had seen the letter, he with a convenient number came to the Manor of Caywood the 4th day of November, and when he was brought to the Cardinal in his chamber, he said to him, 'my lord I pray you take patience, for here I arrest you.'
>
> 'Arrest me' said the Cardinal, 'yea' said the earl, 'I have a commandment so to do'
>
> 'you have no such power' said the Cardinal, 'for I am both a Cardinal and a Legate de Latere and a peer of the College of Rome & ought not to be arrested by any temporal power, for I am not subject to that power, wherfore if you arrest me I will withstand it'
>
> 'well,' said the earl, 'here is the kings Commission', (which he showed him), 'and therefore I charge you to obey.'
>
> The Cardinal somewhat remembered himself and said, "well my lord, I am content to obey, but although that I by negligence fell into the punishment of the Praemunire and lost by the law all my lands and goods, yet my person was in the king's protection and I was pardoned that offence, wherefore I marvel

why I now should be arrested & specially considering that I am a member of the sea Apostolic on whom no temporal man ought to lay violent hands, well I see the king lacketh good counsel.'

'well,' said the earl, 'when I was sworn Warden of the Marches, you yourself told me that I might with my staff arrest all men under the degree of a king, and now I am more stronger for I have a commission so to do, which you have seen.'"

Hall says that "the Cardinal at length obeyed" and was kept in his chamber while his goods were seized and his officers discharged". The cardinal's physician, Venetian Agostino Agostini, was also arrested. He was accused of carrying letters to the French ambassador in London.

Sir William Kingston, Constable of the Tower of London, was sent from London to meet Wolsey in Sheffield as he was escorted to London, but Wolsey never got to London. He died from dysentery while breaking the journey at Leicester Abbey on 29th November 1530.

5 November

On this day in Tudor history, Sunday 5th November 1514, Mary Tudor, sister of King Henry VIII and daughter of the late King Henry VII, was crowned Queen of France by the Bishop of Bayeux at the Abbey Church of Saint-Denis just outside of Paris.

The eighteen-year-old Mary had married the fifty-two-year-old King Louis XII on 9th October 1514, the feast day of Saint Denis, in Abbeville.

Louise of Savoy, whose late husband was Louis' cousin, recorded:

"On the fifth day of November 1514, the Queen Mary was crowned at Saint-Denis between ten and eleven o'clock in the morning, and on the sixth day around four o'clock in the afternoon, she made her entry into Paris."

English chronicler Edward Hall recorded:

"[...] the lady Mary of England the fifth day of Nouember then being Sunday, was with great solemnity crowned Queen of Fraunce in the monastery of Saynte Denee, and the dolphin all the season held the crown over her head, because it was of greate weight to her grievance, at whiche coronation were the lords of England, and according to their degrees well entertained."

The "Dolphyn", or rather, Dauphin, referred to by Hall was Francis, Duke of Valois and Count of Angoulême, the future Francis I. Francis had become heir presumptive to the French throne in 1498 due to his second cousin, the king, not having a surviving son. As Hall says, Francis held Mary's crown above her head during the ceremony because it was deemed too heavy for the eighteen-year-old queen. Mary was invested with the ring, sceptre and rod of justice before hearing high mass and receiving the sacrament.

The coronation was attended by English gentlemen, including Thomas Grey, 2nd Marquess of Dorset, and Charles Brandon, Duke of Suffolk, who would become Mary's second husband in just a few months.

Mary's tenure as queen consort was short-lived because Louis died on 1st January 1515. Francis I became king with his wife Claude (Louis' daughter) becoming queen. Mary married Charles Brandon secretly and without her brother's permission before returning to England. Henry VIII was furious, but his love for his favourite sister and his friendship with Brandon led to him forgiving the couple, and they were officially married at Greenwich Palace on 13th May 1515. Throughout the rest of her life, Mary was always referred to at the English court as the "French Queen", rather than the Duchess of Suffolk.

6 November

On 6th November 1501, Catherine of Aragon, daughter of Ferdinand II of Aragon and Isabella I of Castile, met her betrothed, Arthur, Prince of Wales, eldest son of King Henry VII, at Dogmersfield in Hampshire. This palace belonged to the Bishop of Bath and Wells.

The couple's marriage had been agreed by the Treaty of Medina del Campo, between England and Spain, in March 1489. They were betrothed by proxy at Woodstock in August 1497, then married by proxy at Tickenhall Manor, Bewdley, in 1499.

On 21st May 1501, fifteen-year-old Catherine left her home, the Alhambra Palace in Granada, Andalucia, in southern Spain, to make the gruelling 500+ mile journey to A Coruña, a port in Galicia, on the north-western coast of Spain. Catherine's party set sail for England on 17th August, but strong storms in the Bay of Biscay forced her fleet to land at Laredo, near Bilbao. After hearing of her first failed attempt to reach England, Catherine's future father-in-law sent one of his best captains, Stephen Butt, to steer her ship through the treacherous Bay of Biscay. At 5 o'clock in the afternoon of the 27th September 1501, Catherine's party set sail again. Although violent storms affected their journey again, this time just off the coast of Brittany, the party landed safely at the port of Plymouth, Devon, on 2nd October 1501. They had been due to arrive at Southampton, but at least they were now on English soil.

Catherine's journey was not over yet. She then had to make her way through England's West Country to London, and she must have been exhausted by the time she reached Dogmersfield in Hampshire, having encountered the seasonal November rains on her journey. King Henry VII was impatient to see his son's bride and abandoned plans to meet her at Lambeth and set off from Richmond on 4th November, meeting up with his fifteen-year-old son Arthur at Easthampstead on 5th November.

Their plans to see Catherine were nearly scuppered by Don Pedro de Ayala, Isabella and Ferdinand's diplomat, who insisted that tradition dictated that they could not see the princess before the wedding. As her biographer Julia Fox points out, Catherine "graciously bowed to the inevitable" and agreed to meet with her father-in-law. Henry was happy with what he saw and called Arthur in to see his bride. Catherine then entertained the royal party with minstrels and dancing. Catherine danced with her ladies, and Arthur danced with Lady Guildford.

The next day, Catherine set off from Dogmersfield continuing her journey to London. Catherine and Arthur married in person in a ceremony at St Paul's in London on 14th November 1501. Sadly, Arthur died on 2nd April 1502, and in 1509 Catherine married his younger brother, King Henry VIII.

7 November

On 7th November 1485, just over two months after King Henry VII's forces had defeated those of King Richard III at the Battle of Bosworth Field, Henry VII's first parliament attainted Richard and his supporters.

Here is an account from Raphael Holinshed's chronicle:

"For the establishing of all things, as well touching the preservation of his own estate, as the commendable administration of justice and preferment of the common wealth of his realme, he called his high court of parliament at Westminster the seventh day of November, wherein was attainted Richard late duke of Gloucester, calling and naming himself by usurpation, king Richard the third.

Likewise there was attainted as chief aiders and assistants to him in the battle at Bosworth, advanced against the present king, John late duke of Norfolk, Thomas earle of Surrey, Francis Lovell knight viscount Lovell, Walter Devereux knight late lord Ferrers, john lord Zouch, Robert Harrington, Richard Charleton, Richard Ratcliffe, William Berkeley of Welley, Robert Middleton, James Harrington, Robert Brakenbury, Thomas Pilkington, Walter Hopton, William Catesbie, Roger Wake, William Sapcote of the county of Huntingdon, Humphrey Stafford, William Clerke of Wenlock, Geoffrey St Germain, Richard Watkins herald of arms, Richard Revell of Derbyshire, Thomas Pulter of the county of Kent, John Welsh otherwise called Hastings, John Kendall late secretary to the said Richard late duke of Gloucester, John Bucke, Andrew Rat, and William Brampton of Burford.

In which attainder neverthelesse there were diverse clauses and provisos for the benefit of their wives and other persons, that had or might claim any right, title, or interest lawfully unto any castles, manors, lordships, towns, townships, honours, lands, tenements, rents, services, fée farms, annuities, knights fees, advowsons, reversions, remainders, and other hereditaments; whereof the said persons attainted were possessed or seized to the uses of such other persons: with a special proviso also, that the said attainder should not be prejudicial to John Catesbie knight, Thomas Revell, and William Ashby esquires, in, of, & upon the manor of Kirkebie upon Wretheke [?] in the county of Leicester, nor in, of, and upon any other lands and tenements in Kirkebie aforesaid, Melton, Somerbie, Thropseghfield, and Godebie, which they had of the gift & feoffement of Thomas Davers, & John Lie. And further, notwithstanding this attainder, diverse of the said persons afterwards were not only by the king pardoned, but also restored to their lands and livings."

In "Henry VII's first parliament" on the History of Parliament website, Dr Hannes Kleineke explains that the business of Henry VII's first Parliament "was naturally shaped by recent political events: the king's tenuous title to the throne had to be fortified by parliamentary sanction, his supporters who had been attainted of treason under Edward IV and Richard III rehabilitated, the supporters of the dead Richard III attainted, and their possessions seized" and that in that "it was not very different from the Parliaments that had opened the reigns of Edward IV and Richard III in 1461 and 1484." Supporters had to be rewarded, and enemies had to be punished. Henry VII had to make a strong show of his kingship in a country ravaged by civil war for decades.

8 November

On 8th November 1534, courtier, scholar and literary patron William Blount, 4th Baron Mountjoy, died at Sutton on the Hill in Derbyshire.

Mountjoy had been a pupil of the great humanist scholar Erasmus and had served Henry VIII as Master of the Mint and chamberlain to Catherine of Aragon.

Let me tell you a bit more about this Tudor man.

- William Blount was born around 1478 in Barton Blount and was the son of John Mountjoy, 3rd Baron Mountjoy, and his wife, Lora Berkeley.
- His father died in 1485, so his uncle, Sir James Blount, held custody of his lands and marriage until he came of age. His mother remarried twice more, first to Sir Thomas Montgomery and then to Thomas Butler, 7th Earl of Ormond, great-grandfather of Anne Boleyn and chamberlain to Elizabeth of York.
- In 1497, Mountjoy helped put down the Cornish Rebellion, and the same year, he married Elizabeth Say. The couple had a daughter together, Gertrude, who would go on to marry Henry Courtenay, Marquess of Exeter, who was executed in 1539. Gertrude served Mary I as one of her ladies. In 1497, Mountjoy also went to Paris, where he met Erasmus, a man who became his mentor and friend.
- He returned to England in 1499 and became socius studiorum, or a companion in studies, to Prince Henry, the future Henry VIII. Mountjoy helped organise the prince's education, and he arranged for Erasmus to visit the royal nursery and meet the eight-year-old Henry in 1499.
- Mountjoy acted as Erasmus's patron during his visit to England in 1505 and 1506, and Erasmus declared of Mountjoy "the sun never shone on a truer friend of scholars".
- As well as helping with Prince Henry's education, Mountjoy served on Henry VII's royal council.
- In 1509, in the celebrations for King Henry VIII's coronation, Mountjoy was made a Knight of the Bath, and then he was appointed Master of the Mint. That summer, he also married Inez de Venegas, his first wife having died in 1506. Inez had come over from Spain with Catherine of Aragon in 1501.
- Mountjoy was overjoyed at Henry VIII's accession, writing to Erasmus, "Heaven smiles, earth rejoices; all is milk and honey and nectar. Tight-fistedness is well and truly banished. Generosity scatters wealth with unstinting hand."
- The new king made him Lieutenant of Hammes Castle in October 1509.

- By May 1512, Mountjoy had been appointed as Queen Catherine of Aragon's chamberlain, and in 1513 he served in Henry VIII's campaign in France, being made lieutenant, bailiff, and then governor of the captured city of Tournai. He was replaced in 1517, allowing him to return to England.
- By May 1515, he was married to Alice Keble, widow of William Brown, and the couple went on to have a son, Charles, who'd become 5th Baron Mountjoy and was also a patron of learning, and a daughter, Catherine. Mountjoy and Alice attended the Field of Cloth of Gold in 1520.
- In 1519, Mountjoy's cousin, Elizabeth or Bessie Blount, gave birth to the king's illegitimate son, Henry Fitzroy, Duke of Richmond and Somerset.
- In 1521, Mountjoy served on the commission that tried Edward Stafford, 3rd Duke of Buckingham, and in that same year, his wife Alice died.
- He served in France again in 1523, accompanying the Duke of Suffolk there, and he also married his fourth wife, Dorothy, widow of Robert, Lord Willoughby, and daughter of Thomas Grey, Marquess of Dorset. He and Dorothy had a son, John, and two daughters, Dorothy and Mary.
- Mountjoy was elected as a Knight of the Garter in 1526. In 1530, even though he was Catherine of Aragon's chamberlain, he was one of the signatories of a letter to Pope Clement VII urging him to annul her marriage to Henry VIII. In July 1533, it was Mountjoy who had to tell Catherine of her demotion to Princess Dowager due to the annulment of her marriage and the validity of the king's marriage to Anne Boleyn. Catherine would not accept her new title, and in autumn 1533, Mountjoy wrote to Thomas Cromwell, saying, "it is not my parte, nor for me this often to vex or unquiet her whom the kynges grace caused to be sworne unto and truly to serve her to my power", and wanting to be replaced as her chamberlain. He was not replaced, though.
- In July 1534, his last major service to the king was to serve on the commission trying William, Lord Dacre. Then, on this day in history, 8th November 1534, Mountjoy died at Sutton on the

Hill, near Barton Blount, in Derbyshire. He was laid to rest at Barton Blount.

9 November

This day in Tudor history, 9th November 1569, is the traditional date for the start of the only major armed rebellion of Elizabeth I's reign. It's known as the Northern Rebellion, Rising of the North, or Revolt of the Northern Earls.

Let me tell you a bit more about this Elizabethan rebellion.

In November 1569, Elizabeth I had been on the throne for 11 years, having succeeded her Catholic half-sister, Mary I. Both women had been made illegitimate by King Henry VIII. Still, some Catholics who opposed Elizabeth's religious settlement, which re-established the Church of England's independence from Rome, confirmed Elizabeth's status as supreme governor of the church, and reintroduced the Book of Common Prayer, viewed Elizabeth I as illegitimate and looked to the Catholic Mary, Queen of Scots, as an alternative. Mary had been forced to abdicate as Queen of Scotland in 1567 in favour of her son, who became King James VI. She had fled to England, arriving in 1568, hoping for protection and help to regain the Scottish crown. However, Mary was surrounded by suspicion, with some believing that she had been involved in her second husband, Lord Darnley's murder, and Elizabeth I ordered her to be taken into protective custody.

In the meantime, several powerful Northern lords who were unhappy with Elizabeth's religious changes were also unhappy with how Elizabeth was limiting their powers with her policy of centralization, that is to say, shifting power from regions to central government, a policy that her father had started. Protestants were also being appointed to important offices in the North.

By November 1569, key Northern earls, such as Charles Neville, 6th Earl of Westmorland and Thomas Percy, 7th Earl of Northumberland, had had enough of the situation and began gathering troops. They aimed to depose Elizabeth I and replace her with Mary, Queen of Scots, who would marry Thomas Howard, 4th Duke of Norfolk, and restore Catholicism as the country's faith.

With troops numbering over 4,500 men, they rode to Durham,

where they stormed the cathedral and set about destroying the English Bible and communion table. This was the cathedral of James Pilkington, Bishop of Durham, a staunch Protestant who'd had disagreements with both earls regarding his handling of recusancy in his diocese and his policies in the area. The rebels celebrated an illegal Catholic mass in the cathedral, and masses were said in several other churches in Durham, Darlington, Richmond, Northallerton and Ripon.

By 29th November, the rebels who'd turned south hopeful of raising more support had reached Bramham Moor near Wetherby and numbered 4,000 foot soldiers and a further 1,700 on horseback. However, the Earl of Sussex was marching towards them from York with a force of around 7,000 men, and the Earl of Warwick and Lord Admiral Clinton were also on their way with around 12,000 men. The rebels reacted by breaking up. Northumberland took some troops to his seat, Alnwick Castle, while some headed to Hartlepool, which they took, to wait for assistance from the Continent. Westmoreland marched on Streatham Castle, which he took, and then also took Barney Castle. Their success was short-lived, though. As Sussex's troops arrived in the area, the rebels dispersed and attempted to flee, retreating North.

Many were captured, and an estimated 600 to 800 rebels were executed. Northumberland and Westmoreland fled to Scotland. Westmoreland managed to evade capture and execution by escaping to Flanders, where he lived in exile until he died in 1601. Still, Northumberland was handed over to England and executed at York on 22nd August 1572. He was beatified in 1895 by Pope Leo XIII.

10 November

On 10th November 1556, English explorer and navigator Richard Chancellor was killed.

Chancellor was drowned after saving the Russian ambassador, Osip Napeya, when their ship, the Edward Bonaventure, was wrecked in Pitsligo Bay, just off the Aberdeenshire coast.

Chancellor was the first foreigner to enter the White Sea and establish relations with Russia.

Here are a few facts about Chancellor and his sad end.

- We don't know anything about Chancellor's birth or even his family, but his contemporary Clement Adams recorded that he was brought up in the household of Sir Henry Sidney.
- In 1550, Chancellor sailed on a voyage organised by Sebastian Cabot to the Levant as an apprentice pilot under Roger Bodenham. It was a voyage designed to give English mariners more experience. It certainly helped train Chancellor for his 1553 voyage.
- In 1553, Chancellor was appointed pilot general of a voyage to find a Northeast passage to help the trade of English cloth to the Far East. He was appointed captain of the 160-ton Edward Bonaventure, the largest of the three ships sent.
- This voyage, which Chancellor undertook with Sebastian Cabot and Sir Hugh Willoughby, failed in its aim of finding a Northeast Passage to the Far East, but, instead, in the winter of 1553/4, Chancellor was able to come to a very beneficial trade agreement with Tsar Ivan IV of Russia, Ivan the Terrible.
- Chancellor returned to England in 1554 and was able to give his friend, Clement Adams, lots of information on Russia. He then commanded a voyage for the newly founded Russia Company, or Muscovy Company, which left in May 1555, to take letters of privilege and merchants' factors to Ivan. Two ships, the Philip and Mary, and the Edward Bonaventure, were sent. Chancellor spent the winter of 1555 at Ivan's court at Moscow and then, in July 1556, set off from St Nicholas with his two original ships, along with the Bona Esperanza and Bona Confidentia from the original 1553 voyage, which had been discovered with Willoughby and his crew who had sadly frozen and starved to death. They sailed with rich cargo and also an embassy from Ivan.
- Unfortunately, the Bona Esperanza and Bona Confidentia were both lost in bad weather off the coast of Norway. Then Chancellor's ship, the Edward Bonaventure, which was also carrying the Russian ambassador, Osip Napeya, was caught in a storm and was wrecked in Pitsligo Bay, just off the Aberdeenshire coast of Scotland on this day in 1556. According to the Russian

ambassador, Chancellor saved the ambassador and his entourage using the ship's boat, but sadly drowned.

- We don't know the identity of Chancellor's wife, but the couple had two sons, one of whom, Nicholas, spent several years working for the Muscovy Company in Russia before serving as a purser in navigator Martin Frobisher's three voyages in the late 1570s, and Edward Fenton's 1582 voyage, and as a merchant in a 1580 voyage. Nicholas died of a fever in Sierra Leone in September 1582.
- Chancellor recorded his observations of Russia, including its topography, an account of his first meeting with Ivan IV, and details on the Russian court, in his "booke of the great and mighty Emperor of Russia, etc."

11 November

On 11th November 1541, the Feast of Martinmas, King Henry VIII's council sent Archbishop Thomas Cranmer a letter containing instructions to move Queen Catherine Howard from Hampton Court Palace to Syon House, formerly Syon Abbey.

Here are the instructions the archbishop received:

"First, the King's pleasure is, that the Queen, with convenient diligence, remove to the house of Syon, there to remain, till the matter be further ordered, in the state of a Queen, furnished moderately, as her life and conditions have deserved; that is to say, with the furniture of three chambers hanged with mean stuff, without any cloth of estate; of which three, one shall serve for Mr Baynton, and thothers, to dine in, and thother two, to serve for her use, and with a mean number of servants, according to a book which we send unto you herewith..."

The council's letter stated that Catherine was allowed to have "four gentlewomen, and two chamberers" of her choosing. However, the king wanted Lady Baynton to be one of the ladies and for her husband, Sir Edward Baynton, to be in charge of the household. Nicholas Heath, Bishop of Rochester and the king's almoner, was also sent to Syon.

Although Catherine's jewels had been seized, a letter from Ralph Sadler, one of the king's secretaries of state, to the archbishop states that the queen was sent six French hoods edged with "goldsmith's work", six pairs of sleeves, six gowns, and six kirtles of satin damask and velvet. Catherine was to enjoy these luxuries while further investigations were carried out.

The 11th November also seems to be when Catherine's alleged relationship with Thomas Culpeper came to light. Catherine had mentioned him in her confession in passing, saying that her former beau, Sir Francis Dereham, had asked her, on his return from Ireland, if she was going to marry Culpeper. Still, his name was brought up again by Dereham. Under interrogation about his relationship with the queen, Dereham stated that "Colpepre had succeeded him in the Queen's affections", and this Culpeper was a member of the king's privy chamber! This revelation resulted in Catherine being interrogated again and Thomas Culpeper being questioned on 13th November. Things were getting worse for Catherine.

Trivia: Sir Edward Baynton served as vice chamberlain to Queens Anne Boleyn, Jane Seymour, Anne of Cleves, Catherine Howard and Catherine Parr. His wife, Isabel, was Catherine Howard's half-sister and had been serving Catherine since her marriage to the king.

12 November

On 12th November 1537, the remains of Queen Jane Seymour were transported by chariot from Hampton Court Palace, where she had died on 24th October 1537, to Windsor Castle.

The chariot carrying her remains was followed by a procession led by Charles Brandon, Duke of Suffolk, and Suffolk's son-in-law, Henry Grey, Marquess of Dorset. Lady Mary, the king's daughter by his first wife, Catherine of Aragon, acted as chief mourner in the procession and the service held at St George's Chapel on their arrival at Windsor.

A solemn watch was kept over Queen Jane's remains that night, and the queen was buried in the chapel the next morning. Her heart and entrails had already been buried in the chapel at Hampton Court Palace.

Chronicler and Windsor Herald Charles Wriothesley records the procession and the funeral:

"This year, the 12th of November, being Monday, the corpse of Queen Jane were, with great solemnity, carried from Hampton Court in a chariot covered with black velvet, with a picture of the said Queen richly apparelled like a Queen, with a rich crown of gold on her head, lying above on the coffin of the said corpse, and so was conveyed to Windsor with great lights of torches, with a great multitude of lords and gentlemen riding, all in black gowns and coats, the Lady Mary, the King's daughter, being chief mourner, with a great company of ladies and gentlewomen waiting on her, and riding all in black also; and there, with great solemnity, buried by the Archbishop of Canterbury, with a great company of bishops and abbots being there present in their mitres, with all the gentlemen and priests of the King's chapel, which rode all the way in their surplesses, singing the obsequie for the dead; and the morrow after there was a solemn masse of requiem sung by the Archbishop of Canterbury; and the Bishop of Worcester, called Dr. Latimer, made a notable sermon; and at the offertory all the estates offered rich palls of cloth of gold; and after mass there was a great feast made in the King's palace at Windsor for all the estates and other that had been present at the same burial."

There was also a commemoration for the late queen in London. Charles Wriothesley also records this in his chronicle:

"Also, the said 12th of November, at afternoon, there was a solemn hearse made at Powles [St Paul's] in London, and a solemn dirige done there by Powles choir, the Mayor of London being there present with the aldermen and sheriffs, and all the mayor's officers and the sheriffs sergeants, mourning all in black gowns, and all the crafts of the city of London in their liveries; Also there was a knell rungen in every parish churche in London, from 12 of the clock at noone till six of the clock at night, with all the bells ringing in every parish church solemn peals from 3 of the clock till the knells ceased; and also a solemn dirige sungen in every parish church in London, and in every church of friars, monks, and chanons, about London; and, the morrow after, a solemn masse of requiem in all the said churches, with all the bells ringing, from 9 of the clock in the morning till noon; also there was a solemn mass of requiem done at Powles, and all Powles choir offering at the same masse, the mayor, aldermen, and sheriffs, and the wardens of every craft of the city of London; and, after the said mass, the mayor and aldermen going about the hearse saying 'De profundis', with all the crafts of the city following, every one after their degrees, praying for the soul of the said Queene."

The vault containing Jane's remains was opened in 1547, and her husband's remains were added. They lie together, along with King Charles I and one of the Stuart Queen Anne's babies, in St George's Chapel, Windsor, their resting place marked by a black marble slab.

13 November

On 13th November 1536, mercer and member of Parliament Robert Packington was shot to death by an unknown assailant while he was on his way to mass at St Thomas of Acre Chapel. He was shot with a wheellock pistol.

Packington was laid to rest at St Pancras Church on 16th November, with reformer Robert Barnes preaching at his funeral. He left behind a wife and two young sons.

Chronicler Edward Hall gave an account of Packington's murder. Here is what he wrote:

"In this year, one Robert Packyngton, Mercer of London, a man of good substance, and yet not so rich as honest and wise, this man dwelled in Cheapside at the sign of the leg, and used daily at four of the clock Winter and Summer to rise and go to Mass at a church then called saint Thomas of Acres (but now named the

Mercers chapel) and one morning among all other, being a great misty morning such as hath seldom been seen, even as he was crossing the street from his house to the church, he was suddenly murdered with a gun, which of the neighbours was plainly heard, and by a great number of labourers at the same time standing at Soper lane end, he was both seen go forth of his house, and also the clap of the gun was heard, but the deed doer was never espied nor known, many were suspected, but none could be found faulty: howbeit it is true, that forasmuch as he was known to be a man of a great courage and one that both could speak & also would be heard: and that the same time he was one of the burgesses of the parliament, for the City of London, and had talked somewhat against the covetousness and cruelty of the Clergy, he was had in contempt with them, and therefore most like by one of them thus shamefully murdered as you perceive that Master Hunne was in the sixth year of the reign of this king."

The Master Hunne, to whom Hall was referring, was Richard Hunne, a merchant-tailor arrested for heresy by church officials after he had tried to use the common law courts against the church after a dispute with a priest over his son's burial. He was found dead in his prison cell in 1514, and it was suspected he'd been murdered by church officials.

Martyrologist John Foxe included Robert Packington in his famous Book of Martyrs, although he mistakenly dated his death to 1538. He used Hall's record word for word but added bits, for example:

"Although many in the mean time were suspected, yet none could be found faulty therein, the murderer so covertly was conveyed, till at length, by the confession of Dr. Incent, dean of Paul's, on his death-bed, it was known, and by him confessed, that he himself was the author thereof, by hiring an Italian, for sixty crowns or thereabouts, to do the feat..."

He also wrote that Packington was all the more disdained by the clergy because he "was thought also to have some talk with the king" and that he was murdered "by the said Dr. Incent for his labour".

In an earlier edition of his work, Foxe blamed John Stokesley, Bishop of London.

Foxe also explained that Packington was the brother of Augustine Packington, "who", he explains, "deceived Bishop Tonstal, in buying the new translated Testament of Tyndale".

Edward Hall also writes of Augustine Packington and the Bishop of London, explaining that Packington, who "was a man that highly favoured William Tyndale", helped William Tyndale by getting the Bishop of London to buy a load of New Testaments. Tyndale was in debt at the time and was also in danger, having a lot of copies of his New Testament in his possession, so Packington told the bishop that he could get hold of copies of the New Testament for the bishop to burn as heretical books if the bishop paid for them. Packington then bought them from Tyndale. Hall writes of Tyndale's reaction to this deal: "I am the gladder, said Tyndale, for these two benefits shall come thereof, I shall get money of him for these books, to bring myself out of debt, and the whole world shall cry out upon the burning of God's work. And the overplus of the money that shall remain to me, shall make me more studious to correct the said New Testament, and so newly to imprint the same once again, and I trust the second will much better like you, than ever did the first." What a deal!

Chronicler Raphael Holinshed writes that the murderer was eventually discovered:

> "At length the murderer indeed was condemned at Banbury in Oxfordshire to die for a felony which he afterwards committed, and when he came to the gallows on which he suffered, he confessed that he did this murder, and till that time he was never had in any suspicion thereof."

It's hard to know what happened, but, like his brother, Robert Packington was of the reformed faith, with Protestant Rose Hickman recalling how he "used to bring English Bible from beyond the sea". As merchants who would travel to Antwerp on business, the Packington brothers were in a perfect position to take Bibles and other religious books back to England. It appears that Robert Packington's faith and criticism of the clergy led to his violent death.

Historian and author Derek Wilson points out that "poor Robert Packington probably holds the dubious distinction of being the first person in England to be killed with a handgun." Wilson also used Packington's unsolved murder in his historical thriller "The First Horseman".

14 November

By 14th November 1541, things were not looking good for Thomas Culpeper, a member of the king's privy chamber and a man who Francis Dereham, secretary to Queen Catherine Howard, claimed: "had succeeded him in the Queen's affections". It was on this day that an inventory was taken "of the goods and chattels, lands and fees of Thos. Culpeper, the younger".

On 2nd November 1541, just days after returning from his progress to the North with his fifth wife, Catherine Howard, Henry VIII was informed by Archbishop Cranmer that allegations had been made concerning Catherine's past. It was claimed that during her time in the Dowager Duchess of Norfolk's household, Catherine had had a relationship with her music tutor, which went as far as heavy petting, and a full sexual relationship with the dowager duchess's employee, Francis Dereham. During the subsequent investigation, it came to light that Catherine had had secret meetings during the royal progress with Thomas Culpeper, helped by one of her ladies, Jane Boleyn, Lady Rochford.

Culpeper was arrested around 12th/13th November and interrogated. During the interrogations, he admitted to having a romance with Catherine before she married the king and then this romance was revived after her marriage. He denied having sex with Catherine but confessed that the couple intended to "do ill" with each other. Intention was all that was needed to seal the couple's fate because the 1534 Treason Act stated that traitors were those who "do maliciously wish, will or desire by words or writing, or by craft imagine, invent, practice or attempt any bodily harm to be done or committed to the King's most royal person". Sleeping together, with its risk of pregnancy, would impugn the succession.

Culpeper was in trouble, and on 14th November 1541, while he was imprisoned, an inventory of his possessions was taken. The inventory included his possessions at Westminster Palace, which included "two caps of velvet that the King gave him" along with other items of clothing and "some swords, daggers, and sundries"; his horses, harnesses for the horses, and furniture "at various places"; "Debts and ready money owing to him"; revenues from his lands, which included several manors and a former monastery in Kent; his various offices (the king had been generous with these); his possessions in his house at Greenwich, and his furniture, hangings and possessions "within the great lodge at Southfryth of Master Culpepper".

By this time, an inventory had also been taken of the possessions of the lady who had helped the couple, Jane Boleyn, Lady Rochford. The list included a large amount of plate, jewels including "a broach with an agate, a cross of diamonds with three pearls pendant, a flower of rubies, a flower with a ruby and a great emerald with a pearl pendant, a tablet of gold with black, green, and white enamelled, a pair of bracelets of red cornelyns, a pair of beads of gold and stones, a broach of gold with an antique head and a white face"; and apparel including kirtles of black velvet and black satin, a nightgown of black taffeta, a gown of black damask, and a gown of black satin. It is interesting to note all the items of clothing listed in this inventory are black. Was Jane wearing black to demonstrate her wealth and status, or was she still wearing mourning attire following her husband George Boleyn's execution in 1536? It's hard to know.

Thomas Culpeper was found guilty of "high treason against the Kinges Majestie in mysdemeanor with the Quene", along with Francis Dereham, at a trial at Guildhall, London, on 1st December 1541. Both men were condemned to death and executed at Tyburn on 10th December 1541; Culpeper was beheaded, and Dereham suffered a full traitor's death.

Jane Boleyn, Lady Rochford, was beheaded along with her mistress, Queen Catherine Howard, at the Tower of London on 13th February 1542.

15 November

On 15th November 1532, a rather cross Pope Clement VII threatened King Henry VIII and Anne Boleyn with excommunication.

Over a year earlier, on 5th January 1531, the pope had written to the king forbidding him to remarry and threatening him with excommunication if he took matters into his own hands and disobeyed Rome. Since then, the king had continued his quest for an annulment of his marriage to Catherine of Aragon and had just arrived back from a trip to Calais to seek King Francis I of France's support for his relationship with Anne Boleyn. And, if Edward Hall is to be believed, Henry had even married Anne the day before Pope Clement wrote this letter.

In his letter to the king, Pope Clement VII wrote of how he was "grieved to see that the King, who has always hitherto been a pious son to the Pope and Holy See, has changed his conduct for the last two years without reasonable cause, though the Pope has not altered his affection for him." He wrote of how he was sorry that "his office and justice" had compelled him to do anything that would displease the king, whom he always tried to please, but asked if he was to "neglect justice and the salvation of the King's soul, or prefer their private affection to public interests and the Divine will?" He explained how he was bound to do what was just and honourable, rather than what would please the king at the moment, and went on to say that he "Trusts that when this cloud of error has passed from him, his former attachment will return, and he will confess that his Holiness could do nothing but what he has done, and has sometimes been over-indulgent."

The pope reminded the English king that he, the pope, had committed the case of the king's marriage to two legates four years previously, at Henry's request, even though the pope thought the matter unjust. However, Queen Catherine's appeal then "caused him to commit it, not to the dominions of the Queen's nephew, or other places where she might be favored, but to Rome, the auditory of the Rota, to be referred to himself and the college of Cardinals." In the meantime, wrote the exasperated pope, instead of waiting for a decision from Rome, the king had taken it upon himself to leave Catherine and to publicly co-habit "with a certain Anne".

The pope described this behaviour as "an injury to Divine justice" and cited a letter that he had written about this on 25th January 1532, and wrote of how grieved he was to hear that the king had ignored the pope and was still separated from Catherine and living with Anne. He then got serious, saying that he "Again exhorts him and warns him, on pain of excommunication, to take Katharine back as his Queen, and reject Anne, within one month from the presentation of this letter, until the papal sentence be given. If the King does not do this, the Pope declares both him and Anne to be excommunicated at the expiry of the said term, and forbids him to divorce himself from Katharine by his own authority, and marry Anne or any other, such marriage being invalid."

Of course, Henry VIII completely ignored the pope's warning and began co-habiting properly with Anne on his return to London on 24th November 1532. The couple married in an official but secret ceremony on 25th January 1533, Anne being pregnant by that time. In May 1533, Archbishop Thomas Cranmer declared that Henry and Catherine's marriage was null and void and that Henry's marriage to Anne was valid. Anne was crowned queen on 1st June 1533. On 11th July 1533, the pope declared that Henry VIII's marriage to Anne Boleyn was null and void, as was the annulment declared by Archbishop Thomas Cranmer, and he restored Catherine of Aragon to her "royal state". He ordered the king to return to Catherine, threatening him with excommunication if he didn't. Of course, Henry took absolutely no notice. Still, he escaped excommunication until 17th December 1538, when Pope Paul III excommunicated him following his break with Rome, his persecution of those who did not accept his supremacy, the dissolution of the monasteries and Henry's desecration of religious shrines, including that of Thomas Becket.

16 November

On 16th November 1612, Elizabethan conspirator, William Stafford, died. It is not known where he died or where he was laid to rest.

Let me tell you a little about this man and the plot he was involved in.

William Stafford was the second son of William Stafford, widower of Mary Boleyn, and his second wife, Dorothy, who, in turn, was the daughter of Henry Stafford, 10th Baron Stafford, and Ursula Pole. Our William Stafford had royal blood, being of the Plantagenet line through his maternal grandmother, Ursula, the daughter of Margaret Pole, Countess of Salisbury, and granddaughter of George, Duke of Clarence, brother of Kings Edward IV and Richard III.

When William was just one year old, his family fled England under the rule of Catholic Queen Mary I and went into exile on the Continent. The family knew John Calvin and John Knox during their time in Geneva and then Basel. They returned to Essex in 1559, after Elizabeth I's accession.

William was educated at Winchester College and then New College, Oxford, where he was a fellow from 1573 to 1575. After that, he spent some time at court in London before fighting on the side of the Dutch rebels against the Spanish and then living in Paris for a time with his brother, Edward, who was an ambassador there.

In January 1587, it was claimed that William Stafford had plotted with Baron de Châteauneuf, the French ambassador, and the ambassador's secretary, Des Trappes, to kill Elizabeth I. Also involved in the plot was Michael Moody, William's brother Edward's servant, who came up with the idea of assassinating the queen in her bedchamber by way of a trail of gunpowder. The idea changed to stabbing or poisoning - perhaps the use of a poisoned saddle or gown - after the French pointed out that Stafford's mother, Dorothy, who served in the queen's bedchamber, would probably be killed in such an explosion.

While the Stafford Plot, as it's become known, was ongoing, William Stafford reported the plan to Sir Francis Walsingham, Queen Elizabeth I's spymaster and principal secretary. Des Trappes was then arrested and Châteauneuf questioned. Châteauneuf threw the blame on Stafford but could not explain why he himself had not reported the plot if he'd known about it. Stafford was imprisoned in the Tower but then released without charge in August 1588.

How and why did he escape punishment if he'd plotted to kill his queen?

Well, it's believed that Walsingham and William Cecil, the queen's chief advisor, orchestrated the plot to show Queen Elizabeth I that her life was in danger and to persuade her to act against Mary, Queen of Scots. Stafford was simply acting as an "agent provocateur" and spy. Another theory is that the plot was used to put Châteauneuf under house arrest at the time of the execution of Mary, Queen of Scots, to stop any French protests about it.

In 1593, William Stafford married Anne Gryme, and the couple settled in Norfolk and had two children: Dorothy and William. Their son became an author and pamphleteer.

Stafford died a natural death on this day in 1612, and it seems to have been a quiet end for a man who worked for a queen's spymaster and ended up being imprisoned in the Tower.

17 November

On 17th November 1558, twenty-five-year-old Elizabeth, daughter of King Henry VIII and Anne Boleyn, became Queen Elizabeth I following the death of her half-sister, Queen Mary I.

Today, I want to share a speech recorded by Elizabeth I's godson, Sir John Harington, who described it as "Words spoken by the Queene to the Lordes, at her Accession, 1558".

It is unclear whether she spoke these words on 17th November or when she spoke to the House of Lords on 20th November. Elizabeth's biographer, David Starkey, notes that this speech makes no sense if it's dated to 20th November, adding, "spoken, however, three days earlier, in the fading light of her accession day, it becomes a thing of purpose. It addresses Elizabeth's own immediate concerns in the hours following her sister's death. And it addresses, still more pointedly, the concerns of her audience of ex-Marian councillors, most of whom were 'extremely frightened of what Madame Elizabeth will do with them'." Starkey quotes Ambassador Feria there.

Whether it was spoken on 17th, when Elizabeth found out she was queen, or three days later, it is a wonderful speech:

> "My lords, the law of nature moveth me to sorrow
> for my sister; the burden that is fallen upon me
> maketh me amazed; and yet, considering I am God's

creature, ordained to obey His appointment, I will thereto yield, desiring from the bottom of my heart that I may have assistance of His grace to be the minister of His heavenly will in this office now committed to me.

And as I am but one body naturally considered, though by His permission a body politic to govern, so I shall desire you all, my lords (chiefly you of the nobility, everyone in his degree and power), to be assistant to me, that I with my ruling and you with your service may make a good account to almighty God and leave some comfort to our posterity in earth. I mean to direct all my actions by good advice and counsel.

And therefore, considering that divers of you be of the ancient nobility, having your beginnings and estates of my progenitors, kings of this realm, and thereby ought in honour to have the more natural care for maintaining of my estate and this commonwealth; some others have been of long experience in governance and enabled by my father of noble memory, my brother, and my late sister to bear office; the rest of you being upon special trust lately called to her service only and trust, for your service considered and rewarded; my meaning is to require of you all nothing more but faithful hearts in such service as from time to time shall be in your powers towards the preservation of me and this commonwealth.

And for council and advice I shall accept you of my nobility, and such others of you the rest as in consultation I shall think meet and shortly appoint, to the which also, with their advice, I will join to their aid, and for ease of their burden, others meet for my service. And they which I shall not appoint, let them not think the same for any disability in them, but for that I do consider a multitude doth make rather discord and confusion than good counsel. And of my goodwill you shall not doubt, using yourselves as appertaineth to good and loving subjects."

Like her father and siblings, Elizabeth had a way with words!

I do love the oak tree tradition, though, which places Elizabeth sitting under the oak tree in the parkland of Hatfield when the lords come to tell her of her accession. On hearing the news, she was said to have recited from Psalm 118 in Latin, "This is the LORD'S doing; it is marvellous in our eyes." What I find interesting about Elizabeth's use of the verse from Psalm 118, a psalm of thanksgiving to God for his goodness and mercy, is the previous line. The psalm reads:

"The stone which the builders refused is become the
head stone of the corner.
This is the LORD'S doing; it is marvellous in our eyes.
This is the day which the LORD hath made; we will
rejoice and be glad in it."

Did Elizabeth see herself as the stone that her father and brother refused, a daughter who had been made illegitimate, a daughter and sister who was removed from the succession, a bastard, but who became the headstone of the corner, who became important, who became queen? I think so.

Elizabeth reigned until her death on 24th March 1603. Her achievements as queen included defeating the Spanish Armada and turning England into a strong and dominant naval power, expanding England overseas through colonisation, and founding the Church of England through her religious settlement. She was also a patron of Science and the Arts. Her reign is known for its Golden Age, but it was far from that for some of her Catholic subjects and those of her people living in poverty.

18 November

On 18th November 1559, Bishop of Coventry and Lichfield, Ralph Baynes (Baines), died. He was buried in the church of St Dunstan-in-the-West, London.

At the time of his death, Baynes was imprisoned in the London home of Edmund Grindal, Bishop of London. He'd been deprived of his bishopric and put into Grindal's care in June 1559, but why?

Let me tell you a bit more about this Tudor bishop and how he came to this rather sad end.

- Nothing is known of Baynes' family, and his birthdate is also unknown, but he was a Yorkshireman, probably from Knowsthorpe, and he studied at St John's College, Cambridge, attaining a BA in 1518 and an MA in 1521. He also became a fellow at the college in 1521.
- In 1519, he was ordained as a priest at Ely in Cambridgeshire, and he became rector of Hardwick in the same county at some point, holding the post until he resigned in 1545. In 1527 he was a university preacher.
- In 1532 he attained his Bachelor of Theology, and twenty-three years later, in 1555, he attained his doctorate.
- During Henry VIII's reign, he opposed the annulment of Henry VIII's marriage to Catherine of Aragon. He spoke out against the preaching of Hugh Latimer, who was of the reformed faith, and it appears that he went abroad during Edward VI's reign, working as a professor of Hebrew in Paris. While in Paris, Baynes wrote a Hebrew grammar published in 1550, the first Hebrew grammar book published by an Englishman. He also produced two other books on Hebrew.
- Baynes returned to England when the Catholic Mary I came to the throne, and in November 1554, he was consecrated Bishop of Coventry and Lichfield.
- During Mary's reign, with his chancellor, Anthony Draycot, he examined Protestants, including John Hooper, Robert Glover, John Philpot, and Joan Waste. Waste was a young blind woman burnt at the stake in Derby in 1556 for refusing to recant her Protestant faith. Baynes is mentioned numerous times in this role in martyrologist John Foxe's Book of Martyrs.
- As a staunch Catholic, when Elizabeth I came to the throne in November 1558, he opposed her new religious measures. He was one of the five bishops who defended Catholicism at the 1559 Westminster Conference.
- In June 1559, Baynes was deprived of his bishopric and imprisoned in the home of Protestant Edmund Grindal, Bishop of London. Thomas Betham replaced him as bishop. Baynes was one of eleven bishops imprisoned in this way during Elizabeth I's reign, and their bishoprics given to Protestants.

These imprisoned bishops included Edmund Bonner, Bishop of London; Richard Pate, Bishop of Worcester; Gilbert Scott, Bishop of Chester; Cuthbert Tunstall, Bishop of Durham; Thomas Watson, Bishop of Lincoln, and Nicholas Heath, Archbishop of York, who was temporarily imprisoned.

- On this day in history, 18th November 1559, Baynes died at Grindal's house, according to contemporary John Strype of "the stone", perhaps kidney stones.
- Baynes was laid to rest at St Dunstan-in-the-West in London on 24th November.

19 November

On 19th November 1564, Lord John Grey, youngest son of Thomas Grey, 2nd Marquess of Dorset, died.

Let me tell you a bit more about this Lord John and how he escaped the axeman in 1554.

- John was born around 1523/4 and was the youngest son of Thomas Grey, 2nd Marquess of Dorset, and his second wife, Margaret Wotton. His paternal great-grandparents were Sir John Grey of Groby and Elizabeth Woodville.
- During Edward VI's reign, John was appointed Lord Deputy of Newhaven and granted estates in Leicestershire, Derbyshire and Nottinghamshire.
- At some point, John married Mary Browne, daughter of Sir Anthony Browne, who had served Henry VIII as his Master of the Horse. John and Mary had seven children, three sons and four daughters.
- Following the Catholic Mary I's accession to the throne, John became involved in the 1554 Wyatt's Rebellion led by Sir Thomas Wyatt the Younger and sought to depose Mary and replace her with her half-sister Elizabeth. John's fellow conspirators included his older brothers, Henry Grey, Duke of Suffolk, and Lord Thomas Grey. The rebellion failed after Mary rallied the citizens of London against the rebels, and the Grey brothers were arrested. John was arrested at Astley in Warwickshire on 2nd February 1554 with his brother Suffolk.

- John's brothers, Henry and Thomas, were both executed as traitors in February and April, respectively, and John was tried in May 1554. He was found guilty and condemned to death on 11th June 1554.
- John was saved from execution by the intercession of his wife, Mary, whose brother was the Catholic Viscount Montagu, a man close to Queen Mary. John was released in October 1554 and pardoned on 17th January 1554. Sensibly, he chose a quiet life away from court for the rest of Mary's reign.
- He returned to court on the accession of the Protestant Queen Elizabeth I in late 1558, serving her on her first progress. At New Year 1559, he gave the queen a mother-of-pearl cup.
- Although he'd been pardoned, Lord John was still under attainder and so was suffering financially. After he pleaded poverty to William Cecil, Baron Burghley, he was granted the Essex Manor of Pyrgo in April 1559 and further lands in Somerset. The new queen also released him from the attainder and restored him in blood. Burghley chose John as one of four Protestant nobles to supervise alterations to the Book of Common Prayer.
- In 1563, John's niece, Lady Katherine Grey, sister of Lady Jane Grey, was moved to Pyrgo under John's care. She'd just been released from the Tower of London into house arrest. Katherine had, of course, got into trouble with the queen after her secret marriage to Edward Seymour, Earl of Hertford, in 1560. She'd managed to have two sons with him during her imprisonment. John interceded on his niece's behalf, writing to Burghley pleading for a pardon. Still, unfortunately, in 1564, a man called John Hales wrote and published a book claiming that Katherine was Elizabeth's heir. The queen reacted by removing Katherine from Pyrgo and imprisoning John temporarily. Katherine was imprisoned in the Tower once more.
- John returned to Pyrgo on his release and died there on this day in 1564, reportedly from gout. He was laid to rest in the manor's chapel. He left everything to his wife, Mary, who he'd also named his executor. His only surviving son, Henry, was

made Baron Grey of Groby in July 1603 after the accession of James I.

- John's great-great-grandson was Thomas Grey, Lord Grey of Groby, who committed regicide by being one of the 59 commissioners to sign King Charles I's death warrant in 1649.

20 November

On 20th November 1612, in the reign of King James I, courtier and author Sir John Harington died.

Harington was Queen Elizabeth I's godson, and he invented the Ajax, or "jakes", England's first flush toilet.

Let me tell you more about Harington and his invention, which didn't catch on.

- Sir John Harington was born in 1560. His exact birthdate is not known, but he was baptised on 4th August 1560 at All Hallows, London Wall. Queen Elizabeth I stood as his godmother, while William Herbert, 2nd Earl of Pembroke, stood as his godfather.
- He was the eldest son of courtier John Harington of Kelston in Somerset, and his second wife, Isabella Markham.
- Harington was educated at Eton before moving to King's College, Cambridge, where he attained a BA in 1578 and a Masters in 1581. William Cecil, Baron Burghley, advised him on his studies, as did Sir Francis Walsingham.
- In November 1581, when he was 21, he was admitted to Lincoln's Inn, one of London's inns of the court. However, his father died in 1582, leaving John to inherit the family's estate at Kelston, which he did in 1583.
- In September 1583, Harington married Mary Rogers, granddaughter of Sir Edward Rogers, who had served Henry VIII, Edward VI and Elizabeth I.
- In the 1580s, Harington worked on an English translation of Italian Ludovico Ariosto's epic poem "Orlando Furioso", or "The Frenzy of Orlando". According to one story, Harington had been banished from court by his godmother, the queen, when he'd been caught sharing a rather racy translation of Canto 28 with her ladies, and his penance was to go away and translate

the whole work. He did, and it was published in 1591. It was dedicated to the queen.

- His next work was his 1596 book "A New Discourse of a Stale Subject, called the Metamorphosis of Ajax", in which he outlined his design for a flush toilet. Ajax was a play on "jakes", a slang term for "privy". His invention was inspired by a conversation with a group including Henry Wriothesley, Earl of Southampton, and his sister Mary. The invention incorporated a cistern of water located above a privy, which had a "cock or a washer to yield water with some pretty strength when you would let it in.". I love the fact that in the accompanying diagram of the toilet, the cistern had fish in it! In his book, Harington said that if water "be plenty" then the privy could be flushed as often as it was used, but if water was scant, then once a day was sufficient.

- The invention was just a small part of the book. The work was, as Harington's biographer Jason Scott-Warren describes it, "a complex blend of scatological comedy, moral reflection, and social satire". In this work, he also described himself as a "protesting Catholicke Puritan".

- Unfortunately for Harington, he got into trouble with Elizabeth I due to derogatory remarks he made about her favourite Robert Dudley, Earl of Leicester, in his book, and he was lucky to escape being hauled before the Star Chamber.

- Although his invention didn't take off, he did install one at Richmond Palace and sent one to Robert Cecil to install at his home Theobalds.

- In 1599, Harington served the queen in Ireland under the Earl of Southampton and was knighted there by Robert Devereux, Earl of Essex. Unfortunately, Essex incurred Elizabeth's wrath for his actions in Ireland for leaving without her permission, and Harington was caught up in this. However, he saw the queen privately and explained himself, regaining her favour.

- In December 1600, Harington collated epigrams he'd written in the 1590s into two collections, giving one to the Countess of Bedford and another to his mother-in-law.

- In 1602, Harington completed his "Tract on the Succession to the Crown", which supported the claim of King James VI of Scotland. He also sent the Scottish king a four-volume set of epigrams.
- His final service to his godmother, Elizabeth I, appears to have been entertaining her at Christmas 1602 with readings from his own comic verses. Following her death, he met the new monarch and his wife in Rutland and presented them with congratulatory elegies.
- Harington ended up being imprisoned in the Gatehouse Prison in the summer of 1603 due to being the guarantor for a debt of £4,000 run up by his uncle, Thomas Markham. While in prison, he worked on revising an earlier translation he'd made of Virgil's Aeneid. He presented this to King James in the summer of 1604 to be used in educating the king's son and heir, Prince Henry Frederick. The following year, he presented the prince with a collection of epigrams and then further works in 1608.
- In 1605, Harington put himself forward for the office of Lord Chancellor of Ireland, providing a treatise on how he'd solve the Anglo-Irish problem. He also wanted to be made Archbishop of Dublin. He failed to get either position.
- Sir John Harington died on this day in history, 20th November 1612, at 52, following a few months of illness. He was laid to rest at Kelston on 1st December.

21 November

On 21st November 1495, churchman, Protestant playwright, historian and Bishop of Ossory, John Bale, was born at Cove, near Dunwich, in Suffolk.

Bale wrote twenty-four plays, but his most famous work is his "Illustrium majoris Britanniae scriptorum, hoc est, Angliae, Cambriae, ac Scotiae Summarium..." ("A Summary of the Famous Writers of Great Britain, that is, of England, Wales and Scotland"), which was his effort to record every work by a British author.

Let me tell you about this accomplished Tudor man.

- John Bale was the son of Henry Bale and his wife, Margaret, who were apparently of humble origins.
- He was educated at Norwich's Carmelite priory, from the age of 12, before moving on to Jesus College, Cambridge, and then abroad at Louvain and Toulouse.
- He was awarded a Bachelor of Theology from Cambridge in 1529 and then a Doctorate in Theology around 1531.
- Bale was made prior of the White Friars in Maldon in Essex in 1530, then the Carmelites of Ipswich in 1533, and prior of Doncaster in 1534.
- In the 1530s, Bale converted to Protestantism due to the influence of his patron, East Anglian peer, Thomas, 1st Baron Wentworth of Nettlestead. Bale escaped conviction for heresy in 1534 after being charged with it. He had preached against the invocation of saints in a sermon at Doncaster and was hauled before the Archbishop of York.
- In 1536, he left his posts at Doncaster and Ipswich, renounced his vows and married a widow named Dorothy.
- He became a priest at Thorndon in Suffolk in 1536, and a year later, he was arrested for heresy after denouncing "papistry" in a sermon he preached. Antiquarian John Leland, who was close to Henry VIII and supported Bale and his work, interceded on his behalf, and he was released. Bale was also close to Thomas Cromwell, which may have helped his cause.
- Bale led a troupe of actors who performed allegorical morality plays supporting Protestantism, and Cromwell supported this troupe.
- Bale wrote 24 plays, including "Three Laws of Nature, Moses and Christ, corrupted by the Sodomites, Pharisees and Papists most wicked", "A Tragedy; or interlude manifesting the chief promises of God unto Man", "The Temptation of our Lord", "A brief Comedy or Interlude of Johan Baptist's preaching in the Wilderness, etc." and "King John". King John was performed at the home of Thomas Cranmer, Archbishop of Canterbury, in 1538 and flattered King Henry VIII for attacking papal tyranny and breaking with Rome. Several of his plays were composed under Thomas Cromwell's patronage.

- In 1539, Bale fled into exile abroad with his wife and children following the reversal in Henry VIII's religious policy and the Act of the Six Articles. On the Continent, he wrote several anti-Catholic works, examining the treatment of Protestant martyrs, including Anne Askew. These works were used as a source by martyrologist John Foxe.
- Bale also used his work to attack Stephen Gardiner, Bishop of Winchester, for his persecution of Protestants, and risked trouble by organising the smuggling of religious tracts to England.
- His major work, "Illustrium majoris Britanniae scriptorum" was published in Wesel in 1548.
- Bale returned to England during Edward VI's reign, residing at the Duchess of Richmond's house in London with John Foxe. In 1551, he was granted the living of Bishopstoke in Hampshire and then made vicar of Swaffham in Norfolk.
- In 1552, King Edward VI made him Bishop of Ossory in Ireland, and he was consecrated in Dublin in February 1553, causing controversy by refusing the traditional Catholic consecration rites. He also had boys act out his morality plays in Kilkenny on Sunday afternoons. However, he did manage to do what John Dudley, Duke of Northumberland, Lord President of Edward VI's council, wanted him to do – he converted a number of people with his preaching.
- He lived in Kilkenny until the accession of the Catholic Queen Mary I in the summer of 1553 led to him attempting to flee into exile once more. He set sail from Dublin for the Netherlands in September 1553 but was intercepted and taken prisoner on a Dutch man-of-war. The ship had to dock at St Ives in Cornwall due to bad weather, and Bale was arrested there, accused of treason, but then released. He was arrested once more at Dover when he tried to leave the country again, but although he was held for several weeks, he managed to pay his way out and travel on to the Continent.
- While in exile, he focused on his writing and in Frankfurt, in September 1554, he participated in the disputations among the Protestant exiles there.

- Bale returned to England after the accession of Elizabeth I, and in 1560 he was made a canon of a prebend of Canterbury Cathedral.
- In 1561, he published an attack on Edmund Bonner, the Catholic bishop of London, and in 1563 he attended Convocation. However, he was dead by 26th November 1563 and was laid to rest at Canterbury.

Trivia: for those interested in the Boleyns, John Bale wrote of George Boleyn, Lord Rochford, brother of Queen Anne Boleyn, describing his "rythmos elegantissimos" and how he was the author of some of the most elegant poetry of the age.

22 November

On 22nd November 1594, naval commander, privateer and explorer Sir Martin Frobisher died at Plymouth from gangrene. He had been shot in the thigh during hand-to-hand combat during the Siege of Fort Crozon.

Frobisher is known for the three voyages he made to the New World in search of the Northwest Passage and his service during the Spanish Armada, for which he was knighted. After the Armada, he became one of Elizabeth I's most trusted officers and commanders.

But let me tell you more about this Elizabethan explorer.

Sir Martin Frobisher was born in Altofts, near Normanton, West Yorkshire, in around 1535. He was the son of Bernard Frobisher and Margaret Yorke. After his mother's death, he was sent to live in London with his mother's relative, Sir John Yorke, a merchant adventurer.

Frobisher took part in a voyage to Guinea in 1553, which Yorke had invested in and Thomas Wyndham had led. He acted as assistant to John Beryn, Yorke's factor. A fever wiped out over two-thirds of the crew, including Wyndham, but Beryn and Frobisher survived. In 1554, Frobisher took part in a voyage to Guinea led by John Lok and ended up being taken into custody by the Portuguese and held by them for 2-3 years.

In 1559, Frobisher commanded a voyage to Barbary and then became a privateer. He was imprisoned in 1563 in Launceston gaol after being involved, with his brother John, in the capture of the Katherine, a Spanish ship, but was released in 1564. In 1565, the brothers set off on board the May Flower bound for Guinea to trade but were apprehended on suspicion of piracy and imprisoned. Frobisher was free by October 1566 when Cardinal Châtillon issued him with letters of reprisal, i.e. a licence to attack and capture enemy vessels, to attack French Catholic ships supported by the Guises. Unfortunately, Frobisher didn't just attack these ships and so was arrested in the summer of 1569 and imprisoned, first at the Fleet and then in Marshalsea. He was released following the intervention of Lord Admiral Edward Fiennes de Clinton and William Cecil.

In 1574, Frobisher and Michael Lok, a merchant adventurer and the London agent of the Russia Company, set about planning a voyage to find the Strait of Anian, a northwest passage to the Far East. They set out on 12th June 1576, with Frobisher as commander, after getting the necessary patent from the Russia Company and backing from members of Elizabeth I's privy council, like Ambrose Dudley, Earl of Warwick. Their party consisted of the Gabriel and Michael, two small barks, and a 7-ton pinnace. They lost the pinnace in a storm in the Davis Strait, which lies between mid-western Greenland and Canada's Baffin Island, and the Michael was forced to turn back. However, Frobisher carried on in the Gabriel until a falling out with some Inuit, and the abduction of five Englishmen by the Inuits, combined with bad weather, forced him to return home to England.

Frobisher's second voyage left England on 31st May 1577. Along with the Gabriel and Michael, Frobisher had the Ayde, a former Royal Navy ship provided by Queen Elizabeth I, and 150 men. This time, the aim was not to find the passage but to find ore. Christopher Hall, master of the Gabriel, had found some black ore on what became known as Little Hall's Island on the last voyage, so the plan was to mine for it. Nothing was found when the part inspected Little Hall's Island, but 160 tons were mined from what became known as the Countess of Warwick Mine, on Kodlunarn Island, in Frobisher Bay. They then returned to England.

The hope of finding gold and the need to set up a colony led to a third voyage leaving on 3rd June 1578. This time, Frobisher had a fleet of fifteen ships. The party landed briefly at Friesland, the southern tip of Greenland, before heading to the Countess of Warwick Island. What should have been a short journey took four weeks due to storms, fog and icebergs. Frobisher's biographer, James McDermott, notes that during this treacherous journey, "elements of Frobisher's fleet became the first English ships to enter what is now Hudson Strait". They finally made it to the island and were able to mine 1370 tons of ore to take back to England. Unfortunately, nothing of value was found in the ore, and the colony failed. With all its debts, the enterprise came to a halt, and Frobisher fell from favour.

Frobisher did nothing of note until 1585 when, having managed to get back in royal favour, he was appointed as vice-admiral to Sir Francis Drake for his raiding of Spanish ports and ships in the West Indies. In 1587, he was the commander of a small fleet in the English channel and in April 1588, having been deemed to be one of "those which I think the world doth judge to be men of greatest experience that this realm hath" by Lord Admiral Howard, he was given command of the Triumph, one of Elizabeth I's navy's four "great ships" against the Spanish Armada. James McDermott writes:

"At dawn on 23 July the Triumph and five armed merchantmen were separated from the rest of the English fleet off Portland Bill. Frobisher appears to have intended this. Attacked by the four galliasses of the Armada (probably the best-armed Spanish ships, and highly manoeuvrable in the calm waters of that morning) he conducted a master class in close-in fighting—supposedly the galliasses' forte—which had them fighting in turn for their own survival. Eventually 'rescued' by other English ships, Frobisher had in fact achieved the first tactical victory over vessels of the Armada since Drake's seizure of the Rosario two nights earlier."

The following day, Lord Admiral Howard chose Frobisher as one of four commanders of the English fleet, which had been divided into four squadrons. Frobisher attempted an attack on the San Martin, the Spanish flagship. Things looked bad when a change in wind direction led to the Triumph and two other English ships being isolated and then attacked by the Spanish fleet. Still, another change in the wind and the skills of the English sailors led to them safely returning to the rest of the squadron. Frobisher was knighted the next day on the Ark Royal, the English flagship. The Triumph was also involved in the Battle of Gravelines on 29th July.

Frobisher's service in Elizabeth I's navy made him one of the queen's most trusted officers. Later campaigns and voyages included command of squadrons in the Atlantic to intercept and disrupt Spanish trade and command of the fleet that took Sir John Norreys and the English army to Brittany in 1594. Frobisher was injured in hand-to-hand combat on 7th November 1594, when he led a force against the fortress's main gate at the Siege of Fort Crozon. The injury he sustained was a pistol wound to the thigh. On 22nd November 1594, shortly after the English fleet landed at Plymouth, Frobisher died of gangrene. His entrails were buried at St Andrew's Church, Plymouth, and his body was taken back to London and buried at St Giles-without-Cripplegate.

Trivia: Frobisher Bay in Nunavut, Canada, is named after him.

23 November

On 23rd November 1598, scrivener and sailor Edward Squire was executed. He was hanged, drawn and quartered at Tyburn for treason after being accused of plotting in Seville to poison Elizabeth I and the Earl of Essex.

Nothing is known of Squire's early life, but he moved to Greenwich in 1582, where he worked as a scrivener, i.e. someone who writes or copies documents, and then he married in 1587. Five years later, he was working in the queen's stables.

In August 1595, Squire accompanied explorer Sir Francis Drake on his final voyage. Squire sailed on a small barque, the Francis, which became separated from the rest of Drake's fleet off the coast of Guadeloupe. The Spanish captured the ship, and Squire and his companion, Richard Rolls, were taken prisoner. They were taken to Seville, in southern Spain, where Squire, a Protestant, had contact with English Jesuits at their seminary before being released.

Squire returned to England, arriving there in July 1597, and then accompanied Robert Devereux, Earl of Essex, on his voyage to the Azores.

Squire was back in England by October 1598, when he was

arrested, interrogated and tried for treason. Just a month later, on this day in 1598, Squire was hanged, drawn and quartered at Tyburn as a traitor.

But how did this scrivener and sailor end up being accused of treason?

It was alleged that while he was in Seville in April 1597, the formerly Protestant Squire was converted to Catholicism by Jesuit Richard Walpole and that Squire was released from confinement in Seville to return to England to assassinate the queen. Squire would return to his job working in the royal stables and would poison the queen's saddle. Then, while on the voyage to the Azores, in September 1597, he'd allegedly planned to poison the queen's favourite, the leader of the voyage, the Earl of Essex. Squire confessed to these dastardly deeds under torture.

Contemporary historian William Camden gave an account in his "The history of the most renowned and victorious Princess Elizabeth, late queen of England", writing:

> "This Walpole procured him to be drawn into the Inquisition, as a man guilty of heresy, where after he had endured much affliction, he easily persuaded him to turn to the Romish religion, and afterwards exhorted him several times to attempt something for the cause and service or religion. At length with many circumlocutions he told him (as Squire himself confessed) that it was a meritorious act to kill the Earl of Essex, but more necessary to make away the Queen: which he told him might easily be done, and without any danger, by anointing the pommel of the Queen's saddle with poison, upon which she was to lay her hand as she rode."

Camden goes on to say that Squire gave his assent to the plan, being bound by Walpole "by several vows under pain of damnation" to keep it secret and to commit the dastardly deed, and, in return, being promised eternal salvation.

Camden writes of how Squire did anoint the queen's saddle with poison "crying at the same instant with a loud voice God save the Queen: but by God's mercy, the poison took no effect", and that he also "besmeared" the Earl of Essex's chair with the same poison during their voyage together, but again the poison did not work.

According to Camden, Squire's assassination attempts came to light when Walpole, who suspected that Squire had "deluded him" and broken his vows, took revenge by having someone inform on him. Camden goes on to write of how Squire confessed during interrogations, but at his trial and at the gallows "that though he were put on by Walpole and others to commit the Fact, yet he could never be persuaded in his heart to do it."

This story of Squire and Walpole was disputed by an English priest who'd been in Seville then. He stated that Squire got into trouble with the Inquisition for publicly defending Protestantism but that he escaped and fled home to England rather than being released or sent on an assassination mission by Walpole. Another man, Thomas Fitzherbert, who had served as secretary to Philip of Spain, later claimed that the Jesuits had not been involved in any such plot against Essex and the queen.

Whatever the truth, Squire went to his execution, suffering a full traitor's death, and prayers of thanksgiving were said for the queen's escape from his plot.

24 November

On Saturday 24th November 1487, the coronation procession of Elizabeth of York, queen consort of Henry VII, took place in London.

Henry Tudor had become King Henry VII following the defeat of King Richard III at the Battle of Bosworth Field on 22nd August 1485, and he united the Houses of Lancaster and York when he married Elizabeth of York, daughter of the late King Edward IV, on 18th January 1486. Elizabeth gave birth to their first child, Arthur, in September 1486.

Elizabeth's coronation was postponed due to her pregnancy and then to unrest in the country - the Cornish Rebellion and Perkin Warbeck, for example, but was scheduled for 25th November 1487.

On Friday 23rd November 1487, Elizabeth left Greenwich and travelled by water, along the River Thames, to the Tower of London. She was accompanied by her mother-in-law, Lady Margaret

Beaufort, Countess of Richmond, and a procession of decorated barges containing peers and peeresses, the Lord Mayor, sheriffs and aldermen. One barge stood out in particular as it carried a red dragon that spouted fire! When she got to the Tower, she was welcomed by her husband, the king. Eleven Knights of the Bath were created that night. Then, on this day in history, 24th November 1487, Elizabeth had her coronation procession, processing through the streets of London, from the Tower to Westminster.

The Memoir of Elizabeth York by 19th-century historian Nicholas Harris Nicolas, which appears with the Privy Purse Expenses of Elizabeth of York, which Nicolas edited, gives an account of this day drawn from primary sources:

"[...] On the next day, after dinner, her Majesty being royally apparelled in a kirtle of white cloth of gold damask, and a mantle of the same suit, furred with ermine, fastened before her breast with a great lace, curiously wrought of gold and silk, and rich knobs of gold at the end, tasselled; her fair yellow hair hanging down plain behind her back, with a caul of pipes over it, and wearing on her head a circle of gold, richly garnished with precious stones, quitted her chamber of state. Her train was borne by her sister, the Lady Cecily, and being attended by a great retinue of lords, ladies and others, she entered her litter, in which she was conveyed to Westminster. Most of the streets, which were lined with the city companies in their liveries, were hung with tapestry and arras, whilst in Cheapside, and some other places, rich cloths of gold and velvets and silks were displayed. The houses were filled with spectators, and the crowd is represented as being immense, all eager to see the Queen in her royal apparel, a feeling which had perhaps a deeper source than the gratification of idle curiosity. Children in the dresses of angels and virgins were placed in various parts, who sung the Queen's praises as she passed; and preceded by the Duke of Bedford as Lord Steward, the Earl of Oxford as Great Chamberlain, the Earl of Derby as Constable, and the Earl of Nottingham as Marshal of England, by the Duke of Suffolk, the Lord Mayor, Garter King of Arms, the Heralds, and other official persons, and by the newly made Knights of the Bath, with their banners borne before them, her Majesty proceeded through the city, sitting in a litter, under a canopy borne by the Knights of the body. Her sister Cecily, her aunt the Duchess of Bedford, the Duchesses of Norfolk and Suffolk, the Countess of Oxford, in two chairs, and six Baronnesses, mounted on palfreys, immediately followed the Queen; and in this order the procession arrived at Westminster, where she slept."

Elizabeth needed to rest to prepare for her coronation at Westminster Abbey the next day.

25 November

On 25th November 1487, the Feast of St Catherine, Elizabeth of York, queen consort of Henry VII and mother of one-year-old Arthur Tudor, was crowned queen at Westminster Abbey.

As I explained yesterday, Elizabeth's coronation celebrations had kicked off with a river procession from Greenwich to the Tower of London on the 23rd November, followed by the creation of eleven knights of the bath, and then, on 24th November, a coronation procession through the streets of London from the Tower to Westminster.

19th-century historian Nicholas Harris Nicolas writes of how, on the morning of 25th November 1487, Elizabeth proceeded from her lodgings to Westminster Hall dressed in "a kirtle and mantle of purple velvet, furred with ermine laced in front" and wearing a gold circlet set with pearls and jewels on her head. She processed into the abbey under a canopy of state, walking on new ray cloth, which was ripped to pieces by the crowd to take home as souvenirs after she had walked on it. The Earl of Arundel bore the staff with the dove, the Duke of Suffolk bore the sceptre, and the Duke of Bedford bore the crown. The Bishops of Winchester and Ely flanked Elizabeth, and behind her walked her sister, Cecily, holding her train. Nicolas writes of how she entered Westminster Abbey by the west door and made her way to a seat near the pulpit. Her husband, King Henry VII, watched proceedings from a latticed stage between the pulpit and high altar.

Nicolas states that her coronation "was attended by fifteen bishops, seventeen abbots, two dukes, twelve earls, two viscounts, twenty barons, the heirs apparent of the Earls of Suffolk and Devonshire; the King's mother, and the Lady Cecily, the Queen's sister, three duchesses, four countesses, seven baronesses, thirty-one knight bannerets, one hundred and fifty knights, besides their wives and other gentlewomen; but neither the Queen's mother, nor any of her sisters, excepting Cecily, appear to have been present."

Historian Amy Licence, in her biography of Elizabeth of York, which I would highly recommend, explains that at her coronation, Elizabeth "was anointed twice before the huge assembly of nobles, once on the chest and once on the head before receiving a ring for the fourth finger of her right hand, a gold crown, sceptre and rod of gold." Elizabeth then processed from the abbey to Westminster Hall, where a sumptuous coronation banquet was held in her honour. Henry VII and his mother, Lady Margaret Beaufort, viewed the banquet from a latticed stage which Nicolas says was "erected out of a window on the left side of the hall."

In the book "Elizabeth of York", A. Okerlund lists the food served at the coronation banquet, which a herald recorded. The first course included boar, venison, broth, pheasant, swan, crane, pike, heron, carp, kid (baby goat), rabbit and fruit desserts, and then a "soteltie, with writing of balads", a subtlety usually being an amazing display of marchpane, pastry or spun sugar which would have been moulded into a building or animal. The second course included hippocras, broth, peacock, bittern, partridge, sturgeon, seal, quails, larks, crayfish, quince, marchpane, fritters, jellied desserts, castles made from jelly, and another subtlety.

After the Garter King of Arms had proclaimed Elizabeth's titles and thanks had been given to her, it was time to wrap up the banquet with fruit and wafers and then hippocras and wafers. Then, according to the records, "the queen departed with God's blessing, and to the rejoicing of many a true Englishman's heart".

It was the end of a long day for the queen.

Elizabeth of York was Henry VII's queen consort from their

marriage in January 1486 until her death on 11th February 1503. Henry VII never remarried, and he died in April 1509.

26 November

On 26th November 1585, Catholic priest Hugh Taylor and his friend Marmaduke Bowes were executed in York.

They were both hanged and were the first men executed under the 1585 statute, which made it treason to be a Jesuit or seminary priest in England, or to harbour such a priest. Both men were beatified in 1987 by Pope John Paul II as two of the 85 Martyrs of England, Scotland and Wales.

Let me tell you more about these Catholic martyrs.

- Hugh Taylor was a Durham man who attended the English College, a seminary college, at Reims in May 1582 and became ordained as a priest.
- In March 1585, he returned to England, having been sent there on a mission to convert people to what he viewed as the true faith, Catholicism. However, he was apprehended in York when a search was done of a Catholic man's house, and it appears that the house belonged to Marmaduke Bowes, who was harbouring the priest.
- Bowes was married with children, for whom he had employed a Catholic tutor. He also harboured priests.
- Taylor and Bowes were condemned at York Castle on 24th November 1585 by the Commissioners of the North, and they went to their deaths on Friday 26th November 1585.
- In "Lives of the English Martyrs", Edward Burton and J. H. Pollen quote an account of the execution by a Father Grene:

"At York, Mr. Taylor, having received sentence of death with a layman on a Thursday and on the following day, Friday, having said Mass and his office; ' How happy,' said he, ' should I be, if on this day, on which Christ died for me, I might encounter death for Him '. Scarcely had he said this when the officer unexpectedly came to lead him off to execution, and leaving the layman for Saturday (the usual day for executions) put him immediately to death." The layman mentioned here as dying the next day is Bowes, but some sources state he was executed with Taylor on 26th.

- Taylor was the first priest to suffer under the act against seminary priests, and Bowes was the first layman to suffer for harbouring a priest.
- Elizabeth I and her government had been forced to act against Jesuits and those who helped them following her excommunication in 1570 by Pope Pius V. The pope not only excommunicated the queen, he absolved Catholics from any oaths they had made to her and called on them to disobey her orders, mandates and laws, and threatened excommunication for those who did obey her. This made Jesuits sent on missions to convert English people to Catholicism a real danger and enemies of the state.

27 November

On 27th November 1531 (some say 4th December), Benedictine monk and reformer Richard Bayfield was burnt at the stake at Smithfield for heresy. He'd been caught importing heretical books into England.

Let me tell you a bit more about this Protestant martyr.

- Bayfield was originally from Hadleigh in Suffolk, and his use of the alias Somersam suggests that his family was originally from nearby Somersham.
- He was ordained as a priest in 1518 at Bury St Edmunds Abbey and became chamberlain of the abbey. His role as chamberlain meant that Bayfield was in charge of organising lodgings for visitors, and this was how he met reformer Robert Barnes, who was visiting the abbey. The two men became good friends. During Barnes' time at the abbey, he was visited by brickmakers and Lollards, Lawrence Maxwell and John Stacy, who Bayfield also came to know, and who, like Barnes, influenced his faith. Barnes gave Bayfield a copy of the New Testament in Latin, and the Lollards gave him Tyndale's New Testament in English,

along with "The Wicked Mammon", and "The Obedience of a Christian Man".

- Due to his changing faith, Bayfield ended up imprisoned at the abbey and, according to martyrologist John Foxe, whipped and put in the stocks. Fortunately, Barnes was able to get his friend released and took him to Cambridge on his release. There, Bayfield came into contact with other like-minded men, including Thomas Bilney and Thomas Arthur.
- In 1526, Barnes was apprehended for heresy and imprisoned in the Fleet, and Bayfield was sheltered by his Lollard friends, Maxwell and Stacy, before spending a few months overseas.
- In 1528, Bayfield was arrested and brought before Cuthbert Tunstall, Bishop of London, to answer charges of heresy "for affirming and holding certain articles contrary to the holy church, and especially that all laud and praise should be given to God alone, and not to saints or creatures", and for saying that every priest could preach God's Word by authority of the Gospel, and without the need for a licence. He was convicted of heresy but, according to his later trial, "abjured the said articles" and promised to change his ways and avoid heresy, making a solemn oath on the book. He was ordered to do penance and return to Bury St Edmunds wearing his monk's habit. Bayfield refused to wear his habit but returned to Bury temporarily before fleeing into exile in the Low Countries, avoiding completing his penance. There, he began supplying England with books about the reformed faith, including works by Luther and Zwingli. He sent two consignments in 1530 and another in 1531.
- Unfortunately for Bayfield, his second and third consignments were intercepted by Sir Thomas More, Henry VIII's Lord Chancellor, a staunch Catholic.
- In late 1531, Bayfield was arrested in London while visiting a bookbinder. John Foxe writes of how he was betrayed and followed to the bookbinder's. He was imprisoned first in Lollards' Tower at Lambeth and then in the Coal House Prison. Foxe describes how he was "tied both by the neck, middle, and legs, standing upright by the walls, divers times manacled"

in the hope that he'd share the names of other people involved in importing heretical works but he would not. More interrogated him. On 10ᵗʰ November 1531, at St Paul's, Bayfield was tried by John Stokesley, who'd become Bishop of London the previous year, for his relapse of heresy.

- Bayfield's trial lasted several days, but it was found that he had "abjured certain, errors and heresies, and damnable opinions", and that he had "brought in, divers and sundry times, many books of the said Martin Luther, and his adherents and complices, and of other heretics". The court deprived him of his ecclesiastical office and pronounced him a relapsed heretic due to him going back on his promises to Bishop Tunstall. Foxe describes how Bayfield "with a vehement spirit, (as it appeared,) said unto the bishop of London, "The life of you of the spiritualty is so evil, that ye be heretics; and ye do not only live evil, but do maintain evil living, and also do let, that what true living is, may not be known;" and said that their living is against Christ's gospel, and that their belief was never taken of Christ's church." On 20ᵗʰ November 1531, he was sentenced and turned over to the sheriffs to take him to Newgate Prison. Then, on 27ᵗʰ November 1531, he was taken to St Paul's where, again, the Bishop of London degraded him and, according to Foxe, "took his crosier-staff, and smote him on the breast, that he threw him down backwards, and brake his head, that he swooned". When Bayfield came round, "he thanked God that he was delivered from the malignant church of antichrist, and that he was come into the true sincere church of Jesus Christ, militant here in earth."
- He was led back to Newgate, where he prayed for an hour before being taken to the stake at Smithfield. Foxe writes that Bayfield "went to the fire in his apparel manfully and joyfully, and there, for lack of a speedy fire, was two quarters of an hour alive. And when the left arm was on fire and burned, he rubbed it with his right hand, and it fell from his body, and he continued in prayer to the end without moving."
- Foxe goes on to say that Sir Thomas More set about maligning Bayfield's memory by claiming that he was a bigamist, having a

wife in England and another in Brabant, but there's no evidence to support More's story.

28 November

On this day in Tudor history, 28th November 1499, Edward Plantagenet, styled Earl of Warwick, was executed by beheading on Tower Hill.

Edward was born in February 1475 and was the eldest and only surviving son of George, Duke of Clarence, brother of Edward IV and Richard III, and his wife Isabel, daughter of Richard Neville, Earl of Warwick, the Kingmaker. Edward IV stood as his godfather and proclaimed the infant Earl of Warwick.

His father, the Duke of Clarence, was attainted in 1478, so the Crown seized Edward's inheritance, the Warwick lands. In 1481, his wardship was granted to Thomas Grey, Marquess of Dorset, eldest son of Elizabeth Woodville by her first husband.

Edward attended Richard III's coronation in July 1483 and was knighted in September 1483 when Richard III's son, Edward Middleham, became Prince of Wales. As Edward, Earl of Warwick, was a potential claimant to the throne, he was kept in custody at Sheriff Hutton, a property owned by Richard III. He was moved to the Tower of London on Henry VII's accession.

Chronicler Raphael Holinshed records that the earl "almost from his tender years" was confined "out of all company of men and sight of beasts in so much that he could not discern a goose from a capon" and that he was "a verie innocent". Holinshed states that the pretender Perkin Warbeck, who was imprisoned in the Tower in 1498, "corrupted his keepers, by false persuasions and great promises" and that in 1499 they plotted to free Warbeck and the Earl of Warwick, who did not "himself seek his own death and destruction. But yet by the drift and offence of another he was brought to his death and confusion." According to Holinshed, Warwick, who wanted his freedom, assented and agreed to the plot. The plot was discovered, and on 21st November 1499, Warwick was arraigned at Westminster before the Earl of Oxford, High Steward of England, where he was accused of conspiring to depose King Henry VII. He was condemned to death and executed by beheading on Tower Hill on 28th November 1499 (some sources say 29th November), five days after Perkin Warbeck was hanged at Tyburn.

Warwick may have been involved in Warbeck's plot, but another factor in his execution is the marriage match negotiated between England and Spain. Raphael Holinshed states that Ferdinand II of Aragon, father of Catherine of Aragon, "would make no full conclusion of the matrimony to be had between Prince Arthur and the lady Katharine daughter to the said Ferdinando, nor send her into England as long as this earl lived. For he imagined that so long as any earl of Warwick lived, England should never be purged of civil war and privy sedition, so much was the name of Warwick in other regions had in fear and jealousy."

Whatever the reason, Edward, Earl of Warwick, a potential claimant to the throne of England, was executed on this day in 1499 at 24. He was survived by his sister, Margaret, who had married Sir Richard Pole in 1487. Margaret Pole, Countess of Salisbury, was herself executed by beheading at the Tower of London in 1541 after being attainted for treason, accused of aiding and abetting her son, Cardinal Reginald Pole. The Cardinal was alleged to be planning to marry the king's daughter, Mary, and restore papal supremacy in England.

29 November

On 29th November 1528, nobleman and courtier Anthony Browne, 1st Viscount Montagu, was born.

Montagu was prominent in Mary I's reign, with his offices including Master of the Horse to Philip of Spain, Lord Lieutenant of Sussex and Privy Councillor.

Let me give you a few facts about this Tudor man.

- Anthony was the eldest son of Sir Anthony Browne of Cowdray Park, Sussex, and his first wife, Alice, daughter of Sir John Gage.
- His father had been so trusted by King Henry VIII that he had held a dry stamp of the king's signature. His aunt, Elizabeth, Countess of Worcester, was one of Anne Boleyn's ladies. According to Lancelot de Carle, she made allegations about the

queen's behaviour with Mark Smeaton and her brother, Lord Rochford.

- In 1545, when he was just 16, Anthony served as Member of Parliament for Guildford, in Surrey, due to his father's influence and was joint standard-bearer of England with his father in 1546. He served as equerry of the stable, under his father as Master of the Horse, in early 1547 and was created a Knight of the Bath in Edward VI's coronation celebrations in February 1547.
- Anthony married when he was about 18 in 1546, taking Jane Radcliffe, daughter of Robert Radcliffe, Earl of Sussex, as his wife. They had a son, Anthony and a daughter, Mary. Jane sadly died in July 1552.
- Following his father's death in 1548, Anthony lost his position as standard-bearer. He had been raised Catholic and supported Princess Mary during Edward VI's reign, so he was not given any important offices. However, he served as an MP for Guildford and Petersfield and sheriff for Surrey and Sussex.
- During the succession crisis of July 1553, he did nothing to support Queen Jane, or Lady Jane Grey, and he rose in Mary I's reign.
- He was appointed keeper of Guildford Park in October 1553, then in 1554, steward of Hampton Court chase and a Justice of the Peace for Surrey and Sussex.
- In 1554, he was appointed as Philip of Spain's Master of the Horse, but on his arrival in England, Philip chose to replace Anthony and other Englishmen with Spaniards. However, as part of the celebrations for Mary and Philip's wedding in 1554, he was made Viscount Montagu and then, in 1555, elected as a Knight of the Garter.
- In 1555, Anthony was also sent as an ambassador to Rome to talk to the pope about Mary's restoration of Catholicism in England.
- In 1556, Anthony married his second wife, Magdalen Dacre, daughter of William Dacre, 3rd Baron Dacre. The couple went on to have eight children: five sons and three daughters.

- In 1556, he acted as an executor of the will of Stephen Gardiner, Bishop of Winchester and Mary's Lord Chancellor, and chief mourner.
- In 1557, Anthony served as lieutenant-general under William Herbert, 1st Earl of Pembroke, at Calais and the Siege of St Quentin and was appointed to the queen's privy council.
- Mary I died in November 1558, and Anthony was one of the executors of her will and acted as a chief mourner at her funeral.
- As a Catholic conservative, Anthony was relieved of his position on the privy council on the accession of Elizabeth I, and he went on to oppose Elizabeth's plans for religious reform in 1559. Personally, however, he did manage to keep on the right side of the new queen and acted in a diplomatic capacity for her in Spain in 1560 and 1565, and the Low Countries in 1565.
- By the 1560s, Anthony was a wealthy man, with an annual income of between £2,000-3,000.
- In 1569, at the time of the Rising of the North, he acted as joint Lord Lieutenant of Sussex. Still, he and his son-in-law, Henry Wriothesley, 2nd Earl of Southampton, did become implicated in the rebellion and even set sail for Flanders, being driven back by the wind. However, they went unpunished.
- In 1570, Southampton was arrested and confined to the home of the Sheriff of London after having a secret meeting with the Scottish Bishop of Ross, following Elizabeth I's excommunication. In 1571, he was also implicated in the Ridolfi Plot. However, Anthony was not caught up in it. Southampton was released and allowed to reside at Cowdray House with his father-in-law in 1573.
- In 1585, when trouble began with Spain, Anthony was removed from his office of Lord Lieutenant, but in 1586 he was appointed as one of the commissioners for the trial of Mary, Queen of Scots.
- In 1588, he supported his queen against the Spanish Armada by leading horsemen, aided by his son, Anthony, and grandson, Anthony-Maria.

- In August 1591, he played host to Queen Elizabeth I for six days at his estate at Cowdray, and the queen knighted his second son, George, and his son-in-law, Robert Dormer.
- Anthony Browne, 1ˢᵗ Viscount Montagu, died at his manor of West Horsely in Surrey on 19ᵗʰ October 1592 following what was described as a "tedious, troublesome, and lingering kind of infirmity." He was 63 years of age. His grandson, Anthony Maria Browne, was his heir, inheriting a large fortune worth between £3,600 and £5,400 per year.
- On 6ᵗʰ December 1592, Anthony was laid to rest at Midhurst, but was moved to St Mary's Church in Easebourne, Sussex, in the 19ᵗʰ century. His tomb is marble and alabaster and is topped with a kneeling effigy of Anthony and recumbent effigies of his wives. His second wife died in 1608.

30 November

On 30ᵗʰ November 1601, sixty-eight-year-old Queen Elizabeth I delivered her famous *Golden Speech* to the House of Commons to address their concerns over England's economic state of affairs. It was the last speech she gave to Parliament, and as the National Archives page about this speech points out, the queen had been expected to address members' economic concerns and concerns about rising prices. However, instead, Elizabeth addressed these issues in a royal proclamation and used her speech to the Commons for something completely different. She spoke of her position as queen and her love and respect for her realm, her people, and her members of Parliament.

It was a fitting speech for her final Parliament, given by a queen who had ruled for 43 years.

There are several versions of this speech, and in a version printed in the Harleian Miscellany, the editor writes,

> "This Speech ought to be set in Letters of Gold, that as well the Majesty, Prudence, and Virtue of her gracious Majesty, Queen Elisabeth, might in general most exquisitely appear ; as also that her Religious Love, and tender Respect, which she particularly, and constantly, did bear to her Parliament, in unfeigned

Sincerity, might be nobly and truly vindicated, and proclaimed, with all grateful Recognition to God for so great a Blessing to his People of England, in vouchsafing them heretofore such a gracious Princess, and magnanimous Defender of the Reformed Religion, and heroick Patroness of the Liberty of her Subjects, in the Freedom and Honour of their Parliaments ; which have been, under God, the continual Conservators of the Splendor, and Wealth of this Kingdom, against Tyranny and Oppression."

So perhaps the name of the speech, the Golden Speech, comes from the idea that it should have been printed in gold letters!

Diarist and MP Hayward Townshend gives a version of the speech in his "Commons Journal", printed in "Historical Collections: Or, An Exact Account of the Proceedings of the Four Last Parliaments of Q. Elizabeth". Townshend sets the scene by explaining that 140 members of the Commons attended the Queen at Whitehall at 3 o'clock in the afternoon, plus the Speaker of the House, and that she sat under a cloth of state as she listened to the speaker of the house make a speech to her. In his speech, he thanked her for her "most abundant Goodness, extended and performed to Us", her "sacred ears" that were "ever open" to them and her "blessed hands" that "ever stretched out" to relieve them, and went on to call on the queen to watch over them for their "good". He closed by saying:

"'But, in all Duty and Thankfulness, prostrate at Your Feet, We present our most Loyal and Thankful Hearts; even 'the last Drop of Blood in our Hearts, and the last Spirit of Breath in our Nostrils, to be pour'd out, to be Breathed up for Your Safety."

The Commons then fell to their knees, and the queen addressed them:

"WE have heard your Declaration, and perceive your Care of Our State, by falling into the Consideration of a grateful Acknowledgment of such Benefits as you have Received; and that your Coming is to present Thanks unto Us, which I Accept with no less Joy, than your Loves can have Desire to offer such a Present.

I do assure you, There is no Prince that loveth his Subjects better, or whose Love can countervail Our Love. There is no Jewel, be it of never so Rich a Price, which I set before this Jewel; I mean, your Love: For I do more Esteem of It, than of any Treasure or Riches; for That we know how to prize, but Love and Thanks I count Unvaluable.

And, though God hath raised Me high; yet This I count the Glory of my Crown, That I have Reigned with your Loves. This makes me that I do not so much rejoyce, That God hath made Me to be a Queen, as, To be a Queen over so Thankful a People.

Therefore, I have Cause to wish nothing more, than to Content the Subjects; and that is a Duty which I owe: Neither do I desire to live longer Dayes, than that I may see your Prosperity; and That's my only Desire.

And as I am that Person, that still (yet under God) hath Deliver'd you; so I trust, (by the Almighty Power of God) that I still shall be His Instrument to Preserve you from Envy, Peril, Dishonour, Shame, Tyranny, and Oppression; partly by Means of your intended Helps, which We take very Acceptably, because it manifests the Largeness of your Loves and Loyalty to your Sovereign.

Of My Self, I must say this, I was never any greedy scraping Grasper, nor a straight, fast-holding Prince, nor yet a Waster. My Heart was never set on Worldly Goods, but only for my Subjects Good. What You do bestow on Me, I will not hoard it up, but Receive it to bestow on You again: Yea, My own Proprieties I count Yours, and to be Expended for your Good; and your Eyes shall see the Bestowing of All, for your Good. Therefore, render unto Them from Me, I beseech you, Mr. Speaker, such Thanks as you imagine my Heart yieldeth, but my Tongue cannot express."

The queen then stopped to bid her listeners to get up off their knees, saying "Mr. Speaker, I would wish You, and the Rest to stand up; for I shall yet trouble you with longer Speech..."
And then she continued:

"You give Me Thanks; but I doubt Me, that I have more Cause to Thank You all, than You Me. And I charge you, to Thank them of the Lower-House, from Me: For had I not received a Knowledge from you, I might have fallen into the Lapse of an Errour, only for Lack of True Information.

Since I was Queen, yet, did I never put my Pen unto any Grant, but that, upon Pretext and Semblance made unto Me, it was both Good and Beneficial to the Subject in general; though a private Profit to some of My Ancient Servants, who had deserved well at My Hands. But the Contrary being found by Experience, I am exceedingly beholding to such Subjects, as would move the same at the first. And I am not so Simple to suppose, but that there are some of the Lower-House, whom these Grievances never touched. And for Them, I think they spake out of Zeal for their Countries, and not out of Spleen, or Malevolent Affection, as being Parties grieved. And I take it exceeding Gratefully from them; because it gives Us to know, that no Respects or Interests had moved them other than the minds they bear to suffer no diminution of our Honour, and our subjects Loves unto Us. The zeal of which Affection, tending to ease my People, and Knit their hearts unto Me, I embrace with a Princely care; for (above all earthly Treasure) I esteem my People's Love, more than which I desire not to Merit.

'That my Grants should be grievous to my People, and Oppressions privileged under colour of our Patents; our Kingly Dignity shall not suffer it: yea, when I heard it, I could give no rest unto my Thoughts untill I had Reformed it.

Shall they think to escape unpunished, that have thus Oppressed you, and have been respectless of their Duty, and regardless of Our Honour? No, Mr. Speaker, I assure you, were it not more for Conscience-sake, than for any Glory or Increase of Love, that I desire; these Errours, Troubles, Vexations and Oppressions done by these Varlets and lewd Persons, not worthy the name of Subjects, should not escape without Condigne Punishment. But I perceive they dealt with Me like Physicians, who Administering a Drug, make it more acceptable by giving it a good Aromatical Savour, or when they give Pills, do Gild them all over.

I have ever used to set the last Judgment-Day before my Eyes, as so to Rule, as I shall be Judged to Answer before a higher Judge, to whose Judgment Seat I do Appeal, That never Thought was Cherished in my Heart, that tended not to my People's Good. And now, if my Kingly Bounty have been abused, and my Grants turned to the Hurt of my People, contrary to My Will and Meaning; or if any in Authority under Me, have neglected or perverted what I have Committed to them; I hope God will not lay their Culps and Offences to my Charge; who though there were danger in repealing our Grants, yet what danger would I not rather incur for your Good, than I would suffer them still to continue?

I know the Title of a KING is a Glorious Title. But assure your self, That the Shining Glory of Princely Authority, hath not so dazelled the Eyes of our Understanding; but that we well know and remember that We also are to yield an Account of our Actions, before the Great Judge.

To be a KING, and wear a Crown, is a thing more Glorious to them that see it, than it is pleasing to them that bear it: For my self, I was never so much inticed with the Glorious Name of a KING, or Royal Authority of a QUEEN, as delighted that GOD had made Me his Instrument to maintain his Truth and Glory, and to Defend this Kingdom (as I said) from Peril, Dishonour, Tyranny, and Oppression.

There will never Queen sit in my Seat, with more Zeal to my country, Care for my Subjects, and that sooner with willingness will venture her Life for your Good and Safety, than My Self. For it is not my desire to Live nor Reign longer, than my Life and Reign shall be for your Good. And though you have had, and may have many Princes, more Mighty and Wife, sitting in this State; yet you never had, or shall have any that will be more Careful and Loving.

Shall I ascribe any thing to my Self, and my Sexly Weakness? I were not worthy to Live then; and of all, most unworthy of the great Mercies I have had from God, who hath ever yet given me a Heart, which never yet feared Foreign or Home-Enemy. I speak it to give God the Praise, as a Testimony before you, and not to Attribute any thing to My Self. For I, O Lord, What am I, whom Practices and Perils past should not fear? Or, What can I do? That I should speak for any Glory, God forbid.

This, Mr. Speaker, I pray you deliver to the House, to whom heartily commend Me. And so, I commit you All to your best Fortunes, and further Councels. And I pray you, Mr. Comptroller, Mr. Secretary, and You of My Councel, That before these Gentlemen depart into their Countries, you bring them All to Kiss My Hand."

And there, she ended her speech.

Townshend notes that she said, "For I, O Lord, What am I, whom Practices and Perils past should not fear? Or, What can I do? That I should speak for any Glory, God forbid" with great emphasis.

The speech had a major impact on those listening, with some leaving the room in tears. Elizabeth would never address Parliament again. She died on 24th March 1603, leaving the throne to King James VI of Scotland, son of Mary, Queen of Scots, who became King James I of England

1 December

On 1st December 1541, Thomas Culpeper, a member of King Henry VIII's privy chamber, and Francis Dereham, a secretary to Queen Catherine Howard, were tried for high treason at Guildhall, London. They had both been linked romantically with the queen.

Chronicler and Windsor Herald Charles Wriothesley records:

"This year, the first day of December, was arraigned at the Guild Hall in London, Thomas Culpepper, one of the Gentleman of the King's Privy Chamber, and Francis Dorand, gentleman, for high treason against the King's Majesty in misdemeanor with the Queen, as appeared by their indictments which they confessed, and had their judgments to be drawn, hanged, and quartered […]"

Eustace Chapuys, the imperial ambassador, wrote to his master, Emperor Charles V, of the proceedings:

"This same clerk was again sent on St. Andrews' day to tell me that the day after Colpeper and Durem (Durham) would be tried for high treason, begging me to send one of my secretaries to be present at the trial. The same notice and invitation has been handed round to the ambassador of France, to the Venetian Secretary, and to the gentleman of the duke of Clèves, who is still here. All the privy councillors witnessed the trial, which, after a long discussion lasting six hours, ended in the condemnation of the two abovementioned gentlemen, who were sentenced to be hung and quartered as traitors. Durem (Durham) did confess having known the Queen familiarly before she was either betrothed or promised to the King; but said he did not know that there was any wrong in that, inasmuch as they were then engaged to each other. Colpeper persisted in denying the guilt of which he was accused, maintaining that he never solicited or had anything to do with her; on the contrary, it was she who had importuned him through Mme. de Rochefort, requesting him (Colpeper) to go and meet her in a retired place in Lincolnshire, to which she appointed him, and that on that occasion he (Colpeper) having kept the appointment, she herself told him, as she had on the first instance sent him word through Mme. Rochefort, that she pined for him, and was actually dying of love for his person. It is thought that both will be beheaded to-day."

So, Dereham and Culpeper were both found guilty of treason and sentenced to be hanged, drawn and quartered. Both men were executed at Tyburn on 10th December 1541. Because of his status, Culpeper's sentence had been commuted to beheading, but Dereham had to suffer the full traitor's death of being hanged, drawn and quartered. Their heads were placed on pikes on London Bridge, and the quarters of Dereham's body were displayed around the city as a warning to other would-be traitors. Culpeper's remains were buried at St Sepulchre, Holborn.

But what about the queen and her lady, Jane Boleyn, Lady Rochford? What was happening with them? Well, Chapuys records:

"Dame de Rochefort would have been sentenced at the same time had she not, on the third day after her imprisonment, been seized with a fit of madness (frenesi) by which her brain is affected.

True is it that now and then she recovers her reason, and that the King takes care that his own physicians visit her daily, for he desires her recovery chiefly that he may afterwards have her executed as an example and warning to others.

The Queen is still at Syon House, and it is believed that the King, to show clemency in her case, will make no innovation whatever with regard to her, or do more than he has hitherto done until Parliament meets and decides what her fate is to be."

Catherine was at Syon, and Jane was being nursed back to health at Russell House on the Strand, the London residence of Sir John Russell, Lord Admiral, and his wife Anne, under the supervision of the king's own doctors. The king wanted Jane to be fit enough to execute.

On 21st January 1542, a bill of attainder against Catherine Howard and Lady Jane Rochford was introduced into the House of Lords.

According to this bill, the women were guilty of treason and could be punished without needing a trial. It received the king's assent on 11th February 1542. Jane was taken to the Tower of London on 9th February 1542, and Catherine was taken by barge from Syon to the Tower of London the following day. Both women were beheaded on 13th February 1542.

2 December

On 2nd December 1586, Parliament met following their request for Elizabeth I to sanction the execution of Mary, Queen of Scots, and the commissioners' meeting in the Star Chamber, where they had condemned her to death. A draft proclamation of sentence, written by Elizabeth and her chief advisor, William Cecil, Lord Burghley, was published at the Parliament. This was followed by the drafting of an execution warrant by Sir Francis Walsingham.

Mary, Queen of Scots, had been tried for treason at a trial that opened at Fotheringhay Castle on 14th October 1586. The Crown had provided evidence that not only did Mary know about the Babington Plot, a plot to assassinate Elizabeth and replace her with Mary, she had given it her approval. Mary had proclaimed her innocence, saying, "I would never make shipwreck of my soul by conspiring the destruction of my dearest sister", but after Babington had written to her of the plot, writing that six men, his "private friends", would be in charge of "that tragical execution", referring to the dispatch of Elizabeth, Mary had replied, "then shall it be time to set the gentlemen to work taking order upon the accomplishing of their design". Mary tried to argue that she hadn't specified what that "work" was, but it was no good. Although sentencing was delayed somewhat, she was found guilty on 25th October.

On 29th October 1586. the sixth Parliament of Elizabeth I's reign opened. The queen refused to attend the state opening because this Parliament would be discussing Mary. Mary had been found guilty of treason, but she was an anointed queen, albeit one that had been forced to abdicate, so there were questions regarding the legality of executing her. Elizabeth didn't want to commit regicide, but her privy council wanted Mary gone for good. The History of Parliament website, a wonderful source, explains how privy councillors Sir Christopher Hatton, Sir Walter Mildmay, Sir Ralph Sadler and John Wolley all gave speeches to the Commons in the opening days in support of Mary's execution.

On 5th November, Elizabeth's Lord Chancellor, Sir Thomas Bromley, addressed the Lords, declaring, "he foul and indirect dealings practised by the Queen of Scots against her Majesty and the whole Realm, notwithstanding so many great benefits and favours which the said Queen of Scots had received of her Majesty". On 9th November, "diverse" letters, including ones written by Anthony Babington and Mary were read out, as was the sentence pronounced by the commission that had tried Mary.

After both houses had deliberated, a joint petition from the Lords and Commons calling for Mary's execution was delivered to Elizabeth on 12th November. In it, they described their grief over the "most dangerous and execrable practices" of Mary, Queen of Scots", who had "compassed the destruction of your Majesties sacred and most Royal Person" and wanted "utterly to ruinate and overthrow the happy State and Common Weal of this most Noble Realm". They explained how they had carefully considered the proceedings against Mary and that they believed that if she did not receive "due punishment which by Justice and the Laws of this your Realm she hath so often and so many ways for her most wicked and detestable offences deserved" then Elizabeth "shall be exposed unto many more and those more secret and dangerous Conspiracies than before".

They concluded by writing:

> "We do most humbly beseech your most Excellent Majesty, that as well in respect of the continuance of the true Religion now professed amongst us, and of the safety of your most Royal Person and Estate, as in regard of the preservation and defence of us your most loving, dutiful and faithful Subjects, and the whole Common-Weal of this Realm, It may please your Highness to take speedy Order, That Declaration of the same Sentence and Judgment be made and published by Proclamation, and that thereupon direction be given for further proceedings against the said Scottish Queen according

to the effect and true meaning of the said Statute : Because upon advised and great consultation we cannot find that there is any possible means to provide for your Majesties Safety, but by the just and speedy Execution of the said Queen, the neglecting whereof may procure the heavy displeasure and punishment of Almighty God, as by sundry severe Examples of his great Justice in that behalf left us in the Sacred Scriptures doth appear. And if the same be not put in present Execution, We your most loving and dutiful Subjects shall thereby (so far as mans reason can reach) be brought into utter despair of the continuance amongst us of the true Religion of Almighty God, and of your Majesties Life, and the Safety of all your faithful Subjects, and the good Estate of this most flourishing Common-Weal."

However, the queen wouldn't give a definitive answer and kept stalling, saying that "it was a Cause of great moment, and required good deliberation, and that she could not presently give Answer unto them". It wasn't until this day in history, 2nd December 1586, the final day of the parliament, that she finally agreed to their petition and allowed Mary's death sentence to be proclaimed.

On the 4th December, Mary was publicly proclaimed guilty, and the citizens of London celebrated by lighting bonfires.

Elizabeth finally signed Mary's death warrant on 1st February 1587, although she gave orders for it not to be sent on to Fotheringhay. However, Elizabeth's privy council sent it, and on 8th February 1587, Mary was beheaded.

3 December

On 3rd December 1600, sixty-nine-year-old peer and politician Roger North, 2nd Baron North, died at his London home in Charterhouse Square. He was given a funeral service at St Paul's, followed by a burial at Kirtling in Cambridgeshire.

North was a friend of Robert Dudley, Earl of Leicester, and served Elizabeth I as privy councillor and Treasurer of the Household.

Let me share with you a few more facts about this Tudor man.

- North was born on 27th February 1531 in London, in the parish of St Thomas the Apostle. He was the eldest child of Alice Squire and lawyer Edward North, 1st Baron North, who had served as a privy councillor to Henry VIII, Edward VI and Mary I.
- It's not known where he was educated, but he entered Lincoln's Inn in 1542, and his father introduced him to Henry VIII's court in his youth, and he learned to joust there.
- Around 1547, when he was 16, North married Winifred Rich, a daughter of Richard Rich, 1st Baron Rich, and widow of Sir Henry Dudley. They went on to have four children, three sons and a daughter, but their eldest son died in infancy.
- North was a Member of Parliament for Cambridgeshire in 1555, 1559 and 1563, and a Justice of the Peace for the county in 1558-9.
- In the coronation celebrations for Elizabeth I in January 1559, he was created a Knight of the Bath and jousted as one of the challengers in the Greenwich grand tournament later that year.
- In 1561, North was admitted to Gray's Inn, Then, following the death of his father in 1564, he spent time managing the estates, land and properties he'd inherited in Cambridgeshire, Suffolk and Middlesex. He sold Charterhouse in London to Thomas Howard, 4th Duke of Norfolk, in 1565. This was the mansion where his father had played host to Elizabeth I for six days in 1558, shortly after her accession.
- North's power in Cambridgeshire grew when he was elected alderman and burgess in 1568, then made Lord Lieutenant in 1569 and High Steward in 1572. In 1579, he served as a Justice of the Peace for Suffolk and the Isle of Ely.
- North also served Elizabeth as a diplomat, accompanying the Earl of Sussex to Vienna in 1567 to invest Emperor Maximilian II with the Order of the Garter. Then, in 1574, he was sent to France to congratulate Henri III on his accession and to play a part in negotiating a renewal of the Treaty of Blois. His time in France was mainly positive, but he got angry when a fool at the court dressed up as Henry VIII, the queen's father.
- North played host at his home in Kirtling to the queen during her progress of 1578, and records show that he regularly

played cards with the queen, so he was obviously in favour. He was also good friends with Robert Dudley, Earl of Leicester, and Francis Russell, 2nd Earl of Bedford. He accompanied Leicester on trips to take the waters at Buxton and Bath in 1578 and 1587 and spent other times with him at his properties. He also witnessed Leicester's secret marriage to Lettice Devereux in 1578, had custody of the earl's illegitimate son and stood as godfather to his son by Lettice. North did not get on with Richard Cox, Bishop of Ely. The two argued over a lease, and in 1575 North accused him of ignoring the queen's instructions.

- His wife died in late 1578/early 1579, but although he did start negotiations to marry the daughter of Sir Thomas Rivett, he never remarried.
- The 1584 "Leicester's Commonwealth", a Catholic work of propaganda that attacked Robert Dudley, Earl of Leicester, accused North of converting Leicester to Puritanism, and North did complain in that same year to Baron Burghley regarding a Chief Justice who wasn't sympathetic to Puritan ministers. North was certainly a staunch Protestant.
- In 1585, North and his eldest son, John, accompanied Leicester and English forces to the Netherlands, supporting the Dutch against Philip II of Spain. In 1586, North served as Governor of Flushing, Utrecht and Harlingen and was recorded as showing great courage at the Battle of Zutphen. He'd been shot in the knee but carried on regardless. He was rewarded by being made Knight Banneret by his friend, Leicester. He continued service under Peregrine Bertie when Leicester was recalled but returned to England in April 1588 to do his duty as Lord Lieutenant of Cambridgeshire and prepare for the potential Spanish invasion.
- When the queen visited Tilbury Fort to raise morale in August 1588, North commanded part of her bodyguard.
- In late 1588, he was made Governor of Berwick; in 1596, he was made privy councillor and treasurer of the household.
- Sadly, in 1597, his eldest son, John, died, so when North died on 3rd December 1600, his grandson, Dudley, was his heir and became 3rd Baron North.

- A funeral service for North took place at St Paul's on 22nd December 1600, and his remains were taken to Kirtling, in Cambridgeshire, and buried there on 12th February 1601. In his will, he left a gift of £100 in gold to his beloved queen, stating that it was "in acknowledgment of my love and duety to her Majesty from whom I have receaved advauncement to honor and many and contynuall favours".

4 December

On 4th December 1514, merchant-tailor and leading member of the Lollard community in London, Richard Hunne, died.

Hunne had been arrested for heresy and imprisoned in "Lollards' Tower" at St Paul's on 14th October, following the discovery of a Wycliffite Bible at his home. His body was discovered hanging in his cell from a silk girdle. It was claimed that he had committed suicide, but a coroner's jury ruled that the hanging had been faked and that he had been murdered.

Let me tell you more about Hunne, his arrest and death, but first, let me explain what a Lollard was.

A Lollard was a follower of the teachings of the 14th-century theologian John Wycliffe. Wycliffe denied transubstantiation (the miracle of the Eucharist), emphasised the authority of scripture over all else, and attacked the pope's role, regarding the office as having no scriptural basis and the pope as the Antichrist.

Nothing is known of Hunne's early life, but he worked as a merchant-tailor in the parish of St Margaret New Fish Street in London and was a wealthy man. His wife was the daughter of Thomas Vincent, a leading member of London's Lollards.

In 1511, Hunne and his wife lost their five-week-old son, Stephen, and the usual practice of the time was to give Thomas Drifield, rector of St Mary's, Whitechapel, the baby's bearing sheet from the christening as a mortuary payment. Hunne refused to do this, saying it was not due, and in 1512, the rector sued Hunne for payment at the Archbishop of Canterbury's Court of Audience at Lambeth. Unsurprisingly, the court found in favour of the rector. Then, in December 1512, Hunne turned up at Vespers at St Mary's, only to find that Thomas Marshall, the priest, refused to go on with the service until he had left, crying out, "Hunne, thou art accursed and standest accursed!", meaning that Hunne was excommunicated.

In January 1513, Hunne sued Marshall at the King's Bench for slander, pointing out that the priest's words had damaged his business and reputation. He also sued Marshall, Drifield, and all those involved in Drifield's case against him over the mortuary payment, for praemunire. The case was adjourned, but then heresy proceedings began against Hunne.

On 14th October 1513, a search was carried out on Hunne's home, and a Wyclifite Bible was found. Hunne was arrested and imprisoned at St Paul's Cathedral in the Lollard's Tower. On 2nd December, Hunne was taken to Fulham and examined by Richard Fitzjames, Bishop of London. Martyrologist John Foxe writes that he was questioned regarding six different issues – speaking out against the payment of tithes; saying that bishops and priests were the scribes and pharisees that crucified Christ; saying that bishops and priests were teachers and preaches but not "doers" and that they took "all things" but gave nothing; saying that he defended a woman named Joan Baker and her opinions, a woman who had "abjured of many great heresies", and that he'd said that the Bishop of London and his officers "have done open wrong to the said Joan Baker, in punishing her for heresy; for her sayings and opinions be according to the laws of God; wherefore the bishop and his officers are more worthy to be punished for heresy than she is.". He was also accused of "keeping divers English books, prohibited and damned by the law; as the Apocalypse in English, Epistles and Gospels in English, Wickliff's damnable works, and other books, containing infinite errors, in the which he hath been long time accustomed to read, teach, and study daily."

Following his examination, Hunne was sent back to Lollard's Tower, where, according to Foxe, the bishop's summoner Charles Joseph was relieved of his custody, and bell-ringer John Spalding was put in charge.

On the morning of this day in history, 4th December 1514, Hunne was discovered dead in his cell. Fitzjames and his chancellor, Dr William Horsey, stated that Hunne had committed suicide and that he had hanged himself from a hook in the ceiling using his silk girdle.

They then tried him posthumously for heresy, adding to the charges that he had denied the miracle of the Eucharist and the veneration of saints. On 20th December 1514, Hunne's remains were burnt.

However, a coroner's jury found that Hunne had been murdered due to there being signs of a struggle and Hunne being tortured. They ruled that he had been throttled to death, and then his dead body hanged to make it look like suicide. Dr Horsey and Hunne's gaolers, Charles Joseph and Spalding, were arrested, Joseph, while trying to flee.

Hunne's death caused such a scandal that Henry VIII heard of it and ordered his council to look into it. The people of London were angry and were sympathetic to Hunne's family. So high was feeling in London that Bishop Fitzjames appealed to Cardinal Wolsey to prevent his chancellor from being tried, concerned that he'd be found guilty, "though he was as innocent as Abel". Horsey escaped trial, and John Foxe records that he was sent away from London to Exeter, and sadly Hunne's property was not restored to his widow and children because he had been found guilty of heresy.

Richard Hunne's story is a sad one. Although he did hold beliefs that were deemed heretical then, his arrest and murder appear to have been more about the trouble he was causing for the clergy in London.

5 December

On 5th December 1556, Mildred Cooke, 2nd wife of William Cecil, 1st Baron Burghley, gave birth to a daughter, Anne. Anne was the couple's second daughter, but her older sister did not survive infancy.

The Cecils were an enlightened family and educated their daughters to a high degree. On 6th August 1569, when Anne was 13, a marriage contract was drawn up for her to marry Philip Sidney, son of Sir Henry Sidney and Mary Dudley. However, the contract was broken off, and in the summer of 1571, Anne became betrothed to the twenty-one-year-old Edward de Vere, 17th earl of Oxford. Oxford was a royal ward who had come under the guardianship of Anne's father, William Cecil, who was master of the court of wards, following the death of his father, John de Vere, 16th Earl of Oxford, in 1562. The queen consented to the marriage match and attended Anne and Edward's wedding at Westminster Abbey on 19th December 1571.

Sadly, the marriage was not a happy one. Oxford fell out with his father-in-law over Thomas Howard, 4th Duke of Norfolk's downfall, and may even have been involved in a plot to help Norfolk escape from the Tower. In July 1574, he left England without the queen's permission, bound for Flanders, where Catholic exiles had set up home. He was fetched back to England and was forced to apologise to the queen in the presence of his father-in-law. He was then given royal permission to leave for the Continent. On 2nd July 1575, while he was away, Anne gave birth to a daughter, Elizabeth. Oxford refused to recognise Elizabeth as his daughter, and the couple separated. Burghley was furious and declared that Oxford had been "enticed by certain lewd persons to be a stranger to his wife." In 1576, he returned to England, bringing back a Venetian choirboy, whom he installed in his London residence and lived with for nearly a year. He also had an affair with one of the queen's maids of honour, Anne Vavasour, who gave birth to his son in 1581, which led to him being imprisoned in the Tower for a few months. Shortly after his release, he returned to his wife, who had written to him of her devotion and desire for reconciliation.

Anne went on to have four more children with Oxford: a boy styled Lord Bulbeck, who was born in 1583 but who only lived a few days; and then three girls: Bridget, born in 1584; Susan, born in 1587, and Frances, who died in infancy.

Anne de Vere, Countess of Oxford, died on 5th June 1588 at Greenwich Palace at just 31. She was laid to rest in Westminster Abbey. Her mother, Mildred, was buried with her after her death in 1589. In his inscription on her tomb, Anne's father described her "excellent conduct of life".

Her husband may not have loved her, but Anne received many dedications from scholars, being described in these dedications as "singuler good ladie" with "good inclination to vertue and godlinesse" and a woman who possessed "wit, learning, and authoritie". She was also said to have "zealous love to religion".

6 December

On 6th December 1573, soldier and administrator Sir Hugh Paulet died at his home in Hinton St George in Somerset. He was buried in the parish church there.

Paulet distinguished himself at the Siege of Boulogne under Henry VIII and served Edward VI as Governor of Jersey. In Mary I's reign, he was made Vice-President of the Welsh Marches, and in Elizabeth I's reign he served as a special adviser to Ambrose Dudley, Earl of Warwick, at Le Havre.

Let me tell you a bit more about this Tudor man.

- Sir Hugh Paulet was born in the first decade of the 16th century and was the eldest son of landowner and soldier Sir Amias Paulet and his second wife, Laura Keilway.
- Paulet was admitted to Middle Temple, one of London's four inns of the court, at some point in his youth, and in 1530 he married Philippa Pollard, daughter of Sir Lewis Pollard. The couple went on to have five children, three sons and two daughters.
- In 1532, Paulet served on the commission of peace for Somerset, and in 1534 he became steward to the Bishop of Bath and Wells, a post held previously by his father.
- In 1535, he served as a commissioner for Thomas Cromwell's valor ecclesiasticus, a survey of the church's finances. On 18th July 1536, he was knighted. He came to Cromwell's notice through the influence of his brother-in-law, Richard Pollard.
- In late 1536, at the Pilgrimage of Grace rebellion outbreak, Paulet was called to Ampthill to attend on the king, and then he led 300 men against the rebels. In 1536 and 1537, he also served as sheriff of Somerset and Dorset.
- In 1539, Paulet was appointed to inspect coastal defences in Somerset and served on the council of the west in 1539 and 1540, and as a senior knight of the shire for Somerset at Parliament.
- In the 1540s, he served as sheriff for the counties of Devon, Somerset and Dorset, and in 1544 he served the king in France,

distinguishing himself at the Siege of Boulogne. He then acted as treasurer of Boulogne from 1544 to 1546.

- In 1549, at the fall of Edward VI's uncle, Thomas Seymour, Paulet was sent to Seymour's house at Bromham, in Wiltshire, to take charge of the property. He then served under John Russell, as Knight Marshal, against the rebels of the Prayer Book Rebellion, leading, with Sir Peter Carew, troops that defeated the main body of rebels at King's Weston in Somerset on 27th August 1549.

- After the fall of Edward Seymour, Duke of Somerset and Lord Protector, who had been Governor of Jersey, Paulet was sent to the island, where he dismissed Somerset's lieutenant and reported on the state of the fortifications. In March 1550, Paulet was made Governor of Jersey for life, and he set about using money from the church there to modernise the island's fortifications. He also set about enacting Protestant Reforms there, for example, ordering the Book of Common Prayer to be translated into French, but then the Catholic Mary I came to the throne.

- Even though he appears to have been a staunch Protestant, Paulet was able to put his faith to one side and conform in Mary I's reign. He held on to his governorship under Mary, appointing his conservative brother John as Dean of Jersey, but no Protestants were burnt on the island for heresy.

- From 1559, following the accession of Elizabeth I, Paulet passed the day-to-day administration of Jersey to his son, Amias, who was appointed lieutenant, while he returned to England. In 1559 Paulet served as Vice President of the Welsh Marches.

- In 1560, Paulet, who had been widowed at some point, married Elizabeth Blount, daughter of Walter Blount and widow of Sir Thomas Pope. The marriage was childless.

- In December 1562, Paulet was sent to Le Havre, or Newhaven as the English called it, as special advisor to Ambrose Dudley, Earl of Warwick, following the handing over of Le Havre to Elizabeth by the Huguenots according to the terms of the Treaty of Hampton Court. Unfortunately, Paulet and Warwick had to negotiate the town's surrender to France in July 1563 following a siege and heavy bombardment.

- Following his return from Le Havre, Paulet settled at his home in Hinton St George in Somerset, serving on the commission of the peace for Dorset, Somerset and Devon and as a member of Parliament.
- Sir Hugh Paulet died on 6th December 1573 and was laid to rest in a tomb he'd commissioned for himself and his first wife, Philippa, at the local church.

Trivia: his eldest son, Amias, was the Sir Amias Paulet who served as gaoler to Mary, Queen of Scots, and the man who Elizabeth I wanted to quietly do away with the queen under the Bond of Association, so she didn't have to execute her!

7 December

On 7th December 1549, rebel leader Robert Kett was hanged from the walls of Norwich Castle after being found guilty of treason by a commission of oyer and terminer. His brother William was hanged the same day but at Wymondham Abbey.

Let me tell you a bit more about Robert Kett and his rebellion.

- Robert Kett was born in the 1490s and was the fourth son of Norfolk butcher and landholder Thomas Kett and his wife, Margery.
- Kett was a wealthy man. He worked as a tanner in Wymondham and held lands in the area. His brother, William, was a butcher and mercer in the area, and both men were members of the local St Thomas Becket guild.
- Kett was married, his wife was called Alice, and the couple is thought to have had about five sons.
- The 1540s had seen a rise in the enclosure of common land by local landowners, meaning that villagers and small local farmers didn't have as much land to graze their animals on, which, in turn, led to hardship and poverty. In July 1549, in the Wymondham area, the local people were unhappy with local landowner and lawyer John Flowerdew, who had not only enclosed land but also had upset locals by being involved in the

demolition of Wymondham Abbey following its dissolution. It appears that there had been some feud between Flowerdew and Kett and that Flowerdew paid those attacking his enclosures to move on and attack enclosures that Kett had done. However, Kett listened to the attackers' grievances and was moved by their plight. He helped them remove the fences and hedges and became their leader and spokesperson.

- Kett and the rebels marched on Norwich, where they set up camp on Mousehold Heath. There, under an oak tree, which came to be known as the "oak of reformation", Kett held court for those seeking justice from local landowners. From there, the rebels also drew up a list of grievances, which weren't only about enclosure, but also included Protestant demands and complaints about priests. These grievances were sent to Edward Seymour, Duke of Somerset and Lord Protector. Somerset declared them rebels and offered them a pardon, which they refused.
- Following their refusal of a pardon, Kett and his rebels attacked Norwich on 22nd July 1549, successfully taking the city.
- Protector Somerset sent the Marquess of Northampton to put down the rebellion, but he had to retreat. Then, Somerset sent John Dudley, Earl of Warwick, who, after being sent extra mercenaries on top of his force, was finally able to defeat the rebels at the Battle of Dussindale on 27th August 1549. The rebellion was over, but Robert Kett had managed to flee. He was captured at nearby Swannington the following day, and he and his brother were taken to the Tower of London and imprisoned.
- Robert and William Kett were tried for treason by a commission of oyer and terminer on 26th November 1549, found guilty and condemned to death. They were then taken back to Norfolk.
- On this day in history, 7th December 1549, Robert Kett was hanged from Norwich Castle's walls, and William Kett was hanged from the steeple of Wymondham Church.
- In 1550, the authorities of Norwich made 27th August, the anniversary of the Battle of Dussindale and the defeat of the rebels, a holiday in celebration of the deliverance of Norwich

from the rebels. However, it stopped after a century, and today a plaque on the castle wall reads:

"In 1549 AD Robert Kett yeoman farmer of Wymondham was executed by hanging in this Castle after the defeat of the Norfolk Rebellion of which he was leader. In 1949 AD – four hundred years later – this Memorial was placed here by the citizens of Norwich in reparation and honour to a notable and courageous leader in the long struggle of the common people of England to escape from a servile life into the freedom of just conditions." So by some, he's seen as a rebel and traitor, by others as a protector of the rights of the people.

8 December

On 8th December 1538, Sir William Coffin, courtier and Master of the Horse to Queens Anne Boleyn and Jane Seymour, died at Standon in Hertfordshire.

It is thought that he died of the plague because his wife Margaret wrote to Thomas Cromwell saying that Coffin had "died of the great sickness, full of God's marks all over his body". He was buried at the parish church in Standon, and in his will, he left his hawks and best horses to the king.

Let me tell you a bit more about this Tudor Master of the Horse, but first, let me explain what a Master of the Horse was.

During Henry VIII's reign, the royal household was divided into three departments presided over by the three great officers: the Lord Chamberlain, the Lord Steward and the Master of the Horse, appointed by the king. While the Lord Chamberlain was in charge of the king's chambers, the privy chamber and great chamber, and the Lord Steward was in charge of the household below stairs, including the kitchens, grounds and gardens, the Master of the Horse would have been in charge of the king's horses and stables, all those who worked there, and also the king's hunting dogs. He would provide horses for war and travel and had a ceremonial role at events like coronations.

The queen's household was divided similarly. We know, for

example, that Queen Anne Boleyn had Thomas Lord Burgh as her Lord Chamberlain, Sir Edward Bayntun as her vice-chamberlain, and Coffin as her Master of the Horse. While Sir Nicholas Carew served Henry VIII as his Master of the Horse, Coffin was in charge of the queen's horses and attending her on special occasions.

But who was William Coffin?

William Coffin was born by 1492, probably at Porthledge in Devon, and was the son of Richard Coffin and his wife, Alice Gambon. He first served King Henry VIII as a petty captain in the king's 1513 French campaign. He joined King Henry VIII's privy chamber in 1515 and later that year was part of an embassy that went to Flanders.

In 1517, Coffin wanted to marry the recently widowed Margaret Vernon. Margaret was the daughter of Sir Robert Dymoke of Lincolnshire and the widow of Richard Vernon, son and heir of Sir Henry Vernon of Haddon, who had died in 1515. When Vernon died in 1517, he left Margaret a wealthy woman. The wardship of their son, George, was held by Cardinal Wolsey. Wolsey was planning to arrange a marriage between Margaret and his servant, Sir William Tyrwhit, but Coffin was able to get Sir Nicholas Carew to intercede with the king on his behalf, and he married Margaret. The marriage appears to have been childless.

By 1519, Coffin was one of Henry VIII's gentleman ushers, and while he attended the king at the Field of Cloth of Gold in 1519, his wife served as one of Catherine of Aragon's gentlewomen. Coffin also served the king at his meeting with Emperor Charles V at Gravelines in 1520. That same year, the king rewarded him with the keepership of Combe Martin Park in Devon.

After marrying Margaret, Coffin moved his home from Devon to Derbyshire. He served as a member of Parliament for the county in 1529, a Justice of the Peace from 1524 until his death, and as sheriff of Nottinghamshire and Derbyshire in 1531 and 1532.

By 1526, Coffin had become the sewer of the chamber and served as Anne Boleyn's Master of the Horse at her coronation in 1533. In May 1536, after Queen Anne Boleyn's arrest, Coffin's wife, Margaret, was one of the women appointed by Cromwell to serve Anne Boleyn while she was imprisoned in the Tower of London. The women were not ladies Anne would have chosen, and Anne complained to Sir

William Kingston, Constable of the Tower, saying, "I thynke [much unkindness in the] Kynge to put seche abowt me as I never loved". The ladies appointed were ordered not to speak to Anne unless Lady Kingston, the Constable's wife, was present to remember or record what was said. They were to act as spies.

Following Anne Boleyn's execution and Henry VIII's subsequent marriage to Jane Seymour, Coffin continued his service as Master of the Horse to the new queen. In May 1537, he was sworn in as a knight of the privy chamber, being dubbed in October 1537, following the birth of Prince Edward, the future Edward VI.

In late 1536, during the Pilgrimage of Grace rebellion, Coffin worked for George Talbot, 4th Earl of Shrewsbury, and was involved with interrogating rebels.

On this day in history, 8th December 1538, the same day that he made his will, William Coffin died at the manor of Standon in Hertfordshire, of which he'd just been made bailiff. He named his wife, Margaret, as his executor, and she inherited his goods and leases. His nephews inherited his Devonshire lands, and two servants inherited his lands in Bakewell, Derbyshire. Margaret went on to marry Sir Richard Manners in 1539, and she died in 1550.

9 December

On 9th December 1541, sixty-four-year-old Agnes Tilney, the Dowager Duchess of Norfolk and stepgrandmother of Queen Catherine Howard, was questioned regarding the location of her money and jewels.

Just over two months earlier, on 2nd November 1541, All Souls' Day, Henry VIII had been informed that allegations had been made about his fifth wife's past. His Archbishop of Canterbury, Thomas Cranmer, who "had not the heart to tell it by word of mouth", had shared this shocking news in a letter to the king. He explained that Mary Hall, a member of the Dowager Duchess of Norfolk's household at Lambeth and Horsham with Catherine Howard in the 1530s, had told her brother, John Lassells, that Catherine had been intimate with two men. Firstly, with her music teacher, Henry Mannox, who "knew a privy mark on her body", and secondly with Francis Dereham, who "had lain in bed with her, in his doublet and hose, between the sheets a hundred nights".

The king believed "the matter forged", but ordered an investigation into the allegations. Unfortunately, subsequent interrogations of Mannox, Dereham, and other members of the Dowager Duchess's household, confirmed Mary Hall's story. Witnesses numbering "eight or nine men and women" all "agreed in one tale". Catherine had not been a virgin when she married King Henry VIII in July 1540, and her appointment of Francis Dereham to serve in her household at court suggested to those investigating the case that she wanted to return to that "dissolute living" and cheat on the king. Then, during interrogations, Dereham implicated Thomas Culpeper, a groom of the king's privy chamber, saying that Culpeper "had succeeded him in the Queen's affections". It was found that Catherine had been having secret meetings with Culpeper, helped by her lady, Jane Boleyn, Lady Rochford.

Culpeper and Dereham were tried for treason at Guildhall on 1st December 1541, found guilty and sentenced to death. They were executed at Tyburn on 10th December 1541. Catherine Howard and Jane Boleyn were attainted for treason and beheaded at the Tower of London on 13th February 1542.

But where does Agnes Tilney, Dowager Duchess of Norfolk, come into all this? Why was she confined, and why was she being questioned about her money and jewellery?

It was because it was her household that Catherine was a part of in the 1530s when she had these two intimate relationships. The Crown wanted to understand what went on and how much the dowager duchess had known about it. Had she hidden this information from the king? Was she guilty of misprision of treason?

On 4th December 1541, Thomas Wriothesley and William Fitzwilliam, Earl of Southampton, wrote to Sir Ralph Sadler, Henry VIII's principal secretary, regarding a visit they had made to the dowager duchess. They reported that "she was not so sick as she made out, but able enough to go to my lord Chancellor's", so they advised her to go to Sir Thomas Audley, the Lord Chancellor, because he "had some questions for her". After she arrived at the Lord Chancellor's house, she was then subjected to an interrogation with a long list of questions regarding Dereham's employment, his relationship with Catherine, whether the couple had been precontracted, whether Dereham had asked for her help to get the queen to appoint him, whether she had opened Dereham's coffers and removed anything, and all kinds of other questions.

The poor dowager duchess, who had opened Dereham's coffers and removed items on hearing of him being interrogated, must have been terrified. It is little wonder that the Earl of Southampton recorded the next day, "All things here proceed well...; my lady of Norfolk... hath so meshed and tangled herself that I think it will be hard for her to wind out again". The dowager duchess did, however, deny "having any suspicion of evil between the Queen and Deram", which unfortunately did not match information gathered from other members of the household, who stated that the dowager duchess was aware, although she chastised them. Dereham confessed that she had beaten Catherine on finding her in Dereham's arms, and Katherine Tilney stated that the dowager duchess "gave also Deram a blow".

With regards to opening Dereham's coffer, witnesses stated that the dowager duchess confessed to taking certain writings and ballads and concealing them, which, as Sir Anthony Browne and Sir Ralph Sadler wrote in a report, suggested that "they contained treason, and the likelihood that the Duchess knew of the former naughty life between the Queen and Deram)".

On 8th December 1541, the king ordered the dowager duchess, her son, Lord William Howard, and her daughter, the Countess of Bridgewater, to be committed to the Tower of London for misprision of treason and for their houses and goods to be put in safe custody.

Then, on this day in history, 9th December 1541, members of the king's council in London reported that they had "conceived interrogatories for the duchess of Norfolk" but were "examining the Duchess as to where her money and treasure is, before proceeding further." They also asked other members of the council and the king whether they should indict the dowager duchess seeing "As she is old and testy, and might take her committal to heart so as to endanger her life". She was not in the best of health, and the council were concerned about getting their hands on her money and jewels while she was alive rather than her dying in the Tower before her goods had been forfeit to the Crown.

On 11ᵗʰ December 1541, the dowager duchess was committed to the Tower while a search was carried out at her home, Norfolk House. A large amount of money was found, and plate and jewels were taken.

On 21ˢᵗ December, the Earl of Southampton and Thomas Wriothesley reported that they'd been to see the dowager duchess at the Tower to urge her "to reveal more of the lewd demeanour of the Queen and Deram" but that they found her on her bed "apparently very sickly". According to them, the dowager duchess sorrowfully protested "that she never suspected anything more than a light love between them, and thought that Deram gave her money only because he was her kinsman" and begged for the king's pardon for not telling him before the marriage and for breaking into Dereham's coffer. She also confessed to having more money hidden at her home and begged the king not to give away her home at Lambeth. The two men reported that they now had 5,000 marks in money and 1,000 pounds worth of plate from their searches and that "Wriothesley would sleep better if the King would appoint it to other hands".

On 22ⁿᵈ December 1541, members of the Howard and Tilney family, plus their staff, were tried for misprision of treason for covering up the "unlawful, carnal, voluptuous, and licentious life" of Queen Catherine Howard while she lived with the Dowager Duchess of Norfolk at Lambeth. The sickly dowager duchess was named in the indictments but not tried. She was accused of "knowing the loose conduct of the Queen", "having vehement suspicion of an unlawful intercourse between her and Dereham", and having "falsely" commended and praised "the said Katharine for her pure and honest condition" in the presence of the king and others. She was also accused of breaking open Dereham's coffer, taking out "various chattels, writings and letters", and concealing them.

The dowager duchess was convicted of misprision of treason for her part in concealing Catherine's past but, fortunately for her, was not executed. She remained in the Tower of London until May 1542, when she was pardoned. Some of her properties were restored to her, and she kept her head, so a lucky escape. She died three years later, in 1545, at 68.

Other members of the Howard and Tilney families were pardoned; only Dereham, Culpeper, Catherine and Jane lost their lives. It must, however, have been a terrifying time for all those involved.

10 December

On 10th December 1591, Roman Catholic priest Edmund Gennings and Catholic Swithin Wells were executed on a scaffold outside Wells' house at Holborn.

Let me tell you more about these two Catholic martyrs, St Edmund Gennings and St Swithin Wells.

- Edmund Gennings was born in Lichfield in Staffordshire in 1566 and was the son of innkeeper and bailiff John Gennings.
- He was brought up as a Protestant, but when he was fourteen, he became a page to Richard Sherwood, a Catholic, and acted as a messenger between Sherwood and a man named James Layburne, a Catholic imprisoned in Lancaster. When Sherwood told Edmund of his plans to leave England and train for the priesthood in Reims, Edmund decided to join him.
- In August 1583, when she was 17, Edmund was admitted to the seminary college at Douai. While studying there, he was taken ill with suspected consumption and sent home. He got as far as Le Havre but then prayed and was healed, so he returned to Douai, where he was ordained in March 1590.
- Edmund was a very serious and pious young man. His biographer, Christine J Kelly, writes, "The intensity of his meditations on the responsibilities of priesthood induced a shaking of his body like a palsy that remained with him all his life, yet he spoke constantly of his hope of becoming a martyr."
- In April 1590, just weeks after being ordained, Edmund set off for England accompanied by two other priests. Their journey was rather eventful, with them being robbed, captured for a time by Huguenots, attacked by pirates, and encountering a storm at sea. Still, they eventually landed at Whitby, on the Yorkshire coast. Edmund travelled on to his home at Lichfield, but finding that only his younger brother, John, was still alive and had moved to London, he made his way to the capital.

- Sadly, when he did find John, his brother didn't want anything to do with him because of his faith.
- Edmund stayed in the city working as a priest, and on 2nd November 1591, he was in Holborn, at Swithin Wells' house, celebrating the mass, when the famous priestfinder and torturer Richard Topcliffe found him. Topcliffe was injured in the subsequent struggle with members of the congregation, who wanted the priests to finish mass. Still, Edmund and his fellow priest, Polydore Plasden, surrendered peacefully and were escorted to Newgate Prison with members of their congregation.
- Swithin Wells had not been present at the mass but was arrested the following day when he visited the prison to get his wife released. Wells was a Hampshire man who had been a tutor to Henry Wriothesley, 2nd Earl of Southampton, and a schoolmaster. He'd come under investigation in the early 1580s for his Catholic sympathies and had been forced to give up his school. He'd moved to London in 1585, where he became known for supporting priests. He'd been imprisoned briefly in 1586 after being implicated in the Babington Plot and was examined in 1587 but managed to avoid serious trouble until 1591.
- On 4th December 1591, Edmund, Swithin, Polydore Plasden and several others were tried at Westminster Hall, the priests for treason and the laymen for felony. Following his trial, Edmund was offered a deal by Topcliffe: his life in exchange for conforming to Protestantism. Edmund refused, at which point Topcliffe had him put into the "little ease", a tiny cell that made it impossible for Edmund to stand, sit or lie down.
- On this day in history, 10th December 1591, Edmund Gennings and Swithin Wells were drawn to Wells' house at Holborn. There, Edmund suffered a full traitor's death, being hanged, drawn and quartered, and Wells was hanged. While suffering, Edmund was said to have called upon St Gregory for help, upon which the executioner cried, "God's wounds! His heart is in my hand and yet Gregory is in his mouth!"

- So courageous was Edmund at his execution that his brother John, who witnessed it, converted to Catholicism and wrote a biography of Edmund.
- Edmund's fellow priest, Polydore Plasden, was also executed on this day in 1591, being hanged, drawn and quartered at Tyburn. He was lucky that he was hanged until he was dead, and the rest of his punishment was carried out on his dead body.
- In October 1970, Pope Paul VI canonised Swithin, Edmund, and Polydore as three of the Forty Martyrs of England and Wales.

11 December

On 11th December 1608, one of Queen Elizabeth I's former ladies and a lover of Robert Dudley, Earl of Leicester, was buried at St Margaret's Church, Westminster. Her name was Douglas Sheffield (née Howard), Lady Sheffield

Douglas was born around 1542/1543 and was the eldest daughter of famous naval commander William Howard, 1st Baron Howard of Effingham, and his second wife, Margaret Gamage. Douglas's biographer, Simon Adams, wonders if her name came from Lady Margaret Douglas, Countess of Lennox, who may have been her godmother.

On Elizabeth I's accession, her father, who had served Mary I as Lord High Admiral, was made Lord Chamberlain of the household. Douglas and her sister, Mary, were appointed maids of honour to the new queen.

In 1560, at around 17/18, Douglas married John Sheffield, 2nd Baron Sheffield, son and heir of Edmund Sheffield, 1st Baron Sheffield. They had two surviving children, Edmund and Elizabeth, before John died in December 1568. His son inherited his title.

After her husband's death, Douglas returned to court and became a gentlewoman of the privy chamber (extraordinary), meaning that her position was unsalaried. In the early 1570s, Douglas became Robert Dudley, Earl of Leicester's lover, and, on 7th August 1574, she gave birth to their son, Sir Robert Dudley, the explorer and cartographer. Douglas declared under oath that she and Dudley had married secretly at Esher, her family's home, when she was pregnant in late 1573. Still, she could not provide any evidence to support this when her son sought to claim his father's and uncle's titles in 1604, after Elizabeth I's death.

According to the tract "Leicester's Commonwealth", Douglas and Leicester had begun their romance in 1568 at Belvoir Castle while on royal progress, and Leicester had even had Douglas's husband poisoned. However, there is no evidence to back this up, and there wasn't even a visit to Belvoir.

On 28th November 1579, Douglas secretly married the diplomat Sir Edward Stafford, son of William Stafford, widower of Mary Boleyn, and his second wife, Dorothy. If Douglas had indeed been married to Leicester, this marriage would have been bigamous, but Douglas later claimed that she felt free to remarry as Leicester had married Lettice Devereux. Douglas and Edward had two sons together, but they died young. Douglas accompanied her husband to the French court after he was appointed ambassador there. Simon Adams writes, "Thanks to her place at Elizabeth's court and her command of French, Sheffield was the most socially successful of all the wives of the Elizabethan ambassadors in France. Not only did she get on famously with Catherine de' Medici, but she also made a significant contribution to the administration of the Valois court".

Douglas returned to England in 1588, arriving just after her former lover, the Earl of Leicester's death. Her son, Robert, had been named by Leicester as heir to his estates after his brother, Ambrose. She returned to the queen's employment.

Douglas's husband died in 1605, and on 14th September 1608, Douglas made her will, requesting to be buried with her parents at Reigate or by her sister in St Margaret's, Westminster, which was also Stafford's resting place. She died in December 1608 and was buried at St Margaret's on 11th December 1608.

12 December

On 12th December 1595, Protestant Welsh soldier and author Sir Roger Williams died from a fever with his patron, Robert Devereux, Earl of Essex, at his side. He was buried at St Paul's Cathedral.

Williams served as a soldier in the Low Countries and France and was second in command of the cavalry under Essex at Tilbury Fort in 1588. He also wrote the 1590 "A Briefe Discourse of Warre".

Let me tell you a bit more about him.

- Williams was born around 1539/40 and was the son of Sir Thomas Williams of Penrhos, Monmouthshire in Wales, and his wife, Eleanor Vaughan.
- It is thought that Williams was educated at Brasenose College, Oxford, before entering the service of William Herbert, 1st Earl of Pembroke, as a page.
- He may have accompanied Pembroke to the Low Countries in 1557 in the campaign against the French, on the side of Philip of Spain, husband of Mary I, but it's not certain. It is thought that he served on the Huguenot side in the 1560s during the French Wars of Religion.
- In 1572, in Elizabeth I's reign, he was one of those who volunteered for service under Thomas Morgan in a revolt with the Dutch against Philip of Spain. In 1573, when Morgan returned home, Williams, who had heard a rumour that the Huguenots were raising an army in Rhineland, travelled there but headed home when the news turned out to be wrong. He was arrested by the Spanish while on his journey, luckily being captured by a commander who had served with his patron, Pembroke, in Mary's reign. Williams, who was a keen soldier, accepted the commander's offer to enlist in his regiment, serving in it until 1577.
- In the summer of 1577, following his return to England, Williams was employed as an intelligence gatherer by Sir Francis Walsingham. Perhaps he had used his time serving under Spain to gather intelligence for Elizabeth I's government.
- In 1578, Williams joined a regiment led by John Norris in the Netherlands. Elizabeth's ambassador, William Davison, had to intercede as the Dutch were suspicious of Williams at first due to his recent history of service under Spain. He soon proved himself by fighting a Spaniard single-handedly.
- Williams served Norris loyally as a lieutenant for a few years, although the two men were prone to arguments. The Spanish sadly killed Williams' brother in 1582.

- Williams stayed on serving on the Dutch side after Norris left and became close to William of Orange. He was with the prince when Catholic Balthasar Gerard assassinated him in July 1584 and gave chase, helping to capture Gerard.
- In 1585 he served with Norris once more as lieutenant colonel and continued his service when Robert Dudley, Earl of Leicester, took command. At this time, he got to know the earl's stepson, Robert Devereux, 2nd Earl of Essex.
- Leicester knighted Williams in October 1586 as a reward for his service.
- In 1587, Williams was made governor of Sluys and was there when the Duke of Parma laid siege to the town. Williams and his force resisted for nearly two months before being forced to surrender in August 1587.
- In late 1587, Williams fell out with the Earl of Leicester, but in 1588, at the time of the Spanish Armada's predicted invasion, he served as second in command of the cavalry to the Earl of Essex at Tilbury Fort.
- In 1589, he commanded a regiment during Norris and Sir Francis Drake's expedition to Portugal, incurring the wrath of Queen Elizabeth I when he allowed the Earl of Essex to stow away on his ship after she'd refused to let Essex go. So angry was Elizabeth that Williams went into hiding for a time on his return to England.
- In 1589, Williams also served in France under Henry IV before joining the English army commanded by Peregrine Bertie. His service there helped him win back the queen's favour.
- In 1590, his work "A Brief Discourse of War, with his opinions concerning some part of Martial Discipline" was published, and this was followed, the next year, by "Newes from Sir Roger Williams".
- In early 1591, even though he and his friend Essex had criticised Norris, Williams served under Norris as a colonel in Brittany. That summer, he served as Marshal of the Field under Essex, and, after Essex was recalled in 1592, he became commander of the army.

- In 1594, Elizabeth I granted him a life pension of £300, and in that year and 1595, he served her as special ambassador to the French king.
- Williams died on this day in history, 12th December 1595, after just four days of illness. His patron and friend, the Earl of Essex, was by his side.
- In his will, he instructed for his goods to be given to the Earl of Essex. He had never married.
- He was buried in St Paul's Cathedral on 23rd December 1595 in a funeral paid for by Essex and attended by the earl and Williams' military colleagues.
- In 1618, "Actions of the Low Countries", Williams' account of his time in the Netherlands, was published
- There is a story, probably apocryphal, regarding Williams' relationship with Queen Elizabeth I, which wasn't plain sailing. Tired of his petitioning, the queen said, "'Faugh, Williams, I prithee begone: thy boots stink," to which Williams replied, "Tut, madam, 'tis my suit that stinks".
- Williams has been linked with William Shakespeare's Welsh soldier Fluellan, in Henry V. However, although Fluellan's fiery but witty personality matches that of Williams, Fluellan was a conservative soldier, while Williams was a moderniser.

13 December

On 13th December 1558, civil lawyer and Dean of Chester William Clyffe died.

Clyffe was one of the authors of the 1537 "Bishops' Book" and was consulted by convocation during Henry VIII's Great Matter.

Let me tell you a bit more about William Clyffe.

- Clyffe's background and early life are unknown, but he graduated from Cambridge with a Bachelor of Law in 1514 and a doctorate in 1523.
- In 1522, he was admitted to the Doctors' Commons as an advocate. The Doctors' Commons was a London society of civil lawyers.

- Between 1522 and 1529, Clyffe worked as a commissary of the diocese of London.
- In 1526, he was prebend of Twyford in the diocese of St Paul, and in 1529 was made Archdeacon of London. In 1532, he held the prebend of Fenton in the archdiocese of York.
- In 1533, his expertise in marriage and divorce law led to Convocation seeking his advice regarding Henry VIII's case for an annulment of his marriage to Catherine of Aragon. He heard and determined a number of divorce cases during his career.
- 1533 was also a troubled year for Clyffe because Archbishop Cranmer's vicar general in Ely complained that he was hindering him from administering justice. Later that year, he was involved in litigation due to an accusation of wrongfully interfering in a case in the court of chancery.
- In 1533, Clyffe resigned as Archdeacon of London to become Archdeacon of Cleveland. He also held the living of Waverton, Cheshire, in that year. In 1534 he was precentor of York, then served as treasurer of York in 1538 until the position was suppressed in 1547. At that point, he became Dean of Chester and was subsequently thrown into the Fleet prison after he'd refused to lease chapter lands to the comptroller of the king's household, Sir Richard Cotton, at a preferential rate. It took him changing his mind and leasing Cotton the lands to obtain freedom.
- In 1537, Clyffe was one of the authors of "The Godly and Pious Institution of a Christian Man", more commonly known as the Bishops' Book. This book was compiled by a committee of divines and bishops and was an attempt to outline the religious doctrine of England following the 1536 Ten Articles.
- From 1548, he was prebend of Noxton in Middlesex, and in 1552, he held the living of Standish in Lancashire.
- William Clyffe died on this day in 1558.

14 December

On 14th December 1558, just under a month after her death, Queen Mary I, daughter of King Henry VIII and his first wife, Catherine of Aragon, was buried at Westminster Abbey.

Mary, who had only reigned for just over five years, had died on 17th November 1558, and her half-sister, Elizabeth, had become Queen Elizabeth I.

Although Mary had left instructions in her will for her mother's remains to be exhumed and brought to London, so that mother and daughter could be buried together, her instructions were ignored. Mary was buried by herself at Westminster, with just stones marking her resting place.

On 13th December 1558, Mary's remains were processed from St James's Palace to Westminster. In his diary, Henry Machyn, a merchant-tailor and citizen of London, recorded that her coffin was carried by chariot, and there was a painted effigy of her, which he described as "adorned with crimson velvet and her crown on her head, her sceptre on her hand, and many goodly rings on her fingers."

Machyn records that Mary's coffin was met at the abbey door by "4 bishops and the abbot, mitred in copes and incensing the body". Her remains lay there "all night under her hearse, and her grace was watched. And there were a hundred poor men in good black gowns bearing long torches, with hoods on their heads, and arms on them; and a-bout her the guard bearing staff-torches in blake coats; and all the way chandlers having torches, to give them that had their torches burnt out."

Mary was buried the following day, this day in 1558, and Machyn records her funeral in his diary too:

> "The 14 day of December was the queen's mass; and all the lords and ladies, knights and gentlewomen, did offer. And there was a man of arms and horse offered; and her coat of armour, and sword, and target, and banner of arms, and 3 standards; and all the heroldes about her; and there my lord bishop of Winchester

made the sermon; and there was offered cloth of gold and velvet, whole pieces and other things.

After the mass all done, her grace was carried up to the chapel the king Henry the VII builded, with bishops mitred; and all the officers went to the grave and after they break their staves, and cast them in-to the grave; in the mean time the people plucked down the cloth, every man a piece that could catch it, round a-bout the church, and the arms. And afterwards, my lord bishop of York, after her grace was buried, he declared a collation, and as soon as he had made an end, all the trumpets blew a blast, and so the chief mourners and the lords and knights, and the bishops, with the abbot, went in-to the abbey to dinner, and all the officers of the queen's court."

In 1606, in the reign of King James I, Elizabeth I's remains were moved from their resting place in Henry VII's vault to join her sister Mary's remains. James I erected a monument bearing Elizabeth I's effigy, but not one of Mary, and the Latin inscription on the monument can be translated as:

"Partners both in throne and grave, here rest we two sisters, Elizabeth and Mary, in the hope of the Resurrection."

15 December

On 15th December 1558, Cardinal Reginald Pole, Mary I's Archbishop of Canterbury, was buried at Canterbury Cathedral.

Pole was fifty-eight years old at the time of his death, having been born in March 1500. He was the third son of Sir Richard Pole and his wife, Margaret, Countess of Salisbury. Pole's maternal grandfather was George, Duke of Clarence, brother of Kings Edward IV and Richard III, and his maternal grandmother was Isabella Neville, daughter of Richard Neville, Earl of Warwick, the Kingmaker.

Pole refused to support King Henry VIII in his quest for an annulment of his marriage to Catherine of Aragon and even wrote a treatise against it. He was made a cardinal in 1536 and then papal legate in 1537. His strong and outspoken opposition to Henry VIII and his policies ultimately led to the execution of his brother, Lord Montagu, the imprisonment of his other brother, Geoffrey, and later the execution of his mother, the Countess of Salisbury. The cardinal was also attainted, but he was safely on the Continent.

Cardinal Pole returned to England in late 1554, following the accession of the Catholic queen, Mary I, and on 30th November 1554, Pole, as legate, officially welcomed England back into the Catholic fold. He was consecrated as Archbishop of Canterbury in 1556 and was the queen's chief adviser.

Cardinal Pole became ill in September 1558 and succumbed to his illness on 17th November 1558, the same day as his beloved queen, Mary I.

Raphael Holinshed's Chronicles record his death:

> "Leaving queen Marie being dead & gone, you are to understand and note, that the same evening, or (as some have written) the next day after the said queen's death, Cardinal Pole the bishop of Rome's legate departed out of this life, having been not long afore made archbishop of Canturbury: he died at his house over against Westminster commonly called Lambeth, and was buried in Christs church at Canturbury."

The Chronicles give a not-so-flattering account of Cardinal Pole's life, accusing him of "barbarous" behaviour and blemishing "the honour of his descent".

Diarist and merchant-tailor Henry Machyn records how Cardinal Pole's remains were taken on 10th December from Lambeth to Canterbury in preparation for his burial:

> "The same morning my lord cardinal was removed from Lambeth, and carried toward Canterbury with great company in black; and he was carried in a chariot with banner-rolls wrought with fine gold and great banners of arms, and 4 banners of saints in oil."

In Ecclesiastical Memorials, John Strype writes:

> "Cardinal Pole died the same day that Queen Mary did; and not many hours after her. His last will may be seen in Holinshed's History. Therein he desired his

successor would not sue his executors for dilapidations, seeing he had bestowed more than a thousand pounds within these few years in repairing and making such houses as belonged to the see, since he came to it. The overseers of his will were Nicholas Archbishop of York, lord chancellor; Thomas Bishop of Ely; Ed. Lord Hastings, lord chamberlain; Sir John Boxal, the Queen's secretary; Sir Edward Cordal, master of the rolls; Henry Cole, vicar general of the spiritualities."

Strype goes on to describe how there was "a secret report among Papists, abroad soon after, that both Queen Mary and Cardinal Pole, came to their ends by poison but that Dr. Haddon, 'a knowing man', put their deaths down to "an infectious fever that the nation then laboured under [...] an outrageous burning fever [...]", which would be referring to the influenza epidemic.

Cardinal Pole's rather plain tomb can be found on the north side of the Corona (or Becket's Crown) in Canterbury Cathedral. Pole was the last prelate to be buried in the cathedral.

16 December

On 16th, or possibly the 18th, December 1503, George Grey, 2nd Earl of Kent, died at Ampthill, Bedfordshire. Grey served as a soldier under Henry VII, was on the king's council, and served as Constable of Northampton Castle and as a judge at the trial of Edward, Earl of Warwick in 1499.

Let me give you a few more facts about this member of the Grey family who was also related to the Woodvilles.

- George Grey was the second and eldest surviving son of Edmund Grey, Lord Grey of Ruthin and 1st Earl of Kent, and his wife, Catherine Percy, the daughter of Henry Percy, 2nd Earl of Northumberland.
- George was able to use the courtesy title of Lord Ruthin following the death of his older brother, Arthur, in 1480.
- In July 1483, during the coronation celebrations for King Richard III, George was made a Knight of the Bath, and he was granted manors in Buckinghamshire and Bedfordshire.

- In around 1483, George married Anne Woodville, widow of Sir William Bourchier, daughter of Richard Woodville, Earl Rivers, and his wife, Jacquetta, and sister of Elizabeth Woodville, who'd been married to King Edward IV. George and Anne had one son together, Richard.
- Although he'd been rewarded in 1483 by Richard III, he retained royal favour when Henry VII came to the throne in 1485, being made Constable of Northampton Castle for life in October 1485.
- In 1486, George accompanied Henry VII on his royal progress and was in the king's vanguard fighting against the rebels who supported pretender Lambert Simnel at the Battle of Stoke Field in June 1487.
- In 1489, George was present when Arthur Tudor, Henry VII's eldest son, was created Prince of Wales.
- In May 1490, George's father died, leaving George to inherit his title, the earldom of Kent. In 1490, George married for a second time. He'd lost his first wife, Anne, in 1489, and his second wife was Catherine Herbert, daughter of William Herbert, Earl of Pembroke. The couple had a daughter and three sons together: Anne, Henry, George and Anthony.
- George was a member of the king's council on several occasions, and in 1491, in Bedfordshire, George helped raise money for the French campaign and led a retinue of men there in 1492. He also fought for the king against the Cornish rebels in 1497.
- In 1494, George was present when the king's second son, Henry, was made Duke of York. He also attended Arthur's marriage to Catherine of Aragon in November 1501 and the prince's funeral in 1502. Another royal funeral he attended was that of Elizabeth of York, Henry VII's queen consort, in 1503.
- In 1499, George was appointed as a judge for the trial of Edward, Earl of Warwick. He also served as a commissioner for the peace in several counties.
- In July 1503, he was one of those given the honour of escorting the king's eldest daughter, Margaret, on her trip to Scotland to marry King James IV. He escorted her from the home of her grandmother, Lady Margaret Beaufort, at Collyweston, to York.

- On this day or 18th December 1503, George Grey died at Ampthill in Bedfordshire. He was buried at Warden Abbey, Bedfordshire, where his first wife, Anne, had been laid to rest. Grey's second wife, Catherine Herbert, daughter of William Herbert, 1st Earl of Pembroke, was also buried there after her death not long after her husband's.
- George was succeeded as Earl of Kent by his eldest son, Richard. Sadly, Richard sold off the Grey lands. The Abbot of Warden stated that George's "son and heir would as fast waste and spend his lands as his ancestors purchased them". When Richard died in 1524, there wasn't anything to pass on to his heir, his half-brother Henry, and Henry never formally took the title of earl.
- George's daughter Anne married John Hussey, 1st Baron Hussey of Sleaford.

17 December

On 17th December 1559, fifty-five-year-old Matthew Parker was consecrated as Queen Elizabeth I's Archbishop of Canterbury. It was an office that Parker did not want and would not have accepted if "he had not been so much bound to the mother", that is to say, Anne Boleyn, by a promise he made a few days before Anne's arrest in 1536.

Matthew Parker was born on 6th August 1504, in the parish of St Saviour, Norwich, East Anglia. He was born the son of a worsted weaver, but his destiny wasn't weaving; Parker was destined for the Church and royal service too.

In around 1520, Parker began his studies at Corpus Christi College in Cambridge, graduating with a BA in 1525, and it was there that he met men interested in evangelical reform, like Thomas Bilney, who was martyred in 1531. Parker went on to do a Masters and was elected a fellow of the college in 1527. By this time, he was also a priest.

After gaining a Bachelor of Theology and a doctorate, he was appointed as one of Queen Anne Boleyn's chaplains in 1535. Anne's patronage led to him being appointed Dean of the Collegiate Church of Stoke by Clare, in Suffolk, in November 1535. After her execution in 1536, Parker served as chaplain to King Henry VIII.

In December 1544, Parker was elected master of Corpus Christi College and then vice-chancellor in January 1545. In his article on the Anne Boleyn Files site, "The Cambridge Connections", author Robert Parry explains that "Parker was one of the primary architects of the emerging Anglican Doctrine that shaped the English Reformation, and after the death of Henry VIII, he continued to rise to prominence under the reforming governments of Edward VI and was a close associate of the two most powerful statesmen of Edwards reign – Edward Seymour and John Dudley. He would have been intimately associated, therefore, with the influential Humanist movement of the first part of the 16th century that was centred on Cambridge and consisted of scholars such as John Cheke (1514–1557), William Grindal (d. 1548), Anthony Cooke (1504-1576); Roger Ascham (1515–1568), John Dee (1527–1608/9) and, perhaps most significantly of all, William Cecil (1520–1598)."

Parker's royal favour led to him being made Dean of Lincoln and presented for the prebend of Corringham, Lincolnshire, in 1552. However, things changed when the Catholic Mary I came to the throne in July 1553. As a married churchman, Parker was deprived of his many offices and, instead, focused on writing theological works. His time out of the limelight was short, though, as Mary died in November 1558 and her half-sister, Elizabeth I, came to the throne.

In 1559, Queen Elizabeth I appointed Matthew Parker as her Archbishop of Canterbury. Parker had been offered the post in 1558 but had stalled in accepting it. Parker believed he was not right for the post and, having recently fallen off a horse, also not fit enough. But, Elizabeth I wanted him in that post, and Parker felt that he had no choice; he had made a promise to Elizabeth's mother, Anne Boleyn, back in 1536, and he had to stand by that and serve his queen.

Parker wrote to Sir Nicholas Bacon:

> "[…] though my heart would right fain serve my sovereign lady the Queen's majesty, in more respects than of mine allegiance, not forgetting what words her grace's mother said to me of her, not six days before her apprehension, yet this my painful infirmity will not suffer it in all manner servings…"

He also referred to this promise in a letter to William Cecil, Lord Burghley, in 1572:

"Yea, if I had not been so much bound to the mother, I would not so soon have granted to serve the daughter in this place..."

We don't know what exactly Anne had said to him six days before her arrest, around 26th April, but as Eric Ives points out, "That charge, and the debt he felt he owed to Anne, stayed with him for the rest of his life." It was enough of a promise for him to take a job he didn't want. Did Anne Boleyn know that there was a plot against her? Was it just a coincidence that she spoke to Parker about this just days before her arrest? Was it just Elizabeth's spiritual welfare she was talking about? We will never know because Parker does not give more details about the conversation.

Matthew Parker served as Elizabeth I's Archbishop of Canterbury until his death on 17th May 1575. He is known for being one of the men responsible for the Thirty-Nine Articles of Religion, established in 1563 and seen as "the historic defining statements of Anglican doctrine in relation to the controversies of the English Reformation". He may have been a great theologian and an influential churchman, but for me, he was a man who did something he didn't want to do because of a promise. What a loyal and noble man.

18 December

On 18th December 1555, John Philpott, former Archdeacon of Winchester, was burnt at the stake for heresy at Smithfield. He was about 40 years old at his death.

Philpott was born around 1515/1516 in Hampshire and was educated at Winchester College and then New College, Oxford, becoming a fellow there in 1535. He then continued his studies in Italy, possibly achieving his Bachelor of Civil Law there.

He was back in England by late 1548, and his Protestant stance upset Stephen Gardiner, Bishop of Winchester, who banned Philpott from preaching in his diocese, an order which Philpott ignored. When Edward VI came to the throne, Gardiner lost his office and was replaced by John Ponet, a Protestant, who then made Philpott Archdeacon of

Winchester, a post once promised to him by Gardiner. The latter had gone back on his promise because of Philpott's Protestantism.

In 1553, Catholic Mary I became queen and Gardiner was reinstated as bishop. It wasn't long before Philpott was deprived of his office after speaking out against the doctrine of transubstantiation and excommunicating conservative John White, treasurer of the Winchester diocese. Philpott was also excommunicated and imprisoned in the King's Bench.

He spent his time in prison writing letters to fellow Protestants to encourage them to stay strong in their faith. These letters were later printed by martyrologist John Foxe and Bible translator Miles Coverdale. Philpott was moved to London's Coalhouse Prison and then into solitary confinement in the tower of St Paul's Cathedral.

Philpott was examined many times before being condemned for heresy by Bishop Bonner on 16th December 1555. John Foxe shared the records of these examinations, which Philpott managed to smuggle out of prison, in his famous book "Actes and Monuments". Here is an excerpt about Philpoot's final days:

> "Upon Tuesday at supper, being the seventeenth day of December, there came a messenger from the sheriffs, and bade Master Philpot make him ready, for the next day he should suffer, and be burned at a stake with fire. Master Philpot answered and said, "I am ready; God grant me strength, and a joyful resurrection." And so he went into his chamber, and poured out his spirit unto the Lord God, giving him most hearty thanks, that he of his mercy had made him worthy to suffer for his truth.
>
> In the morning the sheriffs came according to the order, about eight of the clock, and called for him, and he most joyfully came down unto them. And there his man did meet him, and said, "Ah! dear master, farewell." His master said unto him, "Serve God, and he will help thee." And so he went with the sheriffs to the place of execution; and when he was entering into Smithfield, the way was foul, and two officers took him up to bear him to the stake. Then he said merrily, "What! will ye make me a pope? I am content to go to my journey's end on

foot." But first, coming into Smithfield, he kneeled down there, saying these words, "I will pay my vows in thee, O Smithfield!"

And when he was come to the place of suffering, he kissed the stake, and said, "Shall I disdain to suffer at this stake, seeing my Redeemer did not refuse to suffer a most vile death upon the cross for me?" And then with an obedient heart full meekly he said the 106th, the 107th, and the 108th Psalms. And when he had made an end of all his prayers, he said to the officers, "What have you done for me?" and every one of them declared what they had done; and he gave to every of them money.

Then they bound him to the stake, and set fire unto that constant martyr, who the eighteenth day of December, in the midst of the fiery flames, yielded his soul into the hands of Almighty God, and full like a lamb gave up his breath, his body being consumed into ashes."

19 December

On 19th December 1583, twenty-three-year-old convicted conspirator John Somerville was found dead in his cell at Newgate Prison. Death was by strangulation, and it was said to be suicide. His body was buried in Moorfields, and his head was displayed on London Bridge.

Let me tell you more about Somerville, the conspiracy he was accused of being involved in, and his death.

- John Somerville was born in 1560 and was the son of John Somerville of Edstone in Warwickshire, and his wife, Elizabeth Corbett.
- Somerville was educated at Hart Hall, Oxford.
- In 1579, following the death of his father, Somerville inherited properties in the counties of Warwickshire, Gloucestershire and Worcestershire. However, he never took possession of them as they were to be held by his mother until he was 24.

- Somerville married Margaret Arden, daughter of Sir Edward Arden of Park Hall and his wife, Mary Throckmorton. The couple had two daughters.
- The Catholic Somerville was in ill health in October 1583 but set out for London to shoot and kill Queen Elizabeth I, whom he described as "a serpent and a viper". He was arrested after telling fellow guests at an inn of his intentions. He was interrogated, and then his in-laws and their priest were imprisoned in the Tower of London. On 31st October, Somerville spoke of "the trouble of his mind", and it appears that he was mentally ill.
- On 16th December 1583, Somerville and his fellow alleged conspirators were convicted of high treason. On 19th December, Somerville and his father-in-law, Edward Arden, were moved to Newgate Prison, and just hours after their transfer, Somerville was discovered dead in his cell.
- Although Catholics questioned whether he had committed suicide, with William Allen writing that common opinion was that "the poor gentleman were dispatched of purpose and appointment …. for prevention of the discovery of certain shameful practices about the condemnation' of his father-in-law", it appears that Somerville had been unstable. Allen also wrote of his possible "distract of his wits" and "alienation of mind". William Cecil, Elizabeth I's chief advisor, wrote of Somerville in his book "The Execution of Justice in England", calling him a "furious young man of Warwickshire" and explaining that "coming with a full intent to have killed her majesty, whose life God always have in his custody. The attempt not denied by the traitor himself but confessed, and that he was moved thereto in his wicked spirit by enticements of certain seditious and traitorous persons, his kinsmen and allies, and also by often reading of sundry seditious vile books lately published against Her Majesty; and his end was in desperation to strangle himself to death: an example of God's severity against such as presume to offer violence to His anointed."
- It's impossible to know whether Somerville had any true intention of harming the queen and, if so, whether he was mentally ill and manipulated by others.

20 December

Yesterday, I wrote about the death of conspirator John Somerville on 19th December 1583, a man who was said to have committed suicide after being found guilty of treason for conspiring to kill Queen Elizabeth I. He wasn't the only person to have been condemned for high treason for that alleged conspiracy; his father-in-law, Edward Arden, was also found guilty and, on this day in Tudor history, 20th December 1583, was hanged, drawn and quartered at Smithfield and his head displayed on London Bridge along with that of Somerville.

Let me tell you more about Edward Arden and his involvement in the conspiracy.

- Edward Arden was born around 1532/1533 and was the son of William Arden from Warwickshire, a second cousin of William Shakespeare's mother, Mary Arden.
- In 1545, Edward became his grandfather Thomas's heir following the death of his father, William. His grandfather died in 1563, and Edward inherited Park Hall in Warwickshire, an estate now in the West Midlands rather than Warwickshire. There, as a Catholic recusant, he kept a Catholic priest, Hugh Hall, disguised as a gardener.
- Edward was married to Mary Throckmorton, daughter of Sir Robert Throckmorton of Coughton Court, and his first wife, Muriel Berkeley. The couple had three children: Robert, Margaret and Katherine. Their daughter Margaret married John Somerville, the man I introduced yesterday.
- In 1575, Edward served as sheriff of Warwickshire.
- Edward did not get on with fellow Warwickshire landowner Robert Dudley, Earl of Leicester. He refused to wear his livery or sell property to him and disparaged the earl and his marital history. Not a great idea when that earl is close to the queen!
- In October 1583, Edward's son-in-law, John Somerville, who appears to have been mentally ill, was arrested after he had spoken of his intention to shoot and kill the queen. It is said that during interrogations on 31st October, Somerville implicated Edward by saying that he was inspired to assassinate Elizabeth I when he heard Edward's priest speak against the queen in front of

him and Edward. This led to Edward's arrest and imprisonment in the Tower of London on 7th November.

- At a trial on 16th December 1583, Somerville pleaded guilty to treason, while Edward, his wife, Mary, and their priest, Hugh Hall, pleaded innocent. They were all found guilty.
- On the night of 16th December, after bribing the Lieutenant of the Tower's servant, Edward was able to have a last meal with his wife.
- On 19th December 1583, Edward and Somerville were transferred to Newgate Prison, where Somerville was found dead in his cell just hours after their arrival. It was claimed that his death was suicide.
- On this day in Tudor history, 20th December 1583, Edward Arden suffered a full traitor's death at Smithfield. The heads of Edward and Somerville were displayed on London Bridge as a warning of the fate of traitors, and their remains were buried at Moorfields.
- Edward's wife and priest were spared.
- As a traitor, Edward's property was confiscated by the Crown, but his son, Robert, did manage to regain much of it later.
- Edward's biographer, William Wizeman, notes that his contemporaries found the case against him suspicious and blamed it on the Earl of Leicester's vengeance. Wizeman writes, "The dropping of charges against the other defendants and the releasing of Mary Arden only made it more likely that he was the victim of a grave iniquity."

21 December

Today, 21st December is the winter solstice and in Tudor times it was also the feast day of St Thomas the Apostle. His feast day is now commemorated on 3rd July.

Thomas, also known as Didymus, was one of the Twelve Apostles of Jesus Christ. He became known as "Doubting Thomas" because he doubted Christ's resurrection. Here's that story from John's Gospel, and I'm quoting William Tyndale's 16th-century New Testament:

"But Thomas one of the twelve called Didymus was not with them when Jesus came. The other disciples said unto him: we have seen the lord. And he said unto them: except I see in his hands the print of the nails and put my finger in the holes of the nails and thrust my hand into his side, I will not believe. And after eight days again his disciples were within and Thomas with them. Then came Jesus when the doors were shut and stoode in the midst and said: peace be with you. After that said he to Thomas: bring thy finger hither and see my hands and bring thy hand and thrust it into my side and be not faithless but believing. Thomas answered and said unto him: my Lord and my God. Jesus said unto him. Thomas because thou hast seen me therefore thou believest: Happy are they that have not seen and yet believe."

The Saint Thomas Christians in Kerala, India, trace their origins to Thomas's evangelism in the region, as told in the Acts of Thomas in the New Testament Apocrypha and mentioned by 3rd and 4th-century Roman writers. According to the 4th century Christian theologian, Ephrem the Syrian, Thomas was martyred in Chennai in India on St Thomas's Mount on 3rd July AD 72. According to another story, Thomas was killed when a fowler shot at a peacock and missed, hitting Thomas. Following his death, some of his relics were taken to Edessa in Mesopotamia, while others are in the San Thome Basilica in Chennai. In the 13th century, the relics in Edessa were moved to Italy, where they are housed in the Cathedral of St. Thomas the Apostle in Ortona.

St Thomas is also linked to China, Indonesia and Paraguay.

As Sophie Jackson points out in "The Medieval Christmas", Thomas was a carpenter and "was revered for his generosity", so on his feast day, it was traditional for old women, children and the poor to "go a-Thomasing", that is to say, walking the streets collecting alms.

Pie making is another custom associated with the Feast of St Thomas in some countries. The Catholic Culture website explains that in the Tyrol, for example, "A great meat pie is baked for the whole family. It is marked with the Cross and sprinkled with holy water.

Along with the great pie in the hot oven are smaller pies — one for each maid-servant in the house. When the crusts are golden brown, the pies are cooled and frozen. This is very easy to do in the bitter Tyrolean winters. Each maid takes her pie home to her family. On the feast of the Epiphany, the pies are thawed, reheated and eaten. The father of the house makes quite a ceremony of cutting the Christmas pie which is baked in a rectangular pan to resemble the manger."

St Thomas is the patron saint of architects and also India.

22 December

On 22nd December 1557, Protestant martyrs John Rough and Margaret Mearing were burnt at Smithfield for heresy.

Interestingly, although these two people were burnt together and Margaret had gone out of her way to bring Rough comfort while he was in prison, Rough had not liked Margaret at first and had excommunicated her from his congregation.

Let me tell you a bit more about these Protestant martyrs, what we know of them, and how they came to their sad ends.

John Rough was born in Scotland around 1508 and studied at St Leonard's College, St Andrews, before entering the Dominican Friary at Stirling. His Catholic faith was challenged by two visits he made to Rome on business for the friary when he saw people's reaction to the pope in processions and how they gave him more attention and adulation than the Eucharist. Rough began to view the pope as the Anti Christ.

In 1543, James Hamilton, 2nd Earl of Arran, the regent of Scotland, employed Rough as one of his chaplains and obtained a dispensation for him to leave his monastery and to exempt him from wearing his habit. Arran allowed Rough and another of his chaplains, Thomas Gwilliam, to speak out against abuses in the church, superstitious practices and papal authority. Their preaching in Edinburgh nearly led to them being physically attacked, and the Franciscan order branded them heretics, crying out as they preached, "Heresy! Heresy! Gwilliam and Rough will carry the governor to the devil!" Following this trouble and the rise once more of Cardinal Beaton, Gwilliam fled to England, and Rough retreated to Kyle, in Ayrshire.

In 1546, following the assassination of Cardinal Beaton, Rough became chaplain to the Fife lairds responsible for the cardinal's murder. He also began preaching at the parish church in St Andrews, where he came into contact with John Knox and helped support and encourage Knox in his ministry, advising him to become a pastor. Both Knox and Rough successfully converted people in St Andrews to Protestantism. Still, they ended up being called before the vicar-general of St Andrews and barred from preaching at the church.

During the 1540s, Rough had been receiving a pension from King Henry VIII for acting as the king's agent in Scotland. In June 1547, he crossed the border into England, escaping from St Andrew's Castle, which was under siege and which surrendered in July 1547. The French took Knox prisoner. Rough went first to Carlisle, and then, after the intercession of the Earl of Lennox and Lord Wharton with Edward Seymour, the leader of Edward VI's government, Rough was sent to preach at Berwick. His pension was also renewed.

Rough moved to Newcastle, where he married, and then to Hull, where he held a benefice. Then, after the accession of the Catholic Queen Mary I, Rough and his wife fled into exile abroad, settling in Norsden in Friesland, where they knitted caps and stockings to support themselves. Martyrologist John Foxe states that Rough remained abroad until the October before his death, when "lacking yarn and other such necessary provision for the maintenance of his occupation, he came over again into England, here to provide for the same". He arrived in London in November 1557, where he joined a secret congregation of Protestants and was elected as their minister and preacher.

While ministering to this underground congregation, Rough came into contact with his fellow martyr, Margaret Mearing. Foxe writes that Rough "did not well like the sayd Margaret, but greatly suspected her, as many other of them did besides, because she would often times bring in strangers among them, and in her talk seemed (as they thought) somewhat too busy." Foxe goes on to record that the Friday before he was arrested, Rough excommunicated Mearing from the congregation, cutting her off from "their fellowship and society", believing her to be a spy. Foxe describes Mearing's reaction: "Whereat she being moved, did not well take it, nor in good part, but thought her self not indifferently handled among them. Whereupon to one of her friende' in a heat, she threatened to remove them all."

On 12th December 1557, at the Saracen's Head, in Islington, the congregation gathered, pretending that they were going to watch a play. Unfortunately, they were betrayed. Not by Mearing, though, but by tailor Roger Sergeant, who was a spy who had infiltrated their group. Rough, deacon Cuthbert Symson and others were arrested and taken to the Gatehouse Prison in Westminster. There, Rough received a surprise visit. John Foxe records: "none of his friends could come to him to visit him. Then this said Margaret hearing thereof, got her a basket, and a clean shirt in it, and went to Westminster, where she feigning her self to be his Sister, got into the prison to him, and did there to her power not a little comfort him." The very woman he'd thrown out of his congregation, Margaret Mearing, offered Rough comfort in his time of need.

On 15th December 1557, Rough and Symson were taken before the privy council to be examined. Rough was then imprisoned in Newgate Prison, while transcripts of the interrogation were sent to Edmund Bonner, Bishop of London, who then examined Rough. Rough was accused of a long list of heresies. On 19th December, he was brought before Bonner and others but refused to recant. On 20th December, he was brought before the Consistory Court, which attacked him for his heretical beliefs and for marrying and having children even though he was a priest. Rough defended himself, saying his wife and children were lawful and saying that "he would never come to the Church to hear the abominable Mass and other service, being as it was then". The court degraded him and condemned him as a heretic, turning him over to the secular authorities for sentencing.

In the meantime, Margaret Mearing went to the house of Roger Sergeant, the man who had betrayed the congregation. Here is Foxe's account of what happened:

> "Then coming abroad again, she understanding that the Congregation suspected the said Sergeant to be his Promoter, went to his house, and asked whether Judas dwelt not there. Unto whom answer was made, there dwelt no such. No, said she? Dwelleth not Judas here that betrayed Christ? His name is Sergeant."

Margaret was arrested a few days later and imprisoned.

While he was in prison, Rough wrote letters to his congregation "confirming and strengthening them in the truth, which he had before taught." A passage in one of his letters explains why these 16th-century martyrs were willing to die for what they believed:

"I speak to Gods glory: my care was to have the senses of my soul open, to perceive the voice of God, saying: Who so ever denyeth me before men, him will I deny before my father and his angels. And to save the life corporal, is to lose the life eternal. And he that will not suffer with Christ, shall not reign with him. Therefore most tender ones, I have by Gods spirit given over the flesh, with the sight of my soul, and the spirit hath the victory. The flesh shall now ere it be long, leave of to sin: the spirit shall reign eternally. I have chosen the death to confirm the truth by me taught. What can I do more?"

Rough was choosing eternal life. The fate of his immortal soul was far more important to him than his earthly body. Far better to suffer temporary pain in return for eternal life with his Father in Heaven.

On this day in Tudor history, John Rough and Margaret Mearing were taken to Smithfield, where, according to John Foxe, they "most joyfully gave their lives for the profession of Christ's Gospel". Rough was survived by his wife and children, including a two-year-old daughter, Rachel.

The congregation's deacon, Cuthbert Symson (Simpson), was burnt at Smithfield on 28th March 1558.

23 December

On 23rd December 1556, in the reign of Queen Mary I, Nicholas Udall, schoolmaster, cleric, humanist and playwright, was buried at St Margaret's, Westminster.

Udall's play, "Ralph Roister Doister", which combined Latin comedy and English tradition, is regarded as the first English language comedy. He played a part in Anne Boleyn's coronation in 1533, composing verses for the pageant, and in 1534 he published his Latin textbook, "Floures for Latine Spekynge".

In 1541, Udall was imprisoned for a few months at Marshalsea after committing buggery with his pupil Thomas Cheney, but he was back in favour enough the next year to be leading a group of scholars in translating "The Paraphrase of Erasmus upon the New Testament" for Queen Catherine Parr.

Udall's other works included translations of Erasmus's "Apophthegms", Pietro Martire's "Discourse on the Eucharist", Thomas Gemini's "Anatomia", and the play "Respublica".

One of the works he wrote for Queen Anne Boleyn's coronation on 1st June 1533 was a ballad about Anne's falcon badge, and I'll share it with you now in memory of Udall:

"This White Falcon,
Rare and geason,
This bird shineth so bright;
Of all that are,
No bird compare
May with this Falcon White.

The virtues all,
No man mortal,
Of this bird can write.
No man earthly
Enough truly
Can praise this Falcon White.

Who will express
Great gentleness
To be in any wight;
He will not miss,
But call him this
The gentle Falcon White.

This gentle bird
As white as curd
Shineth both day and night;
Nor far ne near

Is any peer
Unto this Falcon White,

Of body small.
Of power regal,
She is, and sharp of sight ;
Of courage hault
No manner fault
Is in this Falcon White,

In chastity,
Excelleth she,
Most like a virgin bright:
And worthy is
To live in bliss
Always this Falcon White.

But now to take
And use her make
Is time, as troth is plight;
That she may bring
Fruit according
For such a Falcon White.

And where by wrong,
She hath fleen long,
Uncertain where to light;
Herself repose
Upon the Rose,
Now may this Falcon White.

Whereon to rest,
And build her nest;
GOD grant her, most of might!
That England may
Rejoice alway
In this same Falcon White."

24 December

On 24th December 1604, Sir Thomas Cornwallis, comptroller of the household of Mary I and member of Parliament, died at about eighty-six.

Cornwallis was active in putting down Kett's Rebellion in 1549, and in 1553, after originally proclaiming Lady Jane Grey as Queen in Ipswich, he swapped sides and swore allegiance to Mary I.

Let me tell you a bit more about this Tudor man.

- Suffolk man Sir Thomas Cornwallis was born around 1518/19 and was the eldest son of Sir John Cornwallis and his wife, Mary Sulyard. Sir John Cornwallis served as steward to the household of Prince Edward, the future Edward VI, from 1538 to 1544.
- In 1539, when he was about 20, Thomas was admitted to Lincoln's Inn, and by 1540, he was married, taking Anne Jerningham, daughter of Sir John Jerningham, as his bride. The couple went on to have two sons: William and Charles, and four daughters, including Elizabeth, who married Sir Thomas Kitson.
- In December 1548, in the reign of King Edward VI, Thomas was knighted, and in 1549 he served under William Parr, Marquess of Northampton, against the rebels of Kett's Rebellion in Norfolk. The rebels took Cornwallis prisoner when they took the city of Norwich, but John Dudley, Earl of Warwick, defeated the rebels and freed their prisoners.
- In 1553, Thomas was sheriff of Norfolk and Suffolk, and in July 1553, following the receipt of a letter from John Dudley, who was now Duke of Northumberland, he proclaimed Lady Jane Grey as Queen Jane at Ipswich. He was accompanied by Lord Thomas Wentworth and some other prominent Suffolk gentlemen. However, while Thomas and the others were still in Ipswich, Thomas Poley, receiver to Mary, daughter of Henry VIII and Catherine of Aragon, came to the marketplace on Mary's orders and proclaimed his mistress "hereditary queen of England". His proclamation was received well by the Ipswich people, and this caused Sir Thomas Cornwallis to have second thoughts. When he heard that the people of London

"were very ill-deposed to Northumberland and the great men of the realm for disinheriting Mary" and that trouble was brewing, Thomas decided to take action. On 12th July, he changed sides and recanted his previous proclamation and proclaimed for Mary. Mary was proclaimed queen in London on 19th July 1553, and she rewarded Thomas by making him a member of her council and his wife a lady of the privy chamber.

- In Mary I's first parliament, Thomas was MP for Gatton in Surrey, and in October 1553, he and Sir Robert Bowes travelled to Berwick to negotiate with Scottish commissioners. That December, they were able to negotiate a code of border laws. In January 1554, Mary I sent Thomas and Sir Edward Hastings to entreat Thomas Wyatt the Younger, who was intent on marching on London, but Wyatt went ahead. In March 1554, Thomas was a member of the commission that tried the rebel leader. In February 1554, Thomas was also sent to Ashridge to fetch Mary's half-sister, Elizabeth, to London because Mary believed she was involved in the rebellion. Elizabeth pleaded illness. Thomas opposed those on the council who pushed for Elizabeth's imprisonment, but she did end up in the Tower for two months.

- In 1554, Thomas also served as MP for Grampound, and in May of that year, he was made treasurer of Calais, serving under his cousin, Sir Thomas Wentworth. In 1557, Thomas reported to Mary on the state of Calais' defences, stating that they were inadequate. In December of that year, following the death of Sir Robert Rochester, Thomas was made comptroller of the household, and in January 1558, the same month that Calais fell to the French, he was elected as MP for Suffolk.

- He was named as one of Mary I's executors. Still, after her death and Elizabeth I's accession, Catholic Thomas lost royal favour and was removed from his position as comptroller and from the privy council. He retired to his home, Brome Hall. However, his quiet life in Suffolk was disturbed when he was arrested with Sir Thomas Kitson, his son-in-law, in 1569 after the Rising of the North. He was interrogated regarding his close links with the Duke of Norfolk, but after a year was released, having sworn loyalty to the queen.

- Thomas conformed in a religious sense for a while, but by 1578 was no longer conforming. He was close friends with William Cecil, Lord Burghley, Elizabeth I's chief advisor, so perhaps that protected him. In 1588, when England was under threat of invasion from Spain, Thomas was confined to the home of his son-in-law, Sir Thomas Kitson, but after that had been dealt with, he was allowed back home. In 1600, his brother, William, a seminary priest who had been imprisoned, was allowed to live with him.
- In March 1604, Thomas made his will, adding to it in November. Sir Thomas Cornwallis died on this day in history, Christmas Eve 1604. Four days later, he was buried at the church at Brome.
- Thomas's eldest son, William, died in November 1611, and Charles died in 1629. Frederick Cornwallis, Thomas's grandson by William, was made 1st Baron Cornwallis and served as Treasurer of the Household to King Charles II.

25 December

On 25th December 1587, Brian Darcy, magistrate, sheriff of Essex, witch-hunter and contributor to the 1582 "A true and just recorde of the information, examination and confession of all the witches, taken at S Oses [St Osyth]", died.

Let me give you a few facts about this witch-hunter.

- Brian Darcy was the son of Thomas Darcy of Tolleshunt Darcy in Essex, and his second wife, Elizabeth Bedingfield.
- Darcy was married to Brigit Corbett, daughter of John Corbett of Sprowston in Norfolk, and the couple had eight children.
- During the 1580s, he lived at the Darcy family seat of St Osyth Priory in Essex and Tiptree Priory.
- In 1581, Darcy served as a Justice of the Peace at Brentwood in Essex at the March assizes.
- In 1582, as a magistrate, he was involved in questioning a group of people suspected of practising witchcraft in the St Osyth area

and who were committed for trial. Darcy's interrogations of each of them were published that same year in the work "A true and just recorde of the information, examination and confession of all the witches, taken at S Oses", which was over 100 pages long. The pamphlet, written by the rather anonymous WW, was dedicated to Darcy: "To the right honourable and his singular good Lorde, he Lord Darcey, W. W. wisheth a prosperous continuance in this lyfe to the glory of God, and a dayly preservation in Gods feare to his endlesse joye."

- Darcy used this work to argue for harsher punishments for those accused of witchcraft, people he viewed as devil worshippers. He wanted the punishment of hanging to be changed to burning. He stated that a normal felon and murderer was hanged and that it was a "great inequality of justice" for a witch to also be hanged, "which deserueth a death so much the more horrible, by how much the honour of God is eclipsed, and the glorye due to his inviolable name most abhominably defaced, euen to the vttermost villanie that they can put in practise." His biographer, Marion Gibson, explains, "The pamphlet's emphasis suggests that Darcy was particularly proud of his use of trick questions against suspected witches, and of his false promises of favourable treatment of anyone who confessed." Perhaps he felt the end justified the means.
- Darcy was personally responsible for the execution of two women and the deaths of four other people who died while in gaol.
- His work was viewed positively by those in authority as he was made sheriff of Essex in 1586.
- Brian Darcy made his will on 19th December 1587 and died six days later, on Christmas Day.

26 December

On 26th December 1526, Rose Lok was born.

Rose is an interesting lady as she was not only a Protestant exile but also a businesswoman, and when she was in her 80s, she wrote an account of her life. In her account, she mentions how her father, a royal mercer, imported religious books for Anne Boleyn.

Let me give you a few facts about Rose.

- Rose was born on this day in 1526 and was the third child of Protestant Sir William Lok, a mercer and merchant adventurer, and his second wife, Katherine Cook. Sir William Lok was also a sheriff, alderman, and gentleman usher of the chamber to King Henry VIII, who also supplied cloth and clothing. Edward VI knighted William.
- Rose was one of at least eleven children.
- Her father was an ancestor of the famous philosopher John Locke.
- Rose was married twice: to merchant Anthony Hickman, in 1543, with whom she had at least two children, and to Simon Throckmorton of Brampton.
- According to Rose's account of her life, "Certaine old stories recorded by an aged gentlewoman … about the yeer our lord 1610", her father, who supported the king's annulment of his first marriage, removed the pope's bull threatening King Henry VIII with excommunication when it was posted in Dunkirk.
- Rose's family were keen Protestants, and Rose's faith was influenced by her mother reading evangelical books to her and her sisters.
- Rose's first husband, Anthony, was a mercer and merchant adventurer who carried out several voyages with Rose's brother, Thomas. They also owned several ships, including the Mary Rose – not the famous one - which they named after their wives.
- Rose and Anthony were friends with Protestants John Hooper, John Foxe and John Knox.
- Rose's husband, Anthony, and her brother, Thomas, were imprisoned in the Fleet in Mary I's reign, accused of heresy and giving aid to imprisoned Protestants. After being released from the Fleet, they then spent time under house arrest at the home of William Paulet, Marquess of Winchester, before they were eventually released. Anthony went into exile in Antwerp. Rose was pregnant and remained in England but chose to give

birth away from London, in Oxfordshire. Her first child was baptised with Catholic rites, following advice from Archbishop Cranmer and Bishops Latimer and Ridley, who would, of course, become the Oxford Martyrs. After recovering from the birth, Rose travelled to Antwerp to be with Anthony. Rose's brother, Thomas, remained in England due to his wife, who, according to Rose, wouldn't let him leave England.

- Rose had her second child while in exile, having the child baptised in the Protestant faith, and she returned to England in 1558, following the accession of Elizabeth I.
- In 1596, according to historian Marilyn Roberts, Rose, her son, William, and his family, bought Gainsborough Old Hall in Lincolnshire, and the property became a focus for Puritans such as William Brewster.
- Rose died at the age of 86 on 21st November 1613.
- Rose is the protagonist of the novel "Tudor Rose" by Sue Allan.

27 December

On 27th December 1583, scholar and Puritan Katherine Killigrew (née Cooke) died after giving birth to a stillborn child.

Let me tell you a bit more about this accomplished Tudor lady.

- Katherine was born around 1542 and was the fifth daughter of scholar and royal tutor Sir Anthony Cooke and his wife, Anne Fitzwilliam. Her sisters included Mildred, who became the wife of William Cecil, Baron Burghley; Anne, who married Sir Nicholas Bacon; and Elizabeth, who married Thomas Hoby and then John, Lord Russell.
- Katherine grew up at the Cooke family home in Essex, Gidea Hall.
- Her father was a humanist who believed that daughters should be educated well, and like her sisters, she was educated in the classics. She later became known for her gift for poetry and her knowledge of Hebrew, Greek and Latin.
- By 1564, Katherine was serving Queen Elizabeth I as a maid of honour.

- In 1565, Katherine married diplomat Sir Henry Killigrew of Cornwall. Henry was often away from home on embassies, and at one point, Katherine wrote to her sister Mildred to intercede with Baron Burghley to excuse Henry from his overseas duties. The message was written in Latin and in verse.
- The Killigrews had four daughters: Anne, Elizabeth, Mary and Dorothy.
- Katherine was a Puritan and was good friends with preacher Edward Dering who visited her at her home at Hendon and corresponded with her. His letters to her in 1575 were published in "The Godly Letters of Mr Dering". In them, Dering writes of her "weak and sickly body", which meant that she could not have as much joy as she should, and seeing it as her cross to bear.
- On this day in history, 27th December 1583, when she was about forty-one years of age, Katherine died following childbirth. The child was stillborn. She was laid to rest in St Thomas the Apostle Church in London, a church which burnt down in 1666 in the Great Fire. Andrew Melvin wrote the following epitaph:
"Apollo's fav'rite and to Pallas dear,
Adorn'd by ev'ry art her works appear.
Parent and sister of the harmonious nine,
All Greece and Rome did in her numbers shine.
The sacred language too she made her own,
Nor eastern learning was to her unknown.
Faith, modest candour, piety resign'd,
Religious zeal, and purity of mind,
Each grace that love or admiration gains,
Her bosom once, and now, her tomb contains."
William Chark wrote:
"Here Kath'rine lies, deriv'd of noble kind,
Of Cooke to Killigrew by marriage join'd,
Enough this notice, for to distant Rhone,
And Rhine, her virtue, and her wit are known,
By fame such lasting monuments are giv'n,
To her, the Muses friend, and saint of Heav'n."

28 December

On 28th December 1510, lawyer, administrator and Lord Keeper of the Great Seal in Elizabeth I's reign, Sir Nicholas Bacon, was born. Bacon was the father of the famous philosopher, statesman, scientist and author, Sir Francis Bacon.

Let me tell you more about this Tudor man.

- Sir Nicholas Bacon was probably born at Drinkstone in Suffolk and was the second son of Robert Bacon, yeoman and sheep-reeve (chief shepherd), and his wife, Isabel Cage.
- Bacon was educated at Bury St Edmunds Grammar School and then Corpus Christi College, Cambridge, where he met men like Matthew Parker, future Archbishop of Canterbury, and future Protestant martyr Thomas Dusgate.
- By 1532, he had been admitted to Gray's Inn and became a barrister in the same year.
- By 1538, Bacon was serving in the court of augmentations, the court that had been set up to deal with monastic property and revenue confiscated during the dissolution of the monasteries. By 1540, he was serving as the solicitor of the augmentations.
- Bacon benefited from the dissolution of the monasteries by being granted former monastic properties as rewards and buying dissolved monasteries and land, particularly in and around Suffolk.
- In 1540, Bacon married Jane Ferneley, daughter of a yeoman from Suffolk. The couple went on to have six surviving children. Jane's sister married Thomas Gresham, the well-known financier and merchant who founded the Royal Exchange.
- By 1542, Bacon was serving as a Member of Parliament for Westmorland, then in 1545 for Dartmouth.
- In 1546, Bacon became attorney to the court of wards and liveries, a position that fit his interest in education for the young.
- Sadly, Jane died in 1552. Just months later, Bacon married Anne Cooke, daughter of scholar Sir Anthony Cooke and sister

of Katherine Killigrew, Mildred Cecil and Elizabeth Russell. They had two sons, Anthony and Francis.

- In 1560, Bacon purchased the manor of Gorhambury in Hertfordshire and built a mansion on the site.
- In 1561, he wrote a paper, "Articles devised for the bringing up ... of the queen's majesty's wards", and he ensured that all five of his sons were well educated. He founded several grammar schools, donated books to Cambridge, and established scholarships.
- In the summer of 1553, during the succession crisis, Bacon's wife, who had been in Mary's service, pledged her allegiance to Mary I. Although they were Protestants, Anne's husband and her brother-in-law, William Cecil, were able to make their peace with the Catholic queen. Anne Bacon continued in Mary's service as a gentlewoman of the privy chamber despite her and her husband's Protestant faith.
- Bacon survived Mary's reign by focusing on his duties at the court of wards and Gray's Inn, but things changed for the better when Elizabeth I came to the throne in November 1558. The new queen sought Bacon's advice on forming her government, and he was able to help her persuade his friend, Matthew Parker, to serve as her Archbishop of Canterbury, even though Parker did not want to.
- In December 1558, Elizabeth knighted Bacon and made him a privy councillor and Lord Keeper of the Great Seal, which was Lord Chancellor in all but name. In that role, he opened the queen's first parliament in 1559, giving an opening speech in which he called for moderation and tolerance regarding religion.
- In 1563, he incurred Elizabeth I's wrath after helping John Hales to gather information and opinion on the case for Lady Katherine Grey being Elizabeth's closest heir to the throne. Hales published "A Declaration of the Succession of the Crowne Imperial of Ingland", and Bacon was temporarily banished from court and the privy council. Still, thanks to the help of his brother-in-law, Cecil, he managed to get back into favour in 1565.

- In 1568, the queen appointed Bacon to preside over the Westminster conference looking into whether Mary, Queen of Scots, was involved in the murder of her second husband, Lord Darnley. In 1569, he was chosen to investigate the Rising of the North and those involved, and then, in 1570, he presided over the York House conference about Mary, Queen of Scots. He was against releasing the imprisoned Scottish queen.
- Bacon was a staunch Protestant, and in 1568 he was described by the Spanish ambassador as "one of the most pernicious heretics in Europe". A tract published abroad called "A Treatise of Treasons againste Queen Elizabeth and the Crowne of England" attacked Bacon and his colleague and brother-in-law, William Cecil.
- Bacon and his wife, Anne, harboured Puritans at their manor of Gorhambury. Matthew Parker reprimanded him for being lenient towards Puritans, but not Catholics, and for maintaining a preacher who encouraged prophesying.
- In 1577, Bacon played host to the queen on her four-day visit to Gorhambury.
- Bacon died in London on 20th February 1579, probably from pneumonia, and was laid to rest at St Paul's. In his will, he left £200 for the building of a new chapel at Corpus Christi.
- As well as being a loyal crown servant, Bacon was a patron to writers and scientists, a keen builder, a keen humanist and student of classical literature, a man who assembled a fine library, and a poet. He was also a real family man, something which is evident in his letters and a poem he wrote for his wife, Anne, when she was ill.

29 December

On 29th (or 30th) December 1605, in the reign of King James I, Elizabethan navigator and explorer John Davis (Davys) died near Bintang, off the coast of Borneo. His ship, The Tiger, was attacked by Japanese pirates who killed Davis in hand-to-hand combat. He was about 55 when he died.

John Davis was born around 1550, in Sandridge, near Dartmouth in

Devon, and was one of the main Elizabethan navigators and explorers. The Davis Strait in the Northwest Passage is named after him. He is also known for being the first Englishman to document a sighting of the Falkland Islands. Davis also wrote "The Seaman's Secrets" (1594) and "The World's Hydrographical Description" (1595).

Let me tell you more about Davis's final voyage and death.

The Tiger, piloted by Davis and commanded by Sir Edward Michelborne, set off from Cowes, a port on the Isle of Wight, on 5th December 1604. It landed at Bantam, or Banten, Java, in October 1605 and then set sail, bound for Patany, on 2nd November. However, they never reached there. According to a contemporary account of the voyage, on 27th December 1605, the crew of The Tiger encountered a Japanese junk while they were anchored in the port of Bintang in the Straits of Malacca. The crew had been pirating along the coasts of China and Cambodia but had lost their pilot and been shipwrecked. The English and Japanese men got on well initially, with a contemporary writer saying that the crew of The Tiger spent "two days, entertaining them with good usage, not taking anything from them" and gifts and feastings were exchanged. However, he goes on to say, "these rogues, being desperate in winds and fortune, being hopeless in that paltry junk ever to return to their own country, resolved with themselves either to gain my ship or to lose their lives." A party led by Davis were sent to search the junk, and Davis, who was "beguiled with their humble semblance", refused to take any weapons. Big mistake. The writer gives an account of Davis's last moments:

> "They passed all the day, my men searching in the Rice and they looking on. At the Sunnesetting, after long search and nothing found, save a little Storax and Benjamin, they, seeing oportunitie, and talking to the rest of their Companie which were in my ship, being neere to their Juncke, they resolved, at a watchword betweene them, to set upon us resolutely in both ships. This being concluded they suddenly killed and drave over-boord all my men that were in their ship; and those which were aboord my ship sallied out of my Cabbin, where they were put, with such weapons as they had, finding certaine Targets in my Cabbin, and other things

that they used as weapons. My selfe being aloft on the Decke, knowing what was likely to follow, leapt into the waste, where, with the Boate Swaines, Carpenter, and some few more wee kept them under the halfe-decke.

At their first comming forth of the Cabbin, they met Captaine Davis comming out of the Gunroome, whom they pulled into the Cabbin, and giving him sixe or seven mortall wounds they thrust him out of the Cabbin before them. His wounds were so mortall that he dyed as soone, as he came into the waste."

The writer explains that the English crew used pikes to try and defend themselves and that they finally drove them off, leaving just one alive, by firing cannons at them through the bulkhead.

In his will, Davis left his worldly goods to his sons, Gilbert, Arthur and Philip, and Judith Havard, his "espoused love" and the woman he intended to marry on his return to England.

John Davis also invented the Davis Quadrant, or the backstaff, which he describes in "The Seaman's Secrets". It was a navigational instrument used to measure the sun's or moon's altitude. The Nautical Instruments website explains that it "was the successor of the cross-staff and the predecessor of the octant", and the National Maritime Museum's description of a Davis quadrant made in the 18th century describes it as follows:

"The backstaff is made from a hornbeam frame with boxwood arcs. The staff has an inlaid ivory plate on the main strut and rivets capped by decorative ivory triangles. There are no vanes. Small decorative stamps, including flowers and fleurs-de-lis, are stamped at the ends of both arcs. The transversal scale on the thirty-degree arc is from 0° to 25° by 5 arcminutes and reads to 0.5 arcminutes. The graduation on the sixty degree arc is from 0° to 65° by 1°."

30 December

On 30th December 1552, in the reign of King Edward VI, Spanish humanist scholar, translator, author and Protestant apologist Francisco de Enzinas (humanist name Francis Dryander) died at Strasbourg from the plague. He was buried there the next day.

Dryander had been a member of the household of Katherine Brandon, Duchess of Suffolk, for a time, possibly teaching her son Charles, and Archbishop Cranmer paid him as a Greek Reader. While at Cambridge in the late 1540s, Dryander translated various ancient texts into Spanish before travelling to the Continent in 1549 to set up a publishing house in Strasbourg. There, he published at least nine classical and Biblical translations.

Let me tell you a bit more about this European scholar.

- Dryander was born Francisco de Enzinas, probably in November 1518 in San Gil, in Burgos, Spain. He was the son of a wealthy wool merchant, Juan de Enzinas. It is thought that his mother was Ana de Sandoval, but his father married again after her death, marrying Beatriz de Santa Cruz from an important Burgos family in 1528.

- By 1539, due to his family's links and business, Dryander was in the Low Countries, where he studied at Louvain's Collegium Trilingue, which was known as a centre of humanist learning. His brother, Diego, also studied there. While in Louvain, he changed his name to Francis Dryander and began studying the classics and the Bible, as well as being influenced by the works of Erasmus and Luther.

- While in Louvain, he became friends with Garbrand Harkes, a bookseller from Oxford, Edmund Crispin from Oriel College, Oxford, and Jan Laski, the Polish reformer.

- In 1541, Dryander travelled to Paris to visit his relative, theologian Pedro de Lerma, dean of theology at the Sorbonne. Then he made his way to Wittenberg, where he began at the university, choosing to study there because of his admiration for Reformer Philip Melancthon. While there, he translated the New Testament into Spanish, the first modern Spanish translation of it, publishing it in 1543. Dryander sought an audience with Emperor Charles V to present him with a copy of his New Testament and to get his protection as plenty of people opposed the translation of the Bible. Unfortunately, this plan didn't work, and the emperor's confessor, Dominican Pedro de

Soto, ordered Dryander's arrest and ordered copies of the work to be confiscated. Accused of heresy, Dryander was imprisoned in Brussels but managed to escape in February 1545, but was then an outlaw.

- Back in Wittenberg, Dryander wrote an account of his imprisonment and escape in his work "De statu Belgico et religione Hispanica". Then, in Basel, in 1546, he published his "Historia de morte sancti viri Ioannis Diazii" about the Spanish Protestant Juan Diaz, who had been murdered. He studied at the university at Basel temporarily but didn't enjoy his studies.
- In 1547, Dryander received news that his brother, Diego, had been burnt as a heretic in Rome. This led to him leaving Basel for Strasbourg, feeling he was safer there.
- In 1548, in Strasbourg, Dryander married exile Marguerite d'Elter, originally from Guelders. Then, in July 1548, after reformer Martin Bucer had advised him to leave the Continent, Dryander and his wife travelled to England, where Protestant Edward VI was on the throne. They resided with Archbishop Thomas Cranmer in Lambeth for a time. Historian Jonathan L Nelson believes that Drander gave the archbishop a copy of Spain's ancient Mozarabic liturgy because the baptism blessing in the 1549 Book of Common Prayer seems to use it.
- Cranmer and Catherine Willoughby, Duchess of Suffolk, whose sons attended Cambridge, helped him move to Cambridge to teach Greek there, although he wasn't an official professor at the university. The duchess was keen on the idea of him teaching her son, Charles. Dryander's first child, Margarita, was born while the couple lived in Cambridge.
- During his time at the university, Dryander worked on translating works by Plutarch, Livy and Lucian into Spanish. His translation of Plutarch's "Lives" was published under the name of Juan Castro de Salinas, which appears to link to the Duchess of Suffolk, whose mother was Maria de Salinas.
- In 1549, Dryander left his wife and daughter in the care of Martin Bucer while he travelled to Basel with his works, as he was unhappy with English printing. He didn't return, and in 1550, his wife and child joined him in Strasbourg,

where Dryander set up his own publishing house. Over the next two years, he published at least nine translations of the Old Testament and classical works.

- In around 1551, Marguerite gave birth to another daughter, Beatriz, but plague hit Strasbourg in 1552, and Dryander died on 30th December 1552, being buried the next day. He was just 34 years of age. Sadly, Marguerite only outlived him a few months, dying on 1st February 1553, also of the plague. Their daughters became wards of the city of Strasbourg, although their paternal step-grandmother Beatriz fought the authorities for custody.
- Dryander's memoirs were published in French a few years after his death. In 1995, his correspondence with reformers Martin Bucer, Philip Melancthon, John Calvin and Heinrich Bullinger was published.

31 December

On 31st December 1559, Owen Oglethorpe, Bishop of Carlisle, died while under house arrest in London. He was buried at St Dunstan-in-the-West on 6th January 1560. In his will, he left provisions for the foundation of a grammar school and almshouse at Tadcaster, Yorkshire

Let me share some facts about this bishop and tell you how he disobeyed a queen and died under house arrest.

- Owen Oglethorpe was born around 1502/3 and was the third son of George Oglethorpe of Newton Kyme, near Tadcaster, Yorkshire.
- He was educated at Magdalen College, Oxford, graduating BA in 1525 and MA in 1529. He then became a lecturer in logic, followed by a lecturer in moral philosophy in 1534.
- He became a priest in 1531.
- In 1536, he graduated with a Bachelor of Theology and then a doctorate of Theology.
- Also, in 1536, he became president of Magdalen College and canon of Lincoln.
- Between 1540 and 1544, he was canon and prebendary of St George's, Windsor

- In 1542, Oglethorpe was canon and prebendary of King Henry VIII College, Oxford, which later became known as Christ Church, and, in the 1540s, served as canon of Ripon and held several benefices in Yorkshire.
- In the late 1540s and early 50s, he corresponded with Heinrich Bullinger, the Swiss reformer.
- In 1551, he was vice-chancellor of Oxford University.
- In September 1552, in Edward VI's reign, he had to resign from his presidency of Magdalen College following problems regarding his conservative Catholic beliefs. He served in that role again in Mary I's reign until 1555.
- Between February 1554 and November 1556, Oglethorpe served as Dean of St George's, Windsor
- In 1555, he became Registrar of the Order of the Garter.
- In August 1556, Oglethorpe was consecrated as Bishop of Carlisle and went on to have benefices in Oxfordshire and Nottinghamshire. However, he didn't take full possession of the bishopric until early 1558, the last year of Mary I's Catholic reign.
- He upset Queen Elizabeth I on Christmas Day 1558 in the Chapel Royal when he elevated the host at Mass. The queen had ordered him not to elevate the host, which suggested the real presence of the body of Christ, but Oglethorpe disobeyed, stating that he could not act contrary to his beliefs and his training in the Church. After the reading of the Gospel, the furious queen left.
- Oglethorpe officiated at Elizabeth I's coronation ceremony on 15th January 1559, but it appears that George Carew, the new dean of her Chapel Royal, led the coronation mass, and he did not elevate the host.
- Oglethorpe was deprived of his bishopric in June 1559 due to his Catholic faith, and in November 1559, while under house arrest, he drew up his will. He died on this day in 1559.
- The boys' grammar school he founded, Tadcaster Grammar School, is still going today, although it moved just outside Tadcaster in 1960. It also merged with Dawson's Girls' School at the beginning of the 20th century.

Bibliography

Acts of the Privy Council of England, Volume 4, 1552-1554, ed.
John Roche Dasent (1892).

Amin, N. The Henry Tudor Society (https://henrytudorsociety.com/)

Andrews, W. E. (1876) *Examination of Fox's Calendar of Protestant Saints, Martyrs*. W. E. Andrews.

The Apprehension and confession of three notorious Witches (1589). Thomas Lawe. https://quod.lib.umich.edu/e/eebo/ A18586.0001.001?rgn=main;view=fulltext#:~:text=The%20 apprehension%20and%20confession%20of%20three%20 notorious%20witches.,thier%20spirits%2C%20whose%20 fourmes%20are%20heerein%20truelye%20proportioned

Benham, W. (1902) *Old St Paul's Cathedral*. Seeley and Co. Ltd.

ed. Bindoff, S. T. (1982) *The House of Commons 1509-1558*. Boydell and Brewer.

Birch, T. (1754) *Memoirs of the reign of Queen Elizabeth, from the year 1581 till her death*. A. Millar.

Bottesford Living History (https://www.bottesfordhistory.org.uk/)

Bragg, M. (Writer and presenter), Cox, Anna (Director). (2013) *The Most Dangerous Man in Tudor England*. BBC.

British Geological Survey (https://www.bgs.ac.uk/)

Brotton, J. (2017) *This Orient Isle: Elizabethan England and the Islamic World*. Penguin.

Brown, M. C. (1911) *Mary Tudor, Queen of France*. Methuen.

Bruce, J. & Perowne, T. T. eds. (1853), *The Correspondence of Matthew Parker, D.D., Archbishop of Canterbury: Comprising Letters Written by and to Him, from A.D. 1535, to His Death, A.D. 1575*. Cambridge University Press.

Burnet, G. (1816) *The History of the Reformation of the Church of England*. Clarendon Press.

Burton, E. H. & Pollen, J. H. (1914) *Lives of the English Martyrs*. Longmans, Green and Co.

Calendar of State Papers Domestic: Edward VI, Mary and Elizabeth, 1547-80, ed. Robert Lemon (1856).

Calendar of State Papers Foreign: Mary 1553-1558, ed. William B Turnbull (1861).

Calendar of State Papers Relating to English Affairs in the Archives of Venice, ed. Rawdon Brown (1871).

Calendar of State Papers, Spain, ed. Pascual de Gayangos (1882).

Calendar of the State Papers relating to Scotland and Mary, Queen of Scots 1547-1603, Vol. I, ed. Joseph Bain (HM General Register House, Edinburgh 1898).

Camden, W. (1635) *Annals, or, The Historie of the Most Renowned and Virtuous Princess Elizabeth Late Queen of England*. Thomas Harper.

Catholic Culture (https://www.catholicculture.org/)

Cavendish, G. (1827) *The Life of Cardinal Wolsey*, 2nd ed. Harding & Lepard.

Cavendish, G. (1825) *The Life of Cardinal Wolsey and Metrical Visions*, Volume II, ed. Samuel Weller Singer. Harding, Triphook & Lepard.

Chaloner, R. (1839) *Memoirs Of Missionary Priests And Other Catholics Of Both Sexes, That Have Suffered Death In England On Religious Accounts, From The Year 1577 To 1684*, Volumes 1-2. John T Green.

Cherry, C. and Ridgway, C. (2014) *George Boleyn: Tudor Poet, Courtier & Diplomat*. MadeGlobal Publishing.

Childs, J. (2014) *God's Traitors: Terror and Faith in Elizabethan England*. Bodley Head.

Chronicle Louis XII, Du Puy MS. No. 107. Robert de la Marck, BNF.

The Chronicle of Queen Jane, and of two years of Queen Mary, and especially of the rebellion of Sir Thomas Wyat. ed. Nichols, John Gough (1850). J.B. Nichols.

'The Chronicle of the Grey Friars: Jane', in Chronicle of the Grey Friars of London Camden Society Old Series: Volume 53, ed. J G Nichols (London, 1852).

Churchyard, T. (1580) *A warning for the wise, a feare to the fond, a bridle to the lewde, and a glasse to the good Written of the late earthquake chanced in London and other places, the. 6. of April 1580. for the glorie of God, and benefite of men that warely can walke, and wisely can iudge. Set forth in verse and prose, by Thomas Churchyard Gentleman. Seen and allowed.* Iohn Allde, and Nicholas Lyng and Henry Bynneman? - https://quod.lib.umich.edu/e/eebo/A18767.0001.001?view=toc

Cobbett, W. (1806) *Cobbett's Parliamentary History of England: from the Norman conquest, in 1066, to the year, 1803.* R. Bagshaw.

Cole, K. (2019-21) *The Witches of Essex.* Essex Voices Past. https://essexvoicespast.thinkific.com/courses/EssexWitches

A Collection of State Papers, Relating to Affairs in the Reigns of King Henry VIII. King Edward VI. Queen Mary, and Queen Elizabeth from the Year 1542 to 1570, Transcribed from Original Letters and other Authentick Memorials Never Before Publish'd, Left by William Cecill, Lord Burghley.... ed. Samuel Haynes (1840).

Doran, S. (2015) *Elizabeth and Her Circle.* Oxford University Press.

Doran, S. (2015) *Monarchy and Matrimony: The Courtships of Elizabeth I.* Routledge.

The Diary of Henry Machyn, Citizen and Merchant-Taylor of London, 1550-1563, ed. J G Nichols (London, 1848), British History Online http://www.british-history.ac.uk/camden-record-soc/vol42

Edwards, J. S. *Thomas Chaloner's 'Elegy on the Death of Lady Jane Grey'.* http://somegreymatter.com/chalonerelegy.htm

Ellis, Sir H. (1825-1846) *Original letters, illustrative of English history.* Harding, Triphook and Lepard.

Emerson, K. *A Who's Who of Tudor Women.* http://www.kateemersonhistoricals.com/

Encyclopædia Britannica (https://www.britannica.com/).

Cavendish. R. (2008, January). The Fall of Calais. *History Today*, Volume 58, Issue 1.

Fox, J. (1851) *Fox's Book of Martyrs: The Acts and Monuments of the Church.* G. Virtue.

Fox, J. (2011) *Sister Queens: Katherine of Aragon and Juana Queen of Castile.* W&N.

Fraser, A. (1992) *The Six Wives of Henry VIII.* Weidenfeld & Nicolson.

Frizzi, A. (1975) *Memorie per la storia di Ferrara.* Arnaldo Forni.

Frye, S. (1992) The Myth of Elizabeth at Tilbury. *The Sixteenth Century Journal,* vol. 23, no. 1, pp. 95–114.

Fuller, T. (1965) *The History of the Worthies of England.* Thomas Tegg.

Godwin, F. (1616) *Rerum Anglicarum Henrico VIII. Edwardo VI. et Maria Regnantibus, Annales.* Ex Officina Nortoniana, APVD Ioan Bill.

"The Golden Speech" https://www.nationalarchives.gov.uk/education/resources/elizabeth-monarchy/the-golden-speech/ Gov.UK (https://www.gov.uk/)

Green, M. A. E. (1849) *Lives of the Princesses of England.* Henry Colburn.

Gunn, S. (2015) *Charles Brandon: Henry VIII's Closest Friend.* Amberley Publishing.

Guy, J. (2004) *My Heart is My Own: The Life of Mary, Queen of Scots.* Fourth Estate.

Hall, E. (1809) *Hall's chronicle: containing the history of England, during the reign of Henry the Fourth, and the succeeding monarchs, to the end of the reign of Henry the Eighth, in which are particularly described the manners and customs of those periods.* J Johnson.

Halley, R. (1872) *Lancashire, its Puritanism and Non-conformity.* Tubbs and Brook.

Harpsfield, N. (1878) *A Treatise on the Pretended Divorce between Henry VIII and Catharine of Aragon.* Camden Society.

ed. Hasler, P. W. (1981) *The House of Commons 1558-1603.* Boydell and Brewer.

Hayward, M. (2008) *Dress at the Court of King Henry VIII.* Routledge.

de Hilster, Nicolàs. 1734 Will Garner Davis Quadrant (reproduction). Nautical Instruments. https://dehilster.info/navigational_instruments/1734_w._garner_davis_quadrant_backstaff.php#:~:text=The%20Davis%20Quadrant%20was%20the%20successor%20of%20the,George%20Waymouth%27s%201604%20manuscript%20%27The%20Jewell%20of%20Artes%27.

Hilton, L. (2014) *Elizabeth Renaissance Prince: A Biography*. Orion.

Hind, J. R. *On the expected return of the great comet of 1264 and 1556*. Leopold Classic Library.

Historical Collections or an Exact Account of the Proceedings of the Four last Parliaments of Queen Elizabeth, 1589-1601, ed. Heywood Townshend (1680).

A History of the County of Lancaster: Volume 8, ed. William Farrer and J Brownbill (London, 1914), British History Online http://www.british-history.ac.uk/vch/lancs/vol8

Holinshed, R. (1807) *Holinshed's Chronicles of England, Scotland, and Ireland*. J. Johnson.

Hooker, J. (1765) *The Ancient History and Description of the City of Exeter*. R. Trewman.

Hotson, J. L. (2015) *The Death of Christopher Marlowe*. Palala Press.

Hoyle, R.W. (2001) *The Pilgrimage of Grace and the Politics of the 1530s*. Oxford University Press.

Hutchinson, R. (2005) *The Last Days of Henry VIII: Conspiracy, Treason and Heresy at the Court of the Dying Tyrant*. Orion.

Ives, E. (2011) *Lady Jane Grey: A Tudor Mystery*. Wiley-Blackwell.

Ives, E. (2004) *The Life and Death of Anne Boleyn*. Blackwell Publishing.

Jackson, S. (2005) *The Medieval Christmas*. The History Press.

James, S. (2009) *Catherine Parr: Henry VIII's Last Love*. The History Press.

Kelly, H. A. (2004) *The Matrimonial Trials of Henry VIII*. Wipf and Stock.

Kingsford, C. L. (1905) *Chronicles of London*. Clarendon Press.

eds. Knighton, C. S., Loades, D. (2011) *The Navy of Edward VI and Mary I*. Routledge.

Kramer, K. C. (2016) *Edward VI in a Nutshell.* MadeGlobal Publishing.

Lambeth Palace Library Guide Reginald Pole (https://www.lambethpalacelibrary.org/wp-content/uploads/sites/37/2021/05/Research-Guide-Reginald-Pole.pdf)

Leland, J. (1774) *Joannis Lelandi Antiquarii De Rebus Britannicis Collectanea*, Volume IV. Benjamin White.

Letters and Papers, Foreign and Domestic, Henry VIII, ed. J. S, Brewer (London, 1920).

Licence, A. (2013) *Elizabeth of York: The Forgotten Queen.* Amberley Publishing.

Lindsey, K. (1996) *Divorced, Beheaded, Survived: A Feminist Reinterpretation Of The Wives Of Henry VIII.* Da Capo Press.

Lisle, L. de (2009) *The Sisters Who Would Be Queen: Mary, Katherine, and Lady Jane Grey: A Tudor Tragedy.* Ballantine Books.

Literary remains of King Edward the Sixth. Edited from his autograph manuscripts, with historical notes and a biographical memoir. ed. Nichols, John Gough (1857). J. B. Nichols.

The Literary Remains of Lady Jane Grey with a Memoir of Her Life ed. Nicholas Harris Nicholas (1825). Harding, Triphook and Lepard.

Loades, D. (2004) *Intrigue and Treason: The Tudor Court, 1547-1558.* Longman.

Loades, D. (2012) *Mary Tudor.* Amberley Publishing.

MacCulloch, D. (2019) *Thomas Cromwell.* Penguin.

trans. MacCulloch, D. (1984, July) Robert Wingfield's Vita Mariae Angliae Reginae. *Camden Miscellany*, XXVIII, CS, 4th ser., 29, pp. 181–301.

The Maner of the Tryumphe of Caleys and Bulleyn: And The Noble Tryumphaunt Coronacyon of Quene Anne, Wyfe Unto the Most Noble Kynge Henry VIII, printed by Wynkyn de Worde, 1532-33, ed. Edmund Goldsmid, Edinburgh, 1885.

The Manuscripts of His Grace the Duke of Rutland: preserved at Belvoir Castle, Volume I, (HMSO, 1888).

Markham, A. H. (1880) *The Voyages and Works of John Davis, the Navigator.* Printed for the Hakluyt Society.

The Mary Rose Trust (https://maryrose.org/)

Mary Sidney Society (http://www.marysidneysociety.org/)

Mattingley, G. (2000) *The Defeat of the Spanish Armada*. Pimlico.

Milton, G. (2003) *Samurai William: The Adventurer Who Unlocked Japan*. John Murray Publisher Ltd.

Miscellaneous Writings and Letters of Thomas Cranmer, Archbishop of Canterbury. ed. Rev. John Edmund Cox for the Parker Society (1846).

Mostly Medieval (https://www.mostly-medieval.com/)

ed. Mueller, J. (2011) *Katherine Parr: Complete Works and Correspondence*. University of Chicago Press.

Munday, A. (1925) *The English Romayne Lyfe*. John Lane The Bodley Head Ltd.

Mush, J. (1849) *The Life and Death of Mistress Margaret Clitherow, the Martyr of York, now first published from the original manuscript, and edited by William Nicholson*. Richardson & Son.

The National Library of Wales (https://www.library.wales/)

National Maritime Museum (https://www.rmg.co.uk/national-maritime-museum)

Neale, J. E. (2005) *Queen Elizabeth I*. Academy Chicago Publishers.

Norton, E. (2011) *Anne of Cleves: Henry VIII's Discarded Bride*. Amberley Publishing.

O'Caellaigh, S. (2017) *Pustules, Pestilence and Pain: Tudor Treatments and Ailments of Henry VIII*. MadeGlobal Publishing.

O'Neill, S. (2012) *Folklore of Lincolnshire*. The History Press.

Okerlund, A. N. (2011) *Elizabeth of York (Queenship and Power)*. Palgrave Macmillan.

ed. Oldys, W. (1744) *The Harleian Miscellany: or, A collection of scarce, curious, and entertaining pamphlets and tracts, as well in manuscript as in print, found in the late Earl of Oxford's Library*. Volume I. T. Osborne.

Oxford Dictionary of National Biography (http://oxforddnb.com/).

Parry, G. (2013) *The Arch Conjuror of England: John Dee*. Yale University Press.

Patten, W. (1879) *The Expedicion into Scotlande of the most woorthely fortunate prince Edward, duke of Soomerset 1548*. Edward Arber.

Rumens, C. (2019, 09 December). Poem of the week: The Flea by John Donne. *The Guardian*. https://www.theguardian.com/books/booksblog/2019/dec/09/poem-of-the-week-the-flea-by-john-donne

Pollen, J. H. H. (1891) *Acts of English martyrs hitherto unpublished*. Burns & Oates.

Porter, L. (2007) *Mary Tudor: The First Queen*. Piatkus.

Porter, S. (2018) *Everyday Life in Tudor London: Life in the City of Thomas Cromwell, William Shakespeare & Anne Boleyn*. Amberley Publishing.

Privy purse expenses of Elizabeth of York: wardrobe accounts of Edward the Fourth. With a memoir of Elizabeth of York, and notes, ed. Nicholas N. H. (1830).

Privy purse expenses of the Princess Mary, daughter of King Henry the Eighth, afterwards Queen Mary:with a memoir of the princess, and notes, ed. Madden F. (1831) William Pickering.

Retief, F. & Cilliers, L. (2010). Diseases and causes of death among the Popes. *Acta Theologica*. 26. 10.4314/actat.v26i2.52576.

Reynolds, E. E. (1960) *Margaret Roper: Eldest daughter of St. Thomas More*. P.J. Kennedy and Sons.

Ridgway, C. (2015) *Tudor Places of Great Britain*. MadeGlobal Publishing.

ed. Robinson, H. (1847) *Original letters relative to the English Reformation: written during the reigns of King Henry VIII, King Edward VI and Queen Mary, chiefly from the archives of Zurich*. Cambridge University Press.

Roud, S. (2008) *The English Year*. Penguin.

The Royal Family, British Monarchy (https://www.royal.uk/)

Shakespeare Documented (https://shakespearedocumented.folger.edu/folger-shakespeare-library)

Skidmore, C. (2008) *Edward VI: The Lost King of England*. W&N.

Smith, L. B. (2011) *Catherine Howard*. Amberley Publishing.

Starkey, D. (2000) *Elizabeth: Apprenticeship*. Vintage Books.

Starkey, D. (2003) *The Six Wives of Henry VIII*. Perennial.

von Staats, B. (2015) *Thomas Cranmer in a Nutshell*. MadeGlobal Publishing.

Stonyhurst College (https://www.stonyhurst.ac.uk/about-us/ stonyhurst-college-historic-collections/exhibitions/relic- exhibition)

Stow, J. (1734) *A survey of the cities of London and Westminster, borough of Southwark, and parts adjacent*, Volumes I and II. J. Read.

Streitz, P. (2001) *Oxford: Son of Queen Elizabeth I*. Oxford Inst. Pr.

Strickland, A. (1864) *Lives of the Queens of England*: Volume II. Bell and Daldy.

Strype, J. (1824) *Annals of the reformation and establishment of religion, and other various occurrences in the Church of England, during Queen Elizabeth's happy reign: together with an appendix of original papers of state, records, and letters*. Clarendon Press.

Strype, J. (1822) *Ecclesiastical memorials relating chiefly to religion and the reformation of it, and the emergencies of the Church of England, under King Henry VIII, King Edward VI and Queen Mary the First*. Clarendon Press.

Tower of London (https://www.hrp.org.uk/tower-of-london/#gs.4ugxb6)

Tudor Rebellions (http://rebellionsa2.blogspot.com/2009/11/ketts- rebellion-1549.html)

Tusser, T. (1810) *A Hundreth Good Pointes of Husbandrie*. Robert Triphook.

Urban, S. (1837). The scull of Sir Thomas More. *The Gentleman's Magazine*, ser. 2, v. 7, p 497.

Wagner, J. and Schmid, S. W. (2011) *The Encyclopedia of Tudor England*. ABC-CLIO.

Walker, J. M. (1998) *Dissing Elizabeth: Negative Representations of Gloriana*. Duke University Press Books.

Warnicke, R. M. (2006) *Mary, Queen of Scots*. Routledge.

Warnicke, R. M. (2011) *The Marrying of Anne of Cleves: Royal Protocol in Tudor England*. Cambridge University Press.

Warnicke, R. M. (2012) *Wicked Women of Tudor England: Queens, Aristocrats, Commoners*. Palgrave MacMillan.

Wedgewood, J. C. (1936) *History of Parliament: Biographies of The Members of The Commons House 1439-1509.* His Majesty's Stationery Office.

Weever, J. (1767) *Antient Funeral Monuments Great-Britain, Ireland, and the Islands adjacent, with the Dissolved Monasteries...* W. Tooke.

Whitelock, A. (2009) *Mary Tudor: Princess, Bastard, Queen.* Random House.

Whitelock, A. (2015, April). Elizabeth I's love life: was she really a 'Virgin Queen'? *BBC History Magazine.*

Wilson, D. (2002) *In the Lion's Court: Power, Ambition, and Sudden Death in the Reign of Henry VIII.* St Martin's Press.

Wilson, D. (2014, June) The Hunt for the Tudor Hitman. *BBC History Magazine.*

Wilson, D. (2013) *The Uncrowned Kings of England: The Black Legend of the Dudleys.* Constable.

ed. Wood, M. A. E. (1846) *Letters of royal and illustrious ladies of Great Britain, from the commencement of the twelfth century to the close of the reign of Queen Mary,* Volume II. Henry Colburn.

Woolley, B. (2002) *The Queen's Conjuror: The Science and Magic of Dr Dee.* Flamingo.

Wriothesley, C. (1875) *A chronicle of England during the reigns of the Tudors, from A.D. 1485 to 1559,* Volume I. Camden Society.

Younghusband, Major-General Sir G. (1919) *The Tower from Within.* The George H. Doran Company.

Zanello, M., Charlier, P., Corns, R., Devaux, B., Berche, P., & Pallud, J. (2015). The death of Henry II, King of France (1519-1559). From myth to medical and historical fact. *Acta neurochirurgica*, 157(1), 145–149. https://doi.org/10.1007/s00701-014-2280-9.

On This Day in Tudor History gives a day-by-day look at events from the Tudor era, including births, deaths, baptisms, marriages, battles, arrests, executions and more.

This must-have book for Tudor history lovers is perfect for:

- Dipping into daily over your morning coffee
- Using in the classroom
- Trivia nights and quizzes
- Finding out what happened on your birthday or special day
- Wowing friends and family with your Tudor history knowledge
- Researching the Tudor period

Written by best-selling Tudor history author Claire Ridgway, On This Day in Tudor History contains a wealth of information about your favourite Tudor monarchs, their subjects and the times they lived in.

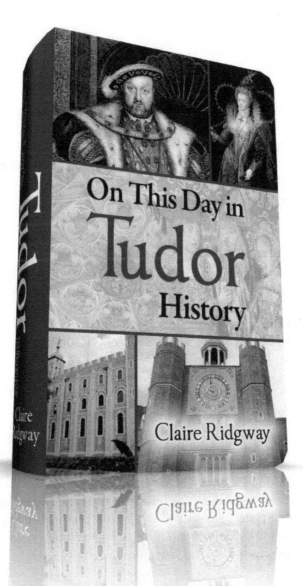

On This Day in
Tudor
History

Claire Ridgway

MadeGlobal Publishing

On This Day in Tudor History - **Claire Ridgway**
Tudor Places of Great Britain - **Claire Ridgway**
The Boleyns of Hever Castle - **Claire Ridgway**
The Life of Anne Boleyn Colouring Book - **Claire Ridgway**
The Fall of Anne Boleyn - **Claire Ridgway**
Illustrated Kings and Queens of England - **Claire Ridgway**
George Boleyn: Tudor Poet, Courtier & Diplomat
- **Ridgway & Cherry**
The Anne Boleyn Collection - **Claire Ridgway**
The Anne Boleyn Collection II - **Claire Ridgway**
The Anne Boleyn Collection III - **Claire Ridgway**
Sweating Sickness in a Nutshell - **Claire Ridgway**
The Tudor Puzzle Book - **Claire Ridgway**
A History of the English Monarchy - **Gareth Russell**
Jasper Tudor - **Debra Bayani**
Two Gentleman Poets at the Court of Henry VIII
- **Edmond Bapst**
A Mountain Road - **Douglas Weddell Thompson**

Please leave a review